Lecture Notes in Computer Science 2781

Edited by G. Goos, J. Hartmanis, and J. van Leeuwen

Springer

Berlin
Heidelberg
New York
Hong Kong
London
Milan
Paris
Tokyo

Bernd Michaelis   Gerald Krell (Eds.)

Pattern
Recognition

25th DAGM Symposium
Magdeburg, Germany, September 10-12, 2003
Proceedings

 Springer

Series Editors

Gerhard Goos, Karlsruhe University, Germany
Juris Hartmanis, Cornell University, NY, USA
Jan van Leeuwen, Utrecht University, The Netherlands

Volume Editors

Bernd Michaelis
Gerald Krell
Otto-von-Guericke-Universität Magdeburg
Institut für Elektronik, Signalverarbeitung und Kommunikationstechnik (IESK)
Postfach 41 20, 39016 Magdeburg, Germany
E-mail: {michaelis;krell}@iesk.et.uni-magdeburg.de

Cataloging-in-Publication Data applied for

A catalog record for this book is available from the Library of Congress.

Bibliographic information published by Die Deutsche Bibliothek
Die Deutsche Bibliothek lists this publication in the Deutsche Nationalbibliografie;
detailed bibliographic data is available in the Internet at <http://dnb.ddb.de>.

CR Subject Classification (1998): I.5, I.4, I.3.5, I.2.10

ISSN 0302-9743
ISBN 3-540-40861-4 Springer-Verlag Berlin Heidelberg New York

Springer-Verlag Berlin Heidelberg New York
a member of BertelsmannSpringer Science+Business Media GmbH

http://www.springer.de

© Springer-Verlag Berlin Heidelberg 2003
Printed in Germany

Typesetting: Camera-ready by author, data conversion by PTP-Berlin GmbH
Printed on acid-free paper   SPIN: 10931486   06/3142   5 4 3 2 1 0

Preface

We are proud to present the proceedings of DAGM 2003, and we want to express our appreciation to the many people whose efforts made this conference such a success. We received about 140 papers from around the world, but we could only accept about half of these submissions for oral and poster presentations so as not to overload the agenda. Each paper was assigned three reviewers who followed a careful anonymous selection procedure. The quality of the research paper and its suitability for presentation were the main criteria in this very difficult selection process. Our 32 reviewers had a tough job evaluating these papers and, of course, the job was even tougher whenever contributions were rejected. We thank the reviewers for their time and effort. The program committee awarded prizes for the best papers, and we want to sincerely thank the donors. The following three invited papers were among the highlights:

- *Anil K. Jain (Michigan State University, USA)*: Who's Who? Challenges in Biometric Authentication
- *Michael Unser (EPFL Lausanne, Switzerland)*: Splines and Wavelets: New Perspectives and Opportunities for Pattern Recognition
- *Bernd Jähne (Heidelberg University, Germany)*: Image Sequence Analysis in Environmental and Life Sciences

We are also very grateful and proud that several well-known experts enhanced our conference by offering tutorial sessions to our participants:

- *Christian Perwass, Gerald Sommer (Christian-Albrechts-University, Kiel, Germany)*: (Clifford) Algebra – Introduction and Applications
- *Hans-Heinrich Bothe (Technical University of Denmark, Oersted-DTU)*: Adaptive Paradigms for Pattern Recognition
- *Peter Kauff, Oliver Schreer (Frauenhofer Institut für Nachrichtentechnik, Heinrich-Hertz-Institute, Berlin, Germany)*: Concepts, Systems and Algorithms for Immersive Video Communication
- *Michael Felsberg (Linköping University, Sweden)*: Systematic Approaches to Image Processing and Computer Vision

Numerous corporations and organizations also deserve our thanks for sponsoring DAGM 2003 with financial support and material contributions: ABW GmbH, DaimlerChrysler AG, Fraunhofer-Inst. für Fabrikbetrieb und -automatisierung, Magdeburg, INB Vision AG, MEGWARE Computer GmbH, Otto-von-Guericke Univ. Magdeburg, Siemens AG, STEMMER IMAGING GmbH, SYMACON Engineering GmbH, and Volkswagen AG. And, last but not least, I want to thank my colleague Klaus Toennies, my co-editor Gerald Krell, and the members of the local organizational team, in particular Werner Liebscher and Regina Pohle, who all really made the DAGM 2003 symposium possible. Everyone did their very best to make the conference a success, and we sincerely hope that all participants profited from the presentations and enjoyed their stay in Magdeburg.

June 2003   Bernd Michaelis

Organization

DAGM e.V.: German Association for Pattern Recognition

General Chair

B. Michaelis   Univ. Magdeburg

Organizing Committee

G. Krell	Univ. Magdeburg
W. Liebscher	Univ. Magdeburg
R. Pohle	Univ. Magdeburg
K. Tönnies	Univ. Magdeburg

Program Committee

J. Buhmann	Univ. Bonn
H. Burkhardt	Univ. Freiburg
W. Förstner	Univ. Bonn
U. Franke	DaimlerChrysler, Stuttgart
S. Fuchs	Univ. Dresden
L. Van Gool	ETH Zürich
G. Hartmann	Univ. Paderborn
B. Jähne	Univ. Heidelberg
B. Kämmerer	Siemens, München
R. Koch	Univ. Kiel
W.G. Kropatsch	TU Wien
F. Leberl	TU Graz
C.E. Liedtke	Univ. Hannover
H. Mayer	Univ.-BW München
R. Mester	Univ. Frankfurt
B. Michaelis	Univ. Magdeburg
H.-H. Nagel	Univ. Karlsruhe
B. Neumann	Univ. Hamburg
H. Ney	RWTH Aachen
H. Niemann	Univ. Erlangen
B. Radig	TU München
H. Ritter	Univ. Bielefeld
G. Sagerer	Univ. Bielefeld
D. Saupe	Univ. Konstanz
B. Schiele	ETH Zürich
C. Schnörr	Univ. Mannheim

G. Sommer	Univ. Kiel
G. Szekely	ETH Zürich
K. Tönnies	Univ. Magdeburg
T. Vetter	Univ. Freiburg
F.M. Wahl	TU Braunschweig
J. Weickert	Univ. Saarland

Since 1978 DAGM (German Association for Pattern Recognition) has organized annual scientific conferences at various venues. The goal of each DAGM symposium is to inspire conceptual thinking, support the dissemination of ideas and research results from different areas in the field of pattern recognition, stimulate discussions and the exchange of ideas among experts, and support and motivate the next generation of young researchers.

DAGM e.V. was founded as a registered research association in September 1999. Until that time, DAGM had been comprised of the following support organizations that have since become honorary members of DAGM e.V.:

DGaO	Deutsche Arbeitsgemeinschaft für angewandte Optik (German Society for Applied Optics)
GMDS	Deutsche Gesellschaft für Medizinische Informatik, Biometrie und Epidemiologie (German Society for Medical Informatics, Biometry, and Epidemiology)
GI	Gesellschaft für Informatik (German Informatics Society)
ITG	Informationstechnische Gesellschaft (Information Technology Society)
DGN	Deutsche Gesellschaft für Nuklearmedizin (German Society for Nuclear Medicine)
IEEE	Deutsche Sektion des IEEE (Institute of Electrical and Electronics Engineers, German Section)
DGPF	Deutsche Gesellschaft für Photogrammetrie und Fernerkundung (German Society for Photogrammetry, Remote Sensing and Geo-Information)
VDMA	Fachabteilung industrielle Bildverarbeitung/Machine Vision im VDMA (Robotics + Automation Division within VDMA)
GNNS	German Chapter of the European Neural Network Society
DGR	Deutsche Gesellschaft für Robotik (German Robotics Society)

DAGM Prizes 2002

The main prize was awarded to

Daniel Cremers and Christoph Schnörr
Univ. Mannheim, Germany
Motion Competition: Variational Integration of Motion Segmentation and Shape
Regularization

Further DAGM prizes for the year 2002 were awarded to

Bernd Fischer and Joachim M. Buhmann
Univ. Bonn, Germany
Resampling Method for Path Based Clustering

Bodo Rosenhahn and Gerald Sommer
Univ. Kiel, Germany
Adaptive Pose Estimation for Different Corresponding Entities
(sponsored by ABW GmbH)

Andrés Bruhn, Joachim Weickert, and Christoph Schnoerr
Saarland Univ., Germany
Combining the Advantages of Local and Global Optic Flow Methods

Spherical Decision Surfaces Using Conformal Modelling

Christian Perwass, Vladimir Banarer and Gerald Sommer

Christian-Albrechts-Universität zu Kiel, Germany

Table of Contents

Postersession I

Invited Paper

Calibration and 3-D Shape

Recognition

Motion

Postersession II

Biomedical Applications

Pose Estimation

Applications

Invited Paper

Author Index

Median Filtering of Tensor-Valued Images

Martin Welk, Christian Feddern, Bernhard Burgeth and Joachim Weickert

Saarland University, Saarbrücken, Germany

Coherence-Enhancing Shock Filters

Joachim Weickert

Mathematical Image Analysis Group
Faculty of Mathematics and Computer Science, Bldg. 27
Saarland University, 66041 Saarbrücken, Germany
weickert@mia.uni-saarland.de
http://www.mia.uni-saarland.de/weickert

Abstract. Shock filters are based in the idea to apply locally either a dilation or an erosion process, depending on whether the pixel belongs to the influence zone of a maximum or a minimum. They create a sharp shock between two influence zones and produce piecewise constant segmentations. In this paper we design specific shock filters for the enhancement of coherent flow-like structures. They are based on the idea to combine shock filtering with the robust orientation estimation by means of the structure tensor. Experiments with greyscale and colour images show that these novel filters may outperform previous shock filters as well as coherence-enhancing diffusion filters.

1 Introduction

Shock filters belong to the class of morphological image enhancement methods. Most of the current shock filters are based on modifications of Osher and Rudin's formulation in terms of partial differential equations (PDEs) [12]. Shock filters offer a number of advantages: They create strong discontinuities at image edges, and within a region the filtered signal becomes flat. Thus, shock filters create segmentations. Since they do not increase the total variation of a signal, they also possess inherent stability properties. Moreover, they satisfy a maximum–minimum principle stating that the range of the filtered image remains within the range of the original image. Thus, in contrast to many Fourier- or wavelet-based strategies or linear methods in the spatial domain [19], over- and undershoots such as Gibbs phenomena cannot appear. This makes shock filters attractive for a number of applications where edge sharpening and a piecewise constant segmentation is desired. Consequently, a number of interesting modifications of the original schemes has been proposed [1,5,9,11,17]. All these variants, however, still pursue the original intention of shock filtering, namely edge enhancement.

Diffusion filters constitute another successful class of PDE-based filters [14, 20]. Compared to shock filters, diffusion filters have stronger smoothing properties, which may be desirable in applications where noise is a problem. While many diffusion filters act edge-enhancing, there are also so-called coherence-enhancing diffusion filters [21,22]. They are designed for the enhancement of oriented, flow-like structures, appearing e.g. in fingerprint images. The basic idea is to diffuse

B. Michaelis and G. Krell (Eds.): DAGM 2003, LNCS 2781, pp. 1–8, 2003.

anisotropically along the flow field such that gaps can be closed. A number of variants exist that have been applied to crease enhancement [18], seismic imaging [7] or flow visualisation [15].

In some of these application areas, noise is not a severe problem. Then the smoothing properties of coherence-enhancing diffusion are less important, while it would be desirable to have stronger sharpening qualities. A first step in this direction was pursued by a filter by Kimmel et al. [8], where backward diffusion is used. Although the results look impressive, the authors mention instabilities caused by the backward diffusion process. Thus the filter could only be used for short times and favourable stability properties as in the case of shock filtering cannot be observed.

The goal of the present paper is to address this problem by proposing a novel class of shock filters, so-called *coherence-enhancing shock filters*. They combine the stability properties of shock filters with the possibility of enhancing flow-like structures. This is achieved by steering a shock filter with the orientation information that is provided by the so-called structure tensor [2,4,16]. As a result, our novel filter acts like a contrast-enhancing shock filter perpendicular to the flow direction, while it creates a constant signal along the flow direction by applying either a dilation or an erosion process.

Our paper is organised as follows. In Section 2 we review some important aspects of shock filtering, and Section 3 describes the structure tensor as a tool for reliable orientation estimation. Both ingredients are combined in Section 4, where we introduce coherence-enhancing shock filters. Numerical aspects are briefly sketched in Section 5. In Section 6 we present a number of experiments in which the qualities of coherence-enhancing shock filtering are illustrated. Section 7 concludes the paper with a summary.

2   Shock Filters

Already in 1975, Kramer and Bruckner have proposed the first shock filter [10]. It is based on the idea to use a dilation process near a maximum and an erosion process around a minimum. The decision whether a pixel belongs to the influence zone of a maximum or a minimum is made on the basis of the Laplacian. If the Laplacian is negative, then the pixel is considered to be in the influence zone of a maximum, while it is regarded to belong to the influence zone of a minimum if the Laplacian is positive. Iterating this procedure produces a sharp discontinuity (shock) at the borderline between two influence zones. Within each zone, a constant segment is created. Iterated shock filtering can thus be regarded as a morphological segmentation method. The method of Kramer and Bruckner has been formulated in a fully discrete way.

The term *shock filtering* has been introduced by Osher and Rudin in 1990 [12]. They proposed a continuous class of filters based on PDEs. The relation of these methods to the discrete Kramer–Bruckner filter became evident several years later [6,17]. To explain the idea behind shock filtering, let us consider a continuous image $f : \mathbb{R}^2 \to \mathbb{R}$. Then a class of filtered images $\{u(x, y, t) \,|\, t \geq 0\}$ of $f(x, y)$ may be created by evolving f under the process

$$u_t = -\text{sign}(\triangle u)\,|\nabla u|, \tag{1}$$
$$u(x, y, 0) = f(x, y), \tag{2}$$

where subscripts denote partial derivatives, and $\nabla u = (u_x, u_y)^\top$ is the (spatial) gradient of u. The initial condition (2) ensures that the process starts at time $t = 0$ with the original image $f(x, y)$. The image evolution proceeds in the following way: Assume that some pixel is in the influence zone of a maximum where its Laplacian $\triangle u := u_{xx} + u_{yy}$ is negative. Then (2) becomes

$$u_t = |\nabla u|. \tag{3}$$

Evolution under this PDE is known to produce at time t a dilation process with a disk-shaped structuring element of radius t; see e.g. [3]. At the influence zone of a minimum with $\triangle u < 0$, equation (2) can be reduced to an erosion equation with a disk-shaped structuring element:

$$u_t = -|\nabla u|. \tag{4}$$

These considerations show that for increasing time, (1) increases the radius of the structuring element until it reaches a zero-crossing of $\triangle u$, where the influence zones of a maximum and a minimum meet. Thus, the zero-crossings of the Laplacian serve as an edge detector where a shock is produced that separates adjacent segments. The dilation or erosion process ensures that within one segment, the image becomes piecewise constant.

A number of modifications have been proposed in order to improve the performance of shock filters. For instance, it has been mentioned in [12] that the second directional derivative $u_{\eta\eta}$ with $\eta \,\|\, \nabla u$ can be a better edge detector than $\triangle u$. In order to make the filters more robust against small scale details, Alvarez and Mazorra [1] replaced the edge detector $u_{\eta\eta}$ by $v_{\eta\eta}$ with $v := K_\sigma * u$. In this notation, K_σ is a Gaussian with standard deviation σ, and $*$ denotes convolution. Taking into account these modifications the shock filter becomes

$$u_t = -\text{sign}(v_{\eta\eta})\,|\nabla u|. \tag{5}$$

3 The Structure Tensor

It is not surprising that the performance of the shock filter (5) strongly depends on the direction η. Unfortunately, in the presence of flow-like structures (e.g. fingerprints) it is well known that the gradient of a Gaussian-smoothed image $K_\sigma * u$ does not give reliable information on the orientation, since parallel lines lead to patterns with opposite gradients [21]. Smoothing them over a window leads to cancellation effects, such that the resulting gradient direction shows very large fluctuations. To circumvent this cancellation problem, a more reliable descriptor of local structure is needed. To this end we replace ∇u by its tensor product

$$J_0(\nabla u) = \nabla u \, \nabla u^\top. \tag{6}$$

This matrix gives the same result for gradients with opposite sign, since $J_0(\nabla u) = J_0(-\nabla u)$. Now it is possible to average orientations by smoothing $J_0(\nabla u)$ componentwise with a Gaussian of standard deviation ρ:

$$J_\rho(\nabla u) = K_\rho * (\nabla u \, \nabla u^\top). \tag{7}$$

This 2×2 matrix is called *structure tensor (second-moment matrix, scatter matrix, Förstner interest operator)*; see e.g. [2,4,16]. It is positive semidefinite, and its orthonormal system of eigenvectors describes the directions where the local contrast is maximal resp. minimal. This contrast is measured by its eigenvalues.

Let w be the normalised eigenvector corresponding to the largest eigenvalue. In the following we shall call w the *dominant eigenvector* of J_ρ. In a flow-like pattern such as a fingerprint it describes the direction where the contrast change is maximal. This is orthogonal to the orientation of the fingerprint lines.

4   Coherence-Enhancing Shock Filtering

Now we are in the position to apply our knowledge about the structure tensor for designing novel shock filters. To this end, we replace the shock filter (5) by

$$u_t = -\mathrm{sign}(v_{ww}) \, |\nabla u| \tag{8}$$

where $v = K_\sigma * u$, and w is the normalised dominant eigenvector of the structure tensor $J_\rho(\nabla u)$. The direction w guarantees that this model creates shocks *orthogonal* to the flow direction of the pattern. In this *shock direction*, contrast differences are maximised. Along the perpendicular *flow direction*, either dilation or erosion takes place. Thus, after some time, structures become constant along the flow direction, and sharp shocks are formed orthogonal to it. Experimentally one observes that after a *finite* time t, the evolution reaches a piecewise constant segmentation where coherent, flow-like patterns are enhanced. Thus it is not required to specify a stopping time.

The *structure scale* σ determines the size of the resulting flow-like patterns. Increasing σ gives an increased distance between the resulting flow lines: Typically one obtains line thicknesses in the range of 2σ to 3σ. Often σ is chosen in the range between 0.5 and 2 pixel units. It is the main parameter of the method and has a strong impact on the result.

The *integration scale* ρ averages orientation information. Therefore, it helps to stabilise the directional behaviour of the filter. In particular, it is possible to close interrupted lines if ρ is equal or larger than the gap size. In order to enhance coherent structures, the integration scale should be larger than the structure scale. One may couple ρ to σ e.g. by setting $\rho := 3\sigma$. Since overestimations are uncritical, setting ρ to a fixed value such as $\rho := 5$ is also a reasonable choice.

The simplest way to perform coherence-enhancing shock filtering on a *multichannel image* $(f_1(x,y), ..., f_m(x,y))^\top$ consists of applying the process channelwise. Since this would create shocks at different locations for the different channels, some synchronisation is desirable. Therefore, we use the PDE system

$$u_{it} = -\text{sign}(v_{ww}) |\nabla u_i| \qquad (i = 1, ..., m) \qquad (9)$$

where $v_{ww} := \sum_{i=1}^{m} v_{iww}$, and w is the normalised dominant eigenvector of the joint structure tensor $J_\rho(\nabla u) := K_\rho * \sum_{i=1}^{m} \nabla u_i \nabla u_i^\top$. Similar strategies are used for coherence-enhancing diffusion of multichannel images [22]. Within finite time, a piecewise constant segmentation can be observed where the segmentation borders are identical for all channels.

5   Discretisation

For the algorithmic realisation of our shock filter, Gaussian convolution is approximated in the spatial domain by discretising the Gaussian, truncating it at tree times its standard deviation and renormalising it such that the area under the truncated Gaussian sums up to 1 again. Exploiting the separability and the symmetry of the Gaussian is used for speeding up the computations.

For the structure tensor, spatial derivatives have been approximated using Sobel masks. Since the structure tensor is a 2×2 matrix, one can easily compute its eigenvalues and eigenvectors in an analytical way.

If $w = (c, s)^\top$ denotes the normalised dominant eigenvector, then v_{ww} is computed from $c^2 v_{xx} + 2cs v_{xy} + s^2 v_{yy}$, where the second-order derivatives v_{xx}, v_{xy} and v_{yy} are approximated by standard finite difference masks.

For computing the dilations and erosions, an explicit Osher-Sethian upwind scheme is used [13]. This algorithm is stable and satisfies a discrete maximum–minimum principle if the time step size restriction $\tau \leq 0.5$ is obeyed. Thus, our shock filter cannot produce any over- and undershoots.

6   Experiments

We start our experimental section by comparing the difference between the conventional shock filter (5) and coherence-enhancing shock filtering. This is illustrated with the fingerprint image in Figure 1. We observe that the directional stabilisation by means of the structure tensor allows a piecewise constant segmentation, where the coherence-enhancing shock filter closes interrupted lines without affecting semantically important singularities in the fingerprint. A conventional shock filter, on the other hand, may even widen the gaps and disconnect previously connected structures.

In Figure 2, we compare our novel shock filter with coherence-enhancing diffusion filtering [21,22]. While both filters have been designed for the processing of flow-like features, we observe that the diffusion filter acts smoothing while the shock filter has very pronounced sharpening properties. In certain applications

Fig. 1. Comparison between conventional and coherence-enhancing shock filtering. **(a) Left:** Fingerprint image, 186×186 pixels. **(b) Middle:** Stationary state using the shock filter (5) with $\sigma = 1.5$. **(c) Right:** Stationary state using coherence-enhancing shock filtering with $\sigma = 1.5$ and $\rho = 5$.

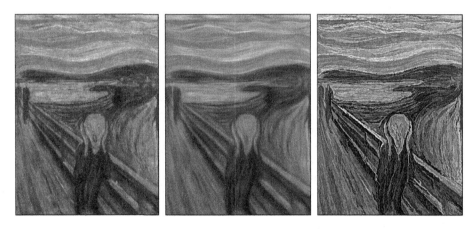

Fig. 2. Comparison between coherence-enhancing diffusion and coherence-enhancing shock filtering. **(a) Left:** Painting by Munch (The Cry, 1893; National Gallery, Oslo), 277×373 pixels. **(b) Middle:** Coherence-enhancing diffusion, $\sigma = 0.5$, $\rho = 5$, $t = 10$. **(c) Right:** Coherence-enhancing shock filtering, stationary state, $\sigma = 0.5$, $\rho = 5$. This is a colour image.

the latter one is thus an interesting alternative to coherence-enhancing diffusion filtering.

Figure 3 shows the influence of the structure scale σ. It is the main parameter of the filter and determines the resulting line thickness. Using values that are larger than the thickness of the initial flow lines, one obtains very interesting, almost artistic simplifications of flow-like images. The CPU time for filtering such a 512×512 colour image on a PC with AMD Athlon 1800+ processor is less than 10 seconds.

Fig. 3. Increasing the structure scale σ creates artistic effects. **(a) Left:** Mandrill, 512×512 pixels. **(b) Middle:** Coherence-enhancing shock filtering, $\sigma = 2$, $\rho = 5$, $t = 10$. **(c) Right:** Ditto with $\sigma = 4$. This is a colour image.

7   Summary and Conclusions

By combing the sharpening qualities of shock filters with the robust orientation estimation of the structure tensor, we have introduced a novel class of image enhancement methods: coherence-enhancing shock filters. These filters are designed for visualising flow-like structures. They inherit a number of interesting stability properties from conventional shock filters. These properties distinguish them from most Fourier- and wavelet-based enhancement methods as well as from classical methods in the spatial domain such as unsharp masking: Gibbs-like artifacts do not occur, a discrete maximum-minimum principle holds, and the total variation is not increasing. Experiments demonstrate that a piecewise constant segmentation is obtained within finite time such that there is no need to specify a stopping time. The process involves one main parameter: the structure scale σ which determines the distance between adjacent flow lines in the resulting image. Our experiments show that coherence-enhancing shock filters produce sharper results than coherence-enhancing diffusion filters, and that they outperform conventional shock filters when flow-like patterns are to be processed.

In out future work we intend to explore a number of application fields for coherence-enhancing shock filters. It can be expected that they are particularly well-suited for some computer graphics applications such as flow visualisation.

References

1. L. Alvarez and L. Mazorra. Signal and image restoration using shock filters and anisotropic diffusion. *SIAM Journal on Numerical Analysis*, 31:590–605, 1994.
2. J. Bigün, G. H. Granlund, and J. Wiklund. Multidimensional orientation estimation with applications to texture analysis and optical flow. *IEEE Transactions on Pattern Analysis and Machine Intelligence*, 13(8):775–790, Aug. 1991.
3. R. W. Brockett and P. Maragos. Evolution equations for continuous-scale morphology. In *Proc. IEEE International Conference on Acoustics, Speech and Signal Processing*, volume 3, pages 125–128, San Francisco, CA, Mar. 1992.

4. W. Förstner and E. Gülch. A fast operator for detection and precise location of distinct points, corners and centres of circular features. In *Proc. ISPRS Intercommission Conference on Fast Processing of Photogrammetric Data*, pages 281–305, Interlaken, Switzerland, June 1987.

5. G. Gilboa, N. A. Sochen, and Y. Y. Zeevi. Regularized shock filters and complex diffusion. In A. Heyden, G. Sparr, M. Nielsen, and P. Johansen, editors, *Computer Vision – ECCV 2002*, volume 2350 of *Lecture Notes in Computer Science*, pages 399–413. Springer, Berlin, 2002.

6. F. Guichard and J.-M. Morel. A note on two classical shock filters and their asymptotics. In M. Kerckhove, editor, *Scale-Space and Morphology in Computer Vision*, volume 2106 of *Lecture Notes in Computer Science*, pages 75–84. Springer, Berlin, 2001.

7. C. Höcker and G. Fehmers. Fast structural interpretation with structure-oriented filtering. *The Leading Edge*, 21(3):238–243, Mar. 2002.

8. R. Kimmel, R. Malladi, and N. Sochen. Images as embedded maps and minimal surfaces: movies, color, texture, and volumetric medical images. *International Journal of Computer Vision*, 39(2):111–129, Sept. 2000.

9. P. Kornprobst, R. Deriche, and G. Aubert. Nonlinear operators in image restoration. In *Proc. 1997 IEEE Computer Society Conference on Computer Vision and Pattern Recognition*, pages 325–330, San Juan, Puerto Rico, June 1997. IEEE Computer Society Press.

10. H. P. Kramer and J. B. Bruckner. Iterations of a non-linear transformation for enhancement of digital images. *Pattern Recognition*, 7:53–58, 1975.

11. S. Osher and L. Rudin. Shocks and other nonlinear filtering applied to image processing. In A. G. Tescher, editor, *Applications of Digital Image Processing XIV*, volume 1567 of *Proceedings of SPIE*, pages 414–431. SPIE Press, Bellingham, 1991.

12. S. Osher and L. I. Rudin. Feature-oriented image enhancement using shock filters. *SIAM Journal on Numerical Analysis*, 27:919–940, 1990.

13. S. Osher and J. A. Sethian. Fronts propagating with curvature-dependent speed: Algorithms based on Hamilton–Jacobi formulations. *Journal of Computational Physics*, 79:12–49, 1988.

14. P. Perona and J. Malik. Scale space and edge detection using anisotropic diffusion. *IEEE Transactions on Pattern Analysis and Machine Intelligence*, 12:629–639, 1990.

15. T. Preußer and M. Rumpf. Anisotropic nonlinear diffusion in flow visualization. In *Proc. 1999 IEEE Visualization Conference*, pages 223–232, San Francisco, CA, Oct. 1999.

16. A. R. Rao and B. G. Schunck. Computing oriented texture fields. *CVGIP: Graphical Models and Image Processing*, 53:157–185, 1991.

17. J. G. M. Schavemaker, M. J. T. Reinders, J. J. Gerbrands, and E. Backer. Image sharpening by morphological filtering. *Pattern Recognition*, 33:997–1012, 2000.

18. A. F. Solé, A. López, and G. Sapiro. Crease enhancement diffusion. *Computer Vision and Image Understanding*, 84:241–248, 2001.

19. F. M. Wahl. *Digitale Bildsignalverarbeitung*. Springer, Berlin, 1984.

20. J. Weickert. *Anisotropic Diffusion in Image Processing*. Teubner, Stuttgart, 1998.

21. J. Weickert. Coherence-enhancing diffusion filtering. *International Journal of Computer Vision*, 31(2/3):111–127, Apr. 1999.

22. J. Weickert. Coherence-enhancing diffusion of colour images. *Image and Vision Computing*, 17(3–4):199–210, Mar. 1999.

Spherical Decision Surfaces Using Conformal Modelling

Christian Perwass, Vladimir Banarer, and Gerald Sommer

Institut für Informatik und Praktische Mathematik
Christian-Albrechts-Universität zu Kiel
Christian-Albrechts-Platz 4, 24118 Kiel, Germany
{chp,vlb,gs}@ks.informatik.uni-kiel.de

Abstract. In this paper a special higher order neuron, the hypersphere neuron, is introduced. By embedding Euclidean space in a conformal space, hyperspheres can be expressed as vectors. The scalar product of points and spheres in conformal space, gives a measure for how far a point lies inside or outside a hypersphere. It will be shown that a hypersphere neuron may be implemented as a perceptron with two bias inputs. By using hyperspheres instead of hyperplanes as decision surfaces, a reduction in computational complexity can be achieved for certain types of problems. Furthermore, it will be shown that Multi-Layer Percerptrons (MLP) based on such neurons are similar to Radial Basis Function (RBF) networks. It is also found that such MLPs can give better results than RBF networks of the same complexity. The abilities of the proposed MLPs are demonstrated on some classical data for neural computing, as well as on real data from a particular computer vision problem.

1 Introduction

The basic idea behind a single standard perceptron is that it separates its input space into two classes by a hyperplane [13]. For most practical purposes such a linear separation is, of course, not sufficient. In general, data is to be separated into a number of classes, where each class covers a particular region in the input space. The basic idea behind classifying using a multi-layer perceptron (MLP), is to use a number of perceptrons and to combine their linear decision planes, to approximate the surfaces of the different class regions. In principle, a MLP can approximate any type of class configuration, which implies that it is an universal approximator [4,7].

However, being an universal approximator alone says nothing about the complexity a MLP would need to have in order to approximate a particular surface. In fact, depending on the structure of the data it may be advantageous to not use perceptrons but instead another type of neuron which uses a non-linear 'decision surface' to separate classes. Such neurons are called *higher-order* neurons. There has been a lot of effort to design higher-order neurons for different applications. For example, there are hyperbolic neurons [3], tensor neurons [12] and hyperbolic SOMs [14]. Typically, the more complex the decision surface a neuron has

B. Michaelis and G. Krell (Eds.): DAGM 2003, LNCS 2781, pp. 9–16, 2003.

is, the higher its computational complexity. It is hoped that a complex decision surface will allow to solve a task with fewer neurons. However, the computational complexity of each neuron should not offset this advantage.

In this paper we present a simple extension of a perceptron, such that its decision surface is not a hyperplane but a hypersphere. The representation used is taken from a conformal space representation introduced in the context of Clifford algebra [11]. The advantage of this representation is that only a standard scalar product has to be evaluated in order to decide whether an input vector is inside or outside a hypersphere. That is, the computational complexity stays low, while a non-linear decision plane is obtained. Furthermore, a hypersphere neuron with sigmoidal activation function can be regarded as a generalization of a classical RBF neuron. Multi-layer networks based on hypersphere neurons are therefore similar to RBF networks of the same complexity. This will be explained in some detail later on. The main advantages of such a hypersphere neuron over a standard perceptron are the following:

- A hypersphere with infinite radius becomes a hyperplane. Since the hypersphere representation used is homogeneous, hyperspheres with infinite radius can be represented through finite vectors. Therefore, a standard perceptron is just a special case of a hypersphere neuron.
- The VC-dimension [1] of a hypersphere neuron for a 1-dimensional input space is three and not two, as it is for a standard perceptron. However, for higher input dimensions, the VC-dimensions of a hypersphere neuron and a standard perceptron are the same.

Although the VC-dimensions of a hypersphere neuron and a standard perceptron are the same for input dimensions higher than one, it is advantageous to use a hypersphere neuron, if the classification of the data is isotropic about some point in the input space. See [2] for more details.

The remainder of this paper is structured as follows. First the representation of hyperspheres used is described in some more detail. Then some important aspects concerning the actual implementation of a hypersphere neuron in a single- and multi-layer network are discussed. The comparison to classical RBF neurons is made. Afterwards some experiments with the Iris data set and the two spirals benchmark are presented. In a further experiment the abilities of a hypersphere multi-layer perceptron as classifier are tested on some real data taken from a particular computer vision problem. Finally, some conclusions are drawn from this work.

2   The Representation of Hyperspheres

There is not enough space here to give a full treatment of the mathematics involved. Therefore, only the most important aspects will be discussed. For a more detailed introduction see [10,11].

Consider the Minkowski space $\mathbb{R}^{1,1}$ with basis $\{e_+, e_-\}$, where $e_+^2 = +1$ and $e_-^2 = -1$. The following two null-vectors can be constructed from this basis,

$e_\infty := e_- + e_+$ and $e_0 := \frac{1}{2}(e_- - e_+)$, such that $e_\infty^2 = e_0^2 = 0$ and $e_\infty \cdot e_0 = -1$. Given a n-dimensional Euclidean vector space $\mathbb{R}^n$, the conformal space $\mathbb{R}^{n+1,1} = \mathbb{R}^n \otimes \mathbb{R}^{1,1}$ can be constructed. Such a conformal space will also be denoted as $\mathbb{ME}^n \equiv \mathbb{R}^{n+1,1}$. A vector $\mathbf{x} \in \mathbb{R}^n$ may be embedded in conformal space as

$$X = \mathbf{x} + \tfrac{1}{2}\mathbf{x}^2 \, e_\infty + e_0, \tag{1}$$

such that $X^2 = 0$. It may be shown that this embedding represents the stereographic projection of $\mathbf{x} \in \mathbb{R}^n$ onto an appropriately defined projection sphere in $\mathbb{ME}^n$. Note that the embedding is also homogeneous, i.e. αX, with $\alpha \in \mathbb{R}$, represents the same vector $\mathbf{x}$ as X. In other words, any vector $A \in \mathbb{ME}^n$ that lies in the null space of X, i.e. satisfies $A \cdot X = 0$, represents the same vector $\mathbf{x}$.

The nomenclature e_0 and e_∞ is motivated by the fact that the origin of $\mathbb{R}^n$ maps to e_0 when using equation (1). Furthermore, as $|\mathbf{x}|$ with $\mathbf{x} \in \mathbb{R}^n$ tends to infinity, the dominant term of the mapping of $\mathbf{x}$ into $\mathbb{ME}^n$ is e_∞.

A null-vector in $\mathbb{ME}^n$ whose e_0 component is unity, is called *normalized*. Given the normalized null-vector X from equation (1) and $Y = \mathbf{y} + \frac{1}{2}\mathbf{y}^2 e_\infty + e_0$, it can be shown that $X \cdot Y = -\frac{1}{2}(\mathbf{x} - \mathbf{y})^2$. That is, the scalar product of two null-vectors in conformal space, gives a distance measure of the corresponding Euclidean vectors. This forms the foundation for the representation of hyperspheres. A normalized hypersphere $S \in \mathbb{ME}^n$ with center $Y \in \mathbb{ME}^n$ and radius $r \in \mathbb{R}$ is given by $S = Y - \frac{1}{2}r^2 e_\infty$, since then

$$X \cdot S = X \cdot Y - \tfrac{1}{2}r^2 \, X \cdot e_\infty = -\tfrac{1}{2}(\mathbf{x} - \mathbf{y})^2 + \tfrac{1}{2}r^2, \tag{2}$$

and thus $X \cdot S = 0$ iff $|\mathbf{x} - \mathbf{y}| = |r|$. That is, the null space of S consists of all those vectors $X \in \mathbb{ME}^n$ that represent vectors in $\mathbb{R}^n$ that lie on a hypersphere. It can also be seen that the scalar product of a null-vector X with a normalized hypersphere S is negative, zero or positive, if X is outside, on or inside the hypersphere. Scaling the normalized hypersphere vector S with a scalar does not change the hypersphere it represents. However, scaling S with a negative scalar interchanges the signs that indicate inside and outside of the hypersphere.

The change in sign of $X \cdot S$ between X being inside and outside the hypersphere, may be used to classify a data vector $\mathbf{x} \in \mathbb{R}^n$ embedded in $\mathbb{ME}^n$. That is, by interpreting the components of S as the weights of a perceptron, and embedding the data points into $\mathbb{ME}^n$, a perceptron can be constructed whose decision plane is a hypersphere.

From the definition of a hypersphere in $\mathbb{ME}^n$ it follows that a null-vector $X \in \mathbb{ME}^n$ may be interpreted as a sphere with zero radius. Similarly, a vector in $\mathbb{ME}^n$ with no e_0 component represents a hypersphere with infinite radius, i.e. a hyperplane.

3   Implementation

The propagation function of a hypersphere neuron may actually be implemented as a standard scalar product, by representing the input data as follows. Let a data vector $\mathbf{x} = (x_1, x_2, \ldots, x_n) \in \mathbb{R}^n$ be embedded in $\mathbb{R}^{n+2}$ (*not* $\mathbb{ME}^n$) as $X = (x_1, \ldots, x_n, -1, -\frac{1}{2}\mathbf{x}^2) \in \mathbb{R}^{n+2}$. Then, representing a hypersphere $S = \mathbf{c} + \frac{1}{2}(\mathbf{c}^2 - r^2)e_\infty + e_0 \in \mathbb{ME}^n$ in $\mathbb{R}^{n+2}$ as $S = (c_1, \ldots, c_n, \frac{1}{2}(\mathbf{c}^2 - r^2), 1)$, one finds that $X \cdot S = \mathbf{X} \cdot \mathbf{S}$. During the training phase of a hypersphere neuron, the components of $\mathbf{S}$ are regarded as independent, such that $\mathbf{S}$ may simply be written as $\mathbf{S} = (s_1, \ldots, s_{n+2})$.

Therefore, a hypersphere neuron may be regarded as a standard perceptron with a second 'bias' component. Of course, the input data must be of a particular form. That is, after embedding the input data in $\mathbb{R}^{n+2}$ appropriately, a decision plane in $\mathbb{R}^{n+2}$ represents a decision hypersphere in $\mathbb{R}^n$. In this respect, it is similar to a kernel method, where the embedding of the data in a different space is implicit in the scalar product.

The computational complexity of a hypersphere neuron is as follows. Apart from the standard bias, which is simply set to unity, the magnitude of the input data vector has to be evaluated. However, for a multi-layer hypersphere network, this magnitude only has to be evaluated once for each layer. In terms of complexity this compares to adding an additional perceptron to each layer in a MLP.

The multi-layer perceptron based on hypersphere neurons (MLHP) can be interpreted as an extended RBF network with an equal number of neurons.

Let the activation function of the hypersphere neuron be the sigmoidal function $\sigma(\lambda, z) = (1 + \exp(-\lambda z))^{-1}$. In general a hypersphere neuron represents a non-normalized hypersphere. Therefore the propagation function becomes $X \cdot \kappa S$, $\kappa \in \mathbb{R}$ (cf. equation (2)), see [2] for more details. Thus the output y of the neuron can be written as

$$ y = \sigma(\lambda, (X \cdot \kappa S)) = \sigma(\lambda, -\tfrac{1}{2}\kappa(\|\mathbf{x} - \mathbf{c}\|_2^2 - r^2)) = \frac{1}{1 + \exp(\frac{1}{2}\lambda\kappa(\|\mathbf{x} - \mathbf{c}\|_2^2 - r^2))} \qquad (3) $$

This equation shows, that the output is an isotropic function similar to a Gauss with extremum at $\mathbf{x} = \mathbf{c}$ and asymptotical behavior for $\|\mathbf{x} - \mathbf{c}\|_2 \to \infty$.

For positive values of κ, y is positive for points lying within the hypersphere and negative for points lying outside the hypersphere. For negative values of κ we obtain the inverse behavior.

Not only the position of the extremum of this functions (center of hypersphere) but also the size of the support area (radius of hypersphere) can be learned.

4   Experiments

In an initial experiment, the simplest form of a multi-layer hypersphere perceptron, a single-layer perceptron, was tested on Fisher's Iris data set [6]. This set consists of 150 four-dimensional data vectors, which are classified into three classes. Visualizing the data [8] shows that one class can be separated linearly from the other two. The two remaining classes are, however, somewhat entangled. The data set was separated into a training data set of 39 randomly chosen data vectors and a test data set of the remaining 111 data vectors. A standard single-layer perceptron (SLP) and a single-layer hypersphere perceptron (SLHP) were then trained on the training data set in two different configurations. In the first configuration (C1) the network consisted of one layer with three neurons, each representing one class. The classes were coded by 3 three-dimensional vectors $(1, 0, 0)$, $(0, 1, 0)$ and $(0, 0, 1)$, respectively. In the second configuration (C2) there was a single layer with only two neurons, whereby the three classes were coded in a binary code. That is, the output of the two neurons had to be $(1, 0)$, $(0, 1)$ and $(1, 1)$, respectively, to indicate the three classes.

Table 1 shows the number of *incorrectly* classified data vectors after training in configuration C1 and C2, respectively, for the training and the test data set using the SLP, the SLHP and RBF networks.

Table 1. Comparison of classification results for SLHP, SLP and RBF on IRIS data.

Network	C1 Train. Data	C1 Test Data	Network	C2 Train. Data	C2 Test Data
SLHP	0	7	SLHP	0	7
SLP	0	2	SLP	9	31
RBF	2	11	RBF	10	20

It can be seen that both the SLP and the SLHP in C1, classify the training data perfectly. However, the SLP is somewhat better in the classification of the test data set. For C2, where only two neurons were used, the SLP cannot give an error free classification of the training data set. This is in contrast to the SLHP where an error free classification is still possible. Also for the test data set the SLHP gives much better results than the SLP. In fact, the SLHP does equally well with two and with three neurons. The results in C2 basically show that the data set cannot be separated into three classes by two hyperplanes. However, such a separation is possible with two hyperspheres. Although RBF networks contain two layers in contrast to the tested single layered models, they classify worse with the same amount of neurons in the hidden layer. In this experiment one needs at least ten neurons in the hidden layer of a RBF network to achieve similar results as with the SLHP.

In the second experiment the two spirals benchmark [5] was used, to compare a MLHP with a classical MLP and a RBF network. The task of this benchmark is to learn to discriminate between two sets of training points, which lie on two distinct spirals in the 2D plane. These spirals coil three times around the origin and around one another. This can be a very difficult task for back-propagation networks and comparable networks [9,15].

Figure 1 shows the results of training for two-layer networks (i.e. one hidden layer) with classical perceptrons (MLP), hypersphere neurons (MLHP) and a RBF network. MLP and MLHP were trained with a backpropagation-algorithm. For each kind of network the minimal amount of neurons needed for almost

Fig. 1. Two spirals benchmark. Visualization of nearly perfect classification for different network types. White and black colors represent the two classes, that are to be learned. Gray color represents an area of unreliable decision. Left - MLHP with 10 neurons in hidden layer; Middle - MLP with 60 neurons in hidden layer; Right - RBF with 80 neurons in hidden layer.

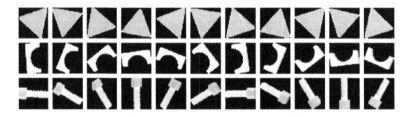

Fig. 2. Each object ist automatically detected, cropped and rescaled to a size of 35×35 pixels.

perfect classification is taken for the visualization. The MLHP with 10 neurons in the hidden layer can do perfect classification (100%). To achieve the same result a RBF network with 80 neurons in the hidden layer is required. A SLP with 60 neurons in the hidden layer can do nearly perfect classification (97%).

In the third experiment the classification abilities of MLHPs were tested on real data. The goal of this experiment was to associate an object (top view) with one of three given classes: screw, bridge or triangle. The data was coded in the following way.

In a preprocessing stage for each object that was to be classified, the data was generated from 360 top views of the object, whereby the object was rotated in one degree steps. The object was automatically detected, cropped and rescaled to a size of 35×35 pixels. Some views of the objects used are shown in figure 2. For further processing the images were interpreted as vectors of length 1225.

For each set of 360 data vectors, a PCA was performed (figure 3). Then all data vectors from all three classes were projected onto the first three principal components of the bridge. The resulting three dimensional data is visualized in figure 4. The associated classes were coded in a two-dimensional binary code $(1,0)$, $(0,1)$ and $(1,1)$. From 1080 data vectors, 360 were taken for training and 720 for testing. Different types of networks were tested.

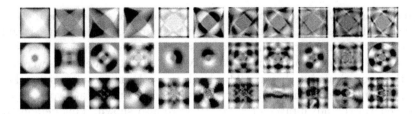

Fig. 3. Mean value and first ten principle components for triangle (top), bridge (middle) and screw (bottom).

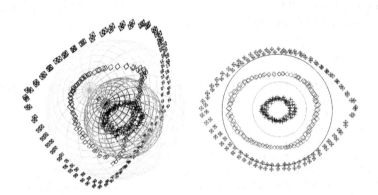

Fig. 4. Left – 3D-visualization of the classification (crosses - triangle, diamonds - bridge, crossed diamonds - screw). The two spheres represent the decision surfaces of the hypersphere neurons. Right – Projecting the data onto two principle components, demonstrates that each of the three classes builds a compact area in the input space and can be easily separated by two hyperspheres.

The best results (in relation to number of neurons) were achieved by a MLHP with two neurons in the hidden layer. For similar results a MLP with three neurons in the hidden layer or a RBF network with 8 neurons was necessary. This result was expected due to the compactness of the classes, that had to be separated.

5   Conclusions

In this paper a higher-order neuron was presented which has the effect of placing a decision hypersphere in the input space, whereas a standard perceptron uses a hyperplane to linearly separate the input data. It was shown that a hypersphere neuron may also represent a hypersphere with infinite radius, i.e. a hyperplane, and thus includes the case of a standard perceptron. Advantages that may be gained by using hypersphere neurons, are the possibility to classify compact regions with a single neuron in n-dimensions, while the computational complexity is kept low. A single-layer hypersphere perceptron was tested and compared to a standard single-layer perceptron on the Iris data of R.A. Fisher. The data could be successfully classified with two hypersphere neurons. At least three standard neurons or a RBF network with ten neurons in the hidden layer were necessary to achieve similar results. Furthermore MLP, MLHP and RBF networks were tested with the two spirals benchmark. Also in this case better results were achieved with hypersphere neurons than with a classical MLP or RBF network. In a real data scenario the advantages of a MLHP were also shown. This demonstrates that using hypersphere neurons is advantageous for certain types of data.

Acknowledgment. This work has been supported by DFG Graduiertenkolleg No. 357 and by EC Grant IST-2001-3422 (VISATEC).

References

1. Y. S. Abu-Mostafa. The Vapnik-Chervonenkis dimension: Information versus complexity in learning. *Neural Computation*, 1(3):312–317, 1989.
2. V. Banarer, C. Perwass, and G. Sommer. The hypersphere neuron. In *11th European Symposium on Artificial Neural Networks, ESANN 2003, Bruges*, pages 469–474. d-side publications, Evere, Belgium, 2003.
3. S. Buchholz and G. Sommer. A hyperbolic multilayer perceptron. In S.-I. Amari, C.L. Giles, M. Gori, and V. Piuri, editors, *International Joint Conference on Neural Networks, IJCNN 2000, Como, Italy*, volume 2, pages 129–133. IEEE Computer Society Press, 2000.
4. G. Cybenko. Approximation by superposition of a sigmoidal function. *Mathematics of Control, Signals and Systems*, 2:303–314, 1989.
5. S. E. Fahlman and C. Lebiere. The cascade-correlation learning architecture. In D. S. Touretzky, editor, *Advances in Neural Information Processing Systems*, volume 2, pages 524–532, Denver 1989, 1990. Morgan Kaufmann, San Mateo.
6. R. A. Fisher. The use of multiple measurements in axonomic problems. *Annals of Eugenics 7*, pages 179–188, 1936.
7. K. Hornik. Approximation capabilities of multilayer feedforward neural networks. *Neural Networks*, 4:251–257, 1990.
8. L. Hoyle. http://www.ku.edu/cwis/units/IPPBR/java/iris/irisglyph.html.
9. K.J. Lang and M.J. Witbrock. Learning to tell two spirals apart. In D.S. Touretzky, G.E. Hinton, and T. Sejnowski, editors, *Connectionist Models Summer School*. Morgan Kaufmann, 1988.
10. H. Li, D. Hestenes, and A. Rockwood. Generalized homogeneous coordinates for computational geometry. In G. Sommer, editor, *Geometric Computing with Clifford Algebra*, pages 27–52. Springer-Verlag, 2001.
11. H. Li, D. Hestenes, and A. Rockwood. A universal model for conformal geometries. In G. Sommer, editor, *Geometric Computing with Clifford Algebra*, pages 77–118. Springer-Verlag, 2001.
12. H. Lipson and H.T. Siegelmann. Clustering irregular shapes using high-order neurons. *Neural Computation*, 12(10):2331–2353, 2000.
13. M. Minsky and S. Papert. *Perceptrons.* Cambridge: MIT Press, 1969.
14. H. Ritter. Self-organising maps in non-Euclidean spaces. In E. Oja and S. Kaski, editors, *Kohonen Maps*, pages 97–108. Amer Elsevier, 1999.
15. A. Wieland and S. E. Fahlman. http://www.ibiblio.org/pub/academic/computer-science/neural-networks/programs/bench/two-spirals, 1993.

Median Filtering of Tensor-Valued Images

Martin Welk, Christian Feddern, Bernhard Burgeth, and Joachim Weickert

Mathematical Image Analysis Group
Faculty of Mathematics and Computer Science, Bldg. 27
Saarland University, 66041 Saarbrücken, Germany
{welk,feddern,burgeth,weickert}@mia.uni-saarland.de
http://www.mia.uni-saarland.de

Abstract. Novel matrix-valued imaging techniques such as diffusion tensor magnetic resonance imaging require the development of edge-preserving nonlinear filters. In this paper we introduce a median filter for such tensor-valued data. We show that it inherits a number of favourable properties from scalar-valued median filtering, and we present experiments on synthetic as well as on real-world images that illustrate its performance.

1 Introduction

Diffusion tensor magnetic resonance imaging (DT-MRI) is a recent medical image acquisition technique that measures the diffusion characteristics of water molecules in tissue. The resulting diffusion tensor field is a positive semidefinite matrix field that provides valuable information for brain connectivity studies as well as for multiple sclerosis or stroke diagnosis [15]. These matrix-valued data are often polluted with noise, hence it is necessary to develop filters to remove this noise without losing too much valuable information. Similar problems also occur in other situations where matrix-valued data are to be smoothed: Tensor fields have shown their use as a common description tool in image analysis, segmentation and grouping [9]. This also includes widespread applications of the so-called structure tensor (Förstner interest operator, second moment matrix, scatter matrix) [8] in fields ranging from motion analysis to texture segmentation. Moreover, a number of scientific applications require to process tensor fields: The tensor concept is a common physical description of anisotropic behaviour in solid mechanics and civil engineering, where stress-strain relationships, inertia tensors, diffusion tensors, and permitivity tensors are used.

For scalar-valued images, the median filter is one of the most frequently used structure-preserving smoothing methods, since it is simple, robust against outliers, and preserves discontinuities. The goal of this paper is to introduce a median filter for matrix-valued images where the matrices are positive (semi-)definite. To this end we will start with a review of the properties of the scalar-valued median in Section 2. In Section 3, we will introduce a median for tensor fields as a solution of a minimisation problem originating from a basic property of the median for scalar-valued data. Algorithmic aspects will be sketched in Section 4.

B. Michaelis and G. Krell (Eds.): DAGM 2003, LNCS 2781, pp. 17–24, 2003.

The fifth section shows experiments on synthetic and real-world images. In the final sixth section we present concluding remarks.

Related work. The search for good smoothing techniques for DT-MRI data and related tensor fields is a very recent research area. Several authors have addressed this problem by smoothing derived expressions such as the eigenvalues and eigenvectors of the diffusion tensor [16,6,17] or its fractional anisotropy [14]. Some methods that work directly on the tensor components use linear [20] or nonlinear [10] techniques that filter all channels *independently*, thus performing scalar-valued filtering again. Nonlinear regularisation methods for matrix-valued filtering with channel coupling have been proposed in [17,19]. Related nonlinear diffusion methods for tensor-valued data have led to the notion of a nonlinear structure tensor [19] that has been used for optic flow estimation [4].

There are several proposals on how to generalise the median filter to vector-valued data; see e.g. [3,13] and the references therein. To our knowledge, however, no attempts have been made so far to design median filters for tensor fields.

2   Properties of Scalar-Valued Median Filters

One of the basic tasks of statistics is the description of some arbitrary sample data $x = \{x_1, x_2, \ldots, x_n\}$ by a single number that is representative of the data. Such a number is commonly called an average. The median $\tilde{x}$ is a prominent example of a position average, in contrast to the arithmetic mean $\bar{x}$ as a computed average. The median is found by locating the place of a value in a sample series. As a measure of central tendency the median $\tilde{x}$ is the value of the middle item in a sample series when the items are ordered according to their magnitude.

It can be formally defined as that value which divides a sample series in such a way that at least 50 percent of the items are equal to or less than it and at least 50 percent of the items are equal to or greater than it. This alludes to the origin of the median as a so-called 50 percent quantile. It is clear that the median depends heavily on the existence of a total order for the sample items. If the number of items in a sample is odd, the median is the value of the middle term. If the number of items in a sample is even, it is usually chosen as the arithmetic mean of the two middle items (though any other average would be formally acceptable). Thus, for an ordered sample with $x_1 \leq x_2 \leq \ldots \leq x_n$, the median is defined as

$$\tilde{x} := \text{med}(x_1, \ldots, x_n) := \begin{cases} x_k & \text{for } n = 2k - 1, \\ \frac{1}{2}(x_k + x_{k+1}) & \text{for } n = 2k. \end{cases} \tag{1}$$

Typical for a position average, the median is highly robust with respect to outliers of the sample. This makes median filtering the method of choice when impulse noise such as salt-and-pepper noise is present, but it is equally popular for other types of noise.

Median filtering in signal processing goes back to Tukey [18]. In image processing, median filtering is usually based on considering a neighbourhood of size

$(2k + 1) \times (2k + 1)$ of some pixel. Median filtering may be iterated. In this case one usually observes that after a relatively small number of iterations, the result becomes stationary (so-called root signal). It is easy to see that median filters preserve straight edges, while they round off corners. For more properties of median filters and their numerous modifications we refer to monographs on statistics [5,11] and nonlinear image processing [7,12].

The median has a very interesting minimisation property: The sum of absolute deviations from the median is smaller than the sum of the absolute deviations from any other point:

$$\sum_{i=1}^{n} |x_i - x| \geq \sum_{i=1}^{n} |x_i - \tilde{x}| = \min. \tag{2}$$

This property has been used in [2,1] to generalise median filters to vector-valued data. It will also be essential for our design of matrix-valued median filters.

3 A Median for Matrix-Valued Images

The definition of a median for matrix-valued functions should inherit as many properties of the standard median described above as possible. We restrict our attention to real 2×2-matrices $A \in \mathbb{R}^{2 \times 2}$ but the extension to larger matrices is straight forward.

We recall the definition of the Frobenius norm $\|A\|$ of a matrix $A \in \mathbb{R}^{2 \times 2}$:

$$\|A\| = \left\| \begin{pmatrix} a_{11} \; a_{12} \\ a_{12} \; a_{22} \end{pmatrix} \right\| := \sqrt{\sum_{i,j=1}^{2} a_{ij}^2}. \tag{3}$$

We use this norm to define a median of an odd number of sample items.

Definition: *The median of the set of matrices $\{A_i : i = 1, \ldots, n\}$ is the matrix $\tilde{A}$ which solves the minimisation problem*

$$\tilde{A} := \underset{X}{\operatorname{argmin}} \sum_{i=1}^{n} \|A_i - X\|. \tag{4}$$

The solution of this minimisation problem is an element of the convex hull of the matrices $\{A_i : i = 1, \ldots, n\}$. If these matrices are positive (semi-)definite, then the median is again a positive (semi-)definite matrix since the set of all such matrices is convex.

There is a new property for the median of a sample of matrices: the median should be rotationally invariant. The matrix

$$R(\varphi) := \begin{pmatrix} \cos\varphi \; -\sin\varphi \\ \sin\varphi \; \cos\varphi \end{pmatrix} \tag{5}$$

describes a rotation with angle $\varphi \in [0, \pi]$ and the requirement of rotational invariance amounts to the equality

$$\text{med}(R(\varphi)A_1 R^\top(\varphi), \dots, R(\varphi)A_n R^\top(\varphi)) = R(\varphi)\,\text{med}(A_1, \dots, A_n)\,R^\top(\varphi) \quad (6)$$

for any $\varphi \in [0, \pi]$ and any choice of matrices $A_1, \dots, A_n$. This property is clearly desirable from the practical point of view, although it has no counterpart in case of scalar-valued data. The median induced by the minimisation problem inherits the rotational invariance of the Frobenius norm:

$$\sum_{i=1}^n \|R(\varphi)AR^\top(\varphi) - R(\varphi)XR^\top(\varphi)\| = \sum_{i=1}^n \|A - X\| \quad (7)$$

holds for all X and also for the minimising $\tilde{A}$. Hence, $\tilde{A} = \text{med}(A_1, \dots, A_n)$ is independent of $R(\varphi)$.

4   Algorithmic Aspects

When computing the median of a set of matrices as defined here, one problem has to be solved. Each of the functions $\|A_i - X\|$ in the definition is differentiable except in A_i itself. Thus their sum is also differentiable except in the matrices of the given set. It is therefore an obvious idea to use a gradient descent method. Unfortunately the gradient vector $\nabla\|A_i - X\|$ has the same length everywhere. Although $-\nabla\|A_i - X\|$ always points in the direction of A_i, it contains no information about the distance to A_i. In the same way the gradient of the sum lacks information on the distance to the minimum. We overcome this problem by implementing a step size control based on the over- and undershoots encountered in the subsequent iteration steps.

The algorithm therefore works as follows. First we find the A_j for which $\sum_{i=1}^n \|A_i - A_j\|$ takes its minimal value within the given set. For that A_j, we compute $\nabla \sum_{i \neq j} \|A_i - A_j\|$. If this gradient is of length 1 or smaller, then $X = A_j$ minimises

$$S(X) = \sum_{i=1}^n \|A_i - X\| \quad (8)$$

and is therefore the median. Otherwise we proceed by gradient descent using the gradient of $S(X)$. After each step in which we change X to

$$X' = X - s\,\nabla S(X) \qquad (s > 0), \quad (9)$$

we compare $\nabla S(X)$ with the projection of $\nabla S(X')$ onto $\nabla S(X)$. This provides an estimate for over- or undershoots which allows us to adapt s for the subsequent step and, in case of extreme overshoots, even to roll back the last step.

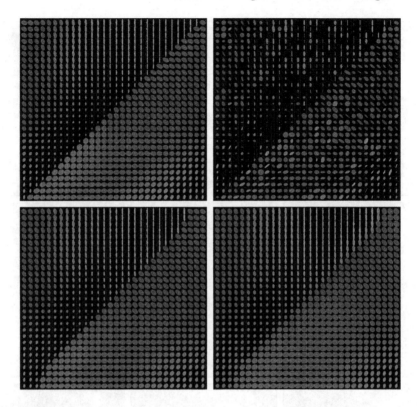

Fig. 1. Edge preservation and noise robustness of matrix-valued median filtering. **(a) Top Left:** Tensor field with a discontinuity. The matrices are visualised by ellipses. Colour indicates orientation and brightness encodes eccentricity. **(b) Top Right:** Degraded version of (a) where the eigenvalues are perturbed by Gaussian noise. **(c) Bottom Left:** Median filtering of (a) shows the discontinuity-preserving qualities (5×5 median, 5 iterations). **(d) Bottom Right:** Median filtering of (b) illustrates the denoising capabilities (5×5 median, 5 iterations).

5   Experiments

Symmetric positive definite matrices $A \in \mathbb{R}^{2 \times 2}$ can be visualised as ellipses

$$\{x \in \mathbb{R}^2 : x^\top A^{-2} x = 1\}. \tag{10}$$

We prefer this representation using the matrix A^{-2} rather than A, since then the larger (smaller) eigenvalue corresponds directly to the semi-major (-minor) axis of the displayed ellipse.

In Figure 1 we illustrate the discontinuity-preserving properties of matrix-valued median filtering by applying it to a synthetic data set that contains a discontinuity. We observe that five iterations of 5×5 median filtering hardly affects this discontinuity. Almost the same results can be obtained when noise

22   M. Welk et al.

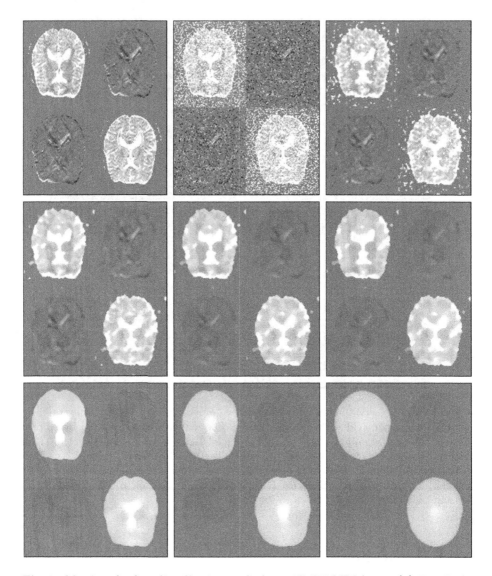

Fig. 2. Matrix-valued median filtering applied to a 2D DT-MRI frame. **(a) Top Left:** The four channels (x,x), (x,y), (y,x), and (y,y) create four subimages of size 92×108. **(b) Top Middle:** Degraded version of (a) where uniform noise is used. **(c) Top Right:** Median filtering of (b) with 1 iteration of a 3×3 median. **(d) Middle Left:** Ditto, 5 iterations. **(e) Middle Middle:** 25 iterations. **(f) Middle Right:** 125 iterations. Note the similarity to (e). **(g) Bottom Left:** 25 iterations with a 5×5 median. **(h) Bottom Middle:** Ditto, 7×7 median. **(i) Bottom Right:** 9×9 median.

is present which perturbs the eigenvalues of the matrix. This illustrates that the median filter inherits its high robustness against outliers from its scalar-valued counterpart. We observe that at the image boundary, the location of the discontinuity is shifted. This effect has been caused by imposing reflecting boundary conditions. This symmetry constraint encourages structures that are perpendicular to the boundary, since deviations from the perpendicular behaviour create corner-like structures.

The behaviour of matrix-valued median filtering on real-world images is studied in Figure 2. In this case we have extracted a 2D frame from a 3D DT-MRI data set of a human head and restricted ourselves to four channels in this plane. 30 % of all data have been replaced by noise matrices. Their angle of the eigensystem was uniformly distributed in $[0, \pi]$, and their eigenvalues are uniformly distributed in the range $[0, 127]$. We observe that the noise robustness and discontinuity preservation that has already been observed in Figure 1 is also present in this case. Moreover, Figure 2(f) suggests that root signals also exist in the matrix-valued case. As can be expected, increasing the stencil size leads to a more pronounced filtering.

6   Conclusions

In this paper we have extended the notion of median filtering to the case of matrix-valued data sets. This has been achieved by seeking the matrix that minimises the sum of the distances to the other sample items in the Frobenius norm. Experiments on synthetic and real-world tensor fields show that the resulting median filter inherits important properties from its scalar-valued counterpart: It is robust against outliers and it preserves discontinuities. In our future work we plan to generalise other nonlinear filters in order to make them applicable to tensor field filtering.

Acknowledgements. We are grateful to Anna Vilanova i Bartrolí (Biomedical Imaging Group, TU Eindhoven) and Carola van Pul (Maxima Medical Center, Eindhoven) for providing us with the DT-MRI data set and for discussing questions concerning data conversion. Susanne Biehl has written our conversion tool and Rico Philipp has developed our tensor visualisation software.

References

1. J. Astola, P. Haavisto, and Y. Neuvo. Vector median filters. *Proceedings of the IEEE*, 78(4):678–689, 1990.
2. T. L. Austin, Jr. An approximation to the point of minimum aggregate distance. *Metron*, 19:10–21, 1959.
3. V. Barnett. The ordering of multivariate data. *Journal of the Royal Statistical Society A*, 139(3):318–355, 1976.
4. T. Brox and J. Weickert. Nonlinear matrix diffusion for optic flow estimation. In L. Van Gool, editor, *Pattern Recognition*, volume 2449 of *Lecture Notes in Computer Science*, pages 446–453. Springer, Berlin, 2002.

5. Y. Chou. *Statistical Analysis*. Holt, Reinehart and Winston, London, 1969.
6. O. Coulon, D. C. Alexander, and S. A. Arridge. A regularization scheme for diffusion tensor magnetic resonance images. In M. F. Insana and R. M. Leahy, editors, *Information Processing in Medical Imaging – IPMI 2001*, volume 2082 of *Lecture Notes in Computer Science*, pages 92–105. Springer, Berlin, 2001.
7. E. R. Dougherty and J. Astola, editors. *Nonlinear Filters for Image Processing*. SPIE Press, Bellingham, 1999.
8. W. Förstner and E. Gülch. A fast operator for detection and precise location of distinct points, corners and centres of circular features. In *Proc. ISPRS Intercommission Conference on Fast Processing of Photogrammetric Data*, pages 281–305, Interlaken, Switzerland, June 1987.
9. G. H. Granlund and H. Knutsson. *Signal Processing for Computer Vision*. Kluwer, Dordrecht, 1995.
10. K. Hahn, S. Pigarin, and B. Pütz. Edge preserving regularization and tracking for diffusion tensor imaging. In W. J. Niessen and M. A. Viergever, editors, *Medical Image Computing and Computer-Assisted Intervention – MICCAI 2001*, volume 2208 of *Lecture Notes in Computer Science*, pages 195–203. Springer, Berlin, 2001.
11. J. Hartung. *Statistik*. R. Oldenbourg Verlag, München, 4 edition, 1985.
12. R. Klette and P. Zamperoni. *Handbook of Image Processing Operators*. Wiley, New York, 1996.
13. A. Koschan and M. Abidi. A comparison of median filter techniques for noise removal in color images. In *Proc. Seventh German Workshop on Color Image Processing*, pages 69–79, Erlangen, Germany, Oct. 2001.
14. G. J. M. Parker, J. A. Schnabel, M. R. Symms, D. J. Werring, and G. J. Barker. Nonlinear smoothing for reduction of systematic and random errors in diffusion tensor imaging. *Journal of Magnetic Resonance Imaging*, 11:702–710, 2000.
15. C. Pierpaoli, P. Jezzard, P. J. Basser, A. Barnett, and G. Di Chiro. Diffusion tensor MR imaging of the human brain. *Radiology*, 201(3):637–648, Dec. 1996.
16. C. Poupon, J. Mangin, V. Frouin, J. Régis, F. Poupon, M. Pachot-Clouard, D. Le Bihan, and I. Bloch. Regularization of MR diffusion tensor maps for tracking brain white matter bundles. In W. M. Wells, A. Colchester, and S. Delp, editors, *Medical Image Computing and Computer-Assisted Intervention – MICCAI 1998*, volume 1496 of *Lecture Notes in Computer Science*, pages 489–498. Springer, Berlin, 1998.
17. D. Tschumperlé and R. Deriche. Diffusion tensor regularization with contraints preservation. In *Proc. 2001 IEEE Computer Society Conference on Computer Vision and Pattern Recognition*, volume 1, pages 948–953, Kauai, HI, Dec. 2001. IEEE Computer Society Press.
18. J. W. Tukey. *Exploratory Data Analysis*. Addison–Wesley, Menlo Park, 1971.
19. J. Weickert and T. Brox. Diffusion and regularization of vector- and matrix-valued images. In M. Z. Nashed and O. Scherzer, editors, *Inverse Problems, Image Analysis, and Medical Imaging*, volume 313 of *Contemporary Mathematics*, pages 251–268. AMS, Providence, 2002.
20. C. Westin, S. E. Maier, B. Khidhir, P. Everett, F. A. Jolesz, and R. Kikinis. Image processing for diffusion tensor magnetic resonance imaging. In C. Taylor and A. Colchester, editors, *Medical Image Computing and Computer-Assisted Intervention – MICCAI 1999*, volume 1679 of *Lecture Notes in Computer Science*, pages 441–452. Springer, Berlin, 1999.

Edge and Junction Detection with an Improved Structure Tensor

Ullrich Köthe

Cognitive Systems Group, University of Hamburg,
Vogt-Köln-Str. 30, D-22527 Hamburg, Germany

Abstract. We describe three modifications to the structure tensor approach to low-level feature extraction. We first show that the structure tensor must be represented at a higher resolution than the original image. Second, we propose a non-linear filter for structure tensor computation that avoids undesirable blurring. Third, we introduce a method to simultaneously extract edge and junction information. Examples demonstrate significant improvements in the quality of the extracted features.

1 Introduction

Since the pioneering work of Förstner [3] and Harris and Stevens [5], the structure tensor has become a useful tool for low-level feature analysis. It gained high popularity for corner detection (see [12] for a review), but applications in edge detection [4], texture analysis [10] and optic flow [9] have also been reported.

However, despite the popularity, applications of the structure tensor for edge and junction detection are facing a number of problems. First, we are showing that the standard method for structure tensor calculation violates Shannon's sampling theorem. Thus small features may get lost, and aliasing may occur. Second, to calculate structure tensors from gradient vectors, spatial averaging is performed by means of linear filters (e.g. Gaussians). The resulting blurring is not adapted to the local feature arrangement and orientation, which may cause nearby features to diffuse into each other. Third, cornerness measures derived from the structure tensor have rather low localization accuracy [12].

A more fundamental problem is the integration of edge and junction detection. From topology we know that a complete boundary description must necessarily incorporate both edges and junctions [7]. Usually, edges and corners/junctions are detected independently. This makes the integration problem quite difficult. Attempts to derive edges and junctions simultaneously from the structure tensor [5,4] have not been very successful. The difficulties are partly caused by the other problems mentioned above, but also stem from the lack of a good method for the simultaneous detection of both feature types.

In this paper we propose three improvements to the structure tensor approach that address the aforementioned problems: we use a higher sampling rate to avoid aliasing; we describe a non-linear spatial averaging filter to improve corner localization and to prevent nearby features from merging; and we develop a new method for the integration of corner/junction and edge detection.

B. Michaelis and G. Krell (Eds.): DAGM 2003, LNCS 2781, pp. 25–32, 2003.

2   The Structure Tensor

Given an image $f(x, y)$, the structure tensor is based on the gradient of f, which is usually calculated by means of Gaussian derivative filters:

$$f_x = g_{x,\sigma} \star f, \qquad f_y = g_{y,\sigma} \star f \qquad (1)$$

where $\star$ denotes convolution, and $g_{x,\sigma}, g_{y,\sigma}$ are the spatial derivatives in x- and y-direction of a Gaussian with standard deviation σ:

$$g_\sigma(x, y) = \frac{1}{2\pi\sigma^2} e^{-\frac{x^2+y^2}{2\sigma^2}} \qquad (2)$$

The gradient tensor Q is obtained by calculating, at each point of the image, the Cartesian product of the gradient vector $(f_x, f_y)^T$ with itself.

$$Q_\sigma = \begin{pmatrix} q_{11} & q_{12} \\ q_{12} & q_{22} \end{pmatrix} = \begin{pmatrix} f_x^2 & f_x f_y \\ f_x f_y & f_y^2 \end{pmatrix} \qquad (3)$$

Spatial averaging of the entries of this tensor, usually with a Gaussian filter, then leads to the structure tensor:

$$S_{\sigma',\sigma} = (s_{ij}), \qquad s_{ij} = g_{\sigma'} \star q_{ij} \qquad (i, j \in \{1, 2\}) \qquad (4)$$

σ' is the scale of spatial averaging. Averaging is necessary because the plain gradient tensor has only one non-zero eigenvalue and thus represents only intrinsically 1-dimensional features (edges). Spatial averaging distributes this information over a neighborhood, and points that receive contributions from edges with different orientations will have two positive eigenvalues, which allows them to be recognized as intrinsically 2D. Cornerness is then measured by the strength of the intrinsically 2D response, for example:

$$c_1 = \frac{\det(S_{\sigma',\sigma})}{\text{tr}(S_{\sigma',\sigma})} \qquad \text{or} \qquad c_2 = \det(S_{\sigma',\sigma}) - 0.04(\text{tr}(S_{\sigma',\sigma}))^2 \qquad (5)$$

The first measure is commonly known as *Förstner's operator* [3], although it was independently proposed by several authors. The second one originates from Harris and Stevens [5] and is called *corner response function*. Rohr [11] later simplified these measures by searching for local maxima of the determinant alone.

3   Improvement I: Correct Sampling

Let us assume that the original image $f(x, y)$ was properly sampled at the Nyquist rate. Setting the pixel distance $\lambda_N = 1$ in the spatial domain, this means that f must be band-limited with cut-off frequency $\omega_N = \pi$:

$$|\omega_1|, |\omega_2| \geq \pi \Rightarrow F(\omega_1, \omega_2) = 0 \qquad (6)$$

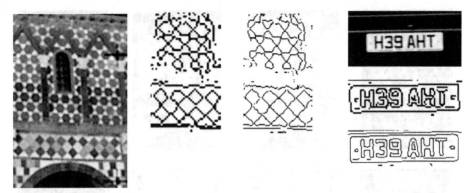

Fig. 1. Original images and their Canny edges at the original and doubled resolutions. The small white tiles in the left image have a diameter of about 3 pixels. Characters in the license plate have a line width of 2 pixels. More examples can be found in [6].

where F denotes the Fourier transform of f, and ω_1, ω_2 are the frequency coordinates. Convolution of f with Gaussian derivative filters corresponds to a multiplication of the spectrum F with the Fourier transforms G_x, G_y of the filters. Since Gaussian derivatives are not band-limited, the derivative images f_x and f_y are still band-limited with $\omega_N = \pi$. Next, we calculate the Cartesian product of the gradient vector with itself. Pointwise multiplication of two functions in the spatial domain corresponds to convolution in the Fourier domain:

$$f_1 f_2 \quad \circ\!\!-\!\!\bullet \quad F_1 \star F_2 \qquad (7)$$

Convolution of two spectra with equal band width *doubles the band width*. Therefore, in order to avoid aliasing and information loss, the elements of the gradient tensor must be represented with *half the sample distance* of the original image. Surprisingly, this important fact has been overlooked so far. As we will see, correct sampling leads to significant improvements in the quality of the edges and corners obtained later on. Oversampling is best realised directly during the calculation of the derivative images. Consider the definition of the convolution of a discrete image f with an analog filter kernel g:

$$(f \star g)(x,y) = \sum_{i,j} f(i,j) g(x-i, y-j) \qquad (8)$$

Despite f being discrete, the right-hand side of this equation is an analog function that can be evaluated at arbitrary points (x,y). We obtain an oversampled derivative image by evaluating $f \star g_x$ and $f \star g_y$ at both integer and half-integer positions.

The problem of insufficient sample density is not limited to structure tensor based methods, it affects all algorithms that take products of derivatives. In fig. 1 we compare edges detected with Canny's algorithm [2] at the original and doubled resolutions. The differences in quality are clearly visible. Of course, oversampling is not necessary if the original image does not contain fine scale structure.

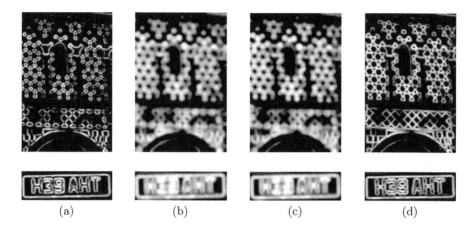

(a)   (b)   (c)   (d)

Fig. 2. (a) Gradient magnitude at original resolution; (b) trace of structure tensor – original resolution, linear averaging; (c) trace of structure tensor – doubled resolution, linear averaging; (d) trace of structure tensor – doubled resolution, non-linear averaging

4   Improvement II: Non-linear Spatial Integration

The gradient tensor has only one non-zero eigenvalue and thus only represents intrinsically 1-dimensional features (edges). Spatial averaging, usually with Gaussian filters, distributes this information over a neighborhood. Unfortunately, location independent filters do not only perform the desirable integration of multiple edge responses into corner/junction responses, but also lead to undesirable blurring of structure information: If two parallel edges are close to each other, they will be merged into a single edge response, and the narrow region between them is lost. Similarly, edges around small circular regions merge into single blobs, which are erroneously signalled as junctions. Figures 2 b and c demonstrate these undesirable effects.

The reason for the failure of the integration step lies in the linear nature of the averaging: the same rotationally symmetric averaging filter is applied everywhere. This is not what we actually want. Structure information should be distributed only *along* edges, not perpendicular to them. Hence, it is natural to use *non-linear* averaging filters. Such filters were proposed in [9] (based on unisotropic Gaussians) and [13] (based on unisotropic diffusion). In both cases the local filter shape resembles an oriented ellipse whose orientation equals the local edge direction. However, in our experiments elliptic filters did not lead to significant improvements over the traditional isotropic integration.

Therefore, we propose to use oriented filters that are shaped like *hour-glasses* rather than ellipses (fig. 3). This type of filter can be interpreted as encoding the likely continuations of a local piece of edge. Our filter was inspired by methods used in perceptual grouping, e.g. tensor voting [8] and curve indicator random fields [1]. In contrast to those, in our application short-range interaction (over

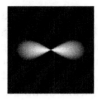

Fig. 3. Hour-glass like filter according to (9), with $\rho = 0.4$ amd $\phi_0 = 0$.

at most a few pixels) is sufficient, and there is no need for separate treatment of straight and curved edges. Thus, we can use a very simple filter design.

We define our non-linear filter kernels as polar separable functions, where the radial part is a Gaussian filter, but the angular part modulates the Gaussian so that it becomes zero perpendicular to the local edge direction $\phi_0(x, y)$:

$$
h_{\sigma', \rho}(r, \phi, \phi_0) = \frac{1}{N} e^{-\frac{r^2}{2\sigma'^2}} e^{-\frac{\tan(\phi - \phi_0)^2}{2\rho^2}} \tag{9}
$$

where ρ determines the strength of orientedness, and N is a normalization constant that makes the kernel integrate to unity. At every point in the image, this kernel is rotated according to the local edge orientation defined by a unit vector $\boldsymbol{n}(x, y) = (\cos(\phi_0), \sin(\phi_0))^T$ which is perpendicular to the gradient. In the local coordinate system defined by $\boldsymbol{n}$ and $\boldsymbol{n}_\perp$, ϕ_0 is zero. Let p, q be Cartesian coordinates in this local coordinate system. Then $r^2 = p^2 + q^2$ and $\tan(\phi - \phi_0) = \frac{q}{p}$. When $r = 0$, we set $\phi := 0$ in order to avoid damping the radial Gaussian at the center of the filter. Given $\boldsymbol{n}$, p and q can be calculated very efficiently from the global coordinates $\boldsymbol{x} = (x, y)$, namely $p = \boldsymbol{n}^T \boldsymbol{x}$ and $q = \boldsymbol{n}_\perp^T \boldsymbol{x}$. In Cartesian coordinates, our kernel thus reads:

$$
h_{\sigma', \rho}(\boldsymbol{x}, \boldsymbol{n}) = \frac{1}{N} \begin{cases} e^{-\frac{\boldsymbol{x}^T \boldsymbol{x}}{2\sigma'^2} - \frac{1}{2\rho^2} \left(\frac{\boldsymbol{n}_\perp^T \boldsymbol{x}}{\boldsymbol{n}^T \boldsymbol{x}} \right)^2} & \text{if } \boldsymbol{n}^T \boldsymbol{x} \neq 0 \\ 0 & \text{if } \boldsymbol{n}^T \boldsymbol{x} = 0, \quad \boldsymbol{n}_\perp^T \boldsymbol{x} \neq 0 \\ 1 & \text{otherwise} \end{cases} \tag{10}
$$

The nonlinear integration operator $\mathcal{T}$ is defined as:

$$
T_{\sigma, \sigma', \rho} = \mathcal{T}_{\sigma', \rho}[Q_\sigma]
$$
$$
t_{ij}(x, y) = \sum_{x', y'} h_{\sigma', \rho}(x - x', y - y', \boldsymbol{n}(x', y')) q_{ij}(x', y') \quad (i, j \in \{1, 2\}) \tag{11}
$$

Fig. 3 depicts this filter for a horizontal edge. The parameter ρ should be as small as possible in order to obtain pronounced orientedness. We have found experimentally that the filter results are not very sensitive to the choice of ρ – values between 0.3 and 0.7 give essentially the same results. However, for $\rho < 0.3$, the filter becomes susceptible to noise in the estimated direction $\boldsymbol{n}$. For $\rho > 0.7$, undesirable blurring becomes visible again. In the examples, we use $\rho = 0.4$. This means that the kernel amplitude at $\phi = \phi_0 \pm 25°$ is half the maximal amplitude at ϕ_0. The parameter σ' must be large enough to ensure sufficient overlap between the different edge contributions coming from the neighborhood of a junction. We have found that the averaging scale should be about twice as large as the scale of the gradient filter. Since the structure tensor is represented with doubled resolution, this means that $\sigma' = 4\sigma$. Experiments were done with $\sigma = 0.7$. A theoretical investigation of optimal choices for ρ and σ' will be conducted. The possibility to improve efficiency by means of steerable filters will also be explored.

Fig. 2 shows the trace of the structure tensor obtained by our new filter and compares it with the trace of the structure tensor calculated with linear integration. It can be seen that nearby edges are merged in the linearly smoothed version, which causes small and narrow regions to disappear. This does not happen with non-linear averaging.

5   Improvement III: Integrated Edge and Junction Detection

In many cases the structure tensor is subsequently used to derive a cornerness measure, e.g. c_1 or c_2 in (5). Since a complete boundary description needs both edges and corners, edges are then detected with another algorithm, such as Canny's [2]. This poses a difficult integration problem of edge and corner responses into a single boundary response. Displacements of the detected corners from their true locations and erroneous edge responses near corners and junctions often lead to topologically incorrect boundaries (gaps, isolated "junction" points etc.). These problems have to be repaired by means of heuristics or dealt with by robust high level algorithms. Obviously, it were better if the errors would be avoided rather than repaired. This should be possible if edges and junctions arose from a unified, integrated process. However, this is not straightforward. For example, Förstner [4] tried to derive edge information from the structure tensor as well, but reliablility was not really satisfying.

The improvements to the structure tensor proposed above open up new possibilities for simultaneous edge and junction detection. We base our new edgeness and cornerness measures on the fact that any positive semi-definite second order tensor can be decomposed into two parts, one encoding the intrinsically 1-dimensional properties of the current location (edge strength and orientation), and the other the intrinsically 2D properties:

$$T = T_{\text{edge}} + T_{\text{junction}} = (\mu_1 - \mu_2)n_1 n_1^T + \mu_2 I \qquad (12)$$

where $\mu_{1,2}$ are the eigenvalues of the tensor, n_1 is the unit eigenvector associated with μ_1, and I is the identity tensor. The eigenvalues are calculated as:

$$\mu_{1,2} = \frac{1}{2}\left(t_{11} + t_{22} \pm \sqrt{(t_{11} - t_{22})^2 + 4t_{12}^2}\right) \qquad (13)$$

and the eigenvector is

$$n_1 = \begin{pmatrix} \cos(\phi_1) \\ \sin(\phi_1) \end{pmatrix} \qquad \text{with} \qquad \phi_1 = \frac{1}{2}\arctan\left(\frac{2t_{12}}{t_{11} - t_{22}}\right) \qquad (14)$$

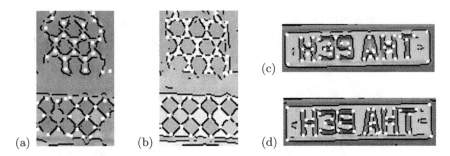

Fig. 4. (a, c) Integrated edge and junction detection – linear structure tensor calculation; (b, d) integrated edge and junction detection – non-linear structure tensor calculation. All images are calculated at doubled resolution.

Corners and junctions can now be detected as local maxima of $\mathrm{tr}(T_{\mathrm{junction}})$, whereas T_{edge} can be transformed back into a gradient-like vector $\sqrt{\mu_1 - \mu_2}\,\boldsymbol{n}_1$ that can be fed into Canny's algorithm instead of the normal gradient. Thus, the detected corners/junctions and edges arise from a decomposition of the same original tensor representation which leads to much fewer errors in the resulting boundary.

Fig. 4 compares edges and junctions derived from the standard structure tensor with those from the improved one. This figure reinforces what fig. 1 already demonstrated for edge detection alone: doubling of the resolution and non-linear tensor filtering indeed improve the boundary quality. In fig. 4a, the most severe error is that junctions are hallucinated in the centers of the small triangular regions, because the edges of these regions are merged into a single blob during blurring. Fig. 4c exhibits low quality of the detected edges, again because nearby edges diffuse into each other. Fig. 5 shows an example where the traditional tensor already performs reasonably. But by looking closer one finds the corners to be displaced by 3 pixels from their true locations, whereas the displacement in the non-linearly smoothed tensor is at most 1 pixel.

6   Conclusions

In this paper we improved structure tensor computation in two important ways: increased resolution and non-linear averaging. These improvements allowed us to define a new integrated edge and junction detection method. The experiments clearly indicate that the new method is superior, especially if the image contains small features near the resolution limit, as is typical for natural images.

In order to improve the method further, a better theoretical understanding of the non-linear averaging is required. It should also be investigated if Canny-like non-maxima suppression is optimal for the linear part T_{edge} of our tensor. Furthermore, quantitative comparisons with existing approaches will be conducted.

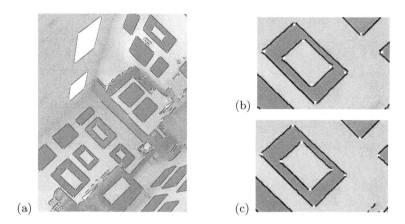

Fig. 5. (a) Integrated edge and junction detection in a lab scene; (b) detail of (a) computed with linear tensor averaging; (c) the same region as (b) obtained with nonlinear averaging. Note the corner displacements in (b).

References

1. J. August, S. Zucker: *Sketches with Curvature: The Curve Indicator Random Field and Markov Processes*, IEEE Trans. Patt. Anal. Mach. Intell., 25(4), 387–400, 2003
2. J. Canny: *A Computational Approach to Edge Detection*, IEEE Trans. Patt. Anal. Mach. Intell., 8(6), pp. 679–698, 1986
3. W. Förstner: *A Feature Based Corresponding Algorithm for Image Matching*, Intl. Arch. of Photogrammetry and Remote Sensing, vol. 26, pp. 150–166, 1986
4. W. Förstner: *A Framework for Low Level Feature Extraction*, in: J.-O. Eklundh (Ed.): Computer Vision – ECCV'94, Vol. II. Springer LNCS 801, pp. 383–394, 1994
5. C.G. Harris, M.J. Stevens: *A Combined Corner and Edge Detector*, Proc. of 4th Alvey Vision Conference, 1988
6. U. Köthe: *Gradient-Based Segmentation Requires Doubling of the Sampling Rate*, Univ. Hamburg, Informatics Dept., Tech. Rep. FBI-HH-M-326/03, 2003, subm.
7. V. Kovalevsky: *Finite Topology as Applied to Image Analysis*, Computer Vision, Graphics, and Image Processing, 46(2), pp. 141–161, 1989
8. G. Medioni, M.-S. Lee, C.-K. Tang: *A Computational Framework for Segmentation and Grouping*, Elsevier, 2000
9. H.-H. Nagel, A. Gehrke: *Spatiotemporally adaptive estimation and segmentation of OF-fields*; in: H. Burkhardt and B. Neumann (Eds.): Computer Vision – ECCV'98, Springer LNCS 1407, pp. 86–102, 1998
10. A. R. Rao, B. G. Schunck: *Computing Oriented Texture Fields*, CVGIP: Graphical Models and Image Processing, vol. 53, no. 2, 1991, pp. 157–185
11. K. Rohr: *Modelling and Identification of Characteristic Intensity Variations*, Image and Vision Computing, vol. 10, 66–76, 1992
12. K. Rohr: *Localization Properties of Direct Corner Detectors*, J. of Mathematical Imaging and Vision, 4, pp. 139–150, 1994
13. J. Weickert, T. Brox: *Diffusion and Regularization of Vector- and Matrix-Valued Images*, in: M. Z. Nashed, O. Scherzer (eds.), Inverse Problems, Image Analysis, and Medical Imaging. Contemporary Mathematics, Vol. 313, AMS, 2002

Who's Who? Challenges in Biometric Authentication

Anil K. Jain

Department of Computer Science and Engineering,
Michigan State University, 3115 Engineering Building, East Lansing, MI 48824
jain@cse.msu.edu, http://biometrics.cse.msu.edu

Abstract. A wide variety of systems require reliable personal recognition schemes to either confirm or determine the identity of an individual requesting their services. The purpose of such schemes is to ensure that only a legitimate user, and not anyone else, accesses the rendered services. Examples of such applications include secure access to buildings, computer systems, laptops, cellular phones and ATMs. In the absence of robust personal recognition schemes, these systems are vulnerable to the wiles of an impostor. Biometric recognition, or simply biometrics, refers to the automatic recognition of individuals based on their physiological and/or behavioral characteristics. By using biometrics it is possible to confirm or establish an individual's identity based on "who she is", rather than by "what she possesses" (e.g., an ID card) or "what she remembers" (e.g., a password). Current biometric systems make use of fingerprints, hand geometry, iris, retina, face, hand vein, facial thermograms, signature, voice characteristics, palmprint, gait, etc. to establish a person's identity [1]. Besides bolstering security and discouraging identity fraud, biometric systems also introduce an aspect of user convenience that may not be possible using traditional security techniques. For example, they alleviate the need for a user to "remember" the PINS and passwords associated with multiple applications.

1 Introduction

A biometric system is essentially a pattern recognition system that operates by acquiring biometric data from an individual, extracting a feature set from the acquired data, and comparing this feature set against the template set stored in the database. Two samples of the same biometric of an individual may not exactly be the same due to imperfect imaging conditions (e.g., sensor noise), changes in the user's physiological or behavioral characteristics (e.g., cuts and bruises on the finger), ambient conditions (e.g., temperature and humidity) and improper interaction with the sensor (e.g., incorrect finger placement). On the other hand, two samples of the same biometric obtained from two different individuals may appear to be the same (e.g., face images of twins). Thus, a biometric system is prone to two types of errors: (i) mistaking biometric measurements from two different persons to be from the same person (called false match), and (ii) mistaking two biometric measurements from the same person to be from two different persons (called false non-match).

B. Michaelis and G. Krell (Eds.): DAGM 2003, LNCS 2781, pp. 33–35, 2003.
© Springer-Verlag Berlin Heidelberg 2003

Among all the biometric indicators, fingerprints have one of the highest levels of reliability and have been extensively studied and used by forensic experts in criminal investigations [2]. Although not scientifically established, fingerprints are believed to be unique across individuals, and across fingers of the same individual. Even identical twins having similar DNA, are believed to have different fingerprints. The process of automatic fingerprint matching is affected by the non-linear deformation introduced in the fingerprint impression during sensing. The non-linear deformation causes the features consisting of minutiae points and ridge curves to be distorted. We have developed an ''average" deformation model (given several impressions of a finger) to account for the non-linear deformation present in fingerprints. The proposed method first establishes ridge curve correspondence between pairs of fingerprint impressions and then employs thin-plate splines (TPS) to model the warping. The average deformation model is utilized to align the template and query fingerprint images before matching. It is shown that the use of the deformation model based on ridge correspondence leads to a better alignment between two fingerprint images. An index of deformation is also proposed for choosing the best deformation model (with the smallest variance) arising from a set of impressions corresponding to a finger.

Face images are the most common biometric characteristic used by humans. A robust automatic face recognition system should be able to recognize a face in the presence of facial variations caused by varying illumination, and change in head poses and facial expressions [3]. However, these variations are not sufficiently captured in the small number of face images usually acquired for each subject to train an appearance-based face recognition system. In the framework of analysis by synthesis, we have developed a scheme to synthesize these facial variations from a given face image for each subject. A 3D generic face model is aligned onto a given frontal face image. A number of synthetic face images of a subject are then generated by imposing changes in head pose, illumination, and facial expression on the aligned 3D face model. These synthesized images are used to augment the training data set for face recognition. The pooled data set is used to construct an affine subspace for each subject. Face recognition is achieved by minimizing the distance between the subspace of a test subject and that of each subject in the database.

A biometric system that uses a single biometric trait for recognition has to contend with problems related to non-universality of the trait, spoof attacks, limited degrees of freedom, large intra-class variability, and noisy data. Some of these problems can be addressed by performing recognition after combining the evidence presented by multiple biometric traits of a user (e.g., face and iris, fingerprint and hand geometry). Such systems, known as multimodal biometric systems, fuse information at the feature extraction level, matching score level or decision level of a biometric system [4]. A variety of fusion techniques have been suggested in the literature. We have performed fusion at the matching score level using the face, fingerprint and hand geometry features of an individual. A simple sum rule is used to integrate the matching scores. We have also employed user-specific parameters during fusion to improve recognition performance. In addition, we have explored the possibility of combining evidence presented by multiple samples of the same biometric, multiple matchers operating on the same biometric, and in the case of fingerprints, multiple fingers of the same user.

References

[1] A. K. Jain, R. Bolle, and S. Pankanti (editors), Biometrics: Personal Identification in Networked Society, Kluwer Academic Publishers, 1999.

[2] D. Maltoni, D. Maio, A. K. Jain, and S. Prabhakar, Handbook of Fingerprint Recognition, Springer, NY, 2003.

[3] P.J. Philips, P. Grother, R. J. Micheals, D. M. Blackburn, E. Tabassi, and J. M. Bone, "FRVT 2002: Overview and Summary", Available from http://www.frvt.org/FRVT2002/

[4] A. Ross and A. K. Jain, " Information Fusion in Biometrics", Pattern Recognition Letters, Special Issue on Multimodal Biometrics, 2003.

Optimal Scale Selection for Circular Edge Extraction

Ji-Young Lim and H. Siegfried Stiehl

Universität Hamburg, Fachbereich Informatik, Arbeitsbereich Kognitive Systeme
Vogt-Kölln-Str. 30, 22527 Hamburg, Germany
{lim, stiehl}@informatik.uni-hamburg.de
http://kogs-www.informatik.uni-hamburg.de/~lim

Abstract. This paper addresses the issue of optimal scale selection for circular edge extraction in the context of higher dimensional multiscale edge extraction. Based on a classification of higher dimensional edges according to local curvature, we exemplarily establish a 2-D circular edge model. Through a careful mathematical derivation, we transform the circular edge model from Cartesian coordinates for which the analytical solution is unknown into polar coordinates. Utilizing this edge model we develop a novel theoretical framework for optimal scale selection for circular edge extraction through which the effects of curvature as related to scale can be analyzed. Moreover, we carry out a validation study in order to investigate on the level of principal performance how well the experimental results obtained from application of the developed framework to 2-D synthetic images match the theoretical results.

1 Introduction

Edge extraction is one of the key issues in image analysis and computer vision. The goal of edge extraction is to obtain a rich and meaningful description of an image by characterizing its intensity changes. Image intensity changes occur with many spatial scales depending on their physical origin. Only some of these stand out locally and seem to be more significant than others. Therefore, a natural requirement is to measure the local scale for each edge. This is the main motivation behind multiscale approaches to edge extraction on the basis of the linear scale-space theory (see e.g. [11]). A multiscale analysis for the purpose of coping with the problem associated with *fixed* scale approaches to edge extraction can reveal precious information about the nature of the underlying physical process which gives rise to edges in the image. Provided that any a priori knowledge about the local edges to be extracted is unknown, it is necessary to select the scale (or support) of the edge operator which optimally adapts to the local scale of the edge in order to perform edge extraction correctly.

Most existing approaches to higher dimensional edge extraction have used the 1-D step or, respectively, the 1-D sigmoid edge profile as a model in an either implicit or explicit way (see e.g. [5], [6], [9]). However, the 1-D sigmoid edge model represents an ideally smooth 1-D intensity change and by generalizing it to

B. Michaelis and G. Krell (Eds.): DAGM 2003, LNCS 2781, pp. 36–43, 2003.
© Springer-Verlag Berlin Heidelberg 2003

higher dimensions its scale cannot be always accurately determined. This can be easily seen for the case when a large scale operator has to be necessarily applied to a 2-D high-curvature contour undergoing a large Gaussian blurring: The large scale of the operator conflicts with the high curvature. As a consequence, only for the case of a linear replication of the 1-D sigmoid along the second orthogonal dimension a large scale operator can be safely applied as yet. A typical example of high curvature contours is a corner, and arbitrary Gaussian smoothing of its curve results in destroying its salient properties (see e.g. [10]).

In this paper, we consider the issue of optimal scale selection for circular edge extraction in the context of higher dimensional multiscale edge extraction and we focus on the principal way of how to analyze the effects of curvature as related to scale in multiscale edge extraction. First, based on a classification of higher dimensional edges according to local curvature, we exemplarily establish a 2-D circular edge model. Utilizing this model, we develop a theoretical framework for optimal scale selection and we analyze the effects of curvature as related to scale. Then, we present the results of a validation study of our optimal scale selection approach, where we investigate how well the experimental results obtained from application of the developed framework to 2-D synthetic images match the theoretical results. Note that we here deal with the 2-D case only, however, the basic approach can be potentially generalized to the higher dimensional case.

2   Towards Higher Dimensional Edge Models

We coarsely classify higher dimensional edges according to their local curvature into three types, i.e. *straight edges*, *circular edges*, and *corners*, while assuming a sigmoid-like profile. In more concrete terms, for a given radius R of a circular edge its corresponding curvature K is given by the reciprocal of the radius (i.e. $|K| = 1/R$), and the curvature is assumed to be constant. Furthermore, we assume edge points on an edge contour of descending curvature to form straight or straight-like edges and edge points on an edge contour of ascending curvature to represent corners or corner-like structures.

As a matter of fact, one can differently classify higher dimensional edges according to other alternative criteria. Our classification for establishing higher dimensional edge models is the first attempt to approach higher dimensional edge extraction theoretically in order to analyze the effects of curvature as related to scale in multiscale edge extraction, although our 2-D edge models based on this classification may not be sufficiently general to represent all edge types in real images. In this paper, we concentrate on the circular edge case.

2.1   Circular Edge Model

A unit circular edge of radius R is described by $\mathcal{H}(R^2 - x^2 - y^2)$, where $\mathcal{H}$ denotes the Heaviside function. Similar types of the circular edge model based upon the Heaviside function have been used for modeling curved edges with constant curvature e.g. in [4]. The sigmoid unit circular edge with edge width t_E is represented by convolution of the Heaviside function with a Gaussian, i.e.

$$E_c(x,y;t_E) = \mathcal{H}(R^2 - x^2 - y^2) * G(x,y;t_E)$$

$$= R \int_{-1}^{1} G(x - R \cdot \gamma; t_E) \left(\Phi\left(y + R\sqrt{1 - \gamma^2}; t_E\right) - \Phi\left(y - R\sqrt{1 - \gamma^2}; t_E\right) \right) d\gamma,$$

where Φ is the normalized error integral function and the edge width t_E corresponds to the scale of edge. Unfortunately since the general analytical solution of $\int G \cdot \Phi$ is unknown ([4]), $E_c(x,y;t_E)$ cannot be determined analytically. However, we can transform $E_c(x,y;t_E)$ represented in Cartesian coordinates into polar coordinates without loss of generality since $\mathcal{H}(R^2 - x^2 - y^2)$ and $G(x,y;t_E)$ are rotationally symmetric in Cartesian coordinates.

2.2   The Gradient in Polar Coordinates

For a multiscale analysis, we derive the scale-space representation of a sigmoid circular edge, which we denote $L_{E_c}(x,y;t)$ and this is given by convolution with the Gaussian of variance t. For the further derivation, $L_{E_c}(x,y;t)$ in Cartesian coordinates must be transformed into $L_{E_c}(r;t)$ in polar coordinates ($r^2 = x^2 + y^2$):

$$L_{E_c}(r;t) = \mathcal{H}(R - r) * G(r;t_E + t) \quad (t_E, t > 0), \tag{1}$$

where t_E and t, respectively, correspond to the edge width of a circular edge and the scale parameter, and $G(r;t_E + t) = \frac{1}{2\pi(t_E+t)} e^{-\frac{r^2}{2(t_E+t)}}$.

Considering the polar coordinates (r, θ), for any point $P = (x, y)$ in Cartesian coordinates we have

$$\begin{cases} x = r\cos\theta \\ y = r\sin\theta \end{cases}, \quad \begin{cases} r = \sqrt{x^2 + y^2} \\ \theta = \tan^{-1}\left(\frac{y}{x}\right) \end{cases}, \quad \text{and} \quad \begin{cases} \frac{\partial r}{\partial x} = \frac{x}{\sqrt{x^2+y^2}} = \frac{r\cos\theta}{r} = \cos\theta \\ \frac{\partial r}{\partial y} = \frac{y}{\sqrt{x^2+y^2}} = \frac{r\sin\theta}{r} = \sin\theta \end{cases}.$$

Then, the gradient of $L_{E_c}(r;t)$ is given by

$$\nabla L_{E_c}(r;t) = \left(\frac{\partial L_{E_c}(r;t)}{\partial x}, \frac{\partial L_{E_c}(r;t)}{\partial y} \right)^T = \left(\frac{\partial L_{E_c}(r;t)}{\partial r} \cdot \cos\theta, \frac{\partial L_{E_c}(r;t)}{\partial r} \cdot \sin\theta \right)^T,$$

and the gradient magnitude of $L_{E_c}(r;t)$ is given by

$$|\nabla L_{E_c}(r;t)| = \sqrt{\left(\frac{\partial L_{E_c}(r;t)}{\partial r}\right)^2 \cdot \cos^2\theta + \left(\frac{\partial L_{E_c}(r;t)}{\partial r}\right)^2 \cdot \sin^2\theta} = \left| \frac{\partial L_{E_c}(r;t)}{\partial r} \right|.$$

In sum, we obtain

$$|\nabla L_{E_c}(r;t)| = \frac{R}{t_E + t} e^{-\frac{r^2+R^2}{2(t_E+t)}} I_1\left(\frac{R \cdot r}{t_E + t}\right) \tag{2}$$

(see Appendix for the detailed derivation), where I_1 denotes the modified Bessel function of integer order 1, which is a monotonously increasing function. Note that the modified Bessel function of integer order n is defined by $I_n(z) = \frac{1}{2\pi} \int_0^{2\pi} \cos(n\theta) e^{z\cos\theta} d\theta$ (cf. [1]).

3   Scale Selection in Circular Edge Extraction

Using the circular edge model in polar coordinates, we attempt to analyze the behavior of circular edges over scales for the purpose of selecting their optimal scale values. Let $M(t)$ be a response function of the gradient magnitude given in (2) at edges ($r = R$); that is, $M(t) = |\nabla L_{E_c}(R;t)|$. $M(t)$ is a monotonously decreasing function of t, which means that the edge operator response becomes weaker as the scale parameter increases, and thus $M(t)$ is not suitable for optimal scale selection.

On the other hand, by utilizing $M(t)$ we intend to find a response function from which an optimal scale (i.e. the edge width t_E) is uniquely selected. Although finding such a response function is quite difficult due to the complexity of $M(t)$, fortunately one can simplify $M(t)$ in a special case. Let $S(t)$ be a response function obtained from multiplying $M(t)$ with e^R as given by

$$S(t) = \frac{R}{t_E + t} e^{\frac{-R^2 + R(t_E + t)}{t_E + t}} I_1 \left(\frac{R^2}{t_E + t} \right), \tag{3}$$

from which one can observe that, when $t_E + t = R$, $S(t)$ reduces to $I_1(R)$ (i.e. $S(t)|_{t_E+t=R} = \frac{R}{R} e^{\frac{-R^2+R^2}{R}} I_1(R) = I_1(R)$), which implies that $S(t)$ gives the response $I_1(R)$ when $t_E + t = R$. That is, the scale value satisfying $S(t) = I_1(R)$ corresponds to $t = R - t_E$. For a given R, $I_1(R)$ is known, from which one can uniquely obtain the value t satisfying $S(t)=I_1(R)$. The obtained value t, in turn, can be used to derive the optimal scale value t_E (i.e. $t_E = R - t$).

It is worth noting that there does not exist any t in the response of $S(t)$ satisfying $S(t)=I_1(R)$ where $R \leq t_E$. As a matter of fact, from a theoretical and practical viewpoint it is meaningless to consider the case for which the radius of a given circular edge is smaller than its edge width (see Sect. 4.1 for the unit of R, t, and t_E). Our theoretical derivation shows that $R \leq t_E$ corresponds to $t \leq 0$. We denote the relationship $R \leq t_E$ the *curvature-scale constraint*. This constraint can be used as a natural limit condition of curvature as related to the edge width for a given circular edge. Consequently, the optimal scale value for circular edges can be uniquely selected using the response function $S(t)$ given in (3) such that the optimal scale value of a given circular edge with the radius R is given by $t_E = R - t$, where t satisfies $S(t) = I_1(R)$.

4   Validation of the Optimal Scale Selection Approach

In this section, we validate the developed theoretical framework using synthetic images through investigating how well the experimental results obtained from application of the developed framework to an image match the theoretical results. Through this validation study, i) we aim to check experimentally for the correctness of our theoretical derivation, ii) we demonstrate in practice the principal performance of optimal scale selection, and (iii) we can probe the limits for some extreme cases. Since the optimal scale value (i.e. the edge width) must be known a priori for our validation study, we use synthetic images and control the degree of edge width as well as the level of noise in the experiments. Note that the full range of experiments, e.g. by fine-sampling of the continuous parameter space, is beyond the scope of this paper and thus left open for future work.

4.1   Experimental Setting

For edge extraction, we use the discrete scale-space (DSS) kernel as well as its first-order odd-number-sized differencing kernel (i.e. $T_{\triangle_{odd}}$) both of which are validated as best performing kernels in [7] and [8], and we employ the non-maxima suppression method by Canny [3].

We apply the developed framework for optimal scale selection to blurred noisy synthetic images and observe whether the theoretically expected scale is selected correctly. For a given synthetic image, we control the degree of edge width by convolving the image with the DSS kernel, the variance (t_E) of which varies from $\frac{1}{3}$ to $\frac{13}{3}$ (i.e. $t_E = \frac{k}{3}, k = 1, 2, \ldots, 13$) in our experiments. Given a blurred synthetic image, we add two different levels of Gaussian noise. We use three synthetic images C_i representing three different types of a circular edge (see Fig. 1). For a given degree of edge width k, let us denote $\tau(k)$ a selected scale value resulting from the application of the developed framework for optimal scale selection to C_i of Fig. 1. With respect to $\tau(k)$, we consider the mean ($\bar{\tau}(k)$) and the standard deviation ($\tau_\sigma(k)$) of $\tau(k)$ along the edge contour. According to the optimal scale selection scheme theoretically derived in the previous section, $\frac{\tau(k)}{3} = R - \frac{k}{3}$ viz. $\tau(k) = 3R - k$ must hold.

Fig. 1. Synthetic images C1 (left), C2 (middle), and C3 (right) representing three different types of circular edge. The radius of a circle is $R = 10$ (occupying 10 pixels) in our experiment. The in-between-distance of neighboring circles in C2 corresponds to the diameter of the given circle, while that in C3 corresponds to the radius of the given circle. The white contour marks the edge loci to be observed.

4.2   Experimental Results and Assessment

Fig. 2 gives a graphical illustration of the experimental results for C1, C2, and C3 in terms of $\{\bar{\tau}, \tau_\sigma\}$ compared with the theoretical result. One can notice several remarkable aspects from Fig. 2. First, the obtained experimental results are in general very close to the theoretical results. The slight deviation of the experimental results from the theoretical ones may be rightfully assumed to be caused by an inevitable gap between a well-founded continuous theory and the implemented discrete case. In other words, even though the circular edge contours of the synthetic images used in our experiment were obtained from the mathematical equation of a circle, strictly speaking, they are not perfectly circular in a digital image. Second, the experimental results are affected by noise only little. This is because that the radius value of a circular edge plays a decisive role in the developed framework for optimal scale selection, where the selected optimal scale value mainly depends on the radius value, and thus the level of noise has less influence. Moreover, the degree of the in-between-distance has little effect on the result of optimal scale selection, where 'little' is only valid with respect to our experiment regarding the condition that the in-between-distance of neighboring circles should be larger than 10 pixels (see Fig. 1).

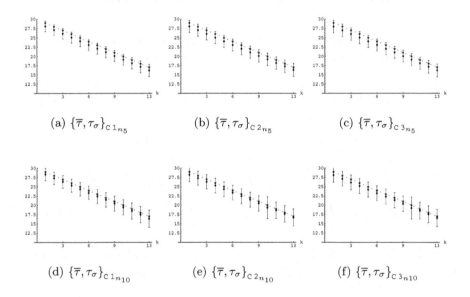

(a) $\{\bar{\tau}, \tau_\sigma\}_{C1_{n_5}}$ (b) $\{\bar{\tau}, \tau_\sigma\}_{C2_{n_5}}$ (c) $\{\bar{\tau}, \tau_\sigma\}_{C3_{n_5}}$

(d) $\{\bar{\tau}, \tau_\sigma\}_{C1_{n_{10}}}$ (e) $\{\bar{\tau}, \tau_\sigma\}_{C2_{n_{10}}}$ (f) $\{\bar{\tau}, \tau_\sigma\}_{C3_{n_{10}}}$

Fig. 2. Graphical illustration of experimental results for C1, C2, and C3 compared with the theoretical result. Each column differs in the type of circular edge and each row differs in the level of noise (n_5 and n_{10} denote weak noise and strong noise, respectively). '$\cdots\bigstar\cdots$' corresponds to the theoretical result (i.e. $\tau(k) = 3R - k$ for $R = 10$; see Sect. 4.1), while '$\blacklozenge$' with error bar represents the experimental result.

5   Summary and Conclusions

In this paper, we proposed a theoretical framework for optimal scale selection in circular edge extraction. We established a 2-D circular edge model based on a classification of 2-D edges according to local curvature. By transforming the circular edge model from Cartesian coordinates for which the analytical solution is unknown into polar coordinates, we were able to analyze the effects of curvature as related to scale, which is a novel approach based on a careful mathematical derivation. Moreover, we presented the results of our validation study in which we investigated how well the experimental results obtained from application of the developed framework to 2-D synthetic images match the theoretical results. Our validation study shows that the experimental results are generally close to the theoretical results on the whole. Future work will include an investigation of the 3-D case. Also, it is necessary to consider how robustly and accurately edge extraction based on our developed framework performs in real-world images.

Appendix: Transformation of the Circular Edge Model from Cartesian Coordinates into Polar Coordinates

Provided that $f(r)$ and $g(r)$ are both rotationally symmetric, convolution of $f(r)$ with $g(r)$ in polar coordinates is defined ([2, p. 339]) by

$$f(r) * g(r) = \int_0^\infty \int_0^{2\pi} f(r')g(s)r' \, dr' \, d\theta' \quad \left(s^2 = r^2 + r'^2 - 2rr' \cos \theta'\right),$$

according to which (1) is derived as (denoting $T = t_E + t$)

$$L(r;t) = \mathcal{H}(R - r) * G(r;T) = \int_0^\infty \int_0^{2\pi} r' \mathcal{H}(R - r') \frac{1}{2\pi T} e^{-\frac{r'^2 + r^2 - 2rr' \cos \theta'}{2T}} \, dr' d\theta'$$

$$= \frac{1}{T} \int_0^R r' e^{-\frac{r'^2 + r^2}{2T}} \int_0^{2\pi} \frac{1}{2\pi} e^{\frac{rr' \cos \theta'}{T}} \, d\theta' \, dr' = \frac{1}{T} \int_0^R r' e^{-\frac{r'^2 + r^2}{2T}} I_0 \left(\frac{rr'}{T}\right) \, dr',$$

where $I_0(\cdot)$ is the modified Bessel function of integer order 0 (see Sect.2.2 for the definition). Then $\frac{dL(r;t)}{dr} = \frac{1}{T} \int_0^R r' \frac{d}{dr} \left(e^{-\frac{r'^2 + r^2}{2T}} I_0(\frac{rr'}{T})\right) dr'$ is derived as

$$\frac{1}{T} \int_0^R \left[\frac{r'^2}{T} e^{-\frac{r'^2 + r^2}{2T}} I_1 \left(\frac{rr'}{T}\right) - \frac{rr'}{T} e^{-\frac{r'^2 + r^2}{2T}} I_0 \left(\frac{rr'}{T}\right) \right] dr' \quad (\text{cf. } I_0'(z) = I_1(z))$$

$$= \frac{1}{T} \int_0^R \left[-r' \frac{d \left(e^{-\frac{r'^2 + r^2}{2T}}\right)}{dr'} I_1 \left(\frac{rr'}{T}\right) - \underbrace{e^{-\frac{r'^2 + r^2}{2T}} \frac{rr'}{T} I_0 \left(\frac{rr'}{T}\right)}_{**} \right] dr'.$$

Using the recurrence relations of the Bessel functions $I_n'(z) = \frac{I_{n-1}(z) + I_{n+1}(z)}{2}$ and $I_n(z) = \frac{z}{2n} I_{n-1}(z) - \frac{z}{2n} I_{n+1}(z)$ (see [1] for details), the above term $\frac{rr'}{T} I_0 \left(\frac{rr'}{T}\right)$ denoted by '**' corresponds to

$$\frac{rr'I_0\left(\frac{rr'}{T}\right)+rr'I_0\left(\frac{rr'}{T}\right)}{2T}=\frac{rr'}{2T}I_0\left(\frac{rr'}{T}\right)+I_1\left(\frac{rr'}{T}\right)+\frac{rr'}{2T}I_2\left(\frac{rr'}{T}\right)$$

$$=\frac{I_0\left(\frac{rr'}{T}\right)+I_2\left(\frac{rr'}{T}\right)}{2}\frac{rr'}{T}+I_1\left(\frac{rr'}{T}\right)=r'\frac{d\left(I_1\left(\frac{rr'}{T}\right)\right)}{dr'}+I_1\left(\frac{rr'}{T}\right)\frac{dr'}{dr'}.$$

As a consequence, $\frac{dL(r;t)}{dr}$ is derived as

$$\frac{1}{T}\int_0^R\left[-r'\frac{d\left(e^{-\frac{r'^2+r^2}{2T}}\right)}{dr'}I_1\left(\frac{rr'}{T}\right)-e^{-\frac{r'^2+r^2}{2T}}\left(r'\frac{d\left(I_1\left(\frac{rr'}{T}\right)\right)}{dr'}+I_1\left(\frac{rr'}{T}\right)\frac{dr'}{dr'}\right)\right]dr'$$

$$=\frac{1}{T}\int_0^R-\frac{d\left(r'e^{-\frac{r'^2+r^2}{2T}}I_1\left(\frac{rr'}{T}\right)\right)}{dr'}dr'=-\frac{R}{T}e^{-\frac{R^2+r^2}{2T}}I_1\left(\frac{Rr}{T}\right).$$

Acknowledgement. The financial support by DAAD (German Academic Exchange Service) to the first author is greatly acknowledged. The authors thank Dr. Ullrich Köthe for his valuable help in deriving (2).

References

1. M. Abramowitz and I. A. Stegun, *Handbook of Mathematical Functions*, Dover Publisher, the 9th edition, 1972
2. R. N. Bracewell, *The Fourier Transform and Its Applications*, McGraw-Hill, the 3rd edition, 2000
3. J. F. Canny, "A Computational Approach to Edge Detection", *IEEE Trans. on Pattern Analysis and Machine Intelligence* (PAMI), Vol. 8(6), pp. 679–698, 1986
4. C. Drewniok, *Objektlokalisation durch Adaption parametrischer Grauwertmodelle und ihre Anwendung in der Luftbildauswertung*, Dissertation, Uni. Hamburg, 1999
5. J. H. Elder and S. W. Zucker, "Local Scale Control for Edge Detection and Blur Estimation", PAMI Vol. 20(7), pp. 699–716, 1998
6. A. F. Korn, "Toward a Symbolic Representation of Intensity Changes in Images", PAMI Vol. 10(5), pp. 610–625, 1988
7. J. Y. Lim, *Discrete Scale-Space Formulation and Multiscale Edge Extraction toward Higher Dimensions*, Dissertation (to be published), Uni. Hamburg, 2003
8. J. Y. Lim and H. S. Stiehl, "A Generalized Discrete Scale-Space Formulation for 2-D and 3-D Signals", *The 4th Int. Conf. on Scale-Space Theories in Computer Vision*, Skye/Scotland, 10–12 June, 2003
9. T. Lindeberg, "Edge Detection and Ridge Detection with Automatic Scale Selection", *Int. Journal of Computer Vision*, Vol. 3(2), pp. 117–154, 1998
10. K. Rohr, "Recognizing Corners by Fitting Parametric Models", *Int. Journal of Computer Vision*, Vol. 9(3), pp. 213–230, 1992
11. J. Sporring, M. Nielsen, L. M. J. Florack P. Johansen, *Gaussian Scale-Space Theory*, Kluwer Academic Publishers, 1997

Localization of Piled Boxes by Means of the Hough Transform

Dimitrios Katsoulas

Institute for Pattern Recognition and Image Processing, University of Freiburg,
Georges-Koehler-Allee 52, D-79110 Freiburg, Germany
dkats@informatik.uni-freiburg.de

Abstract. Automatic unloading of piled boxes of unknown dimensions is undoubtedly of great importance to the industry. In this contribution a system addressing this problem is described: a laser range finder mounted on the hand of an industrial robot is used for data acquisition. A vacuum gripper, mounted as well on the robot hand is employed from grasping the objects from their exposed surfaces. We localize the exposed surfaces of the objects via a hypothesis generation and verification framework. Accurate hypotheses about the pose and the dimensions of the boundary of the exposed surfaces are generated from edge information obtained from the input range image, using a variation of the Hough transform. Hypothesis verification is robustly performed using the range points inside the hypothesized boundary. Our system shows a variety of advantages such like computational efficiency accuracy and robustness, the combination of which cannot be found in existing approaches.

1 Introduction

We address the depalletizing problem, in the context of which a number of objects residing on a platform, the pallet, should be automatically localized grasped and unloaded. More specifically, we present a system for automatic unloading of piled boxes of unknown dimensions, since such objects are quite often encountered in industrial sites. Existing systems utilizing intensity cameras for dealing with the problem [8], [4], depend heavily on lighting conditions at the installation sites, and deal primarily only with neatly placed configurations of objects. Systems utilizing range imagery [1], [7] on the other hand, utilize region information to determine object boundaries which makes them not as accurate as desired.

We employ a laser sensor mounted on the hand of an industrial robot for data acquisition. A vacuum gripper mounted as well on the robot hand, grasps the objects from their exposed surfaces. Both boundary and region based information provided by input range images, are used for localizing fully exposed object surfaces. Boundary information creates accurate hypotheses about the pose and the dimensions of the boundaries of the objects' exposed surfaces, which are verified or rejected using the data inside the boundaries. Exposed surfaces are modeled using parametric geometric entities. The problem of efficiently creating

B. Michaelis and G. Krell (Eds.): DAGM 2003, LNCS 2781, pp. 44–51, 2003.
© Springer-Verlag Berlin Heidelberg 2003

accurate hypotheses about the parameters of those surfaces in the pile is solved by decomposition into various subproblems, each recovering a subset of each surface's parameter set. Our system exhibits various advantages the combination of which cannot be found in existing systems: Insensitivity to lighting conditions, since a laser sensor is employed for data acquisition. Accuracy, due the generation of accurate pose hypotheses. Robustness, since acceptance of a hypothesis is determined by statistical tests which take into consideration the uncertainty in the calculation of features. Computational efficiency, due to problem decomposition in subproblems with lower complexity. In addition, our framework allows for parallel implementation, which can reduce its running time to a considerable extent. In the paragraph that follows, our technique is described in detail.

2   Finding Graspable Surfaces of Piled Boxes

One of the most important properties of an automatic unloading system is that during its operation, it does not destroy the objects of the pile. This suggests that unloading operations should be performed in such a way, so that the objects on the top of the pile are grasped first. The particular objects are expected to fully expose one of their surfaces to the laser sensor. These surfaces are three dimensional planar areas with a rectangle boundary. Unloading of objects can be achieved by grasping the objects from the center of gravity of the fully exposed surfaces. The fully exposed surfaces will therefore be hereinafter referred to as graspable surfaces. The rectangle boundaries of graspable surfaces are geometric entities that can be expressed through eight parameters. Six of them represent their pose (translation and rotation) in space, and the remaining two their dimensions (width and length). Our system should ideally be in the position to localize all the graspable surfaces contained in the range image, which could enable the unloading of multiple objects per scan. The problem we deal with, has therefore to do with the recovery of multiple instances of geometric models in range images.

The Hough Transform is the most common method employed for dealing with such problems. However, the technique in its original form (Standard Hough Transform, SHT) has drawbacks: Lets suppose the model sought has N parameters and each image point constrains p of them. For each image point, the SHT increments all the bins comprising a $N - p$ -dimensional manifold of an N - dimensional accumulator. In our case the models ($3d$ rectangles) have $N = 8$ degrees of freedom and each point constrains $p = 2$ model parameters. Applying the SHT, will be both memory consuming, since a $6d$ accumulator is needed, as well as computationally inefficient, since mapping of a single image point requires updating a $4d$ manifold of the accumulator. A second drawback of the SHT is that it does not take into consideration the error in the localization of the image points. This results in both detection of false positives and missing of objects, thus negatively affects the robustness and effectiveness of the transform. The reader is referred to [9] for details on the issue.

We recover the bounding rectangles of the graspable surfaces of our objects from the edge map of the range image by using a variation of the Hough Transform. We overcome the computational inefficiency of the transform by decomposing the recovery problem into two successive subproblems, each dealing with a subset of the boundary parameter set: The recovery of the pose parameters followed by the recovery of the dimensions. In addition, taking into consideration the error in the localization of the edge points when mapping them to the parameter space, results into robustness and accuracy. A detailed description of the pose and the dimensions recovery subproblems is presented in the subsequent paragraphs.

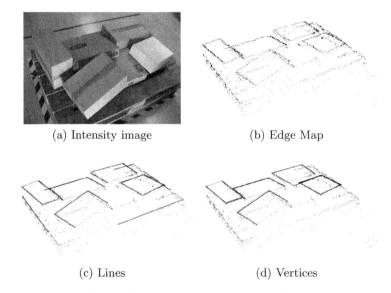

(a) Intensity image   (b) Edge Map

(c) Lines   (d) Vertices

Fig. 1. Vertex detection in range images

2.1   Recovery of Pose

It is since years known in the computer vision community [2], that a visible vertex of a convex object provides the strongest constraints for accurately determining its pose. Object vertices are recovered via the edge map of the range image of the pile. The technique comprises two steps: Firstly, three-dimensional lines corresponding to the linear boundaries of the boxes are extracted. Secondly, all pairs of lines are considered. Pairs of lines found to be orthogonal, along with their intersection point are grouped to a vertex. Line detection in $3d$ is performed via a series of Hough Transforms (see [6] for details). An interesting feature of our vertex detector is that constrains the transform in this way, so that it allows for efficient and accurate propagation of the edge points localization error in the parameter space.

The outcome of the vertex detection process is depicted in Fig.1. Fig.1 (a) is an intensity image of the pile, Fig.1 (b) depicts the outcome of the edge detection operation on the input range image. Line detection in $3d$ and vertex recovery both superimposed on the edge map are presented in Fig.1 (c) and (d) respectively. The reader may have already observed that not all the linear boundaries and as a consequence not all of the vertices of the graspable surfaces have been recovered. The adopted line detection guarantees detection of all boundaries in the image up to a user defined probability of success (see [6],[9]). The execution time of the algorithm depends exponentially on this number. In order to balance computational efficiency and functionality we set the probability of success to a value less than one, namely 0.9. We thus deliberately allow about 10 per-cent of the boundaries to be missed by our algorithm, for the sake of efficiency.

2.2   Recovery of Dimensions

The dimensions of the boundary of a graspable surface of a known pose, can be directly determined from two diagonal vertices of it. In our case, not all the linear boundaries and thereby not two diagonal vertices of each graspable surface can always be detected. To be able to infer the dimensions of the boundary of an exposed surface even in cases when two not diagonal or only one of its vertices is detected, we employ an approach which uses both the already extracted vertices as well as the edge points. The algorithm for finding graspable surfaces of boxes in range images is presented in Fig. 2.

The procedure **findGraspableSurfaces** (see Fig. 2, line 1) attempts to recover the graspable surfaces. Input of the procedure is the set of detected vertices **V**. For every element V_i of the set, a rectangle graspable surface boundary R is initialized (line 2). The pose of R is recovered, by alignment with V_i. Thereby V_i will be hereinafter referred to as the *generating vertex* of R. Then, the algorithm finds the dimensions of R: At first it attempts to do so by finding a scene vertex which lies diagonal to V_i (line 4). If such a vertex cannot be found it attempts to recover the dimensions from edge points (line 7). If one of the two processes is successful R is added to the list of found graspable surface boundaries **R** (line 5,8).

The procedure **dimensionsFromVertices** (line 11) aims at recovering the dimensions of the input rectangle R by finding a scene vertex which is diagonal to the rectangle's generating vertex. Such vertex should be on the same plane to which the generating vertex belongs and its direction vectors should be parallel to the corresponding direction vectors of the generating vertex (line 13). In addition, its intersection point should reside at the first quadrant of the coordinate frame defined by the generating vertex (line 14). When a vertex satisfying the above criteria is encountered, the algorithm updates the width and length parameters of the rectangle R (line 15). There are cases however when a vertex with correct properties is found, which belongs to the boundary of an exposed surface of a different box. In order to identify such cases we regard the range points inside

R. If the average distance of the points to the plane defined by R is small enough, we consider the rectangle successfully localized. This test is realized by the procedure **verify**, invoked in line 16. Points inside R are acquired via a computationally efficient region rasterization framework [10].

1. **findGraspableSurfaces**($\mathbf{V}$, α, p):
2.   *For* every vertex $V_i \in \mathbf{V}$ /* $\mathbf{V}$ is the set of detected vertices*/
3.   consider **Rectangle** R; align R with V_i
4.   *If* **dimensionsFromVertices**(R, $\mathbf{V}$, α) *Then*
5.   add R to $\mathbf{R}$ /* $\mathbf{R}$ is the set of recovered graspable surface boundaries*/
6.   *Else*
7.   *If* **dimensionsFromEdges**(R, α, p) *Then*
8.   add R to $\mathbf{R}$
9.   **select**($\mathbf{R}$) /* Retain the "best" boundaries*/
10.   *Return* $\mathbf{R}$

11. **dimensionsFromVertices**(R, $\mathbf{V}$, α):
12.   *For* every vertex $V_j \in \mathbf{V}$
13.   *If* **coplanar**(R, V_j, α) and **parallel**(R, V_j, α)
14.   *If* **inFirstQuadrantOf**(R, V_j) *Then*
15.   update dimensions of R
16.   *Return* **verify**(R, α)
17.   *Return False*

18. **dimensionsFromEdges**(R, α, p):
19. $\mathbf{P_c} \leftarrow$ **preProcess**(R, α) /* $\mathbf{P_c}$: the set of candidate edge points */
20. $\mathbf{A_x}$, $\mathbf{A_y} \leftarrow$ **accumulate**($\mathbf{P_c}$)/*$\mathbf{A_x}$,$\mathbf{A_y}$: one dimensional accumulators*/
21.   *For* every peak $A_x \in \mathbf{A_x}$
22. $M_x \leftarrow$ parameter value corresponding to A_x (width)
23.   *For* every peak $A_y \in \mathbf{A_y}$
24. $M_y \leftarrow$ parameter value corresponding to A_y (length)
25. $\mathbf{P_i} \leftarrow$ points which contributed to A_x, A_y
26. $\mathbf{P_f} \leftarrow \{$points $P(x,y) \in \mathbf{P_i} : x \leq M_x \wedge y \leq M_y\}$
27.   *If* $\mathbf{P_f}$.**size**() $> p$
28.   dimensions of $R \leftarrow M_x, M_y$
29.   *Return* **verify**(R, α)
30.   *Return False*

Fig. 2. Algorithm for finding graspable surfaces of piled boxes

The procedure **dimensionsFromEdges** (line 18) recovers the dimensions of the input rectangle R, in the event of insufficient vertex information, that is when no diagonal vertex to the generating vertex of R can be found. We infer dimension information from the edge points expected to reside on R. These points should satisfy the following requirements: Firstly they should be coplanar to the plane defined by R. Secondly they should be in the first quadrant of the coordinate frame defined by its generating vertex. Procedure **preProcess** (line 19) realizes these actions. To illustrate, we consider the scene vertex **P** of Fig. 3 (a), which depicts a top down view of Fig. 1 (d), as the generating vertex of R. Fig. 3 (b), shows the coordinate frame defined by the generating vertex and the edge points found to be coplanar to the vertex. **preProcess** will output the set of edge points $\mathbf{P_c}$ on the first quadrant of the frame.

Application of a Hough transform -like technique on this set of edge points will determine the rectangle dimensions: The coordinates of the points in $\mathbf{P_c}$ along the $\mathbf{D_x}$ and $\mathbf{D_y}$ axes of the two dimensional vertex coordinate frame are accumulated in two one dimensional arrays $\mathbf{A_x}$ and $\mathbf{A_y}$ respectively (line 20 of Fig. 2). A search procedure for the rectangle dimensions in the accumulators follows: For each pair A_x, A_y of accumulator peaks, we examine the corresponding parameter values M_x and M_y which form an hypothesis about the width and length of the rectangle (see lines $21-24$). We then consider the set of edge points $\mathbf{P_i}$ which contributed to the current peaks A_x and A_y (line 25). The subset $\mathbf{P_f}$ of this set, containing points which belong to the rectangle should have coordinates lower or equal to the parameter values M_x and M_y (line 26). If the number of elements of $\mathbf{P_f}$ is bigger than a user defined threshold p, we regard the rectangle hypothesis to be successfully supported by boundary information and we update its dimension parameters (line $27-28$). A region based verification approach as in line 16 takes the final decision about the validity of the hypothesis (line 29). The advantage of this technique with regard to a standard implementation of the Hough transform is efficiency, since accumulation and search for peaks is performed in one dimensional structures.

Our framework attempts to recover graspable surface boundaries by examining every detected vertex (see line 2 of Fig. 2). This results to the localization of redundant graspable surfaces when more than one vertices per surface have been detected. The procedure invoked in line 9 selects those recovered boundaries which describe the scene in terms of global accuracy and consistency by applying a minimum description length (MDL) approach. The reader is referred to [5] p.122 for implementation details. In addition, independent graspable surface boundary recovery triggered by each detected vertex allows for parallel implementation of the algorithm: A separate processor can be used for dealing with each vertex of the vertex set.

Throughout our analysis we had to test relations of various geometric entities. We had to find out for example whether a two detected vertices are coplanar (look at line 13 of Fig. 2), if the direction vectors of two vertices are parallel (line 13), if an edge point belongs to a plane defined by a detected vertex (line 19), or if the points inside a hypothesized boundary belong to the plane it defines (lines 16, 29). Introduction of empirically defined thresholds for deciding the validity of the relations leads to a non robust system. This problem can be avoided when taking into consideration the error in calculating the geometric entities and statistically testing the geometric relations. If so, all thresholds can be replaced by a unique value, the significance level. We have performed all tests statistically, using the framework in [3], because of its simplicity and compactness. We denote the

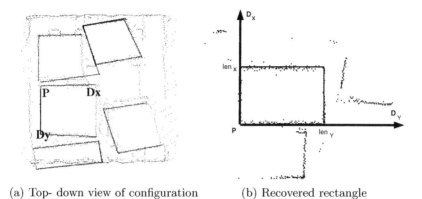

(a) Top- down view of configuration   (b) Recovered rectangle

Fig. 3. Recovery of graspable surface dimensions from edge points

significance level by α in our pseudo code, appearing as input to every procedure where geometric relations are tested (e.g in lines 13,19,16,29).

3   Experimental Results

The output of our algorithm applied on the test case of Fig.1 (a) is given in Fig. 4. Fig. 4 (a) depicts the detected boundaries of the graspable surfaces and Fig. 4 (b) shows the range points inside the detected boundaries, which led to the verification of the particular boundary hypotheses. We have performed a number of experiments of the algorithm using card board boxes. A Pentium 3, $600Mhz$ was used for our experiments. The overall average execution time of the algorithm algorithm was 55 seconds. Edge detection lasted 10 seconds, vertex detection 14 and the dimension recovery about 31 seconds. The average processing time for dimension recovery from a single vertex was 3 seconds. This means that in the event a parallel implementation for object recovery is employed the overall execution time will be less than 30 seconds on the average. In terms of robustness, our experiments demonstrated that the system only occasionally fails to recover all the graspable surfaces in the pile. According to initial accuracy measurements the translational grasping accuracy was less then 1.5 cm, almost equal to the accuracy of the sensor employed. In the future we intend to continue experiments for the system evaluation.

4   Conclusions

We presented a framework for automatic unloading (depalletizing) of piled boxes of unknown dimensions. We employed a laser sensor for data acquisition and detected graspable surfaces of objects from images acquired from the sensor. Major characteristics of our approach is the usage of both boundary and region

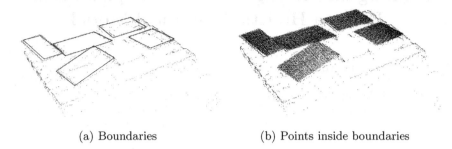

(a) Boundaries   (b) Points inside boundaries

Fig. 4. Recovered graspable surfaces

based sources of information obtained from the range images and the recovery problem decomposition into subproblems. Experiments demonstrated that our system shows advantages such as computational efficiency and robustness. However, our system as is does not recover the height of the objects it grasps. This is a problem when we want to automatically sort the objects grasped. This problem can be solved by the usage of an additional sensor for measuring the objects' height after their grasping.

References

1. A.J. Baerveldt. *Robust Singulation of Parcels with a Robot System using multiple sensors.* PhDthesis, Swiss federal institute of technology, 1993.
2. C.H. Chen and A.C. Kak. A robot vision system for recognizing 3-D objects in low-order polynomial time. *IEEE Transactions on Systems, Man, and Cybernetics,* 19(6):1535–1563, November-December 1989.
3. W. Foerstner, A. Brunn, and S. Heuel. Statistically testing uncertain geometric relations. In G. Sommer, N. Krueger, and Perwass Ch., editors, *Mustererkennung,* pages 17–26. Springer, September 2000.
4. M. Hashimoto and K. Sumi. 3d object recognition based on integration of range image and grey-scale image. In *Britisch Machine Vision Conference,* pages 253–262, 1999.
5. A. Jaklič, A. Leonardis, and F. Solina. *Segmentation and recovery of Superquadrics,* volume 20 of Computational imaging and vision. Kluwer Academic Publishers, Dordrecht, 2000.
6. D. Katsoulas. Robust extraction of vertices in range images by constraining the Hough transform. In *ibPRIA 2003, First Iberian Conference on Pattern Recognition and Image Analysis,* LNCS. Springer, June 2003. To appear.
7. S. Kristensen, S. Estable, M. Kossow, and R. Brosel. Bin-picking with a solid state range camera. *Robotics and autonomous systems,* 35(3–4):143–151, June 2001.
8. D. Newcorn. Robot gains eyesight. *Packaging World,* October 1998.
9. C.F. Olson. A general method for geometric feature matching and feature extraction. *International Journal of Computer Vision,* 45(1):39–54, October 2001.
10. R.W. Swanson and L.J. Thayer. A fast shaded-polygon renderer. In David C. Evans and Rusell J. Athay, editors, *Computer Graphics (SIGGRAPH '86 Proceedings),* pages 95–101, August 1986.

Training and Recognition of Complex Scenes Using a Holistic Statistical Model

Daniel Keysers, Michael Motter, Thomas Deselaers, and Hermann Ney

Lehrstuhl für Informatik VI, Computer Science Department
RWTH Aachen – University of Technology, D-52056 Aachen, Germany
{keysers, motter, deselaers, ney}@informatik.rwth-aachen.de

Abstract. We present a holistic statistical model for the automatic analysis of complex scenes. Here, holistic refers to an integrated approach that does not take local decisions about segmentation or object transformations. Starting from Bayes' decision rule, we develop an appearance-based approach explaining all pixels in the given scene using an explicit background model. This allows the training of object references from unsegmented data and recognition of complex scenes. We present empirical results on different databases obtaining state-of-the-art results on two databases where a comparison to other methods is possible. To obtain quantifiable results for object-based recognition, we introduce a new database with subsets of different difficulties.

1 Introduction

The increasing availability of digital images causes a growing interest in automatic classification of such images. Up to now, approaches to classification, indexing, or retrieval are usually not based on the objects present in the image, but mostly on features derived from color or texture. This is due to the fact that automatic segmentation of objects in presence of inhomogeneous background is still an unsolved problem [7]. Approaches to image object recognition rely on manually pre-segmented data for training. These algorithms also perform best for homogeneous or static background but ignoring background information in automatic recognition can cause classification errors.

In this paper we address the problem of automatically determining object references and object-based classification in the presence of background. We present an appearance-based holistic statistical model for automatic training and recognition of image objects that explicitly takes into account the image background. Starting from Bayes' decision rule, which is the best we can do to minimize the error rate, we avoid explicit segmentation and determination of transformation parameters but instead consider these as integral parts of the decision problem. This is done to avoid incorrect local decisions. This holistic approach takes into consideration experiences in speech recognition, where explicit segmentation of 'objects' (words) and background is neither done in training, nor in recognition. Note that treatment of distortions and transformations is computationally significantly more demanding in 2D (e.g. images) than in 1D (e.g. speech signals).

Related work. The problems addressed here have been considered by other authors with different approaches. We discuss two works that are closely related:

B. Michaelis and G. Krell (Eds.): DAGM 2003, LNCS 2781, pp. 52–59, 2003.

A statistical model for object recognition in the presence of heterogeneous background and occlusions was presented in [6]. The authors use wavelet features to determine the local probabilities of a position in the image belonging to an object or to the background. The background is modeled by a uniform distribution. The assumption of statistical independence of the object features is reported to produce best results. The problem of automatic training in presence of heterogeneous background is not addressed. The authors report 0% error rate on a classification and localization task, in the presence of rotation and translation.

A similar model to the one presented here has been independently proposed in [1]. The authors introduce transformed mixtures of Gaussians that are used to learn representations on different databases of image data. They provide a detailed description of the statistical model. They consider only translations for an image database with background but do not present quantifiable results for this case. Instead, they only compare the results to a Gaussian mixture not regarding transformations. Error rates are only given for a set of synthetic 9×9 images in comparison to Gaussian mixtures.

2   Statistical Model and Decision Making

Principles. To classify an observation $\mathbf{X} \in \mathbb{R}^{I \times J}$ we use Bayes' decision rule

$$\mathbf{X} \longmapsto r(\mathbf{X}) = \operatorname*{argmax}_{k} \left\{ p(k)\, p(\mathbf{X}|k) \right\}, \tag{1}$$

where $p(k)$ is the prior probability of class k and $p(\mathbf{X}|k)$ is the class-conditional probability for the observation $\mathbf{X}$ given class k. For holistic recognition, we extend the elementary decision rule (1) into the following directions:

- We assume that the scene $\mathbf{X}$ contains an unknown number M of objects belonging to the classes $k_1, ..., k_M =: k_1^M$. Reference models $p(\mathbf{X}|\boldsymbol{\mu}_k)$ exist for each of the classes $k = 1, \dots, K$, and μ_0 represents the background.
- We take decisions about object boundaries, i.e. the original scene is implicitly partitioned into $M + 1$ regions I_0^M, where $I_m \subset \{(i,j) : i = 1, ..., I, j = 1, ..., J\}$ is assumed to contain the m-th object and I_0 the background.
- The reference models may be subject to certain transformations (rotation, scale, translation, etc.). That is, given transformation parameters $\boldsymbol{\vartheta}_1^M$, the m-th reference is mapped to $\boldsymbol{\mu}_{k_m} \to \boldsymbol{\mu}_{k_m}(\boldsymbol{\vartheta}_m)$.

The unknown parameters $M, k_1^M, \boldsymbol{\vartheta}_1^M$ and (implicitly) I_0^M must be considered and the hypothesis which best explains the given scene is searched. This must be done considering the interdependence between the image partitioning, transformation parameters and hypothesized objects, where in the holistic concept partitioning is a part of the classification process. Note that this means that any pixel in the scene must be assigned either to an object or to the background class. This model has been introduced in [3], where a restricted version was used in the experiments, only allowing horizontal shift. The resulting decision rule is:

$$r(\mathbf{X}) = \operatorname*{argmax}_{M, k_1^M} \left\{ \max_{\boldsymbol{\vartheta}_1^M} \left\{ p(\boldsymbol{\vartheta}_1^M) \cdot p(k_1^M) \cdot \prod_{m=0}^{M} p(\mathbf{X}_{I_m} | \boldsymbol{\mu}_{k_m}(\boldsymbol{\vartheta}_m)) \right\} \right\}, \tag{2}$$

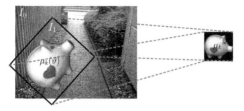

Fig. 1. Implicit partitioning and comparison during the search.

where $\mathbf{X}$ denotes the scene to be classified and $\mathbf{X}_{I_m}$ is the feature vector extracted from region I_m. Instead of performing a summation over the parameters $\boldsymbol{\vartheta}_1^M$, we apply the common maximum approximation here. Invariance aspects can be directly incorporated into the models chosen for the density functions using a probabilistic model of variability. In (2), $p(k_1^M)$ is a prior over the combination of objects in the scene, which may depend on the transformation parameters and the combination of objects.

Constraints. Regarding the components of the presented decision rule (2), we start with the consideration of the interdependence between segmentation and recognition. For the identification of one object in the presence of inhomogeneous background we assume $M = 1$. Thus, (2) reduces to

$$r(\mathbf{X}) = \operatorname*{argmax}_{k} \left\{ \max_{\boldsymbol{\vartheta}} \left\{ p(\boldsymbol{\vartheta})\, p(k)\, p(\mathbf{X}_{I_0}|\mu_0)\, p(\mathbf{X}_{I_1}|\boldsymbol{\mu}_k(\boldsymbol{\vartheta})) \right\} \right\}. \tag{3}$$

We consider 2D-rotation, scaling with fixed aspect ratio, and translation as transformations. The priors $p(\boldsymbol{\vartheta})$ and $p(k)$ are assumed uniform. The object density $p(\mathbf{X}|\boldsymbol{\mu}_k)$ is modeled using Gaussian kernel densities or Gaussian mixture densities. The use of mixture models allows the implicit modeling of further transformations by mapping them to different densities if they are observed in the training data. The part of the image that is not assigned to any object is assigned to the class background. In the experiments, the set of background pixels is modeled by a univariate distribution on the pixel level, where individual pixel values are assumed to be statistically independent. I.e. we assume for the background model $p(\mathbf{X}|\mu_0) = \prod_{x \in \mathbf{X}} p(x|\mu_0)$. The local density $p(x|\mu_0)$ is chosen among univariate Gaussian, uniform distribution, or empirical histograms with different numbers of bins. Note that the correct normalization of the distributions is important because of the changing amount of pixels that are explained for different transformation parameters $\boldsymbol{\vartheta}$. One example partitioning is shown in Fig. 1.

Decision Making. To illustrate the search or decision problem arising from the decision rule (3), we fix the hypothesized class k and assume the maximizing transformation parameters $\hat{\boldsymbol{\vartheta}}$ are to be determined. E.g. considering Gaussian densities $p(\mathbf{X}|\boldsymbol{\mu}_k) = \mathcal{N}(\mathbf{X}|\boldsymbol{\mu}_k, \sigma_1^2 \mathbf{I})$ for the objects and $p(x|\mu_0) = \mathcal{N}(x|\mu_0, \sigma_0^2)$ for the background leads to the search

$$\hat{\boldsymbol{\vartheta}} = \underset{\boldsymbol{\vartheta}}{\operatorname{argmax}} \{p(\boldsymbol{\vartheta})\, p(k)\, p(\mathbf{X}_{I_0}|\mu_0)\, p(\mathbf{X}_{I_1}|\boldsymbol{\mu}_k(\boldsymbol{\vartheta}))\} \tag{4}$$

$$= \underset{\boldsymbol{\vartheta}}{\operatorname{argmin}}\{-\log p(\boldsymbol{\vartheta}) - \log p(k) + \frac{1}{2}|I_0|\log(2\pi\sigma_0^2) + \frac{1}{2\sigma_0^2}\sum_{x\in\mathbf{X}_{I_0}}(x-\mu_0)^2$$

$$+ \frac{1}{2}|S_1|\log(2\pi\sigma_1^2) + \frac{1}{2\sigma_1^2}\|\mathbf{X}_{I_1} - \boldsymbol{\mu}_k(\boldsymbol{\vartheta})\|^2\}$$

The large number of parameter settings $\boldsymbol{\vartheta}$ makes the search for the maximizing arguments a complex problem. Optimization strategies should be considered:

- The Euclidean distances $\|\mathbf{X}_{I_1} - \boldsymbol{\mu}_k(\boldsymbol{\vartheta})\|$ for all translations can be efficiently calculated using the fast Fourier transform reducing the computation effort for this term in the order of $\log|\mathbf{X}| / |\boldsymbol{\mu}_k(\boldsymbol{\vartheta})|$.
- The sums of squares $\sum_{x\in\mathbf{X}_{I_0}}(x-\mu_0)^2$ for all translations can be efficiently computed using precomputed sums of squares. This reduces the effort for this term in the order of $|\boldsymbol{\mu}_k(\boldsymbol{\vartheta})|^{-1}$.
- The search space can be reduced by limiting the number of hypothesized transformations or by restricting the regions I_1 to square regions.
- A significant speedup can be gained by pruning the search space using the results of a complete search in a down-scaled version of the scene.

Training. Algorithms for single object recognition cannot be used to determine the model parameters without given segmentation. The following training algorithm is based on an expectation-maximization (EM) scheme, where the hidden variables are the parameters $\boldsymbol{\vartheta}$ for each object in each training scene:

1. initialize model parameters
2. search maximizing transformation parameters $\boldsymbol{\vartheta}$ in each scene using (4)
3. re-estimate model parameters (e.g. EM algorithm for mixtures)
4. repeat from 2 until convergence

For the training we assume exactly one object to be present in each image. Furthermore, objects are assumed to lie within a square region. The initial model parameters can be based on a constant graylevel estimated from a histogram of the training data or a small set of manually segmented objects. The latter approach facilitates convergence and still leads to a high reduction of manual preprocessing. The hypothesized transformations are translation, scaling with fixed aspect ratio and 2D-rotation.

3   Databases and Results

To evaluate the quality of an image classification approach it is important to compare the obtained results to those of other methods on the same data. One of the drawbacks in the research within this field is that there exists no widely used benchmark database for object-based image recognition or object training. Many groups use their own non-public data which makes it impossible to compare results. A number of databases exist for different purposes, as e.g. face recognition or handwritten digit recognition, or the used databases contain unspecific images on which the results are judged qualitatively by a human observer.

Table 1. Description of databases COIL-20 and ERLANGEN with error rates (ER).

name	ERLANGEN	COIL-20
# classes	5	20
# training images	90	720
# test images	85	180
example images		
other methods (ER [%])	[6] 0.0	[2] 0.0
holistic model (ER [%])	0.0	0.0

The website `http://www-2.cs.cmu.edu/∼cil/v-images.html` lists many databases used in computer vision research, out of which none is suitable for this task. An exception is a database of images collected by the authors of [6], although error rates of 0% can be achieved, making a comparison difficult. Due to this absence of a standard benchmark we created a database for object-based scene analysis based on the well known Columbia Object Image Library (COIL) and a set of real-world backgrounds. This database named COIL-RWTH is publicly available upon request and results are presented in Section 3.3. Tables 1 and 3 show an overview of the databases used in this work.

3.1   ERLANGEN

Database. In [6] the authors used two databases of images containing five different objects, all images of size 256×256. The first of the databases contains images taken with one illumination while in the second case the objects are illuminated with two light sources. Each of the training sets contains 18 images per object taken at different 2D rotation angles on a homogeneous background. Another 17 images per object at rotation angles not occurring in the training set are in the test sets. For each database, three different test sets exist, one with heterogeneous background, and two with two different levels of occlusion. Note that background and occlusions were added to the images artificially. Note also that the background is identical in all of the images and it does not occur in the training images as background (although one image containing only the background exists). The background resolution differs from that of the object images, which might be advantageous when using features based on Gabor filters.

Results. We used the test set with heterogeneous background from the first database and the corresponding training set. In [6] a recognition error rate of 0% is reported. The same error rate was achieved using the proposed holistic model with rectangular prototype models.

3.2   COIL-20

Database. The Columbia Object Image Library (COIL-20) [5] contains 72 graylevel images for each of a set of 20 different objects, taken at intervals of five degrees 3D-rotation. To strictly separate train and test images, we use the odd angles of the 'processed' corpus (size 128×128) for training and the even angles

of the 'unprocessed' corpus (size 448×416) for testing. The two corpora differ
in the lighting conditions (because of the processing) and the size of the object
in the image (cp. Table 1). This procedure ensures at least 5 degrees difference
in 3D position and poses the additional difficulty of differing light conditions.
Other authors use a splitting of the 'processed' corpus into train and test, but
in this case even a Euclidean nearest neighbor classifier leads to a 0% error rate.

Results. On the original COIL-20 database, the holistic approach achieves
a 0% error rate without further tuning than using a Gaussian background model
with mean zero and low variance. This result seems not surprising, as the images
are shown on a homogeneous black background. But as the training and test
images appear at different lighting conditions and on different scales, a nearest
neighbor classifier is not sufficient for completely correct classification and it is
necessary to extend it with elaborate techniques to achieve a 0% error rate [2].

3.3   COIL-RWTH

Database. As the COIL-20 database only contains images with homogeneous
black background, segmentation of the object from the background is a feasible
approach to classification. On the other hand, for real-world images segmentation poses a serious problem. (Although many application areas exist, where a
homogeneous or static background can be assumed and existing methods provide
acceptable solutions.) Therefore, a new dataset was created based on the objects
from the COIL-20 database and a set of new background images. The goal was
to create tasks of increasing difficulty to extend the COIL-20 task that can be
solved perfectly by existing methods. Each test image carries information about
the used transformation parameters for the object images, allowing to separate
the effects of different transformations.

We created two corpora that differ in the background used: The COIL-
RWTH-1 corpus contains objects placed on a homogeneous black background,
whereas the COIL-RWTH-2 corpus contains the objects in front of inhomogeneous real-world background images that were kept separate for training and
test images and vary in resolution. The two training and test sets are based on
the COIL-20 sets as described above. The training images are of size 192×192
and the size of the test images is 448×336. In all sets, we applied the following
uniformly distributed random transformations to the object images: translation,
360 degree 2D-rotation, and 60–100% scaling with fixed aspect ratio.

Results. To investigate the effect of different background models, we tested
univariate Gaussian densities, uniform distributions, and histograms with varying numbers of bins. In about 70% of the evaluated experiments, the univariate
Gaussian densities performed best among these models [4]. In the following we
therefore only discuss results obtained with this background model.

To observe the effect of known transformation parameters on the proposed
training, we trained a Gaussian single density on all images with a fixed 3D-
rotation angle of COIL-RWTH-2. The resulting mean images are shown in Table 2. It can be observed that the algorithm finds visually important parts of the
object searched for. The exact appearance of the mean image differs strongly

Table 2. Training results for Gaussian single densities on COIL-RWTH-2 with fixed 3D-rotation angle shown for one of the objects.

	rotation known		scaling known		no information	
initial mean of Gaussian density						
resulting mean of Gaussian density						

depending on the used initialization and the information supplied to the training algorithm. To evaluate the proposed training algorithm further, we trained Gaussian mixture densities on COIL-RWTH-1 and used these models to classify the original COIL-20 dataset. This resulted in 7.8% error rate. Note that the mixture density now models the different 3D-rotation angles of the objects. If the correct 2D-rotation of the object is supplied to the training algorithm, this error rate can be reduced to 4.4%. To separate the effect of unknown rotation from the other unknown parameters, in the following we only present results, in which the 2D-rotation of the objects in the images is known to the classifier.

We evaluated the classification accuracy of the complete setup on the COIL-RWTH databases in three scenarios. The results are shown in Table 3. As no other results are available, we used a conventional kernel density classifier for comparison. This classifier was supplied with the same information and an object position compensation was implemented using the center of gravity of the images. The results show that the holistic model performs with acceptable error rates for homogeneous background. Recall that scale changes are handled automatically and segmentation is performed implicitly in the model. The high error rates of the kernel density classifier can be explained by the fact that it cannot cope with scale changes. This also explains the improving error rate for the COIL-RWTH-1 test data when switching from the COIL-20 to the COIL-RWTH-1 training data, because the latter already includes variations in scale.

The error rates for the inhomogeneous background are clearly inacceptable. The failure of the algorithm here is based on the coincidence of two problems: 1. Automatic object training with unknown segmentation and variable background is very difficult. The resulting mean vectors show strong blur due to the changing background but capture some characteristic information, which is not enough to achieve lower error rates. 2. Detection of objects of variable scale and position in large inhomogeneous images based on an incomplete object model of graylevels and backgrounds not seen in training is possible only in few cases.

4   Conclusion

We presented a holistic statistical model for appearance-based training and recognition of objects in complex scenes. Experiments on two existing databases show the algorithm to be competitive with other known approaches. A third database with a higher level of difficulty that can be used by other researchers was introduced. The gained results underline the difficulty of training and recognition in the presence of inhomogeneous background. The fact that the presented

Table 3. Error rates for the COIL-RWTH database (20 classes, 180 test images each).

	COIL-20 720 images	COIL-RWTH-1 5760 images	COIL-RWTH-2 5760 images
training data			
test data	COIL-RWTH-1 	COIL-RWTH-1 	COIL-RWTH-2
kernel dens. (ER[%])	38.9	27.2	95.0
holistic (ER[%])	1.1	7.8	92.8

method achieves 0% error rates on two databases used in the literature, but fails on a database of images with highly misleading background shows that the databases on which 0% error rates can be reported are by far not representative for the complexity of the general object-based scene analysis problem.

Most improvement to the presented method can be expected from the inclusion of more descriptive features than only grayvalues, like e.g. wavelet features or local representations of image parts. Furthermore, local variations of the objects may be modeled using tangent distance or appropriate distortion models.

Acknowledgements. We would like to thank the members of the Chair for Pattern Recognition, Department of Computer Science, Friedrich Alexander University of Erlangen-Nürnberg for providing their database, and the members of the Department of Computer Science, Columbia University, New York for sharing their data openly.

References

1. B.J. Frey, N. Jojic: Transformation-invariant clustering using the EM algorithm. *IEEE Trans. Pattern Analysis and Machine Intelligence*, 25(1):1–17, January 2003.
2. D. Keysers, J. Dahmen, H. Ney, M.O. Güld: A Statistical Framework for Multi-Object Recognition. In *Informatiktage 2001 der Gesellschaft für Informatik*, Konradin Verlag, Bad Schussenried, Germany, pp. 73–76, October 2001.
3. D. Keysers, J. Dahmen, H. Ney, B. Wein, T. Lehmann: Statistical Framework for Model-based Image Retrieval in Medical Applications. *J. Electronic Imaging*, 12(1):59–68, January 2003.
4. M. Motter: Statistische Modellierung von Bildobjekten für die Bilderkennung. Diploma thesis, Chair of Computer Science VI, RWTH Aachen University of Technology, Aachen, Germany, December 2001.
5. H. Murase, S. Nayar: Visual Learning and Recognition of 3-D Objects from Appearance. *Int. J. Computer Vision*, 14(1):5–24, January 1995.
6. M. Reinhold, D. Paulus, H. Niemann: Appearance-Based Statistical Object Recognition by Heterogeneous Background and Occlusions. In *Pattern recognition. 23rd DAGM Symposium*, LNCS 2191, Munich, Germany, pp. 254–261, September 2001.
7. A.W.M. Smeulders, M. Worring, S. Santint, A. Gupta, R. Jain: Content-Based Image Retrieval at the End of the Early Years. *IEEE Trans. Pattern Analysis and Machine Intelligence*, 22:1349–1380, December 2000.

Combining White-Patch Retinex and the Gray World Assumption to Achieve Color Constancy for Multiple Illuminants

Marc Ebner

Universität Würzburg, Lehrstuhl für Informatik II
Am Hubland, 97074 Würzburg, Germany
ebner@informatik.uni-wuerzburg.de
http://www2.informatik.uni-wuerzburg.de/staff/ebner/welcome.html

Abstract. The human visual system is able to correctly determine the color of objects irrespective of the actual light they reflect. This ability to compute color constant descriptors is an important problem for computer vision research. We have developed a parallel algorithm for color constancy. The algorithm is based on two fundamental theories of color constancy, the gray world assumption and the white-patch retinex algorithm. The algorithm's performance is demonstrated on several images where objects are illuminated by multiple illuminants.

1 Motivation

The human visual system is able to correctly determine the color of objects irrespective of the actual light reflected by the objects. For instance, if a white wall is illuminated with red light, it will reflect more red light in comparison to the amount of light reflected in the green and blue spectrum. If the same wall is illuminated with green light, then the wall will reflect more light towards the green spectrum. If the scene viewed by a human observer is sufficiently complex, the wall will nevertheless appear white to a human observer. The human visual system is somehow able to discount the illuminant and to estimate the reflectances of the objects in view [24]. This ability is called color constancy, as the perceived color remains constant irrespective of the illuminant. Two different mechanisms may be used by the human visual system to achieve color constancy [20]. We have devised a parallel algorithm which is based on both of these mechanism. Previously, we have only used the gray world assumption [8].

Numerous solutions to the problem of color constancy have been proposed. Land, a pioneer in color constancy research has proposed the retinex theory [19]. Others have added to this research and proposed variants of the retinex theory [2,3,16,18]. Other algorithms for color constancy include gamut-constraint methods [1,13], perspective color constancy [10], color by correlation [11], the gray world assumption [4,17], recovery of basis function coefficients [21], mechanisms of light adaptation coupled with eye movements [7], neural networks [6,15,22], minimization of an energy function [23], comprehensive color normalization [12], committee-based methods which combine the output of several different color

B. Michaelis and G. Krell (Eds.): DAGM 2003, LNCS 2781, pp. 60–67, 2003.

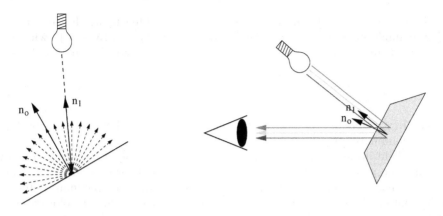

Fig. 1. For a Lambertian surface the amount of reflected light does not depend on viewing angle (left). It only depends on the angle between the surface normal and the direction of the light source. Part of the incoming light is absorbed by the surface, the remainder is reflected equally in all directions. We assume that the sensor's response function is described by a delta function. Thus only three different wavelength (red, green and blue) need to be considered (right).

constancy algorithms [5] or use of genetic programming [9]. Most solutions to color constancy only assume a single illuminant. Our algorithm can also cope with multiple illuminants. It runs on a parallel grid of simple processing elements which only perform local computations. No global computations are made. Thus, it is scalable and lends itself to a VLSI implementation.

2   Color Image Formation

Assume that we have an object with a Lambertian surface. Let a ray of light with intensity $L(\lambda)$ and wavelength λ be reflected by this object. Let $\mathbf{x}_o$ be the position where the ray hits the object. Part of the light is absorbed by the object, the remainder is reflected equally in all direction. For a Lambertian surface the light reaching the eye does not depend on viewing angle. It only depends on the angle between the surface normal and the direction of the light source (Figure 1). The response of a sensor at position $\mathbf{x}_s$ which measures the reflected ray is given by

$$\mathbf{I}(\mathbf{x}_s) = \mathbf{n}_l \cdot \mathbf{n}_o \int_\lambda R(\lambda, \mathbf{x}_o) L(\lambda) \mathbf{S}(\lambda) d\lambda \qquad (1)$$

where $\mathbf{I}(\mathbf{x}_s)$ is a vector of sensor responses, $\mathbf{n}_l$ is the unit vector pointing in the direction of the light source, $\mathbf{n}_o$ is the unit vector corresponding to the surface normal, $R(\lambda, \mathbf{x}_o)$ specifies the percentage of light reflected by the surface, and $\mathbf{S}(\lambda)$ specifies the sensor's response functions [12]. The sensor's response is calculated by integrating over all wavelengths to which the sensor responds.

If we assume ideal sensors for red, green and blue light, the sensor's response function is given by a delta function $(S_i(\lambda) = \delta(\lambda - \lambda_i))$ with $i \in$ {red, green, blue}. If we also assume that the light source illuminates the surface at a right angle, the above equation simplifies to

$$I_i(\mathbf{x}_s) = R(\lambda_i, \mathbf{x}_o)L(\lambda_i) \tag{2}$$

where $I_i(\mathbf{x}_s)$ denotes the i-th component of the vector $\mathbf{I}(\mathbf{x}_s)$. Thus, the light which illuminates the scene is scaled by the reflectances.

The light illuminating the scene can be recovered easily if the image contains at least one pixel for each band which reflects all light for this particular band. We only need to loop over all pixel values, and record the maximum intensity values for all three bands. Using these three values we rescale all color bands to the range $[0, 1]$.

$$R(\lambda_i, \mathbf{x}_o) = \frac{I_i(\mathbf{x}_s)}{L_{\max}(\lambda_i)} \tag{3}$$

with $L_{\max}(\lambda_i) = \max_{\mathbf{x}}\{I_i(\mathbf{x})\}$. This algorithm is called the white-patch retinex algorithm [14].

A second algorithm for color constancy is based on the assumption that the average color is gray. If we assume that the reflectances of the surface are uniformly distributed over the interval $[0, 1]$, the average value will be 0.5 for all bands [9].

$$\frac{1}{N}\sum_{\mathbf{x}}^{N} I_i(\mathbf{x}) = \frac{1}{N}\sum_{\mathbf{x}}^{N} R(\lambda_i, \mathbf{x})L(\lambda_i)$$

$$= L(\lambda_i)\frac{1}{N}\sum_{\mathbf{x}}^{N} R(\lambda_i, \mathbf{x})$$

$$= L(\lambda_i)\frac{1}{2} \tag{4}$$

Thus, space average color can be used to estimate the intensities of the light illuminating the scene. The light illuminating the scene is simply twice the space average color.

$$L(\lambda_i) = \frac{2}{N}\sum_{\mathbf{x}}^{N} I_i(\mathbf{x}) \tag{5}$$

The reflectances can then be calculated as follows.

$$R(\lambda_i, \mathbf{x}_o) = \frac{I_i(\mathbf{x}_s)}{L(\lambda_i)} \tag{6}$$

Both cues, space-average scene color as well as the color of the highest luminance patch may be used by the human visual system to estimate the color of the light illuminating the scene [20].

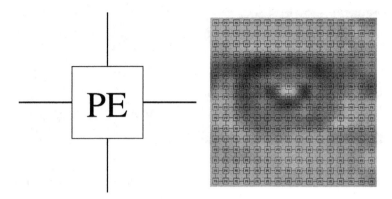

Fig. 2. Each processing element is connected to four neighbors (left). We have one processing element for each pixel of the input image (right).

3   Calculating Local Space Average Color

Our algorithm runs on a parallel grid of processing elements. Each processing element is connected to four other processing elements (Figure 2). We have one element per pixel. A single element is connected to the elements on the left, on the right as well as to the elements above and below the current element. For each color band red, green, and blue, we calculate local space average color by averaging data from the four neighboring elements and slowly fading the intensity of the current band into the result. Let $\mathbf{c}(x,y) = [c_{\text{red}}(x,y), c_{\text{green}}(x,y), c_{\text{blue}}(x,y)]$ be the color of the pixel at position (x,y) and $\mathbf{avg}(x,y) = [\text{avg}_{\text{red}}(x,y), \text{avg}_{\text{green}}(x,y), \text{avg}_{\text{blue}}(x,y)]$ be local space average color estimated by element (x,y). Let p_1 be a small percentage. Local space average color is computed by iterating the following equation indefinitely for all three bands $i \in \{\text{red}, \text{green}, \text{blue}\}$.

$$a_i(x,y) = \frac{1}{4}(\text{avg}_i(x-1,y) + \text{avg}_i(x,y-1) + \text{avg}_i(x+1,y) + \text{avg}_i(x,y+1))$$
$$\text{avg}_i(x,y) = (1-p_1)a_i(x,y) + p_1 \cdot c_i(x,y) \tag{7}$$

In case of a static image, we can stop the calculations after the difference between the old and the new estimate has been reduced to a small value. A sample calculation for a scene illuminated with two different illuminants is shown in Figure 3.

The calculations are done independently for all three color bands red, green, and blue. The first term averages the data from neighboring elements and multiplies the result with $(1-p_1)$. The second term is the local color multiplied by a small percentage p_1. This operation slowly fades the local color into the current estimate of the local space average color. The factor p_1 determines the extent over which local space average color will be computed. As local average color is handed from one element to the next, it will be multiplied by $(1-p_1)$. Thus, if

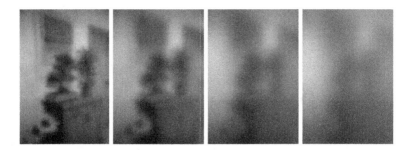

Fig. 3. Space average color after 50, 200, 1000 and 5000 iterations of the algorithm.

p_1 is large, the influence of local space average color will decay very fast from one element to the next. On the other hand, if p_1 is small, then it will decay very slowly.

4   Parallel Dynamic Range Estimation

We now have local average color and the input color available at every processing element. In order to restore the original colors of the image we look at the deviation from local average color. Let $d_i(x, y)$ be the deviation between local average color and the current color at position (x, y). We take the maximum across neighboring elements:

$$d'_i(x, y) = \max\{|\text{avg}_i - c_i|, d_i(x - 1, y), d_i(x, y - 1), d_i(x + 1, y), d_i(x, y + 1)\} \tag{8}$$

Finally, we reduce the maximum deviation by a small percentage p_2.

$$d_i = (1 - p_2)d'_i \tag{9}$$

The factor p_2 determines how fast the deviation decays to zero as it is passed from element to element. This deviation is used to scale the difference between the current color and local space average color.

$$o_i = \frac{(c_i - \text{avg}_i)}{d_i} \tag{10}$$

Finally a sigmoidal activation function is used to transform the computed value to the range [0,1].

$$r_i = \frac{1}{1 + e^{-\frac{o_i}{\sigma}}} \tag{11}$$

If o_i is close to zero, i.e. local average color and the color of the current pixel is very similar, then the output color r_i will be gray. We also experimented with a linear transformation. In this case, output color is computed as follows:

$$r_i = \frac{1}{2}(1 + o_i) \tag{12}$$

Values smaller than 0 are set to zero and values larger than 1 are set to 1. The difference between the sigmoidal and linear transformation are shown in Figure 4. Use of the sigmoidal transfer function produced better results.

Fig. 4. A linear output function was used for the left image. A sigmoidal output function was used for the right image. The colors of the left image look less saturated than the colors of the right image.

5   Results

The above algorithm was tested on several real world images. In each case multiple illuminants were used to illuminate the objects in the scene. The images were taken with an analog SLR camera, developed on film and then digitized. The digitized images were linearized with a gamma correction of 2.2. The algorithm was run on the linearized input images. A gamma correction of $\frac{1}{2.2}$ was applied to the output images. The following parameters were used: $p_1 = 0.0005$, $p_2 = 0.005$, $\sigma = 0.2$. The size of the input images was 256×175 pixels. Results for four different input images are shown in Figure 5. The first row shows the input images. The second row shows local average color, the third row shows the absolute deviation from local average color and the last row shows the output images of our algorithm. The first three images show objects illuminated with two colored light bulbs. For the fourth image, the camera's built in flash was used to illuminate the scene. As can be seen from the output images, the algorithm is able to adjust the colors of the input images. For a scene illuminated with white light the output is almost equivalent to the input image.

6   Conclusion

We have developed a parallel algorithm for color constancy. The algorithm calculates local space average color and maximum deviation of the current color from local average color. Both cues are used to estimate the reflectances of the objects in view. In this respect, the algorithm is a combination of both the gray

Fig. 5. Results for 4 different input images. Two colored illuminants were used for the first three images. A flash was used to illuminate the objects shown in the last image.

world assumption and the white patch retinex algorithm. The algorithm's ability to estimate the reflectances of the objects in view was demonstrated on several real world images taken with multiple illuminants.

References

1. K. Barnard, G. Finlayson, and B. Funt. Color constancy for scenes with varying illumination. *Computer Vision and Image Understanding*, 65(2):311–321, 1997.
2. D. H. Brainard and B. A. Wandell. Analysis of the retinex theory of color vision. In G. E. Healey, S. A. Shafer, and L. B. Wolff, eds., *Color*, pp. 208–218, Boston, 1992. Jones and Bartlett Publishers.
3. M. Brill and G. West. Contributions to the theory of invariance of color under the condition of varying illumination. *Journal of Math. Biology*, 11:337–350, 1981.
4. G. Buchsbaum. A spatial processor model for object colour perception. *Journal of the Franklin Institute*, 310(1):337–350, 1980.

5. V. C. Cardei and B. Funt. Committee-based color constancy. In *Proc. of the IS&T/SID 7th Color Imaging Conference: Color Science, Systems and Applications*, pp. 311–313, 1999.
6. S. M. Courtney, L. H. Finkel, and G. Buchsbaum. A multistage neural network for color constancy and color induction. *IEEE Trans. on Neural Networks*, 6(4):972–985, 1995.
7. M. D'Zmura and P. Lennie. Mechanisms of color constancy. In Glenn E. Healey, Steven A. Shafer, and Lawrence B. Wolff, eds., *Color*, pp. 224–234, Boston, 1992. Jones and Bartlett Publishers.
8. M. Ebner. A parallel algorithm for color constancy. Technical Report 296, Universität Würzburg, Lehrstuhl für Informatik II, Würzburg, Germany, April 2002.
9. M. Ebner. Evolving color constancy for an artificial retina. In J. Miller, M. Tomassini, P. Luca Lanzi, C. Ryan, A. G. B. Tettamanzi, and W. B. Langdon, eds., *Genetic Programming: Proc. of the 4th Europ. Conf., EuroGP 2001, Lake Como, Italy*, pp. 11–22, Berlin, 2001. Springer-Verlag.
10. G. D. Finlayson. Color in perspective. *IEEE Trans. on Pattern Analysis and Machine Intelligence*, 18(10):1034–1038, 1996.
11. G. D. Finlayson, P. M. Hubel, and S. Hordley. Color by correlation. In *Proc. of IS&T/SID. The 5th Color Imaging Conference: Color Science, Systems, and Applications, The Radisson Resort, Scottsdale, AZ*, pp. 6–11, 1997.
12. G. D. Finlayson, B. Schiele, and J. L. Crowley. Comprehensive colour image normalization. In *Fifth Europ. Conf. on Computer Vision*, 1998.
13. D. A. Forsyth. A novel approach to colour constancy. In *2nd Int. Conf. on Computer Vision, Tampa, FL*, pp. 9–18. IEEE Press, 1988.
14. B. Funt, K. Barnard, and L. Martin. Is colour constancy good enough? In *Fifth Europ. Conf. on Computer Vision*, pp. 445–459, 1998.
15. B. Funt, V. Cardei, and K. Barnard. Learning color constancy. In *Proc. of the IS&T/SID 4th Color Imaging Conference*, pp. 58–60, Scottsdale, 1996.
16. B. V. Funt and M. S. Drew. Color constancy computation in near-mondrian scenes using a finite dimensional linear model. In *Proc. of the Comp. Society Conf. on Computer Vision and Pattern Recognition*, pp. 544–549. Comp. Society Press, 1988.
17. R. Gershon, A. D. Jepson, and J. K. Tsotsos. From [r,g,b] to surface reflectance: Computing color constant descriptors in images. In *Proc. of the 10th Int. Joint Conference on Artificial Intelligence*, volume 2, pp. 755–758, 1987.
18. B. K. P. Horn. *Robot Vision*. The MIT Press, Cambridge, Massachusetts, 1986.
19. E. H. Land. The retinex theory of colour vision. *Proc. Royal Inst. Great Britain*, 47:23–58, 1974.
20. K. J. Linnell and D. H. Foster. Space-average scene colour used to extract illuminant information. In C. Dickinson, I. Murray, and D. Carden, eds., *John Dalton's Colour Vision Legacy. Selected Proc. of the Int. Conf.*, pp. 501–509, London, 1997. Taylor & Francis.
21. L. T. Maloney and B. A. Wandell. Color constancy: a method for recovering surface spectral reflectance. *Journal of the Opt. Society of America A3*, 3(1):29–33, 1986.
22. A. Moore, J. Allman, and R. M. Goodman. A real-time neural system for color constancy. *IEEE Trans. on Neural Networks*, 2(2):237–247, 1991.
23. S. Usui and S. Nakauchi. A neurocomputational model for colour constancy. In C. Dickinson, I. Murray, and D. Carden, eds., *John Dalton's Colour Vision Legacy. Selected Proc. of the Int. Conf.*, pp. 475–482, London, 1997. Taylor & Francis.
24. S. Zeki. *A Vision of the Brain*. Blackwell Science, Oxford, 1993.

Method of Creating of Functional Invariants under One-Parameter Geometric Image Transformations

Dmitry Kinoshenko [1], Vladimir Mashtalir [1], Alexander Orlov [2], and Elena Yegorova [1]

[1] Kharkov National University of Radio Electronics, department of information science,
Lenin ave., 14, 61166, Kharkov, Ukraine
{Kinoshenko, Mashtalir, Yegorova}@kture.kharkov.ua
[2] Kharkov Regional Institute of the Ukrainian Academy of Public Administration
at the President of Ukraine, department of information technologies,
Moscow ave., 75, 61050, Kharkov, Ukraine
Orlov@kbuapa.kharkov.ua

Abstract. We propose a regular method for constructing integral invariants under geometric image transformations. The method allows us to find invariant features for arbitrary one-parameter groups of 2D-transformations. Our theoretical results provide a constructive synthesis of functional invariants. We illustrate method by examples involving shear maps and projective transformations. Furthermore, in the same way action of multi-parameter groups can be used for the analysis of image sequences on time intervals when the transformation coefficients are known and constant. The time at which the image appears is also as a parameter. A general form of such one-parameter groups is obtained for six-parameter planar affine transformations. Invariants for one-parameter Euclidean similarity group are found.

1 Introduction

Beginning from earliest studies, see e.g. [1, 2], considerable efforts have been devoted to the improvement of image processing in presence of geometric transformations. In particular, the invariance and equivariance of the image processing algorithms under certain deformations and distortions may be essential for correct interpretation of the images. Traditionally, group theory is used to develop such algorithms [3, 4] because geometric transformations satisfy the axioms of group theory (namely, the closedness, the existence of an inverse, the identity, and the associativity). Methods developed by using group theory demonstrate superior performance. Still this approach is far from being fully explored. In particular, there are no constructive methods providing effective invariant image processing under all possible geometric transformations.

The integral approach to image analysis has many advantages – high noise tolerance, the ability to compensate for several consecutive transformations, the ease of use on parallel computers in real time [5–7]. Many well known and excellent algorithms are based on the integral approach, just to name a few we shall mention correlation methods, moments of different powers, Hough, Fourier, Mellin and others transforms used for motion detection in image sequences, image reconstruction from projections, various forms of template matching [5–9, etc.].

B. Michaelis and G. Krell (Eds.): DAGM 2003, LNCS 2781, pp. 68–75, 2003.
© Springer-Verlag Berlin Heidelberg 2003

The problem of image analysis under geometric transformations, in its generality, can be presented as follows.

Let $B(x, y)$ be a grayscale image, defined on the sensor sight domain $\mathfrak{D} \subset \mathbb{R}^2$. Suppose, r-parameter set $G = \{a_1, a_2, ..., a_r\}$ is given and its action on a plane has form

$$g \in G \quad g : \{x \to \varphi_1(x, y, a_1, a_2, ..., a_r), \; y \to \varphi_2(x, y, a_1, a_2, ..., a_r)\}, \tag{1}$$

where $(x, y) \in \mathfrak{D}$. If some map $\Phi : G \times \mathbb{R}^2 \to \mathbb{R}^2$ is smooth (differentiable in local coordinates) and has properties

$$\forall g', g'' \in G, z = (x, y) \in \mathbb{R}^2, \; \Phi(g' \circ g'', z) = \Phi((g' \circ \Phi(g''), z), \forall z \in \mathbb{R}^2, \Phi(e, z) = z$$

("$\circ$" denotes action of the group, e is identity transformation), then relationships (1) form a Lie group of planar transformations. With the purpose of more strict formalization usually additional restrictions are introduced:

☐ analyzable transformations are effective: if $\forall z \in \mathbb{R}^2, \Phi(g, z) = z$, then $g = e$;

☐ on considered time lag the transforms (1) do not output object image for boundaries of the sight domain, i.e. $\forall (x, y) \in \mathfrak{D} : B(x, y) \neq 0 \Rightarrow (\varphi_1(x, y, a_1, a_2, ..., a_r), \varphi_2(x, y, a_1, a_2, ..., a_r)) \in \mathfrak{D}$.

Translations, rotations, scaling, skewing, Euclidean moving and similarities, affine and projective groups are traditionally used models of image transformations. The action of any group produces images set partition $M = \{B(x, y)\}$ onto classes of equivalence:

$M = \{m_\alpha\}$, $m_\alpha \neq \varnothing$, $\bigcup_\alpha m_\alpha = M$, $\forall m_\alpha, m_\beta \in M \Rightarrow m_\alpha \cap m_\beta = \varnothing$ or $m_\alpha = m_\beta$. At a verbal level the problem of the image analysis by reducing of the coordinate images descriptions is that for any image $B(x, y)$ from a class of equivalence m_α the normal (template) image $B_0(x, y) \in m_\alpha$ must be found. Generally, the choice of the template is arbitrary. Under the fixed template $B_0(x, y) \in M_0 \subset M$ set $\{g \circ B(x, y)\}$, $g \in G$ represents an orbit of this template, and union of all trajectories of all templates is set of images to be processed. Thus, the processing of the images in conditions of geometric transformations frequently is reduced to create a map $F : B \to \square^P$, having one of the properties:

$$\forall g \in G, \forall z \in \mathfrak{D} \subset \mathbb{R}^2, F(B(z)) = F(B(\Phi(g, z))), \tag{2}$$

$$\forall g \in G, \forall z \in \mathfrak{D} \subset \mathbb{R}^2, F(B(\Phi(g, z))) = \tilde{\Phi}_g \circ F(B(z)), \tag{3}$$

where $\tilde{\Phi}_g$ is an action of group G in $\mathbb{R}^P$ possibly distinct from $\Phi(g, z)$ action, but allows to find unknown parameters $a_1, a_2, ..., a_r$ via solution of equations (3) to provide image normalization.

To solve problem (2) we propose a method of invariant features synthesis, applicable to action of any one-parameter transformation group. If $r > 1$, the method can be used for groups decomposed as a commutative product of one-parameter transformations. The method can be applied to image sequences processing on some time interval at constant and known values $a_1, a_2, ..., a_r$ (the time is used as parameter).

2 Theoretical Foundation

In what follows we shall find invariant maps from an image set M into some functional space. If $\mathfrak{F} : B \to f(t)$ is the desired map into space of real variable functions, then considering $f(t)=(f(t_1), f(t_2),\ldots, f(t_p))$ for arbitrary $t_1, t_2,\ldots, t_p$, we shall get invariant map into $\mathbb{R}^p$, i.e. p-dimensional feature vectors.

Firstly, let us reduce a creation of functional invariants to a search for one-parameter set of normalizers. The normalizer is such a map $F : M \to M$ for which the relations $F(B) = \mathfrak{S}(B) \circ B$ and $F(B')=F(B'')$ are fulfilled, where $\mathfrak{S} : M \to G$ is map into the group, the images B', B'' are equivalent with respect to this group action.

Theorem 1. Let F_t be one-parameter set of normalizers and let $\mathfrak{S}_t$ be appropriate set of maps into the group. Then $\mathfrak{F} : B \to f(t)=\mathfrak{S}_1(B)[\mathfrak{S}_t(B)]^{-1}$ is invariant map into space of functions having the values in G.

Proof. Let B', B'' be equivalent images. To prove it is enough to check up that for any t condition $\mathfrak{S}_1(B')[\mathfrak{S}_t(B')]^{-1} = \mathfrak{S}_1(B'')[\mathfrak{S}_t(B'')]^{-1}$ is valid. Assume $B''=g \circ B'$, then $\mathfrak{S}_t(B'')=\mathfrak{S}_t(B')g$. Thus, we get $\mathfrak{S}_1(B'')[\mathfrak{S}_t(B'')]^{-1} = \mathfrak{S}_1(B')g^{-1}[\mathfrak{S}_t(B')g^{-1}]^{-1} = \mathfrak{S}_1(B')[\mathfrak{S}_t(B')]^{-1}$, as was to be shown.

With the purpose of normalizers creating under condition of any one-parameter group action let us introduce a concept of normalizing functional. Note, group parameterization $G=\{g_s\}$ is canonical, if g_0 is unit of group and $g_{s'+s''} = g_{s'}g_{s''}$.

Definition 1. Functional $\mathcal{F} : M \to \mathbb{R}^1 (\mathbb{C}^1)$ is said a normalizing functional with respect to the canonically parameterized group $G=\{g_s\}$, if for some $t \in \mathbb{R}^1 (\mathbb{C}^1)$ the equality $\mathcal{F}(g_s B)=exp\,(ts)\mathcal{F}(B)$ is valid for any value s and any image $B \in M$.

Value t, appearing in definition and being, generally speaking, complex, will be called an index of normalizing functional. The presence of an exponential function in the definition is explained by validity equality $\mathcal{F}(g_s B)=f(s)\mathcal{F}(B)$ which implies the
obvious properties $f(2s)=f(s)^2$, $f(0)=1$, and $exp\,(ts)$ is one of the simplest fun`tions, satisfying these conditions.

Theorem 2. Let $\mathcal{F}$ be a normalizing functional, $\mathcal{F}(B) > 0$ for all $B \in M$, then the map $F : B \to g_\alpha \circ B$, where $\alpha = -ln\,\mathcal{F}(B)/t$, is a normalizer $F : M \to M$.

Proof. It is necessary to be convinced that for the equivalent images B', B'' the equality $g_{\alpha'} \circ B'=g_{\alpha''} \circ B''$, where $\alpha' = -ln\,\mathcal{F}(B')/t$, $\alpha'' = -ln\,\mathcal{F}(B'')/t$ is valid. Let $B''=g \circ B'$, then $g_{\alpha''} \circ B''=(g_{\alpha''}g_s) \circ B'= g_{\alpha'+s} \circ B'=g_{-ln\,\mathcal{F}(B')/t+s} \circ B'$. According to the definition of normalizing functional we have $ln\,\mathfrak{F}(g_s \circ B')/t = s + ln\,\mathfrak{F}(B')/t$. Therefore, $g_{\alpha''} \circ B''=g_{-ln\,\mathcal{F}(B')/t} \circ B'=g_{\alpha'} \circ B'$, as was to be shown.

We shall specify now the way of any index normalizing functional creating in case of arbitrary one-parameter group action. Thus, according to theorems 1 and 2 we shall obtain functional invariants or feature vectors.

For normalizing functional creation let us introduce the following notations. Let $\mathfrak{L}$ be Lie algebra of a group G, and $\varphi \in \mathfrak{L}$ be the generator of this algebra [10]:

$$\mathfrak{L}=\{a\varphi,\ a \in \mathbb{R}^1\},\ \ \varphi = \varphi_1(x,\ y)\partial x + \varphi_2(x,\ y)\partial y.$$

Theorem 3. Let $z = Z(t,\ x,\ y)$ be the first integral of the ordinary differential equations system

$$\begin{cases} \dot{x} = \varphi_1(x,\ y), \\ \dot{y} = \varphi_2(x,\ y), \\ \dot{z} = -\left(t + \dfrac{\partial \varphi_1(x,\ y)}{\partial x} + \dfrac{\partial \varphi_2(x,\ y)}{\partial y}\right) z, \end{cases} \tag{4}$$

then $B(x,\ y)=\iint_{\mathfrak{D}} B(x,\ y)Z(t,\ x,\ y)\,dxdy$ is normalizing functional with the index t.

Proof. Let us consider the external differential 2-form $w = Z(t,\ x,\ y)\,dx \wedge dy$ [10]. The result of applying the transformation $g \in G$ we denote $g \circ w$. To prove the theorem it is necessary to check up, that

$$\iint_{\mathfrak{D}} (g_s \circ B(x,\ y))Z(t,\ x,\ y)\,dxdy = exp\,(ts) \iint_{\mathfrak{D}} B(x,\ y)Z(t,\ x,\ y)\,dxdy.$$

Let us represent the last equality as $\iint_{\mathfrak{D}} B(x,\ y)g_s \circ w = exp\,(ts) \iint_{\mathfrak{D}} B(x,\ y)w$. To take place this equality, validity

$$g_s \circ w = exp\,(-ts)w \tag{5}$$

for all s is necessary and sufficient condition. In particular, should be fulfilled

$$\frac{d}{ds}g_s \circ w + t\,exp\,(-ts)w=0. \tag{6}$$

Since at $s = 0$ the condition (5), obviously, is valid, the conditions (5) and (6) are equivalent. In the case when $s = 0$ from equality (6) we arrive at

$$\frac{d}{ds}\bigg|_{s=0} (g_s \circ w + tw)=0. \tag{7}$$

It appears, that if equality (7) is fulfilled, then the condition (5) is also fulfilled for all s. To be convinced, we shall consider the function $f(s)=g_s \circ w - exp\,(-ts)w$. Differentiating identity $f(s'+s'')=g_{s'} \circ w - exp\,(-t(s'+s''))w$ with respect to s', we get

$$\frac{\partial f(s'+s'')}{\partial s'} = \frac{\partial}{\partial s'}g_{s'} \circ (g_{s''} \circ w)+t\,exp\,(-t(s'+s''))w. \tag{8}$$

Substitute $s' = 0$ in (8) and notice, if (7) hold, then $\frac{\partial}{\partial s'}\big|_{s'=0} g_{s'} \circ (g_{s''} \circ w)=-tg_{s''} \circ w$. Therefore, from (8) follows, that

$$f'(s)=-tg_{s'} \circ w + t\,exp\,(-ts)w = -tf(s). \tag{9}$$

The equality (9) represents the differential equation with respect to $f(s)$. Its general solution has form $f(s)=C\,exp\,(-ts)$, but from the definition of $f(s)$ follows, that $f(0)=0$. Therefore $f(s)$ is identically equal 0, i.e. the condition (5) is fulfilled.

So, the proof of the theorem is reduced to the proof of (7). Let us transform $\frac{d}{ds}\big|_{s=0} g_s \circ w$. As group G is canonically parameterized, then $g_s = exp\,(s\varphi)$, where φ is Lie algebra generator of group G. Expanding $exp\,(s\varphi) \circ w$ by a Taylor series up to the linear term gives

$$exp\,(s\varphi) \circ w = w + s\left\{\left[\frac{\partial Z(t,x,y)}{\partial x}\varphi_1 + \frac{\partial Z(t,x,y)}{\partial y}\varphi_2 + Z\left(\frac{\partial \varphi_1}{\partial x} + \frac{\partial \varphi_2}{\partial y}\right)\right] + o(s^2)\right\} dx \wedge dy .$$

Therefore condition (7) is represented as the equation in partial derivative for the function $Z(t,x,y)$

$$\frac{\partial Z}{\partial x}\varphi_1 + \frac{\partial Z}{\partial y}\varphi_2 + Z\left(\frac{\partial \varphi_1}{\partial x} + \frac{\partial \varphi_2}{\partial y}\right) + tZ = 0 . \tag{10}$$

From (10) it is possible to proceed to the system of the ordinary differential equations (6). If $z=Z(t,x,y)$ is first integral of system (4), then $Z(t,x,y)$ is solution (10). The theorem is proved.

These theorems allow to specify the regular formalized method of functional invariants creating for arbitrary one-parameter group $G=\{g_s\}$.

1. Coordinates of algebra Lie generator are found via

$$\varphi_1(x,y)=\frac{\partial}{\partial s}\Big|_{s=0} h_1(s,x,y), \quad \varphi_2(x,y)=\frac{\partial}{\partial s}\Big|_{s=0} h_2(s,x,y),$$

where $g_s : x \to h_1(s,x,y),\, y \to h_2(s,x,y)$, i.e. $B''(x,y)=B'(h_1(s,x,y),h_2(s,x,y))$.

2. System (4) is integrated with parameter t, that provides search for family of functions $Z(t,x,y)$ and finally, the family of normalizing functionals $\mathcal{F}$.

3. From theorem 2 the set of normalizers, i.e. maps $F:M \to M$ with properties

$$F:B(x,y) \to \mathfrak{S}(B(x,y)) \circ B(x,y), \quad \mathfrak{S}(B(x,y))=g_\alpha, \quad \alpha = -\frac{1}{t}\iint_{\mathfrak{D}} B(x,y)Z(t,x,y)dxdy ,$$

is created.

4. According to theorem 1 functional invariants are obtained

$$\mathfrak{F}:B(x,y) \to f(t) = \frac{1}{t}\iint_{\mathfrak{D}} B(x,y)Z(t,x,y)\,dxdy - \iint_{\mathfrak{D}} B(x,y)Z(1,x,y)\,dxdy . \tag{11}$$

3 Invariants under One-Parameter Transformations

Now we shall find image features, invariant to several one-parameter geometric transformations of a plane, namely, shear maps and projective transformations.

Under one-dimensional skewing with angle $\theta = arctg\,s$, $G = \{x \to x+sy, y \to y\}$ Lie algebra generator is the field $y\partial x$. System (4) has a form $\dot{x}=y$, $\dot{y}=0$, $\dot{z}=-(t+1)z$. With the help of the first integral $z = exp\,(-(t+1)x/y)$ we find functional invariant

$$f(t) = \frac{1}{t}\iint_{\mathfrak{D}} B(x,y)exp\,(-(t+1)x/y)\,dxdy - \iint_{\mathfrak{D}} B(x,y)exp\,(-2x/y)\,dxdy . \tag{12}$$

For projective transformations $G = \{x \to x/(sx+1), y \to y/(sx+1)\}$ Lie algebra generator is the field $\varphi = -x^2\partial x - xy\partial y$. System (4) takes on form $\dot{x}=-x^2$, $\dot{y}=-xy$, $\dot{z}=-(t+x)z$. Integrating it, we get functional invariant

$$f(t) = \frac{1}{t}\iint_{\mathfrak{D}} B(x, y)x exp\left(-t/x\right)dxdy - \iint_{\mathfrak{D}} B(x, y)x exp\left(-1/x\right)dxdy.$$ (13)

Fig.1 illustrates the application of functionals (12) and (13).

Fig. 1. Equivalence classes with respect to skewing (left side) and projective group action (right side) which are obtained via functionals (12) and (13) accordingly

4 Invariants under Transformations with Time Parameter

It is possible to find functional invariants for multi-parameter geometric transformations as well. However, coefficients should be constant and known on some time interval. Then it is necessary to use time as a group parameter for image sequences processing. Consider searching of functional invariants for any one-parameter subgroup of complete group and concretize relations for Euclidean similarity.

4.1 One-Parameter Subgroup of Planar Affine Group

Let $G_1 = \{g_s\}$ be one-parameter subgroup of the planar affine group $Aff(2,\mathbb{R})$, i.e. in a matrix form $z \to Az + b$, $A \in GL(2,\mathbb{R})$, $det\, A \neq 0$, $z, b \in \mathbb{R}^2$. There is an element λ of Lie algebra of group $Aff(2,\mathbb{R})$ such, that $g_s = exp\, s\lambda$. Thus to find any element G_1, it is sufficient to find λ [10]. Let us consider equality $g_1 = exp\,\lambda$, where g_1 is known element. Note, that Lie algebra consists of the vector fields $(c_{11}x + c_{12}y + d_1)\partial x + (c_{21}x + c_{22}y + d_2)\partial y$, then the equation $g_1 = exp\,\lambda$ is equivalent to the equation $exp\begin{pmatrix} C & d \\ 0 & 0 \end{pmatrix} = \begin{pmatrix} A & b \\ 0 & 0 \end{pmatrix}$, $C \in GL(2,\mathbb{R})$, $det\, A \neq 0$, $d \in \mathbb{R}^2$ or

$$E + 1\begin{pmatrix} C & d \\ 0 & 0 \end{pmatrix} + \frac{1}{2!}\begin{pmatrix} C & d \\ 0 & 0 \end{pmatrix}^2 + \frac{1}{3!}\begin{pmatrix} C & d \\ 0 & 0 \end{pmatrix}^3 + \dots = \begin{pmatrix} A & b \\ 0 & 0 \end{pmatrix},$$ (14)

where E is unit matrix. It is easy to prove $\begin{pmatrix} C & d \\ 0 & 0 \end{pmatrix}^k = \begin{pmatrix} C^k & C^{k-1}d \\ 0 & 0 \end{pmatrix}$, therefore from (14) $C = ln\, A$ can be found. To find d we arrive at $\left(E + \frac{1}{2!}C + \frac{1}{3!}C^2 + \dots\right)d = b$. Denote $\mu(z)$ the entire function of complex variable z: $\mu(z) = 1 + \frac{1}{2!}z + \frac{1}{3!}z^2 + \dots$ (it is obvious that the series converges at any $z \in C$). As $\mu(0) \neq 0$, then matrix $\mu(C) = E + \frac{1}{2!}C + \frac{1}{3!}C^2 + \dots$ is nonsingular, as $[\mu(z)]^{-1} = \frac{1}{\mu(z)}\big|_{z=C}$. Then $d = [\mu(C)]^{-1}b$. Taking into account, that from $C\mu(C) = exp\, C - A$, it follows $\mu(C) = C^{-1}(A - E)$, we get $d = ln\, A(A - E)^{-1}b$. Thus, the general relations for subgroup $G_1 = \{g_s\}$ of affine group are found: $x \to a_{11}(s)x + a_{12}(s)y + b_1$, $y \to a_{21}(s)x + a_{22}(s)y + b_2$, where

$$\begin{pmatrix} a_{11}(s) & a_{12}(s) & b_1 \\ a_{21}(s) & a_{22}(s) & b_2 \\ 0 & 0 & 1 \end{pmatrix} = exp \begin{pmatrix} ln\,A & ln\,A(A-E)^{-1}b \\ 0 & 0 \end{pmatrix}. \tag{15}$$

Let us assume that applying (15) Lie algebra generator of $Aff(2,\mathbb{R})$ is found, i.e. $\varphi = (a_{11}x + a_{12}y + b_1)\partial x + (a_{21}x + a_{22}y + b_2)\partial y$. System (4) takes on form

$$\dot{x} = a_{11}x + a_{12}y + b_1, \quad \dot{y} = a_{21}x + a_{22}y + b_2, \dot{z} = -(t + a_{11} + a_{12})z . \tag{16}$$

If proper numbers λ_1, λ_2 of matrix $A = \begin{pmatrix} a_{11} & a_{12} \\ a_{21} & a_{22} \end{pmatrix}$ are real and different then $(x,y) = =T(x_1, y_1)$ transforms (16) to system $\dot{x}_1 = \lambda_1 x_1$, $\dot{y}_1 = \lambda_2 y_1, \dot{z} = -(t + a_{11} + a_{12})z$, i.e.

$$\iint_{\mathfrak{D}} B(x,y)x_1^{-(a_{11}+a_{22}+t)/\lambda_1} dxdy, \quad \iint_{\mathfrak{D}} B(x,y)y_1^{-(a_{11}+a_{22}+t)/\lambda_2} dxdy .$$

Further it is sufficient to replace x_1, y_1 via $(x_1, y_1) = T^{-1}(x,y)$ and apply (11). If proper numbers are complex-conjugate, i.e. $\lambda_1 = \alpha + \beta i$, $\lambda_2 = \alpha - \beta i$, $\beta \neq 0$ then

$$\iint_{\mathfrak{D}} B(x,y)\,exp\,([-(t + a_{11} + a_{22})/\beta][arctg\,(x_1/y_1)])dxdy ,$$

for which the transformation $(x_1, y_1) = T^{-1}(x,y)$ results A in the form $\begin{pmatrix} \alpha & \beta \\ -\beta & \alpha \end{pmatrix}$.

4.2   One-Parameter Euclidean Similarities

We shall apply the obtained above relations for widespread group of Euclidean similarities when rotation, homothety and translations are acting simultaneously. This group is the subgroup of affine transformations. Let $G_1 = \{g_s\}$ be the one-parameter subgroup of Euclidean similarities group and $g_1 : x \to kx\cos\psi + ky\sin\psi + l_1$, $y \to -kx\sin\psi + ky\cos\psi + l_2$, where coefficients k, ψ, l_1, l_2 are known and constant on some time interval. It is clear, that the forming basis of Lie algebra in this case consists of $\varphi = (ln\,kx + \psi y + \gamma_1)\partial x + (-\psi x + ln\,ky + \gamma_2)\partial y$, where

$$\begin{pmatrix} \gamma_1 \\ \gamma_2 \end{pmatrix} = \begin{pmatrix} k\cos\psi - 1 & k\sin\psi \\ -k\sin\psi & k\cos\psi \end{pmatrix}^{-1} \begin{pmatrix} ln\,k & \psi \\ -\psi & ln\,k \end{pmatrix} \begin{pmatrix} l_1 \\ l_2 \end{pmatrix}.$$

Designating $\alpha = (\psi\gamma_2 - ln\,k\gamma_1)/(\psi^2 + ln^2\,k)$, $\beta = (-\psi\gamma_1 - ln\,k\gamma_2)/(\psi^2 + ln^2\,k)$, $\zeta = arctg\,[(x-\alpha)/(y-\beta)]$ one can easily find functional invariant

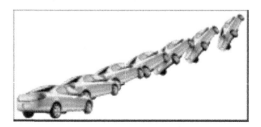

Fig. 2. Images are equivalent with respect to Euclidean similarities

$$f(t) = \iint_{\mathfrak{D}} B(x, y) \exp\left(-\frac{t+2\ln k}{\psi}\zeta\right)dxdy - \iint_{\mathfrak{D}} B(x, y) \exp\left(-\frac{1+2\ln k}{\psi}\zeta\right)dxdy \ . \quad (17)$$

In the fig. 2 the image sequence example is given to be processed on the basis of (17).

5 Conclusion

Under one-parameter image transformations the general method of functional invariants creating has been proposed. Such transformations are special cases of action of eight-parameter projective or six-parameter affine groups, which adequately simulate on a plane change of a relative position and/or orientations of object and sensor. Application of the theory of Lie algebra and groups has allowed to find a constructive method of production of integral invariants under arbitrary group of transformations. At the same time it is necessary to note, that the group approach is not always applicable: generally presence of a background results in distortion of model (1), and the invariance of (11) ceases should be fulfilled. In other words, the efficiency of the analysis and image interpretation in conditions of geometric transformations will depend on accuracy and reliability of segmentation algorithms.

Though in the paper there was no accent on the image normalization problem for template matching, it is necessary to emphasize, that theorem 3 provides search of unknown parameter, and theorem 2 allows to normalize transformations.

References

1. Hu, M.K.: Visual Pattern Recognition by Moment Invariants. IRE Transaction on Information Theory, Vol. IT–8, No. 2 (1962) 179–187
2. Amary, S.: Theory of Normalization of Pattern Signals in Feature Spaces. Electronic and Communication in Japan, Vol. 49, No. 7 (1966) 104–113
3. Richardson, I.M.: Pattern Recognition and Group Theory. In: Watanabe S.: Frontiers of pattern, Academic Press, New York (1972) 453–477
4. Lenz, R.: Group Theoretic Methods in Image Processing. Springer-Verlag, New York: (1990)
5. Wiejak, J.S.: Moment Invariants in Theory and Practice. Image and Video Computing, No. 1 (1983) 79–83
6. Balslev, I.: Noise Tolerance of Moment Invariants in Pattern Recognition. Pattern Recognition Letters, Vol. 19, No. 13 (1998) 1183–1189
7. Burkhardt, H., Siggelkow, S.: Invariant Features in Pattern Recognition – Fundamentals and Applications. In: Kotropoulos C., Pitas I. (eds.): Nonlinear Model-Based Image/Video Processing and Analysis, John Wiley & Sons, New York Chichester Brisbane Toronto Singapore (2001) 269–307
7. Torres-Mendez, L.A., Ruiz-Suarez, J.C., Sucar, L.E., Gomes, G.: Translation, Rotation, and Scale-Invariant Object Recognition. IEEE Transactions on Systems, Man, and Cybernetic, Vol. 30, No. 1 (2000) 125–130
9. Flusser, J., Suk, T.: Pattern Recognition by Affine Moment Invariants. Pattern Recognition, Vol. 26 (1993). 167–174
10. Sternberg, S.: Lecturers on Differential Geometry. Prentice Hall, Inc. Englewood Cliffs, New York (1964)

Gaze Detection System by Wide and Auto Pan/Tilt Narrow View Camera

Kang Ryoung Park

Division of Media Technology, Sangmyung University, 7 Hongji-dong, Jongno-gu,
Seoul, Republic of Korea

Abstract. Gaze detection is to locate the position on a monitor screen where a user is looking. In general, the user tends to move both his face and eyes in order to gaze at a position of monitor. Previous gaze detection system uses a wide view camera, which can capture the whole face of user. However, the image resolution is too low with such a camera and the fine movements of user's eye cannot be exactly detected. So, we implement the gaze detection system with a wide view camera and a narrow view camera. In order to detect the position of user's eye changed by facial movements, the narrow view camera has the functionalities of auto focusing and auto pan/tilt based on the detected 3D facial feature positions. As experimental results, we can obtain the facial and eye gaze position on a monitor and the gaze position accuracy between the computed positions and the real ones is about 3.57 cm of RMS error.

Keyword: Facial and Eye Gaze detection, Auto Focusing and Auto Pan/Tilt

1 Introduction

Gaze detection is to locate the position where a user is looking. Previous studies were mostly focused on 2D/3D facial motion estimation[1][15][20][21], face gaze detection[2-8][16][17][19] and eye gaze detection[9-14][18]. However, the gaze detection considering both face and eye movement has been rarely researched. Ohmura and Ballard et al.[4][5]'s methods have the disadvantages that the depth between camera and feature points in the initial frame must be measured manually and it takes much time(over 1 minute) to compute the gaze direction vector. Gee et al.[6] and Heinzmann et al.[7]'s methods only compute gaze direction vector whose origin is located between the eyes in the face coordinate and do not obtain the gaze position on a monitor. In addition, if 3D rotations and translations of face happen simultaneously, they cannot estimate the accurate 3D motion due to the increase of complexity of least-square fitting algorithm, which requires much processing time. Rikert et al.[8]'s method has the constraints that the distance between a face and the monitor must be kept same for all training and testing procedures and it can be cumbersome to user. In the methods of [10][13][14][16][17], a pair of glasses having marking points is required to detect facial features, which can give inconvenience to a user. The methods of [2][3]

B. Michaelis and G. Krell (Eds.): DAGM 2003, LNCS 2781, pp. 76–83, 2003.
© Springer-Verlag Berlin Heidelberg 2003

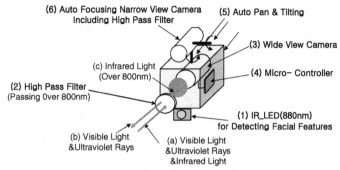

(6) Auto Focusing Narrow View Camera
Including High Pass Filter

(5) Auto Pan & Tilting

(3) Wide View Camera

(c) Infrared Light
(Over 800nm)

(4) Micro- Controller

(2) High Pass Filter
(Passing Over 800nm)

(1) IR_LED(880nm)
for Detecting Facial Features

(b) Visible Light
&Ultraviolet Rays

(a) Visible Light
&Ultraviolet Rays
&Infrared Light

Fig. 1. The Gaze Detecting Camera

shows the gaze detection by facial movements, but have the limits that the eye movements do not happen. The method of [22] shows the gaze detection by facial and eye movements, but uses one wide view camera, which can capture the whole face of user. However, the image resolution is too low with such a camera and the fine movements of user's eye cannot be exactly detected. So, we implement the gaze detection system with a wide view camera and a narrow view camera. In order to detect the positions of user's eye changed by facial movements, the narrow view camera has the functionalities of auto focusing and auto pan/tilt based on the detected 3D facial feature positions.

2   Locating Facial Feature Points

In order to detect gaze position on a monitor, we firstly locate facial features(both eye centers, eye corners, nostrils and lip corners) in an input image. We use the method of detecting specular reflection to detect eyes[22]. It requires a camera system equipped with some hardware as shown in Fig. 1.

In details of Fig. 1, the IR-LED(1) is used to make the specular reflections on eyes[22]. The HPF(2)(High Pass Filter) in front of camera lens can only pass the infrared lights(over 800 nm) and the input images are only affected by the IR-LED(1) excluding external illuminations. So, it is not necessary to normalize the illumination of the input image. We use a normal interlaced wide view CCD camera(3) and a micro-controller(4) embedded in camera sensor which can detect the every VD(the starting signal of even or odd Field as shown in Fig. 2) from CCD output signal. From that, we can control the Illuminator as shown in Fig. 2. In general, when the wavelength of IR-LED is bigger, the sensitivity of such a IR-LED in CCD sensor is lower. In this case, the image sensitivity of IR-LED(880nm) is low, so we use several IR-LEDs as the illuminator for detecting facial features. General human eye can perceive the illumination(below 880nm) and our illuminator does not make inconvenience for user's eye.

In details of Fig. 2, when a user starts our gaze detection system, then the starting signal is transferred into the micro-controller in camera by RS-232C. Then, the micro-controller detects the next VD signals of Even Field and successively

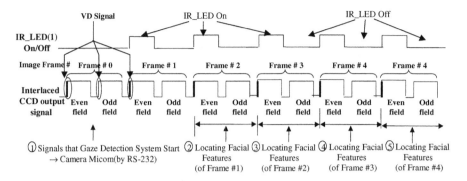

Fig. 2. The IR-LED Controls for Detecting Facial Features

controls IR-LEDs as shown in Fig. 2. The short time(even field) turn-on of IR-LED makes the specular reflection be circle shape even though user's fast x/y movement. In addition, this turn on/off mechanism helps to reduce the effect of ambient light which may pass through the HPF. From that, we can get a difference image between the even and the odd image and the specular points of both eyes can be easily detected in both no glasses and glasses, because its gray level is higher than any other region[22]. In addition, we use Red-Eye effect in order to detect more accurate eye position[22]. When the specular points are detected, then we can restrict the eye region around the detected specular points. With the restricted eye searching region, we locate the accurate eye center by the circular edge matching method. Because we search the restricted eye region, it does not take much time to detect the exact eye center(almost 5-10 ms in Pentium-II 550MHz). After locating the eye center, we detect the eye corner by using eye corner shape template and SVM(Support Vector Machine)[22]. We get 2000 successive image frames(100 frames × 20 persons who have various sitting positions) and from that, 8000 eye corner samples (4 eye corners × 2000 images) are obtained and another 1000 images are used for testing. Experimental results show the generalization error from training data is 0.11% (9/8000) and that from testing data is 0.2%(8/4000). In our experimental results, MLP(Multi-Layered Perceptron) shows the error of 1.58% from training data and 3.1% from testing data. In addition, the classification time is so small as like 13 ms in Pentium-II 550MHz[22]. After locating eye centers and eye corners, the positions of both nostrils and lip corners can be detected by anthropometric constraints in a face and SVM similar to eye corner detection. Experimental results show that RMS error between the detected feature positions and the real ones(manually detected positions) are 1 pixels (of both eye centers), 2 pixels (of both eye corners), 4 pixels (of both nostrils) and 3 pixels (of both lip corners) in 640×480 image[22]. From the detected feature positions, we select 7 feature points $(P_1, P_2, P_3, P_4, P_5, P_6, P_7)$ for estimating 3D facial rotation and translation as shown in Fig. 3. When the user gazes at other point on a monitor, the positions of 7 feature points are changed to $P_1', P_2', \sim P_7'$ as shown in (b) Fig. 3.

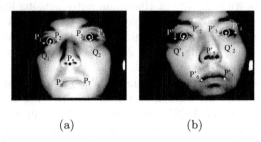

(a)   (b)

Fig. 3. The feature points for estimating 3D facial and eye movements (a)Gazing at monitor center (b)Gazing at some other point on a monitor

3   The 4 Steps in Order to Compute a Gaze Position on a Monitor

After feature detection, we take 4 steps in order to compute a gaze position on a monitor[2][3][22]. At the 1st step, when a user gazes at 5 known positions on a monitor, the 3D positions(X, Y, Z) of initial feature points($P_1, P_2, P_3, P_4, P_5, P_6, P_7$) are computed automatically [2]. Experimental results show that the RMS error between the real 3D feature positions(measured by 3D position tracker sensor) and the estimated one is 1.15 cm(0.64cm in X axis, 0.5cm in Y axis, 0.81cm in Z axis) for 20 person data which were used for testing the feature detection performance. At the 2nd and 3rd step, when the user rotates/translates his head in order to gaze at one position on a monitor like (b) of Fig. 3, the moved 3D positions of those features can be computed from 3D motion estimation. These are explained in chapter 4 and section 5.1 in detail. At the 4th step, one facial plane is determined from the moved 3D positions of those features and the normal vector of the plane represents a gaze vector by facial movements. Here, if the changed 3D positions of initial feature points can be computed at the 2nd and 3th step, they can be converted into the positions of monitor coordinate. From that, we can also convert those feature positions into those of camera coordinate based on the camera parameter, which can be computed at the 1st step. With this information, we can pan/tilt the narrow view camera in order to capture the eye image. In general, the narrow view camera has a small viewing angle(large focal length of about 30 - 45mm) with which it can capture large eye image. So, if the user rotates his face severely, his one eye may disappear in camera view. So, we track only one visible eye with auto pan/tile narrow view camera. For pan/tilting, we use 2 stepping motors with 420 pps(pulse per seconds). In addition, general narrow view camera has small DOF(Depth of Field) and the input image can easily be defocused according to user's Z movement. The DOF is almost the Z distance range in which the object can be captured clearly in the camera image. The DOF shows the characteristics that if the size of camera iris is smaller or the Z distance of object to be captured is larger in front of camera, the DOF is bigger. However, in our case, we cannot make the user's Z distance bigger on purpose because general users sits in 50 - 70 cm in front of monitor. In addition, making iris size smaller lessens the input light to camera CCD sensor and the input image is much darker. So, we use the narrow view camera with iris size of 10mm, an auto focusing lens and a focusing motor(420 pps) in order to capture clearer(more focused) eye image. These auto pan/tilt/focusing are manipulated by micro-controller(4) in camea of Fig. 1. For focusing of narrow view eye image, the Z distance information between the eye and a camera is required. In our research, the Z distance can be computed at the 2nd and 3th step and we can use such information as the seed of auto focusing for eye image. However, the auto focusing in narrow view camera is reported to be difficult due to small DOF and exact auto focusing cannot be achieved only with Z distance. So, we contrive a simple auto focusing algorithm in which checks the pixel disparity in an image. That is, the auto pan/tilt is achieved and the preliminary auto focusing for eye image is accomplished based on the computed Z distance. After that, the captured eye image is transferred to PC and our simple focusing algorithm checks the focus quality of image. If the quality does not meet our threshold, then we send the controlling command of focus lens to camera micro-controller(4) in Fig. 1. Here, when the defocused eye image is captured, it is difficult to determine the movements of focus lens(move forward or backward). For that, we use various heuristic information(for example, image brightness and blind/pyramid lens searching, etc). With this auto focusing mechanism, we can get the focused eye image from narrow view camera. If the focused eye image can be captured, we use a trained neural network(multi-layered perceptron) to detect the gaze position by eye's movement. Then, the facial and eye gaze position on a monitor is calculated from the geometric sum between the facial gaze position and the eye gaze one.

4   Estimating the 3D Facial Rotation and Translation

This section explains the 2nd step shown in chapter 3. Many 3D motion estimation algorithms have been investigated, for example, EKF(Extended Kalman Filter)[1], neural network[21] and affine projection method[6][7], etc. Due to many limitations or problems of previous motion estimation researches[22], we use the EKF for 3D motion estimation algorithm and the moved 3D positions of those features can be estimated from 3D motion estimations by EKF and affine transform[2][22]. Detail accounts can be referred to [1][20][22]. The estimation accuracy of EKF is compared with 3D position tracker sensor. Our experimental results show the RMS errors are about 1.4 cm and 2.98° in translation and rotation.

5   Detecting the Gaze Position on the Monitor

5.1   By Facial Motion

This section explains the 3rd and 4th step explained in chapter 3. The initial 3D feature positions($P_1 \sim P_7$ in Fig. 3) computed in monitor coordinate in chapter 3 are converted into the 3D feature positions in face coordinate[2] and using these converted 3D feature positions(X_i, Y_i, Z_i), 3D rotation[R] and translation[T] matrices estimated by EKF and affine transform, we can obtain the moved 3D feature positions(X'_i, Y'_i, Z'_i) in face and monitor coordinate when a user gazes at a monitor position[2]. From that, one facial plane is determined and the normal vector of the plane shows a gaze vector. The gaze position on a monitor is the intersection position between a monitor and the gaze vector.

5.2 By Eye Motion

In 5.1, the gaze position is determined by only facial movement. As mentioned before, when a user gazes at a monitor position, both the face and eyes can easily be moved simultaneously. So, we compute the eye movements from the detected features points as shown in Fig. 4. Fig. 5 shows the captured eye image with auto pan/tilt/focus narrow view camera. In this figure, the detected eye ball and corner positions are depicted. Here, we use the circular edge detection and the eye corner template with SVM in order to detect eye ball and corner. This method is almost same to those for detecting eye position in wide view camera mentioned in chap.2. As mentioned before, when a user rotates his face severely, his one eye may disappear in narrow view camera. So, we detect both eyes in case the user gazes at a monitor center in (b) of Fig. 5, and when the user rotates his face severely, track only one eye as shown in (a), (c) in of Fig. 5. In general, the eye movements and shape are changed according to a user gaze position. The distance between the eyeball center and left or right eye corner is changed according to user's gaze positions. We use a neural network(Multilayer Perceptron) to train the relations between the eye movements and gaze positions like Fig. 4. Here, the input values for neural network are normalized by the distance between the eye center and the eye corner, which are obtained in case of gazing monitor center. That is why we use only auto focusing lens for narrow view camera without zoom lens and the eye size in image plane(pixel) is bigger when the user approaches the monitor. In our research, the Z distances of user are varied between 50 - 70cm. So, the distance normalizations for neural network are required like Fig. 4. From the neural network for detecting eye gaze position, we locate final gaze positions on a monitor by both face and eye movements with geometric summation of each gaze position(face and eye gaze)[22].

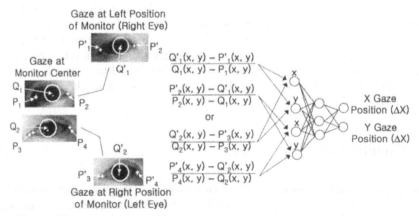

Fig. 4. The neural network for detecting gaze position by eye movements

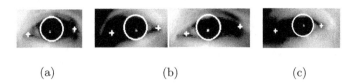

(a)   (b)   (c)

Fig. 5. The captured eye image with auto pan/tilt/focusing narrow view camera (a)Gazing at right position of monitor (b)Gazing at monitor center (c)Gazing at left position of monitor

The gaze detection error of proposed method is compared to our previous methods[2][3][19][22] like table 1, 2. The test data are acquired when 10 users gaze at 23 gaze positions on a 19" monitor. Here, the gaze error is the RMS error between the real gaze position and the computed ones. Shown in table 1, the gaze error of the proposed method is the smallest. However, it is often the case that the facial and eye movements happen simultaneously, when a user gazes at. So, we tested the gaze error including facial and eye movements like table 2.

Table 1. Gaze error about test data including only facial movements (cm)

Method	Linear interpol.[19]	Single neural net[19]	Two neural nets[19]	[2] method	[3] method	[22] method	Proposed method
error	5.1	4.23	4.48	5.35	5.21	3.40	3.1

Table 2. Gaze error about test data including face and eye movements (cm)

Method	Linear interpol.[19]	Single neural net[19]	Two neural nets[19]	[2] method	[3] method	[22] method	Proposed method
error	11.8	11.32	8.87	7.45	6.29	4.8	3.57

Shown in table 2, the gaze error of the proposed method is the smallest. In the second experiment, points of radius 5 pixels are spaced vertically and horizontally at 150 pixel intervals(2.8 cm) on a 19" monitor with 1280×1024 pixels. The test conditions are almost same as Rikert's research[8][22]. The RMS gaze error of between the real and calculated position is 3.61 cm and it is superior to Rikert's method(almost 5.08 cm). In addition, Rikert has the limits that user's Z distance must be always kept same, but we do not. We tested the gaze errors according to the Z distance(55, 60, 65cm). The RMS errors are like; 3.45cm in the distance of 55cm, 3.57cm in 60cm, 3.63cm in 65cm. It shows that our method can permit user with the change of Z-distance. And Rikert's method takes much processing time(1 minute in alphastation 333MHz), compared to our method(about 700ms in Pentium-II 550MHz).

6   Conclusions

This paper describes a new gaze detecting method. The gaze error is about 3.57 cm. Such gaze error can be compensated by the additional facial movement(like mouse dragging).

References

1. A. Azarbayejani., 1993. Visually Controlled Graphics. IEEE Trans. PAMI, Vol. 15, No. 6, pp. 602–605
2. K. R. Park et al., Apr 2000, Gaze Point Detection by Computing the 3D Positions and 3D Motions of Face, IEICE Trans. Inf.&Syst.,Vol. E.83-D, No.4, pp.884–894
3. K. R. Park et al., Oct 1999, Gaze Detection by Estimating the Depth and 3D Motions of Facial Features in Monocular Images, IEICE Trans. Fundamentals, Vol. E.82-A, No. 10, pp. 2274–2284
4. K. OHMURA et al., 1989. Pointing Operation Using Detection of Face Direction from a Single View. IEICE Trans. Inf.&Syst., Vol. J72-D-II, No.9, pp. 1441–1447
5. P. Ballard et al., 1995. Controlling a Computer via Facial Aspect. IEEE Trans. on SMC, Vol. 25, No. 4, pp. 669–677
6. A. Gee et al., 1996. Fast visual tracking by temporal consensus, Image and Vision Computing. Vol. 14, pp. 105–114
7. J. Heinzmann et al., 1998. 3D Facial Pose and Gaze Point Estimation using a Robust Real-Time Tracking Paradigm. Proceedings of ICAFGR, pp. 142–147
8. T. Rikert et al., 1998. Gaze Estimation using Morphable Models. Proc. of ICAFGR, pp. 436–441
9. A.Ali-A-L et al., 1997, Man-machine interface through eyeball direction of gaze. Proc. of the Southeastern Symposium on System Theory, pp. 478–82
10. A. TOMONO et al., 1994. Eye Tracking Method Using an Image Pickup Apparatus. European Patent Specification-94101635
11. Seika-Tenkai-Tokushuu-Go, ATR Journal, 1996
12. Eyemark Recorder Model EMR-NC, NAC Image Technology Cooperation
13. Porrill-J et al., Jan 1999, Robust and optimal use of information in stereo vision. Nature. vol.397, no.6714, pp.63–6
14. Varchmin-AC et al., 1998, image based recognition of gaze direction using adaptive methods. Gesture and Sign Language in Human-Computer Interaction. Int. Gesture Workshop Proc. Berlin, Germany, pp. 245–57.
15. J. Heinzmann et al., 1997. Robust real-time face tracking and gesture recognition. Proc. of the IJCAI, Vol. 2, pp. 1525–1530
16. Matsumoto-Y, et al., 2000, An algorithm for real-time stereo vision implementation of head pose and gaze direction measurement. Proc. the ICAFGR. pp. 499–504
17. Newman-R et al., 2000, Real-time stereo tracking for head pose and gaze estimation. Proceedings the 4th ICAFGR 2000. pp. 122–8
18. Betke-M et al., 1999, Gaze detection via self-organizing gray-scale units. Proc. Int. Workshop on Recog., Analy., and Tracking of Faces and Gestures in Real-Time System. pp. 70–6
19. K. R. Park et al., 2000. Intelligent Process Control via Gaze Detection Technology. EAAI, Vol. 13, No. 5, pp. 577–587
20. T. BROIDA et al., 1990. Recursive 3-D Motion Estimation from a Monocular Image Sequence. IEEE Trans. Aerospace and Electronic Systems, Vol. 26, No. 4, pp. 639–656
21. T. Fukuhara et al., 1993. 3D-motion estimation of human head for model-based image coding. IEE Proc., Vol. 140, No. 1, pp. 26–35
22. K. R. Park et al., 2002. Facial and Eye Gaze detection. LNCS, Vol.2525, pp. 368–376

Distribution Distance Measures Applied to 3-D Object Recognition – A Case Study

Michael Nölle

ARC Seibersdorf research GmbH
Safety & Security
A-2444 Seibersdorf
michael.noelle@arcs.ac.at

Abstract. In this paper we analyse dissimilarity measures for probability distributions which are frequently used in the area of pattern recognition, image processing, -indexing and registration, amongst others. Namely χ^2, Jenson-Shannon divergence, Fidelity and Trace are discussed. We use those measures to tackle the task of recognising three dimensional objects from two dimensional images. The object reference model is defined by (several) feature distributions derived from multiple two dimensional views of each object. The experiments performed on the Columbia Object Image Library indicate that derivatives of Fidelity used as distance measures perform well in terms of recognition rate. If enough views can be provided for modelling (roughly one view per $20°$-$30°$), up to a 100% recognition rate is achievable.

Keywords: Dissimilarity measures, χ^2, Jenson-Shannon divergence, Fidelity type distance measures, Trace, view-based object recognition, invariant transformations, Coil-100 benchmark

1 Introduction

The problem of determining the distance between probability distributions arises frequently in numerous application areas. Examples drawn from image processing related themes are pattern recognition, image indexing and -registration, classification, to list only a few. The common task is to decide whether or not some measured feature distributions are close to each other. Closeness of feature distributions for the entities under consideration indicates that they may have something in common. For example, in the area of image indexing, histograms of colour, contour data, etc. are used to decide on the similarity between two images. One might consider this to be an easy task. However, reviewing the relevant literature becomes frustrating as there are many different approaches and it is far from evident which measure should be employed for a given problem. We do not intend to tackle the general discussion on how good or bad different distance measures for probability distributions are from a theoretical point of view. The contribution of this paper is to compare some of the frequently used measures when applied to a concrete and well defined problem.

B. Michaelis and G. Krell (Eds.): DAGM 2003, LNCS 2781, pp. 84–91, 2003.
© Springer-Verlag Berlin Heidelberg 2003

In particular, we want to solve the task of recognising three dimensional objects from their two dimensional views, which, of course, is a problem on its own. View based object recognition has been studied using a multitude of approaches over a long period. Instead of either using three dimensional geometrically defined models or three dimensional measurement data, multiple two dimensional views of an object are used to built a *reference model* either directly from the images or some features derived from them. The objective then is to recognise a given object by comparing an image of this object with a set of reference models.

The approach, with respect to the recognition task, suggested in this paper uses simple features with some invariant properties. The invariant features derived (measured) from an image result in feature distributions which, interpreted as probability distributions, will be compared by some 'suitable' dissimilarity measure.

The rest of the paper is organised as follows. Section 2 will introduce the general notations. Section 3 briefly describes some methods to extract basic features out of a given image. Finally, in Section 4 we apply these methods to the well known Columbia Object Image Library ([1]).

2   General Notations, Probability, and State Space

This Section will introduce some probability dissimilarity measures frequently used in the literature. It is neither our intention to be exhaustive in terms of all varieties of measures that exist in this area nor on the properties of those mentioned. Where appropriate, we will hint at the literature for in-depth further reading. Let $X = \{x_1, \dots \}$ be a discrete probability variable and p be a probability distribution of X, i.e. $\sum_{x \in X} p(x) = 1$. We may interpret p as a vector of a real vector space $\mathbb{P}$ with positive coordinates whose L_1 norm is equal to one, i.e. $L_1(p) = \sum_{x \in X} |p(x)| = 1$. We call $\mathbb{P}$ the *probability space*. The set of all probability distributions of X is given by:

$$P(X) = \{p \in \mathbb{P}|L_1(p) = 1 \wedge \forall_{x \in X} \; p(x) \geq 0\}. \tag{2.1}$$

Equation 2.1 offers a compact way to address the possible probability distributions of X. The elements of $P(X)$ lie on a hyperplane passing through points with coordinate one on each coordinate axis. It is worthwhile to note that for $p_1, \dots, p_n \in P(X)$ with given a priori probabilities $c_i \geq 0$, $i = 1, \dots, n$, $\sum_{i=1}^{n} c_i = 1$,

$$\sum_{i=1}^{n} c_i \cdot p_i \in P(X). \tag{2.2}$$

Equation 2.2 expresses the well known fact that any convex combination of probability distributions over X with given a priori probabilities, $c_i \geq 0$, results in a new probability distribution over X.

Abusing the quantum information terminology slightly we may derive a new space, called the *state-space*, by:[1]

$$Q = \{q \mid q^2 = p; \; q, p \in \mathbb{P}\}. \tag{2.3}$$

In analogy to Equation 2.1 we define a set

$$Q(X) = \{q \in \mathbb{Q} \mid L_2(q) = 1\}. \tag{2.4}$$

For a given $q \in Q(X)$ the corresponding probability distribution is *generated* by $q^2 = p$. Note that this correspondence is not one to one as more than one q can generate the same p, i.e. all $q' \in \mathbb{Q}$ for which $\forall_{x \in X} q(x) = |q'(x)|$ holds. Thus, all elements of $Q(X)$ lie on a unit hypersphere.

2.1   Some Dissimilarity Measures for Probability Spaces

In order to compare probability distributions frequently the χ^2 measure is used. Let $p_1, p_2 \in P(X)$ and $p = \frac{1}{2}(p_1 + p_2)$. The (relative) χ^2-*measure* is given by ([8])

$$\chi^2(p_1, p_2) = \sum_{x \in X} \frac{(p_1(x) - p(x))^2}{p(x)}. \tag{2.5}$$

Like most of the measures given below the χ^2 measure is not a metric. Usually the triangular inequality as given by

$$d(a, b) \le d(a, c) + d(c, b), \tag{2.6}$$

for all $a, b, c \in \mathbb{A}$ and $d : \mathbb{A} \times \mathbb{A} \to \mathbb{R}$, is not satisfied. Using a counterexample we may convince ourselves that the triangle inequality does not hold for the χ^2 measure:

$$p_1(X) = \{1, 0\}, \; p_2(X) = \{0, 1\}, \; p_3(X) = \{1/2, 1/2\}; \tag{2.7}$$
$$\chi^2(p_1, p_2) = 1 \nleq \chi^2(p_1, p_3) + \chi^2(p_3, p_2) = \frac{2}{3}.$$

The *Jenson-Shannon divergence* ([4]) is given by

$$JS(p_1, p_2) = H(\pi_1 p_1 + \pi_2 p_2) - \pi_1 H(p_1) - \pi_2 H(p_2), . \tag{2.8}$$

$H(p) = -\sum_{x \in X} p(x) \log_2 p(x)$ is Shannon's entropy function and $\pi_1, \pi_2 \ge 0$, $\pi_1 + \pi_2 = 1$. Sometimes the Jenson-Shannon divergence is called Jeffrey-divergence ([8]). π_1, π_2 should be chosen accordingly if a priori the probability of p_1 and p_2 are known. For our purposes we choose $\pi_1 = \pi_2 = 1/2$. Note that $0 \log 0 \equiv 0$. In [4] it is shown that:

$$0 \le JS(p_1, p_2) \le 1.$$

---

[1] For convenience we abbreviate $\forall_{x \in X} q^2(x) = p(x)$, $\forall_{x \in X} q(x) = \sqrt{p(x)}$ by $q^2 = p$, $q = \sqrt{p}$, respectively.

The Jenson-Shannon divergence is the limiting case of the *Jenson-Rényi divergence* as used in [3] for image registration.

Another measure of distance between probability distributions frequently applied in the area of quantum information (as an example see [5], pp. 400ff) is the so called *Fidelity*. The Fidelity is known as Bhattacharyya distance in the image processing field ([2]). Let $p_1, p_2 \in P(X)$. Then the Fidelity of p_1, p_2 is given by

$$F(p_1, p_2) = \sum_{x \in X} \sqrt{p_1(x)} \sqrt{p_2(x)}$$

$$= \sum_{x \in X} q_1(x) \cdot q_2(x) = q_1^T q_2. \tag{2.9}$$

The Fidelity of two probability distributions p_1, p_2 is given by the scalar product of the two state space unit vectors $q_1 = \sqrt{p_1}$ and $q_2 = \sqrt{p_2}$. The Fidelity becomes equal to the cosine of the angle between q_1 and q_2: $\cos \alpha_{q_1, q_2} = q_1^T \cdot q_2 = F(p_1, p_2)$. It is then clear that:

$$0 \le F(p_1, p_2) \le 1. \tag{2.10}$$

Nonetheless, F is not a metric as already $F(p, p) = 1 \ne 0$, $p \in P(X)$, as required by a metric. But we easily may find variations using the Fidelity that comply with definition of a metric (see [7]):

$$\overline{F}(p_1, p_2) = 1 - F(p_1, p_2), \tag{2.11}$$

$$F_{\sqrt{}}(p_1, p_2) = \sqrt{1 - F(p_1, p_2)}, \tag{2.12}$$

$$F_{\log}(p_1, p_2) = \log(2 - F(p_1, p_2)), \tag{2.13}$$

$$F_{\arccos}(p_1, p_2) = \frac{2}{\pi} \arccos F(p_1, p_2), \tag{2.14}$$

$$F_{\sin}(p_1, p_2) = \sqrt{1 - F^2(p_1, p_2)} = \sin \alpha_{\sqrt{p_1}, \sqrt{p_2}}. \tag{2.15}$$

Using the same counterexample (2.7) we verify that the triangle inequality does not hold for JS, $\overline{F}$ and $F_{\log}$. In [7] it was shown that $F_{\sqrt{}}$ and $F_{\sin}$ define metrics on $\mathbb{P}(X)$. Following the same argument as given in [7] it is relatively easy to prove that $F_{\arccos}$ defines a metric on $\mathbb{P}(X)$ as well by noting that the triangle inequality holds for the sides of a spherical triangle.

The *Trace-distance* is given by

$$T(p_1, p_2) = \frac{1}{2} \sum_{x \in X} |p_1(x) - p_2(x)|, \tag{2.16}$$

$$0 \le T(p_1, p_2) \le 1.$$

The Trace is sometimes known as Manhattan distance or variational distance ([4]). Moreover, it is a special form of the so called *Minkowski distance* used for example in [8]. As the Trace-distance is, up to a constant factor, defined as the L_1 norm on the space $\mathbb{P}$, it gives us a metric.

The dissimilarity measures introduced above will be investigated further in Section 4. In the next section we will describe some features of images we will use to build up feature distributions distribution dissimilarity measures work upon.

3   Image Features

As we want to recognise three-dimensional objects out of their two-dimensional views, we have to define the features within the images that shall be used. Basically, we could use any features derivable from the images for this purpose. But some will describe the objects better than others. Therefore, it is worthwhile to put some effort into the selection of meaningful features. The objects to be distinguished are shown in Figure 1. Colour is easily recognised as a predominant aspect in the Coil-100 data-set. But colour is not likely to be sufficient to distinguish some of the object as for example the wooden objects. Therefore, we have to include some features that describe the 'structure' of the objects as well. Our choice has been to derive features from the contours of the objects in addition to colour.

Two-dimensional colour images will be represented by a mapping

$$f : M \times N \to \mathbb{R}^3_{[a,b]}, M = \{1, \ldots, M\}, \ N = \{1, \ldots, N\}. \tag{3.1}$$

$\mathbb{R}^3_{[a,b]}$ defines a set of possible colour values, $I = M \times N$ gives the index space f is defined on.

To cover some of the structural aspects of the object we compute edges on the images. Let $C \subset I$ be a set of edge point coordinates, then $f|C \equiv f(C) = \{f(c), c \in C\}$ describes the image f under the restriction C, i.e. all pixel values that lie on edge points in the image. Conversely, $\overline{C} = I\backslash C$, denotes all coordinates of I that are not in C, i.e. lie not on edge points.

We will always use normalised histograms with equally spaced bins. There will be one histogram per colour channel for each feature. Three types of feature histograms will be determined. For a given image f and a set C of edge points of f compute

- $P^A = P^A_{1,2,3}(f|\overline{C})$, the marginal distributions of colour stemming from interior pixels (non edge pixels) of f,
- $P^E = P^E_{1,2,3}(f|C)$, the marginal distributions of colour on edge pixels of f,
- $P^{rel_{r,s}} = P^{Inv_{r,s}}_{1,2,3}(F_{r,s}(f|C))$, the marginal distributions of the *rel* invariant feature (as suggested in [9]) restricted to edge pixel centres.

The subindex in $P_{1,2,3}$ refers to the colour channel. P^A and P^E as given above are naturally invariant against rotations and translations of an image. Due to space limitations we omit a further discussion on invariant features and refer to [10], [9] for a more details. The particular *rel* function used here is defined as

$$rel_{r,s}(a,b) = 1 + 1/2 \begin{cases} -\overline{F}((a, 1-a), (b, 1-b)), \ a \le b \\ \overline{F}((a, 1-a), (b, 1-b)), \ a > b \end{cases}$$

Taking each edge point of C as the centre of a sample circle with radius r we evaluate $rel_{r,s}(a,b)$ on opposite circle samples. s refers to the number of samples on the circle.

The reason to restrict the distributions on areas and contour points, respectively is that we gain robustness against scale. Both attributes grow (shrink) at different rates when we scale the images. Ideally, the number of area pixels grows with the area of the image whereas the number of contour pixels grows with the perimeter of the image.

3.1   Object Classes and Image to Object Distance

In general an object model will be described by feature distributions of several images of this object. Let $M = \{f_1, ...\}$ be a set of images of a certain object. Then the object class is given by

$$O_M = \left\{ \left(P_{1,2,3}^A(f|\overline{C}), P_{1,2,3}^E(f|C), P_{1,2,3}^{Inv_{r,s}}(F_{r,s}(f|C)) \right), f \in M \right\}. \qquad (3.2)$$

We can think of an element of $o \in O_M$ as a nine-tuple of distributions. To dissimilarity measure of two of these nine-tuples o_1, o_2 we calculate the mean of the dissimilarity measures of corresponding distributions of o_1, o_2. Finally, the dissimilarity of o to an object O is the minimum of the dissimilarity measures o to each member of O.

4   Experiments

For the experiments we are using the Columbia Object Image Library (Coil-100) which consists of 100 objects (see Figure 1). A description of this object recognition benchmark can be found in [6]. The images were taken at $5°$ rotations of each object. A diffuse and more or less stable illumination was used. Moreover, all pictures are taken in front of a roughly homogeneous background and at a size that the longest object axis fits into a 128×128 square. Although not strictly true, from a practical point of view we may consider the Coil-100 images to be segmented. Figure 1 shows the 100 objects from their $0°$ view. All experiments carried out are using from 1 to 20 views. If a reference model contains the views $\{v_0, \dots, v_{n-1}\}$ of the Object O_x, they refer to

$$\{O_{x\_v_i}\} \subset Coil100, \ x = 1, \dots, 100 \text{ and} \qquad (4.1)$$
$$v_i = mod(20 + 5i\lfloor 72/n \rfloor, 360), \ i = 0, \dots, n - 1$$

of the Coil-100 data set. All distributions are built upon 64 bin histograms.

Table 1 gives the recognition rate for all distance measures and features reviewed here. Overall the results indicate that the features were well chosen with respect to the objects to be recognised. Already marginal colour histograms give us a recognition rate starting from 75.92% up to 99.83% depending on the dissimilarity measure and the number of views employed. In general using more views improves the results as can be expected. Adding contour information enhances the results considerably in all cases, even up to 100% in some of the experiments. Adding further invariant information improves the recognition rate as well, but to a lesser extent. Most notably the number of views drop for the 100% recognition rate.

As in almost all the cases the Fidelity based measures, especially $F_{\sqrt{}}$, F_{arccos} and F_{sin}, give notably better results than the 'classically' used dissimilarity measures like Trace, χ^2 and Jenson-Shannon divergence.

Fig. 1. Columbia Object Image Library (Coil-100). The library contains 7200 images of 100 objects. For each object images are taken at every $5°$ rotation.

Table 1. Recognition rate ([%])of several dissimilarity measures. **V** views are used to build the reference models, leaving **T** test images. A boldface setting indicates the best result. The feature distributions used are given in the head line of the corresponding table.

T	**V**	P^A							
		$\bar{F}$	$F_{\sqrt{}}$	$F_{\sin}$	$F_{\arccos}$	$F_{\log}$	T	χ^2	JS
7100	1	80.94	81.23	**81.41**	81.20	80.97	75.92	79.92	80.45
7000	2	84.64	84.87	**84.93**	84.83	84.61	78.90	83.56	84.16
6900	3	94.52	94.74	**94.83**	94.74	94.54	91.81	94.30	94.43
6500	7	97.71	98.05	**98.11**	98.00	97.68	96.97	97.72	97.74
6300	9	99.03	**99.17**	99.14	99.16	99.03	98.27	98.92	99.06
6000	12	99.00	**99.20**	99.18	99.18	99.00	98.35	99.03	98.98
5600	16	99.57	99.71	**99.73**	99.71	99.63	99.46	99.61	99.59
5200	20	99.73	99.79	**99.83**	99.79	99.77	99.56	99.77	99.77

T	**V**	$(P^A+P^E)/2$							
		$\bar{F}$	$F_{\sqrt{}}$	$F_{\sin}$	$F_{\arccos}$	$F_{\log}$	T	χ^2	JS
7100	1	88.55	**89.24**	**89.24**	89.14	88.80	87.46	88.62	88.56
7000	2	91.04	**91.46**	**91.46**	91.33	91.07	89.51	90.71	90.80
6900	3	96.39	**96.96**	**96.96**	**96.96**	96.46	96.42	96.42	96.36
6500	7	99.03	**99.05**	**99.05**	99.03	**99.05**	98.89	99.02	**99.05**
6300	9	99.63	99.71	**99.73**	99.71	99.65	99.51	99.62	99.62
6000	12	99.77	**99.87**	**99.87**	**99.87**	99.77	99.77	99.75	99.75
5600	16	99.82	99.96	**99.98**	99.96	99.82	99.96	99.86	99.82
5200	20	99.94	**100.00**	**100.00**	**100.00**	99.96	99.98	99.96	99.96

T	**V**	$(P^A+P^E+P^{rel5,8})/3$							
		$\bar{F}$	$F_{\sqrt{}}$	$F_{\sin}$	$F_{\arccos}$	$F_{\log}$	T	χ^2	JS
7100	1	89.54	**89.97**	89.96	89.96	89.79	88.70	89.61	89.56
7000	2	91.51	**91.90**	91.81	**91.90**	91.60	90.67	91.19	91.36
6900	3	96.97	97.41	**97.48**	97.41	97.03	96.83	97.04	97.01
6500	7	99.14	99.37	**99.40**	99.35	99.17	99.17	99.14	99.15
6300	9	99.71	**99.83**	**99.83**	99.81	99.73	99.67	99.67	99.70
6000	12	99.82	99.93	**99.97**	99.93	99.82	99.83	99.82	99.82
5600	16	99.88	**100.00**	**100.00**	**100.00**	99.88	99.95	99.89	99.88
5200	20	99.98	**100.00**	**100.00**	**100.00**	99.98	99.98	**100.00**	99.98

5   Discussion and Conclusion

In this paper we analysed dissimilarity measures for probability distributions. We introduced some of the most used measures mentioned in the literature, some measures used mainly in other areas, like quantum information, and derived some measures based on the Fidelity. These measures, as given by Equation 2.12, 2.14 and 2.15, are actually metrics on the 'probability space', which makes them highly attractive as this might considerably speed up search methods on the related feature spaces. Moreover, all of these metric measures outperform the classically used ones in terms of recognition rate. Quite surprising the overall performance on the public domain benchmark Coil-100 data base resulted in a perfect recognition rate of 100% using 16 and more out of 72 available views. Especially after consulting the relevant work in the literature in this area this suggests that adapted features as well as suitable distance or dissimilarity measures may play an important role in the recognition task.

References

1. www.cs.columbia.edu/CAVE/coil-100.html.
2. F. J. Aherne, N. A. Thacker, and P.I. Rockett, *The Bhattacharyya metric as an absolute similarity measure for frequency coded data*, Kypernetika **32** (1997), no. 4, 001–007.
3. Yun He, Ben Hamza, and Hamid Krim, *An information divergence measure for isar image registration*, "Proceedings of the IEEE Workshop on Statistical Signal Processing", "August" "2001".
4. J. Lin, *Divergence measures based on the Shannon entropy*, IEEE Transactions on Information Theory **37** (1991), no. 1, 145–151.
5. A. Nielsen Michael and Isaac L. Chuang, *Quantum computation and quantum information*, Cambridge University Press, 2000.
6. S. Nene, S. Nayar, and H. Murase, *Columbia object image library: Coil*, S. A. Nene, S. K. Nayar and H. Murase. Columbia Object Image Library: COIL-100. Technical Report CUCS-006-96, Department of Computer Science, Columbia University, February, 1996.
7. M. Nölle, *Dissimilarity metrics for probability distributions*, Proceedings of the 27th Workshop of the Austrian Association for Pattern Recognition, Oesterreichische Computer Gesellschafft, 2003, pp. 259–265.
8. Puzicha, J., Rubner, Y., Tomasi, C., and Buhmann, J. M., *Empirical Evaluation of Dissimilarity Measures for Color and Texture*, Proc. of the International Conference on Computer Vision (ICCV'99), 1999, pp. 1165–1173.
9. M. Schael and H. Burkhardt, *Automatic detection of errors in textures using invariant grey scale features and polynomial classiers*, M. Schael and H. Burkhardt. Automatic Detection of Errors in Textures Using Invariant Grey Scale Features and Polynomial Classiers. In M.K. Pietikainen, editor, Texture Analysis in Machine Vision, volume 40, pages 219–229. World Scientic, 2000.
10. R. Veltkamp, H. Burkhardt, and H. Kriegel, *State-of-the-art in content-based image and video retrieval*, R. Veltkamp, H. Burkhardt, and H.-P. Kriegel, editors. State-of-the-Art in Content-Based Image and Video Retrieval. Kluwer Academic Publishers, 2001.

Classification with Controlled Robustness in High-Resolution SAR Data

Wolfgang Middelmann

FGAN-FOM Research Institute for Optronics and Pattern Recognition, Germany
W.Middelmann@fom.fgan.de

Abstract. Ground target classification in high-resolution SAR data has become increasingly important over the years. Kernel machines like the Support Vector Machine (SVM) and the Relevance Vector Machine (RVM) afford a great chance to solve this problem. But it is not possible to customize these kernel machines. Therefore the main objective of this work has been the development of a mechanism that controls the classification quality versus the computational effort. The investigations have been carried out with usage of the MSTAR public target dataset. The result of this work is an extended RVM, the RVMG. A single parameter is controlling the robustness of the system. The spectrum varies from a machine 15 times faster and of 10% lower quality than the SVM, goes to a 5 times faster and equal quality machine, and ends with a machine a little bit faster than the SVM and of better quality than the Lagrangian Support Vector Machine (LSVM).

1 Introduction

Ground surveillance and automatic target recognition are important tasks in military applications. The importance of SAR data has grown in this sector over the last decades. To solve these tasks high-performance classifiers are required. Kernel machines like the Support Vector Machine (SVM), see [9, 5, 2], the Lagrangian Support Vector Machine (LSVM), see [3], and the Relevance Vector Machine (RVM), see [6, 7] afford a great chance to solve this problem. For these investigations we use the Moving and Stationary Target Acquisition and Recognition (MSTAR) public target dataset, see [10].

In previous investigations [4] we have analyzed the utilizability of the mentioned kernel classifiers for the MSTAR dataset. The result of our former examination was an assessment of the classifiers. We measured the classification quality and the number of Support Vectors (SVs) which is directly proportional to the computational effort of evaluating the test function. An important drawback of the existing methods could be identified. Therefore we have formulated: *The main future objective should be the development of a mechanism for controlling the classification quality versus the number of Support Vectors. It should be preferable to design a kernel machine that could be directly or indirectly customized by a control parameter.* In this paper we want to describe one possible solution of this controlling via a special kind of parameterized generator that is integrated directly into the RVM. It fortifies boundary

B. Michaelis and G. Krell (Eds.): DAGM 2003, LNCS 2781, pp. 92–99, 2003.
© Springer-Verlag Berlin Heidelberg 2003

regions in dependency of the parameter, i.e. it strengthens the robustness of the original class structure for the classification training. The result is a classifier with indirectly controlled trade-off between speed and quality.

In section two an introduction of the MSTAR dataset and the experimental setup is given. In section three we recapitulate some previous results of [4]. The extension of the RVM follows in section four. A general extensibility of the RVM is described and a first shot is done to yield an upper limit of high classification quality and low computational effort for the considered family of kernel machines. In section five we introduce the main result, the RVM with a special kind of generator. The experimental results are given in section six followed by the conclusion in the last section.

2   MSTAR Data

The MSTAR dataset consists of training and test data. The training dataset was taken under a depression angle of 17°, the test data under 15°. The vehicles taken into consideration are organized in the three classes BMP2, BTR70, and T72, see Table 1.

Table 1. MSTAR - 1622 training and 1365 test chips organized in three classes

Class	Types	Train 17° (1622)	Test 15° (1365)
BMP2	9563, 9566, C21	698 (233+232+233)	587 (195+196+196)
BTR70	C71	233	196
T72	132, 812, S7	691 (232+231+228)	582 (196+195+191)

We use the magnitude of the complex data (128x128 pixel per chip) for classification purposes. Neither further preprocessing has been done like using superresolution methods (e.g. CLEAN, see [8]), nor feature-enhanced SAR processing has been taken into account, see [1]. In this paper we are interested in pure classification quality and computational effort of evaluating the test function of the classifiers. The experimental setup described above is the same as in [4]. Therefore the investigations are in a straight forward manner of the previous work.

3   Preliminary Investigations

In previous investigations the three mentioned kernel machines SVM, LSVM, and RVM are used with the Radial Basis Function (RBF) kernel. This kernel is defined by

$$K(x_1, x_2) = \exp\left(- \| x_2 - x_1 \|_2^2 / \sigma\right)$$ (1)

with kernel parameter $\sigma > 0$. Its main advantage is that the topology of the 2-norm Voronoi diagram is invariant under the kernel generating function $\Psi : X \rightarrow F$, $\Psi(x) = z$ that holds

$$K(x_1, x_2) = < \Psi(x_1), \Psi(x_2) >$$ (2)

with $< ., . >$ the l_2-inner product, for further details see [2].

The kernel classifiers are tested with the MSTAR dataset. The results of classification quality (in % of the 1365 test chips) and support vectors (in % of the 1622 training chips) are given in Figure 1. There are displayed the maximums relative to the kernel parameter, i.e. the results with highest value for the weakest class.

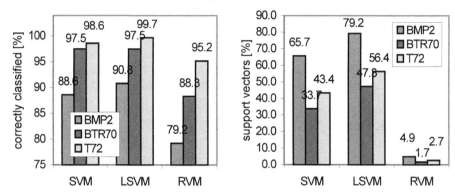

Fig. 1. Classification quality and number of SVs / RVs for the SVM, LSVM, and RVM.

The kernel machines are of quite different nature. The SVM results in a good quality using a lot of SVs. The LSVM is a little bit better using more SVs than the SVM. The RVM yields in a lower classification quality, but the number of Relevance Vectors (RVs) is a few times lower, i.e. the evaluation of the test function is a few times faster. In this example it is more than 15 times faster.

The objective should be to unify the advantages of the machines. We consider that SVM and RVM use the same test function, a linear combination of basis functions:

$$y(x; w) = \sum_{i=1}^{n} w_i K(x, x_i) + w_0 \tag{3}$$

$x_i \in \mathfrak{R}^m$, $i = 1,...,n$ are the training vectors. The weights $w_i \in \mathfrak{R}$, $i = 0,...,n$ have to be computed while training the kernel machine classifier. Taking a look at the test function, RVs or SVs are the same, i.e. the naming results from different methodologies of the underlying optimization problem. The LSVM has another test function, i.e. it is used as reference only. All kernel machine classifiers taken into consideration solve two-class problems internally, i.e. the multi-class problem is divided into two-class problems via the 1-to-rest heuristic.

4   Extended Relevance Vector Machine

To modify the training algorithm we take a look at the RVM training. The RVM is using a system matrix $\Phi \in \mathfrak{R}^{n \times l}$, see (4). The training process only uses this system matrix, the class labels, the l so-called hyper-parameters $\alpha_i \in \mathfrak{R}$, and the l weights $w_i \in \mathfrak{R}$ for the test function.

$$\Phi = \begin{bmatrix} 1 & K(x_1,x_1) & \cdots & K(x_1,x_{l-1}) \\ \vdots & \vdots & \ddots & \vdots \\ 1 & K(x_n,x_1) & \cdots & K(x_n,x_{l-1}) \end{bmatrix} \in \Re^{n \times l}. \tag{4}$$

At the beginning of the training it holds $l = n + 1$. During the iteration basis functions like $K(x, x_{i_0})$ have to be eliminated to guarantee a numerically stable algorithm. The necessity of this elimination is indicated by the respective hyper-parameter α_{i_0} that is growing towards infinity. On the other hand a growing hyper-parameter results in $w_{i_0} \rightarrow 0$, i.e. the basis function has no influence on the value of the test function (3), so it can be eliminated. The update of the system is done by eliminating the corresponding column of the system matrix Φ, the corresponding α_{i_0}, and w_{i_0}. Further it is set $l = l - 1$. For more details see [6, 7].

The columns of Φ correspond to basis functions. The rows of Φ are not eliminated during the training. They correspond to the training data, i.e. the optimization process is internally controlled by the classification quality for this training dataset.

This described structure of the RVM makes it possible to choose the basis functions and the RVM training dataset independently of each other.

Therefore a first shot is done to yield an upper limit of high classification quality and low computational effort for the considered family of kernel machines. We have chosen the training data for the basis functions and the union of training and test dataset for the RVM training dataset. This setup is done to determine an upper limit only. We have set $l = n_{train} + 1$, $n = n_{train} + n_{test}$, and have calculated the system matrix Φ by evaluating the RBF kernel. The cross-classification result of this experimental RVM (RVME) for the MSTAR dataset is given in Table 2. The percent rates are relative to 1365 test or 1622 training chips respectively.

Table 2. Classification result of RVME with RBF kernel parameter $\sigma = 60$

Class	Correct [%]	RVs [%]
BMP2	99.8	6.0
BTR70	100.0	2.1
T72	99.3	3.8

It is possible to get a kernel classifier for basis functions relative to the MSTAR training dataset that does a quasi 100% classification of the test dataset and that uses all over 11.9% RVs only. This result is a possible limit. It strongly depends on the local correlation between training and test dataset in vector space F. For realistic considerations we do not have any knowledge about the test dataset. But such modification of the RVM is an example of a universal method.

5 RVMG – Relevance Vector Machine with Generator

The advantage of the SVM versus the RVM is its good classification quality. This can be explained by maximizing the margin between classes and the discriminating hyperplane in vector space F, the kernel generating function is mapping into. A description of this is the maximization of spheres of same size around all training points. These spheres have to permit a linear discrimination with respect to the classes. The RVM does not respect a neighborhood of data points in contrast to SVM.

Many generators are possible to build a discrete neighborhood of training points. One type produces additional points around all original points, e.g. within a given distance. Other ones use families of geometrical transformations to the original data. Such generators often have several disadvantages. In contrast to this we define objectives of the generator which has to be defined:

☐ No blurring of class boundaries, so the overlapping of classes does not grow.
☐ It should not increase the class density of irrelevant inner regions of classes.
☐ Producing a manageable number of points that does not make the training impossible on real computers.
☐ A variable distance between original and generated points with respect to the underlying structure of classes.

With the method described in the previous section it is possible to extend the training dataset by such generated data. What kind of generator we use and how to overcome the problem of mapping into F is described as follows.

5.1. Generator – Linear Case

The proposed generator computes possible boundary or near boundary points in the first class and their counterparts in the second class, and the other way. Some of these pairs are rejected if they are not the nearest neighbors of their mean point.

$$P_0 = \{(x_i, x_j) \in C_A \times C_B \mid (x_i \text{ is NN in } C_A \text{ of } x_j \vee x_j \text{ is NN in } C_B \text{ of } x_i)$$
$$\wedge \ x_i \text{ is NN in } C_A \text{ of } m_{ij} \wedge x_j \text{ is NN in } C_B \text{ of } m_{ij}\} \quad (5)$$

with the two training classes C_A and C_B, $m_{ij} = (x_i + x_j)/2$. NN is the Nearest Neighbor with respect to $\|.\|_2$. Additionally it holds $|P_0| \leq n_{train}$.

The generator points are defined using the parameter $0 < \lambda < 0.5$ as follows:

$$G_{A,\lambda} = \{(1-\lambda)x_i + \lambda x_j \mid (x_i, x_j) \in P_0\}$$
$$G_{B,\lambda} = \{\lambda x_i + (1-\lambda)x_j \mid (x_i, x_j) \in P_0\}. \quad (6)$$

The number of training points $n = |C_A| + |C_B| + |G_{A,\lambda}| + |G_{B,\lambda}| \leq 3n_{train}$, inclusive the generated data $G_{A,\lambda}$ and $G_{B,\lambda}$ relative to the two classes, is of moderate size.

5.2. Generator – Kernel Case

The nonlinear case is the interesting one. Therefore we use a kernel K. A kernel generating function $\Psi : X \to F$ theoretically exists that holds (2), but in practice only K is given. In the above subsection the generator is described for the linear case, i.e. it could be interpreted as a generator in vector space F that Ψ is mapping into. The following tasks have to be transferred from linear to kernel case.

NN in C_A or C_B for training points is solved in original vector space X. This is possible because we use the RBF kernel for which the Voronoi topology is invariant. A more efficient solution is to calculate differences of training points using elements of Φ as follows:

$$\| \Psi(x_i) - \Psi(x_j) \|_2^2 = K(x_i, x_i) - 2K(x_i, x_j) + K(x_j, x_j) \qquad (7)$$

Secondly the NN in C_A or C_B of mean value $(\Psi(x_i) + \Psi(x_j))/2$ could not be computed directly. But for the NN we have to calculate the distances between mean values and training points. It could be easily shown:

$$\| (\Psi(x_i) + \Psi(x_j))/2 - \Psi(x_k) \|_2^2 = (K(x_i, x_i) + K(x_j, x_j))/4$$
$$+ K(x_k, x_k) + K(x_i, x_j)/2 - K(x_i, x_k) - K(x_j, x_k) \qquad (8)$$

Thirdly the generated points have to be used as extra training data for RVM. Basis functions are only relative to the original training points. Therefore a generated point is needed to calculate elements of the corresponding new row s of Φ.

$$\Phi_{s,k} = <(1-\lambda)\Psi(x_i) + \lambda\Psi(x_j), \Psi(x_k)> = (1-\lambda)K(x_i, x_k) + \lambda K(x_j, x_k). \qquad (9)$$

Equations (7) and (8) allow to generate $G_{A,\lambda}$ and $G_{B,\lambda}$. These generated points are not processed directly but their corresponding rows of Φ are determined by equation (9). No blurring of class boundaries is done because the generated points are elements of Voronoi cells in F corresponding to same classes. The number of training points inclusive generated data is of manageable size $n = |C_A| + |C_B| + |G_{A,\lambda}| + |G_{B,\lambda}| \leq 3n_{train}$. No other than boundary regions are fortified. The relative strength (distance to boundaries) is controlled by $0 < \lambda < 0.5$.

6   Experimental Results

The experimental setup of the MSTAR dataset has been described in section 2. Several tests have been done with the described kernel machines. The results are given in Fig. 2. To yield appropriate results the machines have been parameterized with different kernel parameter values (of a small set): SVM - $\sigma = 80$, LSVM - $\sigma = 40$, RVM - $\sigma = 60$, RVME - $\sigma = 60$, RVMG - $\sigma = 40$.

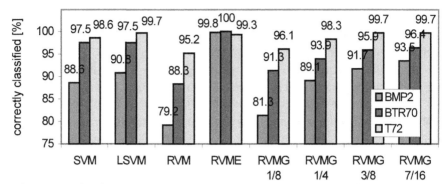

Fig. 2. Classification quality of the tested kernel classifiers (in % of the 1365 test chips).

The RVMG has been tested with several values of control parameter $0 < \lambda < 0.5$. The greater this parameter is, the higher is the classification quality, and the higher is the number of RVs. The number of SVs / RVs in % is given in Fig. 3.

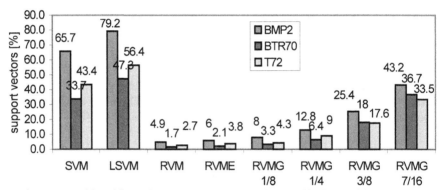

Fig. 3. Number of SVs / RVs of the tested kernel classifiers (in % of the 1622 training chips).

The spectrum varies from a 15 times faster machine than the RVM with 10% lower quality than the SVM, goes to a 5 times faster and equal quality machine – the RVMG ($\lambda = 1/4$), and ends with the RVMG ($\lambda = 7/16$), a machine a little bit faster than the SVM and of better quality than the LSVM. The quality of the RVME could not be reached any more. But for its training it uses the knowledge about the test data.

The greater the parameter λ has been chosen, the harder the training, e.g. the training of the RVMG with $\lambda = 1/4$ has been done in 196 minutes, but with $\lambda = 7/16$ it takes 105 hours. Fortunately the time of training has no influence on the evaluation of the test function. In all cases the cross-classification of the MSTAR test dataset only takes a few minutes on a computer with AMD 1800+.

RVMG is a controllable machine that is adjustable for a higher classification speed while decreasing the classification quality. And it is feasible to reach the quality of the LSVM with lower computational effort.

7 Conclusion

With the described new approach it is possible to construct a kernel machine classifier with indirectly controlled trade-off between speed and quality. For this a single parameter controls the strength of fortification of class boundaries, i.e. the robustness of the original class structure for the classification training. Class boundaries are respected, i.e. no additional class overlapping is produced. The generated extended training dataset is of moderate size. Therefore the proposed RVMG is prepared for a wide range of applications.

Further investigations will be done with other datasets. A preprocessing of data should be taken into consideration. Other generator approaches are possible using the described method and the choice of different kernels should be discussed.

Acknowledgements. The author wishes to thank U. Thönnessen FGAN-FOM for his permanent advice and helpful discussions. Moreover many thanks to A. Ebert FGAN-FOM for his technical assistance in implementing and testing the software system.

References

1. Müjdat Çetin, W. Clem Karl, and David A. Castañon, "Analysis of the Impact of Feature-Enhanced SAR Imaging on ATR Performance", Procedings of SPIE - Algorithms for SAR Imagery IX, E.G. Zelnio (ed.), 4727, 134–145, Orlando, Florida, 2002
2. N. Cristianini, J. Shawe-Taylor, An Introduction to Support Vector Machines and other kernel-based learning methods, Cambridge University Press, 2000
3. O. L. Mangasarian, D. R. Musicant, "Lagrangian Support Vector Machines", Journal of Machine Learning Research, 1, 161–177, 2001
4. W. Middelmann, U. Thönnessen, "Classification in High-Resolution SAR data", Proceedings of SPIE - Algorithms for SAR Imagery, E. G. Zelnio (ed.), to be published
5. B. Schölkopf, Support Vector Learning, PhD Thesis, R. Oldenbourg Verlag, Munich, 1997
6. M. E. Tipping, "The Relevance Vector Machine", Advances in Neural Information Processing Systems, 12, S. A. Solla, T. K. Leen, K.-R. Muller (eds), MIT Press, Cambridge, MA, 2000
7. M. E. Tipping, "Sparse Bayesian Learning and the Relevance Vector Machine", Journal of Machine Learning Research, 1, 211–244, 2001
8. J. Tsao, B. D. Steinberg, "Reduction of Sidelobe and Speckle Artifacts in Microwave Imaging: The CLEAN Technique", IEEE Transactions on Antennas and Propagation, 36, 543–556, 1988
9. V. Vapnik, Statistical Learning Theory, Wiley, New York, 1998
10. MSTAR, Air Force Research Lab., Model Based Vision Lab., Sensor Data Management System, http://www.mbvlab.wpafb.af.mil/public/sdms/datasets/mstar/overview.htm

3D Reconstruction of Human Skeleton from Single Images or Monocular Video Sequences

Fabio Remondino and Andreas Roditakis

Institute for Geodesy and Photogrammetry - ETH Zurich, Switzerland
{fabio,roditak}@geod.baug.ethz.ch

Abstract. In this paper, we first review the approaches to recover 3D shape and related movements of a human and then we present an easy and reliable approach to recover a 3D model using just one image or monocular video sequence. A simplification of the perspective camera model is required, due to the absence of stereo view. The human figure is reconstructed in a skeleton form and to improve the visual quality, a pre-defined human model is also fitted to the recovered 3D data.

1 Introduction

In the last years the generation of 3D models of man made objects has become a topic of interest for several researchers. Particular attention has also been paid on the reconstruction of realistic human models, which could be employed in a wide range of applications such as movies, medicine, surveillance, video games, virtual reality environments or ergonomics applications. A complete human model usually consists of the shape and the movement of the body. Some available systems consider the two modeling processes as separate even if they are very close. Considering the techniques that recover the *shape of static humans*, nowadays a classical approach commonly used relies on *3D scanners* [5, 7, 27]: these sensors (Figure 1, A) are quite expensive but simple to use and various software is available to model the 3D measurements. They work according to different technologies providing for millions of points, often with related color information. Other techniques try to recover the shape of human figures with *image-based* approaches. They can use single camera stereo-view geometry (Figure 1, B) [20], silhouette extraction [11] or single image measurements [3, 16, 23]. *Computer animation software* [1, 18, 21] can instead produce realistic 3D human model subdividing and smoothing polygonal elements, without any measurements (Figure 1, C). These spline-based systems are mainly used for movies or games and the created virtual human is animated using similar animation packages or with motion capture data. Concerning the *motion of the human*, the main problem is the great number of degrees of freedom to be recovered. Existing and reliable commercial systems for capturing human motion typically involve the tracking of human's movements using *sensor-based hardware* [2, 19]. Other approaches instead rely on *2D monocular videos* of human as primary input [12, 22]. They use computer vision techniques, image cues, background segmentation,

B. Michaelis and G. Krell (Eds.): DAGM 2003, LNCS 2781, pp. 100–107, 2003.

blob statistics, prior knowledge about human motion, probabilistic approaches and pre-defined articulated body models to recover motions and 3D information. Finally *multi-cameras approaches* [8, 10, 25] are employed to increase reliability, accuracy and avoid problems with self-occlusions.

Many research activities in this area has focused on the problem of tracking a moving human (human motion analysis) through an image sequence acquired with single/multiple camera(s) and often using pre-defined 3D models. But little attention has been directed to the determination of 3D information of a human directly from a single image or monocular sequence using a camera model (deterministic approach). In this contribution we present a simple and efficient method to find the poses and the 3D model of a human imaged in a single image or in a monocular sequence. Our work is similar to [23], but additional changes and improvements are presented and discussed. The 3D human model is recovered with a deterministic approach and only for visualization purposes a laser scanner 3D model is fitted to the recovered data.

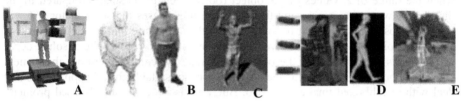

Fig. 1. Different approaches to recover a human body model. A: laser scanner system [27]. B: single-camera stereo-view image sequence [20]. C: computer animation software [21]. D: Multi-camera system [8]. E: Probabilistic approach on monocular sequence [22].

2 The Reconstruction Algorithm

Usually the algorithms that want to recover accurate 3D models from images are based on the collinearity equations [20]. They state that a point in object space, its corresponding point in an image and the projective center of the camera lie on a straight line. If a point is stereo-imaged in more than one frame, its 3D coordinates in the world coordinate system can be recovered e.g. with the bundle method, as well as the camera parameters. Although this method is very accurate, it requires a point to be imaged in at least two images and a good baseline between consecutive frames; therefore it is not possible to use it when a (rotating) monocular sequence or a single image is used. A simplification of collinearity equations leads to the perspective projection that relates the image measurements to the world coordinate system just through the camera constant c:

$$x = -c \cdot \frac{X}{Z}$$
$$y = -c \cdot \frac{Y}{Z}$$
(1)

If we want to recover 3D information from a single uncalibrated view, we have the so called 'ill-posed' problem: for each point, we have two equations and three unknown coordinates, plus the camera constant. Therefore the system is underdetermined and some more assumptions need to be introduced. For man made objects (e.g. buildings), geometric constraints on the object (perpendicularity and orthogonality) and image invariant can be used to solve an ill-posed problem [24]. But in case of free form objects (e.g. the human body) these assumptions are not valid. Therefore equation (1) can be furthermore simplified, describing the relationship between the 3D object coordinates and 2D image measurements with an orthographic projection scaled with a factor s = -c/Z:

$$x = s \cdot X \qquad (2)$$
$$y = s \cdot Y$$

The effect of orthographic projection is a simple scaling of the object coordinates. The scaled-orthographic model amounts to parallel projection, with a scaling added to mimic the effect that the image of an object shrinks with the distance. This camera model can be used if we assume the Z coordinate almost constant in the image or when the range of Z values of the object (object's depth) is small compared to the distance between the camera and the object. In those cases the scale factor c/Z will remain almost constant and it is possible to find a value of s that best fit in equation (2) for all points involved. Moreover it is not necessary to recover the absolute depth of the points with respect to the object coordinate system. Furthermore the camera constant is not required and this makes the algorithm suitable for all applications that deal with uncalibrated images or video. But, as it is generally an ill-posed problem, we still have an undetermined system, as the scale factor s cannot be determined only by means of equation (2) and a single frame. Therefore, supposing that the length L of a straight segment between two object points is known, it can be expressed as $L_{12}{}^2 = (X_1 - X_2)^2 + (Y_1 - Y_2)^2 + (Z_1 - Z_2)^2$. By combining this equations with (2) we end up with an expression for the relative depth between two points:

$$(Z_1 - Z_2)^2 = L_{12}{}^2 - [(x_1 - x_2)^2 + (y_1 - y_2)^2] / s^2 \qquad (3)$$

So, if the scale parameter s is known, we can compute the relative depth between two points as a function of their distance L and image coordinates. Therefore the whole reconstruction problem can be reduced to the problem of finding the best scale factor for a particular configuration of image points. Equation (3) also shows that, for a given scale parameter s, there are two possible solutions for the relative depth of the endpoints of each segment (because of the square root). This is caused by the fact that even if we select point 1 or point 2 to have the smaller Z coordinate, their (orthographic) projection on the image plane will have exactly the same coordinate. In order to have a real solution, we have to impose that:

$$s \geq \frac{\sqrt{[(x_1 - x_2)^2 + (y_1 - y_2)^2]}}{L_{12}} \qquad (4)$$

By applying inequality (4) to each segment with known length one can find the scale parameter that can be used in equation (3) to calculate the relative depth between any two segments endpoints. Because of the orthographic projection assumed, we have to decide an arbitrary depth for the first point and then compute the second point depth relative to the first one. For the next point we use a previous calculated depth and equation (3) to compute its Z coordinate and so on in a segment-by-segment way. Due to the difference in the left side of equation (3), we have also to decide, for each segment, which one is closer to the camera. Then, knowing the scale factor, equation (2) can be used to calculate the X and Y coordinates of the image points. In [23] is mentioned that images with significant perspective effect could not be modeled with this approach. Infect, in some results, because of measurement or assumption errors, a segment that seems to be almost parallel to the image plane can get foreshortened or warped along one axis. But if a segment is almost parallel to the image plane or can be assumed to lie on a plane, then the two points can be treated as being at the same depth. And imposing additional constraints, such as requiring that 2 points must have the same depth, this mistake can be avoided and the resulting 3D model is more accurate and reliable. An example is presented in Figure 2-A where the 3D skeleton recovered with simple orthographic projection is improved using some depth constraints. Other constraints could be the perpendicularity of two segments or a closure constraint, imposing that the two points must coincide (Fig. 2-C).

3   The Human Body Model and Its Representation

The human skeleton system is treated as a series of jointed links (segments), which can be modeled as rigid bodies. For the specific problem of recovering the pose of a human figure, we describe the body as a stick model consisting of a set of thirteen joints (plus the head) connected by thirteen segments (we consider the shoulder girdle as unique segment), as shown in Table 1. The head joint is used to model some figure where it is inclined, as shown in, Fig. 2-C and D. The algorithm needs the knowledge of the relative lengths of the segments, which can be obtained from anthropometric data (motion capture databases or literature). Two sets of length values are used in our tests, leading almost to the same 3D models. The first set of relative distances between human joints is derived from a motion capture database [4] (Table 1, central). The second set is more general and follows the studies performed by Leonardo Da Vinci and Michelangelo on the human figure [13, 26] (Table 1, right). It represents the human figure as an average of eight heads high. Once the program has computed the 3D coordinates of the human joints, they are given to a procedure that uses VRML language to visualize the recovered model. All the joints are represented with spheres and they are joined together with cylinders or tapered ellipsoids (to model the shape of the muscles).

Table 1. Two different sets of relative lengths of the segments used in the computation of the human skeleton. MC = Motion Capture. L = Literature. The coefficient i has been added in the second one to consider the variation of the human size from the average size (i=1). On the right the human model skeleton used in the reconstruction.

Segment	Relative Length (MC) [cm]	Relative Length (L) [unit]	
Height	175	8 i	
Lower arm	35	2 i	
Upper Arm	25	1 ½ i	
Neck-Head	25	1 ¼ i	
Shoulder Girdle	44	2 i	
Torso	53	2 ½ i	
Pelvic Girdle	30	1 ½ i	
Upper leg	46	2 i	
Lower leg	52	2 i	
Foot	22	1 i	

4   Implicit/Explicit Surface Fitting

Fitting a surface on a given set of points is a problem that has been approached in several ways in Computer Graphics literature. The main classification considers the type of the final representation, dividing the fitting methods into explicit and implicit. *Triangular meshes*, *volume grids* [6] and *parametric piecewise functions (NURBS)* [15] are explicit descriptions of the surface, while *soft* or *blobby objects*, also known as *metaballs* [8, 14] describe the surface as the isosurface of a distance function. On one hand the explicit functions appear to be a popular representation in modeling software and are hardware supported, achieving rendering performances of millions of texture mapped polygons per second. Fitting such surfaces on a set of measurements presents, though, the difficulty of finding the faces that are closest to a 3D point, and the disadvantage of non-differentiability of the distance function [14]. Implicit surfaces are more suitable for modeling soft objects as they have been used in modeling clouds [9] or soft tissue objects [14], but present difficulties in deformations and rendering.

In our application, to improve to visual quality of the results, we chose to fit the recovered 3D skeleton with a polygonal mesh [6], using the modeling and animation software Maya [17]. Our skeleton has a hierarchical structure, which is used to calculate the number of joints that influence every point (called influence depth). Large influence depths result in 'softer' objects. We kept a low depth to avoid too soft deformations and after the automatic fitting we adjusted manually the influence weight of some skeleton joints on the polygons to eliminate hard edges. For the movement of the skeleton there are two solutions available in Maya, called *Forward* and *Inverse Kinematics*. The first method requires the rotation and translation of all the joints, starting from the parent and ending to the last child joint, to achieve the final pose. The latter method requires that only the position and rotation of the desired pose, or *target locator*, is given from the user and then the position of the intermediate joints is calculated automatically. In this case, the use of joint rotation constrains is essential in order to achieve a correct solution. In the present paper, we use inverse kinematics, because of the simplicity and automation of the procedure. In Figures 2-E and 3 we present the results of fitting a polygonal model acquired with a Cyberware body scanner [6] to the poses recovered from single image and monocular video sequence.

5   Results on Single Uncalibrated Images

In order to determine the limitations, advantages and accuracy of the method, a series of experiments were performed at the beginning on single images taken from the Internet or extracted from videos.

Fig. 2 show some images and the associated 3D models looked from different viewpoints. In particular, column A shows a 3D model obtain with the simple orthographic projection (central image: 3D model warped and distorted) and after the applied constraints (lower result). Furthermore, measurements occlusions are handled selecting the most adequate point in the image and computing its 3D coordinate using a depth constraint (e.g. right knee in Figure 2-A or right shoulder in Figure 2-B). The accuracy of the reconstruction is demonstrated by the fitting results (Figure 2-E): infect the laser model (that is precise for definition) is just scaled and its segments are rotated to match our skeleton.

Fig. 2. 3D model of human figure recovered from single images. Different representations of the human skeleton are presented: simple cylinders, scaled cylindrical torso and tapered ellipsoids to model the muscles. Note also the head of the figure (C and D), that is represented in the recovered model inclined according to the image data. Column E shows a 3D laser model fitted to our skeleton.

6   Application to Monocular Video Sequences

The reconstruction algorithm has been also extended to solve the reconstruction problem in consecutive frames obtained from videos. The poses and movements of a figure over a short interval of time are recovered and then, by playing the reconstructed poses at an adequate frame rate, we can get a very realistic and observer independent reconstruction of the original motion. However, because the algorithm finds only relative distance in each frame, subsequent poses normally have no object coordinates in common. This is solved assuming that a joint in one frame has the same coordinates (plus a small translation vector) of the corresponding joint in the previous frame. In the example presented in Fig. 3, we digitized 20 frames from an old videotape. The image points were measured semi-automatically with a Least Squares Matching Algorithm. The recovered models show the reliability of the algorithm and its possible application also in case of small perspective effect. In case of good image quality, the corresponding joints could be tracked automatically over the video sequence, as described in [8].

7 Conclusion

In this work we presented the problem of recovering 3D models of humans from single images and monocular video sequences. The problem was solved with a scaled orthographic projection and some additional constraints. The reconstruction and visualization algorithm was tested with several images and sequences and the presented results show the reliability of our extended algorithm, also when some perspective effects are present. As future work we want to add the foot and the hands to the recovered skeleton and we will try to model muscles and shape of some segments using tapered cones. Moreover a perspective camera model will also be tested on human figures imaged in monocular sequences.

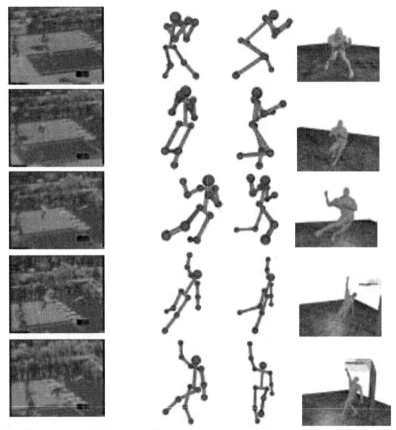

Fig. 3. Reconstructed 3D model of the moving human in the monocular video sequence. The second and third columns show the recovered skeleton viewed from two different viewpoints. The last column shows the fitted laser model to our 3D data.

References

1. 3D Studio Max: http://www.3dmax.com [June 2003]
2. Ascension: http://www.ascension-tech.com/ [June 2003]
3. Barron, C., Kakadiaris, A.: Estimating Anthropometry and Pose from a single uncalibrated image. Computer Vision and Image Understanding, Vol. 81, 269-284, 2001.
4. Biovision: http://www.biovision.com [June 2003]
5. BodySkanner: http://www.scansewsuccess.com [June 2003]
6. Curless, B., Levoy, M.: A volumetric method for building complex models from range images. 23rd Conf. on Computer graphics and interactive techniques, pp. 302-312, 1996.
7. Cyberware: http://www.cyberware.com [June 2003]
8. D'Apuzzo, N., Plankers, R., Fua, P., Gruen, A., Thalmann, D.: Modeling human bodies from video sequences. Videometrics Conference, SPIE Proc., Vol. 3461 (1999), 36-47
9. Dobashi, Y., Kaneda, K., et. al.: A simple, efficient method for realistic animation of clouds. Proc. of 27th Conf. Computer graphics and interactive techniques, pp. 19-28, 2000.
10. Gavrila, D.M, Davis, L.S.: 3-D Model-based Tracking of Humans in Action: a Multi-View Approach. CVPR Proceedings, 1996.
11. Hilton, A., Beresfors, D., Gentils, T., Smith, R., Sun, W., Illingworth, J.: Whole-body modeling of people from multiview images to populate virtual worlds. The Visual Computer, Vol. 16, 411-436, Springer-Verlag, 2001
12. Howe, N., Leventon, M., Freeman, W.: Bayesian reconstruction of 3D human motion from single-camera video. Advances in Neural Information Processing System, Vol. 12, 820–826, MIT Press, 2000.
13. Human Figure Drawing Proportion: www.mauigateway.com/~donjusko/human.htm
14. Ilic, S., Fua, P.: From explicit to implicit surfaces for visualization, animation and modeling, Proc. of Inter. Workshop on visualization and animation of reality based 3D models, Vulpera, Switzerland, 2003.
15. Krishnamurthy, V., Levoy, M.: Fitting smooth surfaces to dense polygon meshes. Proc. of 23rd Conf. on Computer graphics and interactive techniques, pp. 313–324, 1996.
16. Lee, H.J., Chen, Z.: Determination of human body posture from a single view. Computer Vision, Graphics, Image Process, Vol. 30 (1985), 148-168.
17. Learnning Maya 2.5: Alias Wavefront, 1998.
18. Lightwave: http://www.lightwave3d.com [June 2003]
19. Motion Analysis: http://www.motionanalysis.com/ [June 2003]
20. Remondino, F: 3D reconstruction of static human body with a digital camera. Videometrics Conference, SPIE Proc., Vol. 5013, pp. 38–45, 2003.
21. SculpLand: http://www.sanynet.ne.jp/~nakajima/SculpLand.html [June 2003]
22. Sidenbladh, H., Black, M., Fleet, D.: Stochastic Tracking of 3D Human Figures Using 2D Image Motion. ECCV, D. Vernon (Ed.), Springer Verlag, LNCS 1843, pp. 702–718, 2000.
23. Taylor, C.T: Reconstruction of Articulated Objects from Point Correspondences in a Single Uncalibrated Image. Computer Vision and Image Understanding. Vol. 80, 349–363
24. Van den Heuvel, F.A: 3D reconstruction from a single image using geometric constraints. ISPRS Journal for Photogrammetry and Remote Sensing, 53, No. 6, pp. 354-368, 1998.
25. Vedula, S., Baker, S.: Three Dimensional Scene Flow. ICCV '99, Vol. 2, pp. 722-729.
26. Visual Body Proportion: http://www2.evansville.edu/drawinglab/body.html [June 2003]
27. Vitus: http://www.vitus.de [June 2003]

Shape Preservation during Digitization: Tight Bounds Based on the Morphing Distance

Peer Stelldinger and Ullrich Köthe

Cognitive Systems Group, University of Hamburg,
Vogt-Köln-Str. 30, D-22527 Hamburg, Germany

Abstract. We define *strong r-similarity* and the *morphing distance* to bound geometric distortions between shapes of equal topology. We then derive a necessary and sufficient condition for a set and its digitizations to be r-similar, regardless of the sampling grid. We also extend these results to certain gray scale images. Our findings are steps towards a theory of shape digitization for real optical systems.

1 Introduction

In order to make image analysis algorithms more reliable it is desirable to rigorously prove their properties, if possible. As *object shape* is of particular interest, we would like to know to what extend the information derived from a digitized shape carries over to the analog original. In this paper we analyse under which circumstances analog and digital shapes will have the same topology and bounded geometric distortions. For simplicity, we ignore the effect of gray-level quantization, and only consider spatial sampling.

The problem of topology preservation was first investigated by Pavlidis [4]. He showed that a particular class of binary analog shapes (which we will call r-regular shapes, cf. definition 6) does not change topology under discretization with any sufficiently dense square grid. Similarly, Serra [6] showed that the homotopy tree of r-regular sets is preserved under discretization with any sufficiently dense hexagonal grid. Both results apply to binary sets and the so called *subset digitization*, where a pixel is considered part of the digital shape iff its center is element of the given set. Latecki et al. [2] generalized the findings of Pavlidis to other digitizations including the *square subset* and *intersection* digitizations.

Geometric similarity can be measured by the Hausdorff distance. Pavlidis [4] proved a rather coarse bound for the Hausdorff distance between the analog and digital sets. Ronse and Tajine [5] showed that in the limit of infinitely dense sampling the Hausdorff distance between the original and digitized shapes converges to zero. However, they did not analyse topology changes.

In this paper, we combine topological and geometric criteria into two new shape similarity measures, *weak* and *strong r-similarity*. We prove that r-regularity is a necessary and sufficient condition for an analog set (i.e. a binary image) to be reconstructible (in the sense of both measures) by any regular or irregular grid with sampling distance smaller than r. These findings also apply to certain gray-scale images that result from blurring of binary images.

B. Michaelis and G. Krell (Eds.): DAGM 2003, LNCS 2781, pp. 108–115, 2003.

L c c o e

Fig. 1. Examples for weak similarity: L and c have the same topology, but large Hausdorff distance d_H. The two c's have a much smaller d_H (when overlaid). Between c and o, d_H is still quite small, but they differ by topology. The distinction between o and e is not so clear: Their topology is equal, and d_H still relatively small.

2   Shape Similarity and Digitization

Given two sets A and B, their similarity can be expressed in several ways. The most fundamental is topological equivalence. A and B are topologically equivalent if there exists a homeomorphism, i.e. a bijective function $f : A \to B$ with f and f^{-1} continuous. However, this does not completely characterize the topology of a set embedded in the plane $\mathbb{R}^2$. Therefore, [6] introduced the homotopy tree which encodes whether some components of A enclose others in a given embedding. Both notions are captured simultaneously when the homeomorphism f is extended to the entire $\mathbb{R}^2$ plane. Then it also defines a mapping $A^c \to B^c$ for the set complements and ensures preservation of both the topology and the homotopy tree. We call this an $\mathbb{R}^2$-*homeomorphism*.

Geometric similarity between two shapes can be measured by the *Hausdorff distance* d_H between the shape boundaries. We call the combination of both criteria *weak r-similarity*.

Definition 1. *Two bounded subsets* $A, B \subset \mathbb{R}^2$ *are called* weakly r-similar *if there exists a homeomorphism* $f : \mathbb{R}^2 \to \mathbb{R}^2$ *such that* $\boldsymbol{x} \in A \Leftrightarrow f(\boldsymbol{x}) \in B$, *and the Hausdorff distance between the set boundaries* $d_H(\partial A, \partial B) \le r \in \mathbb{R}_+ \cup \{\infty\}$.

In many cases, weak r-similarity captures human perception quite nicely. Fig. 1 demonstrates this for the shape of some letters. However, it is not always sufficient. This can already be seen by comparing the letters "o" and "e" in fig. 1, but fig. 2 shows even more striking examples: These sets are topologically equivalent and have small Hausdorff distance, yet the shapes and meanings are percieved as very different. The reason for the failure of weak r-similarity is the following: Topology preservation is determined by an $\mathbb{R}^2$-homeomorphism that maps each point of A to a unique point of B. In contrast, the Hausdorff distance is calculated by mapping each point of A to the nearest point of B and vice versa. Both mappings are *independent* of each other and, in general, totally different. We can improve the similarity measure by using the same transformation for both the determination of topological equivalence and geometric similarity:

Definition 2. *Two sets* $A, B \subset \mathbb{R}^2$ *are called* strongly r-similar *and we write* $A \overset{r}{\approx} B$, *if they are weakly r-similar and* $\forall \boldsymbol{x} \in \partial A : |\boldsymbol{x} - f(\boldsymbol{x})| \le r$. *Such a restricted homeomorphism is called* r-homeomorphism. *The morphing distance is defined as* $d_M(A, B) := \inf \left(\{\infty\} \cup \{r | A \overset{r}{\approx} B\} \right)$.

(a)   (b)   (c)   (d)

Fig. 2. Failure of weak similarity: (a) and (b) have the same topology and small Hausdorff distance, but large morphing distance. Their shapes and symbolic meanings (s vs. ε) are perceived as very different. Likewise (c) and (d).

Two sets are $\mathbb{R}^2$-topologically equivalent iff they are (strongly or weakly) ∞-similar, and they are equal iff they are (strongly or weakly) 0-similar. The morphing distance is symmetric, and the triangle inequality holds because the triangle inequality of the Euclidien metric applies at every point when two transformations are combined. Therefore, d_M is a metric and an upper bound for the Hausdorff metric d_H. It is easy to show that the existence of an r-homeomorphism that maps ∂A to ∂B implies the existence of an r-homeomorphism for the whole plane. Under strong r-similarity, the topology is not only preserved in a global, but also in a local manner: When we look at the embedding of A into $\mathbb{R}^2$ within a small open region U_A, a corresponding open region U_B with the same topological characteristics exists in the embedding of B, and the distance between the two regions is not greater than r. The shapes in fig. 2 are examples for non-local topology preservation: Morphing of corresponding shapes onto each other requires a rather big r, and $d_H \ll d_M$ in these cases.

Consider a set $A \in \mathbb{R}^2$. Its subset discretization is obtained by storing set inclusion information only at a countable number of points, i.e. on a grid:

Definition 3. *A countable set $S \subset \mathbb{R}^2$ of sampling points where $d_H(\{\boldsymbol{x}\}, S) \leq r$ holds for all $\boldsymbol{x} \in \mathbb{R}^2$ is called an r-grid if for each bounded set $A \in \mathbb{R}^2$ the subset $S \cap A$ is finite. The associated Voronoi regions are called pixels:*

$$\mathrm{Pixel}_S : S \to \mathcal{P}(\mathbb{R}^2), \quad \mathrm{Pixel}_S(\boldsymbol{s}) := \{\boldsymbol{x} : \forall \boldsymbol{s}' \in S \setminus \{\boldsymbol{s}\} : |\boldsymbol{x} - \boldsymbol{s}| \leq |\boldsymbol{x} - \boldsymbol{s}'|\}$$

The intersection of A with S is called the S-digitization of A: $\mathrm{Dig}_S(A) := A \cap S$.

This definition is very broad and captures even irregular grids, provided their Voronoi regions have bounded radius, see fig. 3.

As it is not useful to directly compare discrete sets with analog ones, we reconstruct an analog set from the given digitization. This is done by assigning the information stored at each sampling point to the entire surrounding pixel:

Definition 4. *Given a set $A \subseteq \mathbb{R}^2$ and a grid S, the S-reconstruction of $\mathrm{Dig}_S(A)$ is defined as $\hat{A} = \mathrm{Rec}_S(\mathrm{Dig}_S(A)) = \bigcup_{\boldsymbol{s} \in (S \cap A)} \mathrm{Pixel}_S(\boldsymbol{s})$.*

The results of a reconstruction process will be considered correct if the reconstructed set $\hat{A}$ is sufficiently similar to the original set A. Formally, we get

Definition 5. *A set $A \subseteq \mathbb{R}^2$ is reconstructible by an r-grid S if the S-reconstruction $\hat{A}$ is strongly r-similar to A, i.e. $d_M(A, \hat{A}) \leq r$.*

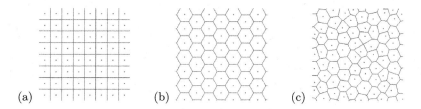

(a)   (b)   (c)

Fig. 3. Many different grid types are covered by our definition based on Voronoi regions, including regular square (a) and hexagonal (b) ones, and irregular grids (c) as found in natural image acquisition devices like the human eye.

3   Conditions for Shape Preserving Digitization

It turns out that shape preserving digitization is only possible if the shape fulfills a regularity requirement developed independently by Pavlidis [4] and Serra [6]:

Definition 6. *A compact set $A \subset \mathbb{R}^2$ is called r-regular iff for each boundary point of A it is possible to find two osculating open balls of radius r, one lying entirely in A and the other lying entirely in A^c.*

Using this definition, we prove the following geometric sampling theorem:

Theorem 1. *Let $r \in \mathbb{R}_+$ and A an r-regular set. Then A is reconstructible with any r'-grid S, $0 < r' < r$.*

In a previous paper [1], we proved the same theorem, but reconstructible sets were defined by means of *weak r-similarity* (simply called *r-similarity* there). Here we will show that the theorem also holds when *strong r'-similarity* is required. Moreover, theorem 2 shows that r-regularity is also a necessary condition.

Proof. From the weak version of the theorem in [1] we already know that the reconstruction is $\mathbb{R}^2$-topologically equivalent to A, and the Hausdorff distance between the boundaries is at most r'. To tighten the theorem for strong r'-similarity it remains to be shown that there even exists an r'-homeomorphism.

Due to the r-regularity of A, no pixel can touch two components of ∂A. Therefore, we can treat each component $\partial A'$ of ∂A and its corresponding component $\partial \hat{A}'$ separately. The proof principle is to split $\partial A'$ and $\partial \hat{A}'$ into sequences of segments $\{C_i\}$ and $\{\hat{C}_i\}$, and show that, for all i, $\hat{C}_i$ can be mapped onto C_i with an r'-homeomorphism. The order of the segments in the sequences is determined by the orientation of the plane, and corresponding segments must have the same index. Then the existence of an r'-homeomorphism between each pair of segments implies the existence of the r'-homeomorphism for the entire boundary. We define initial split points $\hat{c}_i$ of $\partial \hat{A}'$ as follows (see fig. 4a):

Case 1: A split point is defined where $\partial \hat{A}'$ crosses or touches $\partial A'$. *Case 1a:* If this is a single point, it automatically defines a corresponding split point of $\partial A'$. *Case 1b:* If extended parts of the boundaries coincide, the first and last common points are chosen as split points.

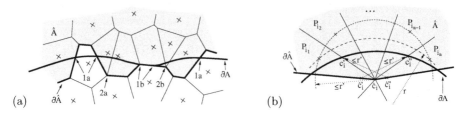

Fig. 4. (a) Different cases for the definition of split points; (b) Partition refinement and mapping for case 2b.

Case 2: A pixel corner which is on $\partial \hat{A}'$ but not on $\partial A'$ becomes a split point if the corner point lies in A (A^c) and belongs to at least two pixels that are in $\hat{A}^c$ ($\hat{A}$). *Case 2a:* If there are exactly two such neighboring pixels, a corresponding split point is defined where $\partial A'$ crosses the common boundary of these pixels. *Case 2b:* Otherwise, the split point is treated specially.

In the course of the proof, the initial partition will be refined. The treatment of case 1b is straigthforward: Here, two segments C_i and $\hat{C}_i$ coincide, so we can define the r'-homeomorphism as the identity mapping.

Next, consider case 2b (fig. 4b). Let the special split point $\hat{c}_i \in A$ (A^c) be a corner of pixels $P_{i_1}, ..., P_{i_n} \in \hat{A}^c$ ($\hat{A}$). The orientation of the plane induces an order of these pixels. The pixels P_{i_2} to $P_{i_{n-1}}$ intersect $\partial \hat{A}'$ only at the single point $\hat{c}_i$. We must avoid that an extended part of $\partial A'$ gets mapped onto the single point $\hat{c}_i$. Thus, we change the initial partitioning: Replace $\hat{c}_i$ with two new split points $\hat{c}_i{}'$ and $\hat{c}_i{}''$, lying on $\partial \hat{A}'$ to either side of $\hat{c}_i$ at a distance ε. Define as their corresponding split points the points c_i' and c_i'' where $\partial A'$ crosses the commen border of P_{i_1}, P_{i_2} and $P_{i_{n-1}}, P_{i_n}$ respectively. Due to r-regularity, $|\overline{c_i'\hat{c}_i}| < r'$ and $|\overline{c_i''\hat{c}_i}| < r'$, and the same is true for all points between c_i' and c_i''. Therefore, ε can always be chosen so that every point between c_i' and c_i'' can be mapped onto every point between $\hat{c}_i{}'$ and $\hat{c}_i{}''$ with a displacement of at most r'. This implies the existence of an r'-homeomorphism between these segments.

After these modifications, the segments not yet treated have the following important properties: Each C_i is enclosed within one pixel P_i, and the corresponding segment $\hat{C}_i$ is a subset of P_i's boundary. To prove the theorem for these pairs, we use the property of Reuleaux triangles with diameter r' that no two points in such a triangle are farther apart than r' (fig. 5a). Due to r-regularity, $\partial A'$ can cross the border of any r'-Reuleaux triangle at most two times. We refine the segments so that each pair is contained in a single triangle, which implies the existence of an r'-homeomorphism. Consider the pair $C_i, \hat{C}_i$ and let the sampling point of pixel P_i be s_i. If this point is not on $\partial A'$ (fig. 5b), C_i splits P_i into two parts, one containing $\hat{C}_i$ and the other containing s_i. We now place r'-Reuleaux triangles as follows: a corner of every triangle is located at s_i, every triangle intersects C_i and $\hat{C}_i$, and neighboring triangles are oriented at $60°$ of each other, so that no three triangles have a common overlap region. Since the pixel radius is at most r', this set of triangles completely covers both

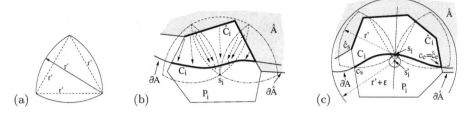

Fig. 5. (a) Any two points in a Reuleaux triangle of size r' have a distance of at most r'; (b) Covering of corresponding segments with Reuleaux triangles; (c) Construction for sampling points lying on $\partial A'$.

C_i and $\hat{C}_i$, and each consecutive pair of triangles shares at least one point of either segment. Thus, we can define additional split points among the shared points, so that corresponding pairs of the new segments lie entirely within one triangle. The existence of an r'-homeomorphism for the refined segments follows.

If the sampling point s_i of P_i is on $\partial A'$ (fig. 5c), this Reuleaux construction does not generally work. In this case, we first place two r'-Reuleaux triangles such that both have s_i as a corner point, one contains the start points $c_s, \hat{c}_s$ of C_i and $\hat{C}_i$ respectively, the other the end points $c_e, \hat{c}_e$, and they overlap $\hat{C}_i$ as much as possible. If they cover $\hat{C}_i$ completely, the Reuleaux construction still works with s_i as split point. Otherwise $\hat{C}_i$ is partly outside of the triangles, and the normal of $\partial A'$ crosses $\hat{C}_i$ in this outside region. We choose a point s'_i on the opposite normal with distance ε from s_i and project each point c of $\hat{C}_i$ not covered by either triangle onto the point where the line $\overline{cs'_i}$ crosses C_i. It can be seen that this mapping is an r'-homeomorphism: Draw circles with radius ε and $r'+\varepsilon$ around s'_i. C_i and $\hat{C}_i$ lie between these circles, so that each point is moved by at most r'. The extreme points of this construction define new split points, and the remaining parts of C_i and $\hat{C}_i$ can be mapped within the two triangles. Thus, there is an r'-homeomorphism in this case as well. □

As the proof makes no assumptions about pixel shape, the geometric sampling theorem applies to *any* regular or irregular r'-grid (cf. fig 3). Moreover, when a set is resonstructible by some grid S, this automatically holds for any translated and rotated copy of S as well. r-regularity is not only a sufficient but also a nessessary condition for a set to be reconstructible:

Theorem 2. *Let A be a set that is not r-regular. Then there exists an r'-grid S with $0 < r' < r$ such that A is not reconstructible by S.*

Proof. We explicitly construct such a grid. There are two cases: *Case 1*: If A is not r''-regular for any $r'' > 0$, then it contains at least one corner or junction. In both cases it is possible to place sampling points so that the reconstruction of a connected set becomes disconnected, and the topology is not preserved (fig. 6 a and b). *Case 2*: Let A be r''-regular with $0 < r'' < r' < r$. Then there is a maximal inside or outside circle of radius r'' with center p_0 that touches ∂A in

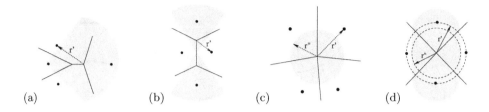

Fig. 6. Examples where the topology of the reconstruction by an r-grid (balls and lines) differs from the topology of the original set (gray area) because it is not r-regular.

at least two points. Draw a circle with radius r' around p_0. *Case 2a*: If the r''-circle coincides with a component of ∂A, a component of A or A^c is completely inside the r'-circle, and we can place sampling points on this circle such that the enclosed component is lost in the reconstruction. *Case 2b*: Otherwise, an r' can be chosen so that part of the r'-circle is in A, part in A^c. If these parts form more than two connected components, we can place a sampling point in each component, and the reconstruction contains a junction whereas the original shape does not. *Case 2c*: If there are exactly two components, we can move the r'-circle a little so that it will either no longer intersect with ∂A, which brings us back to case 2a, or the number of components will increase, which brings us to case 2b. In any case, the topology of A is not preserved (fig. 6 c and d).   □

The geometric sampling theorems do not only hold for binary images, but also for all r-regular level sets of gray-level images. In particular, we proved in [1] that theorem 1 also applies if r-regular sets are subjected to blurring with a circular averaging filter before digitization. Such images are approximations of what could be observed with a real camera (albeit real point spread functions are more complicated). We proved the following theorem:

Theorem 3. *Let A be an r-regular set, k_p a circular averaging filter with radius $p < r$, and $f_A = k_p \star \chi_A$ the blurred image of A (χ_A is A's characteristic function, $\star$ denotes convolution). Further let L_l be any level set of f_A and S an r''-grid with $r'' < r - p$. Then the S-reconstruction $\hat{L}_l$ of L_l is $(p + r'')$-similar to A.*

In [1], reconstruction referred to weak r-similarity, but the theorem can be extended to strong r-similarity. The original proof first showed that any level set L_l of f_A is $(r - p)$-regular and p-similar to A. Then it followed from theorem 1 that L_l is reconstructible by any grid with pixel radius $r'' < r - p$. Since theorem 1 has been tightened for strong r-similarity, it remains to be shown that the first part of the proof can also be tightened:

Proof. We must show that there exists a p-homeomorphism between A and any level set L_l after blurring. We already know that there is an $\mathbb{R}^2$-homeomorphism. Consider a p-wide strip A_p around ∂A. Due to r-regularity, the normals of ∂A cannot cross within A_p. Therefore, every point in A_p is crossed by exactly one normal, and the starting point of the normal is at most at distance p. Since the

level lines ∂L_l always run in the strip A_p without crossing any normal twice (see
[1], lemma 5), we can define a p-homeomorphism from ∂A to any level line by
mapping each point along its normal.   □

4   Findings

In this paper we proved a powerful geometric sampling theorem. In intuitive
terms, our theorem means the following: When an r-regular set is digitized, its
boundaries move by at most half the pixel diameter. The number of connected
components of the set and its complement are preserved, and the digital sets
are directly connected (more precisely, they are well-composed in the sense of
Latecki [3]). Parts that were originally connected do not get separated. As these
claims hold for any regular or irregular r'-grid, they also hold for translated
and rotated versions of some given grid. Thus, reconstruction is robust under
Euclidian transformations of the grid or the shape.

Since strong r-similarity is also a local property, we can still apply our results
if a set is not r-regular in its entirety. We call a segment of a set's boundary
locally r-regular if definition 6 holds at every point of the segment. Theorem 1
then applies analogously to this part of the set because the boundary segment
could be completed into some r-regular set where the theorem holds everywhere,
and in particular in a local neighborhood of the segment.

Our results can be generalized to gray-level images in two ways: First, they
apply to all level sets or parts thereof that are r-regular. This is usually the case
at edge points that are sufficiently far from other edges or junctions. Second,
when a binary image is first blurred by a circular averaging filter, the theorem
still holds with $r = r' + p$, where r' and p are the radii of the pixels and filter
respectively. This is similar to Lateckis work ([2,3]), as his v-digitization amounts
to blurring with a square averaging filter. Our findigs are important steps towards
a geometric sampling theory applicable to real optical systems. In the future, we
will try to extend them to more general filter classes. We will also analyse what
happens in the neighborhood of junctions (where the r-regularity constraint
cannot hold), and under the influence of gray-level quantization and noise.

References

1. Köthe U., Stelldinger, P.: *Shape Preserving Digitization of Ideal and Blurred Binary Shapes*, Univ. Hamburg, Informatics Dept., Tech. Rep. FBI-HH-M-325/03, 2003.
2. Latecki, L.J., Conrad, C., Gross, A.: *Preserving Topology by a Digitization Process.* Journal of Mathematical Imaging and Vision **8**, 131–159, 1998.
3. Latecki, L.J.: *Discrete Representation of Spatial Objects in Computer Vision.* Kluwer Academic Publishers, Dordrecht, 1998.
4. Pavlidis, T.: *Algorithms for Graphics and Image Processing.* Computer Science Press, Rockville, Maryland. 1982.
5. Ronse, C., Tajine, M.: *Discretization in Hausdorff Space.* Journal of Mathematical Imaging and Vision **12**, 219–242, 2000.
6. Serra, J.: *Image Analysis and Mathematical Morphology* Academic Press, New York, 1982.

Evaluation of Uniform and Non-uniform Optical Flow Techniques Using Finite Element Methods

Joan Condell[1], Bryan Scotney[2], and Philip Morrow[2]

[1] School of Computing and Intelligent Systems, University of Ulster, Londonderry, N. I.
[2] School of Computing and Information Engineering, University of Ulster, Coleraine, N. I.
{j.condell, bw.scotney, pj.morrow}@ulster.ac.uk

Abstract. This paper evaluates and compares uniform and non-uniform algorithms that implement the estimation of motion, focusing on the finite element method as a framework for the development of techniques. The finite element approach has the advantages of a rigorous mathematical formulation, speed of reconstruction, conceptual simplicity and ease of implementation via well-established finite element procedures in comparison to finite volume or finite difference techniques. The finite element techniques are implemented through a variety of grid discretisations, with results presented and compared. An important advantage of the non-uniform technique is the capacity to tackle problems in which non-uniform sampling of the image sequence is appropriate.

1 Introduction

Many methods are available in the literature for motion tracking, each with their own characteristics and limitations [1, 2, 6, 7]. One of the main approaches to this optical flow problem is the gradient-based approach which differentiates the image intensity to compute the optical flow. *Horn* and *Schunck* [6] presented a gradient-based approach in the form of an iterative algorithm to find the optical flow pattern in which the derivatives of image intensity are approximated using a finite volume approach. It is one of the most powerful algorithms for optical flow computation, making the simple assumption that image brightness itself does not change during motion. The research in this paper is focused on optical flow estimation in image sequences using a gradient-based approach where finite element methods are used to approximate the image intensity derivatives rather than finite volume methods. Our approach focuses on the development of techniques for computing optical flow based on the observation that the flow velocity has two components and that the basic equation for the rate of change of image brightness provides only one constraint. Smoothness of the flow is introduced as a second constraint with an iterative finite element method being used to solve the resulting equation. The scope of the research involves the improvement in efficiency and decreased computational effort of optical flow estimation through bilinear, triangular and adaptive-triangular finite element grid discretisations in two dimensions. Previous approaches using finite element methods have used uniform bilinear and other finite elements (see literature for extensive review of methods [2]).

B. Michaelis and G. Krell (Eds.): DAGM 2003, LNCS 2781, pp. 116–123, 2003.

2 Finite Element Formulation

The finite volume approach used to develop the *Horn* and *Schunck* algorithm requires a regular sampling of image intensity values stored in simple rectangular arrays [5]. Computational efficiency can be greatly increased by focusing only on those regions in which motion has been detected to be occurring. This requires the ability to work with images in which the intensity values are sampled more frequently in areas of interest, such as localised regions of high intensity gradient or rapid variation of intensity with time, than in areas likely to correspond to scene background. Implementations based on finite difference or finite volume methods become complicated to generalise when the image intensity values are not uniformly sampled because they are based on point differences along regular co-ordinate directions. In contrast, finite element methods are ideally suited for use with variable and adaptive grids, and hence provide a framework for developing algorithms to work with non-uniformly sampled images [2, 4]. Appropriate image partitioning may lead to the use of a variety of element sizes and orientations. It is thus necessary to be able to implement neighbourhood operators systematically in situations involving an irregular discretisation of the image. It has previously been shown that the algorithm of *Horn* and *Schunck* for optical flow estimation may be considered as one of a family of methods that may be derived using an inverse finite element approach [2, 5]. The two-dimensional Galerkin bilinear finite element technique (FETBI) has been developed as well as a triangular finite element technique based on a uniform triangular discretisation (FETTRI) [3, 5]. Also a triangular finite element technique based on a non-uniform triangular discretisation (FETTRI-GR) has been developed [4]. This paper aims to compare these methods, and other methods available in the literature, in terms of efficiency and accuracy.

2.1 Basic Two-Dimensional Formulation

The image intensity at the point (x,y) in the image plane at time t is denoted by $u(x,y,t)$ which is considered to be a member of the Hilbert image space H^1 at any time $t>0$. The optical flow is denoted by $\underline{b} \equiv (b_1(x,y,t), b_2(x,y,t))$ where b_1 and b_2 denote the x and y components of the flow $\underline{b}$ at time $t>0$. In the *inverse* problem with which we are concerned, the image intensity values are known and it is the *velocity function* $\underline{b}$, or *optical flow*, that is unknown and is to be approximated. The optical flow constraint equation is

$$u_x b_1 + u_y b_2 + u_t = 0 \, , \tag{1}$$

where u_x, u_y, u_t are the partial derivatives of the image intensity with respect to x, y and t respectively. This equation cannot fully determine the flow but can give the component of the flow in the direction of the intensity gradient. An additional constraint must be imposed, to ensure a smooth variation in the flow across the image, which is formed by minimising the (square of) the magnitude of the gradient of the optical flow velocity components. It provides a smoothness measure, and may be implemented by setting to zero the Laplacian of b_1 and b_2. The computation of optical flow may then be treated as a minimisation problem for the sum of the errors in the equation for the rate of change of image intensity and the measure of the departure from smoothness in the velocity field. This results in a pair of equations, which along with an approximation of laplacians of the velocity components, allow the optical flow to be computed.

2.2 Uniform Finite Element Bilinear Method (FETBI)

For the uniform bilinear technique, consider a finite element discretisation of the image domain Ω_i based on a rectangular array of pixels. Nodes are placed at the pixel centres, and lines joining these form the edges of elements in the domain discretisation, as shown in Fig. 1. The infinite dimensional function space H^1 cannot be used directly to provide a tractable computational technique, however a function in the image space H^1 may be approximately represented by a function from a finite dimensional subspace $S^h \subset H^1$. From S^h a finite basis $\left\{\phi_j\right\}_{j=0}^N$ is selected, where the support of ϕ_i is restricted to a neighbourhood Ω_i (the domain in which its value is non-zero). The image u may thus be approximately represented at time t_n by a function $U^n \in S^h$, where $U^n = \sum_{j=0}^N U_j^n \phi_j$ and in which the parameters $\left\{U_j^n\right\}_{j=0}^N$ are associated with the image intensity values at time $t = t_n$. A basis for S^h may be formed by associating with each node i, a trial function $\phi_i(x, y)$ such that $\phi_i(x, y) = 1$ at node i, $\phi_i(x, y) = 0$ at node j, $j \neq i$, and $\phi_i(x, y)$ is bilinear on each element. The basis function $\phi_i(x, y)$ is thus a 'tent shaped' function with support limited to those rectangular elements that have node i as a vertex.

If the components of the optical flow are considered to be piecewise constant on each element, then the Galerkin finite element formulation

$$\sum_{j=0}^N \left[\frac{U_j^{n+1} - U_j^n}{\Delta t}\right] \int_\Omega \phi_j \phi_i \, d\Omega + \sum_{j=0}^N U_j^n \int_\Omega b.\nabla\phi_j \phi_i \, d\Omega = 0 \tag{2}$$

provides an approximation to the flow constraint equation in which each equation contains unknown velocity component values. The variables U_j^n and U_j^{n+1} are image intensity values in the nth and $(n+1)^{th}$ images respectively. These equations (2), along with the smoothing constraint, may be rearranged to provide an iteration scheme similar to the *Horn* and *Schunck* equations to approximate the optical flow for each element. A smoothing parameter α is incorporated into the motion equations and an iteration procedure with a tolerance value (toler) is used to ensure convergence to a solution. Specific details of the equation derivations can be found in the literature [2, 5].

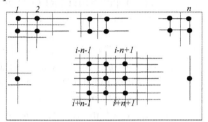
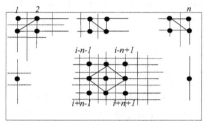

Fig. 1. Regular rectangular array of pixels and nodes for FETBI discretisation

Fig. 2. Regular triangular array of pixels and nodes for FETTRI discretisation

2.3 Uniform Finite Element Triangular Method (FETTRI)

For the uniform triangular finite element technique, it is straightforward to begin with a discretisation of right-angled isosceles triangles. Consider a finite element discreti-sation of the image domain Ω_i based on this triangular array of pixels. Nodes are placed at the pixel centres, and this array of nodes is used by a 2D Delaunay algo-rithm, applied to the row and column co-ordinates of the nodes, to produce a triangu-lar mesh. The resulting mesh allows the partitioning of the image into elements, as illustrated in Fig. 2, with nodes located at the three vertices of the triangular elements. The motion estimation equations may be formed by associating with each element e, a trial function $\Phi_e(x,y)=\phi_1(x,y)+\phi_2(x,y)+\phi_3(x,y)$ such that $\Phi_e(x,y)=1$ over element e, $\Phi_e(x,y)=0$ over all elements other than those surrounding element e, and $\Phi_e(x,y)$ falls linearly from 1 to 0 over the elements that surround element e. The basis function $\Phi_e(x,y)$ is thus a '*plateau*' function and has support limited to those triangular elements which share one of these three vertices of element e.

Using the motion equation in a *Horn* and *Schunck* style iteration, that includes a smoothing term based on laplacians of the velocity components, results in a pair of equations for the optical flow for each triangular element in the mesh. With the tri-angular mesh computed, it is possible to compute the 2D velocity over the image by considering the components of the optical flow to be piecewise constant over each element. We thus have the motion estimation equations:

$$\sum_{j=0}^{N}\left[\frac{U_j^{n+1}-U_j^{n}}{\Delta t}\right]\int_{\Omega}\phi_j\Phi_e\,d\Omega+\sum_{j=0}^{N}U_j^{n}\int_{\Omega}\underline{b}.\nabla\phi_j\Phi_e\,d\Omega=0. \tag{3}$$

As with the FETBI algorithm, a smoothing parameter α is incorporated into the equations and an iteration procedure with a tolerance value (toler) is used to ensure convergence to a solution [2, 3].

2.4 Non-uniform Finite Element Triangular Method (FETTRI-GR)

Another Galerkin finite element approach has been developed (FETTRI-GR) for computing optical flow which uses a non-uniform triangular mesh in which the resolution increases where motion is found to occur. The basic algorithm and motion equations for this FETTRI-GR method are modeled on the FETTRI method. The equations for FETTRI-GR are however applied to a non-uniform mesh whereas the equations for the FETTRI method are applied to a uniform mesh [3]. The non-uniform mesh for this FETTRI-GR method facilitates a reduction in computational effort by enabling processing to focus on particular objects of interest in a scene, specifically those areas where motion is detected. The FETTRI-GR adaptive grid refinement algorithm is applied using an adaptive non-uniform triangular discretisation which increases the density of nodes where motion occurs on non-uniform grids, as illustrated in Fig. 4, as opposed to a uniform FETTRI grid as illustrated in Fig. 3. Initially optical flow is computed over a reasonably coarse uniform FETTRI finite element mesh (see Sect. 2.4 for mathematical formulation [2, 3]) which gives the FETTRI-GR algorithm prior knowledge of where motion is occurring. This is used to construct the optimal adaptive mesh which will be used to recompute the optical flow more efficiently than would be achieved by using the fine triangular grid over the whole image. A fine partition is used only in areas of motion, ensuring a fine resolution of optical flow, and a rough partition is used in areas of little or no motion. This will decrease the numerical complexity and computational effort involved in the solution by reducing both the number of elements and nodes while preserving accuracy [4].

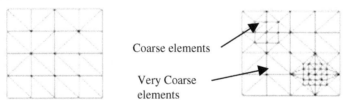

Coarse elements

Very Coarse elements

Fig. 3. Uniform triangular array of elements for FETTRI discretisation   **Fig. 4.** Non-Uniform triangular array of elements for FETTRI-GR discretisation

The meshing principle used is a 'local' meshing where nodes are added locally according to a previously detected motion. Similar to Cohen and Herlin [1] a 'very coarse' tessellation of the grid is used initially but in our approach nodes are added where motion is found to occur whereas Cohen and Herlin subdivided cells of the triangulation depending on the norm of the velocity in the image gradient direction. With Cohen and Herlin's subdivision a limitation existed in that areas were given a fine discretisation due to a high gradient where motion was not occurring and so regions of non-movement may be finely meshed inappropriately [1, 4]. In the proposed FETTRI-GR algorithm the mesh is initially empty and nodes are added at increasing levels of resolution to refine the grid in areas where velocity is found to occur. The levels of resolution used were 'very coarse', 'coarse' and 'fine' (4×4, 2×2, 1×1 pixels respectively).

3   Experimental Results

Results for image sequences are obtained, for the bilinear and uniform/non-uniform triangular implementations of the finite element techniques (FETBI, FETTRI, FETTRI-GR), and comparisons made to the algorithms available in the literature. Due to space limitations, only the real image sequence '*Hamburg Taxi*' is used for analysis, [1, 2, 7]. This sequence is a street scene involving 3 main moving objects, a car moving left to right in lower left (*3* pixels/frame), a taxi in the centre of the image turning the corner (*1* pixel/frame) and a van in the lower right moving right to left (*0.3* pixels/frame). Fig. 5 shows a frame from the *Hamburg Taxi* image sequence.

Fig. 5. *Hamburg Taxi* image sequence

Fig. 6 shows the FETBI and FETTRI results for this sequence with convergence tolerance and smoothing parameters (toler/α) 0.001/275 and 0.001/300 respectively. Fig. 7 shows an adaptive FETTRI-GR mesh and corresponding result for parameters 0.001/800. From these flow diagrams it can be seen that all algorithms give a reasonable flow. The FETTRI-GR result is more consistent as it focuses on the main objects, showing main movement for the taxi in the centre of the image and the van in the lower right moving from right to left. Table 1 shows the number of nodes/elements, computation time and number of iterations to convergence as well as the mean displaced frame difference error value for the FETBI/FETTRI/FETTRI-GR algorithms with other results taken from the literature for comparison [2, 7].

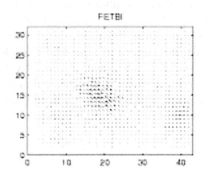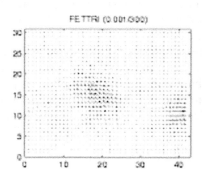

Fig. 6. FETBI and FETTRI flow results for parameters 0.001/275 and 0.001/300 respectively

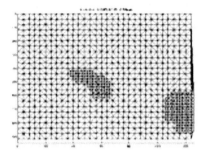 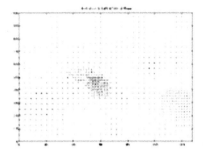

Fig. 7. FETTRI-GR adaptive mesh and FETTRI-GR flow result for parameters 0.001/800

Table 1. Number of Nodes and Elements, Time (seconds) and Number of Iterations to Convergence with Displaced Frame Difference Mean Error Values for *Hamburg Taxi* image sequence with FETBI, FETRI, FETTRI-GR and other algorithms in the literature [2, 7].

Algorithm	toler/α	Nodes	Elts.	Time	Iters.	Dfd Mean
FETBI	0.001/275	12160	11938	6	275	3.53
FETTRI	0.001/300	12160	23876	265	393	3.13
FETTRI-GR	0.001/800	965	1827	4	130	3.24
Anandan						4.35
Fleet Jepson						6.20
Horn Schunck						4.01
Lucas Kanade						3.99
Nagel						4.21
Ong Spann						3.84

Comparing the results for these methods, it can be seen that the FETTRI-GR algorithm shows the lowest number of nodes and elements due to its adaptivity while the FETTRI algorithm shows the largest number of elements (23876 elements). In terms of time and iterations for convergence the FETTRI-GR algorithm is fastest for this experiment and also takes the least iterations to converge. The smallest displaced frame difference error is recorded for the FETTRI algorithm but with a considerable increase in time compared to the FETTRI-GR algorithm. Generally, the FETTRI-GR flow seems most consistent and efficient, and focuses on the main moving objects within the image. It converges very quickly with least iterations, is computationally more efficient (fewest nodes and elements) and has a smaller mean displaced frame difference error value than the other algorithms results taken from the literature.

4   Conclusion

The aim of this research is to enhance the efficiency of flow computation. Different uniform and non-uniform algorithms have been developed based on finite element methods [2, 3, 4, 5]. These have been compared to other uniform/non-uniform algorithms available in the literature, [1, 2, 7]. The finite element method is shown to compare and perform well with particularly promising results shown for the non-uniform algorithm (FETTRI-GR) which has decreased computational complexity compared to the FETBI/FETTRI algorithms in a short time with reduced iterations to convergence. Thus efficiency of flow computation has been improved. The error values also show promising qualitative results suggesting scope for further development. Compared to other state-of-the-art methods in the literature our non-uniform method shows only motion where main movement is known to occur indicating a methodological improvement.

References

1. Cohen, I., Herlin, I.: Non-Uniform Multiresolution Method for Optical Flow and Phase Portrait Models. Int. J. Computer Vision, 33(1) (1999) 1-22
2. Condell, J.V.: Motion Tracking in Digital Images. PhD thesis, Faculty of Informatics, University of Ulster (2002)
3. Condell, J.V., Scotney, B.W., Morrow, P.J.: Estimation of Motion Through Inverse Finite Element Methods with Triangular Meshes. Proc. 9th Int. Confer. Computer Analysis of Images and Patterns (CAIP 2001), Springer-Verlag, LNCS, 2124 (2001) 333-340
4. Condell, J.V., Scotney, B.W., Morrow, P.J.: Detection and Estimation of Motion using Adaptive Grids. IEEE Proc. 14th Int. Confer. Digital Signal Processing (DSP 2002).
5. Graham, J.V., Scotney, B.W., Morrow, P.J.: Evaluation of Inverse Finite Element Techniques for Gradient Based Motion Estimation.. Image Processing III: Mathematical Methods, Algorithms and Applications. Horwood Publishing Series: Mathematics and Applications, Horwood Publishing Ltd, 200-220 (2001)
6. Horn, B.K.P., Schunck, B.G.: Determining Optical Flow. A.I., Vol 17 (1981) 185-203
7. Ong, E.P., Spann, M.: Robust Optical Flow Computation based on Least-Median-of-Squares Regression. Int. J. Computer Vision, 31(1) (1999) 51-82

Colour Image Analysis in 3D-Polar Coordinates

Allan Hanbury[1]* and Jean Serra[2]

[1] Pattern Recognition and Image Processing Group, Vienna University of
Technology, Favoritenstraße 9/1832, A-1040 Vienna, Austria
`hanbury@prip.tuwien.ac.at`, `http://www.prip.tuwien.ac.at/~hanbury/`
[2] Centre de Morphologie Mathématique, Ecole des Mines de Paris,
35 rue Saint-Honoré, F-77305 Fontainebleau cedex, France.

Abstract. The use of 3D-polar coordinate representations of the RGB
colour space is widespread, although many of these representations, such
as HLS and HSV, have deficiencies rendering them unsuitable for quantitative image analysis. Three prerequisites for 3D-polar coordinate colour
spaces which do not suffer from these deficiencies are suggested, and the
results of the derivation of three colour spaces based on these prerequisites are presented. An application which takes advantage of their good
properties for the construction of colour histograms is also discussed.

1 Introduction

Representations of the RGB colour space in terms of 3D-polar coordinates (hue,
saturation and brightness) are often used. Even though this corresponds to a
simple coordinate transform from rectangular to 3D-polar (cylindrical) coordinate systems, the literature abounds with many different ways of performing
this transformation (the HLS, HSV, HSI, etc. colour spaces). Many of these systems were developed with computer graphics applications in mind [1], and have
a number of shortcomings when used for quantitative image analysis.

In this paper, we discuss the deficiencies of commonly used systems (section 2), and suggest three prerequisites for 3D-polar coordinate systems to be
useful for quantitative image analysis (section 3). In section 4, we present three
3D-polar coordinate representations which were derived based on these prerequisites. Finally, an application is discussed (section 5).

2 Deficiencies of the Commonly Used 3D-Polar Spaces

To represent colours in an RGB coordinate system in terms of hue, saturation
and brightness, one begins by placing a new axis, called the *achromatic axis*,
into the RGB space between the pure black and pure white points [2]. The
choice of a function describing the brightness then gives rise to a set of iso-
brightness surfaces, with each surface containing all the points having a specific

---

* This work was supported by the Austrian Science Foundation (FWF) under grants
P14445-MAT and P14662-INF.

B. Michaelis and G. Krell (Eds.): DAGM 2003, LNCS 2781, pp. 124–131, 2003.

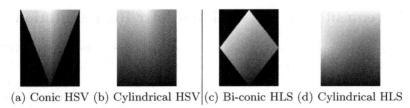

(a) Conic HSV (b) Cylindrical HSV (c) Bi-conic HLS (d) Cylindrical HLS

Fig. 1. Slices through the conic and cylindrical versions of the HSV and HLS colour spaces. The brightness increases from bottom to top, and the saturation increases from the centre (achromatic axis) outwards.

brightness. These surfaces are then projected onto a plane perpendicular to the achromatic axis and intersecting it at the origin, called the *chromatic plane*, where they form hexagons. The *hue* and *saturation* or *chroma* coordinates are determined within this plane. The hue corresponds to an angular coordinate around the achromatic axis, traditionally measured with respect to pure red, and the saturation or chroma to the distance from the achromatic axis.

Two commonly used 3D-polar coordinate colour systems are HSV and HLS. The HSV system is usually described as being in the shape of a hexcone, and the HLS system in the shape of a double-hexcone, as shown in Figures 1a and 1c respectively. However, the commonly used conversion formulae, having been developed to simplify numerical colour selection, produce spaces which have been artificially expanded into cylindrical form (Figures 1b and 1d).

These cylindrically shaped 3D-polar coordinate spaces are not suitable for quantitative image analysis for the reasons presented here. By definition, saturation has a low value for black, white or grey pixels, and a higher value for more colourful pixels. However, the commonly used formulae for the HSV and HLS spaces can assign a maximum saturation value to an almost achromatic pixel. For example, if one calculates the HSV saturation of the RGB coordinates $(0.01, 0, 0)$ with the commonly used $S_{\text{HSV}} = \frac{\max(R,G,B) - \min(R,G,B)}{\max(R,G,B)}$, one obtains a saturation of 1, even though the colour is visually indistinguishable from pure black. In practice, this means that black or white regions in an image often have a very "noisy" saturation, being represented as a mixture of unsaturated and fully-saturated pixels. Figure 3b shows the standard HLS saturation of Figure 3a, in which this problem is well demonstrated.

It is often said that these spaces separate chrominance (hue and saturation) and brightness information. However, the normalisation included to convert the conically-shaped spaces into cylindrically-shaped spaces introduces an interdependence between these coordinates. For example, if one converts the RGB coordinates $\mathbf{c} = (0.5, 0.5, 0)$ into HLS coordinates with the commonly used conversion algorithm, one obtains $(H, L, S) = (60°, 0.25, 1)$. If $\Delta\mathbf{c} = (0.25, 0.25, 0.25)$ is then added to the initial RGB vector $\mathbf{c}$, a modification corresponding uniquely to a change in the brightness, the HLS coordinates become $(60°, 0.5, 0.5)$. In other words, the saturation value has been diminished because of an increase in the brightness value, implying that these values are certainly not independent.

3   Prerequisites for a Useful 3D-Polar Representation

We suggest three prerequisites whose adoption leads to the development of 3D-polar coordinate colour spaces which do not suffer from the shortcomings listed in the previous section, and hence are suitable for quantitative image analysis. We model the RGB space by a Euclidean vector space over $\mathbb{R}^3$, allowing us to make use of its projections, orthogonality, etc., but we equip it successively with different norms. The axes of this space are labelled R, G and B, and the space of valid coordinates is limited to $0 \leq R \leq 1$, $0 \leq G \leq 1$ and $0 \leq B \leq 1$.

The vector space notion associates a point $\mathbf{c} = (R, G, B)$ to the vector $\vec{oc}$. This point can be written in terms of vectors parallel to the R, G and B axes, or $\vec{oc} = \vec{or} + \vec{og} + \vec{ob}$. Equivalently, it can be written as $\vec{oc} = \vec{oc}_d + \vec{oc}_p$, where $\mathbf{c}_d$ and $\mathbf{c}_p$ are the projections of $\mathbf{c}$ onto respectively the achromatic axis and the chromatic plane. We say that $\mathbf{c}_d$ and $\mathbf{c}_p$ are independent if the parameters associated with $\mathbf{c}_p$ (saturation, hue) do not affect those associated with $\mathbf{c}_d$. This is equivalently stated in the following prerequisite:

First prerequisite: Two distinct colours which have the same projection onto the chromatic plane, have the same chromatic parameters.

Use of a vector space also allows us to make use of *norms* and the associated triangular inequality, which says that the norm of the mean vector of two arbitrary vectors $\mathbf{c}$ and $\mathbf{c}'$ cannot be larger than the average of the norms of $\mathbf{c}$ and of $\mathbf{c}'$. For example, two projections onto the chromatic plane which are far from the achromatic axis, but opposite each other, represent colours which are highly saturated. The vector mean of these two colours is, however, achromatic. It therefore makes sense that its norm should not be larger than the norms of the original colours, and hence that the triangular inequality should be satisfied. This leads to the following prerequisite:

Second prerequisite: The intensity parameters associated with colour vector $\mathbf{c}$ (brightness) and with its projection $\mathbf{c}_p$ (saturation) must be norms.

For example, the HLS brightness and saturation parameters are not norms, which leads to some of the undesirable properties discussed in the previous section. Finally, motivated by practical experience, we suggest:

Third prerequisite: Every system for the representation of colour images must be reversible with respect to the RGB standard.

The colour spaces which satisfy the prerequisites presented have the following main advantages over the commonly used 3D-polar coordinate spaces:

- Achromatic or near-achromatic colours always have a low saturation value.
- The saturation and brightness coordinates are independent, as there is no normalisation of the saturation by the brightness.
- Comparisons between saturation values are meaningful, also due to the saturation normalisation having being removed.

4 Three 3D-Polar Coordinate Colour Representations

We present the conversion formulae which result when one limits oneself to using only the L_2 or L_1 norms (the full derivations are in [3]). Lastly, we demonstrate the use of the semi-norm max − min as a measure of saturation. When describing the length of the vector c_p, we make use of two terms, *saturation* and *chroma*. We define chroma as the norm of c_p, as done by Carron [4] (who uses the L_2 norm). It assumes its maximum value at the six corners of the hexagon projected onto the chromatic plane. For the saturation, the hexagon projected onto the chromatic plane is slightly deformed into a circle by a normalisation factor, so that the saturation assumes its maximum value for all points with projections on the edges of the hexagon. Poor choice of this normalisation factor has led to some of the less than useful saturation definitions currently in use.

4.1 L_2 Norm

The conversion equations from the RGB system for the L_2 norm are easy to determine. We call the brightness, chroma and hue determined using this norm M_2, C_2 and H_2 respectively. The M_2 and C_2 norms are scaled to the range $[0, 1]$.

$$M_2 = \frac{1}{\sqrt{3}} \left[R^2 + G^2 + B^2 \right]^{1/2} \tag{1}$$

$$C_2 = \sqrt{\frac{3}{2}} \| c_p \| = \left(R^2 + G^2 + B^2 - RG - RB - BG \right)^{\frac{1}{2}} \tag{2}$$

It is possible to convert the chroma measurement C_2 into a saturation measurement S_2 by dividing $\| c_p \|$ by the distance from the origin to the edge of the hexagon for a given hue H, that is, the maximum value that can be taken by the norm of a projected vector $\| c_p \|$ with hue H [3]. The hue is calculated as

$$H_2 = \begin{cases} 360° - \arccos \left[\frac{r_p \cdot c_p}{\| r_p \| \| c_p \|} \right] & \text{if } B > G \\ \arccos \left[\frac{r_p \cdot c_p}{\| r_p \| \| c_p \|} \right] & \text{otherwise} \end{cases} \tag{3}$$

where r_p is the projection of the vector representing pure red onto the chromatic plane, and $r_p \cdot c_p$ indicates the scalar product of the two vectors.

The advantages of using the L_2 norm are that the Euclidean distance is used and that an accurate value for the hue can be determined, which can also be used in the other representations. The biggest disadvantage is that the inverse transformation back to RGB coordinates is not simple.

4.2 L_1 Norm

As the values of R, G and B are positive, the L_1 norm brightness (M_1) is simply the arithmetic mean of these three components, which can also be written in terms of the maximum, median and minimum component of the RGB vector, notated as max, mid and min. The chroma C_1 is also written in terms of these three values. If one requires an accurate hue value, then the L_2 norm value H_2 should be used. An approximate value H_1, requiring no trigonometric function evaluations can be derived [3]. The full conversion from RGB coordinates is:

$$M_1 = \frac{1}{3}\left(\text{max} + \text{mid} + \text{min}\right) \tag{4}$$

$$C_1 = \begin{cases} \frac{3}{2}\left(\text{max} - M_1\right) & \text{if max} + \text{min} \geq 2\text{mid} \\ \frac{3}{2}\left(M_1 - \text{min}\right) & \text{if max} + \text{min} \leq 2\text{mid} \end{cases} \tag{5}$$

$$H_1 = k\left[\lambda\left(\mathbf{c}\right) + \frac{1}{2} - \frac{\text{max} + \text{min} - 2\text{mid}}{2C_1}\right] \tag{6}$$

where $\lambda\left(\mathbf{c}\right)$ gives the RGB cube sector number (an integer from 0 to 5) in which the vector $\mathbf{c}$ lies [2], and the value of k determines the working units ($k = 60$ for degrees, $k = 42$ for values encodable on 8-bits).

Note that, given variables $R, G, B \geq 0$, every quantity $\alpha R + \beta G + \gamma B$, with weights $\alpha, \beta, \gamma \geq 0$ is still an L_1 norm on the achromatic axis. This is advantageous as it permits the use of psycho-visual *luminance* functions. A further advantage is that the system is easy to invert. However, one should beware of an inbuilt quantisation pitfall. When R, G and B are integer-valued, then C_1 is always a multiple of $1/2$. The rounding of a floating point value of C_1 to the nearest integer therefore behaves extremely erratically, as the 0.5's are sometimes rounded up and sometimes down.

4.3   max − min Semi-norm

The quantity $S_0 = \text{max} - \text{min}$ obviously satisfies the first prerequisite as its value does not change when one shifts an arbitrary RGB vector parallel to the achromatic axis by adding the same amount to each component. In particular, a vector $\mathbf{c}$ in the RGB space and its projection $\mathbf{c}_p$ have the same value for S_0.

It is proved in [3] that S_0 is a norm on the chromatic plane (but only a seminorm over the whole space). Therefore it is ideally suited to describing saturation, and we can take advantage of the independence of the achromatic and chromatic components to choose either the L_1 or L_2 norm on the achromatic axis. It can be shown that S_0 corresponds exactly to the saturation measure derived for the L_2 representation, and it can be derived from the HLS and HSV spaces by removing the saturation normalisation factors [3]. Finally, for the hue, we can use the trigonometric expression (equation 3), replacing it by the approximation (equation 6) if calculation speed is important. We have named this representation the improved HLS (IHLS) space. MATLAB code implementing this conversion is available on the author's home page.

4.4   Comparison of the Saturation and Chroma Formulations

We compare the distributions of three of the saturation and chroma formulations discussed: the $S_0 = \text{max} - \text{min}$ saturation expression, the L_2 norm chroma C_2

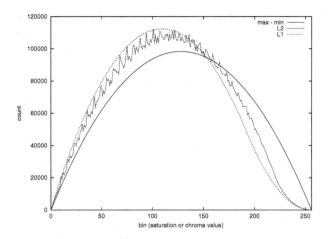

Fig. 2. The saturation and chroma histograms.

(equation 2), and the L_1 norm chroma C_1 (equation 5). We begin with a 256 × 256 × 256 RGB cube with a point at each set of integer-valued coordinates, and look at the 256-level histograms resulting from calculating the saturation and chroma for each of these points. For the max − min and L_2 norms, the S_0 and C_2 values of each point are calculated (as floating point values for the latter, which are then rounded to the nearest integer). To avoid the quantisation problems outlined previously, the values of C_1 were first multiplied by 2 to get a series of integers between 0 and 512, and then adjacent pairs of histogram bins were combined to produce a 256 bin histogram. The histograms are shown in figure 2.

The max − min saturation distribution is regular and symmetric around the central histogram bin because of the normalisation coefficient which deforms the hexagonally shaped sub-region of the chromatic plane into a circle. Conversely, the L_2 chroma has a rather irregular distribution due to the discrete space in which it is calculated. It decreases rapidly as one approaches higher chroma values as it is calculated in hexagonally shaped sub-regions of the chromatic plane. The L_1 norm chroma approximates the L_2 chroma well (if the quantisation effects are taken into account), and its histogram is more regular.

5   Application

A number of applications which take advantage of the good properties of the proposed colour representation have already been suggested, including colour morphology [3] and luminance/saturation histograms [5]. Here we present an application of circular statistics to the calculation of colour image histograms.

As the hue is an angular value, circular statistics [6] should be used to calculate its mean direction. We take advantage of the correlation between colourfulness and saturation value in the suggested colour representation to apply a weighting to the circular mean so that achromatic colours have less influence on the result . The circular mean of a set of angular data is defined as the direction of the resultant vector of the sum of unit vectors in the given directions, and the saturation-weighting is thus easily included by replacing the unit vectors by vectors with lengths proportional to the saturation. One can thus easily determine the saturation-weighted hue mean of a whole image. We next propose that this mean (and its associated variance) be calculated separately for pixels belonging to each luminance level of a colour image, leading to the construction of a colour histogram analogous to the greyscale one.

Given a colour image in the IHLS space, the luminance values are first quantised into $N+1$ levels labeled by $\ell = \{0,1,2,\ldots,N\}$. Then, for each value of ℓ, the following circular statistics descriptors are calculated, where $\overline{H}_{S\ell}$ is the saturation-weighted hue mean for luminance level ℓ, and $\overline{R}_{n\ell}$ is the associated mean length. The latter is essentially the inverse of the circular variance, and assumes values in the range $[0,1]$. A value approaching one indicates that the hue values are more closely grouped. $A_{S\ell}$ and $B_{S\ell}$ are intermediate values.

$$A_{S\ell} = \sum_x S_x \cos H_x \delta_{L_x\ell}, \; B_{S\ell} = \sum_x S_x \sin H_x \delta_{L_x\ell} \tag{7}$$

$$\overline{H}_{S\ell} = \arctan\left(\frac{B_{S\ell}}{A_{S\ell}}\right), \; \overline{R}_{n\ell} = \frac{\sqrt{A_{S\ell}^2 + B_{S\ell}^2}}{\sum_x \delta_{L_x\ell}} \tag{8}$$

where H_x, L_x and S_x are the hue, luminance and saturation at position x in the image, and the sums are over all the pixels in the image. The symbol $\delta_{L_x\ell}$ is the Kronecker delta which limits the calculation to luminance level ℓ.

We now have two histograms of colour information, the mean hue and its associated mean length as a function of luminance. These could conceivably be used directly in image matching and database retrieval applications. For visualisation purposes, these two histograms can very simply be combined into a single histogram, in which the height of the bar at luminance ℓ corresponds to the mean length $\overline{R}_{n\ell}$, and its colour is given by the fully saturated colour corresponding to the mean hue $\overline{H}_{S\ell}$. As the mean hue associated with a very low mean length value does not give much information, we set the colours of the bars with a mean length below a threshold (here 0.05) to the greylevel corresponding to the associated luminance value.

Figure 3f shows the colour histogram (with $N = 100$) of Figure 3a, corresponding to the luminance and IHLS saturation shown in Figures 3d and 3e respectively. One sees that orange dominates at high luminance values, and blue at low luminance values. To show the unsuitability of the standard HLS saturation (Figure 3b) in calculating the colour histogram, this has been done in Figure 3c. In this histogram, at low and high luminance bins, high bars with arbitrary colours, which do not give any pertinent information, are present.

6   Conclusion

We have pointed out the deficiencies of commonly used 3D-polar coordinate colour representations (specifically HLS and HSV, but also applicable to many

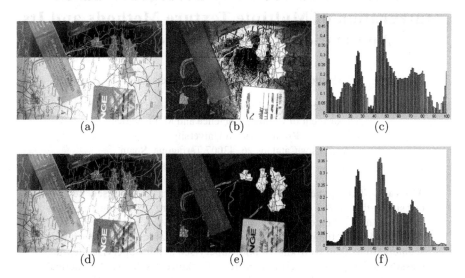

Fig. 3. (a) Colour image (from the University of Washington content-based image retrieval database) and (d) its luminance. (b) and (c): The HLS saturation and the histogram generated when using it. (e) and (f): The suggested saturation and the histogram generated when using it. Larger images in colour are available on http://www.prip.tuwien.ac.at/~hanbury/colour_histogram/

others) rendering them unsuitable for quantitative image analysis. We then list three prerequisites for such colour representations to have useful properties, and summarise three sets of conversion equations between the RGB space and 3D-polar coordinate spaces based on these prerequisites. The good properties of the suggested representations give rise to many applications in image analysis, of which we have described one: the construction of a colour image histogram based on circular statistics. Further work is being undertaken to continue the development of these applications.

References

1. Smith, A.R.: Color gamut transform pairs. Computer Graphics **12** (1978) 12–19
2. Levkowitz, H., Herman, G.T.: GLHS: A generalised lightness, hue and saturation color model. CVGIP: Graphical Models and Image Processing **55** (1993) 271–285
3. Hanbury, A., Serra, J.: A 3D-polar coordinate colour representation suitable for image analysis. Technical Report PRIP-TR-077, TU Wien (2002)
4. Carron, T.: Segmentations d'images couleur dans la base Teinte-Luminance-Saturation. PhD thesis, Université de Savoie (1995)
5. Angulo, J., Serra, J.: Colour feature extraction from luminance/saturation histogram in L_1 representation. Technical Report N-01/03/MM, Centre de Morphologie Mathématique, Ecole des Mines de Paris (2003)
6. Fisher, N.I.: Statistical Analysis of Circular Data. Cambridge University Press (1993)

Pixel Classification by Divergence-Based Integration of Multiple Texture Methods and Its Application to Fabric Defect Detection

Miguel Angel Garcia and Domènec Puig

Intelligent Robotics and Computer Vision Group
Department of Computer Science and Mathematics
Rovira i Virgili University
Av. Països Catalans 26, 43007 Tarragona, Spain
{magarcia,dpuig}@etse.urv.es

Abstract. This paper presents and evaluates a pixel-based texture classifier that integrates multiple texture feature extraction methods through a new scheme based on the Kullback J-divergence. Experimental results show that the proposed technique yields qualitatively better image segmentations than well-known both supervised and unsupervised texture classifiers based on specific families of texture methods. A practical application to fabric defect detection is presented.

1 Introduction

The problem of *pixel-based texture classification* can be stated as the determination of the class to which every pixel of an input image belongs given a set of known texture patterns of interest (models). The final aim is not just segmenting the given image into separate regions, this being the goal of unsupervised texture segmentation algorithms (e.g., [4][7][8][11]), but identifying the texture pattern associated with each distinguishable region. Obviously, such an identification will also lead to the segmentation of the input image into different regions.

In pixel-based texture classification, a certain number of measures (*texture measures*) is computed for every image pixel by applying a set of *texture feature extraction methods* (*texture methods* in short) to its neighboring pixels. This neighborhood is commonly defined as a square pixel window (e.g., 17x17, 33x33) centered at that pixel.

An enormous variety of texture methods have been proposed in the literature (e.g., [12][13]). Unfortunately, no single family of texture methods has been proved to be superior to the others. In fact, some family (e.g., Gabor filters) may be superior for some types of texture patterns, but it may well yield poor results when applied to other textures. This implies that, in order to recognize a wide spectrum of texture patterns, combining different families of texture methods may lead to better classification than if every family is applied on its own, due to the redundant and complementary information that they provide as a whole [5][10].

This work has been partially supported by the Government of Spain under the CICYT project DPI2001-2094-C03-02.

B. Michaelis and G. Krell (Eds.): DAGM 2003, LNCS 2781, pp. 132–139, 2003.
© Springer-Verlag Berlin Heidelberg 2003

This paper presents a supervised pixel-based texture classifier that integrates different families of texture methods. The proposed technique is an improvement over a previous proposal [5][10], by including a new divergence-based scheme in order to combine different texture methods (section 2.2). The technique is open in the sense that it allows the integration of any given family of texture methods.

The organization of this paper is as follows. Section 2 describes the proposed texture classifier. Section 3 shows experimental results of the integration of widely-used texture feature extraction methods with the proposed technique, as well as a comparison with well-known texture classification and segmentation algorithms. Conclusions and further improvements are finally given in section 4.

2   Pixel-Based Texture Classification

Let $\{\tau_1, \dots, \tau_T\}$ be a set of T texture patterns of interest. Every texture τ_j is described by a set of sample images $\mathbf{I}_j$. Let $\mathbf{I}$ be an input image whose pixels must be classified. In order to classify a pixel $\mathbf{I}(x, y)$ based on textural information, a feature vector $(\mu_1(x, y), \dots, \mu_M(x, y))$ is extracted from $\mathbf{I}(x, y)$. Each feature in that vector is obtained by applying a certain texture feature extraction method μ_i to the pixels contained in a neighborhood around $\mathbf{I}(x, y)$. This neighborhood is a square window centered at $\mathbf{I}(x, y)$, whose size is experimentally set for each method. M different texture feature extraction methods are considered.

This section proposes a technique for integrating the M previous features in order to determine whether every pixel $\mathbf{I}(x, y)$ can be classified into one of the T given texture patterns. The technique consists of four stages described below.

2.1   Supervised Training Stage

Each texture method μ_i is evaluated at every pixel of the sample images $\mathbf{I}_j$ associated with each texture pattern τ_j. A frequency table (histogram) of the values returned by that method is computed. $M \times T$ histograms are thus generated, one per texture method and pattern. The values returned by μ_i will range in the interval:

$$\mu_i : \mathbf{I}_j \rightarrow [MIN_{ij}, MAX_{ij}] \subset \mathbf{R} \tag{1}$$

A function $P_i(\mathbf{I}(x, y) | \tau_j)$, which can be interpreted as the likelihood that pixel $\mathbf{I}(x, y)$ belongs to texture τ_j according to method μ_i, is then defined as:

$$P_i(\mathbf{I}(x, y) | \tau_j) = P_{ij}(\mu_i(x, y) \in [MIN_{ij}, MAX_{ij}]) \tag{2}$$

2.2   Integration of Multiple Texture Feature Extraction Methods

Given a set of $M \times T$ basic likelihood functions $P_i(\mathbf{I}(x, y) | \tau_j)$ (2), the likelihoods corresponding to the M texture methods associated with each texture model τ_j: $\{P_1(\mathbf{I}(x, y) | \tau_j), \dots, P_M(\mathbf{I}(x, y) | \tau_j)\}$ are integrated, leading to T combined likelihood functions, $P(\mathbf{I}(x, y) | \tau_j)$.

The combination of different basic likelihood functions, which can be interpreted as different sources of evidence about a certain "state of nature" [1], is modeled as a *linear opinion pool* [1]:

$$P(\mathbf{I}(x,y)|\tau_j) = \sum_{i=1}^{M} w_{ij} \, P_i(\mathbf{I}(x,y)|\tau_j) \tag{3}$$

In order to compute the weights w_{ij} corresponding to each likelihood function, the *Kullback J-divergence* [6][9], which measures the separability between two probability densities, is computed as:

$$KJ_i(\tau_a,\tau_b) = \sum_{\forall u,\,v} (A-B)\log(A/B) \tag{4}$$

with A and B being defined in our context from the probability distributions computed during the supervised training stage (2): $A = P_{ia}(u \in [MIN_{ia}, MAX_{ia}])$ and $B = P_{ib}(v \in [MIN_{ib}, MAX_{ib}])$. Each weight w_{ij} is then defined as the normalized average of the *KJ* divergences between texture τ_j and the other texture models:

$$w_{ij} = d_{ij} \Big/ \sum_{r=1}^{M} d_{rj} \qquad d_{ij} = \frac{1}{T-1} \sum_{k=1,\,k\neq j}^{T} KJ_i(\tau_k,\tau_j) \tag{5}$$

The histograms corresponding to a texture method that does not significantly change its behavior when applied to different texture patterns will have a large overlap. Hence, this method will have a low associated divergence and will receive a low weight in the opinion pool. Conversely, a texture method that behaves differently when applied to several patterns will have a large associated divergence and weight.

2.3   Maximum a Posteriori Estimation

Given a set of T likelihood functions $P(\mathbf{I}(x,y)|\tau_j)$ (3), the posterior probabilities $P(\tau_j|\mathbf{I}(x,y))$ are finally computed by applying the Bayes rule:

$$P(\tau_j|\mathbf{I}(x,y)) = \frac{P(\mathbf{I}(x,y)|\tau_j)P(\tau_j)}{\sum_{k=1}^{T} P(\mathbf{I}(x,y)|\tau_k)P(\tau_k)} \qquad P(\tau_j) = \sum_{i=1}^{M} w_{ij} \Big/ \sum_{k=1}^{T}\sum_{i=1}^{M} w_{ik} \tag{6}$$

T posterior probabilities are generated: $\{P(\tau_1|\mathbf{I}(x,y)), ..., P(\tau_T|\mathbf{I}(x,y))\}$, one per texture model. Pixel $\mathbf{I}(x,y)$ will likely belong to texture class τ_j iff $P(\tau_j|\mathbf{I}(x,y)) > P(\tau_k|\mathbf{I}(x,y)), \forall k \neq j$.

2.4   Significance Test

Let $P(\tau_j|\mathbf{I}(x,y))$ be the maximum posterior probability (6) corresponding to image pixel $\mathbf{I}(x,y)$. In order to finally classify $\mathbf{I}(x,y)$ into texture class τ_j, that probability must be above a certain *significance level* (probability threshold) λ_j computed for that texture as described below.

Let TP be the number of pixels $\mathbf{I}(x,y)$ belonging to a texture pattern that are correctly classified (*true-positives*) and FN the ones that are misclassified (*false-negatives*). Let also FP be the pixels that are incorrectly classified as belonging to that particular pattern (*false-positives*). The significance level is defined based on two ratios that are commonly utilized to characterize the performance of classifiers: *sensitivity,* $S_n = TP/(TP + FN)$, and *specificity,* $S_p = TP/(TP + FP)$. The sensitivity expresses how well the classifier identifies pixels that belong to a given class, while the specificity indicates how well the classifier distinguishes among different patterns. Both ratios are an input parameter to the classifier. Based on them, two thresholds, λ_j^1 and λ_j^2 are defined as follows.

During the training stage, the posterior probabilities $P(\tau_j | \mathbf{I}_j(x, y))$ of the n_j pixels that belong to the sample images associated with τ_j are calculated and sorted in ascending order. A first threshold λ_j^1 is defined as the posterior probability such that the number of sorted posterior probabilities above λ_j^1 (true positives) is $TP_j = n_j S_n$. Similarly, the posterior probabilities $P(\tau_j | \mathbf{I}_k(x, y))$, $k = 1 \ldots T$, $k \neq j$, of the pixels that belong to the sample images corresponding to textures other than τ_j are calculated and sorted in ascending order. A second probability threshold λ_j^2 is defined such that the number of new sorted posteriors above λ_j^2 (false-positives) is $FP_j = TP_j(1 - S_p)/S_p$.

The significance level is finally: $\lambda_j = max(\lambda_j^1, \lambda_j^2)$. If $\lambda_j = \lambda_j^1$, the classifier fulfills the desired sensitivity with a number of false positives small enough as to also fulfill the desired specificity. However, if $\lambda_j = \lambda_j^2$, the classifier only ensures the desired specificity and, hence, limits the number of false positives, implying that the achieved sensitivity is below the desired one. With this formulation, the significance level fulfills the desired sensitivity whenever it does not compromise the desired specificity.

Finally, if $P(\tau_j | \mathbf{I}(x, y)) > \lambda_j$, pixel $\mathbf{I}(x, y)$ will be finally labelled as belonging to texture class τ_j, otherwise it will be classified as an unknown. Once all pixels have been classified in this way, a last denoising stage is applied over the whole labeled image in order to remove very small regions (less than 25 pixels), which are reclassified into the texture associated with their largest neighboring region.

3   Experimental Results

The proposed technique has been evaluated on a set of both composite Brodatz [2] images [e.g., Fig. 1(*a,b,c*)] and real textile images [e.g., Fig. 2(*a,b,c*)]. Taking recent surveys into account [12][13], several widely-used texture feature extraction methods have been chosen to validate the proposed technique: four *Laws filter masks* (*R5R5, E5L5, E5E5, R5S5*), two *wavelet transforms* (*Daubechies-4, Haar*), four *Gabor filters* with different wavelengths (8, 4) and orientations (0°, 45°, 90°, 135°), two *first-order statistics* (*variance, skewness*), a *second-order statistic* (*homogeneity*) based on *co-occurrence matrices* and the *fractal dimension*. Evaluation windows of 17x17 pixels have been utilized.

The proposed classifier has been compared to the texture classifiers included in *MeasTex* [14], a widely recognized texture classification framework, and to two publicly available unsupervised texture segmenters: *JSEG* [4] and *Edge Flow* [7]. Each texture classifier in MeasTex consists of a specific combination of both a pattern classifier and a family of texture methods. Both the proposed technique and Meas-Tex were trained with sample images of the eight texture patterns included in Fig.

1(b). Hence, they allow to classify the pixels of a given image into one of those patterns. In contrast, JSEG and Edge Flow only segment an image into separate regions. The significance test stage of the proposed technique was omitted in this series of experiments since all texture patterns present in the test images are known.

Fig. 1(d,e,f) show the segmentation maps obtained with the proposed technique. Fig. 1(g,h,i) show the maps generated by MeasTex, considering Gabor filters and 5 nearest-neighbors. This is the combination that produced the best classification rates for the set of test images in Fig. 1(a,b,c). The segmentations produced by JSEG and Edge Flow are shown in Fig. 1(j,k,l) and Fig. 1(m,n,o) respectively.

Since JSEG and Edge Flow are not classifiers but segmenters, it is not possible to compute classification rates in order to measure the quality of their results. However, it is possible to compare each segmentation map with the ground-truth segmentation and, for every region in the latter, determine the largest region in the segmentation map. The ratio between the area of that largest region and the one of its corresponding ground-truth region is an indicator of how good the segmentation is. Two quality indicators are thus defined for each image: $\overline{m}$, which is the average of the ratios associated with the various regions of the same ground-truth image (maximum value of 100), and σ, the ratio's standard deviation (minimum value of 0).

The segmentation maps presented in Fig. 1 show that the proposed technique yields significantly better segmentations than the other three tested algorithms. In view of the results, it can be noticed that poorer segmentations are associated with significantly larger values of σ. For instance, the performance of MeasTex considerably degrades when it is applied to the most complex text image, Fig. 1(h). In this case, σ is almost twice the value corresponding to the proposed technique. The two unsupervised texture segmenters produce much worse results, with σ values between two and three times the ones obtained with the proposed technique.

A second set of experiments has been carried out within the context of fabric defect detection in textile images. Fig. 2(a,b,c) show real images of three fabric patterns containing defects. In this case, both the proposed technique and MeasTex were trained with sample images of the same three patterns without defects. In this case, since the texture of a fabric defect may not correspond to any taught texture, it makes sense to apply the significance test stage of the proposed technique. Sensitivity and specificity were both set to 95%. These percentages aim at maximizing the number of true positives while keeping a small number of false positives.

Fig. 2(d,e,f) and Fig. 2(g,h,i) show the defect areas detected by both the proposed technique and MeasTex (Gabor & 5-NN) respectively (the largest classified region is considered to be the correct fabric). In turn, Fig. 2(j,k,l) and Fig. 2(m,n,o) show the regions generated by JSEG and Edge Flow respectively. Again, the proposed technique is the one that produces the best qualitative results.

4 Conclusions

A pixel-based texture classifier based on the integration of multiple texture feature extraction methods from different families has been presented. Experimental results with Brodatz images and real textile images show that this technique produces better

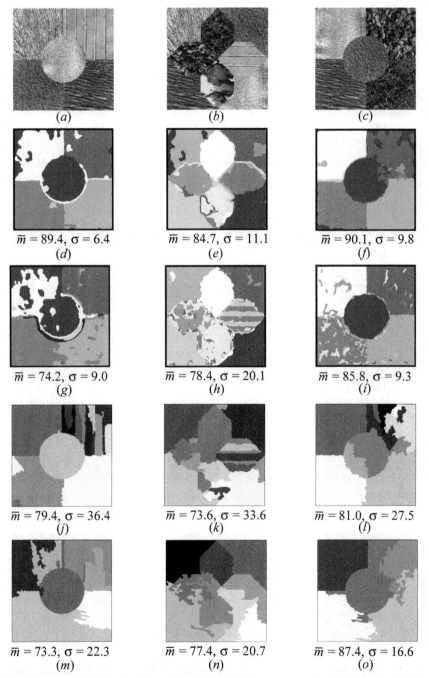

Fig. 1. (*a,b,c*) Test images with portions of Brodatz texture patterns. (*d,e,f*) Segmentation maps with the proposed technique. (*g,h,i*) Maps with MeasTex (Gabor & 5NN). (*j,k,l*) Maps with JSEG. (*m,n,o*) Maps with Edge Flow.

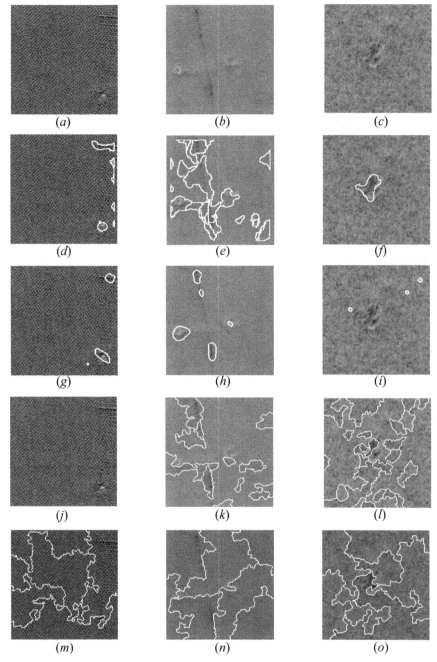

Fig. 2. (*a,b,c*) Real test images corresponding to three different fabrics with manufacturing defects. Detected regions with: (*d,e,f*) proposed technique, (*g,h,i*) MeasTex (Gabor & 5-NN), (*j,k,l*) JSEG and (*m,n,o*) Edge Flow.

quantitative and qualitative results than well-known texture classifiers based on specific families of texture methods and unsupervised texture segmentation algorithms.

The proposed classifier is able to integrate any number of texture feature extraction methods belonging to different families. Future work will consist of developing an automatic selection algorithm that allows to determine which texture methods provide the largest information in order to be able to discriminate a given set of texture patterns. The final aim is to recognize the specified texture patterns by integrating a minimum number of texture methods. We also aim at extending the proposed integration scheme to unsupervised segmentation of textured images. To this end, it is necessary to develop a technique that allows to automatically obtain texture patterns that characterize the different regions of uniform texture present in the input image.

References

[1]   Berger, J.: Statistical Decision Theory and Bayesian Analysis. Springer, (1985).

[2]   Brodatz, P.: Textures: A Photographic Album for Artists and Designers. Dover & Greer Publishing Company, (1999).

[3]   Chang, K.I., Bowyer, K.W., Sivagurunath, M.: Evaluation of Texture Segmentation Algorithms. Proc. IEEE CVPR, Fort Collins, USA, (1999).

[4]   Deng, Y., Manjunath, B.S.: Unsupervised Segmentation of Color-Texture Regions in Images and Video. IEEE Trans. PAMI, 23(8), (2001) 800-813.

[5]   García, M.A., Puig, D.: Improving Texture Pattern Recognition by Integration of Multiple Texture Feature Extraction Methods. 16th IAPR Int. Conf. on Pattern Recognition, Vol. 3, Quebec, Canada, (2002) 7-10.

[6]   Kittler, J.: Feature Selection and Extraction. In: Young, T.Y., Fu, K.S. (eds.): Handbook of Pattern Recog. and Image Proc. Academic Press, (1986) 60-81.

[7]   Ma, W.Y., Manjunath, B.S.: Edge Flow: A Framework of Boundary Detection and Image Segmentation. IEEE Int. Conf. CVPR, Puerto Rico, (1997).

[8]   Malik, J., Belongie, S., Leung, T., Shi, J.: Contour and Texture Analysis for Image Segmentation. In: Boyer, K.L., Sarkar, S. (eds.): Perceptual Organization for Artificial Vision Systems. Kluwer Academic Publishers, (2000).

[9]   Mathiassen, J.R., Skavhaug, A., Bo, K.: Texture Similarity Measure Using Kullback-Leibler Divergence between Gamma Distributions. European Conference on Computer Vision, Copenhagen, Denmark, (2002) 133-147.

[10] Puig, D., García, M.A.: Recognizing Specific Texture Patterns by Integration of Multiple Texture Methods. IEEE ICIP, Vol.1, Rochester, USA, (2002) 125-128.

[11] Puzicha, J., Hofmann, T., Buhmann, J.M.: Non-parametric Similarity Measures for Unsupervised Texture Segmentation and Image Retrieval. IEEE Int. Conf. on Computer Vision and Pattern Recognition, Puerto Rico, (1997) 267-272.

[12] Randen, T., Husoy, J.H.: Filtering for Texture Classification: A Comparative Study. IEEE Trans. PAMI, 21(4), (1999), 291-310.

[13] Reed, T.R., Hans du Buf, J.M.: A Review of Recent Texture Segmentation and Feature Extraction Techniques. CVGIP: Image Underst.,57(3), (1993) 359-372.

[14] Smith, G., Burns, I.: Measuring Texture Classification Algorithms. Pattern Recognition Letters, 18, (1997) 1495-1501. MeasTex Image Texture Database and Test Suite. Centre for Sensor Signal and Information Proc., University of Queensland, Australia, (http://www.cssip.uq.edu.au/staff/meastex/meastex.html).

A Probabilistic Definition of Intrinsic Dimensionality for Images

Michael Felsberg[1][*] and Norbert Krüger[2]

[1] Computer Vision Laboratory, Dept. of Electrical Engineering, Linköping University
SE-58183 Linköping, Sweden, mfe@isy.liu.se
[2] Computational Neuroscience, Department of Psychology, University of Stirling
Stirling FK9 4LA Scotland, UK, norbert@cn.stir.ac.uk

Abstract. In this paper we address the problem of appropriately representing the intrinsic dimensionality of image neighborhoods. This dimensionality describes the degrees of freedom of a local image patch and it gives rise to some of the most often applied corner and edge detectors. It is common to categorize the intrinsic dimensionality (iD) to three distinct cases: i0D, i1D, and i2D. Real images however contain combinations of all three dimensionalities which has to be taken into account by a continuous representation. Based on considerations of the structure tensor, we derive a cone-shaped iD-space which leads to a probabilistic point of view to the estimation of intrinsic dimensionality.

1 Introduction

The aim of this paper is to develop a representation of the intrinsic dimensionality which is well suited for further probabilistic processing. The *intrinsic dimensionality* (iD) is a well known concept from statistics which can be defined as follows: "a data set in d dimensions is said to have an *intrinsic dimensionality* equal to d' if the data lies entirely within a d'-dimensional subspace" [1], p. 314. The term itself goes back to the late sixties [2]. The intrinsic dimensionality was introduced to image processing by Zetsche and Barth [3]. It is obtained by applying the previous definition to the spectrum of an image patch, i.e., the Fourier transform of a neighborhood. The three possible intrinsic dimensionalities in images are defined according to their local spectrum [4] (see also Fig. 1):

i0D – It is concentrated in the origin, i.e., the neighborhood is constant.
i1D – It is concentrated in a line through the origin, i.e., the neighborhood is varying in only one direction. These signals are also called *simple signals* [5].
i2D – It is neither concentrated in the origin, nor in a line.

Typical examples for i1D neighborhoods are edges, lines, sinusoids, whereas corners, junctions, line ends, spots are instances of i2D neighborhoods. As soon as we take noise into account, the discrete definition above becomes useless. Noise is i2D and every signal contains noise. Hence, every image neighborhood is i2D. But how to distinguish between noise and i2D image structures?

---

[*] This work has been supported by DFG Grant FE 583/1-2.

B. Michaelis and G. Krell (Eds.): DAGM 2003, LNCS 2781, pp. 140–147, 2003.
© Springer-Verlag Berlin Heidelberg 2003

Fig. 1. Illustration intrinsic dimensionality. In the image on the left, three neighborhoods with different intrinsic dimensionalities are indicated. The other three images show the local spectra of these neighborhoods.

In recent years, there have been several attempts to define image processing operators which detect the intrinsic dimensionality in images. Note that as long as the intrinsic dimensionality is considered to be a discrete choice from the set {i0D, i1D, i2D}, it is more appropriate to speak of *detection* rather than *estimation*. By switching from a discrete choice to a continuous model for the intrinsic dimensionality, we also switch the terminology from "detection" to "estimation". Looking at the examples for i2D patches, evidently every corner detector is a detector for i2D neighborhoods. Considering image patches at an appropriate scale, all line and edge detectors are detectors for i1D neighborhoods. Besides these two popular fields of image processing, there are other approaches to detect or measure the intrinsic dimensionality, e.g., by Volterra operators [4], tensor methods [6,5], and generalized quadrature filters [7,8].

Since the structure tensor is probably the most well known approach among these, our paper is based on an analysis of the latter approach. From this analysis we derive a new *continuous, triangular* representation of intrinsic dimensionality, making use of *barycentric coordinates*. These coordinates can be interpreted as *confidences* of the measurements or the *likelihood* that the measurement is correct. Hence, they can be used as a prior for further probabilistic processing. The new contribution of this paper compared to [5], p. 253, is the introduction of a coefficient for the i0D case, such that the coefficients add up to one and can therefore be interpreted as probabilities.

In a second step, we introduce orientation information to our model, resulting in a *cone shaped* geometry. This model allows us to average the representation while treating i1D structures with different orientations in an appropriate way, i.e., two i1D neighborhoods with different orientations result in an i2D measurement. This extension of the model makes it independent of the structure tensor: No i2D information is necessary for our model, a simple gradient estimation or quadrature filter response is sufficient. Furthermore, we switch from a deterministic preprocessing to a probabilistic estimation of the barycentric coordinates.

2   A Continuous Definition of Intrinsic Dimensionality

The structure tensor is an approach for the local analysis of images that was first proposed in 1987 [9,10]. For our considerations, however, the derivation in [11] is most appropriate: The structure tensor can be considered as a local approximation of the auto-covariance function in the origin.

The structure tensor is typically interpreted in terms of its eigensystem. Its two eigenvalues correspond to the maximum and minimum 1D frequency spread[1] in the neighborhood of $\mathbf{x}$, i.e.,

$$\lambda_1 \sim \max_{\mathbf{e}_1} \int (\mathbf{e}_1 \cdot \mathbf{u})^2 |F_{\mathbf{x}}(\mathbf{u})|^2 \, d\mathbf{u} \quad \text{and} \quad \lambda_2 \sim \min_{\mathbf{e}_2} \int (\mathbf{e}_2 \cdot \mathbf{u})^2 |F_{\mathbf{x}}(\mathbf{u})|^2 \, d\mathbf{u} \ , \quad (1)$$

where $\mathbf{u} = (u, v)^T$ is the frequency vector and $F_{\mathbf{x}}(\mathbf{u})$ is the local spectrum. The two vectors $\mathbf{e}_1$ and $\mathbf{e}_2$ are perpendicular and $\mathbf{e}_1$ represents the main orientation of the structure. In practice, the structure tensor is typically computed by averaging the outer product of the image gradient:[2]

$$\mathbf{J}(\mathbf{x}) = \int_{\mathcal{N}(\mathbf{x})} (\nabla f(\mathbf{x}'))(\nabla f(\mathbf{x}'))^T w(\mathbf{x} - \mathbf{x}') \, d\mathbf{x}' \ , \quad (2)$$

where $w(\cdot)$ is some weighting function for the neighborhood $\mathcal{N}$ and $\nabla f(\cdot)$ is the image gradient. According to the power theorem [14] and the derivative theorem of the Fourier transform, the tensor $\mathbf{J}$ is proportional to the second moment tensor of the local Fourier spectrum, i.e.,

$$\mathbf{J} \sim \int \mathbf{u}\mathbf{u}^T |F_{\mathbf{x}}(\mathbf{u})|^2 \, d\mathbf{u} \ , \quad (3)$$

such that the eigenvalues of $\mathbf{J}$ are consistent with (1).

A classical technique for estimating the intrinsic dimensionality is to consider the rank of the structure tensor. Theoretically, the number of non-zero eigenvalues corresponds to the rank of the tensor, and therefore, to the intrinsic dimensionality of the neighborhood. In practice the eigenvalues are never zero due to noise and a commonly applied method is to *threshold* the eigenvalues [6]. This approach leads to a discrete categorization of neighborhoods according to their intrinsic dimensionality.

Indeed, it is not only noise that disturbs the evaluation of the rank, but most neighborhoods in real signals consist of combinations of i0D, i1D, and i2D signals. Hence, it is more appropriate to think of the intrinsic dimensionality as a *continuous* measure rather than a discrete set of cases. In order to define a continuous measure, it is necessary to define the *topology* of the measurement

---

[1] The frequency spread is obtained by considering the variance of the squared amplitude response [12].

[2] The are other ways to compute the structure tensor, e.g., polar separable quadrature filter [5] or polynomial expansions [13], but the gradient based approach is best suited in the context of this paper.

space. For the intrinsic dimensionality we observe that the measurement space *cannot be 1D*, since each of the intrinsic dimensionalities is adjacent to the other two. *The intrinsic dimensionality space is thus 2D.*

One approach which at least partially realizes a continuous measure is the *coherence* [6], which takes values in the interval $[0, 1]$ depending on the quotient[3]

$$c = \frac{\lambda_1 - \lambda_2}{\lambda_1 + \lambda_2} \ . \tag{4}$$

The coherence is one for ideal i1D neighborhoods and tends to zero for isotropic structures, i.e., it represents the *confidence* for the presence of an i1D structure. However, the coherence does not take the i0D case into account. In the latter case, we meet a singularity for $A = \lambda_1 + \lambda_2 = 0$ (see Fig. 2, left). Therefore, the coherence is mostly combined with a threshold of A, i.e., the coherence approach is a mixture of a continuous model (i1D–i2D) and a discrete model (i0D–i1D/i2D). Notice that one of the most popular corner detectors, the Harris-Stephens detector [15], is based on the coherence measure.

Another approach to realize a continuous measure is proposed in [5], p. 253, where the tensor is decomposed into a linear combination of tensors with different (non-zero) rank. For images, the linear coefficients are given by $\lambda_1 - \lambda_2$ (i1D) and λ_2 (i2D). Considering these coefficients in an orthonormal basis[4] yields a $\pi/4$ sector (see Fig. 2, center). The same sector shaped space is obtained by multiplying the coherence by A. The center point of the sector corresponds to an i0D neighborhood, one edge corresponds to i1D neighborhoods and the other one corresponds to i2D neighborhoods. Due to the triangular structure, we avoid the problem of evaluating the coherence for $A = 0$. However, the problem with the i0D case is still present, since there is no upper bound of the coordinates. Without having an upper bound, i.e., without having a finite interval for the coordinates, we cannot normalize the coordinates. Hence, we cannot represent confidences for all three cases, and *no probabilistic interpretation* is possible.

In order to map the measured values to finite intervals, we apply a popular technique which is called *soft thresholding*, see e.g. [1,16]. The value A is transformed by a non-linear function:

$$A' = \arctan(a \log(A) + d)/\pi + 1/2 \ \in [0, 1] \ , \tag{5}$$

where a and d are real constants. This transformation results in a finite area for all possible measurements of the intrinsic dimensionality: a *triangle*, see Fig. 2, right, with the coordinates

$$(x, y)^T = (A', A'c)^T \ \in [0, 1] \times [0, 1] \quad \text{and} \quad y \le x \ . \tag{6}$$

The i0D case corresponds to the coordinates $(0, 0)$, the i1D case to $(1, 1)$, and the i2D case to $(1, 0)$. The coordinates (x, y) can easily be transformed to *barycentric*

---

[3] In [6] the coherence is defined as the square of the expression in (4).

[4] The decomposition of a 2D tensor into a rank one tensor and an isotropic tensor is not an orthogonal decomposition, since the angle between a rank one tensor and the identity is $\pi/4$.

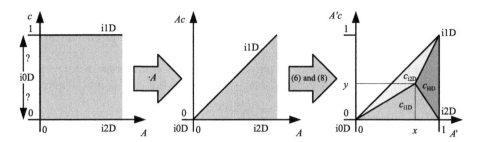

Fig. 2. About the topology of iD-space. Left: the coherence leads to an infinite stripe of width one; center: the tensor decomposition leads to a sector, right: soft thresholding yields a triangle which can be parameterized by barycentric coordinates.

coordinates [17], yielding three coordinates $(c_{i0D}, c_{i1D}, c_{i2D})$ with $c_{ikD} \in [0,1]$ for $k = 0, 1, 2$ and $\sum_{k=0}^{2} c_{ikD} = 1$, i.e., the barycentric coordinates can be interpreted as *likelihoods* or *confidences*. The barycentric coordinates correspond to the areas of the opposite triangles (see Fig. 2, right) and are obtained by the formulas

$$c_{i0D} = 1 - x \qquad c_{i1D} = y \qquad c_{i2D} = x - y \ . \tag{7}$$

Note that although the new representation of the intrinsic dimensionality has been derived from considerations of the structure tensor, it is not necessarily based on its eigenvalues. Any preprocessing method yielding two measurements, which in some way represent the isotropic and the directed part of a signal neighborhood, can be used for building up the triangle representation. Other examples besides the structure tensor are the generalized quadrature filter in [8], a combination of the Canny edge detector [18] and the Harris-Stephens corner detector [15] (both without thresholding), or a combination of local amplitude and local orientation variance [19].

3   The Intrinsic Dimensionality Cone

If we want to process the intrinsic dimensionality information further, we must assure that the representation is *consistent*, i.e., averaging of the representation for two (adjacent) neighborhoods should result in a proper representation for the joint neighborhood. Considering the different possible combinations, one problematic case pops up if two i1D neighborhoods with *different orientations* are considered. The averaged intrinsic dimensionality according to the representation defined above is again i1D, which is wrong. Two i1D neighborhoods with different orientations should give a decreased i1D likelihood and an increased i2D likelihood, depending on the orientation difference, see Fig. 3, right.

Hence, the triangle representation must be modified to be consistent. The required modification has already been mentioned implicitly in terms of linear combination of tensors. A rank one tensor does not only include information about the eigenvalue, but also about the eigenvector, i.e., the local orientation. The rank one tensor represents the orientation in double angle, which is appropriate for averaging orientation information [5]. The triangle representation

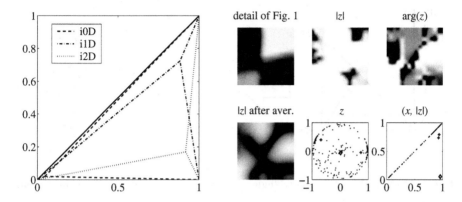

Fig. 3. Left: The triangle representation of the intrinsic dimensionality of the three selected points from Fig. 1. The estimated likelihoods are: 0.95 for the i0D case, 0.72 for the i1D case, and 0.75 for the i2D case. Right: averaging an appropriate i1D representation results in a high i2D likelihood at corners. Bottom row, center and right: histogram representations. The dots indicate the measurements before the averaging, the diamond indicates the estimate at the corner after the averaging, and the pluses indicate the estimates at the edges (five pixels from the corner) after the averaging.

is now modified by multiplying the y-coordinate by the complex double angle representation:

$$z = y \exp(i2\theta) \ , \tag{8}$$

where θ represents the local orientation, see Fig. 4. This modification leads to a *cone-shaped* space for the intrinsic dimensionality, the *iD-cone*.

Measurements for the intrinsic dimensionality are now combined with orientation information and are represented by coordinates inside the iD-cone. Each point in the iD-cone corresponds to a set of local image structures with the same orientation and the same intrinsic dimensionality. Averaging the cone coordinates over some neighborhood leads to a consistent estimate of the intrinsic dimensionality in that neighborhood. If the confidences for the different iD cases are required, we simply evaluate the barycentric coordinates in the plane given by the complex argument, i.e., y is replaced with $|z|$ in (7).

In the cone model, two i1D structures with different orientations give rise to an increased likelihood of a i2D structure. This observation implies that it is not necessary to extract i2D information in the preprocessing, i.e., we do not need coherence information. It is sufficient to estimate the orientation and the intensity, to represent this information in cone coordinates (i.e., on the cone surface), and to apply a local averaging. The i2D information then drops out as a result of the averaging process.[5] The preprocessing can be performed by a simple gradient estimation, by the Riesz transform, or by a spherical quadrature filter [20] which was used to produce the results in Fig. 3.

---

[5] This behavior is similar for the averaging of the outer product of gradients for computing the structure tensor [6].

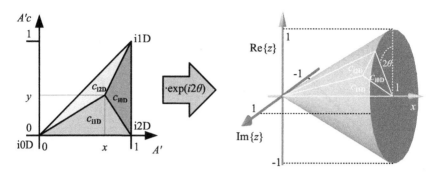

Fig. 4. Modification of the iD-triangle: multiplying y by $\exp(i2\theta)$ yields an iD-cone.

Except for the preprocessing, the described approach for estimating the intrinsic dimensionality contains only three free parameters: the constants a and d in (5) and the size of the neighborhood for the local averaging. In our experiments we set $a = 5$, $d = 0$, and the local averaging is obtained by Gaussian smoothing with variance 2, but the method is very stable with respect to changes in the parameters. Due to the simple analytic description of the approach, it is straightforward to optimize the free parameters for certain applications, e.g., in a similar way as it is done in the back-propagation algorithm [1]. From this point of view and since the barycentric coordinates are obtained from an averaging process, the iD-cone model can be considered as a probabilistic approach. In a larger system the estimated likelihoods for the different intrinsic dimensionalities can be used as priors for the subsequent processing steps. The new model can be applied in a wide range of applications, e.g., corner detection [8][6], edge detection, curve fitting, and segmentation. The introduced definition of intrinsic dimensionality has also been applied as a descriptor for the 'edgeness' or 'junctioness' of local image patches in a new kind of multi-modal image representations [21].

4   Conclusion

In this paper we have derived a continuous representation of the intrinsic dimensionality of images. Although our considerations are based on the structure tensor approach, our model is independent of a specific preprocessing method, which need not even contain i2D information. The derived finite cone-shaped iD-space is easily interpreted in terms of a probabilistic representation by using barycentric coordinates. The model contains only few parameters, which might be obtained by a learning method, depending on a specific application.

Acknowledgment. We like to thank Klas Nordberg for all the discussions on tensor representations.

---

[6] To be precise, we did not make explicit use of the here proposed model in [8], but the applied algorithm is compatible the iD triangle.

References

1. Bishop, C.M.: Neural Networks for Pattern Recognition. Oxford University Press, New York (1995)
2. Trunk, G.V.: Representation and analysis of signals: statistical estimation of intrinsic dimensionality and parameter identification. General System **13** (1968) 49–76
3. Zetzsche, C., Barth, E.: Fundamental limits of linear filters in the visual processing of two dimensional signals. Vision Research **30** (1990)
4. Krieger, G., Zetzsche, C.: Nonlinear image operators for the evaluation of local intrinsic dimensionality. IEEE Transactions on Image Processing **5** (1996) 1026–1041
5. Granlund, G.H., Knutsson, H.: Signal Processing for Computer Vision. Kluwer Academic Publishers, Dordrecht (1995)
6. Jähne, B.: Digitale Bildverarbeitung. Springer, Berlin (1997)
7. Bülow, T.: Hypercomplex Spectral Signal Representations for the Processing and Analysis of Images. PhD thesis, Christian-Albrechts-University of Kiel (1999)
8. Felsberg, M., Sommer, G.: Image features based on a new approach to 2D rotation invariant quadrature filters. In Heyden, A., Sparr, G., Nielsen, M., Johansen, P., eds.: Computer Vision - ECCV 2002. Volume 2350 of Lecture Notes in Computer Science., Springer (2002) 369–383
9. Förstner, W., Gülch, E.: A fast operator for detection and precise location of distinct points, corners and centres of circular features. In: ISPRS Intercommission Workshop, Interlaken. (1987) 149–155
10. Bigün, J., Granlund, G.H.: Optimal orientation detection of linear symmetry. In: Proceedings of the IEEE First International Conference on Computer Vision, London, Great Britain (1987) 433–438.
11. Förstner, W.: Statistische Verfahren für die automatische Bildanalyse und ihre Bewertung bei der Objekterkennung und -vermessung. Number 370 in C. Verlag der Bayerischen Akademie der Wissenschaften (1991)
12. Ramanathan, J.: Methods of Applied Fourier Analysis. Birkhäuser (1998)
13. Farnebäck, G.: Fast and accurate motion estimation using orientation tensors and parametric motion models. In: Proceedings of 15th International Conference on Pattern Recognition. Volume 1., Barcelona, Spain, IAPR (2000) 135–139
14. Bracewell, R.N.: The Fourier transform and its applications. McGraw Hill (1986)
15. Harris, C.G., Stephens, M.: A combined corner and edge detector. In: 4th Alvey Vision Conference. (1988) 147–151
16. Krüger, N.: Learning object representations using a priori constraints within ORASSYLL. Neural Computation **13** (2001) 389–410
17. Coexeter, H.S.M.: Introduction to Geometry. 2nd edn. Wiley & Sons (1969)
18. Canny, J.: A computational approach to edge detection. IEEE Transactions on Pattern Analysis and Machine Intelligence **8** (1986) 679–698
19. Krüger, N., Felsberg, M.: A continuous formulation of intrinsic dimension. In: British Machine Vision Conference. (2003) submitted.
20. Felsberg, M.: Low-Level Image Processing with the Structure Multivector. PhD thesis, Institute of Computer Science and Applied Mathematics, Christian-Albrechts-University of Kiel (2002) TR no. 0203, available at http://www.informatik.uni-kiel.de/reports/2002/0203.html.
21. Krüger, N., Lappe, M., Wörgötter, F.: Biologically motivated multi-modal processing of visual primitives. 'AISB 2003 Convention: Cognition in Machines and Animals', Wales (2003)

Learning Human-Like Opponent Behavior for Interactive Computer Games

Christian Bauckhage, Christian Thurau, and Gerhard Sagerer

Technical Faculty, Bielefeld University, P.O. Box 100131, 33501 Bielefeld, Germany
{cbauckha,cthurau,sagerer}@techfak.uni-bielefeld.de

Abstract. Compared to their ancestors in the early 1970s, present day computer games are of incredible complexity and show magnificent graphical performance. However, in programming intelligent opponents, the game industry still applies techniques developed some 30 years ago. In this paper, we investigate whether opponent programming can be treated as a problem of behavior learning. To this end, we assume the behavior of game characters to be a function that maps the current game state onto a reaction. We will show that neural networks architectures are well suited to learn such functions and by means of a popular commercial game we demonstrate that agent behaviors can be learned from observation.

1 Context, Motivation, and Overview

Modern computer games create complex and dynamic virtual worlds which offer numerous possibilities for interaction and are displayed using incredible computer graphics. Professional game development therefore has become expensive and time consuming and involves whole teams of programmers, authors and artists [2,8]. However, despite all progress in appearance and complexity, when it comes to implementing intelligent virtual characters the game industry largely ignores scientific advances but still reverts to techniques known for more than 30 years [2].

Up to now, the most common techniques to control virtual characters are finite state machines (of admittedly complex topology) and scripts. From a player's point of view this has two major drawbacks: (1) The actions of computer controlled characters often appear artificial since they just cycle through a fixed repertoire; this provokes repetitions and thus causes ennui and frustration. (2) Finite stated or scripted behaviors cannot generalize. Thus, if a human player acts unforeseen, i.e. interaction results in a game state not envisaged by the programmers, virtual characters tend to behave 'dumb' [2].

Therefore –and certainly because of the popularity computer games enjoy among today's students– creating intelligent opponents has attracted attention in AI research [3, 4,11]. Especially Laird identifies a need for human-like behaving characters and heralds games as the 'killer application' of artificial intelligence [8,9]. And indeed, all cited contributions describe ontology based inference machines or reasoning mechanisms and thus are classical AI. In the following, however, we will argue that computer games also offer interesting problems and testbeds for the pattern recognition community. While the next section explains this claim in general, section 3 treats practical issues concerning this idea. In section 4 we present results obtained from several experiments on learning of human-like behavior and finally an outlook concludes this contribution.

B. Michaelis and G. Krell (Eds.): DAGM 2003, LNCS 2781, pp. 148–155, 2003.
© Springer-Verlag Berlin Heidelberg 2003

2   A Pattern Recognition Perspective on Game Characters

Modern computer games create virtual worlds of enormous sizes in which the player slips into the role of a virtual character who has to fulfill a certain task. Depending on the genre, tasks can reach from building and administer cities or civilizations over solving adventurous quests to simply staying alive on a virtual battlefield.

While it is obvious that computer games are not the real world, it is important to note that most of them must not be confused with simulations either. Like in simulations, the states of a game are characterized by a huge set of parameters which encode the current configuration of the virtual world. If this configuration is thought of as a point in a high dimensional state space, the current state of a player's virtual character corresponds to a point in an appropriate subspace and the history of states a character assumes during a game forms a path in the state space. But in contrast to simulations, interactive games merely constrain the actions of a player. Of course there are rules which govern the evolution of game states but they are not necessarily tailored to the real world (in some games, for instance, teleportation is possible). Therefore, paths in the state space neither need to be linear nor smooth. And since there are dynamic interactions between virtual world, computer controlled opponents, and player characters, the state of the player's character is influenced by the player's actions as well as by events in the virtual world. As computer controlled events in the virtual world often are triggered randomly and a players can freely chose their actions, the states of player controlled characters evolve unforeseen rather than predictable.

Given these observations, we see that evolving player states constitute discrete time series. And in a simple approximation, their evolution could be assumed to depend only on the last time step. I.e. if we assume the state of player p at time t to be given by a vector $\underline{\mathbf{s}}_t^p$, the player's state at the next time step $t + 1$ could be modeled as

$$\underline{\mathbf{s}}_{t+1}^p = \underline{\mathbf{s}}_t^p + \underline{\mathbf{e}}_t + \underline{\mathbf{a}}_t^p(\underline{\mathbf{s}}_t^p) \tag{1}$$

where $\underline{\mathbf{e}}_t$ denotes environmental influences at time t and $\underline{\mathbf{a}}_t^p(\underline{\mathbf{s}}_t^p)$ represents the action player p accomplishes according to his current state. If we restate this equation as

$$\underline{\mathbf{a}}_t^p = f(\underline{\mathbf{s}}_{t+1}^p, \underline{\mathbf{s}}_t^p, \underline{\mathbf{e}}_t) \tag{2}$$

we see that player actions correspond to what Arkin calls *reactive behaviors* [1]. I.e. the actions of a player first of all depend on his or her state and on the current environmental influence. Furthermore, we see that, given suitable training data, prototypical actions $\underline{\mathbf{a}}_t^p$ or situated behaviors which we define to be sequences of actions $\{\underline{\mathbf{a}}_{t_i}^p, \underline{\mathbf{a}}_{t_{i+1}}^p, \ldots, \underline{\mathbf{a}}_{t_{i+n}}^p\}$ of a player might be *learnable* using techniques like statistical classifiers, HMMs, or neural networks.

Actually, Markovian approaches and conditional expectation maximization have already been successfully applied to behavior learning in human-machine interaction [5, 7]. Although these methods offer interesting perspectives for computer games, too, we aimed at finding a non-probabilistic approximation of the mapping f in Eq. (2). We thus opted for neural network based approaches. But before we discuss first corresponding results in learning of opponent behavior for commercial games, the next section shall point out that appropriate training data is easily available for most present day games.

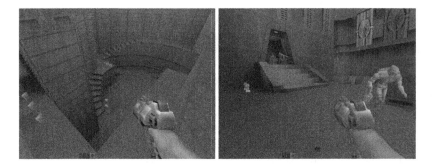

Fig. 1. Screenshots taken from ID's (in)famous FPS game Quake II.

3   Practical Issues in Behavior Learning for Game Characters

For the reminder of this contribution, we will focus on the infamous but nevertheless popular genre of *first person shooter* (FPS) games[1]. In a FPS game, the player moves through a virtual world (called *map* in gamers terminology) which he perceives from the first person perspective (s. Fig.1). Though variations exist, his main task is to battle against every other character on the map. In doing so, the player will loose health, armor, and ammunition which can be compensated by collecting corresponding items distributed all over a map. The state of a FPS character therefore is almost completely determined by its current position and view on the map and its current armament and health conditions.

The ideas discussed below resulted from the fact that nowadays it is actually possible to earn a living from playing computer games. There are professionals who regularly compete at tournaments worth several 10.000 dollars of trophy money. Observing these professionals playing FPS games, one realizes that they do not reflect the situations they encounter in a game but simply react. Their reactions result from long term practice and usually only depend on the current state of their virtual character as well as on its current environmental context. Our reactive behavior model in Eq. (1) thus seems perfectly applicable to this genre. Moreover, game athletes also solve the problem of getting training data for behavior learning: most present day computer games allow to record matches. These so called *demos* can be viewed afterwards and show the game from the perspective of the player who recorded it. A demo therefore encodes the series of states $\underline{s}_0^p, \underline{s}_1^p, \underline{s}_2^p, \ldots, \underline{s}_N^p$ the recording player p underwent during a game.

As there are millions of demos available on the Internet, the idea was to try to use this data to train neural networks which map human-made state vectors to human-made (re)action vectors. Such networks would realize artificial opponents (called *bots* in gamers terminology) which will imitate human players and thus certainly will behave human-like. In order to verify this idea, we experimented with ID's game QUAKE II, which was chosen for the following reasons:

---

[1] Even though ethically controversial, this genre is (pioneered by Laird) commonly to be found in literature on intelligent computer controlled opponents.

Fig. 2. A virtual character's movement depends on its field of view (fov) which is determined by the signed angles YAW and PITCH and on the character's velocity $\underline{\mathbf{v}} = (v_x, v_y)$.

1. Its C++ source code is freely available on the Internet [6].
2. Its network protocol is simple so that it is easy to extract game state data from recorded demos.
3. Though no longer state of the art in computer graphics, it is still popular and demo resources are nearly unlimited.

4   Experiments

In a first series of experiments, we tried to learn moving and aiming behaviors from recorded demos. In doing so, we assumed the state of a QUAKE II character to be comprehensively described by its position $\mathbf{x} \in \mathbb{R}^3$ on a map, its distance $d \in \mathbb{R}$ to the nearest opponent, and the horizontal angle φ and the vertical angle ϑ to this opponent. As QUAKE II encodes angles such that $\varphi, \vartheta \in [0°, 180°]$ both require a signum $\sigma(\varphi), \sigma(\vartheta) \in \{-1, 1\}$ in order to cover the whole angular range. Consequently, in our experiments, a player's state was represented by an 8 dimensional vector $\underline{\mathbf{S}}$.

Since we only considered movement and aiming, we assumed a player's action to be determined by adjustments of its field of view (fov) and its velocity (s. Fig.2). In the experiments reported below, we thus realized virtual opponents by means of at least two neural networks where one was specialized in fov adjustment and the other was responsible for velocity adapting. Correspondingly, the overall reaction of our bots was composed from the output of these expert networks. As QUAKE II represents the fov by means of the angles YAW $\in [0°, 180°]$ and PITCH $\in [0°, 90°]$ with $\sigma(\text{YAW}), \sigma(\text{PITCH}) \in \{-1, 1\}$ and since we assumed the velocity to be given by a vector $\underline{\mathbf{v}}$ where $v_x \in [-400, 400]$ and $v_y \in [-200, 200]$, the networks for adjusting fov and velocity thus map 8 state parameters onto 4 or 2 action parameters, respectively.

Given several training series $\underline{\mathbf{s}}_t^p, t \in \{1, 2, \dots, N\}$ of recorded state vectors, the state parameters $\underline{\mathbf{S}}$ described above can immediately be extracted while the parameters $\underline{\mathbf{A}}^f$ and $\underline{\mathbf{A}}^v$ for corresponding fov and velocity adjustments result from the difference $\underline{\mathbf{s}}_{t+1}^p - \underline{\mathbf{s}}_t^p$. The goal is thus to minimize the square errors

$$E_x = \frac{1}{2} \sum_{t=1}^{N-1} \left\| \hat{\underline{\mathbf{A}}}_t^x(\underline{\mathbf{S}}_t) - \underline{\mathbf{A}}_t^x(\underline{\mathbf{S}}_t) \right\|^2, \quad x \in \{f, v\} \tag{3}$$

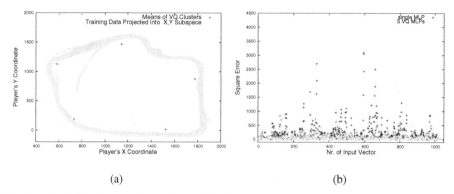

(a)   (b)

Fig. 3. (a) Training data (projected into the (x, y) plane) and means of VQ cluster. (b) Differences between expected and calculated fov adaptions obtained on a test set of 1027 vectors. The plot compares the performance of a single MLP with that of a combination of 5 MLPs.

between automatically generated adjustments $\hat{\mathbf{A}}_t^x$ and known ones. As the next paragraphs indicate, for basic behavior learning tasks this can successfully be done by different combinations of simple multilayer perceptrons (MLPs) based on Levenberg-Marquardt training[2].

Learning Efficient Paths: Experienced FPS players do not move arbitrarily through a game environment. They have learned to cycle a map such that the effort for collecting items is minimal. In a first experiment, we investigated if such paths can be learned from training data. To this end we recorded a demo containing a total of 2064 state vectors which show five efficient runs around a map. Figure 3(a) shows a projection of the corresponding 8 dimensional data into the subspace of the player's (x, y) coordinates.

Integrating MLPs for fov and velocity adjustments into Quake II, i.e. implementing a virtual character, allowed to literally observe their performance. This revealed that a bot based on monolithic MLPs tended to become stuck at certain parts of the map. A solution was provided by clustering the training data using vector quantization. Figure 3(a) also shows the means of clusters that resulted after the number of partitions was chosen to be 5. After MLPs with 12 hidden neurons were trained for each of the resulting clusters, we could observe the bot smoothly pursuing the path encoded in the training data. This is documented in Fig.3(b) and the upper part of Tab.1 which summarize results from an offline evaluation of this experiment. Both compare the performance of the different solutions on an independent test demo of 1027 state vectors.

Learning to Run Crossed Paths: Already in realizing simple running behaviors, the assumption we made in Eq. (1), i.e. the idea that a reaction just depends on the current state, proves to be insufficient. Rather, knowledge of temporal context, e.g. knowing one's last position, can be crucial for intelligent movement behavior. This becomes apparent if we consider Fig.4(a) which superimposes data from two demos. Both demos contain cyclic runs around a map which overlap to a certain extend but happened to be

---

[2] Details on the choice of network topologies discussed in the following can be found in [10].

Table 1. Summary of offline evaluation results.

Experiment	Classifier		Training			Test	
	Task	Network Topology	Epochs	N_{Train}	E_{Train}	N_{Test}	E_{Test}
single path run	adapting fov	single 8-24-4 MLP	150	2064	35.29	1027	190.76
	adapting velocity	single 8-24-2 MLP	150	2064	2455.95	1027	2957.5
	adapting fov	5 VQ 8-12-4 MLPs	150	2064	15.1	1027	140.87
	adapting velocity	5 VQ 8-12-2 MLPs	150	2064	2453.82	1027	2788.75
crossing paths run	adapting fov	10 SOM 8-24-4 MLPs	150	2840	119.22	1513	644.1
	adapting velocity	10 SOM 8-24-2 MLPs	150	2840	3214.18	1513	7214.18
	adapting fov	10 SOM 24-12-4 TDNNs	150	2840	30.56	1513	313.17
	adapting velocity	10 SOM 24-12-2 TDNNs	150	2840	2411.85	1513	6032.1
integrated aim and movement behavior	adapting fov	6 SOM 8-12-4 MLPs	150	2361	18.42	1598	4585.5
	adapting velocity	6 SOM 8-12-2 MLPs	150	2361	1599.94	1598	2834.38
	adapting fov	6 SOM 5-12-4 MLPs	150	2361	15.5	1598	119.06
	adapting velocity	6 SOM 8-12-2 MLPs	150	2361	1599.94	1598	2834.38

directed contrary. Thus, without knowing where it was last a bot that has to move in the overlapping section of the paths would be lost for it simply would randomly choose between velocity adjustments learned from the one or the other demo. This assertion is backed up empirically in Fig.4(b) and the middle rows of Tab.1. Both compare results obtained with combinations of regular MLPs with results from combined time delay neural networks (TDNNs). In these experiments, the training data was separated into 10 clusters using self organizing maps (SOMs). On the one hand, usual MLPs with 24 hidden neurons were trained to learn movement behaviors. On the other hand, we trained TDNNs which not only regarded the current state but also the last two states to derive fov and velocity adjustments. Consequently, the input layer of these networks is of dimension 24. But even if their hidden layers contain only 12 neurons, this architecture lowers the errors E_f and E_v considerably.

Learning to Switch between Movement and Aiming Behaviors: Up to now, we only described neural network architectures that imitate a single human-demonstrated behavior. Figure5(a) depicts a projection of a demo where another character came across the recording player who correspondingly slowed down and aimed at that opponent. What we can see are the (x, y, d) coordinates contained in the demo, i.e. the 8 dimensional state vectors $\underline{S}$ are projected into the subspace describing the player's spatial coordinates as well as his distance to an opponent. An ingame evaluation yielded that a combination of only two MLPs for fov and velocity adjustment cannot really reproduce the switching between behaviors that was implicitly encoded in the training data. SOMs, in contrast, automatically unfold evenly into the space of training data and, in fact, Fig.5(a) shows that one out of 6 SOM neurons emerged as a representative of the situation where the opponent came close. Consequently, the MLPs attached to this neuron automatically assume the role of experts for aiming and the capability to switch between behaviors automatically emerges from input space clustering.

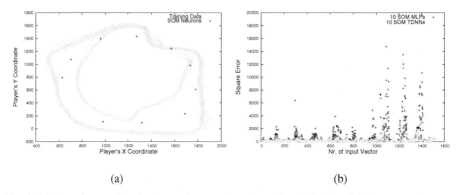

(a)   (b)

Fig. 4. (a) Superimposed projections of crossed, contrary directed paths. **(b)** Corresponding performance in fov adjustment by hybridly coupled regular MLPs and hybridly combined TDNNs

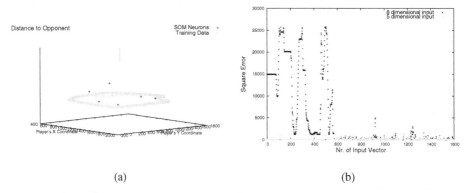

(a)   (b)

Fig. 5. (a) (x, y, d) Space projection of a demo where another player came across. **(b)** Errors in fov adjustment obtained from a combination of SOM clustered MLPs for 8 dimensional input and from the same architecture applied to PCA reduced input.

However, as we see in Fig.5(b), our accustomed technique of assigning MLPs which process 8 dimensional input to SOM neurons does not perform well either. The figure displays the error E_f in fov adjustment. While the first 600 state vectors in the analyzed test data correspond to a situation where an opponent was near, the remaining 998 vectors represent usual player movements. Thus, as for the first phase of this demo the observed error oscillates considerably, the aiming behavior was not learned well. A solution resulted from reducing the input data dimension using PCA. Unsurprisingly, this yielded that mainly field of view parameters are responsible for aiming. And in fact, as the second plot in Fig.5(b) as well as the lower most rows of Tab.1 underline, reducing the input to the fov parameters only improved the quality of aiming.

5   Conclusion and Future Work

Even though computer games have become an enormous business that exhausts considerable intellectual efforts, current commercial realizations of game characters (also called *bots*) are far behind the scientific state of the art. In this contribution, we promoted the idea of understanding bot programming as a learning task. And indeed, first shot experiments with several neural network architectures indicate that it is possible to realize bots which behave human-like simply because they learned from human-generated training data.

Currently, we extend our approaches to more complex behavior and to other games. In doing so, we also investigate online learning for game characters as well as more sophisticated neural network architectures like mixtures of experts. Furthermore, we plan to examine data mining techniques in order to determine which information is relevant to generate and switch between appropriate behaviors. Finally, besides its long-term commercial impact, we believe that the game domain also provides interesting impulses for behavior learning in general. A mid-term vision, for instance, is a robocup-like league where bots from different research groups compete in order to foster the development of intelligently behaving game characters.

References

1. R. C. Arkin. *Behavior-Based Robotics*. MIT Press, 1998.
2. S. Cass. Mind games. *IEEE Spectrum*, pages 40–44, December 2002.
3. K. R. Dixon, R. J. Malak, and P. K. Khosla. Incorporating Prior Knowledge and Previously Learned Information into Reinforcement Learning Agents. Technical report, CMU, 2000.
4. C. Fairclough, M. Fagan, B. MacNamee, and P. Cunningham. Research Directions for AI in Computer Games. Technical report, Trinity College Dublin, 2001.
5. A. Galata, N. Johnson, and D. Hogg. Learning Variable-Length Markov Models of Behaviour. *Computer Visiosn and Image Understanding*, 81(3):398–413, 2001.
6. http://www.idsoftware.com/business/home/techdownloads/.
7. T. Jebara and A. Pentland. Action reaction learning: Automatic visual analysis and synthesis of interactive behaviour. In *Proc. 1st Int. Conf. on Computer Vision Systems*, volume 1542 of *Lecture Notes in Computer Science*, pages 273–292, 1999.
8. J. E. Laird. Using a Computer Game to develop advanced AI. *IEEE Computer*, pages 70–75, July 2001.
9. J. E. Laird and M. v. Lent. Interactice Computer Games: Human-Level AI's Killer Application. In *Proc. AAAI*, pages 1171–1178, 2000.
10. C. Thurau. Untersuchung über Lernverfahren für künstliche Agenten in virtuellen 3D-Umgebungen. Master's thesis, Bielefeld Universtiy, March 2003.
11. J.M.P. van Vaveren. The Quake III Arena Bot. Master's thesis, TU Delft, June 2001.

Rotationally Invariant Wavelet Shrinkage*

Pavel Mrázek and Joachim Weickert

Mathematical Image Analysis Group
Faculty of Mathematics and Computer Science, Building 27
Saarland University, 66123 Saarbrücken, Germany
{mrazek,weickert}@mia.uni-saarland.de
http://www.mia.uni-saarland.de

Abstract. Most two-dimensional methods for wavelet shrinkage are efficient for edge-preserving image denoising, but they suffer from poor rotation invariance. We address this problem by designing novel shrinkage rules that are derived from rotationally invariant nonlinear diffusion filters. The resulting Haar wavelet shrinkage methods are computationally inexpensive and they offer substantially improved rotation invariance.

1 Introduction

Wavelet shrinkage is a fast nonlinear method for discontinuity-preserving image denoising [1]. It is based on the idea to decompose an image in terms of a wavelet basis, to shrink all coefficients with small magnitude, and to reconstruct the filtered image from the shrunken coefficients. The success of this procedure is based on the assumption that the original image can be represented by a relatively small number of wavelet coefficients with large magnitude, while moderate Gaussian noise affects all coefficients, although to a less severe amount.

Several ways have been proposed to improve wavelet shrinkage. One of them is to make the shrinkage translation invariant [2]. Very recently it also became clear that shift-invariant wavelet denoising can be improved substantially by iterating [3,4,5]. While these ideas work well for processing 1D signals, filtering of 2D images creates an additional, but very fundamental problem: the shrinkage should be rotationally invariant. Unfortunately, this is not the case for the frequently used separable approaches. Several attempts to create wavelet transforms with improved rotation invariance have appeared in the literature, including the directional cycle spinning [6], complex wavelets [7], or the elaborated edgelet and curvelet transforms [8]. These ideas are not only relatively difficult to implement, most of them are also computationally significantly more complex than traditional shift-invariant wavelet shrinkage in 2D.

In the present paper we address this problem by proposing a novel class of shift-invariant 2D wavelet shrinkage methods for iterated image denoising with

---

* This research was supported by the project *Relations between Nonlinear Filters in Digital Image Processing* within the DFG–Schwerpunktprogramm 1114: *Mathematical Methods for Time Series Analysis and Digital Image Processing*. This is gratefully acknowledged.

B. Michaelis and G. Krell (Eds.): DAGM 2003, LNCS 2781, pp. 156–163, 2003.

a high degree of rotation invariance. This class is computationally as simple as classical shift-invariant wavelet shrinkage. It is inspired by considering a connection between wavelet shrinkage and nonlinear diffusion filtering that has already proved fruitful in the 1D case [9]. Two-dimensional nonlinear diffusion filtering is based on a continuous differential equation that is rotationally invariant. From numerical analysis it is well-known how to discretise such equations in a consistent way such that rotation invariance is approximated well. By identifying a discrete diffusion filter with a wavelet shrinkage formulation, we can find novel shrinkage rules that lead to substantially improved rotation invariance.

The paper is organised as follows. Sections 2 and 3 provide a brief introduction to translation-invariant Haar wavelet shrinkage, and nonlinear diffusion in 2D. The connections between the two procedures are exploited in Section 4 to establish the conditions on diffusivity and shrinkage functions under which the two methods (restricted to one-step / one-scale) are equivalent. In Section 5 we evaluate the rotation invariance of the new multiscale iterated wavelet filter. The paper is concluded with a summary in Section 6.

2   Wavelet Shrinkage

The discrete wavelet transform represents a one-dimensional signal f in terms of shifted versions of a dilated lowpass scaling function, and shifted and dilated versions of a bandpass wavelet function. In this paper we restrict our attention to the discrete transform with Haar wavelets, well suited for piecewise constant signals with discontinuities. The Haar wavelet transform is described by a low-pass filter L with coefficients $(\frac{1}{\sqrt{2}}, \frac{1}{\sqrt{2}})$, and a high-pass filter H with coefficients $(\frac{1}{\sqrt{2}}, -\frac{1}{\sqrt{2}})$ [10].

The easiest way to design a two-dimensional wavelet transform is to use separable filters [10]. The 2D wavelet transform then describes a 2D signal $\mathbf{f} = (f_{i,j})$ with $i = 0,...,N_x - 1$ and $j = 0,...,N_y - 1$ by its low-pass component at level n, $\mathbf{v}^n$, and three channels of wavelet coefficients $\mathbf{w}_x^l$, $\mathbf{w}_y^l$ and $\mathbf{w}_{xy}^l$ at levels $l = 1, \ldots, n$. This wavelet representation is created by an alternating application of the one-dimensional low-pass and high-pass filters L and H in the directions of axes x and y:

$$\mathbf{v}^{l+1} = L(x) * L(y) * \mathbf{v}^l, \qquad \mathbf{w}_y^{l+1} = L(x) * H(y) * \mathbf{v}^l, \qquad (1)$$

$$\mathbf{w}_x^{l+1} = H(x) * L(y) * \mathbf{v}^l, \qquad \mathbf{w}_{xy}^{l+1} = H(x) * H(y) * \mathbf{v}^l, \qquad (2)$$

with the initial condition $\mathbf{v}^0 = \mathbf{f}$. For image smoothing, the wavelet coefficients $\mathbf{w}_x, \mathbf{w}_y, \mathbf{w}_{xy}$ are subjected to a shrinkage function S, and the filtered image $\mathbf{u}$ is reconstructed from the shrunken coefficients using an inverse procedure to (1)–(2).

Let us now consider a *single* decomposition level, and the wavelet shrinkage steps which contribute to the output pixel $u_{i,j}$. Using the translation-invariant scheme [2], we have to consider four 2×2 neighbourhoods in which the pixel (i, j) is involved. We denote by upper index α the neighbourhood $\{i, i+1\} \times \{j, j+1\}$;

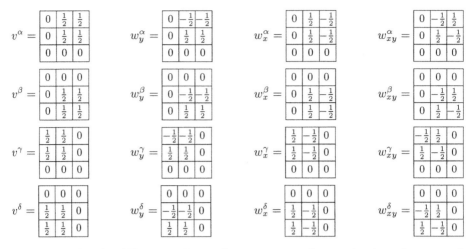

Fig. 1. The first-level Haar wavelet coefficients expressed using 3×3 masks centered at the pixel i, j. The masks represent multiplication of the input signal with the given coefficients, so e.g. $w_x^\alpha = \frac{1}{2} f_{i,j} + \frac{1}{2} f_{i,j+1} - \frac{1}{2} f_{i+1,j} - \frac{1}{2} f_{i+1,j+1}$.

by β the positions $\{i, i+1\} \times \{j-1, j\}$; by γ the neighbourhood $\{i-1, i\} \times \{j, j+1\}$; and, finally, by δ the positions $\{i-1, i\} \times \{j-1, j\}$.

The input signal in neighbourhood α is first transformed into v^α, w_y^α, w_x^α and w_{xy}^α; see Fig. 1 for the definition of the corresponding masks. The wavelet coefficients $w_y^\alpha, w_x^\alpha, w_{xy}^\alpha$ are then subjected to a shrinkage function S, and the (i, j) pixel of the filtered signal belonging to the neighbourhood α is obtained using

$$u_{i,j}^\alpha = \frac{1}{2} \left(v^\alpha + S(w_y^\alpha) + S(w_x^\alpha) + S(w_{xy}^\alpha) \right). \tag{3}$$

Similar expressions can be derived for the results arising from the neighbourhoods β, γ and δ; the necessary masks are shown in Fig. 1. To obtain the final result of a shift-invariant 2D Haar wavelet shrinkage on a single level, the four intermediate results $u_{i,j}^\alpha$, $u_{i,j}^\beta$, $u_{i,j}^\gamma$ and $u_{i,j}^\delta$ have to be averaged. The complete formula for a single-level Haar wavelet shrinkage filter then reads

$$u_{i,j} = \frac{1}{8} \big(v^\alpha + v^\beta + v^\gamma + v^\delta + S(w_y^\alpha) + S(w_x^\alpha) + S(w_{xy}^\alpha) - S(w_y^\beta) + S(w_x^\beta)$$
$$- S(w_{xy}^\beta) + S(w_y^\gamma) - S(w_x^\gamma) - S(w_{xy}^\gamma) - S(w_y^\delta) - S(w_x^\delta) + S(w_{xy}^\delta) \big). \tag{4}$$

3 Nonlinear Diffusion

The basic idea behind nonlinear diffusion filtering [11] is to obtain a family $u(x, y, t)$ of filtered versions of the signal $f(x, y)$ as the solution of a suitable diffusion process

$$u_t = \text{div} \left(g(|\nabla u|^2) \nabla u \right) \tag{5}$$

with f as initial condition: $u(x, y, 0) = f(x, y)$. Here subscripts denote partial derivatives, and the diffusion time t is a simplification parameter: larger values correspond to more pronounced filtering.

The divergence expression on the right hand side of (5) can be decomposed in 2D by means of two orthonormal basis vectors $\boldsymbol{x}_1$ and $\boldsymbol{x}_2$:

$$\text{div}\left(g(|\nabla u|^2)\,\nabla u\right) = \sum_{p=1}^{2} \partial_{\boldsymbol{x}_p}\left(g(|\nabla u|^2)\,\partial_{\boldsymbol{x}_p} u\right). \tag{6}$$

Choosing the diagonal directions $\boldsymbol{x}_1 := (\frac{1}{\sqrt{2}}, \frac{1}{\sqrt{2}})$ and $\boldsymbol{x}_2 := (\frac{1}{\sqrt{2}}, -\frac{1}{\sqrt{2}})$, and replacing the derivatives in (5), (6) by finite differences, we can write the explicit finite difference discretisation of the nonlinear diffusion as

$$u_{i,j}^{k+1} = u_{i,j}^{k} + \tau \sum_{(I,J)\in\mathcal{D}(i,j)} g_{I,J}\, \frac{u_{I,J}^{k} - u_{i,j}^{k}}{2}. \tag{7}$$

Here the upper index k denotes solution at time $k\tau$ with τ standing for the time step, the set $\mathcal{D}(i,j)$ contains the diagonal neighbours of pixel (i,j), and the grid size is assumed to be 1. The term $g_{I,J} \approx g(|\nabla u(x,y)|^2)\big|_{\substack{x=(i+I)/2 \\ y=(j+J)/2}}$ represents the diffusivity belonging to the connection between pixels $u_{i,j}$ and $u_{I,J}$, where the gradient magnitude can be estimated from discrete data using 2×2 masks:

$$
\begin{aligned}
|\nabla u|^2 &= (\partial_x u)^2 + (\partial_y u)^2 \\
&\approx \left(\frac{u_{i,j} + u_{i,J} - u_{I,j} - u_{I,J}}{2}\right)^2 + \left(\frac{u_{i,j} - u_{i,J} + u_{I,j} - u_{I,J}}{2}\right)^2.
\end{aligned} \tag{8}
$$

This diagonal discretisation represents a consistent finite difference approximation to the continuous equation. It has been used successfully by Keeling and Stollberger [12]. Since its spatial consistency can be shown to be of second order, the rotation invariance of the continuous equation is approximated well.

4   Diffusion-Inspired 2D Wavelet Shrinkage

Let us now investigate the connection between a single-level wavelet shrinkage (4) and an explicit diffusion iteration (7). To this end, we consider the first diffusion iteration, starting from the initial signal $\mathbf{f} = (f_{i,j})$ and creating a solution $\mathbf{u} = (u_{i,j})$. We will express the diffusion iteration in the terms of the wavelet coefficients from Section 2.

For the first iteration, (7) becomes

$$u_{i,j} = f_{i,j} + \tau \sum_{(I,J)\in\mathcal{D}(i,j)} g_{I,J}\, \frac{f_{I,J} - f_{i,j}}{2}. \tag{9}$$

The first term on the right-hand side can be rewritten as

$$f_{i,j} = \frac{1}{8}\begin{array}{|c|c|c|}\hline \frac{1}{2} & 1 & \frac{1}{2} \\\hline 1 & 2 & 1 \\\hline \frac{1}{2} & 1 & \frac{1}{2} \\\hline\end{array} + \frac{1}{8}\begin{array}{|c|c|c|}\hline -\frac{1}{2} & -1 & \frac{1}{2} \\\hline -1 & 6 & -1 \\\hline -\frac{1}{2} & -1 & \frac{1}{2} \\\hline\end{array} = \frac{1}{8}\left(v^\alpha + v^\beta + v^\gamma + v^\delta\right) + \frac{1}{8}\left(w_x^\alpha + w_y^\alpha + w_{xy}^\alpha\right.$$

$$\left. + w_x^\beta - w_y^\beta - w_{xy}^\beta - w_x^\gamma + w_y^\gamma - w_{xy}^\gamma - w_x^\delta - w_y^\delta + w_{xy}^\delta\right) \quad (10)$$

where the 3×3 boxes stand for a mask multiplication with the input signal, and the v and w represent the wavelet coefficients for position (i,j); see Fig. 1. Then, the gradient magnitude for the diffusivity calculation can be estimated from the wavelet coefficients w_x and w_y:

$$g_{I,J} = g\big((w_x^\omega)^2 + (w_y^\omega)^2\big) \quad (11)$$

where $\omega = \alpha$ if $(I,J) = (i+1, j+1)$, $\omega = \beta$ for $(I,J) = (i+1, j-1)$, γ for $(i-1, j+1)$, and δ for $(i-1, j-1)$. Finally, the last term from (9) may be expressed using wavelet coefficients as

$$f_{I,J} - f_{i,j} \in \{-w_x^\alpha - w_y^\alpha, \ -w_x^\beta + w_y^\beta, \ w_x^\gamma - w_y^\gamma, \ w_x^\delta + w_y^\delta\} \quad (12)$$

where (I,J) is assigned to the expression involving α, β, γ or δ as above.

To summarise (9)–(12), we can write a single iteration of nonlinear diffusion using the wavelet decomposition components v and w in the form

$$u_{i,j} = \frac{1}{8}\big(v^\alpha + v^\beta + v^\gamma + v^\delta + (w_x^\alpha + w_y^\alpha)(1 - 4\tau g^\alpha) + w_{xy}^\alpha + (w_x^\beta - w_y^\beta)(1 - 4\tau g^\beta)$$

$$- w_{xy}^\beta + (-w_x^\gamma + w_y^\gamma)(1 - 4\tau g^\gamma) - w_{xy}^\gamma + (-w_x^\delta - w_y^\delta)(1 - 4\tau g^\delta) + w_{xy}^\delta\big) \quad (13)$$

where the symbol g^ω stands for $g\big((w_x^\omega)^2 + (w_y^\omega)^2\big)$, $\omega \in \{\alpha, \beta, \gamma, \delta\}$.

Comparing the diffusion iteration (13) and the single-level wavelet shrinkage (4), we observe that the two equations are equivalent under the conditions

$$S(w_x^\omega) = w_x^\omega \left(1 - 4\tau g\big((w_x^\omega)^2 + (w_y^\omega)^2\big)\right), \quad (14)$$

$$S(w_y^\omega) = w_y^\omega \left(1 - 4\tau g\big((w_x^\omega)^2 + (w_y^\omega)^2\big)\right), \quad (15)$$

$$S(w_{xy}^\omega) = w_{xy}^\omega. \quad (16)$$

Equations (14)–(16) connect the diffusivity function g controlling nonlinear diffusion to the shrinkage function S of wavelet shrinkage. If these conditions hold true, the two two-dimensional procedures (limited to a single scale / single iteration) are equivalent.

The equations (14), (15) are similar to the one-dimensional situation which was analysed in detail in [9]. The surprising fact in the 2D equations (14)–(16) is the use of different shrinkage rules for the different channels of wavelet coefficients, while the classical wavelet shrinkage applies the same shrinkage function S to each of them separately. In (14)–(15), the shrinkage of w_x and w_y is interconnected via the common estimation of the image gradient; the third channel, w_{xy}, is left by (16) unshrunken.

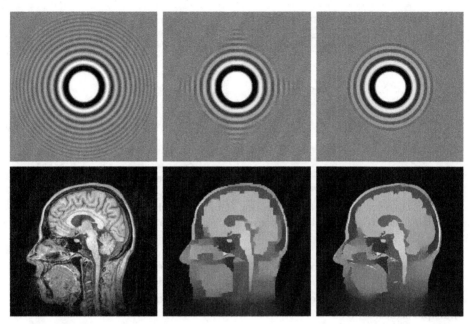

Fig. 2. Experiments on rotation invariance. Left: input image; center: filtered with classical iterated shift invariant wavelet shrinkage; right: method with channels coupled using (14)–(16). Top: ring image, 20 iterations on 8 levels of the wavelet decomposition. Bottom: head image, 100 iterations on 4 levels.

These three shrinkage rules inherit a fundamental property from their diffusion origin: the rotation invariance of the nonlinear diffusion filter. It holds exactly for the grid size tending to zero, but we shall see that this property is also approximated well in realistic discrete situations with non-vanishing grid size. Our diffusion-inspired idea to improve the invariance to rotation by coupling the shrinkage of wavelet channels as in (14)–(16) represents a very simple solution which hardly increases the computational complexity of a wavelet filter.

The diffusion–wavelet connection has been shown for a single iteration of a single-scale filter. In general, nonlinear diffusion is a single-scale iterative process, while wavelet shrinkage finds the solution using a single step on multiple scales. A hybrid multi-scale iterated filter seems a powerful and efficient alternative [5, 4]. It can be understood either as a nonlinear diffusion on the Laplacian pyramid of the signal [13], or as iterated shift-invariant wavelet shrinkage [3]. The rotation invariance of such iterated multiscale filter is tested in the next section.

5   Experiments on Rotation Invariance

In this section we compare the rotation invariance of two wavelet-based filters: the classical iterated translation-invariant 2D wavelet shrinkage (4) with separate shrinkage of the coefficient channels, and the novel filter with shrinkage

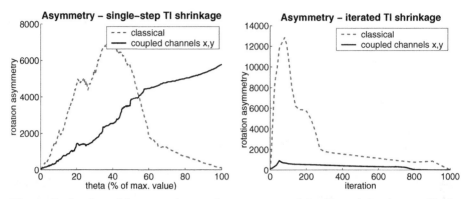

Fig. 3. Evaluation of the errors in rotation symmetry of the filtered ring image. Single-step (left), and iterated (right) shift-invariant wavelet shrinkage.

rules coupled according to (14)–(16). In all cases, we employ the Haar wavelet basis combined with hard thresholding: all coefficients with magnitude below a specified threshold θ are set to zero. The wavelet decomposition is calculated on multiple scales.

In the first experiment, we start from the rotationally symmetric ring image (Fig. 2 top left). Examples of images obtained after 5 iterations of each method are seen in Fig. 2 top. One can observe that using the coupled shrinkage (14)–(16), the filtered result reveals a much better rotational symmetry. The difference between the two methods is further visualised on a medical image at the bottom of Fig. 2. At a comparable level of image simplification, the new method is able to avoid the blocky artefacts of the classical transform.

The graphs in Fig. 3 present a numerical evaluation of the errors in rotational symmetry of the filtered ring image. The measure of asymmetry was calculated as a sum of signal variances along circles of varied diameter, centered at the center of rotation of the input image. In agreement with the design principles, the rotation symmetry of the *iterated* filter with coupled channels is very good (Fig. 3 right), but the coupled shrinkage outperforms the classical transform even using a single step of the multi-scale procedure, if the shrinkage parameter θ is not bigger than 50% of the value which flattens the image completely (Fig. 3 left).

6   Conclusions

In this paper we have addressed one of the main problems that are encountered when 2D wavelet shrinkage methods are to be used: the design of techniques with good rotation invariance. To this end we have established a connection between shift invariant Haar wavelet shrinkage on a single scale and an explicit discretisation of a nonlinear diffusion filter. Since diffusion filtering approximates a rotationally invariant continuous process, we have obtained a technique for constructing shrinkage schemes with a high degree of rotational invariance. It turned out that all one has to do is to modify the shrinkage rules such that two of the wavelet channels are shrunken in a coupled way while the third one is left unaffected. The resulting diffusion-inspired wavelet shrinkage represents a straightforward and computationally efficient solution to the problem of designing rotationally invariant iterated multiscale wavelet shrinkage filters. Our experiments have shown that in this respect it clearly outperforms classical 2D shrinkage methods. In our future work we plan to investigate extensions of this design principle to other wavelets and other discretisations of nonlinear diffusion filters.

References

1. Donoho, D.L., Johnstone, I.M.: Ideal spatial adaptation by wavelet shrinkage. Biometrica **81** (1994) 425–455
2. Coifman, R.R., Donoho, D.: Translation invariant denoising. In Antoine, A., Oppenheim, G., eds.: Wavelets in Statistics. Springer, New York (1995) 125–150
3. Chambolle, A., Lucier, B.L.: Interpreting translationally-invariant wavelet shrinkage as a new image smoothing scale space. IEEE Transactions on Image Processing **10** (2001) 993–1000
4. Mrázek, P., Weickert, J., Steidl, G., Welk, M.: On iterations and scales of nonlinear filters. In Drbohlav, O., ed.: Computer Vision Winter Workshop 2003, Czech Pattern Recognition Society (2003) 61–66
5. Fletcher, A.K., Ramchandran, K., Goyal, V.K.: Wavelet denoising by recursive cycle spinning. In: Proc. IEEE Int. Conf. Image Proc. 2002. (2002)
6. Yu, T., Stoschek, A., Donoho, D.: Translation- and direction- invariant denoising of 2-D and 3-D images: Experience and algorithms. In Unser, M.A., Aldroubi, A., Laine, A.F., eds.: Wavelet Applications in Signal and Image Processing IV. Volume 2825 of SPIE. (1996) 608–619
7. Kingsbury, N.G.: Complex wavelets for shift invariant analysis and filtering of signals. Journal of Applied and Computational Harmonic Analysis **10** (2001) 234–253
8. Starck, J.L., Candès, E.J., Donoho, D.L.: The curvelet transform for image denoising. IEEE Transactions on Image Processing **11** (2002) 670–684
9. Mrázek, P., Weickert, J., Steidl, G.: Correspondences between wavelet shrinkage and nonlinear diffusion. In Griffin, L.D., ed.: Scale-Space Theories in Computer Vision. Lecture Notes in Computer Science. Springer, Berlin (2003)
10. Strang, G., Nguyen, T.: Wavelets and Filter Banks. Wellesley-Cambridge Press (1997)
11. Perona, P., Malik, J.: Scale space and edge detection using anisotropic diffusion. IEEE Transactions on Pattern Analysis and Machine Intelligence **12** (1990) 629–639
12. Keeling, S.L., Stollberger, R.: Nonlinear anisotropic diffusion filters for wide range edge sharpening. Inverse Problems **18** (2002) 175–190
13. Steidl, G., Weickert, J., Brox, T., Mrázek, P., Welk, M.: On the equivalence of soft wavelet shrinkage, total variation diffusion, total variation regularization, and SIDEs. Technical report, Series SPP-1114, Department of Mathematics, University of Bremen, Germany (2003)

Hierarchical Method for Stereophotogrammetric Multi-object-Position Measurement

M. Tornow, B. Michaelis, R.W. Kuhn, R. Calow, and R. Mecke

Otto-von-Guericke-University Magdeburg
Faculty of Electrical Engineering and Information Technology
Institute for Electronics, Signal Processing and Communications (IESK)
PO box 4120, D-39016 Magdeburg, Germany
tornow@iesk.et.uni-magdeburg.de

Abstract. The classical stereophotogrammetric methods based on area correlation are relatively slow if the whole image is analyzed. The new proposed method differs from classical stereophotogrammetric methods in that a hierarchical structure is incorporated in the procedure, so that real-time processing is possible and the relative error is kept reasonably constant even with large variations in one direction (e.g. in road traffic analysis). This is achieved by adapting image resolution to distance. Computation costs are significantly reduced. The method is very suited for implementation in hardware; it runs in real time and can be applied to moving objects that are automatically segmented. The aim of this research project is to reduce the computation power needed although a complex quality criterion is used.

1 Introduction

Area correlation algorithms [1] are typically used for correspondence analysis in stereophotogrammetry. If the algorithms are run with very large variations of distance and if the search area is not restricted in size, the computation cost of the correspondence search will be very high. This is difficult for real-time measurements on quickly changing scenes with the regular occurrence of new objects. Driver-assisting systems [2], [3], [4], [5], [6] for use in road traffic are typical applications.

The position of objects behind an automobile is determined in the application we are dealing with here. We need to establish a mean relative accuracy over a very large measuring range (approximately 10 - 150 m). The detailed structure of the objects can be ignored, as only the mean positions of the objects needs to be calculated. This has to be achieved in a short period (one image capture time) including the new objects too. These requirements cannot be met by using simple tracking algorithms without an exact starting position. Image pairs captured by two cameras are compared using area correlation. The objects are then partitioned out from the distance map by a cluster algorithm and traced over several images (e.g. Kalman filter [7]). The data is then presented to the operator in a convenient format. To allow the driver to react quickly, the system response must be optimized to continually generate the data in real time. In the system the computation power needed is greatly reduced by adapting the image resolution to the distance of the objects in a hierarchical structure.

B. Michaelis and G. Krell (Eds.): DAGM 2003, LNCS 2781, pp. 164–171, 2003.
© Springer-Verlag Berlin Heidelberg 2003

2 Methods of Area Correlation in Stereo Photogrammetry

Image pairs are taken with two calibrated cameras. Each reference block in one image is compared with a search block at different positions in a second image (Fig. 1a). The blocks can be compared with various quality criteria.

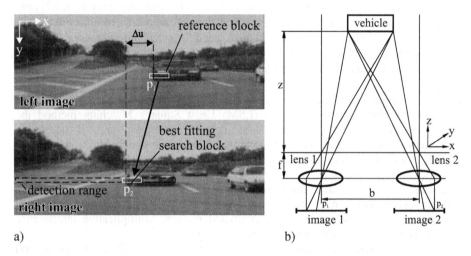

a)   b)

Fig. 1. a) Determining the disparity using area correlation b) The normal case of stereo-photogrammetry

A system of two digital cameras arranged in the normal case of stereophotogrammetry [8] serves for image capture. These two identical gray value cameras take synchronal triggered images in the same plane. The camera axes are aligned parallel to one another. Measurements can only be taken in the common field of view of both cameras. The fields of view of both cameras still overlap at significant distances. Thus, a very large measuring range, which depends to a great extent on the resolution of the cameras, is achieved in one direction (distance z in this case). Fig 1b shows a schematic of such a system.

Selected areas of an image pair are compared to determine the three-dimensional position of an object with respect to the camera positions. The distance to the object can be characterized by the horizontal displacement (disparity) of the best fitting areas in the images. The disparity in the x-direction is called Δu (see Fig. 1) in this paper.

$$\Delta u = |p_1 - p_2| \qquad (1)$$

To reduce the calculation overhead, the images are rectified and compared in one dimension (instead of two dimensions) by the use of epipolar lines. If the camera arrangement cannot be corrected numerically due to constraints on computation power, the cameras must be aligned very accurately with respect to one another, so that the image lines are located sufficiently close to the epipolar lines. It may prove beneficial to take the average of several lines for suitable objects.

Applying the theorem of intersecting lines in the normal case of stereo photogrammetry to the scenario depicted in Fig. 1b, the 3D-position is expressed as

$$z = \frac{f \cdot b}{\Delta u} \; ; \; x = z \cdot \frac{x_{left}}{f} \; ; \; y = z \cdot \frac{y_{left}}{f} \tag{2}$$

Under the specified conditions (additional calibration parameters may be used) only length of base b, focal length f, the x, y -coordinates of the measured object in the left image x_{left}, y_{left} and disparity Δu (Eq. (1)) are needed for calculation purposes. The base b and the focal length are known from the camera setup and calibration, respectively. The x, y -coordinates and Δu are extracted during the calculation.

A quality criterion Q used for finding the corresponding image parts for area correlation is introduced. Using the (LSM) Least Squares Matching method the images are compared by means of an iterative geometric and, if necessary, radiometric transformation between reference block and search block in order to minimize the square sum of the gray value differences between reference block and transformed search block [8].

The simple cross correlation function (KKF) and other quality criteria are subject to additive and multiplicative interference. Additive interference consists of serious differences of intensity between the compared images. Multiplicative interference represents intensity changes within the images.

The normalized zero-mean cross correlation function Eq. (3) (KKFMF) [9] is a good and robust solution to these critical problems. Additive interference between the two images is practically eliminated by the zero-mean representation. Multiplicative interference is greatly reduced by the normalization. The results of the KKFMF are values between -1 and $+1$. A function maximum marks the best affinity.

$$Q = KKFMF(\xi, \eta) = \frac{\sum_{j=0}^{n-1} \sum_{i=0}^{m-1} \left(\overline{F(i,j)} \cdot \overline{P_r(\xi+i, \eta+j)} \right)}{\sqrt{\sum_{j=0}^{n-1} \sum_{i=0}^{m-1} \overline{F(i,j)}^2 \cdot \sum_{j=0}^{n-1} \sum_{i=0}^{m-1} \overline{P_r(\xi+i, \eta+j)}^2}} \tag{3}$$

$\overline{F(j,i)}$ - zero-mean pixel in search block

$\overline{P(j,i)}$ - zero-mean pixel in reference block

m, n - window size

ξ, η - displacement in x, y- direction

Simplifying the normalized zero-mean cross correlation function produces the Moravec criterion [9]. The complex (KKFMF) zero-mean normalized cross correlation function (Eq. (3)) is used for further calculations, as it is most suitable for the application at hand. Because the hardware implementation of the square root function is very difficult, the squared zero-mean normalized cross correlation function is used instead.

3   Reducing the Computation Costs with a Hierarchical Solution

Depending on visibility the measuring range in this application is of the order of some few meters to 150 meters. Whereas far away objects such as automobiles are very small (a few pixels) with correspondingly low disparity values, objects at close range are relatively large with high disparity values.

The use of high resolution for close-range objects can be a hindrance and is normally unnecessary. Therefore we propose to reduce the image resolution for measuring the distance to objects at close range, so that a smaller disparity (measured in pixels for the chosen resolution) reduces the number of correlation values in comparison to that of a full search. The benefits of considerable formalization gained by introducing hierarchical layers [10] are discussed below. The ease of hardware implementation is also covered (Section 4).

3.1   Generating the Hierarchical Layers

Layers with dedicated distance ranges of different resolutions are introduced. Layers are generated by reducing the line resolution by a set factor for each subsequent layer. Fig. 2a shows a typical scheme using ½ as factor. Several neighboring pixels are replaced by one, ratio 2:1 in this example. The resolution can be reduced by means of a weighted function or by calculating the mean value (typical solution). The search area for correlation is increased in higher layers with a constant number of correlation points (Fig. 2b)

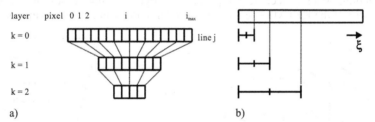

Fig. 2. a) Generating the layers shown in a constructed example b) Search area in different layers

3.2   Correlation and Analysis

To determine the disparity, epipolar lines are correlated, as described above, with their counterparts in the other image of the same resolution. This is always done in each layer in the following order: Rectangular blocks from the reference image and search image are chosen and compared to each other. In the example in Fig. 3, 16x1 pixel dimensioned blocks are used.

The reference block is shifted pixel by pixel over the search region (here 16 pixels) beginning at the start position. An affinity value (preferably: KKFMF, Eq. (3)) is calculated for each resulting pair of patterns. As illustrated in Fig. 3, the pixels are shifted in one line –in this case the epipolar line. The shifting is not done over the full search area. The full search area is only covered by the combination of the correlation results of all layers. The most benefit for hardware implementation is gained when the number of pixels shifted is the same as the size of the reference block. The correlation data from all layers are now assembled for evaluation purposes.

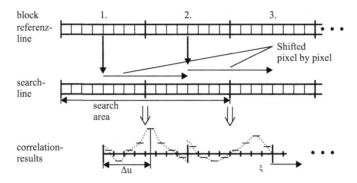

Fig. 3. The correlation procedure (using 8 pixels wide blocks)

The disparity is determined by concatenating the correlation data for a reference block in each layer into a set of results. The procedure can start with either the highest or lowest resolution. In the example shown in Fig. 4 (left) sixteen correlation values are taken for the highest resolution and eight for all other resolutions.

The locations of the corresponding blocks are determined by taking the maxima above a given threshold. This relates to the disparities Δu. Only maxima corresponding with object features (object edges in this case) are used. The denominator of the KKFMF is evaluated in order to determine these positions.

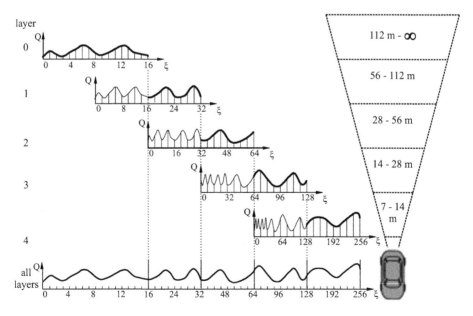

Fig. 4. Concatenating of the quality criterion Q for every layer to one function for estimation of disparities Δu (left), An example of the distance range z covered by every layer (right)

The disparities Δu for the maxima of the quality criterion are then calculated with subpixel accuracy using quadratic interpolation; the 3D coordinates are calculated with Eq. (2). The resulting distance map is then evaluated. Each layer in the hierarchical structure represents a definite measuring range. Measuring ranges for a typical system with a one meter base are shown in Fig 4. (right). It is difficult to define the upper range value for the highest resolution layer because an object has to be at least a few pixels wide. Fig 5. shows a distance map generated by the process described above. Object clustering achieved [11] by using groups of 3D-points. Detailed discussion of other processes such as clustering for segmentation and Kalman filters [7] for tracking is beyond the scope of this paper.

Fig. 5. In this distance map gray values indicate distance (black for close points)

3.3 Accuracy and Errors

Objects at close range are scanned by the coarse resolutions. Objects furthest away (maximum distance for useful measurements) are captured with the initial resolution. Because images from close-range objects are captured with low resolution, the absolute error during 3D-position calculation is increased. The resulting error is inversely proportional to the sensor resolution. The relative measuring error can be plotted as a function of the disparity, as shown in Fig. 6.

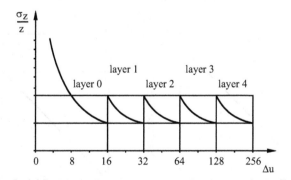

Fig. 6. Plot of relative systematic errors σ_z/z (schematic diagram)

The numerical value of the relative error has been normalized in order to illustrate the general characteristic. Other sources of error include optics, calibration, vibrations from the vehicle, and the like. These values should be added.

4 Suitability for Implementation in Hardware

The above algorithm is suited for implementation in high-speed hardware. Therefore continuous processing and constant dataflow allow constant calculation times to be achieved. This is important for real-time processing of quickly changing scenes. The platform used is the Altera FPGA EPXA10 [12] with approximately 40,000 logic cells and a hardcore ARM 9 processor.

The correlation search can be performed by a single hardware correlator when the algorithm is subdivided and a uniform processing method is chosen. Each layer can be calculated with the same algorithm as the previous layer. The lines of different resolutions described in section 3 can be joined together for correlation – thus allowing linear processing which is more suitable for hardware implementation. The combined line is almost twice as long as the original line. Because of this a doubled pixel clock is needed for the real-time calculation.

The chosen robust quality criterion squared KKFMF (see section 2) can be implemented as a fully parallel and synchronous design in this hardware device. This design enables computation while imaging. The delay between the initial camera pixels and the results is therefore negligible.

The data is then subjected to further complex processing steps in the ARM 9 Processor such as clustering and Kalman filters for tracking. Because the captured imagery depicts rapidly changing scenes, namely fast moving vehicles in road traffic, the incoming data stream needs to be acquired as far as possible in real-time. The hardware-software-co-design described above will achieve this objective.

5 Results

The method was tested under laboratory conditions with a diminished base b as well as in real road scenarios. The results for the z-direction (coordinate of primary interest) for a calibrated system are shown in Figs 7a and 7b.

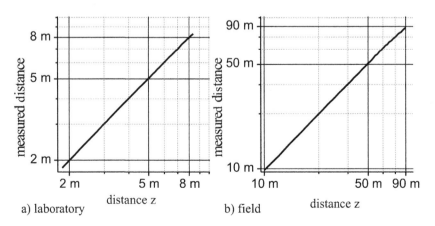

Fig. 7. Laboratory and field tests with different bases b

The mean relative error for the laboratory tests shown in Fig 7a is approximately 0.2 % of the actual distance to the object. The mean relative error from the field tests is in the same order of magnitude. The mechanical adjustment can be corrected by simple calibration equations. Static measurements were taken, whereby the objects were manually moved from position to position. Measurements taken in a moving vehicle confirm the effectiveness of the solution. Further investigations are required to obtain quantitative experimental results with distances from moving objects.

6 Conclusion

The proposed method is very well suited for real-time applications with low percentage errors, where variations in distance are very large. Furthermore, this method yields robust measurements for images containing common image disturbances. Trials have proved the specified attributes. In comparison to a software implementation, investigations have shown that a hardware-software-co-design is a more suitable choice for real-time applications. Driver assistant systems are typical applications.

Acknowledgement. This research project was supported by BMBF grant FKZ 03i1210a, BMBF/LSA grant 0028IF0000 and EU grant 0046KE0000.

References

1. P. Albrecht, B. Michaelis: Improvement of Spatial Resolution of an Optical 3-D Measurement Procedure, IEEE Instrumentation and Measurement vol. 47, 1998, pp. 158-162
2. M. Bertozzi et. al.: Stereo Vision-based Vehicle Detection. Intelligent Vehicle Symposium, 2000, pp. 39-44
3. M. Betke, H. Nguyen: Highway Scene Analysis from a Moving Vehicle under Reduced Visibility Conditions. IEEE International Conference Vehicle, 1998, pp. 131-136
4. B. Ulmer: VITA – An Autonomous Road Vehicle for Collision Avoidance in Traffic, Intelligent Vehicles, 1992 pp. 36-41
5. C. Knppel, U. Regensburger, A. Sc hanz, B. Michaelis, Robuste Erkennung von Straßnfahrzeugen im Rükraum eines   Straßnfahrzeuges DAG Mustererkennung 2000 pp. 35-42
6. U. Franke et. al.: Autonomous Driving Goes Downtown. IEEE Intelligent Systems, Vol. 13, No. 6, 1999, pp. 40-48
7. R. E. Kalman A New Approach to Linear Filtering and Prediction Problems, Sorenson, Kalman-Filtering: Theory and Application IEEE Press 1985
8. T. Luhmann, Nahbereichsphotogrammetrie, Herbert Wichmann Verlag, Heidelberg, 2000 pp. 310, 403, 419
9. P. F. Aschwanden: Experimenteller Vergleich von Korrelationskriterien in der Bildanalyse, Diss. at ETH Zürch, 1993, pp. 20-26
10. M. Tornow, B. Michaelis: Patent Nr. DE 10310849.1 at DPMA.
11. J. van Leuven et. al.: Real-Time Vehicle Tracking in Image Sequences. IEEE Instr. Meas. Technol. Conf., Budapest, Hungary, May 21-23, 2001
12. Altera / ARM :
    http://www.altera.com/products/devices/arm/overview/arm-overview.html

On Robust Regression in Photogrammetric Point Clouds

Konrad Schindler and Horst Bischof

Institute of Computer Graphics and Vision
Graz University of Technology, Austria
{schindl,bischof}@icg.tu-graz.ac.at

Abstract. Many applications in computer vision require robust linear regression on photogrammetrically reconstructed point clouds. Due to the modeling process from perspective images the uncertainty of an object point depends heavily on its location in object space w.r.t. the cameras. Standard algorithms for robust regression are based on distance measures from the regression surface to the points, but these distances are biased by varying uncertainties. In this paper a description of the local object point precision is given and the Mahalanobis distance to a plane is derived to allow unbiased regression. Illustrative examples are presented to demonstrate the effect of the statistically motivated distance measure.

1 Introduction

Several photogrammetric applications require robust surface fitting in 3D point clouds obtained by dense image matching, as for example architectural reconstruction [1] or reverse engineering [2].

Robust fitting algorithms are mostly based on sampling strategies: Hypotheses are generated and their support is measured in the point cloud. Examples for this strategy are the least-median-of-squares (LMS) estimator [3] and different variants of the RANSAC principle [4]. This class of algorithms requires to compute the *support* of each point for a given hypothesis, i.e. the probability that the point is explained by the hypothesis. The simplest form is to assign the probability 1 to all points within a certain threshold distance and 0 to all other points (*voting*). Another popular strategy is to assign each point a probability which is inversely proportional to its distance to the plane (*linear weighting*). The statistically correct procedure is to use the value of the probability density function (*pdf*) at the given distance. In any case computing the support requires a suitable distance measure[1].

We argue that this distance measure must take into account the individual uncertainties of the object points, because they are highly inhomogeneous in

---

[1] It should be mentioned that the same problem exists for robust regression methods which operate in parameter space, namely clustering methods and the Hough transform, where we need a threshold for the clustering radius in the parameter space.

B. Michaelis and G. Krell (Eds.): DAGM 2003, LNCS 2781, pp. 172–178, 2003.

photogrammetric point clouds (see Figure 1). In this paper we treat the basic case of (orthogonal) linear regression. The task to be solved is *optimally fitting an unknown number of planes to a cloud of 3D points with known, individually different variances and covariances.* However the presented ideas are also valid for regression with other parametric surfaces (in fact the distance from a point to a higher-order surface is the distance from the point to the tangent plane through the closest surface point).

NB: Least-squares fitting as a postprocessing step may in many cases alleviate, but not solve the problem, because it requires a correct partitioning of the point cloud into inliers and outliers, and this partitioning is based on the support computed during robust regression. It has been suggested to use a generous threshold for the inliers and compute the fit with an M-estimator [5]. However it seems an awkward strategy to approximately detect inliers with a robust method, re-include some outliers and fit with another robust method, instead of cleanly dividing the task into two steps, one for robust detection of the correct point set and one for optimal fitting.

The paper is organized as follows: in section 2 we briefly review the uncertainty propagation of the photogrammetric reconstruction process. In section 3 we derive the Mahalanobis distance to a plane, and in section 4 we illustrate the difference between the use of the Mahalanobis distance and the geometric distance.

2   Uncertainty of Photogrammetric Points

This section is a brief recapitulation of the uncertainty propagation in the photogrammetric reconstruction process. For lack of space we refer to photogrammetric textbooks, e.g. [6] for details. A measured image point is described by its coordinates and the covariance matrix

$$\mathbf{x} = [x, y]^{\mathsf{T}} \quad , \quad \mathbf{S_{xx}} = \begin{bmatrix} s_{xx} & s_{xy} \\ s_{xy} & s_{yy} \end{bmatrix} \tag{1}$$

Different image points are assumed to be statistically independent. A 3D point $\mathbf{u}$ is constructed from N image points by intersecting their viewing rays, i.e. solving the $2 \times N$ collinearity equations for $\mathbf{u}$. This gives an overdetermined (nonlinear) equation system which is linearized with the Jacobian $\mathbf{A}$ of the collinearity equations

$$\mathbf{Au} = \mathbf{b} \quad , \quad \mathbf{b} = \begin{bmatrix} \mathbf{x}_1 \dots \mathbf{x}_n \end{bmatrix}^{\mathsf{T}} \tag{2}$$

and solved through iterative least-squares adjustment[2]. Error propagation gives a linear approximation $\mathbf{S_{uu}}$ for the covariance matrix of the estimated 3D point coordinates.

---

[2] An elegant formulation in homogeneous coordinates has recently been published by Förstner [7].

$$\mathbf{u} = \mathbf{S_{uu}} \mathbf{A}^T \mathbf{S_{bb}^{-1}} \mathbf{b} \quad , \quad \mathbf{S_{uu}} = (\mathbf{A}^T \mathbf{S_{bb}^{-1}} \mathbf{A})^{-1} \tag{3}$$

From equation 3 we can see that the uncertainty of point $\mathbf{u}$, through the collinearity equations, depends on the camera positions. The uncertainty is low, if the point is close to the cameras and if the intersection angles between different rays are close to 90 degrees. Typically dense point clouds are generated from image sequences with short baselines in order to enable automatic matching with area-based correlation. In such a recording setup the depth has the highest uncertainty. Moreover, if the camera path is (nearly) linear, e.g. in turntable sequences or when recording buildings from ground level, the depth is highly correlated with the direction of camera motion, so that covariances *cannot* be neglected. Figure 1 shows a prototypical setup, which we will use as an example.

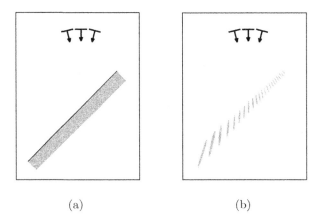

(a)   (b)

Fig. 1. Typical recording setup for automatic reconstruction. (a) Top view of cameras and recorded object plane. (b) Reconstructed points, given by error ellipsoids. The gray ellipses are the projections of the error ellipsoids onto the x, z-plane, computed for a image measurement accuracy of 1:1000. The error ellipsoids are scaled by a factor 10 to make the figure easier to read.

3   Mahalanobis Distance to a Plane

The point coordinates and covariance matrix describe the point position in space with a 3-dimensional probability distribution. The point is thus given by

$$\mathbf{u} = [u, v, w]^T \quad , \quad \mathbf{S_{uu}} = \begin{bmatrix} s_{uu} & s_{uv} & s_{uw} \\ s_{uv} & s_{vv} & s_{vw} \\ s_{uw} & s_{vw} & s_{ww} \end{bmatrix} \tag{4}$$

Let the plane hypothesis in homogeneous coordinates be denoted by $\mathbf{p} = (p_1, p_2, p_3, p_4)$, where $h_{\mathbf{p}} = \sqrt{p_1^2 + p_2^2 + p_3^2}$ is the homogeneous scale. Since the goal of the distance measure is to determine the probability that a point belongs to the plane, the distance measure must take into account the uncertainty of each individual point. This is achieved by the Mahalanobis distance [8] – for a more detailed treatment of its role in optimal geometric fitting see [5]. The Mahalanobis distance from an uncertain point $\mathbf{x}$ to a given point $\bar{\mathbf{x}}$ (in Euclidian coordinates) is defined as

$$d_M^2 = (\mathbf{x} - \bar{\mathbf{x}})^\mathsf{T} \mathbf{S}_{\mathbf{xx}}^{-1} (\mathbf{x} - \bar{\mathbf{x}}) \tag{5}$$

To get the Mahalanobis distance to a plane, we have to apply a whitening transform and normalization to the covariance matrix $\mathbf{S}_{\mathbf{uu}}$ and the plane (geometrically this means warping the error ellipsoid to a unit sphere). The centering is simply a shift from $\mathbf{u}$ to $(0, 0, 0)^\mathsf{T}$. Since the covariance matrix $\mathbf{S}_{\mathbf{uu}}$ is symmetric, its singular value decomposition (SVD) directly gives the rotation R and the scale V.

$$\mathbf{S}_{\mathbf{uu}} = \mathsf{R}^\mathsf{T} \mathsf{V} \mathsf{R} \quad , \quad \mathsf{V} = diag(a^2, b^2, c^2) \tag{6}$$

R aligns the coordinate system with the ellipsoid axes, while the elements a, b, c of V compensate for the non-uniform scale along different axes. We can now write the transformation as a product of homogeneous 4×4 matrices

$$\mathsf{R}_h = \begin{bmatrix} \mathsf{R} & \mathbf{0} \\ \mathbf{0}^\mathsf{T} & 1 \end{bmatrix} \quad , \quad \mathsf{T}_h = \begin{bmatrix} \mathsf{I} & \mathbf{0} \\ -\mathbf{u}^\mathsf{T} & 1 \end{bmatrix} \quad , \quad \mathsf{A}_h = diag(a, b, c, 1) \tag{7}$$

and transform the plane $\mathbf{p}$ to a new plane $\mathbf{q} = \mathsf{A}_h \mathsf{R}_h \mathsf{T}_h \mathbf{p}$. The Mahalanobis distance is the distance from the transformed plane $\mathbf{q}$ to the center of the unit sphere, which lies in the origin of the new coordinate system (see Figure 2).

$$d_M(\mathbf{u}) = \frac{q_4}{\sqrt{q_1^2 + q_2^2 + q_3^2}} \tag{8}$$

Lacking a more qualified *pdf*, we recur to the common approximation of normally distributed image measurement errors (although it is theoretically questionable). In first-order approximation the distances from the points to the plane, being functions of the image point coordinates, also follow a normal distribution. A points support for the plane is thus determined by the percentile rank of $d_M(\mathbf{u})$ in the normalized Gaussian probability density function:

$$S(\mathbf{u}) = 1 - \frac{1}{\sqrt{2\pi}} \int\limits_{-d_M(\mathbf{u})}^{+d_M(\mathbf{u})} e^{-\frac{t^2}{2}} dt = \sqrt{\frac{2}{\pi}} \int\limits_{-\infty}^{-d_M(\mathbf{u})} e^{-\frac{t^2}{2}} dt \tag{9}$$

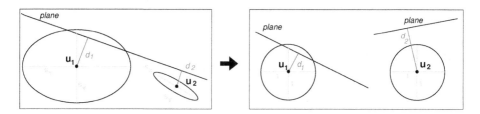

Fig. 2. Comparing distances in the presence of varying point precision. The probability of belonging to the plane is higher for point $\mathbf{u}_1$ than for point $\mathbf{u}_2$ although $d_1 > d_2$. After transforming the error ellipsoids to unit spheres the distance measures correctly reflect the probabilities.

The total support for a plane in a point set $\{\mathbf{u}_1, \mathbf{u}_2, \ldots, \mathbf{u}_n\}$ is the sum of the support values $S(\mathbf{u}_i)$.

$$S_{\mathbf{p}} = \sqrt{\frac{2}{\pi}} \sum_{i=1}^{n} \int_{-\infty}^{-d_M(\mathbf{u}_i)} e^{-\frac{t^2}{2}} dt \qquad (10)$$

4   Examples

In this section we give two examples of how regression with the Mahalanobis distances $d_M(\mathbf{u})$ differs from regression with the plain geometric distances $d(\mathbf{u})$. We will use the synthetic data set shown in Figure 1. Sampling-based regression algorithms instantiate many planes and test their support in the point set. The instantiation is usually done from a minimal set of 3 points. Note however that this is not relevant for the statistical properties. The planes can be arbitrarily derived and are error-free hypotheses.

The first example in Figure 3(a) illustrates the task of separating inliers from outliers. The continuous line marks the plane hypothesis we want to evaluate. If we use the geometric distance, all points within the threshold t are considered inliers, the rest are outliers. The two points marked X and Y are classified as outliers, while the point marked Z is classified as inlier. Statistically this is not correct – the probability of being incident to the plane is higher for X and Y than for Z. Thresholding the Mahalanobis distance is equivalent to a χ^2-test and correctly divides the point set into inliers and outliers according to the probabiliy of being incident to the plane.

The second example illustrates the problem of choosing the correct threshold. The two planes depicted in Figure 3(b) by continuous lines are two possible plane hypothesis. Plane A has been randomly instantiated from the leftmost three points, while plane B has been instantiated from the rightmost 3 points. One can clearly see that plane B is a more probable estimate and should be preferred, as it explains more points within their uncertainty. The discriminative power of the sampling procedure, i.e. the ability to discriminate the better solution from

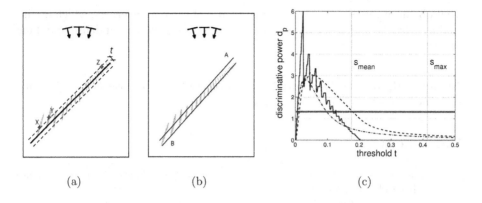

(a)   (b)   (c)

Fig. 3. Geometric distance vs. Mahalanobis distance. See text for explanation.

the worse one when comparing them, depends on the thresholds. It is a critical task to choose a threshold, which selects a good estimate without discarding too many inliers. Figure 3(c) shows the discriminative power as a function of the threshold for different weighting functions. The evaluated functions are

- voting (continuous line): $S(\mathbf{u}) = \{\, 1 \ldots \text{if } d(\mathbf{u}) \leq t \,,\, 0 \ldots \text{else} \,\}$
- linear weighting (dashed): $S(\mathbf{u}) = \max(\, (1 - d(\mathbf{u})/t) \,,\, 0\,)$
- Gaussian weighting (dotted): $S(\mathbf{u}) = 2\, cdf_{\text{Gauss},\mu=0,\sigma=t}(-d(\mathbf{u}))$

The discriminative power is defined as $p_d = (S_B/S_A - 1)$, values close to 0 mean that no reliable discrimination is possible. The horizontal line denotes the constant discriminative power of the Mahalanobis distance, which does not need a threshold. The two vertical lines indicate the mean standard deviation s_{mean} estimated from $S_{\mathbf{uu}}$ (the minimum threshold to make sure that more than half of the inliers are detected) and the maximum standard deviation s_{max} (the threshold we would have to choose to include all inliers). One can clearly see that a threshold with a reasonable discriminative power $d_p > 1$ leads to an incomplete inlier set and thus to a biased fit.

5   Concluding Remarks

We have investigated the influence of uncertainties on sampling-based regression methods in photogrammetric point clouds and derived the Mahalanobis distance from a point to a plane in order to correctly take the uncertainties of individual points into account during regression. Two prototypical examples have been shown to demonstrate the implications of the statistical nature of the point cloud.

We have assumed Gaussian noise of the image measurements. This is a common assumption, however there is no theoretical foundation for it, even less, if the points are derived automatically through a matching procedure. Furthermore it would be desirable to investigate the influence of systematic errors, which are introduced by the smoothness and ordering constraints [9], [10] of dense matching algorithms.

Acknowledgments. This work has been supported by the European Commission under contract No. IST-1999-20273.

References

1. Werner, T., Zisserman, A.: New techniques for automated architecture reconstruction from photographs. In: Proc. 7th ECCV, Copenhagen. (2002)
2. Varady, T., Martin, R., Cox, J.: Reverse engineering of geometric models - an introduction. Computer Aided Design **29** (1997) 255–268
3. Rousseeuw, P., Leroy, A.: Robust Regression and Outlier Detection. John Wiley and Sons (1987)
4. Fischler, M., Bolles, R.: RANSAC random sampling concensus: A paradigm for model fitting with applications to image analysis and automated cartography. Communications of ACM **26** (1981) 381–395
5. Triggs, B.: A new approach to geometric fitting. Available from http://www.inrialpes.fr/movi/people/Triggs (1998)
6. Kraus, K.: Photogrammetrie, Band 1. Dümmler Verlag (1994)
7. Förstner, W.: Algebraic projective geometry and direct optimal estimation of geometric entities. In: Proc. 25th AAPR Workshop, Berchtesgaden. (2001) 67–86
8. Duda, R.O., Hart, P., Stork, D.: Pattern Classification. John Wiley and Sons (2001)
9. Ohta, Y., Kanade, T.: Stereo by intra- and inter-scanline search. Pattern Analsis and Machine Intelligence **7** (1985) 139–154
10. Yuille, A., Poggio, T.: A generalized ordering constraint for stereo correspondence. MIT, A.I. Memo 777 (1984)

A Visual Quality Inspection System Based on a Hierarchical 3D Pose Estimation Algorithm

Clemens von Bank, Dariu M. Gavrila, and Christian Wöhler

DaimlerChrysler Research and Technology, P. O. Box 2360, D-89013 Ulm, Germany

Abstract. This paper presents a quality inspection system based on an efficient model and view based algorithm for locating objects in images and estimating their pose. Off-line, edge templates are generated from a 3D model. On-line, a hierarchical edge template matching technique generates matching solutions from which the pose of the object is derived. This approach tackles the difficult typical trade-off between tesselation size and efficiency. The proposed method works for arbitrarily shaped 3D objects. The accuracy of pose estimation exceeds that of state-of-the-art algorithms even if the objects are viewed on a cluttered background. Since no high-level feature extraction is required, the algorithm is robust against changing ambient conditions such as illumination. The inspection system is successfully tested on two real-world inspection scenarios in the engine production.

1 Introduction

The aim of the visual inspection system described in this paper is to identify an object and to estimate its pose in order to determine whether it has been correctly assembled in the production process. The inputs to the system are the 3D model of the object and an image of the scene. Numerous approaches have been proposed in the literature for solving such a recognition task. These approaches can be categorized in two ways: a) according to the representation of the data, and b) according to the method for matching.

Data representation schemes can be divided into viewer-centered and object-centered representations (for surveys see [3], [6], [9], [13]). In an object-centered representation all features of an object are described with respect to a coordinate system fixed relative to the object. The advantage of such a representation is that only one model is required to fully describe the object. However, the visibility of object features in images is viewpoint dependent due to self occlusion. Viewer-centered representations implicitly account for self occlusion by representing an object as a set of views taken by a (virtual) camera. The main drawback of a viewer-centered representation is the large number of views required to describe an object.

Once the data is represented in a certain scheme, an appropriate matching strategy has to be chosen. Tree searching [11], graph matching [17], and indexing techniques [8] are well known methods for symbolic matching. They have been successfully used to recognize objects in arbitrary poses based on pose-invariant

B. Michaelis and G. Krell (Eds.): DAGM 2003, LNCS 2781, pp. 179–186, 2003.

features (e.g. angle between two planar surfaces). However, symbolic matching has two major drawbacks: a) there is no systematic way to automatically determine robust, pose-invariant features from a 3D model, and b) high-level feature extraction in image data is difficult.

In addition to symbolic matching, there are other techniques for matching low-level features. Geometric Hashing [16] provides an efficient method for setting up a correspondence between a set of characteristic model points and a set of scene points by multiply encoding the model with respect to various normalizations. However, finding points which describe an object sufficiently well and which can be reliably extracted from range images is difficult. Another method for matching two sets of 3D points is the Iterative Closest Point (ICP) algorithm [4] which is often applied to registration. The ICP algorithm requires a good initialization in order to avoid getting stuck in local minima of the error function.

Concerning applications of such methods, template matching techniques are employed for medical purposes for pose estimation of artificial implants [12]. In the field of industrial quality inspection, robot systems are used for optical measurement (e. g. photogrammetry) purposes based on 2D images and 3D range data of industrial parts [5]. CAD data is used to generate the corresponding 3D models. The described applications, however, primarily involve localization and gauging of the inspected objects rather than pose estimation. In [1] a vision-based automatic assembly unit is presented in which a pose estimation of industrial parts is performed by combining an adapted eigenspace method to obtain an initial estimation and a model-based technique for refinement. This algorithm, however, requires that the objects are put on a uniform background.

In this paper a viewer-centered representation of the image data is chosen. The views are generated automatically from a 3D object model with a virtual camera; edge templates are computed for each view. The difficult trade-off between tesselation constant and accuracy of pose estimation is alleviated by a technique for hierarchical template matching [10]. The described method is applied to two real-world industrial quality inspection tasks.

2   The Hierarchical Chamfer Matching Algorithm

The input image first undergoes an edge detection procedure. A Distance Transform (DT) then converts the segmented binary edge image into a so-called distance image. The distance image encodes the distance in the image plane of each image point to its nearest edge point. If we denote the set of all points in the image as $A = \{a_1, \cdots, a_N\}$ and the set of all edge points as $B = \{b_1, \cdots, b_M\}$ with $B \subseteq A$ then the distance $d(a_n, B)$ for point a_n is given by

$$d(a_n, B) = \min(\|a_n - b_m\|, \ \forall \, m = 1, \cdots, M) \tag{1}$$

where $\| \cdot \|$ is a norm on the points of A and B (e.g. the Euclidean norm). For numerical simplicity we use the so called chamfer-2-3 metric [2] to approximate the Euclidean metric.

The chamfer distance $D_C(T, B)$ between an edge template consisting of a set of edge points $T = \{t_1, \cdots, t_Q\}$ with $T \subseteq A$ and the input edge image is given by:

$$D_C(T, B) = \frac{1}{Q} \sum_{n=1}^{Q} d(t_n, B) \tag{2}$$

In applications, a template is considered matched at locations where the distance measure ("dissimilarity") $D(T, I)$ is below a user-supplied threshold θ. To reduce false detections, the distance measure was extended to include oriented edges [10].

In order to recognize an object with unknown rotation and translation, a set of transformed templates must be correlated with the distance image. Each template is derived from a certain rotation of the 3D object. In previous work, a uniform tesselation often involved the difficult choice for the value of the tesselation constant. If one chooses a relatively large value, the views that lie "in between" grid points on the viewing sphere will not be properly represented in the regions where the aspect graph is undergoing rapid changes. This will decrease the accuracy of the measured pose angles. On the other hand, if one chooses a relatively small value for the tesselation constant, this will result in a large number of templates to be matched online; matching all these templates sequentially will be computationally intensive and prohibitive to any real-time performance.

Here, the difficult trade-off regarding tesselation constant is alleviated by a technique for hierarchical template matching, introduced in [10]. That technique, designed for DT-based matching, aims to derive a representation off-line which exploits any structure in a particular template distribution, so that, on-line, matching can proceed optimized. This is done by grouping similar templates together and representing them by two entities: a "prototype" template and a distance parameter. When applied recursively, this grouping leads to a template hierarchy. It is built bottom-up, level by level using a partitional clustering algorithm based on simulated annealing.

Online, matching involves traversing the tree structure of templates. Each node corresponds to matching a (prototype) template $\mathbf{p}$ with the image at some particular locations. For the locations where the distance measure between template and image is below a user-supplied threshold θ_p, one computes new interest locations for the children nodes (generated by sampling the local neighborhood with a finer grid) and adds the children nodes to the list of nodes to be processed. For locations where the distance measure is above the threshold, search does not propagate to the sub-tree; it is this pruning capability that brings large efficiency gains. Further details and applications of this algorithm to object detection in outdoor scenes are described in [10].

In our system, we do not need to estimate scale – the distance to the object is known at an accuracy of better than 3 percent due to the fact that the parts are transported on a conveyor belt. Template matching does not have to search all scales explicitly. Hence, the original pose estimation problem of determining

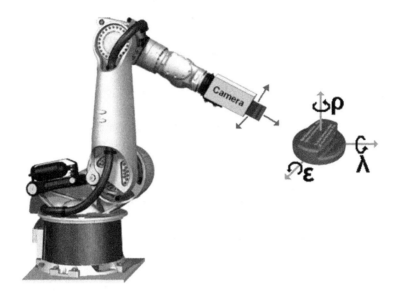

Fig. 1. Sketch of the robot-based inspection system with a definition of the pose angles ϵ (elevation), ρ (rotation), and λ (latitude) in the camera coordinate system.

Table 1. Properties of the three oil cap template hierarchies (ranges of pose angles ρ, ϵ, λ and tesselations constants in degrees). Hierarchy 1 consists of 4550 templates, hierarchies 2 and 3 of 1331 templates, respectively.

no.	ρ range	$\Delta\rho$	ϵ range	$\Delta\epsilon$	λ range	$\Delta\lambda$
1	$0°\dots180°$	$2°$	$18°\dots72°$	$6°$	$-12°\dots+12°$	$6°$
2	$0°\dots20°$	$2°$	$30°\dots50°$	$2°$	$-10°\dots+10°$	$2°$
3	same as 2, but without writing modelled					

6 degrees of freedom (DOF) can be reduced to a 5 DOF (3 pose angles and 2 image position coordinates) problem.

For pose fine tuning, the pose angles are interpolated between the n_b "best" template matching solutions, with $n_b = 30$ in our system. This is justified because in our pose estimation scenario the dissimilarity values of the 30 best solutions usually do not differ by more than about 20% and thus all these solutions contain a significant amount of information about the pose.

In many applications, templates are generated from real-world image data [7]. For inspection tasks, however, one can assume that a CAD model of the object to be inspected is available. We therefore generate realistic 2D templates from CAD data using the public domain software POVRAY [15], simulating the properties of the surface material and the illumination conditions by employing raytracing techniques. The pose of the object is defined by the three angles ρ (rotation), ϵ (elevation), and λ (latitude), as shown in Fig. 1.

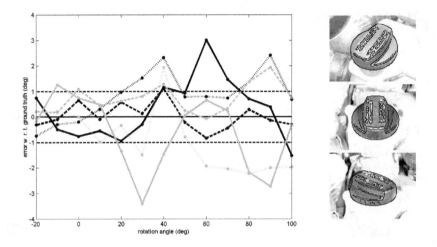

Fig. 2. Left: Deviations of ϵ (solid lines), ρ (dashed lines), and λ (dotted lines) from their ground truth values. Illumination is with cylindric lamp only (black lines) and with both cylindic and halogene lamp (gray lines). The true elevation angle is constantly set to $\epsilon = 70°$. Right: Matching results (best solution) for several poses of the oil cap.

3   Applications

In the oil cap application scenario, we make use of a calibrated robot system. The accuracy of calibration with respect to the world coordinate system is about $0.1°$ with respect to camera orientation and 0.1 mm with respect to camera position. As the engine itself is not part of the robot system, the relation between world coordinate system and engine coordinate system has to be established separately, which reduces the accuracies stated above by about an order of magnitude.

First, the difference between the measured and the true pose of the correctly assembled oil cap is determined depending on the camera viewpoint and the illumination conditions. The scene is illuminated by a cylindric lamp around the camera lens and a halogene spot. The background of the scene may be rather cluttered. For this examination we use template hierarchy 1 (cf. Table 1). For camera viewpoints with $-10° \le \rho \le 10°$ and $50° \le \epsilon \le 60°$, the measured pose lies within the calibration accuracy interval of $1°$ for all three angles. Fig. 2 shows that for $\epsilon = 70°$, this is even true for $-20° \le \rho \le 20°$. This implies that from a correspondingly chosen viewpoint, the algorithm is highly sensitive with respect to deviations from the reference pose. Hence, it is possible to determine the pose of the oil cap to an accuracy of about $1°$. For comparison, the state-of-the-art technique for pose estimation of industrial parts presented in [1] yields pose errors of about $3°$ even when the object is put on a uniform background. Significantly changing the illumination conditions by switching off the halogene lamp does not affect the pose estimation results. The computation time of the system amounts to about 200 ms on a Pentium IV 2.4 GHz processor.

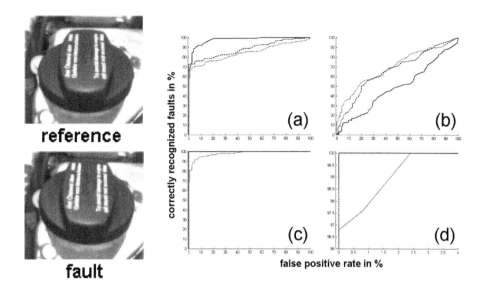

Fig. 3. Left: Reference pose of the oil cap along with the examined typical fault situation. Right: ROC curves of the inspection system, based on measured values of (a) elevation, (b) rotation, (c) latitude, (d) all three pose angles. Solid, dashed, and dotted lines denote three different camera viewpoints. Note that the axis scaling in (d) is different from that in (a)-(c).

As the described system aims at distinguishing incorrect from correct poses, i. e. performing a corresponding classification of the inspected object, the rate of correctly recognized faults (the rate of incorrectly assembled oil caps which are recognized as such by the inspection system) is determined versus the rate of correctly assembled objects erroneously classified as incorrectly assembled (false positive rate). This representation of the system behaviour is called ROC (receiver operating characteristics) curve. We determine the recognition behaviour of the system for three different camera viewpoints. Here, we will concentrate on a typical fault situation showing angle differences $\Delta\rho = 0°$, $\Delta\epsilon = 2.5°$, $\Delta\lambda = -3.5°$ with respect to the reference pose. In the production environment, the engine and thus the attached oil cap is positioned with a tolerance of about 1 cm with respect to the camera. This random positional inaccuracy was simulated by acquiring 125 different frames of each examined fault situation from 125 camera positions inside a cube of 1 cm size which are equally spaced at 2.5 mm in each coordinate direction. This offset is taken into account appropriately in the pose estimation based on the measured position of the oil cap in the image. As a first step, a fault is assigned based on each of the three angles separately if the corresponding angle deviates from the reference value by more than a given threshold. By varying this threshold, a ROC curve is generated for each angle separately as shown in Fig. 3 right, (a)-(c). We then generate a combined ROC curve by assuming that the oil cap is assembled incorrectly if the deviation of

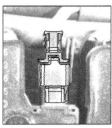

Fig. 4. Ignition plug inspection: Reference configuration (left) and three fault configurations with the corresponding matching results, using two templates. Image scale is 0.2 mm per pixel.

at least one of the pose angles is larger than the corresponding threshold. These thresholds are then adjusted such that the area under the ROC curve becomes maximum. This generally yields a ROC curve showing very few misclassifications on the acquired test set, as illustrated in Fig. 3 right, (d). Both with template hierarchy 1 that covers a wide range of pose angles with a large tesselation constant, and with hierarchy 2 that covers with a small tesselation constant only a region on the viewing sphere close to the reference view (cf. Table 1), very high recognition rates close to 100 percent can be achieved. With hierarchy 3, which is identical to hierarchy 2 except that the writing on top of the oil cap has been omitted, the performance decreases, but not significantly: At a false positive rate of 0%, still a rate of correctly recognized faults of 98.4% is achieved.

For inspection of the ignition plug, we regard in addition to the reference configuration three fault configurations: The clip is not fixed, the plug is loose, and the plug is missing (Fig. 4). The connector and the plug are modelled as two separate objects such that the offset of the plug in y direction can be used to distinguish fault configurations from the reference configuration. The matching results in Fig. 4 show that the y position of the plug relative to the connector can be determined an accuracy of about 0.5 mm, which is sufficient to faithfully distinguish correctly from incorrectly assembled ignition plugs.

4 Conclusion

This paper presented a system for industrial quality inspection based on an approach to object recognition and pose estimation by two-dimensional edge-based template matching, with templates generated from CAD data. The behaviour of the system was robust, without sacrificing for efficiency. The usual high cost of template matching was dramatically reduced by a hierarchical edge matching scheme based on distance transforms, allowing close to real-time performance. Compared to similar techniques used for template matching in intenstiy images, this method has the main advantage that even significant changes in the illumination need not be considered in the matching process as long as the object contours are perceivable. In contrast to most state-of-the-art techniques for pose estimation, no initialization of the algorithm with an approximate pose known a-priori is necessary.

We have regarded two real-world industrial inspection scenarios in the context of engine production. In the first scenario, the system recognizes if an oil cap has been correctly assembled to the engine. The second scenario deals with the inspection of an ignition plug. Our results are encouraging and suggest that the system is suitable for a wide variety of further inspection tasks.

References

1. G. Bachler, M. Berger, R. Röhrer, S. Scherer, A. Pinz. A Vision Driven Automatic Assembly Unit. *Proc. International Conference on Computer Analysis of Images and Patterns*, pages 375–382, Ljubljana, Slovenia, 1999.
2. H. Barrow. Parametric correspondence and chamfer matching: two new techniques for image matching. In *Proc. International Joint Conference on Artificial Intelligence*, pages 659–663, 1977.
3. P. J. Besl and R. C. Jain. Three-dimensional object recognition. *Computing Surveys*, 17(1):75–145, 1985.
4. P. J. Besl and N. D. McKay. A method for registration of 3-d shapes. *IEEE Transactions on Pattern Analysis and Machine Intelligence*, 14(2):239–256, 1992.
5. C. Brenner, J. Böhm, J. Gühring. An experimental measurement system for industrial inspection of 3D parts. *Photonics Fast, Intelligent Systems and Advanced Manufacturing (ISAM)*, vol. 3521, *SPIE*, Boston, 1998.
6. R. T. Chin and C. R. Dyer. Model-based recognition in robot vision. *Computing Surveys*, 18(1):67–108, 1986.
7. C. Demant. Industrial Image Processing. Springer-Verlag, Berlin, 1999.
8. P. J. Flynn and A. K. Jain. 3d object recognition using invariant feature indexing of interpretation tables. *CVGIP: Image Understanding*, 55(2):119–129, 1992.
9. P. J. Flynn and A. K. Jain. Three-dimensional object recognition. In T. Y. Young, editor, *Handbook of Pattern Recognition and Image Processing: Computer Vision*, pages 497–541. Academic Press, 1994.
10. D. Gavrila and V. Philomin. Real-time Object Detection for "Smart" Vehicles. In *Proc. International Conference on Computer Vision*, pages 87–93, Kerkyra, 1999.
11. W. E. L. Grimson. The combinatorics of object recognition in cluttered environments using constrained search. *Artificial Intelligence*, 44(1–2):121–165, 1990.
12. W. A. Hoff, R. D. Komistek, D. A. Dennis, S. Walker, E. Northcut, K. Spargo. Pose Estimation of Artificial Knee Implants in Fluoroscopy Images Using a Template Matching Technique. *Proc. of the 3rd IEEE Workshop on Applications of Computer Vision*, pages 181–186, Sarasota, Florida, 1996.
13. X. Jiang and H. Bunke. *Dreidimensionales Computersehen*. Springer-Verlag, Berlin, 1997.
14. J. J. Koenderink and A. J. van Doorn. The internal representation of solid shape with respect to vision. *Biological Cybernetics*, 32:211–216, 1979.
15. POV-Ray: The Persistence of Vision Raytracer, http://www.povray.org
16. H. J. Wolfson and I. Rigoutsos. Geometric hashing: An overview. *IEEE Computational Science and Engineering*, 4(4):10–21, 1997.
17. E. K. Wong. Model matching in robot vision by subgraph isomorphism. *Pattern Recognition*, 25(3):287–303, 1992.

Using an Active Shape Structural Model for Biometric Sketch Recognition

Stephan Al-Zubi, Arslan Brömme, and Klaus Tönnies

Computer Vision Group
Department of Simulation and Graphics
Otto-von-Guericke University of Magdeburg, Germany
{stephan,arslan.broemme,klaus}@isg.uni-magdeburg.de

Abstract. A deformable shape model called Active Shape Structural
Model (ASSM) is used within a biometric framework to define a biometric sketch recognition algorithm. Experimental results show that mainly
structural relations rather than statistical features can be used to recognize sketches of different users with high accuracy.

1 Introduction

Many deformable shape models have been developed in recent years and used for
segmentation, motion tracking, reconstruction and comparison between shapes:

1. Statistical models use prior knowledge about shape variation for reconstruction [6]. The restriction in statistical models is that they describe the statistical variations of a fixed-structure shape and not structural shape variation.
2. Dynamic models fit shape data using built-in smoothness constraints [10].
   They are able to segment and sample shapes of complex topology like blood
   vessels. They cannot characterize shapes neither statistically nor structurally.
3. Structural models extract structural features to compare and classify shapes
   [13]. The structural models are data driven in that they have no prior knowledge about shape structure. They do not describe shapes they fit statistically.

In our previous work we defined a multi-resolution shape model called Active
Shape Structural Model (ASSM) [1,2] and the core biometric processes within
biometric authentication systems [5]. ASSM defines a-priori knowledge about the
shape both at the structural and the statistical level. It enables statistical models
to represent structural variability and structural models to represent prior shape
knowledge. We have applied ASSM to sketch recognition in [1]. We propose here
to apply ASSM in the field of biometrics as a sketch authentication system.

A biometric authentication system can be considered as a part of an IT in-
frastructure where a person is subjected to a general authentication process for
receiving e.g. access rights to IT system resources, activity regulations and information non-repudiation within electronic business processes, or the permission
to pass a gate or to enter a place or room. The *general authentication process* can

B. Michaelis and G. Krell (Eds.): DAGM 2003, LNCS 2781, pp. 187–195, 2003.

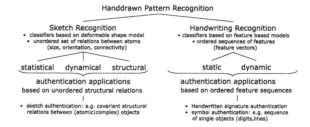

Fig. 1. Classification of Biometric Sketch Authentication Applications

be divided into the five subsequent phases: *enrollment, (biometric) authentication, authorization, access control*, and *derollment and authorization withdrawal* [5]. During the phase of *enrollment* appropriate biometric raw data of a person is captured, the biometric signature (template) for the biometric authentication is computed, and the relevant biometric and personal data is stored in a biometric database [4]. A person's authenticity is checked by an identification (1:c) or verification (1:1) comparison of the actually computed biometric signature with the biometric signature class in the phase of *biometric authentication* potentially being combined with authentication methods based on a person's knowledge, possessions, location, and time. Implicit and explicit authorizations are given to the person in the *authorization* phase with respect to strong and weak authorizations. In the *access control* phase the access to e.g. IT system resources or activity control within electronic business processes is granted by an *access management system*. In the phase of *derollment and authorization withdrawal* a person is derolled and the person's access rights are removed.

Sketches were chosen for the biometric authentication system because they are a very simple and intuitive way to represent secret information. They are easy to remember and draw. Sketches are gaining increasing importance with the shift to pen based interface as palm and tablet computers are proliferating. Currently sketching systems are employed in the field of design such as: Design of user interfaces [9], recognizing mechanical designs [3] and content based image retrieval [11]. Many sketching systems restrict sketch recognition to simple shape primitives like a square, circle, polygons or specific shapes [3,7]. ASSM describes sketches statistically allowing complex and uniform shape description.

We define a sketch as a set of structurally variable and statistically correlated drawing primitives of different complexity. As depicted in fig. 1, the structural component of a sketch (containing rich information in how the shapes relate to each other) is what differentiates sketches from handwritten signatures & symbols (simple fixed drawing) [8,12].

Section 2 will describe the ASSM model mapped to the biometric framework. Section 3 will validate the biometric sketch recognition algorithm statistically (when users draw the same sketch), structurally(when users draw different sketches) and imposter tests with different degrees of knowledge.

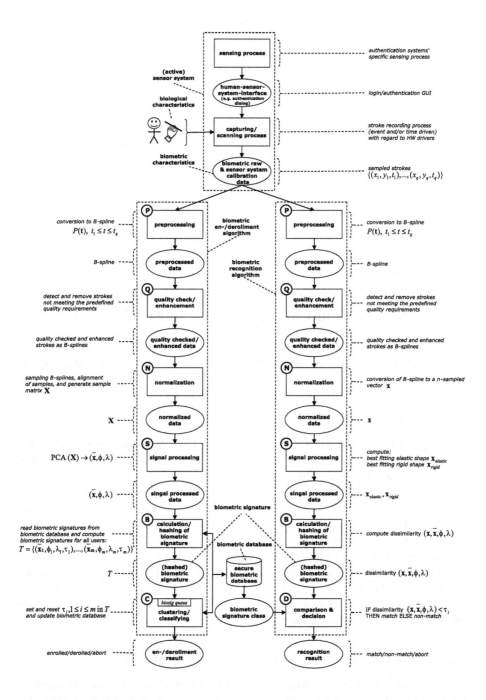

Fig. 2. Biometric Enrollment, Authentication, and Derollment Processes

Fig. 3. The effect of varying the first three shape parameters of an eleven-stroke shape ±3 standard deviations

Fig. 4. Shape types used to construct sketches: bar, wheel, base, and knot

```
1 x̄ ← x₁
2 repeat
3       for i=1 to p
4             find rigid body transform T
                that minimizes ‖T(xᵢ) − x̄‖
5             xᵢ ← T(xᵢ)
6       x̄ ← Σᵢ₌₁ᵖ xᵢ/p
7 until x̄ converges
```

```
1 x₀ ← x̄
2 do
3       find a rigid body transform T
          that minimizes ‖T(x) − x₀‖
4       x₁ ← T(x)
5       b = Φᵀ(x₁ − x̄)
6       x₂ ← x₀
7       x₀ ← x̄ + Φb
8 while‖x₂ − x₀‖ > ε
9 xₑₗₐₛₜᵢ𝒸 ← x₀, xᵣᵢ𝓰ᵢ𝒹 ← x₁
```

Fig. 5. Sample rigid alignment alg.   **Fig. 6.** Deformable shape alignment alg.

2   ASSM Algorithm Mapped to Biometric Processes

Fig. 2 depicts the mapping of ASSM to the biometric framework described by Brömme [5] for enrollment, authentication, and derollment. The following sections describe each step in detail.

2.1   Sensor System Processes

Sensing Process & Human-Sensor System Interface: A tablet screen with a digital pen is used with a sketching program to capture strokes drawn by the user and store it as a table of values.

Capturing / Scanning Process: The program stores a sequence of strokes. A stroke is captured from the moment the user puts his pen on the screen until he lifts it. Device coordinates of every point on the stroke as well as the time in milliseconds from the start of the stroke are recorded. The user can backtrack and delete strokes he is not satisfied with.

Biometric Raw & Sensor System Calibration Data: Every stroke is a sequence of points $((x_1, y_1, t_1), (x_2, y_2, t_2), ..., (x_q, y_q, t_q))$ where (x_i, y_i, t_i), $i = 1...q$ are the (x_i, y_i) pixel coordinates of the pen and t_i is the time in milliseconds from the start of the stroke such that $t_1 = 0$.

2.2   Biometric Enrollment and Derollment Processes

Preprocessing (P): Convert stroke lists to a B-spline representation. During sampling, every stroke is converted to a parametric B-spline curve representation interpolating the sequence of device sampled points $s = ((x_1, y_1, t_1), (x_2, y_2, t_2), ..., (x_q, y_q, t_q)) \rightarrow x(t), y(t), 0 \le t \le t_q$ where t is the time in milliseconds. Time is used as the interpolating variable because it samples more of the curve at points of high curvature and high detail.

Quality check / enhancement (Q): Short strokes drawn by accident and stroke samples which are inferior in quality are removed.

Normalization (N): An n-sampling of the stroke $\mathbf{sp}$ is a vector $\mathbf{x} = (x_1, x_2, ..., x_n, y_1, y_2, ..., y_n)^T$ where $(x_i, y_i) = \mathbf{sp}(\frac{(i-1)t_q}{(n-1)}), 1 \leq i \leq n$. Relations consist of multiple strokes represented as a list of splines $\mathbf{q} = (\mathbf{sp}_1, ..., \mathbf{sp}_m)$. $\mathbf{q}$ is statistically n-sampled by concatenating the corresponding n-sample vectors: $\forall \mathbf{sp}_i : 1 \leq i \leq m : \mathbf{x_n} = (\mathbf{x}_{1,n}^T, \mathbf{x}_{2,n}^T, ..., \mathbf{x}_{m,n}^T)^T$

A group of p stroke or relation samples $S = \{\mathbf{x_1}, \mathbf{x_2}, ..., \mathbf{x_p}\}$ are then iteratively aligned to each other using translation, rotation, or scale. The *rigid body alignment algorithm* is described in fig. 5.

For implementing the normalization of a single user's sketch population, a sample queue within the normalization module (N) will be used to collect the different sketch samples given by the user during the enrollment procedure. After aligning we construct a data matrix $\mathbf{X} = (\mathbf{x_1}^T, \mathbf{x_2}^T, ..., \mathbf{x_p}^T)^T$.

Signal Processing (S): We apply principal component analysis on $\mathbf{X}$ to yield a t matrix of principal components $\mathbf{\Phi} = [\phi_1, \phi_2, ..., \phi_t]$. The shape parameters are described by a vector $\mathbf{b}$ such that $\mathbf{x} = \bar{\mathbf{x}} + \mathbf{\Phi b}$. Figure 3 shows the first three variation modes of a complex 11-stroke shape analyzed from 20 samples. A biometric shape template is $(\bar{\mathbf{x}}, \mathbf{\Phi}, \lambda)$ where λ is the latent roots vector.

Calculation/hashing of biometric signature: Given a population of m users, we calculate biometric signature classes for every user $\{(\bar{\mathbf{x}}_1, \mathbf{\Phi}_1, \lambda_1), (\bar{\mathbf{x}}_2, \mathbf{\Phi}_2, \lambda_2)$, ..., $(\bar{\mathbf{x}}_m, \mathbf{\Phi}_m, \lambda_m)\}$ from his input samples. We also compute the acceptance thresholds for each user $\tau_i, 1 \leq i \leq m$ such that they have minimal overlap.

(Hashed) biometric signature (B): Biometric signature table $\mathbf{T} = \{(\bar{\mathbf{x}}_1, \mathbf{\Phi}_1, \lambda_1, \tau_1), (\bar{\mathbf{x}}_2, \mathbf{\Phi}_2, \lambda_2, \tau_2), ..., (\bar{\mathbf{x}}_m, \mathbf{\Phi}_m, \lambda_m, \tau_m)\}$.

Clustering/Classifying (C): The clustering/classifying step is considered here in two possibilities:

1. Clustering/classifying without accepting a decrease of the authentication system recognition performance. Once the user n will be enrolled to the already $(n-1)$ enrolled users, his biometric signature $(\bar{\mathbf{x}}_n, \mathbf{\Phi}_n, \lambda_n)$ is compared with all enrollment samples of the previous $(n-1)$ users. If the mean dissimilarity is less than three standard deviations from another user's samples, then user n has to re-enroll with a new sketch (pattern).
2. Clustering/classifying with accepting a decrease of the authentication system recognition performance. If the user needs to be enrolled with a fixed set of samples and the dissimilarity is less then three standard deviations, then a higher false match rate can be used to enroll the new user by adjusting τ_n. To maintain the algorithm's performance another sketch can be enrolled - as part of multitemplates [5] - for discriminating users.

En-/derollment result: For derolling a user's biometric signature and enrollment samples will be removed from the biometric database.

2.3   Biometric Authentication Process

The user draws his sketch which is converted to a spline representation and authenticated with the biometric signature he enrolled with.

Preprocessing (P): The input stroke s is converted to B-Spline representation **p** as described in the biometric enrollment process (section 2.2).

Quality check / enhancement (Q): Very short strokes or strokes consisting of a single point are removed from **p** to get **p′** .

Normalization (N): The list of input strokes **p′** is n-sampled and converted to a vector representation **x**.

Signal Processing (S): A fitting process between **x** and the biometric template $(\bar{\mathbf{x}}, \boldsymbol{\Phi}, \lambda)$. The *elastic alignment algorithm* is described in fig. 6 which computes Fitted elastic and rigid shapes $\mathbf{x}_{elastic}, \mathbf{x}_{rigid}$.

Calculation/(hashing) of biometric signature (B): The shape similarity measure is computed as the weighted sum of the deviation of $\mathbf{x}_{elastic}$ from its mean and the maximum distance between $\mathbf{x}_{rigid}$ and $\mathbf{x}_{elastic}$ as follows

$$dissimilarity(\mathbf{x}, \bar{\mathbf{x}}, \boldsymbol{\Phi}, \lambda) = deformation(\mathbf{x}, \bar{\mathbf{x}}, \boldsymbol{\Phi}, \lambda) + \alpha \cdot distance(\mathbf{x}, \bar{\mathbf{x}}, \boldsymbol{\Phi}, \lambda), \quad (1)$$

$$deformation = \sqrt{\sum_{i=1}^{t}(\frac{b_i}{\lambda_i})^2)} \ \ where \ \ \mathbf{b} = \boldsymbol{\Phi}^t(\mathbf{x}_{elastic} - \bar{\mathbf{x}}) = (b_1, b_2, ..., b_t),$$

$$distance = max_{i=1}^{p}\|u_i - v_i\| \ \ where \ \ \mathbf{x}_{elastic} = (u_1, ..., u_p), \mathbf{x}_{rigid} = (v_1, ..., v_p)$$

Comparison & decision (D): Every user i who enrolled into the system has a biometric signature $(\bar{\mathbf{x}}_\mathbf{i}, \boldsymbol{\Phi}_\mathbf{i}, \lambda_\mathbf{i})$ which is compared with his input **x** using the dissimilarity measure. If $dissimilarity(\mathbf{x}, \bar{\mathbf{x}}, \boldsymbol{\Phi}, \lambda) < \tau_i$ we authenticate the user, otherwise we reject him.

Recognition result: The algorithm results in a match or non-match.

3   Evaluation and Tests of the Biometric Sketch Recognition Algorithm

The biometric signatures are used to characterize the input of users in two ways:

1. Statistically (quantitative features): If a population of users is asked to draw exactly the same shape, then the set of biometric signatures can be used to some extent for identification of users based on the characteristic way they draw these shapes. By increasing the complexity of the shape, the identification performance increases.
2. Structurally (qualitative features): A sketch additionally contains connectivity, scale and orientation relations between shapes. These relationships are represented in the biometric templates of single users and substantially improve discrimination performance in comparison to statistical features only.

Three types of experiments were done to examine these two claims:

task	description	objects	error %
1	Draw three connected wheels of different sizes	3	1.3%
2	Draw 3 connected bars one bar is bigger than the others Connect the bars to 3 knots	6	0.9%
3	Draw 2 connected wheels one wheel is bigger than the other Connect the wheels to a small bar Connect bar to a big base	4	0.7%
4	draw Task 2 and task 3 connect them with a knot	11	0.0%

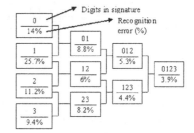

Fig. 7. Sketching tasks given to users and their recognition errors

Fig. 8. Recognition error rates decrease as more digits are combined

1. Handwritten PIN number tests: For testing the statistical claim.
2. Sketch tests: For testing the structural claim.
3. Imposter tests: Test to what extent an intruder with no, partial or full knowledge about user sketches can be falsely authenticated.

Handwritten 4 digit PIN numbers tests: A population of 10 users was asked to draw 30 times the PIN number (0123). Each test used 20 randomly selected samples for training and the remaining 10 for testing. Each test was cross validated 10 times and the average error rate was computed. Each stroke was sampled by 32 points. The number of principle components was set to represent (explain) 98% of the samples and ranged between 11 to 15 principal components.

Figure 8 depicts how the recognition error rate drops from worst case 25.7% for digit 1 to 3.9 for the complete PIN. The conclusion is that the error rate of a combined structure is less than the error rates of its substructures.

Sketch tests: Each user was given four tasks of increasing complexity to complete in his way as shown in fig. 7. Figure 9 shows some mean sketches drawn.

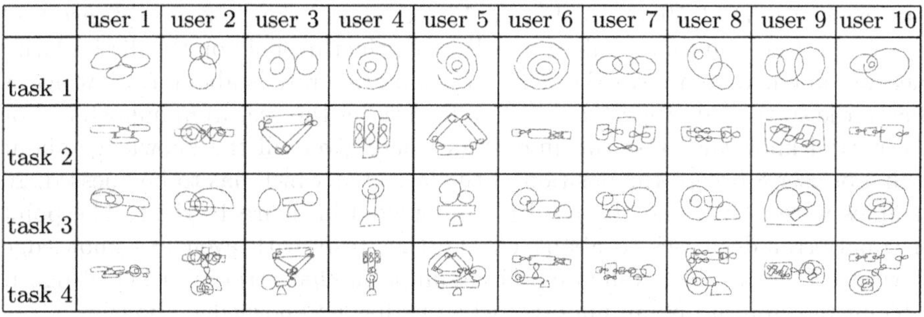

	user 1	user 2	user 3	user 4	user 5	user 6	user 7	user 8	user 9	user 10
task 1										
task 2										
task 3										
task 4										

Fig. 9. Mean sketches drawn by some users

Each stroke was sampled by 16 points. For every sketch, the number of principal components was set to explain 95% of the samples. The number of principal components ranges between 10 for task 1 and 15 for task 4. The experiments

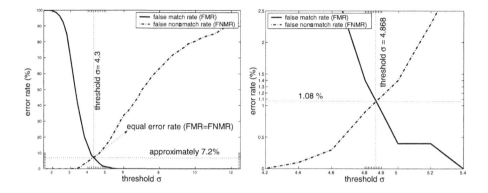

Fig. 10. Imposter tests **left:** direct copying (task 4) **right:** last knot unknown (task 4)

were conducted on 10 users. Each user sketched each task 30 times. For every user task, 20 randomly selected samples were used for training and the remaining 10 were used for testing. The tests were cross validated 10 times and averaged.

As depicted in fig. 7, the average recognition error decreases as the complexity of the structures increases. Task 4 consisting of 11 objects had 0% error.

Imposter tests: verify how much a correct user is falsely rejected for authentication and an Imposter is falsely accepted. Three kinds of tests were considered:

1. That the imposters have full knowledge of the sketch and trying to copy it.
2. They have partial knowledge of the sketch structure.
3. They have no knowledge of the sketch structure at all.

The full knowledge test was conducted with two imposters who tried to copy 20 times task 4 of user 8 (see fig. 9). The results were compared with 10 user samples and cross validated 50 times. Figure 10 left shows the false acceptance and rejection rate graph that resulted by adjusting the threshold on the dissimilarity measure in eq. 1. As we see the point of equal error rate is about 7.2% which is due to the statistical properties which differentiates the user from imposters. For the partial knowledge test two imposters where given all the knowledge about task 4 of user 8 except the position of the last knot which has to be guessed. 20 samples were drawn and the results are depicted in figure 10 right. The point of equal error decreases to about 1%. Further tests with even less knowledge showed 0% error which validates the assumption that structural knowledge is difficult to duplicate by an imposter when he has no knowledge about it.

4   Conclusions and Future Work

ASSM was applied to a biometric sketch recognition algorithm which represents structural covariations of sketches statistically. Experiments demonstrate the roles of dynamic features and structural semantics to identify users and authenticate imposters with different knowledge degrees. The evaluation and testing framework for biometric algorithm enables accurate validation and testing of ASSM. Results show that structural semantics can be used with high accuracy within an authentication system. The intra-user variation of structure over time will be tested in future work.

In future work we will also investigate statistical and structural shape learning in ASSM. This is because the main problem with ASSM is that a large training set is required where all the structural information is defined beforehand.

References

1. S. Al-Zubi and K. Tönnies. *Generalizing the Active Shape Model by Integrating Structural Knowledge to Recognize Hand Drawn Sketches.* CAIP 2003.
2. S. Al-Zubi and K. Tönnies. *Extending Active Shape Models to incorporate a-priori Knowledge about Structural Variability.* DAGM Pattern Recognition, 2002.
3. C. Alvarado and R. Davis. *Resolving ambiguities to create a natural computer-based sketching environment.* Int. Joint Conference on Artificial Intelligence, 2001.
4. A. Brömme. *A Discussion on Privacy Needs and (Mis)Use of Biometric IT-Systems.* IFIP WG 9.6/11.7 SCITS-II, Bratislava, Slovakia, 2001.
5. A. Brömme. *A Classification of Biometric Signatures.* IEEE Int. Conf. on Multimedia & Expo (ICME) 2003, Baltimore, USA, 2003.
6. T. Cootes and C.J. Taylor. *Statistical Models of Appearance for Computer Vision.* Imaging Science and Biomedical Engineering, Univ. Manchester, 2001.
7. M. Fonseca and J. Jorge. *Using Fuzzy Logic to Recognize Geometric Shapes Interactively.* IEEE International Conference Fuzzy Systems (FUZZIEEE), 2000.
8. F. Leclerc and R. Plamondon. *Automatic Signature Verivication: The State of the Art 1989–1993.* Int. Journal of Pattern Recog. and Artificial Intelligence, 1994.
9. J. Lin, M. Newman, and J.I. Hong. *DENIM: Finding a Tighter Fit Between Tools and Practice for Web Site Design.* CHI: Human Factors in Comp. Systems, 2000.
10. T. McInerney and D. Terzopoulos. *Topology Adaptive Deformable Surfaces for Medical Image Volume Segmentation.* IEEE trans. Medical Imaging, Vol 18, 1999.
11. R. Veltcamp and M. Tanase. *Content-Based Image retrieval Systems: A Survey.* Tech. Rep. UU-CS-2000-34. Dep. of Computing Science, Utrecht Univ., 2000.
12. C. Vielhauer. Handschriftliche authentifikation für digitale wasserzeichenverfahren. *Workshop Sicherheit in Netzen und Medienströmen*, 2000.
13. K. Wu and M. Levine. *Segmenting 3D Objects into Geons.* ICIAP 321–334, 1995.

Domain Decomposition for Parallel Variational Optical Flow Computation

Timo Kohlberger[1] Christoph Schnörr[1], Andrés Bruhn[2], and Joachim Weickert[2]

[1] CVGPR-Group, University of Mannheim, 68131 Mannheim, Germany
{tiko,schnoerr}@uni-mannheim.de, www.cvgpr.uni-mannheim.de

[2] MIA-Group, Saarland University, 66041 Saarbrücken, Germany
{bruhn,weickert}@mia.uni-saarland.de, www.mia.uni-saarland.de

Abstract. We present an approach to parallel variational optical flow computation by using an arbitrary partition of the image plane and iteratively solving related local variational problems associated with each subdomain. The approach is particularly suited for implementations on PC-clusters because inter-process communication is minimized by restricting the exchange of data to a lower-dimensional interface. Our mathematical formulation supports various generalizations to linear/non-linear convex variational approaches, 3D image sequences, spatio-temporal regularization, and unstructured geometries and triangulations. Results concerning the effects of interface preconditioning, inexact subdomain solvers, and the number of subdomains are presented. Our approach provides a major step towards real-time 2D image processing using off-the-shelf PC-hardware and facilitates the efficient application of variational approaches to large-scale image processing problems.

1 Introduction

Overview and Motivation. Two decades after the work of Horn and Schunck [1] both the mathematical understanding and algorithmic implementations of variational approaches to optical flow computation have reached a stage where they outperform alternative approaches in many respects. Starting with the work of Nagel [2], more and more advanced versions of the prototypical approach of Horn and Schunck within the rich class of convex functionals have been developed including anisotropic and non-linear regularization preserving motion boundaries [3]. Concerning benchmark experiments [4], they compute accurate optical flow everywhere in the image plane [3]. More robust local evaluation schemes can be exploited within the same mathematical framework [5].

A recurring argument against this class of approaches refers to the computational costs introduced by variational regularization. In our opinion, this argument is strongly misleading since it neglects the costs of alternative approaches related to heuristic post-processing of locally computed motion data (interpolation, segmentation). Moreover, besides computer vision, in many fields of application like medical imaging or remote sensing, variational regularization is the only mathematically sound way for taking into account prior knowledge

B. Michaelis and G. Krell (Eds.): DAGM 2003, LNCS 2781, pp. 196–203, 2003.
© Springer-Verlag Berlin Heidelberg 2003

about the structure of motion fields. This motivates our work on fast algorithms for *variational* optical flow computation.

In this context, the most common approach to accelerate computations is multigrid iteration. Again, starting with early work by Terzopoulos and Enkelmann, much progress has been made during the last years [6,7], and current advanced implementions run in real-time for 200×200 pixel sized image sequences on standard PC-hardware [8]. Nevertheless, since the number of pixels per frame steadily increase in applications – e.g. 1500×700 pixels/frame in fluid mechanics, and even more in 3D medical image sequences – parallelization of computations is inevitable. Due to the *non-local* nature of variational models, however, this is not a trivial task.

Contribution and Organization. We present an approach to the parallelization of variational optical flow computation which fulfils the following requirements: Firstly, suitability for the implementation on PC-clusters through the minimization of inter-process communication. Secondly, availability of a mathematical framework as basis for generalizations to the whole class of linear and non-linear variational models characterized in [3].

Starting points of our work are (i) the variational formulation developed in [9] of the prototypical approach of Horn and Schunck (section 2), and (ii) the general mathematical literature on domain decomposition in connection with the solution of partial differential equations [10,11].

Based on this theory, we derive in section 3 an approach for computing the *global* variational solution in terms of an arbitrary number of *local* variational solutions, each of which can be computed in parallel on the partitioned image plane. An important feature of this approach is that inter-process communication is minimized by restricting the exchange of data to a *lower-dimensional* interface Γ. This requires a careful treatment of the variational models within each subdomain (boundary conditions, discretization). In section 4, we confirm the theoretical properties of our approach by numerical experiments and study the effect of its components on the speed of convergence. The results show that our approach provides a basis for the computation of 2D optical flow in real-time as well as for large-scale applications in other fields including 3D medical imaging, remote sensing and experimental fluid mechanics.

2   Variational Approach and Discretization

Following [9], we summarize the variational formulation of the approach of Horn and Schunck [1] and its discretization. This approach serves as a prototype for a large class of approaches to optical flow computation studied in [3].

Throughout this paper, $x = (x_1, x_2)^\top \in \Omega$ denotes some point in the image plane, $g(x)$ the image function, $\nabla = (\partial_{x_1}, \partial_{x_2})^\top$ the gradient with respect to spatial variables, ∂_t the partial derivative with respect to time, and $u = (u_1, u_2)^\top, v = (v_1, v_2)^\top$ denote vector fields in some linear space V (see [9]).

The variational problem to be solved reads:

$$ J(u) = \inf_{v \in V} \int_\Omega \left\{ (\nabla g \cdot v + \partial_t g)^2 + \lambda \left(|\nabla v_1|^2 + |\nabla v_2|^2 \right) \right\} dx \qquad (1) $$

Vanishing of the first variation yields the variational equation:

$$a(u, v) = f(v) , \quad \forall v \in V , \quad \text{where} \tag{2}$$

$$a(u, v) = \int_\Omega \{(\nabla g \cdot u)(\nabla g \cdot v) + \lambda(\nabla u_1 \cdot \nabla v_1 + \nabla u_2 \cdot \nabla v_2)\} dx \tag{3}$$

$$f(v) = -\int_\Omega \partial_t g \nabla g \cdot v dx \tag{4}$$

Under weak conditions with respect to the image data g, the existence of a constant $c > 0$ was proven in [9] such that $a(v, v) \geq c\|v\|_V^2$, $\forall v \in V$. As a consequence, J in (1) is strictly convex and its global minimum u is the unique solution to the variational equation (2). Partially integrating in (2) by means of Green's formula, we derive the system of Euler-Lagrange equations:

$$Lu = f \quad \text{in} \quad \Omega , \qquad \partial_n u = 0 \quad \text{on} \quad \partial\Omega , \quad \text{where} \tag{5}$$

$$Lu = -\lambda \Delta u + (\nabla g \cdot u)\nabla g, \tag{6}$$

and n denoting the exterior unit normal.

To approximate the vector field u numerically, equation (2) is discretized by piecewise linear finite elements over the triangulated section Ω of the image plane. To minimize notation, we denote the column vectors of nodal variables corresponding to the finite element discretizations of $u_1(x), u_2(x)$ again with u_1, u_2 and arrange them as follows: $u = (u_1^\top, u_2^\top)^\top$. Taking into consideration the symmetry of the bilinear form (3), this induces the following block structure of the discretized version of (2):

$$Au = \begin{pmatrix} A_{11} & A_{12} \\ A_{21} & A_{22} \end{pmatrix} \begin{pmatrix} u_1 \\ u_2 \end{pmatrix} = \begin{pmatrix} f_1 \\ f_2 \end{pmatrix} = f , \tag{7}$$

where for all pixel positions $i, j = 1, \ldots, N$ and corresponding basis functions ϕ_i, ϕ_j:

$$
\begin{aligned}
(A_{11})_{ij} &= a\big((\phi_i, 0)^\top, (\phi_j, 0)^\top\big) & (A_{12})_{ij} &= a\big((\phi_i, 0)^\top, (0, \phi_j)^\top\big) \\
(A_{21})_{ij} &= (A_{12})_{ji} & (A_{22})_{ij} &= a\big((0, \phi_i)^\top, (0, \phi_j)^\top\big) \\
(f_1)_i &= f\big((\phi_i, 0)^\top\big) & (f_2)_i &= f\big((0, \phi_i)^\top\big)
\end{aligned}
$$

We point out that in connection with the decomposition into subproblems (section 3) and parallel implementations, a proper discretization and treatment of boundary conditions is essential to obtain convergence and numerical stability.

3   Problem Decomposition

This section summarizes the representation and parallel solution of the variational approach (1) using a partition of the image section Ω into a number of subdomains. For a detailed exposition we refer to [12]. Our formulation supports the application to more general variational approaches and inherits the flexibility of finite element discretizations with respect to unstructured geometries and triangulations.

Two Subdomains and Interface Equation. Let $\overline{\Omega^1} \cup \overline{\Omega^2}$ be a partition of $\overline{\Omega}$ with a common boundary $\Gamma = \overline{\Omega^1} \cap \overline{\Omega^2}$. We denote the corresponding spaces of vector fields with V^1, V^2. In the following, superscripts refer to subdomains.

We wish to represent u from (5) by two vector fields $u^1 \in V^1, u^2 \in V^2$ by solving two related problems in Ω^1, Ω^2, respectively. The relation:

$$u(x) = \begin{cases} u^1(x) & x \in \Omega^1 \\ u^2(x) & x \in \Omega^2 \end{cases} \tag{8}$$

obviously holds iff the following is true (cf. (5)):

$$Lu^1 = f^1 \quad \text{in } \Omega^1 \qquad \partial_{n^1} u^1 = 0 \quad \text{on } \partial\Omega^1 \cap \partial\Omega \tag{9}$$

$$Lu^2 = f^2 \quad \text{in } \Omega^2 \qquad \partial_{n^2} u^2 = 0 \quad \text{on } \partial\Omega^2 \cap \partial\Omega \tag{10}$$

$$u^1 = u^2 \quad \text{on } \Gamma \qquad \partial_{n^1} u^1 = -\partial_{n^2} u^2 \quad \text{on } \Gamma \tag{11}$$

In order to solve this system of equations, we equate the restriction to the interface Γ of the two solutions u^1, u^2 to (9) and (10) according to the first equation in (11), $u_\Gamma := u^1|_\Gamma = u^2|_\Gamma$, and substitute u_Γ into the second equation in (11). This is accomplished by means of the decomposition $u^i = u_0^i + u_f^i$, $i = 1, 2$, where u_0^i and u_f^i are the unique solutions of the equations:

$$Lu_0^i = 0 \quad \text{in } \Omega^i, \quad \partial_{n^i} u_0^i = 0 \quad \text{on } \partial\Omega^i \setminus \Gamma, \quad u_0^i = u_\Gamma \quad \text{on } \Gamma, \; i = 1, 2 \tag{12}$$

$$Lu_f^i = f^i \quad \text{in } \Omega^i, \; \partial_{n^i} u_f^i = 0 \quad \text{on } \partial\Omega^i \setminus \Gamma, \quad u_f^i = 0 \quad \text{on } \Gamma, \quad i = 1, 2 \tag{13}$$

Defining the *Steklov-Poincaré operators* [11]: $S^i : u_\Gamma \rightarrow \partial_{n^i} u_0^i|_\Gamma$, the second equation in (11) becomes:

$$(S^1 + S^2)u_\Gamma + \partial_{n^1} u_f^1|_\Gamma + \partial_{n^2} u_f^2|_\Gamma = 0 \tag{14}$$

It remains to solve this equation for u_Γ. This will be discussed in the remainder of this section. Once this is done, u in (8) can be computed using (9) and (10) with the boundary conditions replaced by the first equation in (11).

Steklov-Poincaré operator. In order to make explicit the action of the operators S^i on some given boundary data u_Γ, we distinguish in (7) between nodal variables being on and off the interface by indices Γ and I, respectively. Rearranging (7) accordingly for domain $\Omega_i, i = 1, 2$ reads:

$$A^i u^i = f^i \quad \rightarrow \quad \begin{pmatrix} A_{II}^i & A_{I\Gamma}^i \\ A_{\Gamma I}^i & A_{\Gamma\Gamma}^i \end{pmatrix} \begin{pmatrix} u_I^i \\ u_\Gamma^i \end{pmatrix} = \begin{pmatrix} f_I^i \\ f_\Gamma^i \end{pmatrix}$$

Using this representation, the action of S^i in (14) is given by [12]:

$$S^i u_\Gamma = (A_{\Gamma\Gamma}^i - A_{\Gamma I}^i (A_{II}^i)^{-1} A_{I\Gamma}^i)u_\Gamma = \partial_{n^i} u_0^i|_\Gamma \tag{15}$$

The implementation of this equation involves – besides matrix-vector multiplications – the computation of $(A_{II}^i)^{-1}$ which amounts to solve a Dirichlet problem for the operator L in (6) with the right hand side given by the extension of boundary values u_Γ to Ω_i.

The action of $(S^i)^{-1}$, on the other hand, is given by [12]:

$$(S^i)^{-1}\partial_{n^i}u_0^i|_\Gamma = \begin{pmatrix} 0 & I \end{pmatrix} \begin{pmatrix} A_{II}^i & A_{I\Gamma}^i \\ A_{\Gamma I}^i & A_{\Gamma\Gamma}^i \end{pmatrix}^{-1} \begin{pmatrix} 0 \\ I \end{pmatrix} \partial_{n^i}u_0^i|_\Gamma = u_0^i|_\Gamma = u_\Gamma \qquad (16)$$

The implementation of this equation involves (i) to solve a Neumann problem for the operator L in (6) with boundary data $\partial_{n^i}u_0^i|_\Gamma$, and (ii) to extract the values of the solution on the interface Γ afterwards.

Finally, it can be shown [12] that the discretized counterpart of equation (14) reads:

$$(S^1 + S^2)u_\Gamma = f_\Gamma - A_{\Gamma I}^1(A_{II}^1)^{-1}f_I^1 - A_{\Gamma I}^2(A_{II}^2)^{-1}f_I^2 \qquad (17)$$

It is important to note that in order to solve equation (14) or (17), respectively, neither S^i nor $(S^i)^{-1}$ are explicitly computed (which would be expensive). Rather, the action of these operators involves the boundary value problems as explained above which can be separately solved for each domain Ω^i by fast standard methods (e.g., multigrid iteration, see [8]).

Interface preconditioner. Since the operators S^i can shown to be symmetric and coercive [11], preconditioned conjugate gradient iteration is the first choice for solving (17). Among various provably optimal ("spectrally equivalent") possibilities, we have chosen the so-called Neumann-Neumann preconditioner $1/4[(S^1)^{-1} + (S^2)^{-1}]$ [13] because it preserves symmetry and has natural extensions to multiple domains, three-dimensional problems, and problems involving unstructured geometries and/or triangulations.

Multiple domains. Let R^i denote the restriction of the vector of nodal variables u_Γ on the interface Γ to those on $\overline{\Omega^i} \cap \Gamma$. Analogously to the case of two domains, the operator on the left side of eqn. (17) for multiple domains reads:

$$\left(\sum_i (R^i)^\top S^i R^i\right) u_\Gamma = f_\Gamma - \sum_i (R^i)^\top A_{\Gamma I}^i (A_{II}^i)^{-1} f_I^i \qquad (18)$$

The corresponding Neumann-Neumann preconditioner[14,15] is:

$$P_{NN}^{-1} := D \left(\sum_i (R^i)^\top (S^i)^{-1} R^i\right) D, \qquad (19)$$

where D_{jj}^{-1} of the diagonal scaling matrix D is the number of subdomains sharing the nodal variable u_j on Γ. Since it is well known that the convergence becomes worser for an increasing number of subdomains, also the Balancing Neumann-Neumann[16,17] preconditioner is considered:

$$P_{BNN}^{-1} := (I - (R^0)^\top (S^0)^{-1} R^0 S) P_{NN}^{-1} (I - S(R^0)^\top (S^0)^{-1} R^0) + (R^0)^\top (S^0)^{-1} R^0, \qquad (20)$$

introducing a so-called "balancing" step before and after the Neumann-Neumann preconditioning by solving coarse-grid discretization of the Steklov-Poincaré equation, whereas the coarse-grid is identical with the partition into subdomains. The action of the restriction operator R^0 is to calculate the weighted sum of values lying on the shared border of each subdomain. The weights are given by the reciprocal of the number of subdomains sharing each particular node.

4   Parallel Processing, Computational Results, and Discussion

We conducted a number of experiments on regular $n \times n$ partitions in order to investigate (i) the effect of interface preconditioning vs. non-preconditioning, and (ii) the influence of the number of subdomains on the convergence rate both for the non-balancing and the balancing preconditioner.

All results refer to the solution of the interface equation (18) using Conjugate-Gradient Iteration with the preconditioners (19) or (20). (19) involves in each iteration step the solving of local boundary value problems *in parallel* for each subdomain, as explained in connection with equations (15) and (16). (20) additionally introduces the non-parallel calculation of $(S^0)^{-1}$, which is implemented by solving the (small) system $S^0 x = b$ explicitly, using a standard method (see [12] for details). The associated systems to S^i and $(S^i)^{-1}$ were derived from the Finite Element discretization explained in connection with equation (7). The implementation was realized with C/C++ using a MPI-conform inter-process communication library for the parallel parts of the overall algorithm. The regularization parameter λ in (1) was set to 10 in all experiments leading to an amount of smoothing which is adequate for most real applications. As input data an image pair of size 252×252 pixel was used inducing an artifical optical flow field. The overall process started with the zero vector field $(0,0)^\top$.

Effect of interface preconditioning.
    The image plane was partitioned horizontally into two subdomains of size 126×252 and (17) was solved to a relative residual error of 10^{-3} both without and with preconditioning using (19). In the first case 27 PCG-iterations were necessary to reach the given error threshold, whereas using the Neumann-Neumann preconditioner it was only one iteration. A similar experiment was conducted on 4×4 subdomains this time using (20) as preconditioner. Here we obtained similar results: 44 PCG-iterations without and 6 iterations with preconditioning. These and further experiments clearly show that, in agreement with theory [11], the system to be solved for the interface variables u_Γ becomes more and more ill-conditioned if the number of subdomains increases. Using the preconditioners (19) and (20), however, largely compensates this effect and enables shorter computation times through parallelization.

Number of subdomains, effect of parallelization.
    In a second experiment the dependence of the convergence rate on the number of subdomains both for non-balancing and the balancing preconditioner were investigated. In addition, considerations about the overall computation time were made.
    In table 1 the necessary number of PCG-iterations to reach a residual error of 10^{-3} are depicted for both preconditioner types. It shows that with the

Table 1. Number of subdomains, effect of parallelization. Columns 3 and 6 depict the number of outer iterations to reach a relative residual error of 10^{-3}, both for both preconditioner types. Columns 4 and 7 depict the average number of local iterations for an given error threshold of 10^{-5}. Columns 5 and 8 show the total number of sequentially processed pixels as a measure for the total computation time (see text).

Partition (h./v.)	Sub-domain size	Neumann-Neumann			Balancing Neumann-Neumann		
		Outer iter.	Av. inner iter.	$N_s * 10^6$	Outer iter.	Av. inner iter.	$N_s * 10^6$
2×2	126	3	370	35	3	332	63
4×4	63	7	238	13	6	197	19
6×6	42	10	179	6.3	7	141	6.9
9×9	28	14	127	2.8	6	92	1.7
14×14	18	21	86	1.2	6	70	0.5
21×21	12	30	57	0.5	5	42	0.1

non-balancing case the convergence rate depends on the number of subdomains whereas with the balancing case it is nearly independent, due to the coarse-grid correction steps. Furthmore, the average number of inner PCG-iterations for solving the local systems to a residual error of 10^{-5} are shown. Since the computation time for one inner PCG-iteration depends linearly on the number of pixels in one subdomain, the product N_s of the number of pixels in one subdomain, the aver. number of inner iterations, the number of local-system-solvings per one outer iteration (2 with (19) and 4 with (20)) and the total number of outer iteration gives a measure for the overall computation time, if communication time and the time for solving the coarse system in (20) is neglected.

It shows that the non-balancing type needs less time for small number of subdomains (until 6×6), whereas the balancing preconditioner is faster for 9×9 subdomains and above. In comparision to solving the original system (5) non-parallelly in 404 iterations on the whole image plane (252×252), i.e. $N_s \approx 26 \cdot 10^6$, parallelization significantly improves the total computation time for 4×4 subdomains and more (if communication time is neglected). Especially for the case of 21×21 subdomains it can be improved by two orders of magnitude. This factor, of course, becomes even larger for more subdomains, larger image sizes, and 3d image sequences.

5   Conclusion and Further Work

We presented an approach to parallel optical flow computation by decomposing the underlying domain Ω and iteratively solving related local variational problems in each subdomain. Inter-process communication is minimized by restricting the exchange of data to a lower-dimensional interface.

By combining our approach with advanced multigrid iteration as subdomain solvers, real-time 2d image processing will come into reach. This will be confirmed by implementations on dedicated high-speed PC-clusters. Furthermore, we will investigate how coarse-grid corrections can be incorporated into our architecture without compromising efficiency of inter-process communication.

Acknowledgement. TK and AB gratefully acknowledge support by the Deutsche Forschungsgemeinschaft DFG (grant SCHN457/4)

References

1. B.K.P. Horn and B.G. Schunck. Determining optical flow. *Art. Int.*, 17:185–203, 1981.
2. H.H. Nagel. On the estimation of optical flow: Relations between different approaches and some new results. *Artif. Intell.*, 33:299–324, 1987.
3. J. Weickert and C. Schnörr. A theoretical framework for convex regularizers in pde–based computation of image motion. *Int. J. Computer Vision*, 45(3):245–264, 2001.
4. D. J. Fleet J. L. Barron and S. S. Beauchemin. Perfomance of optical flow techniques. *Int. J. Computer Vision*, 1994.
5. A. Bruhn, J. Weickert, and C. Schnörr. Combining the advantages of local and global optic flow methods. In L. van Gool, editor, *Pattern Recognition, Proc. 24th DAGM Symposium*, volume 2449 of *LNCS*, pages 454–462, Zürich, Switzerland, 2002. Springer.
6. D. Terzopoulos. Multilevel computational processes for visual surface reconstruction. *Comp. Vis., Graph., and Imag. Proc.*, 24:52–96, 1983.
7. W. Enkelmann. Investigation of multigrid algorithms for the estimation of optical flow fields in image sequences. *Comp. Vis. Graphics and Imag. Proc.*, 43:150–177, 1987.
8. A. Bruhn, J. Weickert, C. Feddern, T. Kohlberger, and C. Schnörr. Real-time optic flow computation with variational methods. In *Proc. Computer Analysis of Images and Patterns (CAIP'03)*, LNCS. Springer, 2003. in press.
9. C. Schnörr. Determining optical flow for irregular domains by minimizing quadratic functionals of a certain class. *Int. J. Computer Vision*, 6(1):25–38, 1991.
10. T.F. Chan and T.P. Mathew. Domain decomposition algorithms. *Acta Numerica*, pages 61–143, 1994.
11. A. Quarteroni and A. Valli. *Domain Decomposition Methods for Partial Differential Equations*. Oxford Univ. Press, 1999.
12. T. Kohlberger, C. Schnörr, A. Bruhn, and J. Weickert. Domain decomposition for variational optical flow computation. Technical Report 07/2003, Dept. Math. and Comp. Science, University of Mannheim, Germany, May 2003. Submitted to *IEEE Trans. Image Processing*.
13. J.-F. Bourgat, Glowinski R., P. Le Tallec, and Vidrascu M. Variational formulation and algorithm for trace operator in domain decomposition calculations. In T. Chan, Glowinski R., J. Périaux, and O. Widlund, editors, *Domain Decomposition Methods*, pages 3–16, Philadelphia, 1989. SIAM.
14. P. Le Tallec, De Roeck Y.-H., and Vidrascu M. Domain decomposition methods for large linearly elliptic three dimensional problems. *J. Comp. Appl. Math.*, page 34, 1991.
15. Y.-H. De Roeck and P. Le Tallec. Analysis and test of a local domain decomposition preconditioner. In R. Glowinsiki, Y. Kuznetsov, G. Meurant, J Périaux, and Widlund O., editors, *4th Int. Symp. on Domain Decomposition Methods for Part. Diff. Equations*, pages 112–128, Philadelphia, 1991. SIAM.
16. J. Mandel and M. Brezina. Balancing domain decomposition: Theory and performance in two and three dimensions. Technical report, Comp. Math. Group, University of Colorado at Denver, Denver, CO, 1, 1993.
17. J. Mandel. Balancing domain decomposition. *Comm. Numer. Math. Eng.*, 9:233–241, 1993.

Fuzzy Modeling Based Recognition of Multi-font Numerals

Madasu Hanmandlu[1], Mohd. Hafizuddin Mohd. Yusof[2], and
Vamsi Krishna Madasu[3]

[1]Dept. of Electrical Engineering, I.I.T. Delhi, Hauz Khas,
New Delhi – 110016, India.
mhmandlu@ee.iitd.ernet.in
[2]Faculty of Information Technology, Multimedia University, Cyberjaya
64100 Selangor D.E., Malaysia.
hafizuddin.yusof@mmu.edu.my
[3]School of Information Technology and Electrical Engineering, University of Queensland,
QLD 4072, Australia.
madasu@itee.uq.edu.au

Abstract. In this paper, we present a new scheme for off-line recognition of multi-font numerals using the Takagi-Sugeno (TS) model. In this scheme, the binary image of a character is partitioned into a fixed number of sub-images called boxes. The features consist of normalized vector distances (γ) from each box. Each feature extracted from different fonts gives rise to a fuzzy set. However, when we have a small number of fonts as in the case of multi-font numerals, the choice of a proper fuzzification function is crucial. Hence, we have devised a new fuzzification function involving parameters, which take account of the variations in the fuzzy sets. The new fuzzification function is employed in the TS model for the recognition of multi-font numerals.

1   Introduction

The ability to identify the machine printed numbers in an automated or semi automated manner led to the development of an entirely different field of research known as the Optical character recognition (OCR). The earlier computer based OCR systems [1] were confined to recognize only the printed or handwritten characters of fixed size and font. But, the present study aims at producing a system, which could recognize characters, especially numerals of any arbitrary size, shape and fonts.

There are numerous approaches that address the problem of recognition of numerals depending on the type of features extracted and the different ways of extracting them. Although recognition of handwritten numerals is a well-researched topic [2, 3, 4], but not much work has been reported on the recognition of multi-font numerals, in recent times.

Recognition of printed Korean characters of multi-font, multi-size [5] uses a two-stage classification method. Recognition of handwritten numerals using fuzzy logic was first attempted in [6]. Here, the handwritten numeral is decomposed into straight lines, portions of a circle and circles. A more flexible scheme [7] is to decompose the numeral based on the detection of a set of feature points: terminal points, intersection-points and bend- points.

B. Michaelis and G. Krell (Eds.): DAGM 2003, LNCS 2781, pp. 204–211, 2003.
© Springer-Verlag Berlin Heidelberg 2003

An off-line approach to handwritten numeral recognition is presented in [8] using the concept of perturbation. The perturbation is deemed to arise from different writing habits and instruments. The recognition method is able to account for a variety of distortions due to eccentric handwriting.

For unconstrained handwritten numeral recognition, an approach that integrates the statistical and structural information is given in [9]. This approach delves on state-duration adapted transition probability to improve the modeling of state-duration in conventional HMMs and uses macro-states to overcome the difficulty in modeling pattern structures.

A new scheme is presented in [10] for off-line recognition of totally unconstrained handwritten characters using a simple multi-layer cluster neural network trained with the back propagation algorithm. It is shown that the use of genetic algorithms avoids the problem of finding local minima in training the multi-layer cluster neural network with gradient descent technique and improves the recognition rates.

The PCA (Principal Component Analysis) mixture model is used for the recognition of numerals in [11]. This model is motivated by the idea that the classification accuracy is improved by modeling each class into a mixture of several components and by performing the classification in the compact and decorrelated feature space. Each numeral class is partitioned into several clusters and each cluster's density is estimated by a Gaussian distribution function in the PCA transformed space. An iterative EM (Expectation Maximization) algorithm performs the parameter estimation, and model order is selected by a fast sub-optimal validation scheme.

The back-propagation neural network is used in [12] for the recognition of handwritten characters. Feature extraction is done using three different approaches, namely, ring, sector and hybrid. The features consist of normalized vector distances and angles. The same features are adopted in the present work. However, this study is intended for the case when we have a small set of samples. For this reason, we have devised a new fuzzification function as used in [13]. This function contains structural parameters and the Takagi-Sugeno model is used for numeral recognition.

The Takagi-Sugeno model [15] is meant for representing a general class of static or dynamic nonlinear systems. This model is based on a "fuzzy partition" of input space and it can be viewed as the expansion of a piecewise linear partition. Consequent parameters are those used in the output function and antecedent parameters are those that define the fuzzy sets, which partition the input space.

2   Pre-processing

The normalization of the numerals is essential because of the different types of fonts, which result in several variations in the shapes and sizes. Therefore, to bring about uniformity among the input numerals, all of them must be of the same size. For this reason, the numerals are fit into a standard size window of 42 x 32 while preserving the exact aspect ratio of the numerals. This size of window is selected due to the fact that usually height of the numeral is almost 1.5 times more than the width. The un-thinned numeral is normalized first and later thinned.

3   Feature Extraction

Feature extraction is an important phase in any character recognition system and care should be taken to extract distinguishing features that are invariant to transformations applied during the pre-processing stage. When we try to extract the various types of geometric features such as straight-line segments, curve-segments, curvatures etc., and structural features such as number of branches, junction points, tie-points etc., we may land up in spurious features. This is due to the variations in sizes, fonts of the numerals and the pre-processing and thinning procedures adopted. For extracting the features, we have adopted the Box-Method of [13]. The major advantage of this approach stems from its robustness to small variations, easy to implement. The box method encloses a character in a fixed grid structure and from each grid enclosing a portion of the character; the vector distance features are extracted. These features, which are local in nature, are found to be more robust than the geometric (mainly local), and structural features (mainly global).

In this method, the binary array of 42 x 32 is fit into horizontal and vertical grid lines of 6 x 4, yielding 24 boxes. Each box is of the size 7 x 8, so that, the portions of a numeral will lie in some of these boxes. By considering the bottom left corner as the absolute origin (0,0), the vector distances of all the pixels of a box are calculated. Averaging all distances by the number of pixels in a box, a normalized vector distance γ for each box is obtained. All γ 's constitute a feature set based on the vector distances. However, for empty boxes, the value will be zero. The vector distance is calculated for each pixel at coordinates (i, j) with respect to the origin, using the formula, $d_{kb} = (i^2 + j^2)^{1/2}$. Similarly, for all pixels in a box, the vector distances are computed and normalized with the total number of pixels available in that box using the formula, $\gamma_b = \dfrac{1}{n} \sum_{k=1}^{n} d_{kb}$, n being the number of pixels in a box and b refers to the number of boxes.

4   Recognition System

In the recognition process, a database of numerals of different fonts is required to extract the features. These extracted features will then be used to identify the unknown multi-font numerals. For this purpose, we have considered a standard database of multi-font numerals consisting of thirty fonts. Only ten samples of each font are taken into account, as there is not much difference between the individual samples.

The features extracted from the size normalized and thinned binary array, form the input for recognition system. TS model serves as the recognition system taking the membership functions of the unknown numeral as the input. The means and variances of the fuzzy sets of reference numeral database form the Knowledge Base (KB).

4.1   Choice of Membership Function

In order to recognize the unknown numeral set using fuzzy logic, an exponential variant of fuzzy membership function is found appropriate. The fuzzy membership function proposed in [13] is based on the normalized vector distance. The concept of fuzzy sets is clearly explained in [14]. To mention briefly, every feature considered over several samples contributes to a fuzzy set.

The means m_i and variance σ_i^2 for each of the 24 fuzzy sets denoted by "C" are computed from:

$$m_i = \frac{1}{N_i}\sum_{j=1}^{N_i} f_{ij} \tag{1}$$

$$\sigma_i^2 = \frac{1}{N_i}\sum_{j=1}^{N_i}(f_{ij} - m_i)^2 \tag{2}$$

where, N_i is the number of samples in the ith fuzzy set and f_{ij} stands for the jth feature value of reference numeral in the ith fuzzy set where (i=1,2...C).

For an unknown input numeral, the 24 features are extracted using the box method. The membership function is chosen as,

$$\mu_i = \exp-\left\{\frac{|x_i - m_i|}{\sigma_i^2}\right\} \tag{3}$$

where, x_i is the ith feature of the unknown numeral, "u".

If all x_i's are close to m_i's which represent the known statistics of a reference character, then unknown numeral is identified with this numeral because all the membership functions are close 1 and hence the average membership function is almost 1. Let, $m_j(r), \sigma_j^2(r)$ belong to the rth reference numeral with $r = 0,1...9$. We then calculate the average membership as,

$$\mu_{av}(r) = \frac{1}{C}\sum_{j=1}^{C} e^{\frac{-|x_j - m_j(r)|}{\sigma_j^2(r)}} \tag{4}$$

Then the unknown numeral, $u \in r$ if $\mu_{av}(r)$ is the maximum for $r = 0,1...9$.

4.2   Modified Membership Functions

The recognition of numerals by (4) using the fuzzification function (3) does not perform well when we have a limited database such as the case of multi-font numerals, shown in Figure 1. This is because some of the fuzzy sets have a very small variance and others have a large variance. Equation (3) presumes that the unknown features are governed by the known statistics, namely, the means and variances of fuzzy sets. In order to represent the possible deviations from the statistics, we introduce two structural parameters in the membership function (3).

1234567890   **1234567890**   1234567890
1234567890   **1234567890**   1234567890
1234567890 1234567890   1234567890
1234567890   1234567890   1234567890
1234567890   1234567890   1234567890
1234567890   1234567890   1234567890
1234567890 **1234567890**   1234567890
1234567890   1234567890   1234567890
1234567890 1234567890   1234567890
1234567890   1234567890   1234567890

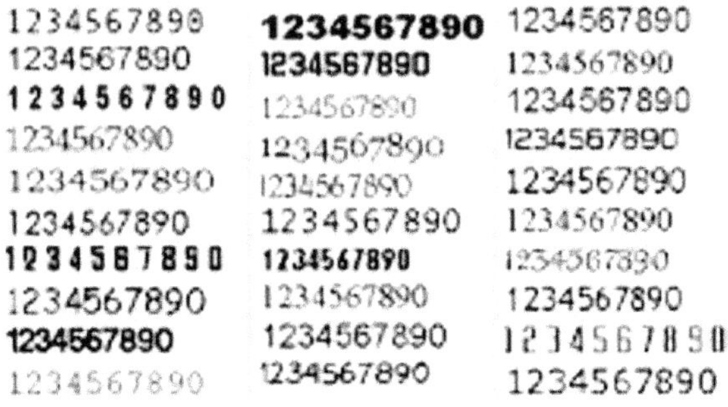

Fig. 1. Database of multi-font numerals

The modified membership function is given by,

$$\mu_k(x_k) = \exp-\left[\frac{(1-s)+s^2|x_k-m_k|}{(1+t)+t^2\sigma_k^2}\right] \tag{5}$$

where, s and t are the parameters of the membership function.

Thus the structural parameters s and t model the variations in the mean and variance over all the 24 clusters (boxes). The choice of these parameters has implicit reasoning in the sense that if $s=1$ and $t=-1$, it yields the original membership function (3). If the values of s and t are perturbed around the above values, it would reflect the changes that take place in the means and variances. Hence (5) is a generalized form of (3). We employ the TS model to act as a recognition system using the function (5) on the basis of the performance index, J (See appendix). The optimization of means and variances does not converge whereas the optimization of structural parameters does converge because their range of variation is small as compared to the range of variation of means and variances.

4.3   Results

We have first implemented the membership function (3) with the recognition scheme (4) and obtained a recognition rate (RR) of 93 %. But with the modified membership function (5) in the TS model, RR has risen to 98.67%. This higher rate is due to the fact that the structural parameters take care of variations in the different fonts of the numerals. These structural parameters and recognition rates are given below in Table 1.

Table 1. Structural Parameters and Recognition Rates.

Digit	s	t	c_0	c_1	RR with function (3)	RR with function (5)
0	1.1999	2.5062	0.0417083	0.0001310	96.7	100
1	1.1981	2.5135	0.0417354	0.0001303	100	100
2	1.1983	2.5137	0.0417402	0.0002321	96.7	100
3	1.1995	2.5089	0.0417195	0.0001672	100	100
4	1.1986	2.5125	0.0417295	0.0001931	93.3	100
5	1.1992	2.5104	0.0417252	0.0001879	90	96.67
6	1.1989	2.5117	0.0417290	0.0002191	90	96.67
7	1.1996	2.5076	0.0417165	0.0001232	96.7	100
8	1.199	2.5103	0.0417234	0.0002315	83.3	96.67
9	1.1985	2.5133	0.0417324	0.0002304	83.3	96.67
					93.00	**98.67**

5   Conclusions

In this paper, we have devised a modified fuzzification function in the TS model for dealing with a small set of numeral data. The means and variances of membership functions are adapted using two structural parameters, which model their variations in the different fonts of the numerals. It is shown that the performance of TS model is improved by the inclusion of structural parameters in the fuzzification function. Suggested future work may include testing of the proposed method with cursive numeral fonts, which have not been considered in the present study.

References

1. Mori, S., Suen, C.Y., Kamamoto, K., Historical review of OCR research and development. Proc. of IEEE. 80 (1992) 1029–1058.
2. Govindan, V.K., Shivaprasad, A.P., Character Recognition - A review. Pattern Recognition. 23 (1990) 671–683.
3. Suen, C.Y., Nadal, C., Legault, R., Mai, T.A., Lam, L., Computer recognition of unconstrained handwritten numerals. Proc. of IEEE. 80 (1992) 1162–1180.
4. Plamondon, R., Srihari, S.N., On-Line and Off-line Hand Writing Recognition: A Comprehensive Survey. IEEE Trans. PAMI. 22 (2000) 63–84.
5. Lee, J.S., Kwon, O.J., Bang, S.Y., Highly accurate recognition of printed Korean characters through an improved two stage classification method. Pattern Recognition. 32 (1992) 1935–1945.
6. Siy, P., Chen, C.S., Fuzzy Logic for handwritten numeral character recognition. IEEE Trans. Systems, Man and Cybernetics. 4 (1974) 570–575.
7. Baptista, G., Kulkarni, K.M., A high accuracy algorithm for the recognition of handwritten numerals. Pattern Recognition. 21 (1988) 287–291.
8. Ha, T.M., Bunke, H., Off-line handwritten numeral recognition by perturbation method. IEEE Trans. on PAMI. 19 (1997) 535–539.

9.   Cai, J., Liu, Z-Q, Integration of structural and statistical information for unconstrained handwritten numeral recognition. IEEE Trans. PAMI. 21 (1999) 263–270.
10. Lee, S.W., Off-line Recognition of totally unconstrained handwritten numerals using Multilayer Cluster Neural Network. IEEE Trans. PAMI. 18 (1996) 48–652.
11. Kim, H.C., Kim, D., Bang, S.Y., A numeral character recognition using the PCA mixture model. Pattern Recognition Letters. 23 (2002) 103–111.
12. Hanmandlu, M., Mohan, K.R.M., Kumar, H., Neural based handwritten character recognition. In: Proceedings of the Fifth IEEE International Conference on Document Analysis and Recognition, Bangalore (1999) 241–244.
13. Hanmandlu, M., Mohan, K.R.M., Chakraborty, S., Goyal S., Roy Choudhury, D., Unconstrained Handwritten Character Recognition based on Fuzzy Logic. Pattern Recognition. 36 (2003) 603–623.
14. Hanmandlu, M., Mohan, K.R.M., Chakraborty, S., Garg, G., Fuzzy modeling based signature verification system. In: Proceedings of Sixth IEEE International Conference on Document Analysis and Recognition, Seattle (2001) 110–114.
15. Takagi, T., Sugeno, M., Fuzzy Identification of Systems and its application to Modeling and Control. IEEE Trans. Systems, Man and Cybernetics. 15 (1985) 116–132.

Appendix: Takagi-Sugeno (TS) Model

Let x_i be the ith feature in a fuzzy set A_i then IF THEN rule in TS model has the following form:

Rule k: IF x_k is A_k

THEN $y_k = c_0 + c_1 x_k$ $\hspace{2cm}$ (A.1)

The fuzzy set A_k is represented by the membership function (5). The strength of the rule in (A. 1) is obtained as

$$w_k = \mu_k(x_k) \hspace{2cm} (A.2)$$

The output is expressed as $\hspace{1cm}$ $$Y = \sum_{l=1}^{L} w_l y_l \hspace{2cm} (A.3)$$

The performance function is defined as $J = (Y_r - Y)^2$ $\hspace{1cm}$ (A.4)

where Y and Y_r denote the output of the fuzzy model and of the real system respectively.

In order to learn the parameters s and t, and the consequent parameters c_0 and c_1. Eqn. (A.4) is partially differentiated with respect to each of these parameters. Accordingly, we have

$$\frac{\partial J}{\partial c_1} = \frac{\partial J}{\partial Y} \cdot \frac{\partial Y}{\partial c_1} = -2(Y_r - Y)\sum_{k=1}^{C} w_k x_k \hspace{2cm} (A.5)$$

$$\frac{\partial J}{\partial c_0} = \frac{\partial J}{\partial Y}\cdot\frac{\partial Y}{\partial c_0} = -2[Y_r - Y]\sum_{k=1}^{C}w_k = -2\delta\sum_{k=1}^{C}w_k \tag{A.6}$$

$$\frac{\partial J}{\partial s} = \frac{\partial J}{\partial Y}\cdot\frac{\partial Y}{\partial s} = -2\delta\sum_{k=1}^{C}y_k\mu_k\left[\{1-2s|x_k-m_k|\}/T\right] \tag{A.7}$$

$$\frac{\partial J}{\partial t} = \frac{\partial J}{\partial Y}\cdot\frac{\partial Y}{\partial t} = -2\delta\sum_{k=1}^{C}y_k\mu_k\{(1-s)+s^2|x_k-m_k|\}\{1+2t\sigma_k^2\}/T^2 \tag{A.8}$$

where $\delta = Y_r - Y$, $T = (1+t)+t^2\sigma_k^2$ and k denotes the rule number

The learning laws are as follows:

$$c_i^{new} = c_i^{old} - \in_1\frac{\partial J}{\partial c_i}; s^{new} = s^{old} - \in_2\frac{\partial J}{\partial s}; t^{new} = t^{old} - \in_3\frac{\partial J}{\partial t} \tag{A.9}$$

where $\in_1, \in_2, \in_3$ are the learning coefficients such that $\in_1, \in_2$ *and* $\in_3 > 0$.

The chosen values are 1.0E-05, 0.1, and 0.01 respectively. The initial values of parameters are $s = 1, t = 2, c_0 = \frac{1}{C} \& c_1 = 0$. Interestingly, it turns out that the recognition scheme (5) is a special case of (A.3) of TS model for $s = 1, t = -1$, in (5) and $c_0 = \frac{1}{C}, c_1 = 0$ in (A.3).

The classification is based using minimum mean square error, which is the performance index, J for determining the identity of unknown characters. The classification scheme is now described. Each character is described by a set of membership functions with known parameters, i.e., means and variances. The known characters are trained to obtain structural and consequent parameters. The unknown character assumes the means and variances of each known character in order to ascertain its identity. Then its consequent and structural parameters are updated and the performance is evaluated. The particular known character that yields the least value of J is taken as the identity of the unknown character.

System Concept for Image Sequence Classification in Laser Welding

Sören Hader

Robert Bosch GmbH, FV/PLF2, P.O. Box 30 02 40,
D-70442 Stuttgart, Germany
soeren.hader@de.bosch.com

Abstract. This work introduces a concept for a challenging classification problem of highly dynamic laser welding image sequences. Under the conditions of the industrial production a decision is required within seconds with a high selectivity. The introduced concept consists of classic elements of image processing, classification, and machine learning. The components are not optimized but as a whole, yielding a high-performance system. It also contains individually a statistical preprocessing for change detection in image sequences. The event hypotheses generated by the algorithm are classified frame-wise by an object classifier. The optimization of recognition performance is based on a feature selection by a modified sequential forward selection. We use the properties of the polynomial classifier for the efficient computation of cross validations.

1 Introduction

Image processing in industrial applications is subject to ever higher demands. In quality control high selectivity is demanded to minimize costs. High-speed two-dimensional sensors acquire more data permitting observation of ever faster processes. The processing of bigger and bigger amounts of data cannot be handled by using faster computers only, it also requires more efficient algorithms.

This paper introduces a system concept for efficient classification of image sequences in laser welding. A HDRC (High-Dynamic-Resolution-CMOS) sensor observes a welding process on metal parts in an area of $10 \times 10\ mm$. The arising sequence contains over 1000 frames with a resolution of 64×64 pixel. The problem consists of observing and evaluating the process within a timing cycle. Defective parts arise from an irregular course of the welding which produces material particles flying off, so-called sputter. These events appear very seldom, below one per mille. The importance of an automatic quality control on high-speed sensors has increased within the last few years thanks to camera engineering with high range of dynamic [7].

The handling of large amounts of data is particularly difficult. The raw image data is several megabytes in size. If an algorithm generates event hypotheses for further steps, a fast processing is possible. A hypothesis $O_{i,j}$ is the jth coherent pixel group which represents a supposed event at the frame t_i.

B. Michaelis and G. Krell (Eds.): DAGM 2003, LNCS 2781, pp. 212–219, 2003.
© Springer-Verlag Berlin Heidelberg 2003

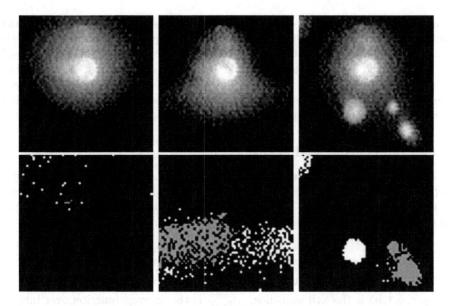

Fig. 1. Top row: Original frames (64 × 64) from laser welding process as prototypical examples. Bottom row: After change detection and binarization, the largest connected objects are represented with gray color. Only the right column contains an error relevant event (sputter).

Another typical property is the strongly asymmetric cost of classification error. Defective parts shall never be classified as faultless because they lead to high follow-up costs. Pseudo errors (false negatives) can be tolerated within certain limits.

A well-known method for the analysis of image sequences is tracking. However, the quality depends strongly on the capability to assign the objects over the sequence. If the movements are so fast that there is no overlap of time neighboring objects, tracking and optical flow contain errors. Despite fast registration, sputters can be observed only in few frames.

In the further course of this work, a statistical approach for change detection [3] is introduced along with other parts of the system concept like segmentation, feature extraction and the two-stage classification (Section 2). An efficient cross validation for the polynomial classifier, the feature selection on a per-frame basis, and the system optimization are described in Section 3. The experimental results are presented in Section 4.

2   Online Mode

In principle, the system contains two chains which are connected to each other. On the one side, the online mode which carries out the processing chain with trained classifier and adapted decision thresholds in the real application domain.

On the other side, for the system optimization the so-called offline mode is carried out using a cross validation. The optimization comprises not only tuning of the classifier, but also choice of feature subsets and parameter settings. The idea is to optimize the complete set of variable quantities as a whole at the recognition performance of the image sequences. Therefore, relatively simple components were chosen, which have low costs in online and also offline mode, because it is possible to test more parameter settings.

2.1 Preprocessing and Segmentation

The relevant information of laser welding images is in the pixel intensity; it represents the temperature. A statistical approach for object-background separation is used. BROCKE [3] introduces an approach in which the image sequence is standardized pixel-wise to a uniform variance.

$$f(x, y, t, n) = \frac{g(x, y, t, n) - \langle g(x, y, t, n)\rangle_{t_s, \Delta t}}{\sqrt{\langle [g(x, y, t, n) - \langle g(x, y, t, n)\rangle_{t_s, \Delta t}]^2\rangle_{t_s, \Delta t}}} \tag{1}$$

$g(x, y, t, n)$ is the nth sequence, $\langle . \rangle_{t_s, \Delta t}$ is the average function over interval Δt starting at t_s. The assumption is that the values are normally distributed $N(0, 1)$. The sputter is of a different nature and is found above a threshold θ which sensibly is in the range of $2.0 \cdots 4.0$ [3].

For sputterless sequences, the number of pixels above threshold is low (see Table 1). However, there is no physically relevant event and the active pixels show no temporal or spatial correlation over the sequence. On the other hand, real events lead to coherent pixel groups.

Exceptions are two-dimensional reflections, which are no welding errors. These must be distinguished in the object classification.

Table 1. For an image sequence of approximately 700 frames at 64×64 pixel resolution, the number of objects is grouped by size in the three middle columns. Last column gives the pixel rate of the smallest objects.

θ	# pixel $f(.) \geq \theta$	# groups $\|O_{i,j}\| = 1 \cdots 5$	# groups $\|O_{i,j}\| = 6 \cdots 25$	# groups $\|O_{i,j}\| > 25$	# pixel $\|O_{i,j}\| = 1 \cdots 5$
2.0	76723	34162	735	166	42078 (54.8 %)
2.5	29025	15121	147	51	17717 (61.0 %)
3.0	12980	5592	88	27	6477 (49.9 %)
3.5	6883	2421	43	27	2840 (41.3 %)
4.0	4149	1098	39	18	1337 (32.2 %)

The idea is to detect more pixels in a first step to detect all sputters subsequently. According to image processing sequence after normalization, binarization, and segmentation connected objects are detected. In a following rough classification the smaller pixel groups are then filtered out, all others are brought to the object classification.

2.2   Feature Extraction

After the segmentation there are objects as hypotheses for class *Sputter*. For the objects we use global features, primarily the 2D central moment based invariants of low order [10]. Also, the function value of $f(x, y, t, n)$ exists as a factor in some features, because it provides information about the significance of the outlier. The list of features is arbitrarily expandable in the concept. It is important to get many simple translation invariant features from 2D image processing without previous knowledge.

2.3   Object Classification with Polynomial Classifier

The 2D hypotheses presented by the algorithm must be classified into two groups *Sputter* and *Non-Sputter*. According to our philosophy of using simple components we choose the polynomial classifier (PC) for the object classification. PC is faster compared with newer classifiers [6]. Unlike neural net parameters which require iterative optimization, an analytic solution is available for the choice of PC parameters. A long adaptation process whose exit condition has a strong influence on the result is not necessary. The recognition rate is comparable with multi-layer perceptron (MLP) [5].

PC is based on polynomial regression [9]. The polynomial structure list $x(v)$ is produced from the feature vector $v = m_o(n, t)$, o for object. It contains all monomials with maximal polynomial degree G. According to [9], a matrix product represents the decision vector, $d_{PC}(v) = A^T x(v)$.

$d_{PC}(v)$ will be clipped to the interval $[0,1]$ and can be interpreted as a membership probability for the two classes. It is only necessary to know $d_{PC,Sputter}(v)$ for class *Sputter*, because $\sum d_{PC}(v) = 1$ holds. Under the assumption that enough observations are available for the estimate of A, there is a higher confidence in predictions with values close to 0 or 1.

2.4   Image Sequence Classification with Aggregate Function

The real aim is the classification of the complete sequence. Therefore, the classification of the object hypotheses must still be condensed into a complete statement. At the beginning we noted that random 2D events are not correlated. In other words, sputter appears in a row of frames.

To use this effect for the second stage classification, the event hypotheses of time neighboring frames are summarized. The window size of time slot, which slides over the frames, is arbitrary. We propose to choose the window not larger than the shortest sputter sequence in the training database. There are also simple link operations for aggregate function like summation.

For each frame we choose the hypothesis with the highest value $d_{PC,Sputter}(v)$. If there is no hypothesis in a frame, the value is set to 0. Finally, the values are summarized in an aggregate function $a(d_1, \cdots, d_w)$. We suggest $\sum_{i=1}^{w} d_i$, $\prod_{i=1}^{w} d_i$ and $Min(d_1, \cdots, d_w)$ as possible realizations. The first both functions can compensate fluctuation within few frames. The last step is to select a class based on a threshold. If there are w successive frames with $a(d_1, \cdots, d_w) > \Theta$, the part is defective, otherwise faultless.

3   System Optimization

Quality control in the industrial production is primarily centered around error recognition. Wrong decisions are weighted differently. The classification is optimized by a loss function that implements the strongly asymmetric costs. It is customary to arrange the loss function into a loss matrix as shown in below equations.

$$L = \begin{vmatrix} L_{IO,IO} & L_{IO,NIO} \\ L_{NIO,IO} & L_{NIO,NIO} \end{vmatrix}, \qquad L_{IO,IO} = L_{NIO,NIO} = 0,$$

$$L_{IO,NIO} \ll L_{NIO,IO}$$

The first argument represents the true class, the second one the estimate class, IO faultless, and NIO defective. The aim is to find a decision function which minimizes the Bayes risk $r = E\{L\}$. In the univariate case, a strong asymmetry means that the decision threshold is moved so far in one direction that all faulty parts are detected. In other words, the worst NIO part influences the decision threshold.

A missed NIO part cannot be compensated in empirical loss $\hat{r}$. $\hat{r}$ will have a very flighty behavior regarding slightly changed parameter settings and feature combinations. A smart feature selection has a great potential for performance improvement. In many complex pattern recognition tasks this aspect is undervalued. In the presence of high complexity, as in our case with a two-stage classification, a feature selection done by the user is only suboptimal and a stochastic search method is more meaningful.

Here the PC suggests itself, because the maximum polynomial degree G is the only control parameter. In this work, the so-called wrapper method [4] is used. The feature subset will be tested directly in combination with the classifier. In other words, the wrapper approach conducts a search for a good subset using the induction algorithm itself as part of the evaluation function. The advantage is that the selection criteria is not abstract which perhaps does not correspond to the nature of the used classifier.

The wrapper method is expensive since it requires full adaptation of the classifier. The complexity of a complete search is $O(2^n)$. The complete search is feasible only for small n. Therefore, a single 10-fold cross validation is used.

3.1   Efficient Cross Validation

The equation for estimation of the coefficient matrix is $E\{xx^T\} \cdot A = E\{xy^T\}$. The input vector is x and the supervised decision vector is y, with $|y| = 1$ and coding only with 0 and 1. Both expectation values are also called moment matrices.

The class wise moment matrices are calculated and weighted[1] [9].

$$E\{xx^T\} = \sum_{k=1}^{K} m_k E\{x_k x_k^T\}, \qquad \sum_{k=1}^{K} m_k = 1, m_k \geq 0 \qquad (2)$$

---

[1] Either it gets equal weighted or proportional to frequency of instances.

$$E\{x_k x_k^T\} = \frac{1}{I} \sum_{i=1}^{I} x(v) \cdot x(v)^T \tag{3}$$

Moments calculated once can be reused in the cross validation. The instances are divided into C subsets. For each subset the moment matrix is computed. After that, the moment matrix for each cross validation combination is computed by summation of all subset moment matrices (see equations 4 and 5). A part of the adaptation costs are saved, in contrast to MLP, which requires a new adaptation for every new feature subset. This reduces the analysis time compared with other methods.

$$E\{x_k x_k^T\} = \frac{1}{C_k} \sum_{i=1}^{C_k} m_k x(v_{C_{k,i}}) \cdot x(v_{C_{k,i}})^T \tag{4}$$

$$E\{xx^T\} = \frac{1}{I} \sum_{k=1}^{C} C_k \cdot E\{x_k x_k^T\} \tag{5}$$

3.2 Modified Sequential Forward Selection

There are two principal sequential search strategies, sequential forward selection (SFS) and sequential backward elimination (SBE) [2]. The first one starts with an empty set which is increased step-by-step with only one additional feature. Only the best combination is selected after every generation. Contrary, SBE begins with the complete feature set and eliminates only one feature at a time. Both SFS and SBE have a reduced complexity of $O(n^2)$ compared to an exhaustive enumeration of all subsets, which has a complexity of $O(2^n)$. One disadvantage of both SFS and SBE is that once a feature is selected/eliminated it is never replaced. In the style of the BEAM-algorithm [1], we use the best k subsets, which will increase or exchange one feature for each new generation of subsets. These will be evaluated through polynomial classifier and after that it will be repeated with next k best subsets until there is no further improvement.

3.3 Simultaneous Optimization of Two-Stage Classification

In the offline mode, the parameters of the system are optimized. No perfect object recognition is attempted for in the first stage. It is assumed that a worse object recognition becomes a better image sequence recognition, because a defective welding consists of several sputters. Cross validation tests and evaluates different polynomial degrees, aggregate functions, time slots, and threshold Θ systematically.

4   Experimental Results

The system has been tested on a dataset of 629 IO and 150 NIO image sequences which include 5294 labeled objects, i.e. the user provides the class information to

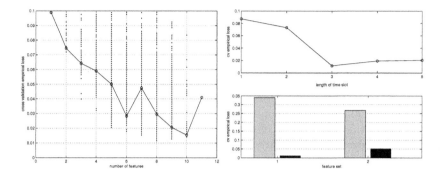

Fig. 2. Left: All tested feature sets with number of features and recognition rate (cross validation empirical loss $\hat{r}$). It shows in addition the results of SFS (solid line). Top Right: Influence of time slot for the optimal feature subset. $(a(d_1, \cdots, d_w) = \sum_{i=1}^{w} d_i)$ Bottom Right: Comparison of empirical loss on object (*gray*) and sequence basis (*black*). Feature set 1 corresponds to the optimal system solution found, feature set 2 to the optimal object classification.

every larger object hypothesis. The settings were $L_{IO,NIO} = 1$ and $L_{NIO,IO} = 100$ with a single 10-fold cross validation. There were 20 features altogether per object. The modified forward search ran for 10 generations with $k = 5$, such that 3131 subsets were tested.

The results are shown in Figure 2. There is a high variance of recognition rate, the optimum is 8 features with a cross validation empirical loss $\hat{r} = 0.012$, that means a recognition rate of 98.8%. Similar results are obtained with SFS ($\hat{r} = 0.015$), but a deterioration arises at 7 features. The choice of the time slot and aggregate function has great influence on the results whereas the summation and window width 3 has proved themselve almost generally. This can be attributed to the used data set.

Surprisingly, the object recognition rate of sputters was low. At an object classification carried out empirical loss was $\hat{r} = 0.341$ with $L_{Non-Sputter,Sputter} = 10$ and $L_{Sputter,Non-Sputter} = 1$ (that is the 29 fold sequence risk). A feature selection executed directly on an object basis yielded a set of 6 features ($\hat{r} = 0.267$). On a sequence basis the PC can separate the image sequences comparatively well, but is considerably worse than the global optimum, 0.051 vs. 0.012.

5   Conclusion and Outlook

In this work, a system concept was introduced for classification of image sequences whose component parameters can be suboptimal because we optimize the whole system by a asymmetric loss function. PC does not have the performance of newer types of classifiers, but due to the low number of control parameters and short adaptation time it is well suited for a complex system like the introduced two-stage classification. A great variety of parameter settings and feature combinations can be tested, exploiting a great optimization potential which was proved in the experiment.

Alternative strategies for feature selection like genetic algorithms are also promising [8]. In practical applications, the appearance of unknown, atypical image sequences plays a role. Additional information about the confidence would be meaningful. The examination of the Hat-matrix which expresses the leverage of influential cases in the regression model especially offers itself in the case of PC. In other cases, a comparison with the distribution of the dataset can be helpful to study the predictive capability.

References

1. Aha, D.W., Bankert, R.L.: *A comparative evaluation of sequential feature selection algorithms*, Fifth International Workshop on Artificial Intelligence and Statistics, editors Fisher, D. & Lenz, H., pp. 1–7, 1995.
2. Boz, O.: *Feature Subset Selection by Using Sorted Feature Relevance*, International Conference on Machine Learning and Applications (ICMLA'02), June 24–27, 2002.
3. Brocke, M.: *Statistical Image Sequence Processing for Temporal Change Detection*, In: Van Gool, L., Mustererkennung 2002, 24.DAGM-Symposium, Zürich.
4. Kohavi, R., John, G.H.: *Wrappers for Feature Subset Selection*, Artificial Intelligence 97(1–2), pp. 273–324, 1997.
5. Kressel, U., Franke, J., Schürmann, J.: *Polynomklassifikator versus Multilayer-Perzeptron*, In: Grosskopf, R.E., Mustererkennung 1990, 12.DAGM-Symposium, Oberkochen.
6. LeCun, Y. et al.: *Comparison of learning algorithms for handwritten digit recognition*, International Conference on Artificial Neural Networks, Fogelman, F. and Gallinari, P. (Ed.), pp. 53–60, 1995.
7. Nordbruch, S., Tschirner, P., Gräser, A.: *Analyse von HDRC-Bildern des Werkstoffübergangs des MSG-Schweissprozesses*, In: Sommer, G., Mustererkennung 2000, 22.DAGM-Symposium, Kiel.
8. Raymer, M.L. et al.: *Dimensionality reduction using genetic algorithms*, IEEE Transactions on Evolutionary Computation, vol. 4(2), pp. 164–171, 2000.
9. Schürmann, J.: *Pattern Classification*. John Wiley and Sons, Inc., New York 1996.
10. Teague, M.R.: *Image Analysis via the General Theory of Moments*, Opt. Soc. of America, vol. 70, no. 8, pp. 920–930, 1980.

3D Parametric Intensity Models for the Localization of Different Types of 3D Anatomical Point Landmarks in Tomographic Images

Stefan Wörz and Karl Rohr

School of Information Technology, Computer Vision & Graphics Group
International University in Germany, 76646 Bruchsal
{woerz,rohr}@i-u.de

Abstract. We introduce a new approach for the localization of 3D anatomical point landmarks based on 3D parametric intensity models which are directly fit to an image. We propose different analytic intensity models based on the Gaussian error function in conjunction with 3D rigid transformations as well as deformations to efficiently model tip-like, saddle-like, and sphere-like structures. The approach has been successfully applied to accurately localize anatomical landmarks in 3D MR and 3D CT image data. We have also compared the experimental results with the results of a previously proposed 3D differential operator. It turns out that the new approach significantly improves the localization accuracy.

1 Introduction

The localization of 3D anatomical point landmarks is an important task in medical image analysis. Landmarks are useful image features in a variety of applications, for example, for the registration of 3D brain images of different modalities or the registration of images with digital atlases. The current standard procedure, however, is to localize 3D anatomical point landmarks manually which is difficult, time consuming, and error-prone. To improve the current situation it is therefore important to develop automated methods.

In previous work on the localization of 3D anatomical point landmarks, 3D differential operators have been proposed (e.g., Thirion [12], Rohr [10]). Recently, an evaluation study of nine different 3D differential operators has been performed by Hartkens et al. [7]. 2D differential approaches for extracting point landmarks in 2D medical images have been described in Briquer et al. [3] and Hartkens et al. [6]. While being computationally efficient, differential operators incorporate only small local neighbourhoods of an image and are therefore relatively sensitive to noise, which leads to false detections and also affects the localization accuracy. Recently, an approach based on deformable models was introduced (Frantz et al. [4], Alker et al. [1]). With this approach tip-like anatomical structures are modeled by *surface* models, which are fit to the image data using an edge-based fitting measure. However, the approach requires the detection of 3D image edges as well as the formulation of a relatively complicated fitting measure.

B. Michaelis and G. Krell (Eds.): DAGM 2003, LNCS 2781, pp. 220–227, 2003.

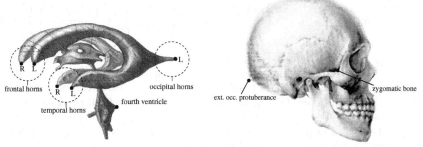

Fig. 1. Ventricular horns of the human brain (from [11]) and the human skull (from [2]). Examples of 3D point landmarks are indicated by black dots.

We have developed a new approach for the localization of 3D anatomical point landmarks. In contrast to previous approaches the central idea is to use 3D parametric *intensity* models of anatomical structures. In comparison to differential approaches, larger image regions and thus semi-global image information is taken into account. In comparison to approaches based on surface models, we directly exploit the intensity information of anatomical structures. Therefore, more a priori knowledge and much more image information is taken into account in our approach to improve the robustness against noise and to increase the localization accuracy. Also, a much simpler fitting measure can be used.

2 Parametric Intensity Models for Anatomical Structures

Our approach uses 3D parametric intensity models which are fit directly to the intensities of the image data. These models describe the image intensities of anatomical structures in a semi-global region as a function of a certain number of parameters. The main characteristic in comparison to general deformable models is that they exhibit a prominent point which defines the position of the landmark. By fitting a parametric intensity model to the image intensities we obtain a *subvoxel* estimate of the position as well as estimates of the other parameters, e.g., the image contrast. As important classes of 3D anatomical point landmarks we here consider tip-like, saddle-like, and sphere-like structures.

3D Intensity Model of Tip-Like Structures. Tip-like structures can be found, for example, within the human head at the ventricular system (e.g., the tips of the frontal, occipital, or temporal horns, see Fig. 1) and at the skull (e.g., the tip of the external occipital protuberance). The shape of these anatomical structures is ellipsoidal. Therefore, to model them we use a (half-)ellipsoid defined by three semi-axes (r_x, r_y, r_z) and the intensity levels a_0 (outside) and a_1 (inside). We also introduce Gaussian smoothing specified by a parameter σ to incorporate image blurring effects. The exact model of a Gaussian smoothed ellipsoid cannot be expressed in analytic form and thus is computationally expensive. To efficiently represent the resulting 3D intensity structure we developed an analytic model as an approximation. This model is based on the Gaussian error function $\Phi(x) = \int_{-\infty}^{x} (2\pi)^{-1/2} e^{-\xi^2/2} d\xi$ and can be written as

$$g_{Ell.}(\mathbf{x}) = a_0 + (a_1 - a_0) \; \Phi \left(\frac{\sqrt[3]{r_x r_y r_z}}{\sigma} \left(1 - \sqrt{\frac{x^2}{r_x^2} + \frac{y^2}{r_y^2} + \frac{(z + r_z)^2}{r_z^2}} \right) \right) \quad (1)$$

where $\mathbf{x} = (x, y, z)$. We define the tip of the ellipsoid w.r.t. the semi-axis r_z as the position of the landmark, which also is the center of the local coordinate system. In addition, we include a 3D rigid transform $\mathcal{R}$ with rotation parameters (α, β, γ) and translation parameters (x_0, y_0, z_0). Moreover, we extend our model to a more general class of tip-like structures by applying a tapering deformation $\mathcal{T}$ with the parameters ρ_x and ρ_y, and a bending deformation $\mathcal{B}$ with the parameters δ (strength) and ν (direction), which are defined by

$$\mathcal{T}(\mathbf{x}) = \begin{pmatrix} x\,(1 + z\,\rho_x/r_z) \\ y\,(1 + z\,\rho_y/r_z) \\ z \end{pmatrix} \quad \text{and} \quad \mathcal{B}(\mathbf{x}) = \begin{pmatrix} x - z^2\delta \cos\nu \\ y - z^2\delta \sin\nu \\ z \end{pmatrix} \quad (2)$$

This results in the parametric intensity model with a total of 16 parameters:

$$g_M(\mathbf{x}, \mathbf{p}) = g_{Ell.}(\mathcal{T}(\mathcal{B}(\mathcal{R}(\boldsymbol{x})))) \quad (3)$$

$$\mathbf{p}_{Ell.} = (r_x, r_y, r_z, a_0, a_1, \sigma, \rho_x, \rho_y, \delta, \nu, \alpha, \beta, \gamma, x_0, y_0, z_0) \quad (4)$$

3D Intensity Model of Saddle-Like Structures. Saddle-like structures can be found, for example, within the human head at the zygomatic bone (see Fig. 1). These structures can be modelled by a bended ellipsoid where the bending is symmetrical w.r.t. the center of the ellipsoid. Therefore, we modify (1) such that the center of the local coordinate system is localized at the tip of the ellipsoid w.r.t the semi-axis r_x. By restricting the direction of the bending deformation $\mathcal{B}$ towards the x-axis, i.e. setting $\nu = 0$ in (2), we achieve a saddle-like structure where the curvature of the bending is maximal at the center of the local coordinate system. This defines the position of the landmark. Besides the bending deformation we also apply a 3D rigid transform $\mathcal{R}$. Here, we do not use a tapering deformation. Applying the transformations, we obtain the parametric intensity model with a total of 13 parameters:

$$\mathbf{p}_{Saddle} = (r_x, r_y, r_z, a_0, a_1, \sigma, \delta, \alpha, \beta, \gamma, x_0, y_0, z_0) \quad (5)$$

3D Intensity Model of Sphere-Like Structures. Sphere-like structures are, for example, human eyes. These structures can be modelled by a sphere with radius R. Fortunately, the exact model of a Gaussian smoothed sphere can be expressed in analytic form (see [8]) and is given by

$$g_{Sphere}(\mathbf{x}) = \Phi_\sigma(R - r) - \Phi_\sigma(-R - r) - \sigma^2 r^{-1}(G_\sigma(R - r) - G_\sigma(R + r)) \quad (6)$$

where $r = \sqrt{x^2 + y^2 + z^2}$, $\Phi_\sigma(x) = \Phi(x/\sigma)$, and $G_\sigma(x) = (\sqrt{2\pi}\sigma)^{-1} e^{-\frac{x^2}{2\sigma^2}}$. We define the center of the sphere as the position of the landmark. In addition, we include the intensity levels a_0 and a_1 as well as a 3D translation. This results in the parametric intensity model with a total of 7 parameters:

$$\mathbf{p}_{Sphere} = (R, a_0, a_1, \sigma, x_0, y_0, z_0) \quad (7)$$

Table 1. Size and resolution of the medical 3D images used in the experiments.

Image	Slices	Size (Voxels)	Resolution (mm³)
Woho (MR)	sagittal	$256 \times 256 \times 256$	$1.0 \quad \times 1.0 \quad \times 1.0$
C06 (MR)	axial	$256 \times 256 \times 120$	$0.859 \times 0.859 \times 1.2$
C06 (CT)	axial	$320 \times 320 \times 87$	$0.625 \times 0.625 \times 1.0$

3 Model Fitting Approach

Estimates of the model parameters in (4), (5), and (7) are found by a least-squares fit of the model to the image intensities $g(x)$ within semi-global regions-of-interest (ROIs), thus minimizing the objective function

$$\sum_{x \in \text{ROI}} \left(g_M(x, p) - g(x)\right)^2 \qquad (8)$$

Note, the fitting measure does not include any derivatives. This is in contrast to previous fitting measures for surface models which incorporate the image gradient as well as 1st order derivatives of the model (e.g., [4]).

For the minimization we apply the method of Levenberg-Marquardt, incorporating 1st order partial derivatives of the intensity model w.r.t. the model parameters. In [9] such type of approach has been used for localizing 2D corner and edge features. The partial derivatives can be derived analytically using the generalized chain rule. Note, we do not need to compute the image gradient as is the case with surface models. We need 1st order derivatives of the intensity model only for the minimization process, whereas the surface model approach requires 2nd order derivatives for the minimization.

4 Experimental Results: 3D Synthetic Data

We applied our approach to synthetic 3D image data generated by the three intensity models itself with added Gaussian noise. For the ellipsoidal model, we carried out about 3000 experiments with different parameter settings and achieved a very high localization accuracy with a maximum error in the estimated position of less than 0.15 voxels (except in one case we got 0.35 voxels). We also found that the approach is robust w.r.t. the choice of initial parameters. Additionally, for about 2000 experiments with similar settings but very intense Gaussian noise down to a signal-to-noise ratio of ca. 1, the maximum localization error turned out to be less than 0.53 voxels. For the saddle model, we carried out about 5000 similar experiments. The resulting localization errors turned out to be about twice as large as for the ellipsoidal model. For the spherical model, the results of 5000 similar experiments are much better than the results of the other two models, i.e. the localization error is less than 0.17 voxels even with very intense Gaussian noise down to a signal-to-noise ratio of ca. 0.1.

5 Experimental Results: 3D Medical Images

We also applied the new approach to three real 3D tomographic images of the human head (datasets Woho and C06, see Table 1).

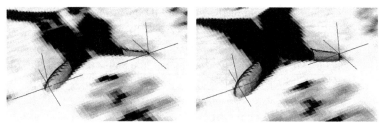

Fig. 2. 3D contour plots of the fitted intensity models for the left and right frontal horn within an MR image (Woho). The result is shown for two different slices of the original data. The marked axes indicate the estimated landmark positions.

We considered seven tip-like landmarks, i.e. the frontal, occipital, and temporal horns (left and right) as well as the external occipital protuberance, and two saddle-like landmarks, i.e. the zygomatic bone (left and right). For these landmarks in all three images we used as ground truth, positions that were manually determined in agreement with up to four persons. For the CT image, we did not consider the temporal horns since either the ground truth position was missing due to very low signal-to-noise ratio (left horn) or it was not possible to successfully fit the intensity model (right horn). Particularly with this landmark the image quality was very bad. In addition, we considered two sphere-like landmarks in the MR images, i.e. the left and right eye.

Parameter Settings. The fitting procedure described above requires the determination of suitable initial parameter values. The specification of these values is not a trivial task. Often all values are initialized manually, which is time-consuming. In case of the ellipsoidal model, we automatically initialize half of the model parameters. Values for the most important parameters, namely, the translation parameters (x_0, y_0, z_0) defining the position of the landmark were obtained by a 3D differential operator. Here we used the operator $Op3 = det C_g / trace C_g$, where C_g is the averaged dyadic product of the image gradient ([10]). This initialization was successfull for model fitting except in two cases, where the positions of Op3 were relatively far away from the ground truth positions (see Table 4). In these two cases, we initialized the translation parameters manually. The smoothing parameter σ was always initialized with 1.0 and the deformation parameters ρ_x, ρ_y, δ, and ν were all initialized with 0.0, thus, the intensity model was always initialized as an ellipsoid without deformation. The remaining parameters and the size of the ROI were initialized manually. For the saddle and spherical model, all parameters were so far initialized manually.

Results. Tables 2, 3, and 4 show the fitting results for the considered landmarks. In case of the ellipsoidal model, model fitting needed 75 iterations on average. We have visualized the fitting results of the left and right frontal horn within an MR image in Figure 2 and of the external occipital protuberance for the C06 image pair in Figure 3 using 3D Slicer ([5]). The average distance between the estimated landmark positions and the ground truth positions for all 19 tip-like landmarks computes to $\bar{e} = 1.14mm$. In comparison, using the 3D differential

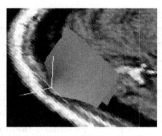

Fig. 3. 3D contour plots of the fitted intensity model for the external occipital protuberance within the original image pair C06 (left MR and right CT). Note, the size of the ROI and the used deformations are different.

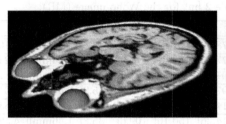

Fig. 4. 3D contour plots of the fitted intensity model for the eyes within an MR image (Woho) and for the left zygomatic bone within an CT image.

Table 2. Fitting results for the ventricular horns and the external occipital protuberance (ellipsoidal model), for the zygomatic bone (saddle model), and for the eyes (spherical model) for the C06 image (MR). The estimated landmark position, intensity levels, and the distance e to the ground truth position are given. For comparison, the distance e_{Op3} of the differential operator $Op3$ to the ground truth position is listed.

C06 (MR)	$\hat{x}_0$	$\hat{y}_0$	$\hat{z}_0$	$\hat{a}_0$	$\hat{a}_1$	e	e_{Op3}
Left frontal horn	150.65	79.58	68.14	91.6	22.3	1.27mm	1.92mm
Right frontal horn	112.34	76.85	69.02	93.9	18.8	0.58mm	1.72mm
Left occipital horn	143.91	200.85	53.01	84.9	15.2	0.15mm	3.32mm
Right occipital horn	107.82	195.98	56.04	86.6	20.0	0.70mm	1.72mm
Left temporal horn	164.01	117.26	45.38	82.4	12.8	1.20mm	1.71mm
Right temporal horn	98.98	112.23	40.63	80.0	18.8	0.97mm	2.10mm
Ext. occipital protub.	130.05	230.94	32.97	61.6	8.7	0.06mm	1.21mm
					Mean	0.70mm	1.96mm
Left zygomatic bone	192.29	62.81	34.46	121.7	20.8	1.42mm	1.21mm
Right zygomatic bone	70.94	60.95	31.66	128.2	14.9	0.99mm	1.48mm
Left eye	167.16	41.69	44.42	90.4	24.7		
Right eye	98.00	40.68	43.50	97.5	25.4		

operator Op3, we obtain an average distance of $\bar{e}_{Op3} = 2.18mm$. Thus, the localization accuracy with our new approach turns out to be much better.

The results for the saddle model are worse in comparison to the ellipsoidal model. The average distance between the estimated landmark positions and the ground truth positions for all 6 saddle-like landmarks computes to $\bar{e} = 1.84mm$.

Table 3. Same as Table 2 but for the C06 image (CT).

C06 (CT)	$\hat{x}_0$	$\hat{y}_0$	$\hat{z}_0$	$\hat{a}_0$	$\hat{a}_1$	e	e_{Op3}
Left frontal horn	192.80	93.94	77.04	1043.5	996.8	1.33mm	0.63mm
Right frontal horn	135.31	90.46	78.14	1036.7	1001.8	1.26mm	2.10mm
Left occipital horn	184.07	260.57	69.21	1038.5	989.7	0.66mm	0.00mm
Right occipital horn	129.50	255.77	72.88	1045.0	994.0	0.94mm	1.33mm
Ext. occipital protub.	161.20	309.43	48.01	1007.9	2679.0	1.10mm	1.72mm
					Mean	1.06mm	1.16mm
Left zygomatic bone	245.91	77.37	49.73	976.1	2829.0	1.49mm	0.63mm
Right zygomatic bone	79.17	75.24	50.80	977.1	2918.0	1.81mm	1.00mm

Table 4. Same as Table 2 but for the Woho image (MR).

Woho	$\hat{x}_0$	$\hat{y}_0$	$\hat{z}_0$	$\hat{a}_0$	$\hat{a}_1$	e	e_{Op3}
Left frontal horn	111.26	78.26	101.84	124.0	23.8	2.22mm	3.16mm
Right frontal horn	111.49	77.54	132.27	117.3	20.1	1.44mm	2.24mm
Left occipital horn	189.38	101.53	91.62	107.3	23.3	2.31mm	4.12mm
Right occipital horn	182.63	97.42	150.02	112.7	15.9	0.68mm	3.61mm
Left temporal horn	134.90	111.86	88.81	95.1	44.3	1.80mm	2.83mm
Right temporal horn	129.24	114.36	150.16	109.6	35.8	1.46mm	4.58mm
Ext. occipital protub.	232.14	149.73	120.96	84.2	26.8	1.48mm	1.41mm
					Mean	1.63mm	3.14mm
Left zygomatic bone	96.46	125.64	58.69	167.2	47.1	2.22mm	3.00mm
Right zygomatic bone	89.59	128.50	179.83	197.8	12.1	3.12mm	2.45mm
Left eye	73.49	107.70	82.47	114.8	29.9		
Right eye	70.16	105.95	151.44	122.2	30.4		

In comparison, using the 3D differential operator Op3, we obtain an average distance of $\bar{e}_{Op3} = 1.63mm$. In addition, it turned out that the saddle model depends more on the initial parameter values than the other models. The results for the spherical model are very good. The fitted model describes the image intensities fairly well and also the model fitting is very robust w.r.t. the initial parameters. Figure 4 shows the fitting result for both eyes within an MR image.

The execution time of our algorithm is mainly dependent on the size of the ROI, the chosen variant of the deformation, and the quality of the initial parameters. As a typical example, the fitting time for the right temporal horn in the Woho image including tapering and bending deformations and a diameter of the ROI of 19 voxels is ca. 1s (on a AMD Athlon, 1.7GHz, running Linux).

6   Discussion

The experiments verify the applicability of our new approach, which yields sub-voxel positions of 3D anatomical landmarks. The intensity models describe the anatomical structures fairly well as can be seen from the 3D contour plots. Also, the figures demonstrate that the spectrum of possible shapes of our intensity models is relatively large. An issue for further work is the automatic initialization of all model parameters, e.g., based on differential properties of the image.

Acknowledgement. The original MR and CT images have kindly been provided by Philips Research Hamburg and W.P.Th.M. Mali, L. Ramos, and C.W.M. van Veelen (Utrecht University Hospital) via ICS-AD of Philips Medical Systems Best.

References

1. M. Alker, S. Frantz, K. Rohr, and H.S. Stiehl, "Improving the Robustness in Extracting 3D Point Landmarks from 3D Medical Images Using Parametric Deformable Models", *Proc. MICCAI'2001*, Utrecht, The Netherlands, Oct. 14–17, 2001, *Lecture Notes in Computer Science* 2208, W.J. Niessen and M.A. Viergever (Eds.), Springer-Verlag Berlin Heidelberg 2001, 582–590

2. R. Bertolini and G. Leutert, *Atlas der Anatomie des Menschen. Band 3:Kopf, Hals, Gehirn, Rückenmark und Sinnesorgane*, Springer-Verlag, Berlin, 1982

3. L. Le Briquer, F. Lachmann, and C. Barillot, "Using Local Extremum Curvatures to Extract Anatomical Landmarks from Medical Images", *Medical Imaging 1993: Image Processing*, 16–19 Febr. 1993, Newport Beach, California/USA, Proc. SPIE 1898, M.H. Loew (Ed.), 549–558

4. S. Frantz, K. Rohr, and H.S. Stiehl, "Localization Of 3D Anatomical Point Landmarks In 3D Tomographic Images Using Deformable Models", *Proc. MICCAI'2000*, Pittsburgh, Pennsylvania/USA, Oct. 11–14, 2000, *Lecture Notes in Computer Science* 1935, S.L. Delp, A.M. DiGioia, and B. Jaramaz (Eds.), Springer-Verlag Berlin Heidelberg, 2000, 492–501

5. D.T. Gering, A. Nabavi, R. Kikinis, W.E.L. Grimson, N. Hata, P.Everett, F. Jolesz, and W.M. Wells, "An Integrated Visualization System for Surgical Planning and Guidance using Image Fusion and Interventional Imaging", *Proc. MICCAI'99*, Cambridge England, Sep. 19–22, 1999, *Lecture Notes in Computer Science* 1679, C. Taylor and A. Colchester (Eds.), Springer-Verlag Berlin Heidelberg, 1999, 808–819

6. T. Hartkens, K.Rohr, and H.S. Stiehl, "Evaluierung von Differentialoperatoren zur Detektion charakteristischer Punkte in tomographischen Bildern", *Proc. 18. DAGM-Symposium Mustererkennung (DAGM'96)*, 11.–13. Sept. 1996, Heidelberg/Germany, *Informatik aktuell*, B. Jähne, P. Geißler, H. Haußecker, and F.Hering (Eds.), Springer-Verlag Berlin Heidelberg, 1996, 637–644

7. T. Hartkens, K.Rohr, and H.S. Stiehl, "Evaluation of 3D Operators for the Detection of Anatomical Point Landmarks in MR and CT Images", *Computer Vision and Image Understanding* 85, 2002, 1–19

8. R.M. Kessler, J.R. Ellis, Jr., and M. Eden, "Analysis of Emission Tomographic Scan Data: Limitations Imposed by Resolution and Background", *Journal of Computer Assisted Tomography* 8:3, 1984, 514–522

9. K. Rohr, "Recognizing Corners by Fitting Parametric Models", *International J. of Computer Vision* 9:3, 1992, 213–230

10. K. Rohr, "On 3D differential operators for detecting point landmarks", *Image and Vision Computing* 15:3, 1997, 219–233

11. J. Sobotta, *Atlas der Anatomie des Menschen. Band 1: Kopf, Hals, obere Extremität, Haut*, Urban & Schwarzenberg, München, 19th edition, 1988

12. J.-P. Thirion, "New Feature Points based on Geometric Invariants for 3D Image Registration", *Int. J. of Computer Vision* 18:2, 1996, 121–137

Comparing Clustering Methods for Database Categorization in Image Retrieval

Thomas Käster, Volker Wendt, and Gerhard Sagerer*

Applied Computer Science, Faculty of Technology,
Bielefeld University, P.O. Box 100131, 33501 Bielefeld, Germany
{tkaester,vwendt,sagerer}@techfak.uni-bielefeld.de

Abstract. Applying image retrieval techniques to large image databases requires the restriction of search space to provide adequate response time. This restriction can be done by means of clustering techniques to partition the image data set into subspaces of similar elements. In this article several clustering methods and validity indices are examined with regard to image categorization. A subset of the COIL-100 image collection is clustered by different agglomerative hierarchical methods as well as the k-Means, PAM and CLARA clustering algorithms. The validity of the resulting clusters is determined by computing the Davies-Bouldin-Index and Calinski-Harabasz-Index. To evaluate the performance of the different combinations of clustering methods and validity indices with regard to semantically meaningful clusters, the results are compared with a given reference grouping by measuring the Rand-Index.

1 Introduction

In recent years, caused by the explosive growth of digital stored image data and the necessity of its efficient management, content-based image retrieval has become an important research topic. Pre-computed image features are used to retrieve the imagery without any manual annotation of image content and keyword-based strategies.

In many cases, retrieval is performed as a simple step by step process where the query image is compared to each image of the data set. This straight-forward strategy suffers from computational costs indicated by the proportional ratio of the search time to the number of images and the dimension of the extracted features. Therefore this technique is limited to small databases and is not feasible for scaling to large image data sets. Scalability to large databases requires image grouping to restrict the search space and to avoid exhaustive comparisons. Clustering techniques are approved methods to organize multi-dimensional data and can be used to group similar images based on their visual features. Thus, a hierarchical retrieval process can be performed: First, the clusters which are most similar to the query image are selected. Second, the query image is compared to all elements of the chosen subset. Krishnamachari et al. [9] and Chen et al. [2] illustrate that a high retrieval accuracy can be achieved and that the search time does not increase linearly for a given accuracy. However, image clustering is processed in feature space, using low-level features without any supervision. Therefore correspondence to semantic classes cannot be ensured. But, providing a high-level image organization seems to be a

---

* This work has been supported by the BMB+F under contract 01IB 001B.

B. Michaelis and G. Krell (Eds.): DAGM 2003, LNCS 2781, pp. 228–235, 2003.
© Springer-Verlag Berlin Heidelberg 2003

desirable property because it offers a good initial database overview and improves the effectivity of image retrieval.

To address this issue we analyze different clustering methods and validity indices with regard to their suitability for image categorization. An evaluation scheme based on a high-level reference grouping is proposed that offers the possibility to check which combinations of clustering methods and indices are the most powerful to group the given image data set into semantically meaningful clusters. The adjusted Rand-Index [5] is applied to measure the correspondence between the formed clusters and the given reference grouping. The clustering methods considered in this article are various agglomerative methods [6], the k-Means clustering [4] as well as the PAM and CLARA algorithms which have been proposed by Kaufman and Rousseeuw [8]. The resulting partitionings are evaluated by the Davies-Bouldin-Index [3] and Calinski-Harabasz-Index [1] which are well-suited for assessing the performance of clustering methods [11].

The remainder of the paper is organized as follows: In the next section the applied clustering techniques are described. Afterwards the used indices are discussed in section 3 and the evaluation scheme is outlined in section 4. In section 5 the experimental results are presented and finally our concluding remarks are summarized.

2   Clustering Methods

Any image from an image collection is represented by a feature vector, containing information about its visual content. Therefore a collection of images is represented by a finite subset $X = \{x_1, \dots, x_N\}$ of the feature space. The purpose of image clustering is to find an appropriate grouping $G = \{C_1, \dots, C_K\}$ of this set, so that similar images are assigned to the same group. The clustering methods used in this study are discussed in the following paragraphs.

Agglomerative clustering starts with an initial set of clusters each one containing a single data element. Stepwise the two closest clusters are merged into one cluster. This process may be repeated until only one cluster remains which contains all elements. Agglomerative methods require measuring the distance between two clusters. Within our examinations the following popular inter-cluster distance measures are used: single, complete, average, centroid, median linkage and Ward's method. The mathematical definition of these measures are explained by Jain and Dubes [6]. For instance,

$$d(C_i, C_j) = \min_{x_i \in C_i, x_j \in C_j} d(x_i, x_j) \tag{1}$$

describes the distance between two clusters C_i and C_j using single linkage, where $d(x_i, x_j)$ is any distance measure between two vectors. For this calculation we have focused on the euclidean, manhattan and maximum distance [6]. In combination with the listed inter-cluster distance measures there is a total of 18 variants of agglomerative hierarchical methods we examined.

The **k-Means algorithm** [4] is an iterative process which aims to minimize the sum of the mean square errors

$$E = \sum_{i=1}^{K} \sum_{x \in C_i} ||x - m_i||^2 \tag{2}$$

of all clusters $\{C_1, \ldots, C_K\}$, where m_i is the centroid of cluster C_i. Based on a given number of clusters K the initial cluster prototypes are selected randomly. Afterwards each vector is assigned to the cluster of the closest prototype and a new prototype for each cluster is calculated as the centroid of all vectors within the same cluster. The process of vector assignment and prototype update is repeated until either the centroids do not shift or E does not change significantly in two successive steps.

The **PAM** (Partitioning Around Medoids) algorithm developed by Kaufman and Rousseeuw [8] is a variation of the well-known k-Means algorithm, motivated by the intention to handle outliers efficiently. Instead of choosing the cluster centroids to represent each cluster the most centrally positioned element within a cluster is chosen, the *medoid*. Initially the algorithm starts with a random selection of K medoids and clusters are formed by assigning the non-selected elements to the closest medoid. Then the medoids and the non-medoids are swapped successively as long as the quality of the clustering can be improved. However, the PAM algorithm suffers from its computational complexity. Therefore **CLARA** (Clustering LARge Applications) was proposed [8]. This algorithm randomly draws a sample of the data set, applies the PAM method and presents the resulting medoids of the sample set. To achieve a good approximation of the medoids of the whole data set several sample sets are drawn and only the medoids of the best clustering are returned.

3 Validity Indices and the Adjusted Rand-Index

Applying the above clustering algorithms with various parameterizations leads to different groupings of the data set. To distinguish good partitionings from worse ones, indices are necessary. Next, the quantities which were utilized in our study are described.

The **Davies-Bouldin-Index** [3] is motivated by the demand for strongly separated clusters. The separation of two clusters C_i and C_j is defined by the distance $m_{ij} = ||m_i - m_j||$ of the cluster centroids m_i and m_j as well as their average expansion e_i and e_j, respectively:

$$R_{ij} = \frac{e_i + e_j}{m_{ij}}, \quad \text{where} \quad e_k = \frac{1}{|C_k|} \sum_{x \in C_k} ||x - m_k||. \tag{3}$$

The greater R_{ij} the lower is the separation of both clusters C_i and C_j. Thus, the DB-Index of a grouping $G = \{C_1, \ldots, C_K\}$ is defined by

$$I_{DB} = \frac{1}{K} \sum_{i=1}^{K} R_i, \quad \text{with} \quad R_i = \max_{i \neq j} R_{ij}. \tag{4}$$

The smaller the index I_{DB} the better is the separation of clusters within the grouping G.

The **Calinski-Harabasz-Index** [1] is a quantity describing the degree of inter-cluster separation and intra-cluster homogeneity. It is derived from the dispersion matrix T of a data set $X = \{x_1, \ldots, x_N\}$ with mean $\bar{x}$, which can be separated into $T = B + W$:

$$B = \sum_{C_i \in G} |C_i|(m_i - \bar{x})(m_i - \bar{x})^{\mathrm{T}} \tag{5}$$

and

$$W = \sum_{C_i \in G} \sum_{x \in C_i} (x - m_i)(x - m_i)^{\mathrm{T}}. \tag{6}$$

Matrix B describes the dispersion of the cluster centroids and matrix W is the sum of the intra-cluster dispersions. Clearly a good clustering result should minimize dispersion within clusters and maximize separation between clusters, so the CH-Index is written as

$$I_{CH} = \frac{\mathrm{tr}(B)}{K - 1} \cdot \frac{N - K}{\mathrm{tr}(W)}, \tag{7}$$

where N is the number of data elements and K is the number of clusters. To describe the matrices B and W by means of a scalar quantity the traces are calculated to estimate dispersion and homogeneity.

In contrast to the discussed validity indices determining the **adjusted Rand-Index** [5] makes it possible to compare clustering results against a given semantically meaningful reference grouping. Therefore the resulting measure of agreement indicates how adequate is a clustering algorithm to form clusters of semantic similar images.

Calculating the Rand-Index requires two groupings $G = \{C_1, \dots, C_K\}$ and $G_R = \{C_1^R, \dots, C_L^R\}$ of the same data set $X = \{x_1, \dots, x_N\}$ so that $\bigcup_{k=1}^{K} C_k = X = \bigcup_{l=1}^{L} C_l^R$ and $C_k \cap C_{k'} = \emptyset = C_l^R \cap C_{l'}^R$ for $1 \le k \ne k' \le K$ and $1 \le l \ne l' \le L$.

Thereby G_R represents a reference grouping based on an external criterion and G is a clustering result. Let n_{kl} denote the number of elements that are common to cluster C_k and class C_l^R. Furthermore the number of elements in C_k and C_l^R are represented by $|C_k|$ and $|C_l^R|$, respectively. Based on this notation the adjusted Rand-Index is defined by

$$I_R = \frac{\sum_{kl} \binom{n_{kl}}{2} - \left[\sum_k \binom{|C_k|}{2} \sum_l \binom{|C_l^R|}{2} \right] / \binom{N}{2}}{\frac{1}{2} \left[\sum_k \binom{|C_k|}{2} + \sum_l \binom{|C_l^R|}{2} \right] - \left[\sum_k \binom{|C_k|}{2} \sum_l \binom{|C_l^R|}{2} \right] / \binom{N}{2}} \in [0, 1]. \tag{8}$$

The greater the value of the Rand-Index the greater is the correspondence between the reference grouping and the considered clustering result.

4 Evaluation Scheme

For each clustering method there should be an index to decide which result of the applied method is best. Any clustering algorithm can be expressed as a function $C_\theta : \mathcal{X} \to \mathcal{G}$ that gets a data set $X \in \mathcal{X}$ as input and results in a grouping $G \in \mathcal{G}$ of X. The result G depends on the parameterization θ of the algorithm. Any validity index gets a data set X and a grouping G as input and returns a scalar quantity as its result: $I_V : \mathcal{G} \times \mathcal{X} \to \mathbb{R}$. The process of finding the best cluster solution can be expressed formally as the solution of the optimization problem

$$\theta_V(X) = \arg \max_\theta I_V(C_\theta(X), X), \tag{9}$$

where $\theta_V(X)$ denotes the parameterization that yields the optimal result according to the index I_V.

To check whether a combination of a cluster algorithm and a validity index is suitable to form semantically meaningful clusters, the result is compared to a reference grouping $G_R \in \mathcal{G}$ by applying the Rand-Index which is a function $I_R : \mathcal{G} \times \mathcal{G} \to \mathbb{R}$. The greater the correspondence between the groupings the greater is the value of the Rand-Index. The parameterization yielding the best cluster result concerning the reference grouping G_R is given by

$$\theta_R(X, G_R) = \arg \max_\theta I_R(C_\theta(X), G_R), \tag{10}$$

which is very similar to equation 9. Normally no reference grouping is given. Therefore a validity index is the only possibility to make a decision about which parameterization leads to the best cluster result according to adequacy for semantic classification. To approximate this behavior, a suitable combination of cluster algorithm and validity index must fulfill

$$\theta_V(X) \approx \theta_R(X, G_R), \tag{11}$$

and consequently

$$I_R(C_{\theta_V}(X), G_R) \approx I_R(C_{\theta_R}(X), G_R). \tag{12}$$

Furthermore the number of clusters given by the optimal parameter θ_V should nearly match the number of groups within the reference grouping:

$$|C_{\theta_V}(X)| \approx |G_R|. \tag{13}$$

In addition any suitable clustering method should provide a large value of the Rand-Index. If all these three conditions are fulfilled for a given combination of validity index and clustering method it can be treated as suitable for clustering the image domain.

5   Experimental Results

Clustering images by their visual content requires the computation of visual features. We have computed features for a subset of the Columbia Object Image Library (COIL-100) [12]. This subset consists of $N = 1440$ color images of 20 objects each shown from 72 different perspectives and each representing a semantic class (s.Fig. 1). Every image is described by the following high-dimensional signatures which are components of the image retrieval system INDI [7]:

1. Color moments: 9-D feature which has been proposed by Stricker and Orengo [13]
2. Color distribution: 24-bin color histogram calculated in the HSV color space
3. Structure: 102-D feature calculated in the HSI color space by rastering the image and determining the mean value inside the resulting grids for each color channel

To avoid computational expensive image clustering we performed a principal component analysis of the above signatures. Within our examination each feature is represented by three principal components which are joined to one overall feature vector of nine dimensions.

Fig. 1. Subset of COIL-100 which forms 20 semantically disjoint classes. The chosen colored objects correspond to the grey-level objects of the COIL-20.

To apply our evaluation scheme, finding an appropriate parameterization θ is required. The parameterization which controls the clustering obviously depends on the used method. In case of the clustering methods examined in this study, the parameterization consists of the number of clusters the method should produce, so $\theta \equiv K$. For each clustering method the number of clusters were varied from $K_{min} = 2$ to $K_{max} = \sqrt{N} \approx 38$ as proposed by Maulik and Bandyopadhyay [10]. To conform to equation 9 the values of the DB-Index are inverted.

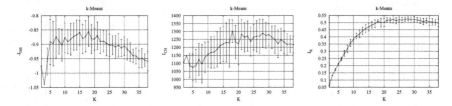

Fig. 2. Plots of the inverted DB-Index, the CH-Index and the Rand-Index (from left to right) for the k-Means clustering method. Since each clustering was repeated 30 times for a given K the resulting standard deviations are indicated by error bars.

Applying the discussed clustering methods and indices to the explained data set leads to the results shown in table 1. Based on the proposed evaluation scheme this data offer the possibility to rate the different clustering methods and to decide which validity index should be used with a specific clustering method. For instance, the data of the method 'k-Means' in table 1 show, that the number of clusters at the maxima of the CH-Index $K(I_{CH}^{max})$ and the DB-Index $K(-I_{DB}^{max})$ is very close to the real number of classes in the data set (which is 20, see above). Furthermore the Rand-Index at these points $I_R(I_{CH}^{max})$ and $I_R(-I_{DB}^{max})$ is nearly as large as the total maximum of the Rand-Index I_R^{max}. Although the number of clusters at the location of the total maximum of the Rand-Index $K(I_R^{max})$ is significantly greater than the number of classes the large values of $I_R(I_{CH}^{max})$ and $I_R(-I_{DB}^{max})$ legitimates rating this method as suitable. This is approved by the corresponding plots (s.Fig. 2).

As can be seen from table 1 the single, centroid and the median linkage methods are not suitable for clustering the given domain: For these methods neither of the examined validity indices yield a suitable number of clusters, independent of the selected distance measure. Compared with all other methods, the single linkage method also provides very small maximum values of the Rand-Index. Most of the other methods are suitable but only in combination with the CH-Index.

Table 1. Experimental Results: The shaded rows mark the clustering methods selected to be suitable to cluster the test data set adequately, because they fulfill the conditions of the proposed evaluation scheme (s.Sec. 4). The names of the 18 hierarchical method variants are coded with the prefix 'agglom' followed by the used distance measure and linkage method, respectively. The columns $K(-I_{DB}^{max})$ and $K(I_{CH}^{max})$ contain the number of clusters at the location of the maximum of the validity indices. The columns $I_R(-I_{DB}^{max})$ and $I_R(I_{CH}^{max})$ provide the value of the Rand-Index at those locations. I_R^{max} contains the absolute maximum of the Rand-Index within the inspected range of K. $K(I_R^{max})$ denotes the number of clusters at this location.

Method	$K(-I_{DB}^{max})$	$I_R(-I_{DB}^{max})$	$K(I_{CH}^{max})$	$I_R(I_{CH}^{max})$	$K(I_R^{max})$	I_R^{max}
k-Means[1]	18	0.51	18	0.51	28	0.53
CLARA	7	0.36	15	0.49	31	0.54
PAM	12	0.49	23	0.53	31	0.55
agglom-manhattan-single	2	0.01	2	0.01	37	0.08
agglom-euclidean-single	2	0.01	2	0.01	29	0.04
agglom-maximum-single	2	0.01	2	0.01	38	0.07
agglom-manhattan-complete	4	0.25	26	0.52	38	0.56
agglom-euclidean-complete	14	0.42	26	0.56	33	0.57
agglom-maximum-complete	17	0.48	21	0.52	20	0.52
agglom-manhattan-centroid	2	0.08	13	0.41	35	0.58
agglom-euclidean-centroid	2	0.02	6	0.25	37	0.54
agglom-maximum-centroid	2	0.09	10	0.32	37	0.53
agglom-manhattan-median	2	0.08	4	0.16	38	0.45
agglom-euclidean-median	2	0.02	5	0.17	34	0.48
agglom-maximum-median	2	0.01	6	0.21	37	0.46
agglom-manhattan-average	9	0.41	10	0.43	32	0.62
agglom-euclidean-average	2	0.08	22	0.55	37	0.55
agglom-maximum-average	2	0.09	21	0.55	20	0.55
agglom-manhattan-ward	12	0.48	37	0.59	19	0.62
agglom-euclidean-ward	7	0.32	23	0.55	21	0.57
agglom-maximum-ward	7	0.31	25	0.54	23	0.54

The methods which may be combined with the DB-Index are the k-Means algorithm and the complete linkage method when using the maximum distance measure. In general, the agglomerative methods perform best with the maximum distance measure followed by the euclidean distance measure. Moreover the presented results indicate that the CH-Index tends to provide better cluster solutions than the DB-Index.

6   Conclusion

The necessity to restrict the search space for scaling image retrieval techniques to large databases requires image grouping which can be done by applying clustering methods.

---

[1] The k-Means algorithm was limited to a maximum of 100 iterations. Since this method depends on a random selection of the initial prototypes the algorithm was repeated 30 times and average values were computed for all indices.

Furthermore an image grouping should reflect the high-level concepts desired by the user. Motivated by these requirements we proposed a scheme which allows to evaluate various combinations of clustering methods and validity indices with regard to their ability to form semantic meaningful clusters. This is achieved by comparing quantitatively the unsupervised clustering results with a given high-level reference grouping. Consequently, based on a small classified subset of an image data set the most powerful combination of clustering method and validity index to categorize the whole image data set can be determined systematically.

To obtain more general answers about semantically meaningful results from image data clustering, the scheme has to be applied to imageries of other visual content, for instance the COREL data set. Since visual content of such data sets is more complex than the considered COIL-100, images may belong to more than one semantically meaningful cluster. This motivates the examination of fuzzy clustering techniques which allow handling of overlapping clusters.

References

1. R. Calinski and J. Harabasz. A Dendrite Method for Cluster Analysis. *Communications in Statistics*, 3:1–27, 1974.
2. J.-Y. Chen, C.A. Bouman, and J.C. Dalton. Hierarchical Browsing and Search of Large Image Databases. *IEEE Transactions on Image Processing*, 9:442–455, 2000.
3. D. Davies and D. Bouldin. A Cluster Separation Measure. *IEEE Transactions on PAMI*, 1:224–227, 1979.
4. J.A. Hartigan and M.A. Wong. A K-Means Clustering Algorithm. *Applied Statistics*, 28:100–108, 1979.
5. L. Hubert and P. Arabie. Comparing Partitions. *Journal of Classification*, 2:193–218, 1985.
6. A. Jain and R. Dubes. *Algorithms for Clustering Data*. Prentice Hall Inc., Englewood Cliffs, NJ, 1988.
7. T. Kämpfe, T. Käster, M. Pfeiffer, H. Ritter, and G. Sagerer. INDI – Intelligent Database Navigation by Interactive and Intuitive Content-Based Image Retrieval. In *IEEE ICIP*, volume III, pages 921–924, Rochester, USA, September 2002.
8. L. Kaufman and P. Rousseeuw. *Finding Groups in Data: An Introduction to Cluster Analysis*. Wiley, New York, 1990.
9. S. Krishnamachari and M. Abdel-Mottaleb. Hierachical Clustering Algorithms for Fast Image Retrieval. In *IS&T/SPIE Conference on Storage and Retrieval for Image and Video Databases VII*, pages 427–435, San Jose, California, January 1999.
10. U. Maulik and S. Bandyopadhyay. Performance Evaluation of Some Clustering Algorithms and Validity Indices. *IEEE Transactions on PAMI*, 24(12):1650–1654, 2002.
11. G. Milligan and M. Cooper. An Examination of Procedures for Determining the Number of Clusters in a Dataset. *Psychometrika*, 50(2):159–179, June 1985.
12. S. Nene, S. Nayar, and H. Murase. Columbia Object Image Library (COIL-100). Technical report, Department of Computer Science, Columbia University, February 1996.
13. M.A. Stricker and M. Orengo. Similarity of Color Images. In *Storage and Retrieval for Image and Video Databases (SPIE)*, volume III, pages 381–392, 1995.

Locally Optimized RANSAC[*]

Ondřej Chum[1], Jiří Matas[1,2], and Josef Kittler[2]

[1] Center for Machine Perception, Czech Technical University, Faculty of Electrical Engineering
Dept. of Cybernetics, Karlovo nám. 13, 121 35 Prague, Czech Republic
[2] CVSSP, University of Surrey, Guildford GU2 7XH, United Kingdom

Abstract. A new enhancement of RANSAC, the locally optimized RANSAC (LO-RANSAC), is introduced. It has been observed that, to find an optimal solution (with a given probability), the number of samples drawn in RANSAC is significantly higher than predicted from the mathematical model. This is due to the incorrect assumption, that a model with parameters computed from an outlier-free sample is consistent with all inliers. The assumption rarely holds in practice. The locally optimized RANSAC makes no new assumptions about the data, on the contrary - it makes the above-mentioned assumption valid by applying local optimization to the solution estimated from the random sample.

The performance of the improved RANSAC is evaluated in a number of epipolar geometry and homography estimation experiments. Compared with standard RANSAC, the speed-up achieved is two to three fold and the quality of the solution (measured by the number of inliers) is increased by 10-20%. The number of samples drawn is in good agreement with theoretical predictions.

1 Introduction

Many computer vision algorithms include a robust estimation step where model parameters are computed from a data set containing a significant proportion of outliers. The RANSAC algorithm introduced by Fishler and Bolles in 1981 [3] is possibly the most widely used robust estimator in the field of computer vision. RANSAC has been applied in the context of short baseline stereo [13,12], wide baseline stereo matching [9,15,10,6], motion segmentation [13], mosaicing [7], detection of geometric primitives [2], robust eigenimage matching [5] and elsewhere.

In a classical formulation of RANSAC, the problem is to find all inliers in a set of data points. The number of inliers I is typically not known a priori. Inliers are data points consistent with the 'best' model, e.g. epipolar geometry or homography in a two view correspondence problem or line or ellipse parameters in the case of detection of geometric primitives. The RANSAC procedure finds, with a certain probability, all inliers and the corresponding model by repeatedly drawing random samples from the input set of data points.

---

[*] The authors were supported by the European Union under projects IST-2001-32184, ICA 1-CT-2000-70002 and by the Czech Ministry of Education under project LN00B096 and by the Czech Technical University under project CTU0306013. The images for experiments **A**,**B**, and **E** were kindly provided by T. Tuytelaars (VISICS, K.U.Leuven), **C** by M. Pollefeys (VISICS, K.U.Leuven), and **E** by K. Mikolajczyk (INRIA Rhône-Alpes).

B. Michaelis and G. Krell (Eds.): DAGM 2003, LNCS 2781, pp. 236–243, 2003.

RANSAC is popular because it is simple and it works well in practice. The reason is that almost no assumptions are made about the data and no (unrealistic) conditions have to be satisfied for RANSAC to succeed. However, it has been observed experimentally that RANSAC runs much longer (even by an order of magnitude) than theoretically predicted [11]. The discrepancy is due to one assumption of RANSAC that is rarely true in practice: it is assumed that a model with parameters computed from *an uncontaminated sample* is consistent with *all* inliers.

In this paper we propose a novel improvement of RANSAC exploiting the fact that the model hypothesis from an uncontaminated minimal sample is almost always sufficiently near the optimal solution and a local optimization step applied to selected models produces an algorithm with near perfect agreement with theoretical (i.e. optimal) performance. This approach not only increases the number of inliers found and consequently speeds up the RANSAC procedure by allowing its earlier termination, but also returns models of higher quality. The increase of average time spent in a single RANSAC verification step is minimal. The proposed optimization strategy guarantees that the number of samples to which the optimization is applied is insignificant.

The main contributions of this paper are (a) modification of the RANSAC that simultaneously improve the speed of the algorithm and and the quality of the solution (which is near to optimal) (b) introduction of two local optimization methods (c) a rule for application of the local optimization and a theoretical analysis showing the local optimization is applied at most $\log k$ times, where k is the number of samples drawn. In experiments on two image geometry estimation (epipolar geometry and homography) the speed-up achieved is two to three fold.

The improvement proposed in this paper requires no extra input information or prior knowledge, and it does not interfere with other modifications of the algorithm, the MLESAC [14], R-RANSAC [1] and NAPSAC [8]. MLESAC, proposed by Torr and Zisserman, defines a cost function in the maximal likelihood framework.

The structure of this paper is as follows. First, in Section 2, the motivation of this paper is discussed in detail and the general algorithm of locally optimized RANSAC is described. Four different methods of local optimization are proposed in Section 3. All methods are experimentally tested and evaluated through epipolar geometry and homography estimation. The results are shown and discussed in Section 4. The paper is concluded in Section 5.

2   Algorithm

The structure of the RANSAC algorithm is simple but powerful. Repeatedly, subsets are randomly selected from the input data and model parameters fitting the sample are computed. The size of the random samples is the smallest sufficient for determining model parameters. In a second step, the quality of the model parameters is evaluated on the full data set. Different cost functions may be used [14] for the evaluation, the standard being the number of inliers, i.e. the number of data points consistent with the model. The process is terminated [3,13] when the likelihood of finding a better model becomes low, i.e. the probability η of missing a set of inliers of size I within k samples falls under predefined threshold

$$\eta = (1 - P_I)^k. \tag{1}$$

Repeat until the probability of finding better solution falls under predefined threshold, as in (1):

1. Select a random sample of the minimum number of data points S_m.
2. Estimate the model parameters consistent with this minimal set.
3. Calculate the number of inliers I_k, i.e. the data points their error is smaller than predefined threshold θ.
4. If new maximum has occurred ($I_k > I_j$ for all $j < k$), run **local optimization**. Store the best model.

Algorithm 1: A brief summary of the LO-RANSAC

Symbol P_I stands for the probability, that an uncontaminated sample of size m is randomly selected from N data points

$$P_I = \frac{\binom{I}{m}}{\binom{N}{m}} = \prod_{j=0}^{m-1} \frac{I-j}{N-j} \approx \varepsilon^m, \tag{2}$$

where ε is the fraction of inliers $\varepsilon = I/N$. The number of samples that has to be drawn to ensure given η is

$$k = \log(\eta)/\log(1 - P_I).$$

From equations (1) and (2), it can be seen, that termination criterion based on probability η expects that a selection of a single random sample not contaminated by outliers is followed by a discovery of whole set of I inliers. However, this assumption is often not valid since inliers are perturbed by noise. Since RANSAC generates hypotheses from minimal sets, the influence of noise is not negligible, and the set of correspondences the size of which is smaller than I is found. The consequence is an increase in the number of samples before the termination of the algorithm. The effect is clearly visible in the histograms of the number of inliers found by standard RANSAC. The first column of Figure 2 shows the histogram for five matching experiments. The number of inliers varies by about 20-30%.

We propose a modification that increases the number of inliers found near to the optimum I. This is achieved via a local optimization of so-far-the-best samples. For the summary of the locally optimized RANSAC see Algorithm 1. The local optimization step is carried out only if a new maximum in the number of inliers from the current sample has occurred, i.e. when standard RANSAC stores its best result. The number of consistent data points with a model from a randomly selected sample can be thought of as a random variable with unknown (or very complicated) density function. This density function is the same for all samples, so the probability that k-th sample will be the best so far is $1/k$. Then, the average number of reaching the so-far-the-best sample within k samples is

$$\sum_{1}^{k} \frac{1}{x} \leq \int_{1}^{k} \frac{1}{x} \, dx + 1 = \log k + 1.$$

Note, that this is the upper bound as the number of correspondences is finite and discrete and so the same number of inliers will occur often. This theoretical bound was confirmed experimentally, the average numbers of local optimization over an execution of (locally optimized) RANSAC can be found in Table 3. For more details about experiments see Section 4.

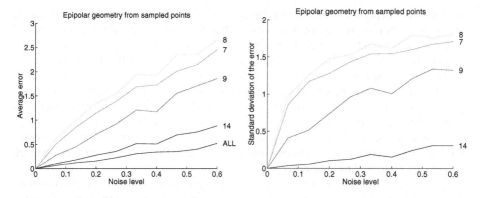

Fig. 1. The average error (left) and the standard deviation of the error for samples of 7,8,9, 14 and all 100 points respectively with respect to the noise level.

3   Local Optimization Methods

The following methods of local optimization have been tested. The choice is motivated by the two observations that are given later in this section.

1. Standard. The standard implementation of RANSAC without any local optimization.

2. Simple. Take all data points with error smaller than θ and use a linear algorithm to hypothesize new model parameters.

3. Iterative. Take all data points with error smaller that $K \cdot \theta$ and use linear algorithm to compute new model parameters. Reduce the threshold and iterate until the threshold is θ.

4. Inner RANSAC. A new sampling procedure is executed. Samples are selected only form I_k data points consistent with the hypothesised model of k-th step of RANSAC. New models are verified against whole set of data points. As the sampling is running on inlier data, there is no need for the size of sample to be minimal. On the contrary, the size of the sample is selected to minimize the error of the model parameter estimation. In our experiments the size of samples are set to $\min(I_k/2, 14)$ for epipolar geometry (see results in Section 3) and to $\min(I_k/2, 12)$ for the case of homography estimation. The number of repetitions is set to ten in the experiments presented.

5. Inner RANSAC with iteration. This method is similar to the previous one, the difference being that each sample of the inner RANSAC is processed by method 3.

The local optimization methods are based on the two following observations.

Observation 1: The Size of Sample

The less information (data points) is used to estimate the model parameters in the presence of noise, the less accurate the model is. The reason for RANSAC to draw minimal samples is that every extra point exponentially decreases the probability of selecting an outlier-free sample, which is approximately ε^m where m is the size of the sample (i.e. the number of data points included in the sample).

It has been shown in [13], that the fundamental matrix estimated from a seven point sample is more precise than the one estimated form eight points using a linear algorithm [4]. This is due to the singularity enforcement in the eight point algorithm. However, the following experiment shows, that this holds only for eight point samples and taking nine or more points gives more stable results than those obtained when the fundamental matrix is computed from seven points only.

Experiment: This experiment shows, how the quality of a hypothesis depends on the number of correspondences used to calculate the fundamental matrix. For seven points, the seven point algorithm was used [13] and for eight and more points the linear algorithm [4] was used. The course of experiment was as follows. Noise of different levels was added to the noise-free image points correspondences divided into two sets of hundred correspondences. Samples of different sizes were drawn from the first set and the average error over the second was computed. This was repeated 1000 times for each noise level. Results are displayed in Figure 1.

This experiment demonstrates, that the more points are used to estimate the model (in this case fundamental matrix) the more precise solution is obtained (with the exception of eight points). The experiment also shows that the minimal sample gives hypotheses of rather poor quality. One can use different cost functions that are more complicated than simply the number of inliers, but evaluating this function only at parameters arising from the minimal sample will get results at best equal to the proposed method of local optimization.

Observation 2: Iterative Scheme
It is well known from the robust statistic literature, that pseudo-robust algorithms that first estimate model parameters from all data by least squares minimization, then remove the data points with the biggest error (or residual) and iteratively repeat this procedure do not lead to correct estimates. It can be easily shown, that a single far–outlying data point, i.e. leverage point, will cause a total destruction of the estimated model parameters. That is because such a leverage point overweights even the majority of inliers in least-squares minimization. This algorithm works only well, when the outliers are not overbearing, so the majority of inliers have bigger influence on the least squares.

In local optimization method 3 there are no leverage points, as each data point has error below $K \cdot \theta$ subject to the sampled model.

4   Experimental Results

The proposed algorithm was extensively tested on the problem of estimation of the two view relations (epipolar geometry and homography) from image point correspondences. Five experiments are presented in this section, all of them on publicly available data, depicted in Figures 3 and 4. In experiments A and B, the epipolar geometry is estimated in a wide-baseline setting. In experiment C, the epipolar geometry was estimated too, this time from short-baseline stereo images. From the point of view of RANSAC use, the narrow and wide baseline problems differ by the number of correspondences and inliers (see Table 1), and also by the distribution of errors of outliers. Experiments D and E try to recover homography. The scene in experiment E is the same as in experiment A and this experiment could be seen as a plane segmentation. All tentative correspondences were detected and matched automatically. Algorithms were implemented in C and the experiments were ran on AMD K7 1800+ MHz processor. The terminating criterion based on equation (1) was set to $\eta < 0.05$. The threshold θ was set to $\theta = 3.84\sigma^2$ for

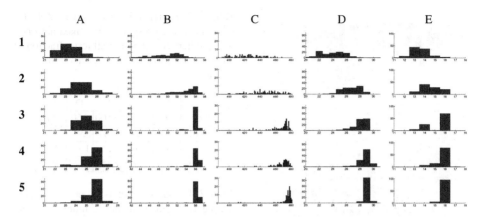

Fig. 2. Histograms of the number of inliers. The methods 1 to 5 (1 stands for standard RANSAC) are stored in rows and different dataset are shown in columns (A to E). On each graph, there is a number of inliers on the x-axis and how many times this number was reached within one hundred repetitions on the y-axis.

the epipolar geometry and $\theta = 5.99\sigma^2$ for the homography. In both cases the expected σ was set to $\sigma = 0.3$.

The characterization of the matching problem, such as number of correspondences, the total number of inliers and expected number of samples, are summarized in Table 1. The total number of inliers was set to the maximal number of inliers obtained over all methods over all repetitions. The expected number of samples was calculated according to the termination criterion mentioned above.

Performance of local optimization methods 1 to 5 was evaluated on problems A to E. The results for 100 runs are summarized in Table 2. For each experiment, a table containing the average number of inliers, average number of samples drawn, average time spent in RANSAC (in seconds) and efficiency (the ratio of the number of samples drawn and expected) is shown. Table 3 shows both, how many times the local optimization has been applied and the theoretical upper bound derived in Section 2.

The method 5 achieved the best results in all experiments in the number of samples and differs slightly from the theoretically expected number. On the other hand standard RANSAC exceeds this limit 2.5 – 3.3 times. In Figure 2 the histograms of the sizes of the resulting inliers sets are shown. Each column shows results for one method, each row for one experiment. One can observe that the peaks are shifting to the higher values with the increasing identification number of method.

Method 5 reaches the best results in terms of sizes of inlier sets and consequently in number of samples before termination. This method should be used when the fraction of inliers is low. Resampling, on the other hand, might be quite costly in the case of high number of inliers, especially if accompanied by a small number of correspondences in total) as could be seen in experiment A (61 % of inliers out of 94 correspondences). In this case, method 3 was the fastest. Method 3 obtained significantly better results than the standard RANSAC in all experiments, the speed up was about 100%, and slightly worse than for method 5. We suggest to use method 5. Method 3 might be used in real-time procedures when a high number of inliers is expected. Methods 2 and 4 are inferior to methods with iteration (3 and 5 respectively) without any time saving advantage.

Fig. 3. Image pairs and detected points used in epipolar geometry experiments (A - C). Inliers are marked as dots in left images and outliers as crosses in right images.

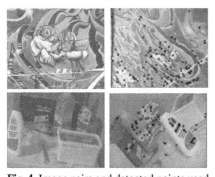

Fig. 4. Image pairs and detected points used in homography experiments (D and E). Inliers are marked as dots in left images and outliers as crosses in right images.

Table 1. Characteristics of experiments A-E. Total number of correspondences, maximal number of inliers found within all tests, fraction of inliers ε and theoretically expected number of samples.

	A	B	C	D	E
# corr	94	94	1500	160	94
# inl	57	27	481	30	17
ε	61%	29%	32%	19%	18%
# sam	115	34529	8852	2873	3837

Table 2. The summary of local optimization experiments: average number of inliers (inl) and samples taken (sam), average time in seconds and efficiency (eff). The best values for each row are highlighted in bold. For more details see the description in text in Section 4.

		1	2	3	4	5
A	inl	49.7	53.9	55.9	56.0	**56.2**
	sam	383	205	129	117	**115**
	time	0.018	0.010	**0.007**	0.010	0.019
	eff	3.35	1.79	1.12	1.02	**1.01**
B	inl	23.3	24.4	25.0	25.5	**25.7**
	sam	90816	63391	49962	44016	**39886**
	time	3.911	2.729	2.154	1.901	**1.731**
	eff	2.63	1.84	1.45	1.27	**1.16**
C	inl	423.5	446.2	467.5	468.9	**474.9**
	sam	25205	16564	11932	10947	**9916**
	time	4.114	2.707	1.971	1.850	**1.850**
	eff	2.85	1.87	1.35	1.24	**1.12**
D	inl	23.9	26.7	28.1	28.8	**29.0**
	sam	8652	5092	3936	3509	**3316**
	time	0.922	0.543	0.423	**0.387**	0.391
	eff	3.01	1.77	1.37	1.22	**1.15**
E	inl	13.5	14.6	15.3	15.7	**15.9**
	sam	12042	8551	6846	5613	**5254**
	time	0.979	0.696	0.559	0.463	**0.444**
	eff	3.14	2.23	1.78	1.46	**1.37**

5   Conclusions

An inprovement of the RANSAC algorithm was introduced. The number of detected inliers increased, and consequently the number of samples drawn decreased. In all experiments,

Table 3. The average number of local optimizations ran during one execution of RANSAC and logarithm of average number of samples for comparison.

	1		2		3		4		5	
A	3.0	5.9	2.6	5.3	2.0	4.9	1.9	4.8	1.8	4.7
B	6.4	11.4	6.1	11.1	5.9	10.8	6.0	10.7	5.9	10.6
C	7.7	10.1	6.8	9.7	6.5	9.4	6.7	9.3	6.5	9.2

	1		2		3		4		5	
D	5.2	9.1	4.8	8.5	4.5	8.3	4.4	8.2	4.0	8.1
E	4.8	9.4	4.3	9.1	4.2	8.8	4.0	8.6	3.9	8.6

the running-time is reduced by a factor of at least two, which may be very important in real-time application incorporating a RANSAC step. It has been shown and experimentally verified that the number of local optimization steps is lower than logarithm of the number of samples drawn, and thus local optimization does not slow the procedure down. Four different methods of local optimization were tested and the efficiency of method 5 is almost 1. The proposed improvement allows to make precise quantitative statements about the number of samples drawn in RANSAC. The local optimization step applied to selected models produces an algorithm with near perfect agreement with theoretical (i.e. optimal) performance.

References

1. O. Chum and J. Matas. Randomized ransac with T(d,d) test. In *Proceedings of the British Machine Vision Conference*, volume 2, pages 448–457, 2002.
2. J. Clarke, S. Carlsson, and A. Zisserman. Detecting and tracking linear features efficiently. In *Proc. 7th BMVC*, pages 415–424, 1996.
3. M. Fischler and R. Bolles. Random sample consensus: A paradigm for model fitting with applications to image analysis and automated cartography. *CACM*, 24(6):381–395, June 1981.
4. R. Hartley. In defence of the 8-point algorithm. In *ICCV95*, pages 1064–1070, 1995.
5. A. Leonardis and H. Bischof. Robust recognition using eigenimages. *Computer Vision and Image Understanding: CVIU*, 78(1):99–118, Apr. 2000.
6. J. Matas, O. Chum, M. Urban, and T. Pajdla. Robust wide baseline stereo from maximally stable extremal regions. In *Proc. of the BMVC*, volume 1, pages 384–393, 2002.
7. P. McLauchlan and A. Jaenicke. Image mosaicing using sequential bundle adjustment. In *Proc. BMVC*, pages 616– 62, 2000.
8. D. Myatt, P. Torr, S. Nasuto, J. Bishop, and R. Craddock. Napsac: High noise, high dimensional robust estimation - it's in the bag. In *BMVC02*, volume 2, pages 458–467, 2002.
9. P. Pritchett and A. Zisserman. Wide baseline stereo matching. In *Proc. International Conference on Computer Vision*, pages 754–760, 1998.
10. F. Schaffalitzky and A. Zisserman. Viewpoint invariant texture matching and wide baseline stereo. In *Proc. 8th ICCVon, Vancouver, Canada*, July 2001.
11. B. Tordoff and D. Murray. Guided sampling and consensus for motion estimation. In *Proc. 7th ECCV, Copenhagen, Denmark*, volume 1, pages 82–96. Springer-Verlag, 2002.
12. P. Torr, A. Zisserman, and S. Maybank. Robust detection of degenerate configurations while estimating the fundamental matrix. *CVIU*, 71(3):312–333, September 1998.
13. P. H. S. Torr. *Outlier Detection and Motion Segmentation*. PhD thesis, Dept. of Engineering Science, University of Oxford, 1995.
14. P. H. S. Torr and A. Zisserman. MLESAC: A new robust estimator with application to estimating image geometry. *Computer Vision and Image Understanding*, 78:138–156, 2000.
15. T. Tuytelaars and L. Van Gool. Wide baseline stereo matching based on local, affinely invariant regions. In *Proc. 11th British Machine Vision Conference*, 2000.

Splines and Wavelets: New Perspectives for Pattern Recognition

Michael Unser

Biomedical Imaging Group,
Swiss Federal Institute of Technology Lausanne (EPFL),
CH-1015 Lausanne Switzerland
Michael.Unser@epfl.ch

Abstract. We provide an overview of spline and wavelet techniques with an emphasis on applications in pattern recognition. The presentation is divided in three parts. In the first one, we argue that the spline representation is ideally suited for all processing tasks that require a continuous model of the underlying signals or images. We show that most forms of spline fitting (interpolation, least-squares approximation, smoothing splines) can be performed most efficiently using recursive digital filtering. We also discuss the connection between splines and Shannon's sampling theory. In the second part, we illustrate their use in pattern recognition with the help of a few examples: high-quality interpolation of medical images, computation of image differentials for feature extraction, B-spline snakes, image registration, and estimation of optical flow. In the third and last part, we discuss the fundamental role of splines in wavelet theory. After a brief review of some key wavelet concepts, we show that every wavelet can be expressed as a convolution product between a B-spline and a distribution. The B-spline constitutes the regular part of the wavelet and is entirely responsible for its key mathematical properties. We also describe fractional B-spline wavelet bases, which have the unique property of being continuously adjustable. As the order of the spline increases, these wavelets converge to modulated Gaussians which are optimally localized in time (or space) and frequency.

1 Splines and Continuous/Discrete Signal Processing

What follows is a brief synopsis of the presentation, with some pointers to the relevant literature.

Splines provide a unifying framework for linking the continuous and discrete domains. They are well understood theoretically, and are ideally suited for performing numerical computations [6]. This makes them the perfect tool for solving a whole variety of signal and image processing (or pattern recognition) problems that are best formulated in the continuous domain but call for a discrete solution [21]. This leads to a class of computational techniques that we refer to as "continuous/discrete signal processing", and which may be best summarized by the motto "*think analog, act digital*".

The cardinal splines, which are the type of splines considering here, were invented by Schoenberg almost 60 years ago [14]. These polynomial splines are 1D functions that

B. Michaelis and G. Krell (Eds.): DAGM 2003, LNCS 2781, pp. 244–248, 2003.
© Springer-Verlag Berlin Heidelberg 2003

are defined on a uniform grid with knots at the integers when the degree is odd, or at the mid-integers when the degree is even. For each segment defined by two successive knots, the spline is a polynomial of degree n; the polynomial pieces are patched together at the knots in a way that guarantees the continuity of the function and of all its derivative up to order $(n\text{-}1)$. Schoenberg in his landmark paper showed that these splines could be represented most conveniently in terms of basis functions that are integer translates of a generating function: the B-spline of degree n. These B-splines have a number of very desirable properties. They have a simple analytical form (piecewise polynomial of degree n) that facilitates their manipulation [6, 23]. In our earlier work, we have shown that most B-spline computations can be made using digital filters [22, 23], provided that the grid is regular, which is always the case in image/signal processing.

The B-splines satisfy a two-scale relation which makes them prime candidates for constructing wavelet bases [24]. In this respect, B-splines form a category apart since the scaling relation holds for any positive integer m—and not just powers of two; this property can be used advantageously for designing fast multi-scale filtering algorithms [26] .

Splines have excellent approximation properties, mainly because the underlying B-spline basis functions are very regular [19, 4, 3]. They are also optimal in the sense that they provide the signal interpolant with the least oscillating energy [13]. Finally, the spline framework allows for a progressive transition between the two extreme signal representations: the piecewise-constant model (spline of degree zero) that uses the most localized, but least regular, basis functions, and the bandlimited model that corresponds to a spline of infinite degree [1]. Also note that there are recent extensions of Shannon's sampling theory that consider spline-like representations of functions instead of the traditional bandlimited model [20].

2   Splines: Applications in Pattern Recognition

The primary applications of splines in pattern recognition are sampling and interpolation, feature extraction, image matching, and motion analysis. In the presentation, we briefly discuss the following topics:

2.1 High-Quality Image Interpolation

When compared to other interpolation algorithms, splines provide the best tradeoff in terms of quality and of computational cost. In other words, if you want to improve interpolation quality, your best choice over any other method is to increase the order of the spline. This is a finding that has been confirmed independently by several research teams [16, 11, 10, 9].

2.2 Feature Extraction

After fitting the image with a spline, it is straightforward to compute exact image derivatives to derive gradients or Hessians for the detection of various image features such as contours or ridges [22]

2.3 Snakes and Active Contour Models

The B-spline representation is also well suited for describing 2D curves [2]. These parametric curves can be optimized to detect object boundaries in images using snake-like algorithms [12, 5]. An advantage of the spline model is that it gives a direct control on the smoothness of the curve.

2.4 Image Registration

There are various versions of spline-based algorithms for the registration of intra-modal or inter-modal medical images [18, 17]. These can correct for rigid-body deformations with subpixel accuracy, even when the noise level is very high. Variants of these algorithms for elastic deformation are also available [7, 8]. Note that, in these latter works, both the image and the deformation function are represented by splines.

2.5 Motion Analysis

A good illustration of this topic is an optical flow algorithm that computes cardiac movement from ultrasound images of the heart [15]. This technique estimates the parameters of a local affine motion model over a sliding B-spline window. The method is implemented within a multi-scale framework using a wavelet-like algorithm for the efficient computation of weighted B-spline inner-products and moments.

3   Fractional Splines and Wavelet Theory

The polynomial splines have also been extended to fractional degrees [27]. The basic constituents of these fractional splines are piecewise power functions of degree α. One constructs the corresponding B-splines through a localization process similar to the classical one, replacing finite differences by fractional differences. The fractional B-splines share virtually all the properties of the classical B-splines, including the two-scale relation. One of their key property is that these functions are closed under fractional differentiation; in other words, the fractional derivative of order s (i.e., the multiplication by $(j\omega)^s$ in the frequency domain) of a spline of degree α yields a spline of degree $(\alpha\text{-}s)$.

 We have shown recently that these fractional B-splines play a fundamental role in wavelet theory [28]. Their presence as a convolutional factor is necessary for the wavelet transform to be mathematically well-defined. More precisely, we can show that five key wavelet properties—vanishing moments, order of approximation, reproduction of polynomials, smoothness of the basis functions, multi-scale differentiation—are all to be attributed to the B-spline that lies hidden within. In other words, there cannot be wavelets without splines.

Fractional B-splines can also be used to construct new fractional wavelet basis functions that are unique in several respects. These basis functions are adjustable in a continuous manner. This gives the user a full control over all key wavelet properties:

the parametric form of the basis functions, their smoothness, the order and multi-scale differentiability properties of the transform, and, finally, the number of vanishing moments. Interestingly, the spline degree α also controls the size (i.e., the spatial extent) of the basis functions. For instance, for the B-spline family, the basis functions (resp., the wavelets) converge to Gaussians (resp., modulated Gaussians or Gabor functions) with a standard deviation (or an equivalent window size) that is proportional to $\sqrt{\alpha + 1}$. This also means that these functions, for α sufficiently large (say, $\alpha > 2$), will tend to be optimally localized in the sense of the Heisenberg uncertainty principle; in other words, the product of their space and frequency uncertainties will tend to the minimum that is achievable. This result constitutes a fractional generalization of an earlier theorem for polynomial B-spline wavelets with integer order [25].

More information on splines and on fractional wavelets, including software (C and Java), demos, and papers, can be found at: **http://bigwww.epfl.ch/**

References

[1]   A. Aldroubi, M. Unser and M. Eden, *Cardinal spline filters: Stability and convergence to the ideal sinc interpolator*, Signal Processing, 28 (1992), pp. 127–138.

[2]   R. H. Bartels, J. C. Beatty and B. A. Barsky, *Splines for use in computer graphics*, Morgan Kaufmann, Los Altos, CA, 1987.

[3]   T. Blu and M. Unser, *Quantitative Fourier analysis of approximation techniques: Part II—wavelets*, IEEE Transactions on Signal Processing, 47 (1999), pp. 2796–2806.

[4]   T. Blu and M. Unser, *Quantitative Fourier analysis of approximation techniques: Part I—interpolators and projectors*, IEEE Transactions on Signal Processing, 47 (1999), pp. 2783–2795.

[5]   P. Brigger, J. Hoeg and M. Unser, *B-spline snakes: a flexible tool for parametric contour detection*, IEEE Transactions on Image Processing, 9 (2000), pp. 1484–1496.

[6]   C. de Boor, *A practical guide to splines*, Springer-Verlag, New York, 1978.

[7]   J. Kybic, P. Thévenaz, A. Nirkko and M. Unser, *Unwarping of unidirectionally distorted EPI images*, IEEE Transactions on Medical Imaging, 19 (2000), pp. 80–93.

[8]   J. Kybic and M. Unser, *Fast Parametric Elastic Image Registration*, IEEE Transactions on Image Processing (in press).

[9]   T. M. Lehmann, C. Gönner and K. Spitzer, *Addendum: B-spline interpolation in medical image processing*, IEEE Transactions on Medical Imaging, 20 (2001), pp. 660–665.

[10] T. M. Lehmann, C. Gönner and K. Spitzer, *Survey: Interpolation methods in medical image processing*, IEEE Transactions on Medical Imaging, 18 (1999), pp. 1049–1075.

[11] E. H. W. Meijering, W. J. Niessen and M. A. Viergever, *Quantitative evaluation of convolution-based methods for medical image interpolation*, Medical Image Analysis, 5 (2001), pp. 111–126.

[12] S. Menet, P. Saint-Marc and G. Medioni, *B-snakes: implementation and application to stereo*, Image Understanding Workshop, DARPA, 1990, pp. 720–726.

[13] P. M. Prenter, *Splines and variational methods*, Wiley, New York, 1975.

[14] I. J. Schoenberg, *Contribution to the problem of approximation of equidistant data by analytic functions*, Quart. Appl. Math., 4 (1946), pp. 45–99, 112–141.

[15] M. Sühling, M. Arigovindan, C. Jansen, P. Hunziker and M. Unser, *Myocardial motion analysis and visualization from echocardiograms*, SPIE Medical Imaging (MI'03), SPIE, San Diego, CA, 2003, pp. 306–313.

[16] P. Thévenaz, T. Blu and M. Unser, *Interpolation revisited*, IEEE Transactions on Medical Imaging, 19 (2000), pp. 739–758.

[17] P. Thévenaz and M. Unser, *Optimization of mutual information for multiresolution image registration*, IEEE Transactions on Image Processing, 9 (2000), pp. 2083–2099.

[18] P. Thévenaz and M. Unser, *A pyramid approach to sub-pixel image fusion based on mutual information, IEEE Int. Conf. on Image Processing*, IEEE, Lausanne, Switzerland, 1996, pp. 265–268.

[19] M. Unser, *Approximation power of biorthogonal wavelet expansions*, IEEE Trans. Signal Processing, 44 (1996), pp. 519–527.

[20] M. Unser, *Sampling—50 years after Shannon*, Proceedings of the IEEE, 88 (2000), pp. 569–587.

[21] M. Unser, *Splines: A perfect fit for signal and image processing*, IEEE Signal Processing Magazine, 16 (1999), pp. 22–38.

[22] M. Unser, A. Aldroubi and M. Eden, *B-spline signal processing: Part II—efficient design and applications*, IEEE Trans. Signal Processing, 41 (1993), pp. 834–848.

[23] M. Unser, A. Aldroubi and M. Eden, *B-spline signal processing: Part I—theory*, IEEE Trans. Signal Processing, 41 (1993), pp. 821–833.

[24] M. Unser, A. Aldroubi and M. Eden, *A family of polynomial spline wavelet transforms*, Signal Processing, 30 (1993), pp. 141–162.

[25] M. Unser, A. Aldroubi and M. Eden, *On the asymptotic convergence of B-spline wavelets to Gabor functions*, IEEE Trans. Information Theory, 38 (1992), pp. 864–872.

[26] M. Unser, A. Aldroubi and S. J. Schiff, *Fast implementation of the continuous wavelet transform with integer scales*, IEEE Trans. Signal Processing, 42 (1994), pp. 3519–3523.

[27] M. Unser and T. Blu, *Fractional splines and wavelets*, SIAM Review, 42 (2000), pp. 43–67.

[28] M. Unser and T. Blu, *Wavelet theory demystified*, IEEE Transactions on Signal Processing, 51 (2003), pp. 470–483.

Robust Camera Calibration from Images and Rotation Data

Jan-Michael Frahm and Reinhard Koch

Institute of Computer Science and Applied Mathematics
Herman-Rodewald-Str. 3,
24098 Kiel, Germany
{jmf,rk}@mip.informatik.uni-kiel.de

Abstract. The calibration of cameras from external orientation information and image processing is addressed in this paper. We will show that in the case of known rotation the calibration of rotating cameras is linear even in the case of fully varying parameters. For freely moving cameras the calibration problem is also linear but underdetermined for fully varying internal parameters. We show one possible set of contraints to reach a fully determined calibration problem. Furthermore we show that these linear calibration techniques tend to fit to noise for some of the intrinsics. To avoid this fit to noise we introduce a statistical calibration technique which uses the robust components of linear calibration and prior knowledge about cameras. This statistical calibration is fully determined even for freely moving cameras.

1 Introduction

We have seen a lot of research on camera calibration from image sequences over the last decade. These approaches calibrate the cameras by observing unknown scenes and therefore they may suffer under degeneracies caused by the scenes respectively the image information. We will introduce a technique for selfcalibration from image sequences together with external orientation information. This information is available in many applications. Today's cars are already equipped with orientation sensors for Electronic Stability systems (ESP) for example. Future cars will also have smart cameras. Another popular application is the surveillance with rotating and zooming cameras. In this case we have rotation information of the camera but normally lack correct zoom data.

In this contribution we will discuss the possibilities to use this external orientation information for selfcalibration of arbitrary moving and zooming cameras. We will first review the literature in section 2. Selfcalibration from image and rotation data will be discussed in detail in section 3. Finally we will discuss some experiments and conclude.

2 Previous Work

Camera calibration has always been a subject of research in the field of computer vision. The first major work on selfcalibration of a camera by simply observing

B. Michaelis and G. Krell (Eds.): DAGM 2003, LNCS 2781, pp. 249–256, 2003.

an unknown scene was presented in [9]. Since that time various methods have been developed. Methods for the calibration of rotating cameras with unknown but constant intrinsics were first developed in [11]. The approach was extended for rotating cameras with partially varying intrinsic parameters in [5]. This work uses the infinite homography constraint and has the disadvantage that not all parameters are allowed to vary. The calibration process has three major steps: linearized calibration, nonlinear calibration, and statistical calibration. Sometimes the first calibration step may fail due to noisy data. Camera selfcalibration from unknown general motion and constant intrinsics has been dicussed in [12]. For varying intrinsics and general camera motion the selfcalibration was proved by [8]. All these approaches for selfcalibration only use the images of the cameras themselves for the calibration.

Only few approaches exist to combine image analysis and external rotation information for selfcalibration. In [10] cameras with constant intrinsics and known rotation were discussed. They use unconstrained nonlinear optimization to estimate the camera parameters. This lack of attention is somewhat surprising since this situation occurs frequently in a variety of applications: cameras mounted in cars for driver assistence, robotic vision heads, surveillance cameras or PTZ-cameras for video conferencing often provide rotation information.

In this paper we will address one of the few cases which have not yet been explored, that of a rotating camera with varying intrinsics and known rotation information. We will show that orientation information is helpful for camera calibration. Furthermore it is possible to detect degenerate cases for calibration like rotation about only one axis or about the optical axis.

3   Selfcalibration with Known Rotation

In this section we will develop novel techniques to use available external orientation information for camera selfcalibration. We will address both cases of purely rotating and arbitrarily moving cameras.

3.1   Rotating Cameras

We can exploit given rotational information to overcome the limitations on the number of varying intrinsics and the problems caused by noise during computation in [5]. The homography $H_{j,i}^{\infty}$ between two images i and j of a rotating camera is given by

$$H_{j,i}^{\infty} = K_i R_{j,i} K_j^{-1} \text{ with } K = \begin{bmatrix} f & s & c_x \\ 0 & a \cdot f & c_y \\ 0 & 0 & 1 \end{bmatrix}, \qquad (1)$$

where f is the focal length of the camera expressed in pixel units. The aspect ratio a of the camera is the ratio between the size of a pixel in x-direction and the size of a pixel in y-direction. The principal point of the camera is (c_x, c_y) and s is a skew parameter which models the angle between columns and rows of the CCD-sensor. $R_{j,i}$ is the relative rotation of the camera between image j and i. If $R_{j,i}$ is known from an external orientation sensor, then equation (1) can be rewritten as

$$K_i R_{j,i} - H_{j,i}^{\infty} K_j = 0_{3x3} \quad \text{or} \quad K_i^{-1} m_{i,k} - \alpha(m_{j,k}) R_{j,i} K_j^{-1} m_{j,k} = 0_{3x3}, \quad (2)$$

where $\alpha(m_{j,k})$ is the factor to homogenize $R_{j,i} K_j^{-1} m_{j,k}$. $(m_{i,k}, m_{j,k})$ is in the set of point correspondences between a point m_k in image j and a point m_k in image i. The homography $H_{j,i}^{\infty}$ can be estimated from the image point correspondences [3]. Therefore, (2) is linear in the components of K_i and K_j and provides nine linear independent contraints on the intrinsics of the cameras.

The estimated homographies are determined only up to scale $\rho_{j,i}$. Therefore we can estimate only $\tilde{H}_{j,i}^{\infty} := \rho_{j,i} H_{j,i}^{\infty}$ from the images. For the estimated homographies $\tilde{H}_{j,i}^{\infty}$ equation (2) is modified to

$$0_{3x3} = \tilde{K}_i R_{j,i} - H_{j,i}^{\infty} K_j \text{ with } \tilde{K}_i = \rho_{j,i}^{-1} K_i, \quad (3)$$

which is also linear in the intrinsics of the camera j and linear in the elements of $\tilde{K}_i$. Note that due to the unknown scale we have now six unknowns in $\tilde{K}_i$. Eq. (2) provides nine linearly independent equations for each camera pair for the five intrinsics contained in K_j and the five intrinsics of K_i plus the scale $\rho_{j,i}^{-1}$ contained in $\tilde{K}_i$. If there are no constraints available for the intrinsics, (2) has no unique solution for a single camera pair. With two constraints for the intrinsics or the scale $\rho_{j,i}^{-1}$ the solution is unique. Alternatively, if we consider a camera triplet (i, j, k) with estimated homographies $\tilde{H}_{j,i}^{\infty}$ and $\tilde{H}_{j,k}^{\infty}$, (3) provides

$$\tilde{K}_i R_{j,i} - H_{j,i}^{\infty} K_j = 0_{3x3} \quad \text{and} \quad \tilde{K}_k R_{j,k} - H_{j,k}^{\infty} K_j = 0_{3x3}, \quad (4)$$

with 17 unknowns and up to 9 independent equations for each camera pair. Therefore, for each camera triplet the solution for the intrinsics and scales is unique and can be solved even for fully varying parameters. In contrast to the approach in [5] this calibration can always be computed even in the case of strong noise.

Evaluation for rotating cameras: To measure the noise robustness of the calibration we test the approach with synthetic data. The center of the rotating camera is at the origin , the image size is 512x512. The camera rotates about x-axis and y-axis with up to six degrees and observes a scene in front of the camera. The location of the projected points is disturbed by Gaussian noise with variance of 2 pixel. The known camera orientation is also disturbed by noise of up to 2 degrees per axis. We varied both pixel and rotational noise. The homographies $\tilde{H}_{j,i}^{\infty}$ are estimated from point correspondences by least squares estimation. The measurements for the first camera with focal length $f = 415$ and $c_y = 201$ are shown in figure 1. The measured errors for the other images are similar to these results.

It can be seen from figure 1 that the estimated focal length f is rather stable if the pixel noise is less than one pixel and the orientation data are noisy by angular errors of less than one degree. The measured variance of the linear estimation is below 10% for angle noise of up to 1 degree. The estimation for the aspect ratio shows similar stability. The estimated principle point component c_y is not as stable as focal length f. It fits to noise for angular noise greater than 0.5 degrees. The estimation for the other principal point component c_x and the skew s is similar to the values of the principal point component c_y. Furthermore the influence of the orientation noise is much larger since the absolute rotation angle between the cameras is in the range of the noise (6 degree camera rotation with up to 2 degree noise). In the next subsection we will introduce a statistical calibration method for robust calibration of all intrinsics.

3.2   Statistical Calibration with Known Rotation

The above linear approach (4) is able to robustly estimate the focal length and the aspect ratio. The estimation of the principal point is an ill posed problem [5]. For the most cameras the principal point is located close to the image center and the skew is zero. Therefore the use of prior knowledge about the distribution of the principal point and the skew can be used to reduce the estimation problems of the linear approach (4).

Let us consider that the noise n on the measured image positions is additive and has a Gaussian distribution with mean zero and standard deviation σ. Then an approximation of the Maximum Likelihood estimation is given by:

$$\text{MLE} = \arg \min_{K_i, R_i} \sum_{i=1}^{\#cameras} \sum_{k=1}^{\#points} \| K_i^{-1} m_{i,k} - \alpha(m_{j,k}) R_{j,i} K_j^{-1} m_{j,k} \|^2 \quad (5)$$

To compute an exact Maximum Likelihood we have to weight the backprojection error with the inverse variance of the image measurement. The approximation error is small because we use normalized coordinates [2] for the computation. If we model the expectation pp_{prior} that the principal point probably lies close to the center of the camera and has also a Gaussian distribution whose mean is the image center, a Maximum a Posterori estimation of the intrinsics is simply

$$\text{MAP}_{pp} = \text{MLE} + \lambda_{pp} \sum_{i \in cameras} (c^i - pp_{prior})^T \begin{bmatrix} \sigma_x^2 & 0 \\ 0 & \sigma_y^2 \end{bmatrix} (c^i - pp_{prior}). \quad (6)$$

where λ_{pp} is the weight of the prior knowledge and σ_x^2, σ_y^2 the distribution parameters for the components of the principal point. Furthermore we are able to use the given sensor orientation as a prior knowledge:

$$\text{MAP}_{ori} = \text{MAP}_{pp} + \lambda_{ori} \sum_{i \in cameras} (1 - < r_{j,i}, r_{est} >) + |\phi_{i,j} - \phi_{est}|. \quad (7)$$

where $r_{j,i}$ is the rotation axis of $R_{j,i}$ and $\phi_{j,i}$ is the rotation angle about $r_{j,i}$. The estimated rotation axis is r_{est} and ϕ_{est} is the estimated rotation angle about r_{est}. Now we are able to optimize the orientation information concurrently with the calibration. This can be used to improve the orientation data. The statistical optimization is started with the linearily estimated focal length and aspect ratio and the prior knowledge about principal point and skew.

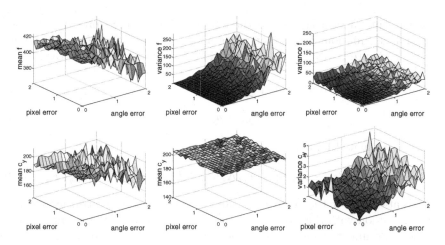

Fig. 1. Noise robustness measurements. Top from left to right: mean of linear estimated focal length f, variance of linear estimated focal length f, variance of MAP estimated focal length f. Bottom from left to right:mean of linear estimated principal point component c_y, mean of MAP estimated c_y, variance of MAP estimation

Evaluation for rotating cameras: To measure the noise robustness of the calibration technique (7) we test the approach with the above described synthetic data. The measurements are shown in figure 1. The principal point varies with about eight percent around the image center. As prior knowledge we use the principal point at the image center. It can be seen that the statistical estimation is more robust if the data is noisy. The variance of the focal length is much better than in the linear case. The estimation of the principal point is much more stable than in the linear case. The results for the other intrinsics are very similar. Since the error of orientation sensors like the InertiaCube[2] from InterSense is normally in the range below one degree, we can rely on the rotation information. The homography estimation can also be estimated with an error of less than 1 pixel for the features' positions in most situations. This shows that the proposed calibration with (7) is robust for most applications.

3.3 Calibration for Freely Moving Cameras

We will investigate how to combine rotational information and the Fundamental matrix $F_{j,i}$ in the general motion case. The Fundamental matrix as opposed to projection matrix is not affected by projective skew, therefore we will use $F_{j,i}$ in the following to calibrate the cameras.

Without loss of generality[3] each Fundamental matrix $F_{j,i}$ can be decomposed to

$$F_{j,i} = [e]_x K_i R_{j,i} K_j^{-1} \Leftrightarrow [e]_x K_i R_{j,i} - F_{j,i} K_j = 0_{3 \times 3}. \qquad (8)$$

This is linear in the intrinsics of camera i and camera j. Please note the relationship to Eq. (2). One can see that (8) is an extension of (2) which contains the unknown camera translation t in the epipole. Equation (8) provides six linear independent equations for the intrinsics of the cameras. So we need five image pairs to compute the camera calibration in case of fully varying intrinsics.

The Fundamental matrices $\tilde{F}_{j,i}$ that have to be estimated from the images are scaled by an arbitrary scale $\rho_{j,i}$

$$\tilde{F}_{j,i} = \rho_{j,i} F_{j,i}. \tag{9}$$

For these estimated Fundamental matrices $\tilde{F}_{j,i}$ (8) is

$$0_{3\times3} = [e]_x K_i R_{j,i} - \tilde{F}_{j,i} K_j = [e]_x \tilde{K}_i R_{j,i} - F_{j,i} K_j \text{ with } \tilde{K}_i = \rho_{j,i}^{-1} K_i, \tag{10}$$

which is also linear in the intrinsics of camera j and the scaled intrinsics of camera i in conjunction with the scale $\rho_{j,i}^{-1}$. It provides six linear independent equations for the scale and the intrinsics of the cameras. From the counting argument follows that the solution is never unique if no constraints for the scales $\rho_{j,i}^{-1}$ or the intrinsics of the cameras are available.

If we use prior knowledge about the principal point of the cameras we are able to compute the camera calibration from an image triplet (j, i, k) with (10). To get a full camera calibration we use an approach similar to (7).

Evaluation for freely moving cameras: To measure the noise robustness of the proposed calibration for arbitrarily moving cameras we use synthetic data with known noise and ground truth information. Six cameras are positioned on a sphere, observing the same scene as used before in case of purely rotated cameras. The cameras also have a resolution of 512x512 pixels. The noise is the same as above. We calculate the Fundamental matrices $\tilde{F}_{j,i}$ for the image pairs by least squares estimation. The computed Fundamental matrices $\tilde{F}_{j,i}$ are used for the robustness measurements. The results for the case of known principal point (c_x, c_y) and known skew s are shown in figure 2 for the first camera with focal length $f = 415$. The errors and variances for the other images are very similar to these measurements.

It can be seen that for orientation noise of up to 1 degree and pixel noise of up to 1 pixel the calibration is rather stable. The noise sensitivity for this calibration is very similar to the rotational case, but one can see a slightly larger influence of pixel noise for F-estimation.

4   Experiments

In this section we show some experiments on real data for rotating cameras and for simulator scenes for fundamental matrix calibration.

4.1   Calibration of Rotating Camera

We tested the calibration techniques for rotating cameras with a sequence taken by a consumer pan-tilt-zoom camera as used in video conferencing (Sony DV-31).

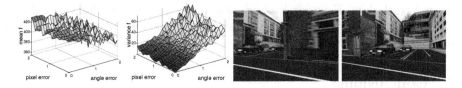

Fig. 2. Noise robustness measurements. Left: mean of estimated focal length f, and variance of estimated focal length f. Right: images from the sequence for Fundamental matrix calibration.

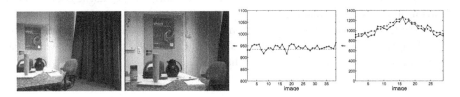

Fig. 3. Left:Images from the zoom-pan sequence for rotation calibration, right: calibration results for constant and varying focal length

The camera is panning, and zooming during the sequence. Some frames of the sequence are shown in figure 3. The camera rotation is taken from the camera control commands, which means that we used the angles which are sent to the camera. Therefore the rotation error depends on the positioning accuracy of the pan-tilt head which is in the range of below 0.5 degrees for each axis. As reference for the zoom we manually measured the focal length of the different zoom positions to calculate approximate ground truth. The focal length of the camera varied between 875-1232 (in pixel). We also compensated the zoom-dependent radial distortion beforehand. This can be done for the different zooming steps of the camera without knowledge of the correct zoom.

The sequence was processed by tracking feature points with a KLT-tracker [13]. From these tracks we calculated the homographies for the sequence with RANSAC and least-squares-estimation over the inliers. The reprojection error gave a mean pixel error of 0.8 pixel. Calibration estimates for the focal length were computed from triples of images.

Figure 3 shows results for focal length estimation. The dashed line gives the true values, the solid line the estimated values. The left chart shows the estimated focal length (in pixel) for constant focal length $f_{true} = 940$ pixel, the right chart contains a zooming camera. The average relative estimation error is around 3% for fixed zoom and 7% for changing zoom.

We tested the calibration of a moving and rotating camera by using images rendered from a photorealistic car driving simulator. A camera in the car is looking sideways and is panning while the car is driving forward (see figure 2). The focal length was fixed to 415 (in pixel). From this sequence we estimated the fundamental matrix with RANSAC. The rotation is the given rotation of the ground truth data. However, we were able to detect this situation easily due to the known rotation information. The estimated focal length has a relative error of 3% w.r.t. the true focal length.

5   Conclusions

We introduced a novel linear calibration technique for rotating and moving cameras which uses external orientation information. This orientation information is already avaible in many applications. Furthermore the robustness of this calibration approach was discussed.

The analysis of the linear calibration technique leads to a statistical approach for calibration. We showed that the statistical approach is more robust and can be used for a wide range of applications.

References

1. R. Franklin, "Efficient Rotation of an Object", IEEE Transactions on Computing, 1983.
2. R. Hartley, " In defence of the 8-Point-Algorithm", *ICCV95*
3. R. Hartley and A. Zisserman, "Multiple View Geometry in Computer Vision" *Cambridge university press, Cambrige, 2000*
4. H. Shum and R.Szeliski, "Panoramic Image Mosaics" *Microsoft Research*, Technical Report MSR-TR-97-23, 1997.
5. L. de Agapito and E. Hayman and I. Reid, "Self-calibration of a rotating camera with varying intrinsic parameters" *British Machine Vision Conference 1998*
6. H. Sawhney, S.Hsu and R. Kumar, "Robust Video Mosaicing through Topology Inference and Local to Global Alignment" *ECCV*, 1998.
7. C. E. Pearson, *Handbook of Applied Mathematics*, S.898, Second Edition, Van Nostrand Reinhold Company, 1983.
8. B. Triggs,"Autocalibration and the Absolute Quadric", Proceedings Conference on Computer Vision and Pattern Recognition, pp. 609–614, Puerto Rico, USA, June 1997.
9. O. D. Faugeras and M. Herbert, "The representation, recognition and locating of 3-D objects," *Intl. J. of Robotics Research*, 1992.
10. G. Stein, "Accurate internal camera calibration using rotation, with analysis of sources of error," *ICCV*, 1995.
11. R. I. Hartley, "Self-calibration from multiple views with a rotating camera" *ECCV*, 1994.
12. S.J. Maybank and O. Faugeras, "A therory of self-calibration of a moving camera," *Int. J. of Computer Vision*, 1992.
13. Bruce D. Lucas and Takeo Kanade, " An Iterative Image Registration Technique with an Application to Stereo Vision," *International Joint Conference on Artificial Intelligence, pages 674–679*, 1981.

FFT-Based Disparity Estimation for Stereo Image Coding

Udo Ahlvers, Udo Zoelzer, and Stefan Rechmeier

Department of Signal Processing and Communications
University of the German Federal Armed Forces
Hamburg, Germany
udo.ahlvers@unibw-hamburg.de

Abstract. In stereovision systems, the depth information of objects in the scene can be obtained by estimating the disparity, i.e. the displacement of corresponding pixels in the image pair. In this paper a new FFT-based algorithm for disparity estimation is proposed. The phase difference between the two images is calculated at several frequencies for each pixel. These phase differencies have a linear coherence which can be used to make the approach robust and to avoid local errors. The resulting disparity can then be estimated from the gradient of these phase differences. In the second part, these disparity maps are used for an efficient stereo image coding approach. Here, the transmission of both left and right image is not necessary. At the receiver, e.g. the right image can be reconstructed having only the left image and the disparity map.

1 Introduction

By observing a 3D-Scene with a camera, a 2D-image on the camera target is produced. Thus the depth information of the scene is lost [1]. To estimate this depth information, a calibrated stereoscopic camera-set can be used. This approach is called *Fronto-Parallel Binocular Vision*. Between the resulting two images, there is a shift between corresponding pixels, which is called *disparity*. With the relation

$$A \sim \frac{1}{d} \tag{1}$$

it is possible to get object distances A from the disparity values d. Furthermore, to create a realistic 3D-impression of a scene, a stereoscopic image pair is necessary. On the other hand, both images contain lots of identical information. For a transmission of 3D visual information and reconstruction at the receiver it should be more reasonable to use the disparity map for an efficient image coding approach.

In section 2 a new FFT-based algorithm for disparity estimation is introduced. A quality measure for comparing the new method with existing approaches is presented in section 3. In section 4, the application of the disparity map for stereo image coding is shown. At last, a conclusion of the work and an outlook are given.

B. Michaelis and G. Krell (Eds.): DAGM 2003, LNCS 2781, pp. 257–264, 2003.

2   FFT-Based Disparity Estimation

There are different algorithms available for disparity estimation. In contrast to the correlation-based or feature-based approaches, which suffer from high computational load or classification problems, the approach in the Fourier domain, where disparity can be calculated directly from local phase differences, has been proven advantageous.

To obtain dense disparity maps, the following calculations have to be carried out for each pixel $px(n_1, n_2)$ in the image pair. In a calibrated camera-set, corresponding pixels lie in the same row (*epipolar constraint* [1]), so there exists only horizontal disparity. Due to that reason we have a one-dimensional problem with only the column index n_2 as a parameter. For simplification, we write $n = n_2$ for the column index from here on. $x(n)$ with $n = 0, 1, \ldots, N-1$ denotes a local area of a row of the image centered at $px(n_1, n_2)$. Using the local discrete Fourier Transform $(k = 0, 1, \ldots, N-1)$

$$X(k) = \sum_{n=0}^{N-1} x(n) \cdot e^{-j\frac{2\pi}{N}kn} = |X(k)| \cdot e^{j\varphi(k)} \tag{2}$$

a general spatial shift yields

$$x(n-d) \;\circ\!\!-\!\!\bullet\; X(k) \cdot e^{-j\frac{2\pi}{N}kd} \tag{3}$$
$$= |X(k)| \cdot e^{j\varphi(k)} \cdot e^{-j\frac{2\pi}{N}kd} . \tag{4}$$

Applying this to two local areas of a stereoscopic image pair yields

$$x_L(n) = x_R(n-d) \tag{5}$$
$$\circ \atop \bullet \tag{6}$$
$$|X_L(k)| \cdot e^{j\varphi_L(k)} = |X_R(k)| \cdot e^{j\varphi_R(k)} \cdot e^{-j\varphi_D(k)} . \tag{7}$$

For identical contents, the magnitude spectra $|X_L(k)|$ and $|X_R(k)|$ are identical, too. So from the phase terms

$$\varphi_L(k) = \varphi_R(k) - \varphi_D(k) \Rightarrow \varphi_D(k) = \varphi_R(k) - \varphi_L(k) \tag{8}$$

and the formal definition of $\varphi_D(k)$ in Eq. (4) we get the frequency-dependent disparity

$$d(k) = \varphi_D(k) \cdot \frac{N}{2\pi k}, \; k = 0, 1, \ldots, N-1 . \tag{9}$$

First phase-based algorithms used Gabor-Filters [2,3], where the disparity was evaluated only for one frequency (i.e. for one $k = $ const). However, distortions at that frequency lead to errors in the disparity estimation. In our approach, we use a FFT to calculate a **set** of frequency-dependent phase differencies $\varphi_D(k)$, from which we derive the final disparity value $d(n_1, n_2)$ for the observed pixel (see Fig.1). The fundamental advantage lies in the fact that the phase shift

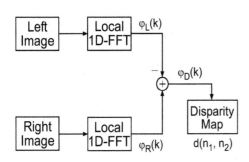

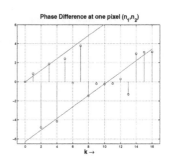

Fig. 2. Calculated set of phase differencies $\varphi_D(k)$ (*stems*) with the resulting disparity as the gradient (*solid line*).

Fig. 1. Principle of FFT-based disparity estimation.

$\varphi_D(k)$ is linear frequency dependent (see Eq. (4)). For all this set of frequencies k, the resulting disparity d can be found as the gradient of the phase shift $\varphi_D(k)$ [4]. Due to the periodicity of the phase, values lie between -2π and $+2\pi$. To obtain the final gradient, we use an approach of two straight lines, which are fit in the phase values with a linear regression procedure [5] (see Fig.2). Applying this approach to each pixel in the image, we get dense disparity maps. Since the disparity d is calculated directly from the phase difference, even subpixel accuracy is possible, which is an additional advantage compared to the correlation-based approaches. Fig. 3 shows the results of this algorithm for a random-dot stereo image pair. The process of disparity through the object fits the reference nearly perfect, and the background with zero-disparity has no local errors.

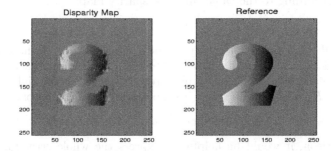

Fig. 3. FFT-based disparity estimation for an artificial image pair. Left:*calculated result*, right:*reference* [6].

To show this in detail, in Fig. 4 only one line of the image is plotted. Here we see again the good conformity between reference and calculated result.

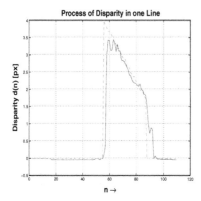

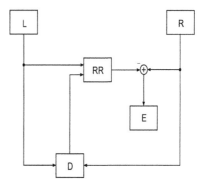

Fig. 4. Process of Disparity $d(n)$ for one row of the artificial image. Plotted are the calculated result (*solid*) and the reference (*dashed*).

Fig. 5. Principle of the quality measurement for disparity maps (*L:left image, R:right image, D:disparity map, RR:reconstruction of the right image, E:error image*).

3   Introduction of a Quality Measure

In most cases, especially when dealing with natural images, a reference disparity map is not available. So a criterion has to be found to evaluate the quality of a calculated disparity map. As the disparity map itself is obtained from a stereoscopic image pair, one can reconstruct e.g. the right image by only using the left image and the disparity map. The comparison between the original and the reconstructed right image then directly yields a measurement for the quality of the disparity map (see Fig. 5). Considering the fact that the disparity map d contains the spatial shifts between corresponding pixels in the stereoscopic image pair, the reconstruction of the right image is performed by "back-shifting" the left image according to the values in the disparity map:

$$\hat{x}_R(n_1, n_2 - d(n_1, n_2)) = x_L(n_1, n_2) .\tag{10}$$

Here n_1 and n_2 again denote the row and column indices of the image. Since we obtained a dense disparity map with our FFT-based approach, performing Eq.(10) for each pixel yields a complete reconstruction of the right image. The error image E is then produced by a simple pixelwise subtraction:

$$x_E(n_1, n_2) = |x_R(n_1, n_2) - \hat{x}_R(n_1, n_2)| .\tag{11}$$

For comparison, it would be helpful to express the whole error image by one scalar. Due to the substraction in Eq. (11), errors are shown as intensities in the error image. A summation of all pixels and a consequent normalization on the image size produces the error criterion

$$ErrorCrit = \frac{\displaystyle\sum_{n_1=0}^{N_1-1}\sum_{n_2=0}^{N_2-1} |x_R(n_1, n_2) - \hat{x}_R(n_1, n_2)|}{N_1 \cdot N_2 \cdot Res} .\tag{12}$$

In the denominator of Eq. (12) also the resolution *Res* of the image appears. For the most common $8 - bit$ grayscale type, the resolution is $2^8 = 256$ grayscale values. As the error image E has the same range as the original image pair, this range has to be considered for the normalization, too.

Applying Eq. (12) to several image pairs we obtained values for

$$ErrorCrit \leq 0.05 \,. \tag{13}$$

This means that the right image can be reconstructed with a reliability of over 95%. In addition to Fig. 3 these values confirm the performance and the good results of our FFT-based approach.

It has to be noticed that a perfect reconstruction without any errors is not possible. At locations in the image, where jumps in the disparity process occur, you will have very small remaining errors caused by reconstruction errors. This will be discussed extensively in the next chapter.

4   Stereo Image Coding Using Disparity Maps

For the transmission of camera signals, a stereoscopic image pair is necessary at the receiver to create visual depth information. However, the transmission of both original images (left and right) is to costly. Here the fact can be used that the stereoscopic image pair contains a lot of redundancy. Both images show objects of the same visual scene, except at the very brink of the images. So, with transmitting only one image (e.g. the left one) and the calculated disparity map [7], a reconstruction of the other image is possible at the receiver (see Eq. (10)). As already mentioned in the previous chapter, a perfect reconstruction is not possible with that approach. In most areas of the image pair, there will be a steadily changing disparity process. However, e.g. at object edges, the disparity will have branches. These jumps lead to errors in the reconstruction process. Fig. 6 shows the two possible situations.

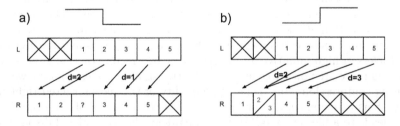

Fig. 6. Possible errors in the reconstruction occur at locations with jumps in the disparity process (*a: falling disparity, b: rising disparity*).

For falling disparity (Fig. 6a), there remains a pixel without any assignment. This influence can be handled by an interpolation of the neighborhood pixels. For rising disparity (Fig. 6b), we have a double assignment leading to an allocation problem.

On the other hand, the error image produced for the quality measure exactly contains locations and values of the errors produced in the reconstruction. The solution therefore is the transmission of the the error image E additional to the left image and the disparity map. In the reconstruction procedure at the receiver, the error image is superposed to eliminate the reconstruction errors:

$$\hat{x}_R(n_1, n_2 - d(n_1, n_2)) = x_L(n_1, n_2) \tag{14}$$

$$\tilde{x}_R(n_1, n_2) = \hat{x}_R(n_1, n_2) + x_E(n_1, n_2). \tag{15}$$

In Eq. (15), $\tilde{x}_R(n_1, n_2)$ denotes the final reconstruction result after the superposition of the error image. Fig. 7 shows the resulting stereo image coding approach with Eq. (15) applied for the whole image.

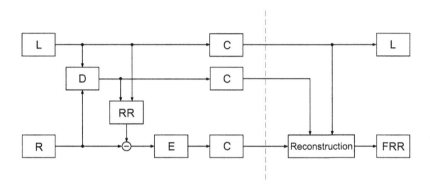

Fig. 7. Principle of stereo image coding using the disparity map (*L:left image, R:right image, D:disparity map, RR:reconstruction of the right image, E:error image, C:coding and compression, FRR:final reconstruction at the receiver*).

Fig. 8 shows the results of this approach. In the upper row, the original stereo image pair and the corresponding disparity map are mapped. The error image, the reconstruction at the receiver and the final error image are displayed below. Disparity map and error image have been compressed using a JPEG-Coder. Nonetheless, a high-qualitive and nearly error-free reconstruction is possible [8]. Although there are now three images to be transmitted instead of two, we have a resulting compression gain. Taking the quality of the reconstructed right image in Fig. 8 as a reference, an "ordinary" JPEG-compression of the original right image leads to a file size of 6 KB. In comparison, the transmitted disparity map and the error image together only have a size of 2 KB! So for stereoscopic image pairs, we obtain a compression gain of over 60% compared to a single JPEG-compression with the same quality.

Additionally, the information content of the transmitted data is higher with the disparity based approach. Besides the possibility to create 3D-impressions, a depth map is available at the receiver, from where explicit object distances can be derived easily.

Furthermore, information from the reconstruction process can be used to improve

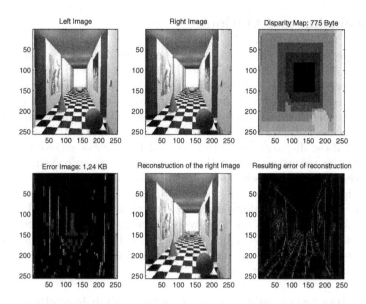

Fig. 8. Results of stereo image coding. Original uncompressed images have a file size of 65 KB. Disparity map and error image have been maximum compressed by a JPEG-Coder. The resulting error image (*lower right*) has been derived from Eq. (11).

the disparity estimation at the coder itself. As we have seen in the previous section, the error image indicates where errors appear in the disparity map. This information about the position of errors can be included in a feedback-loop to the disparity map itself (see Fig. 9). This analysis-by-synthesis approach could

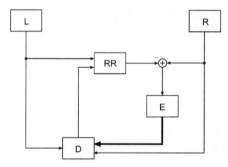

Fig. 9. Principle of an analysis-by-synthesis approach. Notice the feedback from the reconstructed right image to the disparity map in contrast to Fig. 5 (*L:left image, R:right image, D:disparity map, RR:reconstruction of the right image, E:error image*).

perhaps avoid the transmission of the error image and therefore lead to a further improvement in the efficiency of the stereo image coding approach.

5   Conclusion and Outlook

We have presented a FFT-based algorithm for disparity estimation using local phase differences at several spatial frequencies. Here the linear context between phase difference and disparity is used for the suppression of estimation errors. Having one image and the disparity map, a reconstruction of the other image is possible. This was first used to produce an error image and a quality measurement to evaluate the estimated disparity maps. Furthermore, we have shown that these disparity maps can be used for efficient stereo image coding. Here again the reconstruction of the right image was performed, this time at the receiver. The transmission of only the left image, the disparity map and the error image has proven to be advantageous. The disparity map and the error image contain less information and can thus be compressed much more efficiently. Furthermore an analysis-by-synthesis approach has been presented. The feedback-loop from the error image back to the disparity estimation helps to eliminate remaining errors and can be used for improving the efficiency of the stereo image coding approach.

Future work focuses on improvements of the analysis-by-synthesis approach, in order to avoid the transmission of the error image at all. Concerning the disparity estimation, the relationship of the magnitude spectra of the two local image areas can be taken into account as well. As these spectra should be identical, this relationship can be taken as a confidence value for the corresponding phase differencies.

References

1. Liedtke, C.-E.: Computer Aided Scene Analysis. Script for Lecture, University of Hannover, 1998.
2. Nuerenberg, B.: Development and Application of a phase-based Method for fast Disparity Estimation in Stereoscopic Image Pairs. Masters Thesis, Ruhr-University Bochum, 1998.
3. Sanger, T.: Stereo Disparity Computation using Gabor Filters. Biological Cybernetics, **59** (1988) 490–498.
4. Vernon, D.: Fourier Vision. Kluwer Academic Publishers, 2001.
5. Kreyszig, E.: Statistical Methods and their Applications. Vandenhoeck & Ruprecht, 7th ed., 1985.
6. Henkel, R.: Rolf Henkel's Homepage. http://axon.physik.uni-bremen.de/r̃dh/research/.
7. Siggelkow, S.: Stereo Image Coding. Internal Report, Albert-Ludwigs-University Freiburg, 1997.
8. Rechmeier, S.: Coding and Reconstruction of Stereoscopic Image Pairs. Masters Thesis, University of Federal Armed Forces Hamburg, 2002.

Projective Reconstruction of Surfaces of Revolution

Sven Utcke[1] and Andrew Zisserman[2]

[1] Arbeitsbereich Kognitive Systeme, Fachbereich Informatik,
Universität Hamburg, Germany
utcke@informatik.uni-hamburg.de
[2] Visual Geometry Group, Department of Engineering Science,
University of Oxford, United Kingdom
az@robots.ox.ac.uk

Abstract. This paper addresses the problem of recovering the generating curve of a surface of revolution from a single uncalibrated perspective view, based solely on the object's outline and two (partly) visible cross-sections. Without calibration of the camera's internal parameters such recovery is only possible up to a particular transformation of the true shape. This is however sufficient for 3D reconstruction up to a 2 DOF transformation, for recognition of objects, and for transfer between views. We will describe the basic algorithm and show some examples.

1 Introduction

This paper describes a method for the recovery of the generating function of a Surface of Revolution (SOR) from a single image. Ignoring the usual unknowns scale and position the generating function could be used for a reconstruction up to a particular subgroup of 3D-projective transformations with only 2 degrees of freedom (DOF). Additionally, the generating function can be used directly for recognition of the SOR from an arbitrary view point, provided the method of matching plane curves is invariant to a projective transformation. Transfer of the contour between views finally can be used for verification.

Most algorithms for the reconstruction of SORs (or, more generally, Straight Homogeneous Generalised Cylinders, SHGCs) go back to [1], where a possible algorithm for the identification of a SHGC's axis from its outline was given, on to an algorithm for the identification of a SHGC's ending cross-sections in [2], and [3,4,5,6] who all gave algorithms for the reconstruction of SHGCs from orthographic views (e. g. approximated by a tele-lens). For SORs the approach in [5,6] was recently extended to work with any calibrated camera [7]. All of these algorithms require knowledge about the actual camera used, and mostly even a particular camera geometry, in addition to the object's outline and at least one (partly) visible cross-section. The cross-section could be a discontinuity in the SOR's generating function such as the flat top or bottom of an object, or surface markings. Our novel algorithm by contrast requires the outline and two partly visible cross-sections, but no additional information about the imaging process

B. Michaelis and G. Krell (Eds.): DAGM 2003, LNCS 2781, pp. 265–272, 2003.

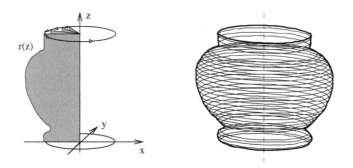

Fig. 1. SORs as either a rotational surface or as a stack of circular cross-sections.

— it is in fact invariant not only to perspective transformation, but the entire projective group.

Other methods for the reconstruction of SORs previously employed by us were e. g. based on a number of distinguished points [8,9]. In [10] we gave an algorithm for the computation of an SOR's projectively (quasi-) invariant signature and in [11] these methods demonstrated a recognition-rate similar to that of appearance-based approaches. Since we already demonstrated in [12,6] that the identification and grouping of potential SORs in cluttered images is possible, we will in this paper concentrate on simple images so as not to confound the issues.

This paper is structured as follows: we will recall the basic properties of an SOR in Sec. 2; Section 3 gives a description of the actual algorithm used for the projective reconstruction as well as some examples, and applications to recognition and transfer will be discussed in Sec. 4.

2   Object Model

There are two traditional models for the construction of Surfaces of Revolution. Most commonly used is that of a *generating function* $r(z)$ being rotated around the axis of revolution, resulting in a surface

$$\boldsymbol{S} = \left(r(z)\cos(\phi), r(z)\sin(\phi), z\right)^{T} , \qquad (1)$$

compare Fig. 1. Our intentions, however, are best served if we understand an SOR as a special case of a Straight Homogeneous Generalised Cylinder, namely one with a circular cross-section where the axis goes through the centre of the cross-section, and the cross-section is orthogonal to the axis. In such a model the circular cross-section is swept along the SOR's axis and scaled according to a *scaling function* (equivalent to the planar generating function mentioned above); further simplifying this model a little, we can imagine an SOR to be constructed out of (infinitely) many circular cross-sections stacked on top of each other. Figure 1 illustrates both models. The idea of forming the SOR outline as an envelope of circles is the backbone of the novel method presented here.

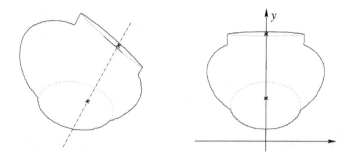

Fig. 2. Projectively distorted outline of an SOR in arbitrary position, and the rectified version symmetric around the y-axis

3   Projective Reconstruction

In this section we will show how, from a single image, an SOR's generating function $r(z)$ can be recovered up to a 2 DOF subgroup of the plane projective transformations (discounting the usual overall scale ambiguity and an offset along the axis). All that is needed is the image of an SOR's outline and two of its cross-sections, C_1 and C_2, two conics.

The algorithm proceeds by first identifying and grouping possible SORs in the image and computing a transformation into a rectified frame where the outline as well as the image of the two cross-sections C_1 and C_2 will be symmetric around the y-axis; this can always be done using the algorithms described in [10,12, 6] and will not be discussed in any detail. From there a planar homography into a distinguished frame is found where the image of each cross-section will be a circle; this immediately results in a projective reconstruction $\varrho(y)$ of the generating function $r(z)$. We will now describe the process in more detail, but touching only lightly on most of the previously published results mentioned above.

The identification and grouping of an SOR's outline draws heavily on the fact that the two sides of its outline (i.e. on both sides of the projection of the axis) are related by a planar harmonic homology, which can be calculated quite accurately using one of [10,12]. Once this homology has been found it is always easily possible to rectify the outline in such a way that it will be symmetric around the y-axis of a 2D-plane. Figure 2 gives an example of a severely distorted image of an SOR and its rectified version, which is symmetric around the y-axis.

The outline or contour of an SOR is the image of the so called *contour generator*, the set of points where rays through the viewpoint are tangent to the object; this will generally be a space-curve in 3D, and no straightforward invariant transformation exists between the outline as observed in the image and the generating function. For each individual cross-section however such a transformation is easily found, and since all cross-sections were originally completely contained within the SOR they will, after projection, be completely contained

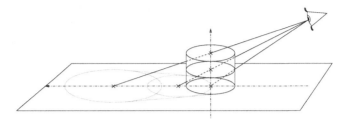

Fig. 3. Independent of viewpoint a planar homography from the image plane onto a distinguished plane exists such that the images of all cross-sections become circles

within the SOR's projected 2D-outline — this means that the outline is nothing else but the envelope of all these projected cross-sections.

For each view the position of the centre of projection uniquely determines the view-cone and therefore the contour-generator. However, it does not determine the position of the image-plane, and it is possible to generate the information on any such plane from the information on any other plane by a simple plane to plane projective transformation, a so called planar homography. This means that we are free to put a virtual image plane wherever we like. There exist in particular a set of distinguished image planes that maintain the y symmetry and where the projection of each circular cross-section will again be a circle; these are the planes which are parallel to the cross-sections in 3D, and in particular any plane containing a cross-section. In Fig. 3 this is illustrated for a cylinder.

How do we find the homography from the image-plane into one of these distinguished planes? Since the rectified outline is symmetric around the y-axis this must also hold for the images of the two cross-sections, which can therefore be parameterised as conics of the form $\boldsymbol{x}^T \boldsymbol{C} \boldsymbol{x} = 0$ with

$$
\boldsymbol{C}_i = \begin{pmatrix} 1 & 0 & 0 \\ 0 & C_i & \frac{E_i}{2} \\ 0 & \frac{E_i}{2} & F_i \end{pmatrix}. \tag{2}
$$

The homography we are looking for needs to apply some projective skew in y-direction such that the aspect ratios of both conics will be the same, as well as some anisotropic scaling along one of the two axes (we choose the x-axis) such that both conics will become circles, it therefore has the form

$$
\boldsymbol{H} = \begin{pmatrix} s & 0 & 0 \\ 0 & 1 & 0 \\ 0 & b & 1 \end{pmatrix}. \tag{3}
$$

If $\boldsymbol{x}' = \boldsymbol{H}\boldsymbol{x}$ is the image of the point $\boldsymbol{x}$ under the homography $\boldsymbol{H}$, then

$$
\boldsymbol{C}'_i = \boldsymbol{H}^{-T} \boldsymbol{C}_i \boldsymbol{H}^{-1} = \begin{pmatrix} \frac{1}{s^2} & 0 & 0 \\ 0 & C_i - bE_i + b^2 F_i & \frac{E_i}{2} - bF_i \\ 0 & \frac{E_i}{2} - bF_i & F_i \end{pmatrix} \tag{4}
$$

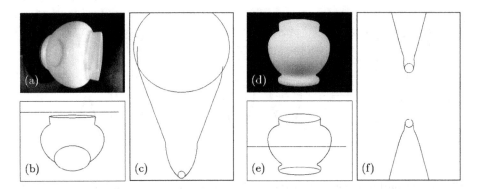

Fig. 4. Original photographic image (a), (d); outline, conics, and the conics' vanishing line (b), (e); outline and conics transferred onto a distinguished plane (c), (f). Note that (a) displays serious non-linear distortions, which have a negative impact on the calculations — the top conic appears to sit above the object in (c)

is how the two conic-cross-sections C_1 and C_2 will transform, and based on our requirement that both conics should have the same aspect-ratio after transformation, we can calculate two possible values for b as

$$b_{I/II} = \frac{(E_1 - E_2) \pm \sqrt{(E_1 - E_2)^2 - 4(C_1 - C_2)(F_1 - F_2)}}{2(F_1 - F_2)}. \tag{5}$$

The line $\ell = (0, 1, 1/b)^T$ is the planes' vanishing line within the rectified image. The two different values for b code the two different cases where either both conics are viewed from the same side, i. e. the viewpoint is completely above or below both conics, and the line ℓ will be outside the object, and the case where one conic is viewed from above and one from below, i. e. the viewpoint is somewhere between the two conics, and so is the line ℓ, which intersects the object. Figure 4(a)+(d) show two pictures of real objects, each corresponding to one of the two cases for b in (5), as well as the objects' outlines, conics and the lines $\ell = (0, 1, 1/b)^T$ in Fig. 4(b)+(e).

Once b has been found it is then easy to find a solution for s based on the stipulation that the conics should be circles after scaling; this solution is

$$s = (C_i - bE_i + b^2 F_i)^{-1/2}. \tag{6}$$

Since the knowledge of b and s uniquely determines the homography H in (3) we can next transfer the outline into this distinguished plane. We also know that here the images of all cross-sections are circles and that the outline is the envelope of all these circles; we can therefore in reverse find the images of all intermediate cross-sections as circles which are 1) fully contained within the outline, have 2) their centres on the image of the SOR's axis, and are 3) tangent at two corresponding points of the outline. The left image of each set in Fig. 5

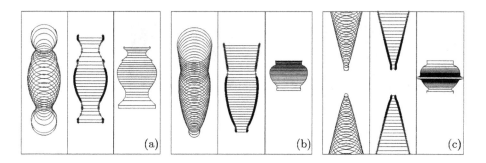

Fig. 5. The outline of an SOR as the envelope of cross-sections (*left* image of each set), a projective reconstruction of the generating function (*middle* image of each set), and an alternative representation of the generating function (*right*)

shows the image of an SOR's outline on the distinguished plane, as well as some of the inscribed cross-sections.

Once the centre $(0, y)^T$ and radius ϱ have been computed for each circle we immediately have a projective reconstruction $\varrho(y)$ of the generating function. From Fig. 3 it can be seen that y is related to the true distance along the axis z by a line to line projective transformation; the complete 3×3 plane projective transformation can be represented as $(r, z, 1)^T = \boldsymbol{G} \cdot (\varrho, y, 1)^T$ with

$$G = \begin{pmatrix} a & 0 & 0 \\ 0 & as_y & t_y \\ 0 & c & 1 \end{pmatrix} \tag{7}$$

which is of the same basic form as (3) and — ignoring the usual overall scale ambiguity and choice of origin ($a = 1$ and $t_y = 0$) — has 2 DOF, which code the vertical vanishing point (in c) and aspect-ratio (in s_y). Examples are shown in the middle image of each set in Fig. 5.

However, while being projectively equivalent to the original generating function it will in general not be very similar by human standards — this is particularly true for Fig. 5(c). We have therefore used the inverse of (3) to project the reconstructed outline back into the rectified image, where the projective reconstruction will generally look more realistic. The right image of each set in Fig. 5 shows this projection. How close these are to an Euclidean reconstruction depends on the viewing-position. For near orthographic projections ($c = 0$) the reconstruction will already be true up to anisotropic scaling, but in that case we could have used one of [5,6], requiring only one cross-section instead of two.

4   Applications

The recovered generating function can be used to reconstruct the surface up to the particular projective ambiguity $\boldsymbol{G}$ given in (7) above. However, it can also be

 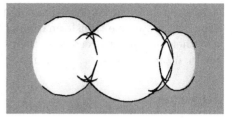

Fig. 6. Examples of transfer from one particular view of an SOR into a second view

used directly (despite the projective ambiguity) for two other tasks: recognition and transfer, and we describe these now.

Ignoring self-occlusion, the recovered generating curve is within a projective transformation of the true generating curve, so any method for projectively invariant curve representation may be used to recognise it. This is more powerful than the distinguished points previously used by us [8,9], since the entire generating curve can be matched rather than just the isolated points available on the original outline; a number of possible representations are cited in [13,14,15].

The result could then e.g. be verified using *transfer*, i.e. given an SOR's outline and two cross-sections in one image, and the corresponding two cross-sections in a second image, we are trying to predict the contour in that second image; the predicted and measured outline have to agree. Although for each view the generating function can only be recovered up to a 2 (4) DOF ambiguity as described in (7), it is still possible to compute the map between the generating function and the image contour for any view in which the two cross-sections have been specified, using the construction of Sec. 3 in reverse, generating the contour as the envelope of cross-sections. The position and radii of the two cross-sections serve to uniquely compute the missing parameters in (7).

Figure 6 gives an example of the transfer of a contour from one view of an SOR into a different view of the same SOR, this demonstrates nicely the correctness of the reconstruction. The cusps on the second contour (as, indeed, all contours inside the object-outline) correspond to parts of the contour generator which, for opaque objects, can not be observed in that second, slightly more tilted view. This effect is called self-occlusion. The part of the contour generator corresponding to the self-occluded bit of the contour can never be reconstructed from contour-information alone (although it might be possible to use grey-level cues) and will consequently be missing from the reconstruction, something which an algorithm for the recognition of SORs would need to take into account.

5   Conclusion

We have demonstrated a simple method which, based on the outline of an SOR and two cross-sections, can easily create a projective reconstruction for all parts of the generating function where the object is not (self-) occluded. This method does not require any knowledge about the camera but does in fact work for an arbitrary projective transformation of the contour. The resulting reconstruction can then be used to recognise the object by any of a number of projectively invariant approaches, or to calculate the transfer into additional views.

References

1. Ponce, J., Chelberg, D., Mann, W.B.: Invariant properties of straight homogeneous generalized cylinders and their contours. IEEE Trans Pattern Anal Mach Intell **11** (1989) 951–966
2. Sato, H., Binford, T.O.: On finding the ends of SHGCs in an edge image. In: Image Understanding Workshop, San Diego, CA, DARPA, Morgan Kaufmann Publishers, San Mateo, CA (1992) 379–388
3. Gross, A.D., Boult, T.E.: Recovery of SHGCs from a single intensity view. IEEE Trans Pattern Anal Mach Intell **18** (1996) 161–180 errata in [16].
4. Sato, H., Binford, T.O.: Finding and recovering SHGC objects in an edge image. Comput Vision, Graphics & Image Processing: Image Understand **57** (1993) 346–358
5. Zerroug, M., Nevatia, R.: Volumetric descriptions from a single intensity image. Int J Comput Vision **20** (1996) 11–42
6. Abdallah, S.M., Zisserman, A.: Grouping and recognition of straight homogeneous generalized cylinders. In: Asian Conf Comput Vision, Taipei (2000) 850–857
7. Wong, K.Y.K., Mendonça, P.R.S., Cipolla, R.: Reconstruction of surfaces of revolution from single uncalibrated views. In: Brit Mach Vision Conf. (2002) 93–101
8. Forsyth, D.A., Mundy, J.L., Zisserman, A., Rothwell, C.A.: Recognising rotationally symmetric surfaces from their outlines. In Sandini, G., ed.: Proc Eur Conf Comput Vision. LNCS, Springer Verlag (1992) 639–647
9. Liu, J., Mundy, J., Forsyth, D., Zisserman, A., Rothwell, C.: Efficient recognition of rotationally symmetric surfaces and straight homogeneous generalized cylinders. In: Proc Conf Comput Vision Pattern Recognit, New York City, New York, USA, IEEE CS, IEEE CS Press (1993) 123–128
10. Pillow, N., Utcke, S., Zisserman, A.: Viewpoint-invariant representation of generalized cylinders using the symmetry set. Image Vision Comput **13** (1995) 355–365
11. Mundy, J., Liu, A., Pillow, N., Zisserman, A., Abdallah, S., Utcke, S., Nayar, S., Rothwell, C.: An experimental comparison of appearance and geometric model based recognition. In: Proc. Object Representation in Computer Vision II. LNCS 1144, Springer-Verlag (1996) 247–269
12. Zisserman, A., Mundy, J., Forsyth, D., Liu, J., Pillow, N., Rothwell, C., Utcke, S.: Class-based grouping in perspective images. In: Proc Int Conf Comput Vision, Cambridge, MA, USA, IEEE CS, IEEE CS Press (1995) 183–188
13. Carlsson, S., Mohr, R., Morin, L., Rothwell, C., Van-Gool, L., Veillon, F., Zisserman, A.: Semi-local projective invariants for the recognition of smooth plane curves. Int J Comput Vision **19** (1996) 211–236
14. Reiss, T.H.: Object recognition using algebraic and differential invariants. Signal Processing **32** (1993) 367–395
15. Holt, R.J., Netravali, A.N.: Using line correspondences in invariant signatures for curve recognition. Image Vision Comput **11** (1993) 440–446
16. Gross, A.D., Boult, T.E.: Correction to "recovery of SHGCs from a single intensity view". IEEE Trans Pattern Anal Mach Intell **18** (1996) 471–479

Illumination Insensitive Template Matching with Hyperplanes

Christoph Gräßl*, Timo Zinßer*, and Heinrich Niemann

Lehrstuhl für Mustererkennung, Universität Erlangen-Nürnberg, Martensstraße 3,
91058 Erlangen, Germany
{graessl, zinsser}@informatik.uni-erlangen.de

Abstract. Data-driven object tracking is very important for many vision based applications, because it does not require any previous knowledge about the object to be tracked. In the literature, template matching techniques have successfully been used to solve this task. One promising descendant of these techniques is the hyperplane approach, which is both fast and robust. Unfortunately, like other template matching algorithms, it is inherently sensitive to illumination changes. In this paper, we describe three methods that considerably improve the illumination insensitivity of the hyperplane approach, while retaining the capability of real-time tracking. Experiments conducted on real image sequences prove the efficiency of our enhancements.

1 Introduction

In recent years, visual tracking has emerged as an important component of vision-based systems. It is used in many different application areas like medical imaging [1] and video surveillance [2]. The main purpose of visual tracking is to compute the position of a target object in each image of an image sequence. Additionally, it might be interesting to recover the orientation of the object. The main problem of visual tracking is that the appearance of an object can change dramatically in the 2-D image sequence. This is not only caused by object motion in conjunction with projective geometry, but also by occlusions, highlight effects and changes in illumination. One way to overcome these difficulties is to use model-based tracking algorithms, which require a priori knowledge about the objects. For example, the approach presented in [3] applies lightfield models and a particle filter for estimating the pose of an object.

One shortcoming of model-based tracking approaches is that they cannot be used when dealing with unrecognized or unknown objects. In this case, data-driven tracking, for example with template matching, is the only viable alternative. The template matching algorithm proposed by Hager and Belhumeur in [4] approximates the relation between variations in intensities and variations in pose by computing the Jacobian matrix of the initial template. Recently, Jurie

---

* This work was funded by the European Commission 5th IST Programme - Project VAMPIRE. Only the authors are responsible for the content.

B. Michaelis and G. Krell (Eds.): DAGM 2003, LNCS 2781, pp. 273–280, 2003.

and Dhome [5] have improved the basin of convergence of Hager's algorithm by replacing the Jacobian approximation with a hyperplane approximation.

As both algorithms directly operate on image intensities, they are inherently sensitive to changes in illumination. Belhumeur and Kriegman [6] have shown that the image of an object can be reconstructed under arbitrary lighting conditions if a small number of base images is available. Hager incorporated this method into his algorithm [4], basically transforming it into a model-based algorithm and thus losing the possibility of working with unknown objects.

In this paper, we present and compare three methods for reducing the illumination sensitivity of Jurie's hyperplane tracker without using prior knowledge about the tracked objects. Our first method does not work on the original images, but on edge images created with an adapted Sobel filter. The other two methods estimate linear illumination compensation parameters, either with a least square minimization technique or by computing the mean and variance of the template intensities. Especially the last two methods do not inhibit the real-time capability of the original approach and vastly improve its illumination insensitivity.

Our paper is structured as follows. In the next section, a short review of template matching is given. We present three methods for reducing the illumination sensitivity of the hyperplane tracker in Sect. 3. In the subsequent section, the results of our experimental evaluation with real image sequences are detailed. After a summary of our work, possible future extensions are discussed in Sect. 5.

2   Template Matching for Data-Driven Tracking

Template matching algorithms for data-driven tracking work on a sequence of images, which we represent as vectors of gray-level intensities. Additionally, a *reference template* must be specified in the first image. The reference template is defined by vector $r = (x_1, x_2, \ldots, x_N)^T$, which contains the 2-D coordinates of the template points. The gray-level intensity of a point $x_i = (x_i, y_i)^T$ at time t is given by $f(x, t)$. Consequently, vector $f(r, t)$ contains the intensities of template r at time t. The transformation of the reference template r at time t can be modeled by $r_t = g(r, \mu(t))$, where vector $\mu(t) = (\mu_1(t), \mu_2(t), \ldots, \mu_n(t))^T$ contains the *motion parameters*. Examples of tracking with different motion parametrizations are shown in Fig. 1. Template matching can now be described as computing the motion parameters $\mu(t)$ that minimize the least-square intensity difference between the reference template and the current template:

$$\mu(t) = \underset{\mu}{\operatorname{argmin}} \| f(r, t_0) - f(g(r, \mu), t) \|_2 \ . \tag{1}$$

Non-linear minimization in a high-dimensional parameter space involves extremely high computational cost and cannot be performed in real-time [7]. It is more efficient to approximate μ by a linear system

$$\hat{\mu}(t + 1) = \hat{\mu}(t) + A(t + 1) \left(f(r, t_0) - f(g(r, \mu(t)), t + 1) \right) \tag{2}$$

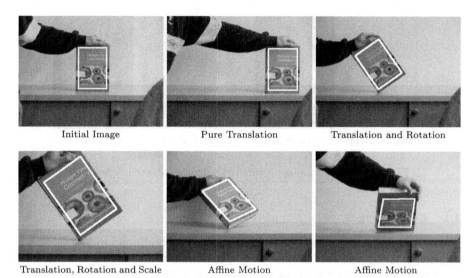

| Initial Image | Pure Translation | Translation and Rotation |

| Translation, Rotation and Scale | Affine Motion | Affine Motion |

Fig. 1. Some examples of tracking with different motion parametrizations. The reference template was taken from the initial image. The templates are marked by white rectangles.

as presented in [4,5]. There are two approaches for computing matrix $A(t)$ from equation (2). Hager and Belhumeur [4] propose the use of a Taylor approximation. The hyperplane approach presented in [5] acquires matrix A by a least-square estimation. In the latter approach, matrix A is independent from time t, but has to be computed in a separate training step when the initial image and the reference template are available. As the hyperplane approach has a superior basin of convergence, we will use it throughout the rest of this paper.

3   Illumination Insensitive Template Matching

The template matching algorithm presented in the last section is inherently sensitive to illumination changes, because it directly uses gray-level differences of the templates to compute the motion parameters. These illumination changes are a common problem in real images; they can be caused by automatic exposure adjustments of the camera, changes of light source irradiance, appearance of shadows or movement of the tracked objects [8]. We have investigated two different methods for countering the effects of illumination changes. One possibility is to preprocess the captured images in such a way that most of the adverse lighting effects are eliminated. In the next subsection, we will present such an approach based on edge images, which were created by applying a modified Sobel filter. Another technique is to estimate illumination compensation parameters for the current template, in order to adjust its gray-level values with respect to the reference template. Two algorithms employing this approach are described below.

original image   edge image   original image   edge image
            bright   dark

Fig. 2. Two edge images computed with the adapted Sobel filter.

3.1   Edge Images

In this subsection, we present a method for increasing illumination insensitivity by preprocessing the captured images. This approach has the advantage that there is no need to change the internal structure of the tracking system. Instead, only a preprocessing step has to be performed before passing the images to the tracker.

As it is independent of image brightness, the Sobel edge detection filter is an obvious choice for the preprocessing step. But using the Sobel filter also introduces new problems. Firstly, image noise is amplified by edge detection filters like the Sobel filter. Furthermore, if fast moving objects are temporarily blurred in the captured image, their appearance in the edge image changes considerably.

In order to counteract the problems described above, we suggest to compute the edge images according to

$$\boldsymbol{f}_{\text{edge}} = \text{blur}\left(\text{abs}\left(\text{sobel}_x\left(\text{blur}(\boldsymbol{f})\right)\right) + \text{abs}\left(\text{sobel}_y\left(\text{blur}(\boldsymbol{f})\right)\right)\right) , \qquad (3)$$

where $\text{blur}(\cdot)$ is a 3×3 box filter operation, $\text{sobel}_x(\cdot)$ and $\text{sobel}_y(\cdot)$ are 3×3 horizontal and vertical Sobel filter operations and $\text{abs}(\cdot)$ computes the absolute values of the input image intensities. The inner blurring operation reduces the noise in the captured image. After applying both Sobel filters, the absolute values of the intensities are computed and the resulting edge images are combined. This operation ensures that similar images are obtained even if the tracked object rotates in the image plane. At last, the edge image is blurred in order to smooth the edges, thus making the final image more suitable for the hyperplane tracker. The input images of our adapted Sobel filter consist of 8 bit unsigned integer values. After internally computing with larger data types, the final values are again saturated to this range.

Figure 2 shows two images captured in varying illumination conditions. Although the brightness of the original images is clearly differing, the computed edge images look very similar. However, in areas where the intensities of the original images are saturated, edges may appear weaker in the corresponding edge image. This example clearly demonstrates that the presented approach can compensate for changes of brightness, but not for changes of contrast.

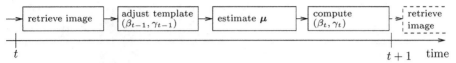

Fig. 3. One iteration cycle for the illumination insensitive hyperplane tracker using illumination compensation parameters

3.2 Intensity Difference Minimization

The influence of illumination changes on the gray-level values of an image is generally of non-linear nature. Nevertheless, previous work has shown that approximating these changes by a linear model is sufficiently accurate for our purposes [8]. Using the linear model

$$f_{\text{new}}(\boldsymbol{x}) = \beta f(\boldsymbol{x}) + \gamma \quad \forall \boldsymbol{x} \in \boldsymbol{r} \tag{4}$$

with illumination compensation parameters β and γ, we can represent variations of contrast and brightness.

When corresponding points of the initial template $\boldsymbol{f}(\boldsymbol{r}, t_0)$ and the current template $\boldsymbol{f}(\boldsymbol{g}(\boldsymbol{r}, \boldsymbol{\mu}(t)), t)$ are given, the illumination compensation parameters are a solution to the least-squares minimization problem

$$(\beta_t, \gamma_t) = \operatorname*{argmin}_{(\beta, \gamma)} \sum_{\boldsymbol{x} \in \boldsymbol{r}} \left[\beta \, f(\boldsymbol{g}(\boldsymbol{x}, \boldsymbol{\mu}(t)), t) + \gamma - f(\boldsymbol{x}, t_0) \right]^2 . \tag{5}$$

For brevity, we replace $\boldsymbol{g}(\boldsymbol{x}, \boldsymbol{\mu}(t))$ with $\tilde{\boldsymbol{x}}(t)$. Differentiating equation (5) with respect to the motion compensation parameters yields the linear system

$$\left[\sum_{\boldsymbol{x} \in \boldsymbol{r}} \begin{pmatrix} f^2(\tilde{\boldsymbol{x}}(t), t) & f(\tilde{\boldsymbol{x}}(t), t) \\ f(\tilde{\boldsymbol{x}}(t), t) & 1 \end{pmatrix} \right] \begin{pmatrix} \beta_t \\ \gamma_t \end{pmatrix} = \sum_{\boldsymbol{x} \in \boldsymbol{r}} \begin{pmatrix} f(\boldsymbol{x}, t_0) f(\tilde{\boldsymbol{x}}(t), t) \\ f(\boldsymbol{x}, t_0) \end{pmatrix} . \tag{6}$$

When using equation (6) directly, the matrix on the left has to be computed at every time step. To avoid this time consuming operation, we swap the reference template with the current template and thus obtain the motion compensation parameters $\tilde{\beta}$ and $\tilde{\gamma}$ for adapting the reference template to the current template. Consequently, the matrix in equation (6) has to be computed only once. As we still want to adapt the current template, we revert to the original illumination compensation parameters $\beta = 1/\tilde{\beta}$ and $\gamma = \tilde{\gamma}/\tilde{\beta}$.

One iteration cycle for the illumination insensitive hyperplane tracker is shown in Fig. 3. During the initialization, the illumination compensation parameters are set to $\beta_{t_0} = 1$ and $\gamma_{t_0} = 0$.

3.3 Intensity Distribution Normalization

Another approach for illumination compensation is presented in [9]. All templates are normalized by subtracting the mean value and dividing by the standard deviation of their intensities:

$$f_{norm}(\boldsymbol{r}) = \frac{\boldsymbol{f}(\boldsymbol{r}) - m}{\sigma}, \quad m = \frac{1}{N} \sum_{\boldsymbol{x} \in \boldsymbol{r}} f(\boldsymbol{x}), \quad \sigma^2 = \frac{1}{N} \sum_{\boldsymbol{x} \in \boldsymbol{r}} (f(\boldsymbol{x}) - m)^2 . \tag{7}$$

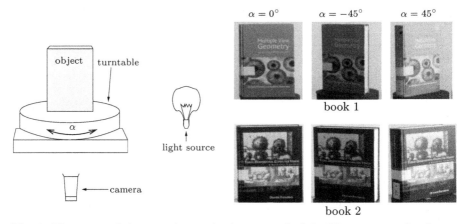

Fig. 4. The setup of the experiments is shown on the left. The camera takes images from two different books, which are placed on a turntable and illuminated from the right side. Three images for each book from different turntable positions are shown on the right to demonstrate the correlation of turntable position and illumination.

In this approach, adapting the current template to the reference template can also be written with linear illumination compensation parameters

$$\beta_t = \frac{\sigma_{t_0}}{\sigma_t} \text{ and } \gamma_t = \frac{\sigma_{t_0}}{\sigma_t} m_t - m_{t_0} . \tag{8}$$

These parameters are applied exactly as in the previous subsection. In contrast to the intensity difference minimization approach, where the intensities of corresponding points are analyzed, the intensity distribution normalization approach considers the distribution of intensities in the templates. Consequently, we expect it to be more robust when the motion parameter estimation is slightly inaccurate, as the distribution of intensities will be affected less than the individual point intensities.

4   Experimental Results

The following experiments with real image sequences demonstrate that our proposed methods significantly reduce the illumination sensitivity of Jurie's hyperplane tracker. Our experimental setup is shown in Fig. 4. This setup is used to generate K image sequences where the turntable moves from $0°$ to α_k ($k = 1, 2, \ldots, K$) and back to $0°$. Turntable angle α directly influences the illumination of the object. The values of α_k range from $-90°$ to $90°$ in steps of $5°$. The image resolution is 640×480 pixels and the turntable speed is $20.8°/\text{sec}$. The frame rate of the Sony DFW-VL500 firewire camera is 30 frames per second.

The initial position of the book was obtained manually and was used for the reference template. The tracker used a general affine motion parametrization and was initialized with $N = 100$ reference template points, which were selected at random. An image sequence is successfully tracked if the initial motion parameter

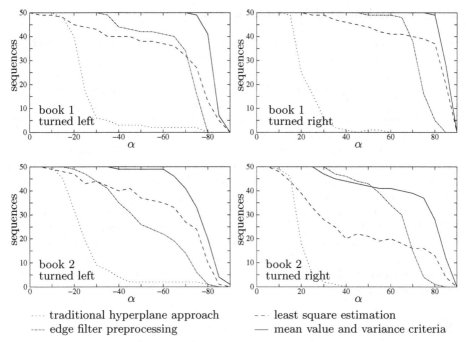

Fig. 5. The four graphs show the number of successfully tracked image sequences in dependency of the turntable angle α. The used objects (*book 1* and *book 2*) have been presented in Fig. 4.

is approximately the same as the motion parameter in the last frame. With these image sequences, we tested the traditional hyperplane approach (Sec. 2), the hyperplane approach with the edge filter preprocessing step (Sec. 3.1) and both illumination compensation methods (Sec. 3.2 and 3.3).

The results of the experiments, which are presented in Fig. 5, show that all of our suggested methods significantly improve the tracker's insensitivity to illumination changes. Using intensity distribution normalization clearly leads to the best results. This is what we expected, as small errors in the estimation of the motion parameter have only a small impact on the intensity distribution of the templates, and thus the illumination parameter estimation is very stable. This is not the case for the intensity difference minimization, which generally seems to be more unstable. The edge image method performs quite respectably, but as it does not compensate for contrast changes, it cannot cope with extreme illumination changes.

All presented methods are real-time capable on an Intel Pentium 4 processor system with 2.4 GHz and 1GB of memory. Motion estimation takes about 2.3msec per frame with the traditional hyperplane approach. This value increases to 3.8msec per frame for both illumination compensation approaches. With 10.4msec per frame, the edge image method is slowest.

5   Conclusion and Further Work

We have presented three approaches for reducing the illumination sensitivity of Jurie's hyperplane tracker. The first approach uses an adapted Sobel filter for preprocessing and does not require further changes to the tracking algorithm. The two remaining approaches estimate linear illumination compensation parameters for adjusting the templates to the reference template, either by considering corresponding points or by equalizing the intensity distributions. Experiments conducted with real image sequences prove the efficiency of the proposed algorithms, as all of them clearly enhance the illumination insensitivity of the hyperplane tracker. Among the presented algorithms, the intensity distribution normalization approach achieves the best results. Additionally, all approaches retain the tracker's real-time capability.

Our further work will concentrate on dealing with partial occlusions and highlights. For this purpose, the use of an iteratively reweighted least-square technique as shown in [4] seems to be very promising. We will also try to find a more intelligent way for choosing the points in the template, as they are currently selected at random. By doing so, we hope to reduce the number of points needed for reliable tracking.

References

1. Kang, D., Kweon, I.: Fast and Stable Snake Algorithm for Medical Images. Pattern Recognition Letters **20** (1999) 507–512
2. Ziliani, F., Reichel, J.: Effective Integration of Object Tracking in a Video Coding Scheme for Multisensor Surveillance Systems. In: Proceedings of the IEEE International Conference on Image Processing (ICIP), Rochester, USA, IEEE Computer Society Press (2002) 521–524
3. Zobel, M., Fritz, M., Scholz, I.: Object Tracking and Pose Estimation Using Light-Field Object Models. In Greiner, G., Niemann, H., Ertl, T., Girod, B., Seidel, H., eds.: Vision, Modeling, and Visualization 2002, Erlangen, Germany, Infix (2002) 371–378
4. Hager, G., Belhumeur, P.: Efficient region tracking with parametric models of geometry and illumination. IEEE Transactions on Pattern Analysis and Machine Intelligence **20** (1998) 1025–1039
5. Jurie, F., Dhome, M.: Hyperplane approach for template matching. IEEE Transactions on Pattern Analysis and Machine Intelligence **24** (2002) 996–1000
6. Belhumeur, P., Kriegman, D.: What is the set of images of an object under all possible lighting conditions. In: IEEE Confernce on Computer Vision and Pattern Recognition, IEEE Computer Society Press (1996) 270–277
7. Betke, M., Makris, N.: Fast object recognition in noisy images using simulated annealing. Technical Memo AIM-1510, Massachusetts Institute of Technology, Artificial Intelligence Laboratory (1995)
8. Jin, H., Favaro, P., Soatto, S.: Real-Time Feature Tracking and Outlier Rejection with Changes in Illumination. In: International Conference On Computer Vision, Los Alamitos, IEEE Computer Society (2001) 684–689
9. Fusiello, A., Trucco, E., Tommasini, T., Roberto, V.: Improving Feature Tracking with Robust Statistics. Pattern Analysis and Application **2** (1999) 312–320

Robust Orientation, Calibration, and Disparity Estimation of Image Triplets

Helmut Mayer

Institute for Photogrammetry and Cartography, Bundeswehr University Munich
Helmut.Mayer@UniBw-Muenchen.de,
http://www.BauV.UniBw-Muenchen.de/institute/inst10

Abstract. This paper addresses robust automatic orientation, calibration, and disparity estimation for generating visualizations from image triplets. Here, robust means, that meaningful results are obtained for a larger number of triplets without changing any parameter. This is achieved, e.g., by using as initial search space the whole image and by automatically estimating the search width for disparity estimation. The approach works for wider baselines than standard approaches for sequences. Results for visualization based on the trifocal tensor show the validity of the approach.

1 Introduction

Visualization of real world scenes is needed for a variety of applications ranging from video communications to the generation of movies. In the next section a robust approach for the automatic (projective) orientation of image triplets is presented, which is the first step towards visualization. Image triplets are employed instead of pairs, because their redundancy helps to rule out blunders and helps to robustly determine important parameters such as the search width for disparity estimation. The orientation builds on the estimation of the trifocal tensor based on the Carlsson-Weinshall duality, RANSAC (random sample consensus), and hierarchical matching including tracking through the pyramid. Section 3 presents a robust approach for the determination of the principal distances. An approximate calibration is a prerequisite for a meaningful navigation during visualization. From epipolar resampled images we generate a disparity map with a cooperative approach improved by several means and extended to three images given in Section 4. Results for trifocal tensor based visualization in Section 5 demonstrate the validity of our approach. The whole approach is robust in that sense that for a larger number of triplets meaningful results are obtained with all parameters fixed. The paper ends with conclusions.

2 Robust Orientation of Image Triplets

2.1 Estimation of the Trifocal Tensor

Where not stated otherwise, the algorithms employed are taken from [1]. Our basic building block for the orientation of an image sequence is the trifocal tensor

B. Michaelis and G. Krell (Eds.): DAGM 2003, LNCS 2781, pp. 281–288, 2003.

$\mathcal{T}$. Its basic advantage is, that it renders it possible to linearly transfer points from two images into a third, helping to rule out blunders. To estimate the trifocal tensor from a minimum of six point triplets, we employ the Carlsson-Weinshall duality. Utilizing an algorithm which gives a solution for a minimum number of points is important, because it considerably reduces the solution space for robust estimation based, e.g., on RANSAC.

Even though we reduce mismatches by hierarchical matching (cf. Section 2.2), there are usually far too many, e.g., for an efficient least squares solution. As we only have relatively few parameters and a high redundancy, RANSAC is a good choice. As proposed in [2], we have fixed the problem, that by neglecting statistical correlations the procedure to determine adaptively the number of samples gives a much too low number, by multiplying the number of samples with a larger factor. We use 500 for the fundamental matrix and 50 for the trifocal tensor, which gives satisfying results.

2.2   Hierarchical Matching

We significantly reduce the search space by means of a hierarchical approach based on image pyramids. With this not only the efficiency, but also the robustness is improved considerably. Highly precise conjugate points are obtained from a least-squares matching of points obtained from the sub-pixel Förstner operator [3]. On the coarsest level of the pyramids, which we define to consist of about 100×100 pixels, no reduction of the search space, e.g., by means of epipolar lines, is yet available. To reduce the complexity of the matching induced by setting the search space to the full image size for the coarsest pyramid level, several measures are taken. First, before least-square matching, we sort out many points by thresholding and maximizing, respectively, the correlation score among image windows. What is more, we restrict ourselves in the first image to only a few hundred points by regional non-maximum suppression.

Because of the higher combinatorial complexity of the trifocal tensor than of fundamental matrices, we compute on the coarsest pyramid level fundamental matrices from the second to the first and to the third image. We have found that it suffices to track the points through the image pyramid, after having obtained a solution for the trifocal tensor on the second coarsest level of the pyramid. For each level, we scale the point coordinates by a factor of two and then match the point by least-squares matching sub-pixel precisely. This was found to be much faster and equally reliable than extracting points and matching them on each level. The tracking of two hundred points is a matter of a few seconds even for images with a size of five mega-pixels.

2.3   Robust Projective Bundle Adjustment

For the linear solution with the trifocal tensor there is no need for approximate values. To obtain a precise solution, we compute a (projective) bundle adjustment. For the actual optimization the Levenberg-Marquardt algorithm implemented in the MINPACK public domain package is used.

Even though RANSAC together with other measures more or less guarantees, that the solution is valid, there is still a larger number of blunders in the data. To get rid of them, we eliminate observations with the largest residuals as long they are n times larger than the average standard deviation of the observations $\sigma_0 = v^\mathsf{T}v/redundancy$, with v the residuals and all observations weighted equally. We have found that a factor n of 5 to 8 times σ_0 leads to reasonable results. This is in accordance with values derived from robust statistics.

The approach was implemented in C++ based on the commercial image processing package HALCON and the public domain linear algebra package LA-PACK interfaced by the template numerical toolkit (TNT). The left three images of Figure 1 show the orientation of a triplet, which we have named Cathedral. The dataset is given in [4] as an example for a wider baseline triplet which cannot be oriented by the usual image sequence programs. We are not only able to orient this triplet, but as we use the full image as initial search space, it is possible to do this with one and the same parameter set for a wider range of imagery.

Fig. 1. Left: Wide baseline triplet Cathedral from [4] with matched points and epipolar lines from first to second and third image after calibration. σ_0 was 0.051 pixels before and 0.51 pixels after calibration; Right: First image of triplet Desk.

3 Robust Calibration

We have implemented standard procedures for auto-calibration, particularly, based on the absolute dual quadric, also including the constraint, that the skew is zero, and stratified auto-calibration [5]. Unfortunately, we found our implementation to be unstable for image triplets. Therefore, we have developed a simple, but robust means for the calibration of image triplets.

Start point is the projective, robustly optimized image orientation. From the trifocal tensor the fundamental matrix F_{12} from image one to two can be computed and from it the essential matrix and the calibrated projection matrix for the second camera. After defining the metric coordinate frame by this means, three-dimensional (3D) Euclidean points are calculated and the third projection matrix is determined linearly from the 3D points via the direct linear transform.

For the metric bundle adjustment we employ $P_i = K[R\,|\,t]$. There are five parameters to be optimized for the second projection matrix and six for the third: three translations in t (only two for the second projection matrix) and three rotations in R. To make the problem well-behaved, rotations are represented via quaternions.

The unconstrained optimization of the calibration parameters leads to local minima and thus to unsatisfactory results. Therefore, we assume that the principal point is in the center of the image, the skew is zero, and the ratio of the principal distance in x- and y- direction is approximately the ratio of the width and the height of the image. We further assume that principal distances range from 0.5 to 2.5. Then, the idea is to sample the principal distance in x-direction, α_x logarithmically by $2.5 * 0.95^n$ with $0 \le n \le 30$ and to take the σ_0 of the of the least squares adjustment as criterion. For the α_x resulting in the lowest σ_0, α_y is varied starting from $1.15 * \alpha_x$ with $1.15 * \alpha_x * 0.98^n$ and $0 \le n \le 15$.

The approach gave a meaningful result for all runs of the experiments presented here, but also in all other experiments. The camera used for the triplet shown in Figure 1, right side, is a Rollei D7 metric camera with highly precisely known parameters $\alpha_x = 0.8317$, $\alpha_y = 1.1055$, $x_0 = 0.0329$ and $y_0 = -0.0095$, and no skew. For this triplet $\alpha_x = 0.778 \pm 0.020$ and $\alpha_y = 1.079 \pm 0.033$ were obtained for ten runs. This is not too good but still in accordance with the given calibration data. Our implementation of calibration based on the absolute dual quadric gave reasonable results for this triplet, but only with the constraint on the skew. Also our implementation of stratified auto-calibration did not lead to a useful result for many of the runs. For the above triplet Cathedral we do not have ground-truth. We have obtained $\alpha_x = 2.37 \pm 0.11$ and $\alpha_y = 1.93 \pm 0.14$ for ten runs. Both methods based on the absolute dual quadric failed for all ten runs. The stratified auto-calibration gave a totally different result for two runs and for the rest $\alpha_x = 2.18 \pm 0.10$ and $\alpha_y = 1.91 \pm 0.06$, which is in the same range as our result. Similar results were obtained also for other image triplets.

4   Improved Cooperative Disparity Estimation

For disparity estimation we generate epipolar images based on the essential matrix. An essential step to make the whole procedure independent of user-supplied parameters is the determination of offset and search width for disparity estimation. As the employed approach uses a 3D array, this is not only important for robustness, but also due to computational complexity. The idea is to take the most reliable points that we can get hold of, namely those which survive the robust least squares adjustment for the image triplet, and project them into the epipolar image. As we have the redundant triplets, this step generates a meaningful search width in most cases. Because of the computational complexity, we scale down the images to a range of 200×300 pixels for disparity estimation.

Our approach on disparity estimation is based on [6]. It is described in more detail in [7]. The basic idea is to employ explicitly stated global constraints on uniqueness and continuity of the disparities. 3D support regions are employed to enforce continuity by fusing support among disparity estimates. Matching scores are calculated for the search width and then stored in a 3D array made up of image width and height as well as search width. Assuming opaque, diffuse-reflecting surfaces, the uniqueness constraint requires that on one ray of view only one point is visible. This implies an inhibition which is realized by weighting down all scores besides the strongest. Support and inhibition are iterated. We have chosen [6] because it can deal with strong occlusions and large search widths and have extended it by the following means:

- By a recursive implementation of the 3D box-filter we have sped up the computation. Opposed to the original approach, we employ symmetric support. This considerably improves the performance. By a small preference for smaller disparities we increase the probability, that occluded regions, for which no match is possible, obtain correct, smaller disparities.
- As proposed by [8], we use for the matching scores besides cross-correlation absolute differences with truncation. We have extended it by combining both. This is based on the idea, that correlation works best for horizontally textured regions. To generate unambiguous matches, the matching scores are weighted down when a special type of auto-correlation, which is only evaluated outside the matching window and inside the search width, is large.
- By combining image gradient and disparity gradient to control the amount of smoothing as proposed by [9], we avoid blurring disparity discontinuities and the elimination of narrow linear structures. Detecting occlusions and reducing the probabilities for large disparities in these regions is another means to obtain in occluded regions more meaningful, smaller disparities.

An excellent recent survey [8] on disparity estimation has not only grouped existing approaches into a taxonomy, but also introduced an evaluation metric as well as test data to compare different approaches. Our results for an evaluation according to [8] are given at www.middlebury.edu/stereo. The improved algorithm is listed on third place as of June 4, 2003, while the original algorithm is ranked thirteenth. The computation time for all four images is 102 seconds on a 2.5 GHz PC.

For the results in this paper we use this algorithm with the modification, that the absolute differences are made invariant against a different average brightness of the image windows. Opposed to the data set in www.middlebury.edu/stereo, many other images have a significantly different gray value for homologous windows.

To make use also of the information in the third image, we have implemented the following procedure: For all iterations but the first, for each pixel in the first image the disparity is selected, for which the score is maximum. Using this disparity, the herewith defined point is transferred via the trifocal tensor into the third image. There, the cross-correlation with the corresponding region in the first image is calculated and the element in the 3D array corresponding to the given disparity is weighted with it. We found that this procedure improves the results slightly for some images, but in most cases it does not only make each iteration much slower, but it takes also more iterations until convergence.

5   Results

Figure 2 shows the result for the image triplet Cathedral. The disparity map clearly reflects the depth-structure and the visualizations show that the metric structure was at least approximately reconstructed. The disparity map for the triplet Desk (cf. Figure 3 upper row) is not totally satisfying, but it should be considered that there are larger textureless parts in the image. The image triplet Kitchen stems from the web page at Microsoft maintained by Antonio Criminisi and Phil Torr. The results show the high quality achievable with the approach. Please note that all results shown in this paper where produced with one set of parameters. Similar results were obtained also for a larger number of other images, though there are, naturally, also a couple of images where the results are not (yet) satisfactory.

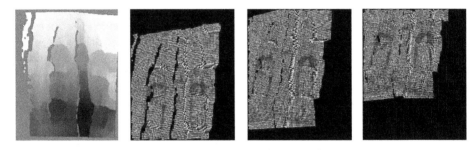

Fig. 2. Disparity map (left; non-overlapping and occluded regions in red/gray) and visualizations (center and right; occluded regions in black) for Cathedral from [4]

6   Conclusions and Problems

Our method for (projective) orientation of image triplets is robust in that sense that it generates results, which can be reproduced, with one set of parameters for a larger set of triplets. The cameras can have a considerably larger baseline than usual video sequences.

As we do not yet use homographies as a second option instead of fundamental matrices, such as in [10], we cannot deal with planar scenes. Our approach also fails, if the overlap between the three images is not large enough. This problem and also our failure to orient images, which are rotated around the camera axis could probably be overcome by an extension of our approach with importance sampling, such as in [11]. Though, the additional modeling will also increase the complexity considerably.

The tracking of points through the pyramid relies on two conditions: Basically, the sizes of objects or, from another point of view, the frequencies in the

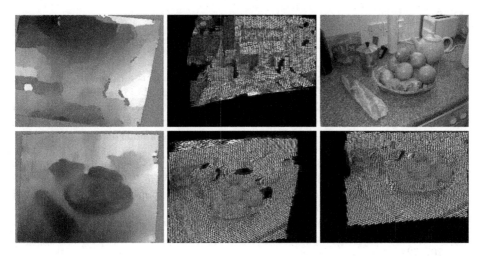

Fig. 3. Upper row – left: disparity map for Desk (non-overlapping and occluded regions in red / light gray); center: visualization (occluded regions in black) for Desk; right: first image for Kitchen from web page Antonio Criminisi and Phil Torr; lower row – left: disparity map for Kitchen; center and left: visualizations

images, have to be more or less uniformly distributed. More specifically, point objects, in the most instances corners, must exist, which are visible and keep their characteristics over the lower parts of the pyramid. We have found, that these conditions are fulfilled by many images, though there are also counterexamples. For instance, the circular targets usually employed in close range photogrammetry result into prominent points at coarse resolutions, while at finer resolutions, they can only be detected in the form of ellipses.

The calibration procedure based on sampling yields acceptable results, which can be reproduced and are in accordance with given calibration data. Though, it will probably fail, if the principal point is farther away from the image center. Therefore, it might be useful to implement the approach for constrained autocalibration proposed by [10].

Our means to improve the cooperative approach for disparity estimation give good results for a variety of images. Other approaches such as [12] perform partly better, but they also have an even higher computational complexity. Our simple experiments of a generalization of the approach with the trifocal tensor to triplets were not too successful. We think that a better way would be to project the results of cooperative disparity estimation from stereo pairs via the known orientation parameters in a Euclidean 3D array and then feed back cooperating points to cooperative disparity estimation. This would be similar to the voxel walls in [13].

Acknowledgment. We want to thank Peter Krzystek from Fachhochschule München for making us available his code for least squares matching.

References

1. Hartley, R., Zisserman, A.: Multiple View Geometry in Computer Vision. Cambridge University Press, Cambridge, UK (2000)
2. Tordoff, B., Murray, D.: Guided Sampling and Consensus for Motion Estimation. In: Seventh European Conference on Computer Vision. Volume I. (2002) 82–96
3. Förstner, W., Gülch, E.: A Fast Operator for Detection and Precise Location of Distinct Points, Corners and Centres of Circular Features. In: ISPRS Intercommission Conference on Fast Processing of Photogrammetric Data, Interlaken, Switzerland (1987) 281–305
4. Van Gool, L., Tuytelaars, T., Ferrari, V., Strecha, C., Vanden Wyngaerd, J., Vergauwen, M.: 3D Modeling and Registration under Wide Baseline Conditions. In: The International Archives of the Photogrammetry, Remote Sensing and Spatial Information Sciences. Volume (34) 3A. (2002) 3–14
5. Pollefeys, M., Van Gool, L.: Stratified Self-Calibration with the Modulus Constraint. IEEE Transactions on Pattern Analysis and Machine Intelligence 21 (1999) 707–724
6. Zitnick, C., Kanade, T.: A Cooperative Algorithm for Stereo Matching and Occlusion Detection. IEEE Transactions on Pattern Analysis and Machine Intelligence 22 (2000) 675–684
7. Mayer, H.: Analysis of Means to Improve Cooperative Disparity Estimation. In: Photogrammetric Image Analysis (PIA). (2003)
8. Scharstein, D., Szeliski, R.: A Taxonomy and Evaluation of Dense Two-Frame Stereo Correspondence Algorithms. International Journal of Computer Vision 47 (2002) 7–42
9. Zhang, Y., Kambhamettu, C.: Stereo Matching with Segmentation-Based Cooperation. In: Seventh European Conference on Computer Vision. Volume II. (2002) 556–571
10. Pollefeys, M., Verbiest, F., Van Gool, L.: Surviving Dominant Planes in Uncalibrated Structure and Motion Recovery. In: Seventh European Conference on Computer Vision. Volume II. (2002) 837–851
11. Torr, P., Davidson, C.: IMPSAC: Synthesis of Importance Sampling and Random Sample Consensus. IEEE Transactions on Pattern Analysis and Machine Intelligence 25 (2003) 354–364
12. Sun, J., Shum, H.Y., Zheng, N.N.: Stereo Matching Using Belief Propagation. In: Seventh European Conference on Computer Vision. Volume II. (2002) 510–524
13. Koch, R., Pollefeys, M., Van Gool, L.: Robust Calibration and 3D Geometric Modeling from Large Collections of Uncalibrated Images. In: Mustererkennung 1999, Berlin, Germany, Springer-Verlag (1999) 413–420

Fast Feature Selection in an HMM-Based Multiple Classifier System for Handwriting Recognition

Simon Günter and Horst Bunke

Department of Computer Science, University of Bern
Neubrückstrasse 10, CH-3012 Bern, Switzerland
{sguenter,bunke}@iam.unibe.ch

Abstract. A novel, fast feature selection method for hidden Markov model (HMM) based classifiers is introduced in this paper. It is also shown how this method can be used to create ensembles of classifiers. The proposed methods are tested in the context of a handwritten text recognition task.

Keywords: feature selection, hidden Markov model (HMM), handwritten word recognition, ensemble creation method.

1 Introduction

The problem of feature selection has been a focus of research in pattern recognition for a long time [9]. In general, the choice of features to be used in a classifier is application dependent and often very difficult. A possible way to solve this problem is to start with a set of candidate features and either modify or reduce them. There exist many ways to reduce a given set of features [12]. Feature set reduction is typically based on an objective function to validate the quality of the considered subset of features. Often a validation set is used on which the recognition rate is measured. An optimal approach is to calculate the objective function for all possible subsets. But this approach is only feasible for a rather small number of features. Branch & Bound algorithms [17] use a priori knowledge to reduce the search space. However, often there is no such a priori knowledge available and a suboptimal approach, such as Sequential Forward/Backward Search [4], Floating Search [18] or Oscillating Search [20], is used.

In this paper we propose a novel procedure for feature subset selection. Our approach is intended to work with hidden Markov models (HMMs). HMMs have originally emerged in speech recognition. Recently they have become very popular in the domain of handwritten word recognition [15,21]. Some feature selection algorithms which take advantage of the architecture of HMMs have been proposed. In [14] a feature selection method for classification problems where the classes have Gaussian distributions was presented. By regarding each state of an HMM as a class this approach may be also applied to HMM classifiers. In [3] a method was presented that allows fast feature selection for HMM classifiers.

B. Michaelis and G. Krell (Eds.): DAGM 2003, LNCS 2781, pp. 289–296, 2003.

In [7] an approach working with semi-continuous HMM systems was presented which calculates the discriminative power of such systems without testing on a validation set.

Recently a number of classifier combination methods, called ensemble methods, have been proposed in the field of machine learning [5]. It has been shown in many applications that systems consisting of multiple classifiers have the potential of improving recognition rate over single classifier systems. Given a single classifier, called the base classifier, a set of classifiers is automatically generated, e.g. by changing the training set [2] or the input features [8], A summary of ensemble methods is given in [5].

The field of off-line handwriting recognition has been a topic of intensive research for many years. Most of the systems reported in the literature until today consider constrained recognition problems based on vocabularies from specific domains, e.g. postal addresses [10]. Free handwriting recognition, without domain specific constraints and large vocabularies, was addressed only recently in a few papers [11,15]. The recognition rate of such systems is still low, and there is a need to improve it.

The contribution of this paper is twofold. First a fast feature selection algorithm for HMM classifiers is introduced that allows to validate a large number of feature sets very quickly. Secondly, a new ensemble method using this search algorithm is proposed.

The rest of the paper is organized as follows. In Section 2 the fast feature selection method is described. The following section introduces the new ensemble method. Section 4 contains information about the handwritten word recognizer, which is used in the experiments. Those experiments are then discussed in Section 5 and, finally, conclusions are drawn in Section 6.

2   Fast Feature Selection Algorithm

Normally feature selection algorithms use an objective function that assigns a measure of quality to each feature set. Often this function calculates the recognition rate of the classifier using the considered feature set on a validation set. For many applications the time complexity of a feature selection algorithm is very high, because the validation set must be large in order to get reliable results and because the number of validated feature sets is large. In the current paper we propose a new objective function that quickly computes an approximation of the recognition rate on a validation set.

An HMM based classifier system usually incorporates one individual HMM for each class where each HMM is built up from a set of states. For all these states output distributions, and for all pairs of states transition probabilities are defined. The input to an HMM classifier is a sequence of feature vectors $x_1, \ldots, x_n$. In the recognition, or decoding, phase the input sequence $x_1, \ldots, x_n$ is mapped to a sequence of states $s_{i1}, \ldots, s_{in}$ and for each such mapping a likelihood value is defined by the HMM. The optimal mapping, which maximizes the likelihood, is usually found by means of the Viterbi algorithm [19]. This optimal mapping is equivalent to an optimal path through a graph that is defined by the product of the sequence of input vectors and the states of the HMM.The likelihood of the optimal path is the score of the sequence of feature vectors for the considered HMM. The class corresponding to the HMM with the highest score is the output class. For a more detailed treatment of HMMs see for example [19].

It was empirically observed that two HMM classifiers using different feature sets but the same HMM topology often have similar (or identical) optimal paths of the HMM of the correct class, even when the outputs of the two classifiers differ from each other. Consequently, our fast feature selection algorithm is based on the assumption that the optimal path for a given input sequence and a given HMM is the same for all feature sets. The assumption will be only approximately true in most applications, but it leads to a speed-up in feature selection, because the optimal paths of the HMMs must be calculated once only for all feature sets. Normally this is done with the full set of features. For all other feature sets only the score for this path must be re-calculated for each HMM. A similar approach was proposed in [3].

It was also observed that the HMM with the highest score given one feature set is also very often among the HMMs with very high scores using another feature set. This observation leads to another assumption where we suppose that the output of the classifier using any feature set is among the classes with the N best score values obtained with the full set of features. Using this simplification only the scores of HMMs that are in the N-best list of the test with the classifier using the full set of features must be calculated. A pattern is regarded as correct if the HMM corresponding to the correct class has a higher score than any other HMM in this list[1].

The two simplifications mentioned above allow us to very quickly calculate an approximation of the recognition rate of the classifier for any feature set. The method requires the testing of the classifier on the validation set producing an N-best list for each pattern.

In this paper we examine two approaches to select the final feature set

- The feature set with the highest approximate recognition rate is selected for the final classifier.
- For each feature set size the classifier using the feature set with the highest approximate recognition rate is tested on the validation set (without any simplifications). The feature set that achieves the highest (real) recognition rate on the validation set is selected for the final classifier.

The motivation for the second approach is that the approximate recognition rate depends strongly on the size of the feature set. Especially for small values of N small feature sets obtain often too large values. By validating the best feature sets for each feature set size these effects can be overcome.

---

[1] In the experiments of Section 5 N denotes the number of incorrect HMMs compared to the correct HMM, i.e. a $(N+1)$-best list is used.

Note that the new feature selection method may also be used in the conjunction with classical feature selection methods by using the approximated instead of the real recognition rate as objective function.

3   New Ensemble Method

An ensemble method automatically produces a set of classifiers, the ensemble, given a single classifier. It has been shown in many applications that the recognition rate can be increased by using an ensemble rather than a single classifier. The best known ensemble methods are Bagging [2], AdaBoost [6] and Random Subspace Method [8].

In Section 2 a method for the calculation of an approximate recognition rate of the classifiers using a given feature set was introduced. As a by-product of this method we obtain the HMM with the highest score for each pattern of the validation set. The idea of the method described in this section is to find an ensemble of classifiers where each individual classifier has a different set of features and all classifiers together have a good performance when combined. To simulate the output of the classifiers using different feature sets the methods introduced in Section 2 are used. In this paper the classifiers are always combined by voting, i.e. the class which receives most votes is the final output. Unlike other methods which measure criteria such as diversity among the individual classifiers, this method directly measures an approximation of the performance of the ensemble.

Two approaches are considered to find a good performing ensemble of classifiers:

- A sequential search approach (*seq*). Starting with the empty set S of classifiers always the classifier leading to the best performance of the ensemble is added to S until the desired number of classifiers is reached.
- A sequential search approach with replacement (*seq replace*). This algorithm also starts with the empty set S. After adding the best classifier, it is repeatedly checked if the replacement of any existing classifier by any other classifier results in a better performance of the ensemble.If no replacement improves the solution then the next classifier is added.

It was observed that the method of Section 2 assigns too high recognition rates to small feature sets Therefore only feature sets of size 3 or larger will be considered in the experiments described in Section 5.

4   Handwritten Word Recognizer

The application considered in this paper is the off-line recognition of cursively handwritten words. As basic classifier an HMM-based recognizer is used. This recognizer is similar of the one described in [15]. We assume that each handwritten word input to the recognizer has been normalized with respect to slant, skew, baseline location and height (for details of the normalization procedures see [15]). A sliding window of one pixel width is moved from left to right over the word and nine geometric features are extracted at each position of the window. The geometric features used in the system include the fraction of black pixels in the window, the center of gravity, and the second order moment. These features characterize the window from the global point of view. The other features give additional information. They represent the position of the upper and lowermost pixel, the contour direction at the position of the upper and lowermost pixel, the number of black-to-white transitions in the window, and the fraction of black pixels between the upper and lowermost black pixel.

For each upper- and lowercase character, an HMM is built. For all HMMs the linear topology is used, i.e. there are only two transitions per state, one to itself and one to the next state. The character models are concatenated to word models. There is exactly one model for each word from the underlying dictionary. This approach makes it possible to share training data across different words. That is, each word in the training set containing character x contributes to the training of the model of x. Thus the words in the training set are more intensively utilized than in the case where an individual model is built for each word as whole.

The implementation of the system is based on the Hidden Markov Model Toolkit (HTK), which was originally developed for speech recognition. This software tool employs the Baum-Welch algorithm for training and the Viterbi algorithm for recognition [19].

5   Experiments

For the experiments, words from the handwritten sentence database described in [16] were used. Training and test sets contain 8795 and 1066 words, respectively, and a validation set of 1066 words was used. The number of writers contributing to these sets is larger than 80. The validation and the training set contain words from the same writers, whereas the writers of the test set are disjoint from the writers of the validation and training set. This means that the experiments described in this paper are writer independent. The vocabulary underlying the data set used in the experiments is 2296. That is, a classification problem with almost 2300 classes is considered. The feature selection is done using classifiers trained on the training set and the performance of these classifiers is measured on the validation set. The feature sets found by the proposed method are then used to train the classifiers on the combination of the training and validation set and those classifiers are finally tested on the test set. Note that the test set is not used for the feature sel ection.

In Table 1 the results of an evaluation of the methods described in Section 2 are shown. The goal of the experiments was to find subsets of features that lead to an improvement of the recognition rate over the original full set of features. In the table, the approximate recognition rate on the validation set (*approx*), the real performance on the validation (*valid*) and on the test set (*test*), and also the

Table 1. Results of the tests of the fast feature selection methods. The recognition rate of the base classifier is 70.5 % on the validation and 66.2 % on the test set.

	1. approach					2. approach					fs	bs
N	1	2	3	4	5	1	2	3	4	5	-	-
approx	77.2	74.6	74.4	74.3	74.3	75.8	73.4	73.2	73.2	73.2	-	-
valid	62.6	71.5	70.8	71.5	70.8	72.2	73.1	73.1	73.1	73.1	71.5	73.1
test	58	67.8	68.1	67.8	68.1	67.5	67.7	67.7	67.7	67.7	68.8	67.7
time	1.6	1.75	1.8	1.85	1.9	9.6	9.75	9.8	9.85	9.9	45	25

Table 2. Results of the tests with the ensemble methods. The recognition rate of the classifier using the full set of features is 66.2 % on the test set.

	1. approach					2. approach					Ada	rsm
N	1	2	3	4	5	1	2	3	4	5	-	-
vote (score)	68.9	70.6	70.9	69.8	70.3	67.8	69.3	69.9	70.3	70.1	68.4	67.7
time	1.8	1.95	2	2.05	2.1	2.8	2.95	3	3.05	3.1	-	-

time complexity (*time*) are given. The time complexities are given as multiples of the time used for the testing of one classifier on the validation set (which is 4 hours on a Pentium 500 MHz PC). The recognition rate of the system using the full set of features is 70.5 % on the validation and 66.2 % on the test set. As a comparison two standard feature selection methods similar to the "plus 1 - take away 1" algorithm [18] were also tested. The results of the method which starts with the empty set of features is shown in column *fs* and the results of the method which starts with the full set is given in column *bs*.

Except for $N = 1$, the first approach produced higher recognition rates on the test set than the second. An improvement over the classifier using all features from 66.2 % to 68.1 % was achieved. In the second approach the same feature set was found for values of N larger than 1. The classifiers found by the new feature selection method have a slightly lower performance than the ones produced by the standard method (see columns *fs* and *bs*), but the time complexity of the new method is much lower, especially for the first approach.

In Table 2 the results of experiments with the classifier ensemble methods of Section 3 are shown. Always 10 classifiers were produced for an ensemble. The values in row *vote (score)* show the performance of the ensemble when ties are broken by the maximum rule, i.e. in case of a tie the class with the highest score among the tied classes is the output of the combined classifier. In the last row of Table 2 the complexity is given As a comparison, ensembles of 10 classifiers were also produced by two classical ensemble methods, viz. AdaBoost [6] and random subspace method [8]. The results of these methods are shown in columns *Ada* and *rsm*, respectively. All recognition rates reported in Table 2 are measured on the test set.

The results of the first approach are in general better than the results of the second approach, although a much simpler algorithm is used. The reason for this is that the second algorithm tends to overfit. This overfitting effect is stronger for low values of N, because in this case the ensemble is optimized on the basis of an inaccurate approximation of the recognition results. For values of N between 3 and 5 both methods produced very good results. The improvements over the single classifier using the full set of features ranged from 3.6 % to 4.7 %. As it is obvious from the results of Table 2 all results of the new ensemble method with $N > 2$ have much higher recognition rate than both classical ensemble methods. Note that the classical ensemble methods do not need any testing on the validation set.

6 Conclusions

Two new, fast feature selection methods for HMM classifiers were proposed. In addition, two new approaches to creating ensembles of classifiers based on the new feature selection methods were introduced. All methods were evaluated in the context of a handwritten word recognition task and their results were compared to an HMM classifier that uses the full set of features.

For both feature selection methods and the two ensemble methods the first approach, which is the simpler one, achieved the best results. The feature selection method was able to increase the recognition rate of the classifier using all features from 66.2 % to 68.1 %. Two other feature selection methods, known from the literature, achieved slightly better recognition rates, but their time complexities are much higher. The best recognition rate achieved by the ensemble methods was 70.9 %. From the experimental results it can be concluded that both methods proposed in this paper are potentially very useful to improve the performance of HMM-based recognition systems.

Note that neither the feature selection method nor the ensemble method are restricted to handwriting recognition, but may also be applied to other recognition tasks where HMM based classifiers are used. In future research we will aim at a further improvement of the ensemble method by employing more sophisticated objective functions to evaluate the performance of an ensemble. We also plan to address the restricted ability of the validation set to represent the test set by applying cross-validation schemes.

Acknowledgment. This research was supported by the Swiss National Science Foundation (Nr. 20-52087.97). The authors thank Dr. Urs-Victor Marti for providing the handwritten word recognizer and Matthias Zimmermann for the segmentation of a part of the IAM database. Additional funding was provided by the Swiss National Science Foundation NCCR program "Interactive Multimodal Information Management (IM)2" in the Individual Project "Scene Analysis".

References

1. *Proc. of the 8th International Workshop on Frontiers in Handwritting Recognition,* Niagara-on-the Lake, Ontario, Canada, 2002

2. L. Breiman. Bagging predictors. *Machine Learning*, (2):123–140, 1996.
3. D. Charlet and D. Jouvet. Optimizing feature set for speaker verification. *Pattern Recognition Letters*, 18:873–879, 1997.
4. P. A. Devijver and J. Kittler. *Pattern Recognition: A Statistical Approach*. Prentice-Hall, 1982.
5. T. G. Dietterich. Ensemble methods in machine learning. In *[13]*, pages 1–15.
6. Y. Freund and R. Schapire. A decision-theoretic generalisation of on-line learning and an application to boosting. *Journal of Computer and Systems Sciences*, 55(1):119–139, 1997.
7. F. Grandidier, R. Sabourin, M. Gilloux, and C.Y. Suen. An a priori indicator of the discrimination power of discrete hidden markov models. In *Proc. of the 6th Int. Conference on Document Analysis and Recognition*, pages 350–354, 2001.
8. T. K. Ho. The random subspace method for constructing decision forests. *IEEE Trans. on Pattern Analysis and Machine Intelligence*, 20(8):832–844, 1998.
9. A. Jain and D. Zongker. Feature selection: evaluation, application, and small sample performance. *IEEE Trans. on Pattern Analysis and Machine Intelligence*, 19(2):153–158, 1997.
10. A. Kaltenmeier, T. Caesar, J.M. Gloger, and E. Mandler. Sophisticated topology of hidden Markov models for cursive script recognition. In *Proc. of 2nd Int. Conf. on Document Analysis and Recognition, Tsukuba Science City, Japan*, pages 139–142, 1993.
11. G. Kim, V. Govindaraju, and S.N. Srihari. Architecture for handwritten text recognition systems. In S.-W. Lee, editor, *Advances in Handwriting Recognition*, pages 163–172. World Scientific Publ. Co., 1999.
12. J. Kittler, P. Pudil, and P. Somol. Advances in statistical feature selection. In S. Singh, N. Murshed, and W. Kropatsch, editors, *Advances in Pattern Recognition - ICAPR*, pages 425–434, 2001.
13. J. Kittler and F. Roli, editors. *1st Int. Workshop on Multiple Classifier Systems*, Cagliari, Italy, 2000. Springer.
14. S. Krishnan, K. Samudravijaya, and P. Rao. Feature selection for pattern classification with gaussian mixture models: A new objective function. *Pattern Recognition Letters*, 17:803–809, 1996.
15. U. Marti and H. Bunke. Using a statistical language model to improve the performance of an HMM-based cursive handwriting recognition system. *Int. Journal of Pattern Recognition and Art. Intelligence*, 15:65–90, 2001.
16. U. Marti and H. Bunke. The IAM-database: an English sentence database for offline handwriting recognition. *Int. Journal of Document Analysis and Recognition*, 5:39–46, 2002.
17. M. P. Narendra and K. Fukunaga. A branch and bound algorithm for feature subset selection. *IEEE Trans. Comp.*, 26(9):917–922, 1977.
18. P. Pudil, J. Novovičovà, and J. Kittler. Floating search methods in feature selection. *Pattern Recognition Letters*, 15(11):1119–1125, 1994.
19. L. Rabiner. A tutorial on hidden Markov models and selected applications in speech recognition. *Proc. of the IEEE*, 77(2):257–285, 1989.
20. P. Somol and P. Pudil. Oscillating search algorithms for feature selection. In *Proc. of 15th Int. Conference on Pattern Recognition*, pages 406–409, 2000.
21. W. Wang, A. Brakensiek, and G. Rigoll. Combination of multiple classifiers for handwritten word recognition. In *[1]*, pages 117–122.

Empirical Analysis of Detection Cascades of Boosted Classifiers for Rapid Object Detection

Rainer Lienhart, Alexander Kuranov, and Vadim Pisarevsky

Microprocessor Research Lab, Intel Labs
Intel Corporation, Santa Clara, CA 95052, USA
Rainer.Lienhart@intel.com

Abstract. Recently Viola et al. have introduced a rapid object detection scheme based on a boosted cascade of simple feature classifiers. In this paper we introduce and empirically analysis two extensions to their approach: Firstly, a novel set of rotated haar-like features is introduced. These novel features significantly enrich the simple features of [6] and can also be calculated efficiently. With these new rotated features our sample face detector shows off on average a 10% lower false alarm rate at a given hit rate. Secondly, we present a through analysis of different boosting algorithms (namely Discrete, Real and Gentle Adaboost) and weak classifiers on the detection performance and computational complexity. We will see that Gentle Adaboost with small CART trees as base classifiers outperform Discrete Adaboost and stumps. The complete object detection training and detection system as well as a trained face detector are available in the Open Computer Vision Library at sourceforge.net [8].

1 Introduction

Recently Viola et al. have proposed a multi-stage object classification procedure that reduces the processing time substantially while achieving almost the same accuracy as compared to a much slower and more complex single stage classifier [6]. This paper extends their rapid object detection framework in two important ways: Firstly, their basic and over-complete set of haar-like features is extended by an efficient set of 45° rotated features, which add additional domain-knowledge to the learning framework and which is otherwise hard to learn. These novel features can be computed rapidly at all scales in constant time. Secondly, we empirically show that Gentle Adaboost outperforms with respect to object detection accuracy and computational complexity Discrete and Real Adaboost. Also, the usage of small decision trees instead of stumps as weak classifiers further improves the detection performance at a comparable detection speed.

2 Features

Our feature pool was inspired by the over-complete haar-like features used in [5,4] and their very fast computation scheme proposed in [6], and is a generalization of their work. Let us assume that the basic unit for testing for the presence of an object is a window of $W \times H$ pixels. A rectangle is specified by the tuple $r = (x, y, w, h, \alpha)$ with $0 \le x, x + w \le W$, $0 \le y, y + h \le H$, $x, y \ge 0$, $w, h > 0$, $\alpha \in \{0°, 45°\}$, and its pixel sum is denoted by $RecSum(r)$. Two examples of such rectangles are given in Figure 1. Our raw feature set is then the set of all possible features of the form

$$feature_I = \sum_{i \in I = \{1, ..., N\}} \omega_i \cdot RecSum(r_i),$$

where the weights $\omega_i \in \Re$, the rectangles r_i, and N are arbitrarily chosen. This raw feature set is (almost) infinitely large. For practical reasons, it is reduced as follows:

B. Michaelis and G. Krell (Eds.): DAGM 2003, LNCS 2781, pp. 297–304, 2003.

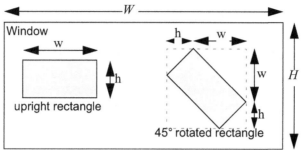

Fig. 1. Example of an upright and 45° rotated rectangle.

1. Only weighted combinations of pixel sums of two rectangles are considered.
2. The weights have opposite signs, and are used to compensate for the difference in area size between the two rectangles.
3. The features mimic haar-like features and early features of the human visual pathway such as center-surround and directional responses.

These restrictions lead us to the 14 feature prototypes shown in Figure 2: Four edge features, eight line features, and two center-surround features, and a special diagonal line feature. These prototypes are scaled independently in vertical and horizontal direction in order to generate a rich, over-complete set of features. Note that the line features can be calculated by two rectangles only. Hereto it is assumed that the first rectangle r_0 encompasses the black and white rectangle and the second rectangle r_1 represents the black area. Only features (1a), (1b), (2a), (2c) and (4a) of Figure 2 have been used by [4,5,6]. In our experiments the additional features significantly enhanced the expressional power of the learning system and consequently improved the performance of the object detection system. This is especially true if the object under detection exhibit diagonal structures such as it is the case for many brand logos.

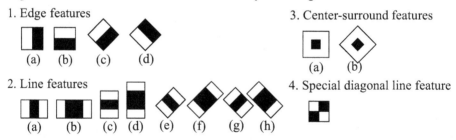

Fig. 2. Feature prototypes of simple haar-like and center-surround features. Black areas have negative and white areas positive weights.

NUMBER OF FEATURES. The number of features derived from each prototype is quite large and differs from prototype to prototype and can be calculated as follows. Let $X = \lfloor W/w \rfloor$ and $mY = \lfloor H/h \rfloor$ be the maximum scaling factors in x and y direction. An upright feature of size $w \times h$ then generates $XY(W+1-w(X+1)/2)(H+2-h(Y+1)/2)$ features for an image of size $W \times H$, while a 45° rotated feature generates $XY(W+1-z(X+1)/2)(H+1-z(Y+1)/2)$ with $z=w+h$. The number of features for a window size of 24x24 totals to 117,941.

Fast Feature Computation. All features can be computed very fast in constant time for any size by means of two auxiliary images. For upright rectangles the auxiliary image is the *Summed Area Table* $SAT(x, y)$. $SAT(x, y)$ is defined as the sum of the pixels of the upright rectangle ranging from the top left corner at (0,0) to the bottom right corner at (x,y) (see Figure 3a) [6]:

$$SAT(x, y) = \sum_{x' \le x, y' \le y} I(x', y').$$

It can be calculated with one pass over all pixels from left to right and top to bottom by means of $SAT(x, y) = SAT(x, y-1) + SAT(x-1, y) + I(x, y) - SAT(x-1, y-1)$ with $SAT(-1, y) = SAT(x, -1) = SAT(-1, -1) = 0$ From this the pixel sum of any upright rectangle $r = (x, y, w, h, 0)$ can be determined by four table lookups (see also Figure 3(c):

$$RecSum(r) = SAT(x-1, y-1) + SAT(x+w-1, y+h-1)$$
$$- SAT(x-1, y+h-1) - SAT(x+w-1, y-1)$$

This insight was first published in [6]. For 45° rotated rectangles the auxiliary image is the *Rotated Summed Area Table* $RSAT(x, y)$. It is defined as the sum of the pixels of a 45° rotated rectangle with the bottom most corner at (x,y) and extending upwards till the boundaries of the image (see Figure 3b):

$$RSAT(x, y) = \sum_{y' \le y, y' \le y - |x-x'|} I(x', y').$$

It can be calculated also in one pass from left to right and top to bottom over all pixels by

$$RSAT(x, y) = RSAT(x-1, y-1) + RSAT(x+1, y-1)(-RSATx, y-2) + I(x, y) + I(x, y-1)$$

with $RSAT(-1,y)=RSAT(x,-1)=RSAT(x,-2)=RSAT(-1,-1)=RSAT(-1,-2)=0$. From this the pixel sum of any rotated rectangle $r = (x, y, w, h, 45°)$ can be determined by 4 table lookups:

$$RecSum(r) = RSAT(x-h+w, y+w+h-1) + RSAT(x, y-1)$$
$$- RSAT(x-h, y+h-1) - RSAT(x+w, y+w-1) \cdot$$

Fast Lighting Correction. The special properties of the haar-like features also enable fast contrast stretching of the form $\check{I}(x, y) = (I(x, y) - \mu)/(c\sigma)$, $c \in R^+$. μ can easily be determined by means of $SAT(x,y)$. Computing σ, however, involves the sum of squared pixels. It can easily be derived by calculating a second set of SAT and $RSAT$ auxiliary images for $I^2(x, y)$. Then, calculating σ for any window requires only 4 additional table lookups. In our experiments c was set to 2.

3 (Stage) Classifier

We use boosting as our basic classifier. Boosting is a powerful learning concept. It

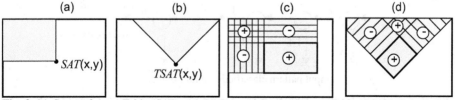

Fig. 3. (a) *Summed Area Table (SAT)* and (b) *Rotated Summed Area Table (RSAT)*. Calculation scheme of the pixel sum of upright (c) and rotated (d) rectangles.

combines the performance of many "weak" classifiers to produce a powerful 'committee' [1]. A weak classifier is only required to be better than chance, and thus can be very simple and computationally inexpensive. Many of them smartly combined, however, result in a strong classifier, which often outperforms most 'monolithic' strong classifiers such as SVMs and Neural Networks. Different variants of boosting are known such as Discrete Adaboost, Real AdaBoost, and Gentle AdaBoost [1]. All of them are identical with respect to computational complexity from a classification perspective, but differ in their learning algorithm. All three are investigated in our experimental results. Learning is based on N training examples $(x_1, y_1), ..., (x_N, y_N)$ with $x \in \Re^k$ and $y_i \in \{-1, 1\}$. x_i is a K-component vector. Each component encodes a feature relevant for the learning task at hand. The desired two-class output is encoded as -1 and $+1$. In the case of object detection, the input component x_i is one haar-like feature. An output of $+1$ and -1 indicates whether the input pattern does contain a complete instance of the object class of interest.

4 Cascade of Classifiers

A cascade of classifiers is a degenerated decision tree where at each stage a classifier is trained to detect almost all objects of interest (frontal faces in our example) while rejecting a certain fraction of the non-object patterns [6] (see Figure 4). For instance, in our case each stage was trained to eliminated 50% of the non-face patterns while falsely eliminating only 0.1% of the frontal face patterns; 20 stages were trained. Assuming that our test set is representative for the learning task, we can expect a false alarm rate about $0.5^{20} \approx 9.6e - 07$ and a hit rate about $0.999^{20} \approx 0.98$. Each stage was trained using one out of the three Boosting variants. Boosting can learn a strong classifier based on a (large) set of weak classifiers by re-weighting the training samples. Weak classifiers are only required to be slightly better than chance. Our set of weak classifiers are all classifiers which use one feature from our feature pool in combination with a simple binary thresholding decision or which are small CART trees with up to 4 features. At each round of boosting, the feature-based classifier is added that best classifies the weighted training samples. With increasing stage number the number of weak classifiers, which are needed to achieve the desired false alarm rate at the given hit rate, increases.

5 Experimental Results

All experiments were performed on the complete CMU Frontal Face Test Set of 130 grayscale pictures with 510 frontal faces [7]. A hit was declared if and only if

- the Euclidian distance between the center of a detected and actual face was less than 30% of the width of the actual face as well as
- the width (i.e., size) of the detected face was within ±50% of the actual face width.

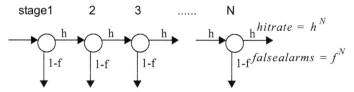

input pattern classified as a non-object

Fig. 4. Cascade of classifiers with N stages. At each stage a classifier is trained to achieve a hit rate of h and a false alarm rate of f.

Every detected face, which was not a hit, was counted as a false alarm. Hit rates are reported in percent, while the false alarms are specified by their absolute numbers in order to make the results comparable with related work on the CMU Frontal Face Test set. Except otherwise noted 5000 positive frontal face patterns and 3000 negative patterns filtered by stage 0 to n-1 were used to train stage n of the cascade classifier. The 5000 positive frontal face patterns were derived from 1000 original face patterns by random rotation about ±10 degree, random scaling about ±10%, random mirroring and random shifting up to ±1 pixel. Each stage was trained to reject about half of the negative patterns, while correctly accepting 99.9% of the face patterns. A fully trained cascade consisted of 20 stages.

During detection, a sliding window was moved pixel by pixel over the picture at each scale. Starting with the original scale, the features were enlarged by 10% and 20%, respectively (i.e., representing a rescale factor of 1.1 and 1.2, respectively) until exceeding the size of the picture in at least one dimension. Often multiple faces are detect at near by location and scale at an actual face location. Therefore, multiple nearby detection results were merged. Receiver Operating Curves (ROCs) were constructed by varying the required number of detected faces per actual face before merging into a single detection result. During experimentation only one parameter was changed at a time. The best mode of a parameter found in an experiment was used for the subsequent experiments.

Feature Scaling. Any multi-scale image search requires either rescaling of the picture or the features. One of the advantage of the Haar-like features is that they can easily be rescaled. Independent of the scale each feature requires only a fixed number of look-ups in the sum and squared sum auxiliary images. These look-ups are performed relative to the top left corner and must be at integral positions. Obviously, by fractional rescaling the new correct positions become fractional. A plain vanilla solution is to round all relative look-up positions to the nearest integer position. However, performance may degrade significantly, since the ratio between the two areas of a feature may have changed significantly compared to the area ratio at training due to rounding. One solution is to correct the weights of the different rectangle sums so that the original area ratio between them for a given haar-like feature is the same as it was at the original size. The impact of this weight adaptation on the performance is amazing as can be seen in Figure 8(a)."*-Rounding" show the ROCs for simple rounding, while "*-AreaRatio" shows the impact if also the weight of the different rectangles is adjusted to reflect the weights in the feature at the original scale.

Comparison Between Different Boosting Algorithms. We compared three different boosting algorithms: Discrete Adaboost, Real Adaboost, and Gentle Adaboost. Three 20-stage cascade classifiers were trained with the respective boosting algorithm using the basic feature set (i.e., features 1a, 1b, 2a, 2c, and 4a of Figure 2) and stumps as the weak classifiers. As can be seen from Figure 5, Gentle Adaboost outperformed the other two boosting algorithm, despite the fact that it needed on average fewer features (see Table 1, second column). For instance, at a an absolute false alarm rate of 10 on the CMU test set, RAB detected only 75.4% and DAB only 79.5% of all frontal faces, while GAB achieved 82.7% at a rescale factor of 1.1. Also, the smaller rescaling factor of 1.1 was very beneficial if a very low false alarm rate at high detection performance had to be achieved. At 10 false alarms on the CMU test set, GAB improved from 68.8% detection rate with rescaling factor of 1.2 to 82.7% at a rescaling factor of 1.1. Table 1 shows in the second column (nsplit =1) the average number of features needed to be evaluated for

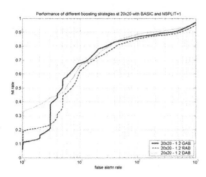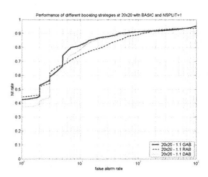

Fig. 5. Performance comparison between identically trained cascades with 3 different boosting algorithms using the basic feature set and stumps as weak classifiers.

background patterns by the different classifiers. As can be seen GAB is not only the best, but also the fastest classifier. Therefore, we only investigate a rescale scaling factor 1.1 and GAB in the subsequent experiments.

Table 1. Avg. # of features evaluated per background pattern at a pattern size of 20x20.

NSPLIT	1	2	3	4
DAB	45.09	44.43	31.86	44.86
GAB	30.99	36.03	28.58	35.40
RAB	26.28	33.16	26.73	35.71

5.1 Input Pattern Size

Many different input pattern sizes have been reported in related work on face detection ranging from 16x16 up to 32x32. However, none of them have systematically investigated the effect of the input pattern size on detection performance. As our experiments show for faces an input pattern size of 20x20 achieves the highest hit rate at an absolute false alarms between 5 and 100 on the CMU Frontal Face Test Set (see Figure 6). Only for less than 5 false alarms, an input pattern size of 24x24 worked better. A similar observation has been made by [2].

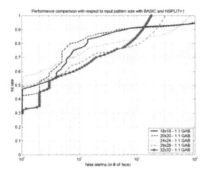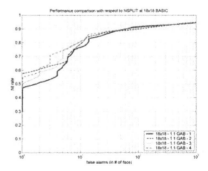

Fig. 6. Performance comparison (a) between identically trained cascades, but with different input pattern sizes using GAB, the basic feature set, and stumps as weak classifiers (nsplit=1), (b) with respect to the order of the weak CART classifiers. GAB, the basic features, and a pattern size of 18x18 was used.

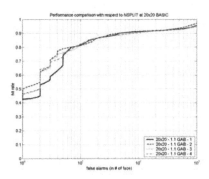
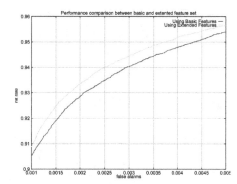

Fig. 7. Performance comparison with respect to (a) the order of the weak CART classifiers. GAB was used together with the basic feature set and a pattern size of 20x20. (b) Basic versus extended feature set: On average the false alarm rate of the face detector exploiting the extended feature set was about 10% better at the same hit rate (from [3]).

Tree vs. Stumps. Stumps as weak classifier do not allow learning dependencies between features. In general, N split nodes are needed to model dependency between N-1 variables. Therefore, we allow our weak classifier to be a CART tree with NSPLIT split nodes. Then, NSPLIT=1 represents the stump case. As can be seen from Figure 6(b) and Figure 7 stumps are outperformed by weak tree classifiers with 2, 3 or 4 split nodes. For 18x18 four split nodes performed best, while for 20x20 two nodes were slightly better. The difference between weak tree classifiers with 2, 3 or 4 split nodes is smaller than their superiority with respect to stumps. The order of the computational complexity of the resulting detection classifier was unaffected by the choice of the value of NSPLIT (see Table 1). The more powerful CARTs proportionally needed less weak classifiers to achieve the same performance at each stage.

Basic vs. Extended Haar-like Features. Two face detection systems were trained: One with the basic and one with the extended haar-like feature set. On average the false alarm rate was about 10% lower for the extended haar-like feature set at comparable hit rates. Figure 7(b) shows the ROC for both classifiers using 12 stages. At the same time the computational complexity was comparable. The average number of features evaluation per patch was about 31 (see [3] for more details). These results suggest that although the larger haar-like feature set usually complicates learning, it was more than paid of by the added domain knowledge. In principle, the center surround feature would have been sufficient to approximate all other features, however, it is in general hard for any machine learning algorithm to learn joint behavior in a reliable way.

Training Set Size. So far, all trained cascades used 5000 positive and 3000 negative examples per stage to limit the computational complexity during training. We also trained one 18x18 classifiers with all positive face examples, 10795 in total and 5000 negative training examples. As can be seen from Figure 8, there is little difference in the training results. Large training sets only slightly improve performance indicating that the cascade trained with 5000/3000 examples already came close to its representation power.

6 Conclusion

Our experimental results suggest, that 20x20 is the optimal input pattern size for frontal face detection. In addition, they show that Gentle Adaboost outperforms Discrete and

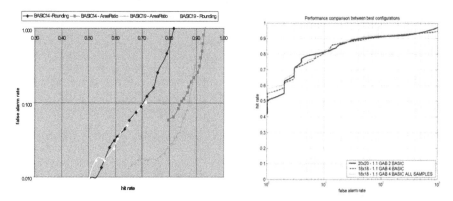

Fig. 8. Performance comparison (a) between different feature scaling approaches. "*-Rounding" rounds the fractional position to the nearest integer position, while "*-AreaRatio" also restores the ratio between the different rectangles to its original value used during training. (b) with respect to the training set size. One 18x18 classifier was trained with 10795 face and 5000 non-face examples using GAB and the basic feature set.

Real Adaboost. Logitboot could not be used due to convergence problem on later stages in the cascade training. It is also beneficial not just to use the simplest of all tree classifiers, i.e., stumps, as the basis for the weak classifiers, but representationally more powerful classifiers such as small CART trees, which can model second and/or third order dependencies. We also introduced an extended set of haar-like features. Although frontal faces exhibit little diagonal structures, the 45 degree rotated features increased the accuracy. In practice, the have observed that the rotated features can boost detection performance if the object under detection exhibit some diagonal structures such as many brand logos. The complete training and detection system as well as a trained face detector are available in the Open Computer Vision Library at http:/sourceforge.net/projects/opencvlibrary/ [8].

References

[1] Y. Freund and R. E. Schapire. Experiments with a new boosting algorithm. In Machine Learning: Proceedings of the Thirteenth International Conference, Morgan Kauman, San Francisco, pp. 148-156, 1996.
[2] Stan Z. Li, Long Zhu, ZhenQiu Zhang, Andrew Blake, HongJiang Zhang, and Harry Shum. Statistical Learning of Multi-View Face Detection. In Proceedings of The 7th European Conference on Computer Vision. Copenhagen, Denmark. May, 2002.
[3] Rainer Lienhart and Jochen Maydt. An Extended Set of Haar-like Features for Rapid Object Detection. IEEE ICIP 2002, Vol. 1, pp. 900-903, Sep. 2002.
[4] A. Mohan, C. Papageorgiou, T. Poggio. Example-based object detection in images by components. IEEE Transactions on Pattern Analysis and Machine Intelligence, Vol. 23, No. 4, pp. 349 -361, April 2001.
[5] C. Papageorgiou, M. Oren, and T. Poggio. A general framework for Object Detection. In *International Conference on Computer Vision*, 1998.
[6] Paul Viola and Michael J. Jones. Rapid Object Detection using a Boosted Cascade of Simple Features. IEEE CVPR, 2001.
[7] H. Rowley, S. Baluja, and T. Kanade. Neural network-based face detection. In IEEE Patt. Anal. Mach. Intell., Vol. 20, pp. 22-38, 1998.
[8] Open Computer Vision Library. http:/sourceforge.net/projects/opencvlibrary/

Local Representations for Multi-object Recognition

Thomas Deselaers[1], Daniel Keysers[1], Roberto Paredes[2*],
Enrique Vidal[2*], and Hermann Ney[1]

[1] Lehrstuhl für Informatik VI, Computer Science Department
RWTH Aachen - University of Technology, D-52056 Aachen, Germany
{deselaers, keysers, ney}@informatik.rwth-aachen.de
[2] Instituto Tecnológico de Informática
Departemento de Sistemas Informáticos y Computación
Universidad Politécnica de Valencia, E-46022 Valencia, Spain
{rparedes,evidal}@iti.upv.es

Abstract. Methods for the recognition of multiple objects in images using local representations are introduced. Starting from a straight forward approach, we combine the use of local representations with region segmentation and template matching. The performance of the classifiers is evaluated on four image databases of different difficulties. All databases consist of images containing one, two or three objects and differ in the backgrounds which are used. Also, the presence or absence of occlusions of the objects in the scenes is considered. Classification results are promising regarding the difficulty of the task.

1 Introduction

The problem of recognition of single objects in images has been thoroughly studied and satisfactory solutions exist for many applications such as face recognition (e.g. [10]), character recognition (e.g. [7]), and some classification tasks in medical applications (e.g. [5]). The methods used for these tasks are not applicable to the classification of more general images or complex scenes like general images from the world wide web. These images usually contain more than one object, and the objects may be subject to image transformations. A solution to this more general problem is desirable but so far no satisfying approach is known [13]. Methods not explicitly considering objects have been presented, e.g. [2]. In this paper, we examine some new algorithms based on local representations for multi-object recognition which are inherently invariant against translations. Considering the difficulty of the task, the results are promising, but not satisfactory. This implies that further research in this area is needed.

---

* Work supported by the Spanish "Ministerio de Ciencia y Tecnología" under grant
TIC2000-1703-CO3-01 and the Valencian OCYT under the grant CTIDIA/2002/80.

B. Michaelis and G. Krell (Eds.): DAGM 2003, LNCS 2781, pp. 305–312, 2003.

2   Local Representations for Classification

The local representation approach is based on the representation of the image by a set of small square subimages taken from different relevant positions of the original image (e.g. determined by the image variance). This method achieves translation invariance and also partially compensates for image occlusions. Using this local representation scheme, each image is represented by several smaller images that are also called local feature images. To classify each test image, a nearest neighbor classifier is applied using a suitable voting scheme. Given a test image, the k-nearest neighbors of all extracted local feature images are searched among the feature vectors computed for the training images. Each neighbor votes for its own class and a vector of votes (per class) is obtained by counting all votes. Following a direct voting scheme, the test image is classified into the most voted class. This sum rule of the votes of each local feature image is similar to the sum rule used in classifier combination theory [3].

The reference training set, consisting of all the local feature images of each training image, usually contains a large number of prototypes. To search the nearest neighbors efficiently, the well known KD-tree data structure is used. An approximate nearest neighbor search is performed instead of the exact search. The search is based on the $(1 + \epsilon)$-approximate nearest neighbor search [1].

Local representations of image objects have the advantage to be invariant against translations of the whole object and of parts of the objects with respect to each other. The local representations approach considered here has been successfully applied to different image object classification tasks [9,10].

Different approaches for local representations have been proposed, mainly in the image database retrieval literature [11,12]. In that field, the images are generally completely unconstrained, and representations invariant to translation, scale and rotation, among others, are needed.

3   Multi-object Recognition Using Local Representations

We propose to use local representations to analyze images which contain more than one object and objects which are placed on complex backgrounds. Note that these tasks are considerably harder than the tasks considered so far, where one object is placed on a uniformly colored background.

We consider the following scenario: In training, segmented images representing the objects are given. The test images contain occurrences of these objects in arbitrary position and combination. The difficulty of the test is influenced by occurrence of occlusion and inhomogeneous background.

3.1   Direct Transfer to Multiple Objects

The first idea to use local representations for multi-object recognition would be a direct transfer of the well understood and effective algorithm for single object

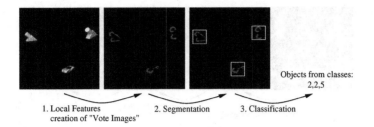

Objects from classes:
2,2,5

1. Local Features   2. Segmentation   3. Classification
creation of "Vote Images"

Fig. 1. Step 1: Obtaining the vote image from the test image. Positions where local representations have been extracted are marked white in the vote image. Step 2: The regions of votes are segmented into 3 regions. One for each object. Step 3: A majority vote for each of the 3 regions yields the classification result.

recognition. We slightly modify the classification algorithm and arrive at the following method.

The training process is unchanged and yields a KD-tree with local representations of the training images. Processing of the test images is performed as for single object recognition, arriving at a number of votes for each class. If the number of votes for one of the classes exceeds a certain threshold, the image is assumed to contain an object from this class. Obviously, one of the immediate drawbacks of this method is the inability to classify an image correctly which contains more than one object from one class.

Apart from this drawback, this method also leads to high error rates even on simple classification tasks, although the underlying principle is very effective for classification of single objects.

3.2   Combination with Region Segmentation

Local feature images belonging to an object that is present in the test image are localized within a specific region corresponding approximately to the size of the object in that image. Therefore, it should be required that only votes that are sufficiently close together lead to a joint vote for one object. To fulfill this constraint, we consider a region segmentation process for the votes.

The training process remains the same as for the single object recognition approach. The test image is processed in three steps, creation of vote images, region segmentation, and classification, as illustrated in Fig. 1.

Test images are processed as described for the single object case, yielding votes for one of the classes. Each vote can be uniquely associated with a position in the test image, representing the position the classified local representation was extracted from. The class number voted for can thus be associated with that position, yielding a new image with 'grey' values in the range $1, \ldots, K$, called vote image. These vote images are then segmented into d-connected regions. Regions with a size below a certain threshold are deleted, as they are probably resulting from noise. Those regions which are close enough together and from the same class are joined to one region. Each region is then classified by determining

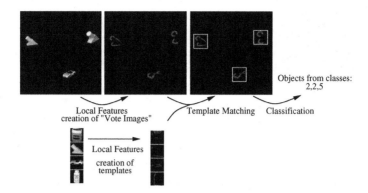

Fig. 2. The training data is processed to obtain the templates for the template matching process. The vote image is calculated from the test image and the template matching process is applied. The classification result is computed from this result.

the winner class using a majority vote procedure and this class is added to the list of classes assumed to be contained in the image.

3.3   Combination with Template Matching

To further refine the algorithm, we propose to use the information about the location of the local representations extracted in the training phase. As this information may enhance discrimination between classes, we apply the following template matching approach.

The extraction of local representations in the training phase is performed as described above. Additionally, for each training image the positions from which local representations are extracted are stored in a template that is equivalent to a binary image marking positions of high variance.

Processing of the test images is again a three step process. First, the vote images are produced in the same way as described above. Second, the template matching is performed by determining the correlation value between the templates produced in training and the vote images. These values are determined for each class and each position in the test image. A completely black template is included as a competing reference to model the background in the case of homogeneous black background. For each position, the highest correlation value and the correlation value for the black template are stored. In the third step, the information gained so far is used to obtain a classification result. If the correlation value for a class is higher than the correlation value for the background, no further detection of an object is allowed within the direct neighborhood and the corresponding class is added to the list of classes of objects assumed to be contained in the image. Template matching can be regarded as implicitly including segmentation, since the regions that are not classified as objects are considered as background. The whole process is illustrated in Fig. 2.

Fig. 3. One training image from each class of the COIL database

This approach and the approach laid out in section 3.2 implicitly detect the object. For classification, a summation of appropriate scores over all positions should be performed, but here the maximum approximation is used instead.

4 Databases

As standardized image databases for multiple object recognition are not publicly available, we generated appropriate databases with different levels of difficulty based on the well known COIL-20 database (Columbia Object Image Library, [8]). It consists of images taken from 20 different 3D-objects viewed from varying positions. Each image contains a single object subject to different illumination conditions. There are 1,440 reference images of size 128×128 pixels available. Examples are shown in Fig. 3.

Four databases were created, two with homogeneous black background and two with complex backgrounds. Each database consists of 400 images with 400×400 pixels. (The databases are available upon request.)

To create the test and training databases, the 1440 images from the COIL training set were split into two parts of 720 images each. The 720 images with even 3D-rotation angles were used as training images and the remaining 720 images were used to create the four test databases. This was done to avoid the occurrence of exactly the same objects in the test and the training dataset.

The databases with homogeneous background are named `black-noocc` and `black-occ`. Every image contains 1, 2, or 3 objects. The background is completely black. The difference between `black-occ` and `black-noocc` is that the objects in `black-occ` may occlude each other and in `black-noocc` not.

The databases with complex background are `dark-occ` and `normal-occ`. The images contain 1, 2, or 3 objects each and occlusions are allowed. The backgrounds are taken from a set of 110 background images. In the `dark-occ` database the images are darkened by 50% to reduce the background variability. Sample images for all databases are shown in Fig. 4.

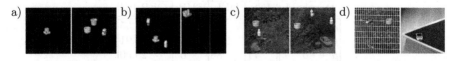

Fig. 4. Examples from a) `black-noocc` b) `black-occ` c) `dark-occ` d) `normal-occ`.

5   Results

For multi-object recognition the error rate known from single object recognition is not a sufficient error measure. This is because images that are classified partly correctly should be distinguished from those classified entirely incorrectly. Therefore, we compute two different error rates inferred from the measures used in speech recognition known as sentence error rate and word error rate. We use the *image error rate* (IER) where an image is only counted as correctly classified if all objects in the image have been recognized (and not more). This measure corresponds to the sentence error rate in speech recognition. The *object error rate* (OER) is similar to the word error rate in speech recognition and we distinguish between insertion (INS), deletion (DEL), and substitution (SUB) errors. The object error rate itself is then defined as the ratio of the minimum number of insertions, deletions, and substitutions to the number of objects in the image. The object error rate can be above 100% if there are more objects detected than actually contained in the image.

With the approach laid out in Section 3.1 the results given in Table 1 were obtained. The results are not satisfactory even on this simple classification task although the approach used performs well for single object classification. With this approach many errors occur because it is obiously not possible to classify an image correctly which contains two objects from the same class and because the position information of the local features is completely disregarded. These experiments were only performed with the database `black-occ` because results were not satisfactory even on this easy task. The threshold given in Table 1 is the threshold used to decide whether an object from one class is in the image given the number of votes per class. Here μ is the mean over the whole vector of votes and σ is the standard deviation. Several experiments were performed, but the best error rate of 28.07% is not sufficient for a task of this low complexity, which can be processed at a low error rate using background segmentation and a nearest neighbor classifier. If no occlusions are allowed, this approach even leads to 0% error rate. Nevertheless, segmentation is an unsolved problem in the presence of complex background and therefore this method is only applicable to images with homogeneous background.

The approach of local representations and region segmentation laid out in Section 3.2 as well as the approach of local representations and template matching described in Section 3.3 were applied to all of the four databases presented in

Table 1. Results for naive approach on `black-occ`. The threshold of minimum number of votes is given in terms of the mean μ and the standard deviation σ for each image.

threshold	INS	DEL	SUB	OER [%]
μ	177	49	96	41.65
$\mu + \sigma$	10	195	34	30.91
$\mu + \frac{1}{4}\sigma$	71	88	65	29.00
2μ	39	106	72	28.07

Table 2. Summary of the results on the different databases using local representations with region segmentation and local representations with template matching.

	region segmentation					template matching				
database	INS	DEL	SUB	OER [%]	IER [%]	INS	DEL	SUB	OER [%]	IER [%]
black-noocc	7	60	14	9.69	19.25	3	64	4	7.89	16.25
black-occ	29	70	18	14.66	26.75	1	132	2	13.66	25.75
dark-occ	458	90	118	88.33	75.00	170	320	11	64.23	60.00
normal-occ	1943	28	315	290.84	97.01	57	534	40	80.79	88.22

Section 4. Table 2 contains the results where the free parameters were manually optimized. The approach of local representations and region segmentation suffers mainly from insertion errors while the template matching approach suffers mainly from deletions. The figures show that the computationally more expensive template matching solution yields better results in all cases.

Interestingly, nearly all insertions in `dark-occ` result from just three test images with very high background variance. When using only the 397 test images that do not contain this background, only one insertion remains, with the same number of deletions and only 5 substitutions. This results in an OER of 42.45% and an IER of 59.64%. An impression of the amount of background noise in the vote images is given in Fig. 5. This high amount of noise stresses the need for a better background model.

6   Discussion and Conclusion

We presented an approach to classifying images containing multiple objects using local representations and different enhancements. The results may serve as a starting point for further work in the field of multi-object recognition and need further improvement.

Different improvements to the methods may be considered: In the segmentation step it would be possible to use class and direction dependent distances for joining regions. We also observed that there are some objects which are very similar in some regions (e.g. the two cups). This often results in some parts of the objects being classified as part of an object of another class. This information might also be learned from the training data and used for joining regions.

As suggested in [6] it may lead to better results to consider the whole image and not only some parts in taking the classification decision (holistic approach),

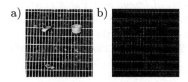

Fig. 5. a) an image from database `normal-occ` b) the vote image to the image from a)

which also includes a better background model. The training phase is not yet fully automated. Here, well segmented data is used for training, which is not always available. It is desirable to learn the representations of the objects from a number of given scenes. First steps into this direction are described in [4,6].

References

1. S. Arya, D.M. Mount, N.S. Netanyahu, R. Silverman, and A.Y. Wu. An optimal algorithm for approximate nearest neighbor searching. *Journal of the ACM*, 45(6):891–923, November 1998.
2. H. Burkhardt and S. Siggelkow. Invariant features in pattern recognition – fundamentals and applications. In C. Kotropoulos and I. Pitas, editors, *Nonlinear Model-Based Image/Video Processing and Analysis*, pages 269–307, Wiley, 2001.
3. R.P. Duin, J. Kittler, M. Hatef, and J. Matas. On combinig classifiers. *IEEE Trans. Pattern Analysis and Machine Intelligence*, 20(3):226–239, March 1998.
4. B.J. Frey and N. Jojic. Transformation-invariant clustering using the EM algorithm. *IEEE Trans. Pattern Analysis and Machine Intelligence*, 25(1):1–17, January 2003.
5. D. Keysers, J. Dahmen,H. Ney, B. Wein, and T. Lehmann. Statistical framework for model-based image retrieval in medical applications. In *Journal of Electronic Imaging*,12(1):59–69, January 2003
6. D. Keysers, M. Motter, T. Deselaers, and H. Ney. Training and recognition of complex scenes using a holistic statistical model. In *DAGM 2003, Pattern Recognition, 25th DAGM Symposium, Magdeburg, Germany*, September 2003. This volume.
7. D. Keysers, R. Paredes, H. Ney, and E. Vidal. Combination of tangent vectors and local representations for handwritten digit recognition. In *SPR 2002, Int. Workshop on Statistical Pattern Recognition, Lecture Notes in Computer Science*, Vol. 2396, pp. 538–547, Windsor, Ontario, Canada, August 2002.
8. S. Nene, S. Nayar, and H. Murase. Columbia object image library: COIL-100. Technical Report CUCS-006-96, Department of Computer Science, Columbia University, New York, February 1996.
9. R. Paredes, D.Keysers, T. Lehmann, B. Wein, H. Ney, and E. Vidal. Classification of medical images using local representations. In *Bildverarbeitung für die Medizin*, pp. 171–174, Leipzig, Germany, March 2002.
10. R. Paredes, J. Perez-Cortes, A. Juan, and E. Vidal. Local representations and a direct voting scheme for face recognition. In *Workshop on Pattern Recognition in Information Systems*, pp. 71–79, Setúbal, Portugal, July 2001.
11. C. Schmid and R. Mohr. Local grayvalue invariants for image retrieval. *IEEE Trans. Pattern Analysis and Machine Intelligence*, 19(5):530–535, May 1997.
12. C. Shyu, C.E. Brodley, A.C. Kak, A. Kosaka, A. Aisen, and L. Broderick. Local versus global features for content-based image retrieval. In *Proc. IEEE Workshop on Content-Based Access of Image and Video Libraries*, pp. 30–34, June 1998.
13. A.W.M. Smeulders, M. Worring, S. Santint, A. Gupta, and R. Jain. Content-based image retrieval at the end of the early years. *IEEE Trans. Pattern Analysis and Machine Intelligence*, 22(12):1349–1380, December 2000.

A Generative Model Based Approach to Motion Segmentation*

Daniel Cremers[1] and Alan Yuille[2]

[1] Department of Computer Science
University of California at Los Angeles

[2] Department of Statistics and Psychology
University of California at Los Angeles

Abstract. We address the question of how to choose between different likelihood functions for motion estimation. To this end, we formulate motion estimation as a problem of Bayesian inference and compare the likelihood functions generated by various models for image formation. In contrast to alternative approaches which focus on noise in the measurement process, we propose to introduce noise on the level of the velocity, thus allowing it to vary around a given model. We show that this approach generates additional normalizations not present in previous likelihood functions. We numerically evaluate the proposed likelihood in a variational framework for segmenting the image plane into domains of piecewise constant motion. The evolution of the motion discontinuity set is implemented using the level set framework.

1 Introduction

The problem of estimating motion from an image sequence has been addressed by minimizing appropriate cost functionals, which depend on the gray values of the image sequence and its spatial and temporal derivatives. Since the seminal work of Horn and Schunck [5], a wealth such variational methods have been proposed (cf. [9,14,7,15]). Commonly these functionals consist of a fidelity term which measures how well the local gray values are in accordance with a specific motion, and of a prior which enforces a certain regularity of the estimated motion field.

Yet, the question remains: Which cost functional is appropriate for the given task? As for the regularity term, it clearly depends on the prior knowledge about what kinds of motion fields can be expected. In particular, one can impose smoothness of the estimated motion fields [5], smoothness with discontinuities [12,15], parametric [1] and piecewise parametric motion models [2], or higher-level regularity constraints derived from fluid mechanics [6].

In this paper, we are concerned with the fidelity term. This likelihood can be derived from a generative model of image formation (cf. [16]). One makes certain assumptions about how the image sequence is generated – for example one may

---

*Supp: ONR N00014-02-1-0720, NSF SBR-9631682,0240148, NIH R01EY013875-01A1.

B. Michaelis and G. Krell (Eds.): DAGM 2003, LNCS 2781, pp. 313–320, 2003.

assume that a static scene is transformed according to a certain velocity. As we will see, it is of particular importance to address the question at which level noise is allowed to enter this image formation process: Different models of noise will induce different normalizations (i.e. scalings or weightings) of the data term in the resulting cost functional.

Commonly noise is introduced as additive Gaussian noise to the measurements [16,13,10]. In contrast, we argue that one should allow statistical variation of the quantity which is to be estimated and introduce noise directly on the velocity. As a consequence, we derive a novel fidelity term for motion estimation.

Based on this fidelity term, we propose a variational method which permits to segment the image plane into domains of piecewise constant motion. Segmentation and motion estimate are obtained by minimizing the proposed energy functional jointly with respect to the motion vectors for each region and with respect to the boundary separating these regions. We implement this motion boundary by the level set method [11], since this implicit representation facilitates topological changes of the evolving boundary such as splitting and merging. Energy minimization amounts to alternating the two fractional steps of solving an eigenvalue problem for the motion vectors in each region, and of evolving the level set function which encodes the motion boundaries.

Numerical results demonstrate that the proposed likelihood function induces accurate segmentations of the image plane based exclusively on the motion information extracted from two consecutive images of a sequence. Our approach is computationally efficient and tracking applications are conceivable.

2   Motion Estimation as Bayesian Inference

Let $\Omega \subset \mathbb{R}^2$ denote the image plane and let $I : \Omega \times \mathbb{R} \to \mathbb{R}$ be a gray value image sequence. In the following, we will assume that this image sequence represents an unknown scene function $s : \Omega \to \mathbb{R}$ which undergoes a motion $v : \Omega \to \mathbb{R}^2$ at each point $x \in \Omega$.[1] The motion field v can be estimated by maximizing the conditional probability

$$\mathcal{P}(v \mid I) = \frac{\mathcal{P}(I \mid v)\, \mathcal{P}(v)}{\mathcal{P}(I)}, \qquad (1)$$

with respect to v. Here $\mathcal{P}(v)$ represents the prior on the velocity field.

The focus of the present paper lies on modeling the conditional probability $\mathcal{P}(I \mid v)$ for an image sequence I given a velocity field v. To this end, we will revert to generative models of image formation.

3   Generative Models with Measurement Noise

Let us assume that the image sequence is obtained from a scene function $s : \Omega \to \mathbb{R}$ by applying a certain velocity field v:

$$I(x + vt, t) = s(x), \qquad (2)$$

---

[1] Since we are only concerned with the velocity at a fixed time instance, we will ignore the temporal variation of the velocity field.

where $s(x) = I(x, 0)$. Given a particular model of how noise enters this image formation process, one can derive the conditional distribution $\mathcal{P}(I \,|\, v, s)$ for the intensity function I given the velocity field v and the (unknown) scene function s. The desired likelihood $\mathcal{P}(I \,|\, v)$ can then be obtained by marginalization with respect to the scene function:

$$\mathcal{P}(I \,|\, v) = \int \mathcal{P}(I \,|\, v, s) \, \mathcal{P}(s) \, ds. \tag{3}$$

In the following, we will review three different approaches to introduce noise into the above image formation process. In all three cases, the noise enters on the level of the measurements. Each noise model entails a different likelihood function $\mathcal{P}(I \,|\, v)$.

3.1 Additive Gaussian Noise in the Measurement Equation

Weiss and Fleet [16] suggested to introduce additive Gaussian noise to the measurement equation: $I(x + vt, t) = s(x) + \sigma\eta$, where η represents zero mean Gaussian noise with variance 1. It follows that the conditional distribution is given by

$$\mathcal{P}(I \,|\, v, s) \propto \exp\left(-\frac{1}{2\sigma^2} \int (I(x + vt, t) - s(x))^2 \, dx \, dt\right). \tag{4}$$

Assuming a uniform prior over the scene functions s and given a fixed time interval for observation, the marginalization in (3) can be carried out analytically, one obtains [16]:

$$\mathcal{P}(I \,|\, v) \propto \exp\left(-\frac{1}{2\sigma^2} \int (I(x, t) - \hat{s}(x - vt))^2 \, dx \, dt\right), \tag{5}$$

where the function $\hat{s}(x)$ turns out to be the mean of $I(x + vt, t)$ over the time window of observation.

3.2 Additive Gaussian Noise on the Temporal Derivative

If the velocity in (2) is sufficiently small and the intensity function sufficiently smooth, then one can perform a first-order Taylor expansion which yields the well-known optic flow constraint equation:

$$v^T \nabla I + I_t = 0. \tag{6}$$

Due to this approximation, the resulting conditional density no longer depends on the unknown scene function such that the marginalization in (3) becomes trivial. Simoncelli [13] suggested to introduce additive Gaussian noise to the temporal derivative in (6). This yields the conditional probability

$$\mathcal{P}(I \,|\, v) \propto \exp\left(-\frac{1}{2\sigma^2} \int (v^T \nabla I + I_t)^2 \, dx \, dt\right), \tag{7}$$

which has become a popular likelihood function for motion estimation since the work of Horn and Schunck [5].

3.3   Additive Gaussian Noise on Spatial and Temporal Derivatives

Extending the above model, one can assume that both the spatial and the temporal derivative in (6) are corrupted by zero-mean additive Gaussian noise. As shown in [10], this assumption results in a conditional probability of the form

$$\mathcal{P}(I \,|\, v) \propto \exp\left(-\frac{1}{2\sigma^2} \int \frac{(v^T \nabla I + I_t)^2}{1 + |v|^2}\, dx\, dt\right). \tag{8}$$

Compared to the previous likelihood, this introduces an additional normalization with respect to the length of the homogeneous velocity vector. However, it was pointed out in [8] that the noise on the spatio-temporal derivatives may not be independent, since the latter are calculated from digitized images.

4   A Generative Model with Noise on the Velocity Field

The above generative models incorporate noise on different levels of the measurement process. In the following, we will argue that it may be favorable to consider noise models for the quantity which is to be estimated, namely the velocity field itself. Consider the general case of an image sequence in which different regions are moving according to different velocity models (for example parametric motion models). In order to partition the image plane into regions of homogeneous velocity, we need to be able to measure how well a certain velocity is in accordance with a given model.

   To this end, we assume that the true velocity $\hat{v}$ may deviate from the model velocity v according to a noise model of the form:

$$\hat{v} = v + g(v)\, \sigma\, \bar{\eta}, \tag{9}$$

where $\sigma\bar{\eta} \in \mathbb{R}^2$ is 2-d Gaussian noise of width σ, scaled by a factor $g(v) = \sqrt{1 + |v|^2/|v_o|^2}$, which implies that the noise increases with the magnitude of the velocity and is non-zero for zero velocity. For simplicity, we set the normalization constant to $v_0 = 1$. As in equation (2), we assume that the image sequence is generated from a static scene $s(x)$ deformed according to the velocity field $\hat{v}$. Assuming the noise to be sufficiently small and the intensity function to be sufficiently smooth, we can perform a Taylor expansion with respect to the noise:

$$s(x) = I(x + \hat{v}t, t) \approx I(x + vt, t) + t\, g(v)\, \sigma\, \bar{\eta}^T \nabla I. \tag{10}$$

Rearranging terms, we obtain:

$$\frac{I(x + vt, t) - s(x)}{t\, g(v)\, |\nabla I|} \approx \sigma\eta, \tag{11}$$

where η denotes 1-d Gaussian noise. This corresponds to a likelihood function of the form:

$$\mathcal{P}(I \,|\, s, v) \propto \exp\left(-\frac{1}{2\sigma^2} \int \frac{(I(x + vt, t) - s(x))^2}{t^2\, g^2(v)\, |\nabla I|^2}\, dx\, dt\right). \tag{12}$$

Compared to the likelihood (4) for additive noise in the measurement equation, this likelihood includes normalizations with respect to the spatial gradient, the magnitude of the homogeneous velocity and time.

For sufficiently small velocity v, we can expand the intensity function even further:

$$I(x + \hat{v}t, t) \approx I(x, 0) + t\, g(v)\, \sigma\, \bar{\eta}^T \nabla I + t\, v^T \nabla I + t\, I_t. \tag{13}$$

Making use of the fact that $s(x) = I(x, 0)$, we obtain a conditional probability which is independent of the underlying scene function s:

$$\mathcal{P}(I \,|\, v) \propto \exp\left(\frac{-1}{2\sigma^2} \int \frac{(v^T \nabla I + I_t)^2}{g^2(v)|\nabla I|^2} dx dt\right) = \exp\left(\frac{-1}{2\sigma^2} \int \frac{(\bar{v}^T \nabla_3 I)^2}{|\bar{v}|^2 |\nabla I|^2} dx dt\right). \tag{14}$$

Here $\nabla_3 I \in \mathbb{R}^3$ and $\bar{v} \in \mathbb{R}^3$ represent the spatio-temporal image gradient and the homogeneous velocity vector, respectively.

Note that, compared to the likelihood for noise on the spatial and temporal derivative in equation (8), this likelihood function includes an additional normalization with respect to the image gradient. A similar likelihood function (normalized with respect to the spatio-temporal gradient rather than the spatial one) was derived in [2] based on purely geometric considerations. Here the likelihood function with both normalizations is derived from a generative model with noise on the velocity field as introduced above.

In numerical evaluation, we found that these normalizations are important in the case of motion *segmentation* which differs from motion *estimation* in that one needs to associate each image location with one or the other motion hypothesis.

5   Variational Motion Segmentation

In the previous section, we derived the fidelity term (14) for motion estimation. In the present section, we will incorporate this fidelity term into a variational framework for motion segmentation. To this end, we revert to the Bayesian approach introduced in Section 2 and specify a prior $\mathcal{P}(v)$ on the velocity field which enforces the formation of piecewise constant velocity fields. Extensions to models of piecewise parametric motion are conceivable (cf. [3]), they are however beyond the scope of this paper.

We discretize the velocity field over a set of disjoint regions $R_i \subset \Omega$ with constant homogeneous velocity $\bar{v}_i \in \mathbb{R}^3$. We now assume the prior probability on the velocity field to only depend on the length of the boundary C separating these regions. Maximizing the conditional probability (1) is equivalent to minimizing its negative log likelihood. Up to a constant, the latter is given by the energy:

$$E(C, \{\bar{v}_i\}) = \sum_{i=1}^{n} \int_{R_i} \frac{(\bar{v}_i^T \nabla_3 I)^2}{|\bar{v}_i|^2 \, |\nabla I|^2} \, dx \; + \nu\,|C|. \tag{15}$$

Since we only consider the spatio-temporal image derivatives at a given time instance calculated from two consecutive frames of the sequence, the temporal integration in the likelihood (14) disappears. For an extension of a related approach to the problem of spatio-temporal motion segmentation we refer to [4].

6   Energy Minimization

In order to generate a segmentation of the image plane into areas of piecewise constant motion, we minimize energy (15) by alternating the two fractional steps of updating the motion vectors $\bar{v}_i$ and evolving the motion boundary.

For fixed boundary C, minimization with respect to $\bar{v}_i$ results in the eigenvalue problem:

$$\bar{v}_i = \arg\min_{\bar{v}} \frac{\bar{v}^T M_i \bar{v}}{\bar{v}^T \bar{v}}, \quad \text{with } M_i = \int_{R_i} \frac{\nabla_3 I^T \nabla_3 I}{|\nabla I|^2}\, dx \qquad (16)$$

The solution of (16) is given by the eigenvector corresponding to the smallest eigenvalues of M_i, normalized such that its third component is 1.

Conversely, for fixed motion vectors, the gradient descent equation on the boundary C is given by:

$$\frac{dC}{dt} = (e_j - e_k) \cdot n - \nu\kappa, \qquad (17)$$

where n denotes the normal vector on the boundary, κ denotes the curvature, the indices 'k' and 'j' refer to the regions adjoining the contour, and e_i is the energy density given by the integrand in the functional (15).

We implemented this evolution using the level set method [11], since it is independent of a particular parameterization and permits to elegantly model topological changes of the boundary such as splitting and merging. For details, we refer to [2].

7   Numerical Results

7.1   Simultaneous Segmentation and Motion Estimation

Figure 1 presents several steps during the energy minimization for two consecutive images from a sequence showing a rabbit which moves to the right. By minimizing a single cost functional both the boundaries and the estimated motion are progressively improved. The final segmentation gives both an accurate reconstruction of the objects location and an estimate of the motion of object and background.

7.2   Segmenting Multiple Motion

The cost functional (15) permits a segmentation into multiple differently moving regions. Figure 2 shows segmentation results obtained for an image sequence showing two cars moving to the top right, while the background is moving to the bottom left. The original sequence was recorded with a static camera by D. Koller and H.-H. Nagel.[2] To increase its complexity, we artificially translated the

---

[2] KOGS/IAKS, Univ. of Karlsruhe, `http://i21www.ira.uka.de/image_sequences/`

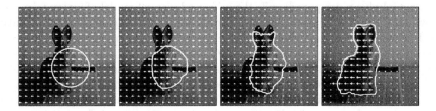

Fig. 1. Motion segmentation obtained by minimizing functional (15) simultaneously with respect to the motion models and the separating motion boundary. During minimization the boundary location and estimated motion are progressively improved. Thus the object's location and motion are simultaneously reconstructed. In contrast to the approach proposed in [3], the present formulation does not require a posterior normalization of the driving terms in the evolution equation.

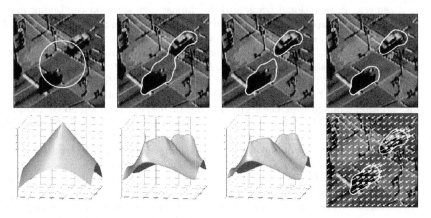

Fig. 2. Evolution of motion boundary (**top**) given by the zero crossing of the level set function (**bottom**) for moving cars on moving background. While the two cars cannot be segmented based on intensity criteria such as edges or gray value homogeneity, the motion segmentation gives an accurate reconstruction of the object location and its motion (**bottom right**).

second frame thereby simulating a moving camera. An accurate reconstruction of the object location and an estimate of the motion of objects and background (bottom right) is obtained by minimizing the proposed functional. Due to the representation of the boundary as the zero level set of the function shown in the bottom row, the boundary is free to undergo splitting and merging.

8   Conclusion

We addressed the question of choosing appropriate likelihood functions for variational motion segmentation. Motion segmentation differs from gray value segmentation in that the velocity field is not identical with the measured signal, but rather a derived quantity. For this reason, we argued that one needs to break with

the "signal plus noise paradigm". We proposed a novel model of image formation
in which the velocity is permitted to vary statistically. In contrast to alternative
models, we assume that the effect of noise in the measurements is dominated
by the effect caused by variations of the true velocity around a particular model
velocity. As a consequence, the resulting likelihood function contains additional
normalizations with respect to the velocity magnitude and the image gradient.
This novel likelihood function is shown to induce highly accurate segmentations
of the image plane, obtained purely on the basis of motion information.

References

1. M. J. Black and P. Anandan. The robust estimation of multiple motions: Parametric and piecewise–smooth flow fields. *Comp. Vis. Graph. Image Proc.: IU*,
63(1):75–104, 1996.
2. D. Cremers. A variational framework for image segmentation combining motion
estimation and shape regularization. In C. Dyer and P. Perona, editors, *IEEE Int.
Conf. on Comp. Vis. and Patt. Recog.*, Madison, Wisconsin, June 2003. To appear.
3. D. Cremers and C. Schnörr. Motion Competition: Variational integration of motion
segmentation and shape regularization. In L. van Gool, editor, *Pattern Recognition*,
volume 2449 of *LNCS*, pages 472–480, Zürich, Sept. 2002. Springer.
4. D. Cremers and S. Soatto. Combining motion estimation and surface regularization
for variational image sequence segmentation. In *ICCV*, Nice, Oct. 2003. To appear.
5. B.K.P. Horn and B.G. Schunck. Determining optical flow. *A.I.*, 17:185–203, 1981.
6. T. Kohlberger, E. Memin, and C. Schnörr. Variational dense motion estimation
using the Helmholtz decomposition. In L. Griffin, editor, *Int. Conf. on Scale Space
Theories in Comp. Vis.*, LNCS. Springer, 2003. To appear.
7. P. Kornprobst, R. Deriche, and G. Aubert. Image sequence analysis via partial
differential equations. *J. Math. Im. Vis.*, 11(1):5–26, 1999.
8. H.H. Nagel. Optical flow estimation and the interaction between measurement
errors at adjacent pixel positions. *Int. J. of Comp. Vis.*, 15(3):271–288, 1995.
9. H.H. Nagel and W. Enkelmann. An investigation of smoothness constraints for
the estimation of displacement vector fields from image sequences. *IEEE Trans.
on Patt. Anal. and Mach. Intell.*, 8(5):565–593, 1986.
10. O. Nestares, D.J. Fleet, and D.J. Heeger. Likelihood functions and confidence
bounds for total-least-squares problems. In *Proc. Conf. Computer Vis. and Pattern
Recog.*, volume 1, pages 760–767, Hilton Head Island, SC, June, 2000.
11. S. J. Osher and J. A. Sethian. Fronts propagation with curvature dependent speed:
Algorithms based on Hamilton–Jacobi formulations. *J. of Comp. Phys.*, 79:12–49,
1988.
12. C. Schnörr. Computation of discontinuous optical flow by domain decomposition
and shape optimization. *Int. J. of Comp. Vis.*, 8(2):153–165, 1992.
13. E.P. Simoncelli. *Distributed Representation and Analysis of Visual Motion.* PhD
thesis, Dept. of Elect. Eng. and Comp. Sci., MIT, Cambridge, 1993.
14. E.P. Simoncelli, E.H. Adelson, and D.J. Heeger. Probability distributions of optical
flow. In *Proc. Conf. Comp. Vis. Patt. Rec.*, pages 310–315, Hawaii, June 1991.
15. J. Weickert and C. Schnörr. A theoretical framework for convex regularizers in
PDE–based computation of image motion. *IJCV*, 45(3):245–264, 2001.
16. Y. Weiss and D.J. Fleet. Velocity likelihoods in biological and machine vision.
In M.S. Lewicki R.P.N. Rao, B.A. Olshausen, editor, *Probabilistic Models of the
Brain: Perception and Neural Function*, pages 81–100. MIT Press, 2001.

A New View at Differential and Tensor-Based Motion Estimation Schemes

Rudolf Mester

Institute for Applied Physics, University of Frankfurt, Robert-Mayer-Str. 2–4,
D-60054 Frankfurt, Germany
mester@iap.uni-frankfurt.de, www.uni-frankfurt.de/fb13/iap/cvg

Abstract. This paper contributes to the recent attempts to generalize classical differential and tensor-based motion estimation methods; it provides means for a better adaptation to the statistical structure of signal and noise. We show that conventional differential constraint equations often used for motion analysis capture the essence of translational motion only partially, and we propose more expressive formulations using higher order derivatives, finally leading to steerable nulling filters. Such filters consist of a 'static' prefilter and a steerable filter; we show how the prefilter can be optimized for given autocovariance structure of signal and noise, and how the steerable filter can be related to classical tensor-based approaches, leading to a constrained eigensystem problem.

1 Introduction

After an initial phase during which many different proposals for motion estimation have been made, a certain tendency to join different classes of motion algorithms in a common framework can be observed in the recent years. It is a sign of growing maturity of the field that modern approaches to motion analysis more and more deal with the theoretical background of the motion analysis task, and increasingly exploit the perfected methods of numerical analysis, signal theory and statistics, which are standard tools in modern signal processing.

This paper shall contribute to the theoretical foundations of motion analysis. We start in section 2 with a short review on the differential approach to motion analysis, which can be understood as a special case of tensor-based methods [1]. We model signal and noise probabilistically and formulate the motion estimation problem as a statistical estimation problem. If, furthermore, prior knowledge on the average distribution of the entity to be estimated (i.e. the motion vector) is available, our problem can be tackled using Bayesian theory. From a statistical point of view, there is no other way to use the information contained in the image data in a better way, but of course, there are quite many design parameters in the process that make it difficult to devise *the* optimum motion estimator. Therefore, this paper is more the exposition of a theoretical framework rather than the description of a specific algorithm.

B. Michaelis and G. Krell (Eds.): DAGM 2003, LNCS 2781, pp. 321–329, 2003.

2   Differential Approaches to Motion Analysis

The general principle behind all differential approaches to motion estimation is
that the conservation of some local image characteristic throughout its temporal
evolution is reflected in terms of differential-geometric descriptors. In its simplest form, the assumed conservation of brightness along the motion trajectory
through space–time leads to the well-known *brightness constancy constraint
equation* (BCCE), where $\mathbf{g}(\mathbf{x})$ is the gradient of the gray value signal $s(\mathbf{x})$:

$$\left(\frac{\partial s}{\partial x_1}, \frac{\partial s}{\partial x_2}, \frac{\partial s}{\partial x_3}\right) \cdot \mathbf{r} = 0 \quad \Leftrightarrow \quad \mathbf{g}^T(\mathbf{x}) \cdot \mathbf{r} = 0. \tag{1}$$

Since $\mathbf{g}^T(\mathbf{x}) \cdot \mathbf{r}$ is proportional to the directional derivative of s in direction $\mathbf{r}$,
the BCCE states that this derivative vanishes in the direction of motion.

In order to cope with the *aperture problem* , and in order to decrease the
variance of the motion vector estimate, usually some kind of weighted averaging
is performed in a neighborhood V, using a weight function $w(\mathbf{x})$.

$$\int_V w(\mathbf{x}) \cdot \left|\mathbf{g}^T(\mathbf{x}) \cdot \mathbf{r}\right|^2 d\mathbf{x} \longrightarrow \min$$

$$\Rightarrow \quad \mathbf{r}^T \cdot \mathbf{C}_g \cdot \mathbf{r} \longrightarrow \min \quad \text{with} \quad \mathbf{C}_g := \int_V \mathbf{g}(\mathbf{x}) \cdot w(\mathbf{x}) \cdot \mathbf{g}^T(\mathbf{x}) \, d\mathbf{x}$$

The solution vector $\hat{\mathbf{r}}$ is the eigenvector corresponding to the minimum eigenvalue of the *structure tensor* [1] $\mathbf{C}_g$ (cf. [4], [5], p.366; [6]). The minimization
criterion according to eq.2 can be replaced by modified criteria which yield exactly the same solution $\mathbf{r}$ in case of ideal rank-2 signals, but different solutions
for the realistic case of perturbations in matrix $\mathbf{C}_g$. One motivation for doing
so is for compensating the typically complicated error statistics in the vector
$\mathbf{g}$ which are due to anisotropic image statistics, colored noise, and overlapping
filter support. Furthermore, since the matrix $\mathbf{C}_g$ is built from outer products of
the vectors $\mathbf{g}$, the covariances between elements of $\mathbf{C}_g$ are hard to analyze [7].

In the classical theory, the (discrete!) implementation of the derivative operators itself is a formidable problem, even though some early authors apparently
overlooked the crucial importance of this point. Both [8,9,10] as well as [11] treat
this explicitly as an optimization problem; ELAD ET AL. [11] point out that the
closeness of the derivatives to the 'ideal' derivatives is not the correct goal, but
rather the quality of the direction estimate obtained by using them. Furthermore, they show that prior knowledge on the distribution of motion vectors
significantly changes the shape of the computed filter masks.

In the present contribution, the same problem is approached with a different
strategy: we stay with the conventional scheme of building the gradient operators
with a prefilter and a subsequent derivative operator, but we let the prefilter be
completely determined by the image statistics (see section 5).

---

[1] The tensor approach to motion analysis and representation has been extensively
investigated by Granlund, Knutsson, Bigün and many others at Linköping university,
Sweden. For two rather recent accounts on that subject, see [2] and [3].

2.1 How Conventional Differential Approaches Can Be Generalized

The differential formulation of brightness constancy along the motion trajectory is not the unique and presumably $\underline{\text{not}}$ the most expressive way of specifying a relation between the entity that is sought (the motion vector $\mathbf{r}$) and the data that can be observed.   What is definitely to be taken into account are   the *spectral characteristics of the image signal* and the *spectral characteristics of the noise.* Following the principles introduced into signal processing by Nobert Wiener already in the 1940ies, those spectral components where the signal-to-noise ratio is high should be paid more attention than those with a low S/N ratio. As this is shown in section 5, this can be understood also as consequently applying weighted-least-squares theory to the given estimation problem, using the autocovariance functions of signal and noise.

Quite obviously, since any   pure rank-2 signal s may be prefiltered by (almost) any filter with arbitrary transfer function $P(\mathbf{f})$ (except complete nullification of the signal) without changing the *direction* of the eigenvectors of $\mathbf{C_g}$, the interpretation of $\mathbf{g}$ as being the local gradient is much too narrow. There is also more to these prefilters than just a 'regularization' of gradient computation: they can (and should) be designed according to Wiener's criteria, i.e. minimizing the S/N ratio of the gradient estimates.

The same applies also to the classical (and mostly undisputed) usage of 1st order derivatives in optic flow algorithms: Assuming brightness constancy along the motion trajectory, all higher order directional derivatives vanish in the motion direction:

$$\frac{\partial s}{\partial \mathbf{r}} \overset{!}{=} 0 \;\bigcap\; \frac{\partial^2 s}{\partial \mathbf{r}^2} \overset{!}{=} 0 \;\bigcap\; \ldots \tag{2}$$

For an ideally oriented signal, anything that could be said is already expressed by the 1st order condition, but for real signals *none* of the requirements in eq. 2 is met. A condition which is less stringent than eq. 2, but nevertheless comprises as much as possible from these multitude of conditions in a single linear equation can be obtained by summing up the constraints:

$$\alpha_1 \frac{\partial s}{\partial \mathbf{r}} + \alpha_2 \frac{\partial^2 s}{\partial \mathbf{r}^2} + \alpha_3 \frac{\partial^3 s}{\partial \mathbf{r}^3} + \ldots \overset{!}{=} 0 \tag{3}$$

The left hand side of this equation is nothing else than a generator for a very rich class of filter operators, parameterized by direction vector $\mathbf{r}$:

$$h(\mathbf{x} \mid \mathbf{r}) * s(\mathbf{x}) \overset{!}{=} 0$$

This means that all linear operators that do not let an ideal oriented signal $s(\mathbf{x})$ pass have the structure of eq. 3. Since all oriented signals have power spectra that are concentrated on lines or planes in the Fourier domain [12], we can denote these filters as *oriented nulling filters*, and the Fourier transform of eq.3 describes the Taylor series expansion of the transfer function of such an oriented nulling filter.

If a signal $s(\mathbf{x})$ has a single dominant orientation (i.e. if it is a rank-2 signal), it may be prefiltered by any filter $p(\mathbf{x})$ with radially symmetric transfer function

$P(\mathbf{f})$ without changing the *direction* of the eigenvectors of $\mathbf{C}_g$ (the non-vanishing eigen*values* will in general change). Even the application of an (almost) arbitrary *anisotropic* linear filter $p(\mathbf{x})$ on $s(\mathbf{x})$ will not change the orientation (except that $p(\mathbf{x})$ nullifies $s(\mathbf{x})$ totally). This means that the interpretation of $\mathbf{g}$ in eq.2 as being the local gradient is much too narrow and we can use the pre-filter $p(\mathbf{x})$ for tuning the approach. Coming back to eq.3, we can replace $s(\mathbf{x})$ by $s(\mathbf{x}) * p(\mathbf{x})$, and the orientation remains invariant (for rank 2 signals!) Thus we may formulate a new type of constraint equation:

$$\left(\alpha_1 \frac{\partial}{\partial \mathbf{r}} + \alpha_2 \frac{\partial^2}{\partial \mathbf{r}^2} + \ldots \right) * (s(\mathbf{x}) * p(\mathbf{x})) \overset{!}{=} 0 \quad \Rightarrow \quad \tilde{h}(\mathbf{x} \mid \mathbf{r}) * (s(\mathbf{x}) * p(\mathbf{x})) \overset{!}{=} 0$$

Of course, the more degrees of freedom we obtain in formulating constraint equations from which (hopefully) the motion direction can be deduced, the more parameter values have to be selected. For real image data neither the traditional BCCE nor any generalization will hold; instead of insisting in the left hand side to *vanish*, the requirement is relaxed to *minimizing it on an average*. This is exactly the point where the precise design of the various imaginable constraint equations makes a difference: it implicitly defines a metric on the space of direction vectors $\mathbf{r}$. We obtain now: which, subsuming all the reasoning made before, can be generalized to

$$\int_{\mathbf{x}} w(\mathbf{x}) \cdot |h(\mathbf{x} \mid \mathbf{r}) * s(\mathbf{x})|^2 \, d\mathbf{x} \quad \longrightarrow \quad \min \tag{4}$$

where $h(\mathbf{x} \mid \mathbf{r})$ comprises the combination of directional derivatives of different order, and an optional *pre-filter* $p(\mathbf{x})$. This means: *The frequency-weighted directional variation of the signal is minimized in the direction of motion.* Since we are aiming at estimates for $\mathbf{r}$ which are optimum with respect to e.g. minimizing the variance of the residual error in the estimate $\hat{\mathbf{r}}$, the parameterized filter $h(\mathbf{x} \mid \mathbf{r})$ should be selected in a way that considers the known statistics of signal and noise. We have recently proposed [13] a motion analysis scheme that incorporates a steerable directional approximation of the given signal and can be extended in the spirit of Wiener filtering. The approach in the present paper is to split $h(\mathbf{x} \mid \mathbf{r})$ into a *pre-filter* which is optimally designed estimating the 'true' image signal by minimizing the mean squared error, and a *directional post-filter*. This leaves the possibility to design the (steerable) post-filter according to signal-independent optimality requirements discussed extensively elsewhere (e.g. in [10]).

3   Generalizing Structure Tensors Using Steerable Filters

We proceed by restating the relation between directional derivatives and steerable filters, which have been explored e.g. in [8,14,9]. The partial derivative in a direction specified by a unit vector $\mathbf{e}_r \in \mathbb{R}^3$ parameterized via spherical angles $\theta = (\theta_1, \theta_2)$ as $\mathbf{e}_r = (a_1(\theta), a_2(\theta), a_3(\theta))$ is given by $\frac{\partial}{\partial \mathbf{e}_r} s(\mathbf{x}) = \mathbf{e}_r^T \cdot \mathbf{g}(x) = \mathbf{e}_r^T \cdot \nabla s(\mathbf{x}) = \sum_{i=1}^{3} a_i(\theta) \cdot \frac{\partial s(\mathbf{x})}{\partial x_i}$

3.1   Generalized Directional Derivatives

Following the reasoning on pre-filters presented in section 2.1, we   may insert a prefilter $p(\mathbf{x})$ (see e.g. [8,10])

$$\frac{\partial}{\partial \mathbf{e}_r}(s(\mathbf{x}) * p(\mathbf{x})) = \left(\sum_{i=1}^{3} a_i(\theta_1, \theta_2) \cdot \left(\frac{\partial}{\partial x_i} p(\mathbf{x}) \right) \right) * s(\mathbf{x}) \qquad (5)$$

For $p(\mathbf{x})$ there are therefore many more functions under consideration than only a simple Gaussian kernel[2].   We can design $p(\mathbf{x})$ in a way that optimizes the signal/noise ratio at the output of the prefilter; this is the *Wiener-type prefilter approach* [15]. On the other hand, we may generalize the structure of the analysis scheme described by eq.5 and arrive at a generalized class of structure tensors, as will be shown in the following.

3.2   Steerable Oriented Signal Energy Determination

We abstract now from derivative filters and regard a family of steerable filter operators which can be written in the form [14] $h(\mathbf{x} \mid \theta) = \sum_{i=1}^{N} a_i(\theta) \cdot b_i(\mathbf{x})$ Since the original signal is *sheared* instead of being rotated by motion, it is appropriate to design $h(\mathbf{x} \mid \theta)$ accordingly; however, we will not deal here with details of such *shearable filters*. The symbol θ stands for a general parameter (or parameter vector) that controls the direction in which the filter operator is being steered. The $b_i(\mathbf{x})$ are basis functions; $a_i(\theta)$ and $b_i(\mathbf{x})$ are subject to certain conditions discussed in [14]. This operator will now be applied to a signal $s(\mathbf{x})$:

$$h(\mathbf{x} \mid \theta) * s(\mathbf{x}) = \sum_{i=1}^{N} a_i(\theta) \cdot (b_i(\mathbf{x}) * s(\mathbf{x}))$$

As before, the local energy of the resulting signal will be computed. The localization of the computation is again ensured by the weight function $w(\mathbf{x})$:

$$Q(\theta) = \int_{\mathbf{x}} w(\mathbf{x}) \cdot (h(\mathbf{x} \mid \theta) * s(\mathbf{x}))^2 \, d\mathbf{x}$$

A closer look reveals (using $g_i(\mathbf{x}) \equiv s(\mathbf{x}) * b_i(\mathbf{x})$):

$$(h(\mathbf{x} \mid \theta) * s(\mathbf{x}))^2 = \left(\sum_{i=1}^{N} a_i(\theta) \cdot (b_i(\mathbf{x}) * s(\mathbf{x})) \right)^2$$

$$= \left(\sum_{i=1}^{N} a_i(\theta) \cdot g_i(\mathbf{x}) \right)^2 = \sum_{i=1}^{N} \sum_{k=1}^{N} a_i(\theta) \cdot a_k(\theta) \cdot g_i(\mathbf{x}) \cdot g_k(\mathbf{x})$$

---

[2] In general, a binomial filter does much better than a sampled (and truncated) Gaussian.

If now a local integration is performed across this squared signal we obtain the quadratic form:

$$Q(\theta) = \sum_{i=1}^{N} \sum_{k=1}^{N} a_i(\theta) \cdot a_k(\theta) \int_{\mathbf{x}} w(\mathbf{x}) \cdot g_i(\mathbf{x}) \cdot g_k(\mathbf{x}) \, d\mathbf{x} \quad = \quad \mathbf{a}^T(\theta) \cdot \mathbf{J} \cdot \mathbf{a}(\theta) \quad (6)$$

In the standard structure tensor approach, $N = 3$, and $h(\mathbf{x} \mid \theta)$ is the first order directional derivative which can be represented by a steerable set of $N = 3$ filters (each of them representing the directional derivative in one of the principal directions of space-time). It is not very surprising that in this case $\mathbf{a}(\theta)$ is a unit vector in $\mathbb{R}^3$, and the determination of $Q(\theta) \longrightarrow$ min boils down into a simple eigensystem problem, as given already in eq.2. For synthesizing and steering a more general filter operator $h(\mathbf{x} \mid \theta)$, we know that the basis functions $b_i(\mathbf{x})$ should be polar-separable harmonic functions. The coefficient functions $a_i(\theta)$ will then be trigonometric functions of different (harmonic) frequencies [16], and the optimization problem eq.(3.2) will not be so simple to solve, though well-behaved. The design of the localization function $w(\mathbf{x})$ and the generalization of the directional derivative can be adapted to the signal and noise power spectra, respectively. Within this framework, a wide class of orientation selective steerable filters can be used to find principal orientations; if necessary they can equipped with a much more pronounced selectivity, offering the potential for higher accuracy.

4   Covariance Structure of Video Signals

Since the autocovariance structure of the image and the noise are needed for designing the Wiener prefilter, we have to obtain that information for the class of image sequences under consideration. In order to obtain the required model for the (auto)covariance function *(acf)* of video signals, it turns out to be useful to analyze the video acquisition process in the continuous domain.

Let us assume that the image signals we are dealing with are generated by shifting a given twodimensional image with constant speed (v_x, v_y) in an certain direction. We assume that the twodimensional image can be characterized by a *twodimensional* autocovariance function $\tilde{\varphi}_{ss}(x, y)$. Obviously, the resulting three-dimensional autocovariance function $\varphi_{ss}(x, y, t)$ is then

$$\varphi_{ss}(x, y, t) = \tilde{\varphi}_{ss}(x - v_x t, \ y - v_y t)$$

If the motion vector (v_x, v_y) itself is a generated by a random process (as it is reasonable to assume for real video signals), there is a distribution for the new position $(x(t), y(t))$ at time instant t of the point which was located at $x = 0, y = 0$ at time instant 0. This distribution $\zeta(x, y, t)$ depends on t, and under normal circumstances its variance in x, y-direction will increase with increasing time t. The overall 3D autocovariance results from a convolution of the *purely spatial* autocovariance function $\tilde{\varphi}_{ss}(x, y)$ with the *position distribution function* $\zeta(x, y, t)$.

5 The Prefilter as a Least Squares (Wiener) Restoration Operator for Image Blocks

Our model states that the observed image signal z in a spatio-temporal block of dimension $N \times N \times N$ is given by

$$z(i, j, k) = s(i, j, k) + v(i, j, k) .$$

Here, $v(i, j, k)$ denotes the observation (measurement) noise and we assume that this is discrete white noise, also denoted as *independent identically distributed (i.i.d.)* noise. For the subsequent steps, it is convenient to arrange the elements of the blocks s, v, and z in vectors $\mathbf{s}, \mathbf{v}$, and $\mathbf{z}$.

5.1 The Canonical Basis

The canonical basis is the coordinate frame of vectors $\mathbf{y}$ which are obtained from vectors $\mathbf{s}$ by a rotation $\mathbf{A}$ according to

$$\mathbf{y} = \mathbf{A} \cdot \mathbf{s}, \quad |\mathbf{y}| = |\mathbf{s}|$$

such that the covariance matrix $\mathbf{C}_y \equiv \mathsf{Cov}\,[\mathbf{y}]$ is diagonal. It is well known that this rotation is performed by the *principal component analysis (PCA)* or *Karhunen-Loève transform (KLT)*. In this new coordinate frame, we have

$$\mathbf{C}_y \stackrel{def}{=} \mathsf{Cov}\,[\mathbf{y}] = \mathsf{diag}\,\{\sigma_{yi}^2\} \tag{7}$$

The row vectors of the orthonormal (i.e. rotation) matrix $\mathbf{A}$ are given by the unit norm eigenvectors of the covariance matrix $\mathbf{C}_s \equiv \mathsf{Cov}\,[\mathbf{s}]$, i.e. $\mathbf{A}$ is the solution to the eigensystem problem

$$\mathbf{A} \cdot \mathsf{Cov}\,[\mathbf{s}] \cdot \mathbf{A}^T = \mathsf{diag}\,\{\lambda_i\} \quad | \quad \mathbf{A} \cdot \mathbf{A}^T = \mathbf{I}$$

In the new coordinate frame, we have

$$\text{signal vector (unobservable):} \quad \mathbf{y} = \mathbf{As} \tag{8}$$
$$\text{noise vector (unobservable):} \quad \mathbf{u} = \mathbf{Av} \tag{9}$$
$$\text{observed vector:} \quad \mathbf{w} = \mathbf{y} + \mathbf{u} = \mathbf{Az} \tag{10}$$

Since the original noise covariance matrix was a scaled unit matrix, and since $\mathbf{A}$ is a rotation, the covariance matrix of the noise vector $\mathbf{u}$ contained in $\mathbf{w}$ remains simple:

$$\mathbf{C}_u \stackrel{def}{=} \mathsf{Cov}\,[\mathbf{u}] = \sigma_v^2 \cdot \mathbf{I} \tag{11}$$

Estimating the value of $\mathbf{y}$ means now to minimize the loss function

$$J(\hat{\mathbf{y}}) = (\hat{\mathbf{y}} - \mathsf{E}\,[\mathbf{y}])^T \mathbf{C}_w^{-1} (\hat{\mathbf{y}} - \mathsf{E}\,[\mathbf{y}]) + (\hat{\mathbf{y}} - \mathbf{w})^T \cdot \mathbf{C}_v^{-1} \cdot (\hat{\mathbf{y}} - \mathbf{w})$$

The *minimum mean squared error (MMSE)* estimate of $\mathbf{y}$ is then given by

$$\hat{\mathbf{y}} = \left(\mathbf{C}_y^{-1} + \mathbf{C}_u^{-1}\right)^{-1} \cdot \left(\mathbf{C}_y^{-1} \cdot \mathsf{E}\left[\mathbf{y}\right] + \mathbf{C}_u^{-1} \cdot \mathbf{w}\right) \tag{12}$$

It is relatively simple to compute (and to interpret!) this estimate in the canonical coordinate frame. For the white noise case, the covariance matrix of the noise term remains proportional to a unity matrix under any arbitrary rotation of the coordinate frame. With the specific covariance matrices which we have here (see eq.(7) and eq.(11)), we obtain:

$$\hat{\mathbf{y}} = \left(\text{diag}\left\{\frac{1}{\sigma_{yi}^2}\right\} + \frac{1}{\sigma_v^2} \cdot \mathbf{I}\right)^{-1} \cdot \left(\mathbf{C}_y^{-1} \cdot \mathsf{E}\left[\mathbf{y}\right] + \mathbf{C}_u^{-1} \cdot \mathbf{w}\right) \tag{13}$$

Assuming $\mathsf{E}\left[\mathbf{y}\right] = \mathbf{0}$, this leads to

$$\hat{\mathbf{y}} = \left(\text{diag}\left\{\frac{1}{\sigma_{yi}^2} + \frac{1}{\sigma_v^2}\right\}\right)^{-1} \cdot \frac{1}{\sigma_v^2}\mathbf{w} \quad \Rightarrow \quad \hat{\mathbf{y}} = \text{diag}\left\{\frac{\sigma_{yi}^2}{\sigma_v^2 + \sigma_{yi}^2}\right\} \cdot \mathbf{w} \tag{14}$$

Since σ_{yi}^2 is the power of the signal and σ_v^2 the power of the noise in the regarded 'spectral component', this result is also according to our intuitive expectation. Using eq.(10) we obtain:

$$\hat{\mathbf{s}} = \mathbf{A}^{-1}\hat{\mathbf{y}} = \mathbf{A}^{-1}\text{diag}\left\{\frac{\sigma_{yi}^2}{\sigma_v^2 + \sigma_{yi}^2}\right\} \cdot \mathbf{w} = \mathbf{A}^T\text{diag}\left\{\frac{\sigma_{yi}^2}{\sigma_v^2 + \sigma_{yi}^2}\right\} \cdot \mathbf{A} \cdot \mathbf{z} \tag{15}$$

This means that for obtaining a MMSE estimate of the signal, the observed signal vector $\mathbf{z}$ has to be transformed (rotated) into the canonical coordinate frame, the canonical coordinates have to be attenuated according to the fraction $\sigma_{yi}^2/(\sigma_v^2 + \sigma_{yi}^2)$ and finally rotated back into the original coordinate frame.

6   Conclusions

I have presented two main contributions to motion analysis in this paper. The first one is the generalization of the differential constraint equation, the exposition of its relation to directional variation measures, and its usage in terms of generalized tensor-based methods.

The second contribution is the prefilter design approach based on classical Wiener theory. It provides the possibility to adapt differential or tensor-based motion estimation schemes to the specific statistics of the given signal and the noise contained in it. This explicitly includes the design of different filters for the case of prior knowledge on the typical range of motion vectors; the spatio-temporal distribution of the displacement is directly reflected in the autocovariance function, and thus also considered in the optimum pre-filter derived from the autocovariance function.

References

1. Johansson, B., Farnebäck, G.: A theoretical comparison of different orientation tensors. In: Proceedings SSAB02 Symposium on Image Analysis, Lund (2002) 69–73
2. Knutsson, H.: What is so special about quadrature filters? In: International Conference on Image Processing, ICIP, Barcelona, IEEE Computer Society Press (2003)
3. Nordberg, K., Farnebäck, G.: An overview of methods for estimation and representation of local orientation. In: International Conference on Image Processing, ICIP, Barcelona, IEEE Computer Society Press (2003)
4. Bigün, J., Granlund, G.H.: Optimal orientation detection of linear symmetry. In: First International Conference on Computer Vision, ICCV, Washington, DC., IEEE Computer Society Press (1987) 433–438
5. Haussecker, H., Spies, H.: Motion. In: Handbook of Computer Vision and Applications, Academic Press (1999)
6. Jähne, B.: Digital Image Processing. 4th edn. Springer Verlag (1998)
7. Mühlich, M., Mester, R.: Subspace methods and equilibration in computer vision. In: Proc. Scandinavian Conference on Image Analysis. (2001)
8. Simoncelli, E.P.: Design of multi-dimensional derivatives filters. In: Intern. Conf. on Image Proc., Austin TX (1994)
9. Farid, H., Simoncelli, E.P.: Optimally rotation-equivariant directional derivative kernels. In: 7th Intern. Conf. on Computer Analysis of Images and Patterns, Kiel, Germany (1997)
10. Scharr, H.: Optimal Operators in Digital Image Processing. PhD thesis, Interdisciplinary Center for Scientific Computing, Univ. of Heidelberg (2000)
11. Elad, M., Teo, P., Hel-Or, Y.: Optimal filters for gradient-based motion estimation. In: Proc. Intern. Conf. on Computer Vision (ICCV'99). (1999)
12. Granlund, G.H., Knutsson, H.: Signal processing for computer vision. Kluwer (1995)
13. Mester, R.: A system-theoretic view on local motion estimation. In: Proc. IEEE SouthWest Symposium on Image Analysis and Interpretation, Santa Fé (NM), IEEE Computer Society (2002)
14. Freeman, W.T., Adelson, E.H.: The design and use of steerable filters. IEEE Transactions on Pattern Analysis and Machine Intelligence **13** (1991)
15. Mester, R.: A generalization of differential optical flow estimation using 3D covariance functions of signal and noise. In: Submitted in Nov. 2002 to IEEE Conf. on Computer Vision and Pattern Recognition. (2003)
16. Yu, W., Daniilidis, K., Sommer, G.: A new 3D orientation steerable filter. In: DAGM 2000, Springer (2000)
17. Dong, D.D., Atick, J.J.: Statistics of natural time-varying images. Computation in Neural Systems **6(3)** (1995) 345–358
18. Therrien, C.W.: Discrete random signals and statistical signal processing. Prentice Hall (1992)

Real-Time Texture-Based 3-D Tracking

Wolfgang Sepp and Gerd Hirzinger

Institute of Robotics and Mechatronics,
German Aerospace Center (DLR),
82234 Wessling, Germany
wolfgang.sepp@dlr.de

Abstract. We present a tracking approach for textured surfaces which recovers the object motion in 6 degrees of freedom. We assume an arbitrary but known surface shape, and an image of the object at a known reference pose. We extend the 2-D tracking framework of Hager et al. [1] to tracking in 3-D and under full perspective projection. The algorithm is evaluated to ground-truth motion and shows high accuracy. Thanks to problem-specific optimizations we achive tracking at video-rate.

1 Introduction

Three-dimensional pose estimation of objects is a recurrent problem in robotics, computer graphics, and computer vision. Especially applications for visual servoing, augmented reality, and human-machine interfaces benefit from real-time tracking methods for arbitrary objects in 6 degrees of freedom (DoF). While the task seems to be solved for 2-D motion [1], research is still ongoing in the field of 3-D tracking in video images.

Existing solutions are mainly based on the localization of a-priori known artificial or natural landmarks. Many approaches rely on the correspondence between edges on the object and edges in the perceived intensity image [2], which are generally absent for free form surfaces. Other approaches employ range images computed by stereo algorithms [3] with all uncertainties and problems associated with surface reconstruction methods. Also optical flow coupled to 3-D surface models is used for pose tracking [4].

Some approaches exist which apply a distortion model to a reference image to recover the rigid object movement. Diehl et al. [5] developed a fast method for tracking of 4 DoF motion of planar objects. Cernuschi-Frias et al. presented in [6] a model for estimating the parameters of simple parameterized surface models. The approach is based on an orthographic imaging model and the method has been evaluated only for up to 4 DoF geometric surfaces.

The approach of Sepp et al. [7] is capable of tracking arbitrary shaped surface patches in 6 DoF in stereo images without any prior knowledge of surface texture and under varying illumination conditions. This universality proves to be computational much more expensive than approaches that assume a reference image of the object. For instance, La Cascia et al. [8] have developed an algorithm which determines a head's pose by minimizing the residual error of the surface

B. Michaelis and G. Krell (Eds.): DAGM 2003, LNCS 2781, pp. 330–337, 2003.

texture seen from a single camera to a reference image. Their approach differs from [1] in the numerical approximation of the Jacobian matrix of the surface texture. Also Jurie et al. [9] approximate the Jacobian matrix by using simulations of the surface texture under small pose variations. The tracking approach of Belhumeur et al. [10] requires several images of the object taken at different poses to establish the basis vectors for an optical-flow subspace. The coefficients to these vectors are mapped onto a 6-DoF object motion under the orthographic projection model. Lately, Buenaposada et al. [11] presented a tracking method for planar objects under full perspective projection in real-time.

We extend the affine tracking model of Hager et al. [1] to arbitrary shaped objects under full perspective projection. The increased computational requirements are tamed by applying problem-specific optimizations. Therefore, tracking in real-time is achieved not only for planar objects but also for general 3-D shapes.

2   Tracking Framework

Our approach is based on the framework for efficient tracking developed by Hager et al. [1] for 2-D motion. Accordingly, tracking is formulated as a minimization problem for a least-squares objective function.

2.1   2-D Tracking Model

Let $I(\mathbf{u}, t)$ be a brightness value at image position $\mathbf{u} \in \mathbb{R}^2$ and time t. The region to be tracked is defined by the set of two-dimensional coordinates $X = \{\mathbf{x}_0, \mathbf{x}_1, .., \mathbf{x}_N\}$. For a vector $\mu \in \mathcal{M}$ of motion parameters, an image region is warped to a template

$$I(\mathbf{x}, \mu, t) = I(f(\mathbf{x}, \mu), t) \quad \forall \mathbf{x} \in X \ , \tag{1}$$

where the motion model is expressed by the parametric function $f : \mathbb{R}^2 \times \mathcal{M} \to \mathbb{R}^2$. In the following, the warped image is denoted by the column vector

$$\mathrm{I}(\mu, t) = \left(I(\mathbf{x}_0, \mu, t), \ I(\mathbf{x}_1, \mu, t), \ \ldots, \ I(\mathbf{x}_N, \mu, t) \right)^{\mathrm{T}} \ . \tag{2}$$

The goal of the tracking process is to find a pose vector μ wich minimizes the dissimilarity between the warped image and the reference image, which is

$$O(\mu) = \left\| \mathrm{I}(\mu, t) - \mathrm{I}(\mu^0, t^0) \right\|^2 \quad t > t^0 \ . \tag{3}$$

A linearization of I around μ, t simplifies this nonconvex objective function (3) and leads to the set of linear equations

$$\mathrm{I}_\mu(\mu, t)^{\mathrm{T}} \mathrm{I}_\mu(\mu, t) \ \delta\mu = \mathrm{I}_\mu(\mu, t)^{\mathrm{T}} \left(\mathrm{I}(\mu^0, t^0) - \mathrm{I}(\mu, t + \tau) \right) \ , \tag{4}$$

which has to be solved at every tracking iteration for the pose increment $\delta\mu$ to the previous pose estimation μ. Here, $\mathrm{I}_\mu(\mu, t)$ denotes the jacobian of I and $\mathrm{I}(\mu, t + \tau)$ is the current image warped under the previous pose estimation μ.

The efficiency for solving this system of equations is closely related to the efficiency for computing the jacobian $I_\mu(\mu, t)$. Hager et. al rewrite the jacobian under the image-constancy assumption $I(\mathbf{x}, \mu, t) = I(\mathbf{x}, \mu^0, t^0)$ and obtain

$$I_\mu(\mathbf{x}, \mu, t) = I_\mathbf{x}(\mathbf{x}, \mu^0, t^0) \, f_\mathbf{x}^{-1}(\mathbf{x}, \mu) \, f_\mu(\mathbf{x}, \mu) \ , \tag{5}$$

which is a term independet of the current image. Further simplifications apply, if a factorization

$$f_\mathbf{x}^{-1}(\mathbf{x}, \mu) \, f_\mu(\mathbf{x}, \mu) = \Gamma(\mathbf{x}) \cdot \Sigma(\mu) \tag{6}$$

can be found, where Γ depends only on the surface points and Σ depends only on the current pose estimate. The set of linear equations (4) then reads

$$\Sigma(\mu)^\mathrm{T} \left(\mathrm{M}_0^\mathrm{T} \mathrm{M}_0 \right) \Sigma(\mu) \, \delta\mu = \Sigma(\mu)^\mathrm{T} \mathrm{M}_0^\mathrm{T} \left(\mathrm{I}(\mu^0, t^0) - \mathrm{I}(\mu, t+\tau) \right) \ , \tag{7}$$

where M_0 can be computed at startup based on the reference template, that is

$$\mathrm{M}_0 = \left(I_\mathbf{x}(\mathbf{x}_0, \mu^0, t^0) \, \Gamma(\mathbf{x}_0), \ I_\mathbf{x}(\mathbf{x}_1, \mu^0, t^0) \, \Gamma(\mathbf{x}_1), \ \cdots, \ I_\mathbf{x}(\mathbf{x}_N, \mu^0, t^0) \, \Gamma(\mathbf{x}_N) \right)^\mathrm{T} . \tag{8}$$

2.2   3-D Tracking Extension

In our model, the three-dimensional surface patch to be tracked is modeled as an arbitrary set of three-dimensional points $X = \{\mathbf{x}_0, \mathbf{x}_1, .., \mathbf{x}_N\}$. The rigid body transformation for a point $\mathbf{x} \in \mathrm{IR}^3$ is described by

$$g(\mathbf{x}, \mu) = R(\mu_0, \mu_1, \mu_2) \, \mathbf{x} + t(\mu_3, \mu_4, \mu_5) \tag{9}$$

where $R(\mu_0, \mu_1, \mu_2)$ is a rotation matrix and $t(\mu_3, \mu_4, \mu_5)$ the translation for the pose vector $\mu = \{\mu_0, \mu_1, \mu_2, \mu_3, \mu_4, \mu_5\}$. A point in space is mapped to the image under the full perspective projection

$$h(\mathbf{x}) = \left(\frac{\mathbf{k}_1^\mathrm{T} \cdot \mathbf{x}}{\mathbf{k}_3^\mathrm{T} \cdot \mathbf{x}}, \frac{\mathbf{k}_1^\mathrm{T} \cdot \mathbf{x}}{\mathbf{k}_3^\mathrm{T} \cdot \mathbf{x}} \right)^\mathrm{T} \ , \quad K = \begin{pmatrix} \mathbf{k}_1^\mathrm{T} \\ \mathbf{k}_2^\mathrm{T} \\ \mathbf{k}_3^\mathrm{T} \end{pmatrix} \tag{10}$$

for the matrix $K \in \mathrm{IR}^{3 \times 3}$ of intrinsic camera parameters. The model f for motion of the 3-D surface points in the 2-D image plane is defined by

$$f(\mathbf{x}, \mu) = h(g(\mathbf{x}, \mu)) \ . \tag{11}$$

Note that function f is not invertible and therefore, the 2-D tracking model does not apply any longer. We examine the derivatives of the surface-texture images

$$I_\mathbf{x}(\mathbf{x}, \mu, t) = I_1(h(g(\mathbf{x}, \mu)), t) \cdot h_1(g(\mathbf{x}, \mu)) \cdot g_1(\mathbf{x}, \mu) \tag{12}$$

$$I_\mu(\mathbf{x}, \mu, t) = I_1(h(g(\mathbf{x}, \mu)), t) \cdot h_1(g(\mathbf{x}, \mu)) \cdot g_2(\mathbf{x}, \mu) \ . \tag{13}$$

where I_1, h_1, and g_1 denote the derivative of the corresponding function with respect to the first argument. Therefore, the counterpart to (5) reads

$$I_\mu(\mathbf{x}, \mu, t) = I_\mathbf{x}(\mathbf{x}, \mu^0, t^0) \, g_1^{-1}(\mathbf{x}, \mu) \, g_2(\mathbf{x}, \mu) \ , \tag{14}$$

where $I_\mathbf{x}$ is now a three-dimensional derivative of the surface texture. In our tracking-model approach, the derivatives for g are

$$g_\mathbf{x}(\mathbf{x}, \mu) = R(\mu_0, \mu_1, \mu_2) \ , \tag{15}$$

$$g_\mu(\mathbf{x}, \mu) = \left(R_{\mu_0}\mathbf{x} | R_{\mu_1}\mathbf{x} | R_{\mu_2}\mathbf{x} | I_{3\times3} \right) \ , \tag{16}$$

where subscript arguments denote the associated partial derivative. Analogous to (6) a factorization of $g_\mathbf{x}^{-1}(\mathbf{x}, \mu)\, g_\mu(\mathbf{x}, \mu)$ can be found, where

$$\Gamma(\mathbf{x}) = \begin{pmatrix} \mathbf{x}^\mathrm{T} & \mathbf{0} & \mathbf{0} & \mathbf{x}^\mathrm{T} & \mathbf{0} & \mathbf{0} & \mathbf{x}^\mathrm{T} & \mathbf{0} & \mathbf{0} & 1\,0\,0 \\ \mathbf{0} & \mathbf{x}^\mathrm{T} & \mathbf{0} & \mathbf{0} & \mathbf{x}^\mathrm{T} & \mathbf{0} & \mathbf{0} & \mathbf{x}^\mathrm{T} & \mathbf{0} & 0\,1\,0 \\ \mathbf{0} & \mathbf{0} & \mathbf{x}^\mathrm{T} & \mathbf{0} & \mathbf{0} & \mathbf{x}^\mathrm{T} & \mathbf{0} & \mathbf{0} & \mathbf{x}^\mathrm{T} & 0\,0\,1 \end{pmatrix}, \ \Sigma(\mu) = \begin{pmatrix} s_0 & \mathbf{0} & \mathbf{0} & \mathbf{0} \\ \mathbf{0} & s_1 & \mathbf{0} & \mathbf{0} \\ \mathbf{0} & \mathbf{0} & s_2 & \mathbf{0} \\ \mathbf{0} & \mathbf{0} & \mathbf{0} & R^{-1} \end{pmatrix}.$$
$$\tag{17}$$

Here and in the following, $\mathbf{0}$ denotes a zero submatrix of appropriate size and

$$s_i = \mathrm{vec}\big(R^{-1}(\mu_0, \mu_1, \mu_2)\, R_{\mu_i}(\mu_0, \mu_1, \mu_2)\big) \tag{18}$$

with vec(.) being the operator which concatenates all rows of the matrix argument to a column vector.

2.3   3-D Tracking Optimizations

The matrix M_0 in (7) is of size $N \times 30$ and $\Sigma(\mu)$ is of size 30×6, where usually $N \gg 30$. Therefore, the right-hand side of (7) requires the major computation effort. The analysis of the structure of the matrices $\Gamma(\mathbf{x})$ and $\Sigma(\mu)$, however, leads to the following optimizations.

First, thanks to the repetitive structure of $\Gamma(\mathbf{x})$ the matrix M_0 can be written as

$$M_0 = \left(\check{L}_0 \mid \check{L}_0 \mid \check{L}_0 \mid L_0 \right) \tag{19}$$

where the $N \times 9$ matrix $\check{L}_0$ and the $N \times 3$ matrix L_0 correspond to

$$\check{L}_0 = \begin{pmatrix} I_\mathbf{x}\big(\mathbf{x}_0, \mu^0, t^0\big)\, \mathrm{F}(\mathbf{x}_0) \\ I_\mathbf{x}\big(\mathbf{x}_2, \mu^0, t^0\big)\, \mathrm{F}(\mathbf{x}_1) \\ \cdots \\ I_\mathbf{x}\big(\mathbf{x}_N, \mu^0, t^0\big)\, \mathrm{F}(\mathbf{x}_N) \end{pmatrix}, \ L_0 = \begin{pmatrix} I_\mathbf{x}\big(\mathbf{x}_0, \mu^0, t^0\big) \\ I_\mathbf{x}\big(\mathbf{x}_2, \mu^0, t^0\big) \\ \cdots \\ I_\mathbf{x}\big(\mathbf{x}_N, \mu^0, t^0\big) \end{pmatrix}, \ \mathrm{F}(\mathbf{x}) = \begin{pmatrix} \mathbf{x}^\mathrm{T} & \mathbf{0} & \mathbf{0} \\ \mathbf{0} & \mathbf{x}^\mathrm{T} & \mathbf{0} \\ \mathbf{0} & \mathbf{0} & \mathbf{x}^\mathrm{T} \end{pmatrix}.$$
$$\tag{20}$$

Then, considering the sparsity of $\Sigma(\mu)$, we can substitute on the left-hand side of (7)

$$\Sigma(\mu)^\mathrm{T}\left(M_0^\mathrm{T}M_0\right)\Sigma(\mu) = \begin{pmatrix} s_0^\mathrm{T}\big(\check{L}_0^\mathrm{T}\check{L}_0\big)\, s_0 & s_0^\mathrm{T}\big(\check{L}_0^\mathrm{T}\check{L}_0\big)\, s_1 & s_0^\mathrm{T}\big(\check{L}_0^\mathrm{T}\check{L}_0\big)\, s_2 & s_0^\mathrm{T}\big(\check{L}_0^\mathrm{T}L_0\big)\, R^\mathrm{T} \\ \cdot & s_1^\mathrm{T}\big(\check{L}_0^\mathrm{T}\check{L}_0\big)\, s_1 & s_1^\mathrm{T}\big(\check{L}_0^\mathrm{T}\check{L}_0\big)\, s_2 & s_1^\mathrm{T}\big(\check{L}_0^\mathrm{T}L_0\big)\, R^\mathrm{T} \\ \cdot & \cdot & s_2^\mathrm{T}\big(\check{L}_0^\mathrm{T}\check{L}_0\big)\, s_2 & s_2^\mathrm{T}\big(\check{L}_0^\mathrm{T}L_0\big)\, R^\mathrm{T} \\ \cdot & \cdot & \cdot & R\big(L_0^\mathrm{T}L_0\big)\, R^\mathrm{T} \end{pmatrix}, \tag{21}$$

where the redundant entries of the symmetric matrix are omitted. Furthermore, on the right-hand side of (7) we can simplify

$$M_0\,\Sigma(\mu) = \left(\check{L}_0\, s_0 \mid \check{L}_0\, s_1 \mid \check{L}_0\, s_2 \mid L_0\, R^{-1} \right) \ . \tag{22}$$

Since the matrices $\check{L}_0$ and L_0 are computed only once for the reference image, the above problem-specific optimizations reduce the number of operations involved in the computation of the linear equation system (7) substantially (see Table 1).

Table 1. Number of floating point multiplications and additions for the computation of (7) prior and after sparcity optimizations. N denotes the number of surface points.

	before optimizations		after optimizations	
	#mult.	#add.	#mult.	#add.
$\Sigma(\mu)^{\mathrm{T}}\left(\mathrm{M}_0^{\mathrm{T}}\mathrm{M}_0\right)\Sigma(\mu)$	6480	2462	459	390
$\Sigma(\mu)^{\mathrm{T}}\mathrm{M}_0^{\mathrm{T}}$	$180N$	$174N$	$36N$	$30N$

3   Experimental Results

We show in the following two typical experiments with real world surface patches. Our setting consists of a camera with a 56.5° horizontal and with a 48.8° vertical aperture angle, and with known distortion coefficients. The resolution is set to PAL with 576 lines per 768 columns at 25Hz. The camera is mounted on a passive manipulator which is synchronized with the capturing device to deliver the exact position and orientation of the camera. The illumination on the object is constant as we move the camera while the object stands still.

The first surface patch to be tracked is an 5.7cm × 4cm × 4cm edge of a book. The patch is sampled at intervals of 1mm leading to 4756 three-dimensional surface points.

The first step of the experiment consists of taking a reference image of the surface patch and determining its initial pose. For this purpose, we manually select 4 coplanar points on the surface at known object coordinates and employ a least-squares minimization method to calculate the surface pose. Figure 1 shows the reference image with the localized surface points.

Given the reference image and reference pose of the surface patch, we bring the camera once again close to the reference pose to start the tracking procedure.

Fig. 1. Reference images superimposed by the outlines of the surface patch to be tracked. Left: surface patch for the book. Right: surface patch for the bottle.

Fig. 2. Left: history of the mean squared error for an exemplary camera motion of the book (top) and bottle (bottom). Middle: tracked model points for a rotation close to selfocclusion. Right: tracked model points in a closeup with an arbitrary rotation.

Thanks to our efficiency optimizations, we measure only $4-5$ms for a single iteration of the tracking algorithm on a standard Pentium4 computer running at 2GHz. This corresponds to a high tracking rate of 200Hz. The $4-5$ms also include the correction of 4756 screen coordinates for the lens distortion with a polynomial of degree 3. We perform 5 minimization steps per full frame to cope with the substantial object displacement between frames. The remaining time is used for the online visualization.

Figure 2 shows the mean squared error achieved at the end of each frame for an exemplary motion.

The second surface patch to be tracked is part of the label of an ordinary 1.5l soda bottle. The body of the object is modeled as a cylinder with a radius of 4.615cm. The patch itself is of size 6.7cm × 6.7cm which is equivalent to a segment of 83.17° of the cylindrical body. We choose the origin to be in the center of the surface patch with the y-axis pointing to the top of the bottle and the z-axis pointing in the direction of the surface normal. The surface patch is sampled at intervals of 1mm leading to 4624 three-dimensional surface points.

The accuracy of the tracking results and the pull-in range of the minimization method strongly depends on the objective function in the local neighbourhood of the true pose. The plots shown in Fig. 3 reveal the precise location of the minimum of this patch with respect to all parameters for the reference pose.

Figure 4 shows the estimated trajectories of a tracking session together with the real movement of the surface patch. Real motion is calculated based on the reference pose and the camera movement as measured by the passive manipulator mentioned above. The tracked translation shows a mean error of 3mm while the

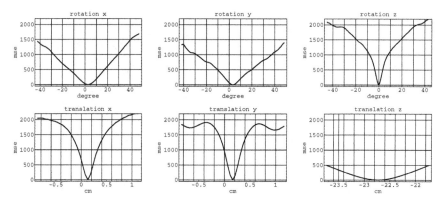

Fig. 3. Mean squared error over the bottle reference patch plotted around the reference pose for rotations and translations along the x-, y-, z-axis.

tracked parameters for object centered rotation reveal some outliers but only a mean error of $1°$ over the sequence.

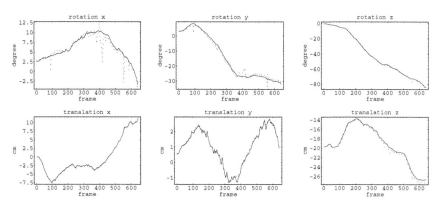

Fig. 4. Trajectories for an exemplary motion of the bottle surface patch. The solid line depicts the ground-truth motion while the dotted line shows the tracked motion.

Two tracked poses for each of the exemplary surface patches are documented in the snapshots of Fig. 2 and demonstrate good tracking results even for a pose close to selfocclusion.

4   Conclusion and Outlook

We present an extension of the tracking model of Hager et al. [1] capable of tracking arbitrary shaped surfaces at a rate up to 200Hz on a standard personal computer.

The tracking results are validated to ground-truth motion with a passive mechanical arm which measures the camera pose while the object remains fixed.

The tracked motion shows a mean residual error of 1° in rotation and 3mm in the translation parameters.

Currently, our method works primarily in settings with stationary object and moving camera, that is, under constant illumination conditions. Such settings are usually encountered in visual servoing applications. Future work is directed towards the extension to moving objects, where illumination changes have to be considered. Since image variation can be decomposed into pose and illumination changes [10] the algorithm can be augmented by a simple compensation algorithm like [1] for complex shapes or [10] for nearly convex objects.

References

1. Hager, G., Belhumeur, P.: Efficient region tracking with parametric models of geometry and illumination. IEEE Trans. on PAMI **20** (1998) 1025–1039
2. Wunsch, P., Hirzinger, G.: Real-time visual tracking of 3-d objects with dynamic handling of occlusions. In: Proc. IEEE ICRA. (1997)
3. Harville, M., Rahimi, A., Darrell, T., Gordon, G., Woodfill, J.: 3d pose tracking with linear depth and brightness constraints. In: ICCV99. (1999) 206–213
4. Basu, S., Essa, I., Pentland, A.: Motion regularization for model-based head tracking. In: Proc. ICPR. (1996) C8A.3 Vienna, Austria.
5. Diehl, N., Burkhardt, H.: Planar motion estimation with a fast converging algorithm. In: Proc. 8th ICPR. (1986) 1099–1102
6. Cernuschi-Frias, B., Cooper, D.B., Hung, Y.P., Belhumer, P.N.: Toward a model-based bayesian theory for estimating and recognizing parameterized 3-d objects using two or more images taken from different positions. IEEE Trans. on PAMI **11** (1989) 1028–1052
7. Sepp, W., Hirzinger, G.: Featureless 6dof pose refinement from stereo images. In: Proc. ICPR. Volume IV. (2002) 17–20 Quebec, Canada.
8. Cascia, M.L., Sclaroff, S., Athitsos, V.: Fast, reliable head tracking under varying illumination: an approach based on registration of texture-mapped 3d models. IEEE Trans. on PAMI **22** (2000) 322–336
9. Jurie, F., Dhome, M.: A simple and efficient template matching algorithm. In: Proc. ICCV. Volume II. (2001) 544–549 Vancouver, Canada.
10. Belhumeur, P.N., Hager, G.D.: Tracking in 3d: Image variability decomposition for recovering object pose and illumination. Pattern Analysis & Applications **2** (1999) 82–91
11. Biencinto, J.M.B., Molina, L.B.: Real-time tracking and estimation of plane pose. In: Proc. ICPR. Volume II. (2002) 697–700 Quebec, Canada.

Hierarchy of Partitions with Dual Graph Contraction*

Yll Haxhimusa and Walter Kropatsch

Pattern Recognition and Image Processing Group 183/2,
Institute for Computer Aided Automation, Vienna University of Technology, Austria
{yll,krw}@prip.tuwien.ac.at

Abstract. We present a hierarchical partitioning of images using a pairwise similarity function on a graph-based representation of an image. This function measures the difference along the boundary of two components relative to a measure of differences of component's internal differences. This definition attempts to encapsulate the intuitive notion of contrast. Two components are merged if there is a low-cost connection between them. Each component's internal difference is represented by the maximum edge weight of its minimum spanning tree. External differences are the cheapest weight of edges connecting components. We use this idea to find region borders quickly and effortlessly in a bottom-up 'stimulus-driven' way based on local differences in a specific feature, like as in preattentive vision. The components are merged ignoring the details in regions of high-variability, and preserving the details in low-variability ones.

1 Introduction

Wertheimer [19] has formulated the importance of wholes (Ganzen) and not of its individual elements , and introduced the importance of perceptual grouping and organization in visual perception. Low-level cue image segmentation cannot and should not produce a complete final "good" segmentation. The low-level coherence of brightness, color, texture or motion attributes should be used to come up sequentially with hierarchical partitions [18]. Mid and high level knowledge can be used to either confirm these groups or to select some for further attention. A wide range of computational vision problems could make use of segmented images, where such segmentation relies on efficient computation. For instance motion estimation requires an appropriate region of support for finding correspondence. Higher-level problems such as recognition and image indexing can also make use of segmentation results in the problem of matching.

It is important that a grouping method has the following properties [3]:
- captures perceptually important groupings or regions, which reflect global aspects of the image,
- is highly efficient, running in time linear in the number of image pixels,
- creates hierarchical partitions [18].

* This paper has been supported by the Austrian Science Fund under grants P14445-MAT and P14662-INF

B. Michaelis and G. Krell (Eds.): DAGM 2003, LNCS 2781, pp. 338–345, 2003.

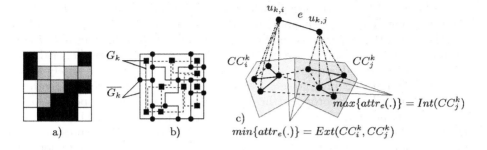

Fig. 1. a) Partition of pixel set into cells. b) Representation of the cells and their neighborhood relations by $(G_k, \overline{G_k})$ of plane graphs. c) Internal and External contrast.

In a regular image pyramid the number of pixels at any level k, is r times higher than the number of pixels at the next reduced level $k+1$. The so called reduction factor r is greater than 1 and it is the same for all levels k. If s denotes the number of pixels in an image I, the number of new levels on top of I amounts to $log_r(s)$. Thus, the regular image pyramid may be an efficient structure for fast grouping and access to image objects in top-down and bottom-up processes [17].

However, regular image pyramids are confined to globally defined sampling grids and lack shift invariance. Bister [1] concludes that regular image pyramids have to be rejected as general-purpose segmentation algorithms. In [9] it was shown how these drawbacks can be avoided by irregular adaptive image pyramids, where the hierarchical structure (vertical network) of the pyramid was not a priori known but recursively built based on the data. Moreover in [16,13,5] it was shown that irregular pyramids can be used for segmentation and feature detection.

The construction of an irregular pyramid is iteratively local [15]. This means that only local properties build the hierarchy of the pyramid. Each level represents a partition of the pixel set into cells [11], i.e. connected subsets of pixels. On the base level (level 0) of an irregular image pyramid the cells represent single pixels and the neighborhood of the cells is defined by the 4 (8)-connectivity of the pixels. A cell on level $k+1$ (parent) is a union of neighboring cells on level k (children). This union is controlled by so called contraction kernels (decimation parameters [12]). Every parent computes its values independently of other cells on the same level. This implies that an image pyramid is built in $O[log(image\_diameter)]$ time. Neighborhoods on level $k+1$, are derived from neighborhoods on level k. Two cells c_1 and c_2 are neighbors if there exist pixels p_1 in c_1 and p_2 in c_2 such that p_1 and p_2 are 4-neighbors (Fig. 1a). We assume that on each level $k+1$ ($k \geq 0$) there exists at least one cell not contained in level k. In particular, there exists a highest level h . We represent the levels as dual pairs $(G_k, \overline{G_k})$ of plane graphs G_k and its dual (plane) graph $\overline{G_k}$ [6] (Fig. 1b). To achieve the planar embedding of graphs we use the 4-connectivity. The sequence $(G_k, \overline{G_k})$, $0 \leq k \leq h$ is called (dual) graph pyramid. Moreover the graph is attributed, $G(V, E, attr_v, attr_e)$, where $attr_v : V \rightarrow \mathbb{R}^+$ and $attr_e : E \rightarrow \mathbb{R}^+$. We use weights for $attr_e$ depending on dissimilarity criteria.

The aim of this paper is to build a minimum weight spanning tree (MST) of regions of an image combining the advantage of regular pyramids (logarithmic tapering) with the advantages of irregular graph pyramids (their purely local construction and shift invariance). The aim is reached by the selection method for contraction kernels proposed in [6] to achieve logarithmic tapering, local construction and shift invariance. Borůvka's algorithm [2] with dual graph contraction (DGC) [12] is used for building MST of the region and to preserve the graph topology. The topological relation seems to play an even more important role for vision tasks in natural systems than precise geometrical position. We build the MST to find region borders based on local differences in a specific feature. See the book of Jolion [10] for an extensive overview of the pyramid framework for early vision.

The plan of the paper is as follows. In Sec. 2 we give the merging decision criteria and we prove that the proposed algorithm builds a nested hierarchy of parititons. Sec. 3 reports on experimental results.

2   A Hierarchy of Partitions

Hierarchies are a significant tool for image partitioning as they are naturally combined with homogeneity criteria. Horowitz and Pavlidis [8] define a consistent homogeneity criteria over a set V as a boolean predicate P over its parts $\Phi(V)$ that verifies the consistency property:

$$\forall (x, y) \in \Phi(V) \quad x \subset y \Rightarrow (P(y) \Rightarrow P(x)). \tag{1}$$

In image analysis Eq. 1 states that the subregions of a homogeneous region are also homogeneous. It follows that if Pyr is a hierarchy and P a consistent homogeneity criteria on V then the set of maximal elements of Pyr that satisfy P defines a unique partition of V. Thus the combined use of a hierarchy and homogeneity criteria allow one to define partitioning in a natural way.

The goal is to find partitions $P_k = \{CC_1^k, CC_2^k, ..., CC_n^k\}$ such that these elements satisfy certain properties. We use the pairwise comparison of neighboring vertices, i.e. partitions to check for similarities [3,4,5]. A pairwise comparison function, $Comp(CC_i^k, CC_j^k)$ is true, if there is evidence for a boundary between CC_i^k and CC_j^k, and false when there is no boundary. Note that $Comp(CC_i^k, CC_j^k)$ is a boolean comparison function for pairs of partitions. The definition of $Comp(CC_i^k, CC_j^k)$ depends on the application.

The pairwise comparison function $Comp(\cdot, \cdot)$ measures the difference along the boundary of two components relative to the differences of component's internal differences. This definition tries to encapsulate the intuitive notion of contrast: a contrasted zone is a region containing two components whose inner differences (**internal contrast**) are less then differences between them (**external contrast**). We define an **external contrast** between two components and an **internal contrast** of each component. These measures are defined in [3,4, 5], analogously.

Every vertex $u \in G_k$ is a representative of a connected component CC^k of the partition P_k. The equivalent contraction kernel [12] of a vertex $u \in G_k$, $N_{0,k}(u)$ is a set of edges on the base level that are contracted, i.e. applying $N_{0,k}(u)$ on the base level contracts the subgraph $G' \subseteq G$ onto the vertex u. The **internal contrast** of the $CC^k \in P_k$ is the **largest dissimilarity** inside the component CC^k i.e. the largest edge weight of the $N_{0,k}(u_k)$ of vertex $u_k \in G_k$, that is

$$Int(CC^k) = max\{attr_e(e), e \in N_{0,k}(u_k)\}. \tag{2}$$

Let $u_{k,i}, u_{k,j} \in V_k$ be the end vertices of an edge $e \in E_k$. The **external contrast** between two components $CC_i^k, CC_j^k \in P_k$ is the **smallest dissimilarity** between component CC_i^k and CC_j^k i.e. the smallest edge weight connecting $N_{0,k}(u_{k,i})$ and $N_{0,k}(u_{k,j})$ of vertices $u_{k,i}, u_{k,j} \in G_k$:

$$Ext(CC_i^k, CC_j^k) = min\{attr_e(e), e = (u_{k,i}, u_{k,j}) : u_{k,i} \in N_{0,k}(u_{k,i}) \wedge w \in N_{0,k}(u_{k,j})\}. \tag{3}$$

This definition is problematic since it uses only the "smallest" edge weight between the two components, making the method very sensitive to noise. But in practice this limitation works well as shown in Sec. 3. In Fig. 1c an example of $Int(CC^k)$ and $Ext(CC_i^k, CC_j^k)$ is given. The $Int(CC_i^k)$ of the component CC_i^k is the *maximum* of weights of the solid edges (analogously for $Int(CC_j^k)$), whereas $Ext(CC_i^k, CC_j^k)$ is the *minimum* of weights of the dashed edges connecting component CC_i^k and CC_j^k. Vertices $u_{k,i}$ and $u_{k,j}$ are representative of the components CC_i^k and CC_j^k. By contracting the edges $N_{0,k}(u_{k,i})$ (see solid edges in Fig. 1c) one arrives to the vertex $u_{k,i}$, analogously $N_{0,k}(u_{k,j})$ for the vertex $u_{k,j}$.

The pairwise comparison function $Comp(\cdot, \cdot)$ between two connected components CC_i^k and CC_j^k can now be defined as:

$$Comp(CC_i^k, CC_j^k) = \begin{cases} \text{True if } Ext(CC_i^k, CC_j^k) > PInt(CC_i^k, CC_j^k), \\ \text{False} \qquad\qquad\qquad \text{otherwise,} \end{cases} \tag{4}$$

where $PInt(CC_i^k, CC_j^k) = min\{Int(CC_i^k) + \tau(CC_i^k), Int(CC_j^k) + \tau(CC_j^k)\}$ is the minimum internal contrast difference between two components. For the function $Comp(CC_i^k, CC_j^k)$ to be true i.e. for the border to exist, the external contrast difference must be greater than the internal contrast differences. The reason for using a threshold function $\tau(CC^k)$ is that for small components CC^k, $Int(CC^k)$ is not a good estimate of the local characteristics of the data, in extreme case when $|CC^k| = 1$, $Int(CC^k) = 0$. Any non-negative function of a single component CC^k, can be used for $\tau(CC^k)$. Choosing criteria other than minimun and maximum will lead to an NP-complete algorithm [3].

2.1   Building Hierarchy of Partitions

Let $P_k = CC_1^k, CC_2^k, ..., CC_n^k$ be the partition on the level k of the pyramid. The algorithm to build the hierarchy of partitions is as follows:

Algorithm 1 – Hierarchy of Partitions

Input: Attributed graph G_0.

1: $k = 0$

2: **repeat**

3:     **for all** vertices $u \in G_k$ **do**

4:         $E_{min}(u) = argmin\{attr_e(e) \,|\, e = (u, v) \in E_k$ or $e = (v, u) \in E_k\}$

5:     **end for**

6:     **for all** $e = (u_{k,i}, u_{k,j}) \in E_{min}$ with $Ext(CC_i^k, CC_j^k) \leq PInt(CC_i^k, CC_j^k)$ **do**

7:         include e in contraction edges $N_{k,k+1}$

8:     **end for**

9:     contract graph G_k with contraction kernels, $N_{k,k+1}$: $G_{k+1} = C[G_k, N_{k,k+1}]$.

10:     **for all** $e_{k+1} \in G_{k+1}$ **do**

11:         set edge attributes $attr_e(e_{k+1}) = min\{attr_e(e_k) \,|\, e_{k+1} = C(e_k, N_{k,k+1})\}$

12:     **end for**

13:     $k = k + 1$

14: **until** $G_k = G_{k-1}$

Output: A region adjacency graph (RAG) pyramid.

Each vertex $u_k \in G_k$ i.e. CC^k represents a connected region on the base level of the pyramid, and since the presented algorithm is based on Borŭvka's algorithm [2], it builds a $MST(u_k)$ of each region, i.e $N_{0,k}(u_k) = MST(u_k)$ [7]. The idea is to collect the smallest weighted edges e (4th step) that could be part of the MST, and then to check if the edge weight $attr_e(e)$ is smaller than the internal contrast of both of the components (MST of end vertices of e) (6th step). If these conditions are fulfilled then these two components will be merged (7th step). Two regions will be merged if the internal contrast, which is represented by its MST, is larger than the external contrast, represented by the weight of the edge, $attr_e(e)$. All the edges to be contracted form the contraction kernels $N_{k,k+1}$, which are then used to create the graph $G_{k+1} = C[G_k, N_{k,k+1}]$ [14], so that the topology is preserved. In general $N_{k,k+1}$ is a forest. We update the attributes of those edges $e_{k+1} \in G_{k+1}$ with the minimum attribute of the edges $e_k \in E_k$ that are contracted into e_{k+1} (11th step). The output of the algorithm is a pyramid where each level represents a RAG, i.e a partition. Each vertex of these RAGs is the representative of a MST of a region in the image. The algorithm is greedy since it collects only the nearest neighbor with the minimal edge weights and merges them if Eq. 4 is false.

Proposition 1. *For any connected attributed graph $G(V, E, attr_e, attr_v)$, Alg. 1 produces a* **hierarchy** *over* V.

Proof. All individual vertices $v \in V$ on the base level form a partition. It is only needed to check that partitions are partially ordered by the inclusion relation. Assume this is not the case, i.e. $\exists (CC_i^k, CC_j^k) \in P_k$ such that $CC_i^k \cap CC_j^k \neq \phi$ but neither $C_i^k \subset C_j^k$ nor $C_j^k \subset C_i^k$. There are at least two edges, e' connecting CC_i^k and $CC_j^k \setminus CC_i^k$ and the other edge e'' connecting CC_j^k and $CC_i^k \setminus CC_j^k$, from which it follows that $CC_i^k \in P_k \Rightarrow PInt(CC_i^k, CC_j^k) < Ext(CC_i^k, CC_j^k) = attr_e(e')$, and for the edge e'' one shows that $attr_e(e'') = Ext(CC_j^k, CC_i^k) \leq$

$PInt(CC_j^k, CC_i^k)$, since $PInt(CC_j^k, CC_i^k) = PInt(CC_i^k, CC_j^k)$ (Eq. 2) and $e'' \in CC_i^k$ it follows $Ext(CC_j^k, CC_i^k) \leq PInt(CC_i^k, CC_j^k) < Ext(CC_i^k, CC_j^k) \leq PInt(CC_j^k, CC_i^k) \Rightarrow CC_j^k \notin P_k$, contradicting the assumption $CC_j^k \in P_k$. □

Proposition 2. *For any connected attributed graph $G(V, E, attr_e, attr_v)$, Alg. 1 produces the **partitions** which are **invariant** under any monotone transformation of the $attr_e$ (dissimilarity measure).*

Proof. It should be checked that the order by which the edges are contracted is not changed by a monotone transformation. The monotone transformation does not change the total order of edges incident on a vertex. This implies that the edge with the minimum weight is also not changed after this monotone transformation in the 4th step of Alg. 1. Moreover this transformation does not change the total order of the edges in a connected component CC_i^k and CC_j^k, implying that the minimum of maximum edge weight of the CC_i^k and CC_j^k is on the same edge (7th step). Edges marked in the 4th and 7th step of the Alg. 1 are not changed by the transformation, which results in the invariance of the partitions. □

Proposition 3. *For any connected attributed graph $G(V, E, attr_e, attr_v)$, the **hierarchy** over V is **invariant** under monotone transformation of attributes.*

Proof. The proof is straightforward using Prop. 2. □

3   Experiments on Image Graphs

We attribute edges with the intensity difference $att_e(u_i, u_j) = |I(u_i) - I(u_j)|$, where $I(u_i)$ is the intensity of the pixel p_i. For color images we run the algorithm by computing the distances in color space. To compute the hierarchy of partitions the function $\tau(CC^k) = f(CC^k)$ is defined as $\tau(CC^k) = \alpha/|CC^k|$, where $\alpha = const$ and $|CC^k|$ is the number of elements in CC^k, i.e. the size of the region. The algorithm has one running parameter α. A larger constant α sets the preference for larger components. A more complex definition of $\tau(CC^k)$, which is large for certain shapes and small otherwise, would produce a partition which prefers certain shapes. To speed up the computation, vertices are attributed $(attr_v)$ with the internal differences, average color and the size of the region it represents. Each of these attributes is computed for each level of the hierarchy. Note that the height of the pyramid depends only on the image content.

We use indoor RGB images 'Lena'[1] (512×512) and 'Object 45'[2] (128×128) and an outdoor image 'Monarch'[1] (768×512) for experiments. We found that $\alpha = 300$ produces the best hierarchy of partitions of the images shown in Fig. 2. Fig. 2b,c,e,h show some of the partitions on different levels of the pyramid and the number of components. In all of the images there are regions of large intensity variability and gradient. This algorithm is capable of grouping perceptually important regions dispite of large intensity variability and gradient. Since the algorithm preserves details in low-variability regions, a noisy pixel would survive

---

[1] Waterloo image database
[2] Coil 100 image database

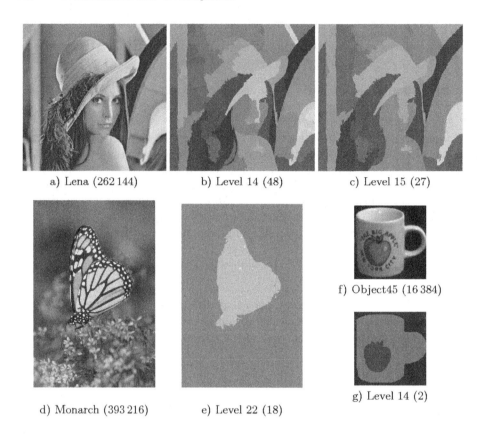

a) Lena (262 144)   b) Level 14 (48)   c) Level 15 (27)

f) Object45 (16 384)

g) Level 14 (2)

d) Monarch (393 216)   e) Level 22 (18)

Fig. 2. Some levels of the partitioning produced with $\alpha = 300$.

throughout the hiearchy (Fig.2e). Image smoothing in low variability regions would overcome this problem. We do not smooth the images, because that would introduce another parameter in the method. The hierarchy of partitions can also be built from an oversegmented image to overcome the problem of noisy pixels. Note that the influence of τ in the decision criterion is smaller as the region gets bigger. For an oversegmented image the algorithm becomes parameterless.

4   Conclusion and Outlook

In this paper we have introduced a method to build hiearchical partitions of an image by comparing in a pairwise manner the difference along the boundary of two components relative to the differences of component's internal differences. Even though the algorithm makes simple greedy decisions locally, it produces perceptually important partitions in a bottom-up 'stimulus-driven' way based only on local differences. It was shown that the algorithm can handle large variation and gradient intensity in images. Since our framework is general enough, we can use RAGs of any oversegmented image and build the hierarchy of partitions. External knowledge can help in a top-down segmentation technique. A drawback is that the maximum and minimum criterion is very sensitive to noise, although in practice it has a small impact. Other criteria, such as median, would lead to an NP-complete algorithm. The algorithm has only one running parameter which controls the sizes of the regions.

References

[1] M. Bister, J. Cornelis, and A. Rosenfeld. A critical view of pyramid segmentation algorithms. *Pattern Recognition Letters*, Vol. 11(No. 9):p.605–617, 1990.

[2] O. Borůvka. O jistém problému minimálnim. *Práce Mor. Přírodvěd. Spol. v Brně (Acta Societ. Scienc. Natur. Moravicae)*, (3):p.37–58, 1926.

[3] P. F. Felzenszwalb and D. P. Huttenlocher. Image Segmentation Using Local Variation. In *Proc. of IEEE Conf. on CVPR*, p.98–104, 1998.

[4] B. Fischer and J. M. Buhmann. Data Resampling for Path Based Clustering. *Proc. 24th DAGM Symp.*, LNCS 2449 p.206–214, 2002.

[5] L. Guigues, L. M. Herve, and J.-P. Cocquerez. The Hierarchy of the Cocoons of a Graph and its Application to Image Segmentation. *Patt. Recog. Lett.*, 24(8) p.1059–1066, 2003.

[6] Y. Haxhimusa, R. Glantz, M. Saib, G. Langs, and W. G. Kropatsch. Logarithmic Tapering Graph Pyramid. *Proc. 24th DAGM Symp.*, LNCS 2449, p.117–124, 2002.

[7] Y. Haxhimusa and W. G. Kropatsch. Hierarchical Image Partitioning with Dual Graph Contraction. *Techical Report PRIP-TR-81*,TU Wien, Austria 2003, http://www.prip.tuwien.ac.at.

[8] S. Horowitz and T. Pavlidis. Picture Segmentation by a Tree Traversal Algorithm. *J. Assoc. Compt. Math.*, Vol. 2(23):p.368–388, 1976.

[9] J.-M. Jolion and A. Montanvert. The adaptive pyramid, a framework for 2D image analysis. *Comp. Vis., Graph., and Im. Process.*, 55(3):pp.339–348, 1992.

[10] J.-M. Jolion and A. Rosenfeld. *A Pyramid Framework for Early Vision*. Kluwer Acadademic Pub., 1994.

[11] V. A. Kovalevsky. Finite topology as applied to image analysis. *Comp. Vis., Graph., and Imag. Process.*, Vol. 46:pp.141–161, 1989.

[12] W. G. Kropatsch. Building Irregular Pyramids by Dual Graph Contraction. *IEE-Proc. Vision, Image and Signal Processing*, Vol. 142(No. 6):pp.366–374, 1995.

[13] W. G. Kropatsch and S. BenYacoub. A general pyramid segmentation algorithm. *Intl. Symp. on Opt. Scie., Eng., and Instr.*, Vol. 2826:p.216–224. SPIE, 1996.

[14] W. G. Kropatsch, A. Leonardis, and H.Bischof. Hierarchical, Adaptive and Robust Methods for Image Understanding. *Surv. on Math. for Ind.*, No.9:p.1–47, 1999.

[15] P. Meer. Stochastic image pyramids. *Computer Vision, Graphics, and Image Processing*, Vol. 45(No. 3):pp.269–294, 1989.

[16] P. Meer, D. Mintz, A. Montanvert, and A. Rosenfeld. Consensus vision. In *AAAI-90 Workshop on Qualitative Vision*, p. 111–115, 1990.

[17] A. Rosenfeld, editor. *Multiresolution Image Processing and Analysis*. Springer, Berlin, 1984.

[18] J. Shi and J. Malik. Normalized Cuts and Image Segmentation. In *Proceedings IEEE Conf. Comp. Vis. and Patt.*, pp:731–737, 1997.

[19] M. Wertheimer. Über Gestaltheorie. *Philosophische Zeitschrift für Forschung und Aussprache*, 1:30–60, 1925.

One-Class Classification with Subgaussians

Amir Madany Mamlouk[1], Jan T. Kim[1], Erhardt Barth[1],
Michael Brauckmann[2], and Thomas Martinetz[1]

[1] Institute for Neuro- and Bioinformatics, University of Lübeck
[2] ZN Vision Technologies AG, Bochum
{madany,kim,barth,martinetz}@inb.uni-luebeck.de

Abstract. If a simple and fast solution for one-class classification is required, the most common approach is to assume a Gaussian distribution
for the patterns of the single class. Bayesian classification then leads to
a simple template matching. In this paper we show for two very different applications that the classification performance can be improved
significantly if a more uniform subgaussian instead of a Gaussian class
distribution is assumed. One application is face detection, the other is
the detection of transcription factor binding sites on a genome. As for
the Gaussian, the distance from a template, i.e., the distribution center,
determines a pattern's class assignment. However, depending on the distribution assumed, maximum likelihood learning leads to different templates from the training data. These new templates lead to significant
improvements of the classification performance.

1 Introduction

In many applications a one-class classification problem has to be solved, i.e. the
separation of a single class of patterns from the rest of the pattern space. A
typical example is the detection of faces in images: the class of human faces
has to be separated from all the other possible patterns [3,6,12]. Usually, the
single class occupies only a negligible volume compared the rest of the pattern
space, and only positive examples for this class are useful or even given for
training a classifier. The huge rest of the pattern space can hardly be represented
by examples. Another typical one-class classification problem can be found in
bioinformatics. Gene regulation is controlled by sequence-specific DNA binding
proteins, the so-called transcription factors [2]. Molecular biologists want to know
the sites where these factors bind on a genome. Sequence patterns where binding
takes place form the single class that has to be separated from the rest of all
possible sequence patterns.

Our investigation is further motivated by the computational requirements
for an industrial face detection system that has to find faces in a video stream
in real time. A common and simple approach is to assume a Gaussian distribution for the single class. More complex would be a mixture of Gaussians or the
application of a support vector machine [6,10]. Therefore simple approaches are
needed, but what performance can be achieved by simple template matching?
As we will see below, Bayesian classification with a Gaussian class distribution
leads to template matching. However, the same is true for every radial symmetric

B. Michaelis and G. Krell (Eds.): DAGM 2003, LNCS 2781, pp. 346–353, 2003.

and monotonic class distribution, with the form of the distribution determined only by the template. We focused our investigation on a class of subgaussian distributions that vary from the Gaussian to the rectangular distribution. Obviously, the subgaussian model which fits most adequately to the distribution of the given data will yield the best template.

2 One-Class Classification with Gaussians

We assume patterns $\mathbf{x} \in \mathbb{R}^N$. Given a pattern $\mathbf{x}$, we ask whether this pattern belongs to the class c. For example, whether an image pattern is a face. Bayes decision rule answers this based on the posterior class probability $P(c|\mathbf{x})$ of the given pattern to belong to class c. $P(c|\mathbf{x})$ can be derived from the pattern distribution of class c, $P(\mathbf{x}|c)$, with the Bayes theorem $P(c|\mathbf{x})P(\mathbf{x}) = P(\mathbf{x}|c)P(c)$. $P(c)$ is the prior class probability, and $P(\mathbf{x})$ denotes the prior probability for the occurrence of pattern $\mathbf{x}$.

A simple model for the probability distribution $P(\mathbf{x}|c)$ of patterns from class c is the Gaussian. Assuming the same prior probability $P(\mathbf{x})$ for all patterns, we obtain for the posterior class probability

$$P(c|\mathbf{x}) = Ce^{-(\mathbf{x}-\mathbf{w})^2/2\sigma^2} \tag{1}$$

with $\mathbf{w}$ as the center of the Gaussian, σ^2 as its variance, and C as a normalization constant that includes the prior class probability $P(c)$.

We assume that a query pattern $\mathbf{x}$ belongs to class c, if $P(c|\mathbf{x})$ exceeds a prespecified value $P_{\min}$. Hence, all the patterns that lie within a sphere with a certain radius R around $\mathbf{w}$ are assumed to belong to class c. Thus, the distribution center $\mathbf{w}$ can be regarded as a template for the class c.

Usually, the prior class probability $P(c)$ is not known, and, hence, a prespecified $P_{\min}$ can not explicitly be translated into a respective radius R. But one knows that $P_{\min}$ increases with decreasing R. By varying R one controls the specificity/sensitivity of the classifier.

Starting with $R = 0$ and increasing R against infinity, one obtains the so-called specificity-sensitivity- or receiver-operating-curve (ROC) of the classifier.

2.1 Determining the Template by Maximum Likelihood Estimation

To estimate the template, i.e., the center of the Gaussian distribution, based on example patterns $X = \{\mathbf{x}_1, ..., \mathbf{x}_p\}$ for class c (the training set), we assume that the training patterns are independently drawn from the class distribution $P(\mathbf{x}|c)$. Then the likelihood $L(X|\mathbf{w})$ that a Gaussian class distribution with center $\mathbf{w}$ generates the data X is given by

$$L(X|\mathbf{w}) = \prod_{\mathbf{x}\in X} e^{-(\mathbf{x}-\mathbf{w})^2/2\sigma^2}. \tag{2}$$

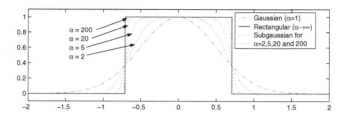

Fig. 1. Shape of the distribution functions $P_\alpha(\mathbf{x}|c)$ with $\mathbf{w} = 0$ and $\sigma = 0.5$ for $\alpha = 1$, which is the Gaussian (dash-dotted line), $\alpha = 2, 5, 20, 200$ (dotted lines), and for $\alpha = \infty$, which is the rectangular distribution (solid line).

Maximum likelihood estimation (MLE) looks for the $\mathbf{w}$ that maximizes this likelihood and yields as solution

$$\mathbf{w}^* = \frac{1}{p} \sum_{\mathbf{x} \in X} \mathbf{x}. \tag{3}$$

Given a Gaussian distribution, the center-of-gravity of the training data is the MLE for its center, i.e., one takes the average pattern as a template.

3   One-Class Classification with Subgaussians

Instead of being a Gaussian, we now assume the distribution of the patterns of class c to be a subgaussian

$$P(\mathbf{x}|c) = C_\alpha e^{-[(\mathbf{x}-\mathbf{w})^2/2\sigma^2]^\alpha}. \tag{4}$$

For $\alpha = 1$ we obtain the standard Gaussian distribution discussed above. Now we are interested in α-values larger than one. Fig. 1 illustrates how the shape of the distribution $P(\mathbf{x}|c)$ changes with an increasing α towards a more and more rectangular (spherical in higher dimensions) distribution. For $\alpha \to \infty$ the distribution $P(\mathbf{x}|c)$ becomes a (hyper)sphere with $P(\mathbf{x}|c) = 1$ inside the sphere, i.e., for $(\mathbf{x} - \mathbf{w})^2 < 2\sigma^2$, and zero outside.

As above, with the assumption of a homogeneous prior $P(\mathbf{x})$ the posterior class probability $P(c|\mathbf{x})$ has the same shape as the class pattern distribution $P(\mathbf{x}|c)$. Again, all the patterns inside a hypersphere of radius R and center $\mathbf{w}$, are assigned to class c. By varying R, the false acceptance rate (FAR) and the false rejection rate (FRR) can be influenced along the respective ROC. Compared to the standard Gaussian distribution, we now obtain different distribution centers $\mathbf{w}$, i.e., different templates. Should the real pattern distribution rather have the shape of a sphere than of a Gaussian, the classification performance will improve with increasing α.

3.1   Determining the Center of the Subgaussian Distribution

As for the Gaussian distribution we determine the center of the subgaussian by MLE. The likelihood $L(X|\mathbf{w})$ of generating the data X is

Fig. 2. Face detection templates. From left to right the average face ($\alpha = 1$) and the subgaussian templates are shown for $\alpha = 10, 20, 100$ and $\alpha \to \infty$.

$$L(X|\mathbf{w}) = \prod_{\mathbf{x} \in X} e^{-[(\mathbf{x}-\mathbf{w})^2/2\sigma^2]^\alpha}. \tag{5}$$

Maximizing $L(X|\mathbf{w})$ is equivalent to minimizing

$$S(\mathbf{w}) = \sum_{\mathbf{x} \in X} (\mathbf{x} - \mathbf{w})^{2\alpha}. \tag{6}$$

The maximization of the likelihood with respect to $\mathbf{w}$ is independent of the σ that is assumed for the model distribution. If we set the derivative of $S(\mathbf{w})$ to zero, we obtain an equation for the distribution center $\mathbf{w}^*_\alpha$. However, this equation can be solved explicitly only for $\alpha = 1$. In this case the solution is, as expected, the center-of-gravity of the training data. For $\alpha > 1$, $\mathbf{w}^*_\alpha$ can be obtained iteratively by gradient descent. The new estimate $\mathbf{w}^*_\alpha(t+1)$ then follows from the old estimate according to

$$\mathbf{w}^*_\alpha(t+1) = \mathbf{w}^*_\alpha(t) + \epsilon \sum_{\mathbf{x} \in X} ||\mathbf{x} - \mathbf{w}^*_\alpha(t)||^{2(\alpha-1)} (\mathbf{x} - \mathbf{w}^*_\alpha(t)), \tag{7}$$

with ϵ as the step size of the gradient descent.

4 Face Detection

As a first example we present the results we obtained for face detection. For these experiments we used a public database[1] of gray-scale images with (19×19) pixel resolution. This database is a standard for the evaluation of face detection systems [3,6,8,10], and thus, is a good basis for comparisons. The database provides 2,429 faces as a training set, and 472 faces and 23,573 non-faces as a test set. We flipped the training images horizontally to increase the training set to 4,858 faces. As in [8], the pixel intensities of each image were normalized to zero-mean and unit variance.

With the training faces the templates $\mathbf{w}^*_\alpha$ were calculated for different α. For $\alpha = 1$ we simply had to calculate the average face. Starting from this average face, α was increased step by step. For each α, 100 iterations of the gradient descent ($\epsilon = 0.01$) were performed. In Fig. 2 we see how the template $\mathbf{w}^*_\alpha$ changed with increasing α.

---

[1] http://www.ai.mit.edu/projects/cbcl/software-datasets/FaceData2.html

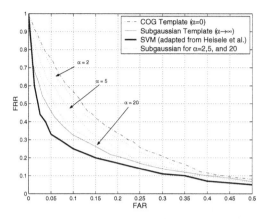

Fig. 3. Face detection performance for different templates. The dash-dotted line shows the ROC for the average face as a template ($\alpha = 1$). The small solid line shows the ROC for the template one obtains if a uniform spherical pattern distribution is assumed ($\alpha \rightarrow \infty$). The performance increases with increasing α. The thick solid line is the ROC for a SVM classifier adapted from Heisele et al. [3].

Figure 3 presents the ROC for different templates. The closer such a curve bends towards the origin, the better the classifier works. Interestingly, the performance increases significantly with increasing α. For the common Gaussian ($\alpha = 1$) we obtain the worst performance. The best performance is obtained for $\alpha \rightarrow \infty$, which yields the center of the spherical distribution as template. Obviously, the distribution of faces in the pixel space is rather spherical than Gaussian.

To illustrate the gain in performance in a more global context, we adapted a ROC obtained with a state-of-the-art approach for face detection by Heisele et al. [3]. A support vector machine (SVM) with a 2nd degree polynomial kernel was trained not only on the 2,429 faces that we used, but in addition also on 4,450 non-face images. As a preprocessing step, the histogram of each image was equalized. Interestingly, with our extremely simple approach of template matching within the raw pixel space, we obtain a classification performance which is remarkably close to this much more sophisticated approach of Heisele et al. (Fig. 3).

5   Detection of Protein-DNA Binding Sites

Genetic information in most biological systems is stored in DNA sequences, consisting of base pairs which are denoted by A (adenine), C (cytosine), G (guanine) and T (thymine). Regulation of gene expression is mediated by specialized proteins, called transcription factors, which bind to specific regulatory sites on the genome more tightly than to all other sites. A transcription factor "recognizes" a binding site by the local sequence, called the binding word.

For understanding and modelling gene regulation, it is necessary to know at which words a certain transcription factor binds and executes its function. Classification of words into binding words and non-binding words is therefore an important task in bioinformatics. Since for experimental reasons non-binding words have only rarely been described, we have to solve a one-class classification problem in which only positive samples from the class of binding words are given.

For representing DNA sequence information by vectors with real-valued components, a method called "orthogonal coding" is typically used. Let $\mathcal{A} =$

$\{A, C, G, T\}$ denote the alphabet of base pairs. Orthogonal coding is a mapping from $\mathcal{A}^L$ to $\mathbb{R}^{4L}$ which represents a sequence of L nucleotide symbols as a vector $\mathbf{x} = (x_{A,1}, x_{C,1}, x_{G,1}, x_{T,1}, x_{A,2}, \dots, x_{T,L})$, where $x_{b,l} = 1$ if the l-th symbol is b and $x_{b,l} = 0$ otherwise. As an example, the orthogonal coding of the sequence GAT is $(0, 0, 1, 0, 1, 0, 0, 0, 0, 0, 0, 1)$. By this construction, symbols are represented by quartets of components, and different symbols correspond to different, orthogonal quartets.

5.1   Classification of Words

The concept presented above to choose a template and to use the distance to the template as a basis for classification is now applied to the problem of detecting binding words. A word (pattern) $\mathbf{x}$ is assumed to be a binding word if the distance $||\mathbf{x} - \mathbf{w}||$ of the word to the template $\mathbf{w}$ is smaller than a maximum distance R. Since $||\mathbf{x}||^2 = L$ is valid within the orthogonal coding scheme, we obtain $||\mathbf{x} - \mathbf{w}||^2 = L + ||\mathbf{w}||^2 - 2\mathbf{w}^T\mathbf{x}$. Hence, the condition of a maximum distance R then is equivalent to the condition that the so-called score $\mathbf{w}^T\mathbf{x}$ of a word has to exceed a threshold $S_{\min}$ for being a binding word.

The template $\mathbf{w}$ is called a "scoring matrix" in the bioinformatics literature, where the term "matrix" refers to the common practice to arrange the $4L$ components of $\mathbf{w}$ in a $4 \times L$ table. The scoring matrix is a good approximation for calculating the protein-DNA binding energy [1,5] and, therefore, it is structurally adequate for capturing the binding behaviour of a transcription factor. The maximum likelihood template now depends on the assumed distribution of the binding words.

Here we assume the subgaussian class distributions as introduced in Section 3. For $\alpha = 1$, the case of a Gaussian class distribution, we obtain for the template $\mathbf{w}$ the arithmetic mean of the experimentally known binding words. Interestingly, this is equivalent to the so-called profile matrix, the most commonly used approach for binding word detection in bioinformatics [2,9].

As an alternative, we now consider the template resulting from $\alpha \to \infty$ and ask, whether this yields improvements similar to those we have seen for face detection. This template is equivalent to the so-called binding matrix which has been introduced recently [5].

5.2   Sample Application

Since non-binding words are not available, it is not possible to determine ROCs as for the face detection problem. Instead, we split up the known binding words into a training set and a test set. The training set is then used to calculate the templates for $\alpha = 1$ and $\alpha \to \infty$. The respective thresholds are then set to the largest value that still provides a zero FRR on both the test set and the training set (i.e. we require that all binding words are classified correctly). The corresponding FAR cannot directly be determined, because false positives are not known. However, from theoretical analyses and empirical observation it is known that the ratio of k, the number of words accepted by the transcription factor, to $K = 4^L$, the number of all words, has to be small [7,4]. Quantitatively,

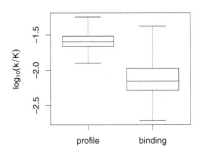

Fig. 4. Box plot showing the gain in specificity achieved with the assumption of a subgaussian instead of a Gaussian distribution. From the 73 binding words for the SOX-9 transcription factor, 1000 subsets of 48 binding words were independently drawn at random and k/K was determined as described in the text. Boxes encompass the middle quartiles, the bar depicts the median and the whiskers extend to the extreme values.

$k/K \approx 10^{-3}$ is, on average, a reasonable estimate and $k/K < 10^{-2}$ can definitely be expected to be satisfied. Thus, the amount by which the k/K ratio obtained for the classifier exceeds 10^{-3} is a measure for the FAR which corresponds to the zero FRR.

Of course, it would be easy to achieve a low k/K at FRR=0, if we could choose a classifier of arbitrary structure. However, we want to minimize the k/K ratio with a template (matrix) classifier since this approach is structurally adequate from biochemical and biophysical considerations. As we will see, within this approach it is not easy to achieve a k/K ratio which is in the right order of magnitude. In particular, the profile matrix typically leads to a k/K ratio which indicates a large FAR. Finding a template (matrix) that allows for a lower k/K value would therefore be a significant improvement.

Fig. 4 shows the results we achieved for $\alpha = 1$ and $\alpha \to \infty$ on a set of 73 binding words of the SOX-9 transcription factor provided by the TRANSFAC database [11] (TRANSFAC matrix M00410). We created training sets by randomly drawing 2/3 of the binding words. Templates were computed based on these training sets, and for each template, the threshold was set to the maximum value at which all known binding words, including those not used for training, are classified correctly. Then the corresponding k/K ratios were determined. For an extreme subgaussian distribution ($\alpha \to \infty$) we achieve a reduction of k/K by half an order of magnitude in comparison to the classifier based on the Gaussian distribution ($\alpha = 1$), which corresponds to the common profile matrix.

6   Conclusions

We have shown that the assumption of a subgaussian class distribution can increase one-class classification performance significantly compared to the widespread assumption of a Gaussian class distribution. This is obtained with simple and fast template matching as in case of the traditional Bayesian approach for Gaussian class distributions. It is just that the template that results from assuming the subgaussian class distribution seems to be more appropriate. With the framework presented in this paper, the shape of the distribution is steered by a single continuous parameter α, with $\alpha = 1$ for the standard Gaussian and

$\alpha \to \infty$ for a rectangular distribution. The corresponding templates can be determined by simple gradient descent. The performance increase was shown for two example problems as different as face finding and DNA-binding site detection. For face detection, the increase was robust against different methods of image preprocessing like histogram normalization, subtraction of best-fit linear plane, and edge extraction. This suggests that there might be quite a number situations and problems where the assumption of a subgaussian instead of a Gaussian pattern distribution would be more appropriate and thus lead to superior results without additional computational costs for the classification task.

Acknowledgements. The authors would like to thank Carsten Hinckfuss and Frank Prill for preparing the data for the face detection analysis as well as Jan Gewehr for his preparation of the TRANSFAC data. This work has been supported by the MORPHA project of the BMBF, FKZ01IL902Q/0.

References

1. P. V. Benos, M. L. Bulyk, and G. D. Stormo. Additivity in protein-DNA interactions *Nucleic Acids Research*, 30:4442–4451, 2002.
2. K. Frech, K. Quandt, and T. Werner. Finding protein-binding sites in DNA sequences: The next generation. *TIBS*, 22:103–104, 1997.
3. B. Heisele, T. Poggio, and M. Pontil. Face detection in still gray images. Technical Report AI Memo 1687, Massachusetts Institute of Technology, 2000.
4. J. T. Kim, T. Martinetz, and D. Polani. Bioinformatic principles underlying the information content of transcription factor binding sites. *Journal of Theoretical Biology*, 220:529–544, 2003.
5. T. Martinetz, J. E. Gewehr, and J. T. Kim. Statistical learning for detecting protein-DNA-binding sites. In *Int. Joint Conf. on Neural Networks 2003*. IEEE Press, 2003.
6. E. Osuna, R. Freund, and F. Girosi. Training support vector machines: an application to face detection. *Proceedings of CVPR'97*, 1997.
7. T. D. Schneider, G. D. Stormo, and L. Gold. Information content of binding sites on nucleotide sequences. *J.Mol.Biol.*, 188:415–431, 1986.
8. H. Schneiderman and T. Kanade. Probabilistic modeling of local appearance and spatial relationships for object recognition. *Proceedings of CVPR'98*, 1998.
9. G. D. Stormo. DNA binding sites: Representation and discovery. *Bioinformatics*, 16:16–23, 2000.
10. K.K. Sung and T. Poggio. Example-based learning for view-based human face detection. *IEEE PAMI*, 20:39–51, 1998.
11. E. Wingender, X. Chen, R. Hehl, H. Karas, I. Liebich, V. Matys, T. Meinhardt, M. Prüß, I. Reuter, and F. Schacherer. TRANSFAC: An integrated system for gene expression regulation. *Nucl. Acids Res.*, 28:316–319, 2000.
12. M-H. Yang, D. Kriegman, and N. Ahuja. Detecting faces in images: A survey. *IEEE PAMI*, 24:34–58, 2002.

A Hybrid Distance Map Based and Morphologic Thinning Algorithm

Klaus Donath, Matthias Wolf*, Radim Chrástek, and Heinrich Niemann

FORWISS, Knowledge Processing Research Group, Haberstr. 2, 91058 Erlangen,
donath@forwiss.de,
http://www-wv.informatik.uni-erlangen.de/~donath

Abstract. A lot of applications need that an object is transformed into its medial axis while preserving its topology. In this paper we present a thinning algorithm based on special masks preserving connectivity. The thinning process is controled by a distance map to overcome problems of a former approach. As a result we obtain a skeleton that has minor artefacts only and which is suitable in the field of blood vessel analysis. We are providing results on synthetic and real images that are compared with another approach.

1   Introduction

Many computer vision applications need characteristics of an object. Mainly elongated 2D objects are usually transformed into their 1D medial axis while preserving the topology. A point in a binary image whose deletion does not destroy the topology is called a simple point. Thus, a process deleting simple points is called a thinning algorithm. Typical fields of application are found in optical character recognition or medical image analysis. I.e. in blood vessel analysis the skeleton of the vessel system can be used for computing the length of all vessels.

A thinning algorithm is a method that transforms an object into a 1 pixel thin line in the middle of the object while preserving its topology. Such a method should meet the following requirements:

- The skeleton must preserve the topology of the original object,
- The end points of the object should be part of its skeleton,
- The skeleton should be situated in the middle of the object that means every skeleton point has the same distance from at least 2 object borders,
- Rotation invariance: Skeletonisation and object rotation should correspond. Due to spatial discretisation this should be approximately satiesfied for arbitrary rotations.
- Noise invariance: The skeleton should be insensitive to noise.

However, it is known that these requirements cannot be fulfilled simultaneously. In particular, it is difficult to distinguish a large artefact from a little feature.

---

* Now with: Siemens Medical Solutions USA, Inc., 51 Valley Stream Parkway, Malvern, PA 19355, USA

B. Michaelis and G. Krell (Eds.): DAGM 2003, LNCS 2781, pp. 354–361, 2003.

1.1 Thinning Algorithms

In literature a large number of thinning algorithms can be found that meet these requirements more or less. Regarding their basic ideas they can be roughly divided into the following groups:

- Morphological methods: Those are local processes based on several masks typically of size 3×3 or 5×5. For that matter they are rather fast but due to the locality of small masks there are often artefacts remaining.
- Border tracking algorithms: For each border point a corresponding point at the opposite border is searched. The skeleton is found in the middle of the line connecting both points. Beginning with two corresponding border points the object borders are then tracked by using additional information, e.g. the direction. At last the skeleton points are connected. The resulting curve is rather smooth but concave objects or bifurcations can cause problems of finding corresponding pixels.
- Extractions from distance maps: The approach starts out from computing a distance map (DM) containing distances of object points to their closest object border according to a given metric. Then the skeleton is extracted from the DM by searching local maximums and connecting them to a closed curve.

There is no universal algorithm combining all advantages and meeting all requirements but for most applications a suitable skeleton algorithm can be found. In case of blood vessel analysis the number of skeleton points are assumed to correspond to the vessel length whereas the positions of skeleton points in the DM correspond to the radii of blood vessels. Therefore skeleton points should be identical with maximums of the DM.

In the following we will focus on morphological approaches. Usually, a morphological thinning algorithm is an iterative process. In a sequential approach a pixel is deleted in each iteration. Due to the locality of the data, only the values of some neighbours are necessary. Thus, an algorithm can be implemented as a parallel process which deletes a number of pixels in each iteration. The number of iterations itself depends on the maximum thickness of an object.

While earlier approaches mainly focused on the quality of the algorithm, nowadays there seems to be a focus on speed and complexity as well. Such an algorithm can be found in [3] published recently. This approach does not only give good results but it is also very fast and well founded. But unfortunately the requirement for 1 pixel thin midlines is not satisfied.

2 Algorithm

2.1 Former Algorithm

In [2] a morphological thinning algorithm is proposed for analyzing blood vessel images of the chicken yolk sack membrane. The method is an iterative conditional erosion based on 8 masks of size 3×3 (Fig. 1) adapted to thin elongated objects

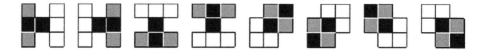

Fig. 1. Morphological thinning algorithm: 3×3 masks for conditional erosion.

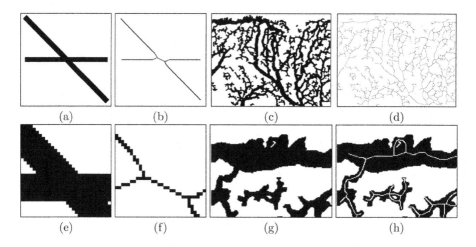

(a)	(b)	(c)	(d)
(e)	(f)	(g)	(h)

Fig. 2. Results of thinning method: (a) synthetic image and skeleton (b), (c) real image and skeleton (d), and subimages (e, f, g, h), (h) skeleton is superimposed onto image.

preserving connectivity and with nearly no remaining artefacts. The approach uses an 8-topology for the object and a 4-topology for the background. Every iteration consists of 2 steps. At first, all object points which meet the condition of a mask are marked and in the second step all marked pixels are erased. These iterations are repeated until there are no more pixels to be erased.

An object point can be marked if at least one of its neighbours is an unmarked object point and the two neighbours on the left and on the right side are marked or unmarked object points and the 3 opposite points belong to the background (see Fig. 1).

In this way an object will be thinned to a 1 pixel thin line that might contain only little artefacts. The results are shown in Fig. 2.

2.2   Problems

In spite of the appearently good results the algorithm causes some problems. Because of the masks in Fig. 1 a single background pixel inside an object cannot be eroded thus yielding a skeleton which is not in the middle of the object. Furthermore the skeleton seems to be incorrect on image borders. Normally skeleton lines do not end on object borders but in a distance of a about vessel radius within the object. This is tolerable for vessels ending within an image but not for vessels on image borders (Fig. 2 (h)).

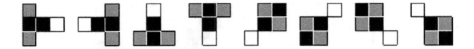

Fig. 3. Additional 3 × 3 masks that are used in the first iteration

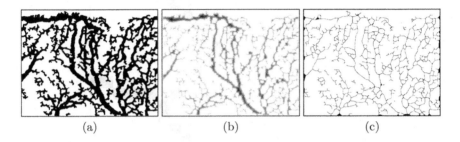

Fig. 4. Results of thinning method in combination with distance map: (a) binary image, (b) distance map and (c) interim skeleton image.

Sometimes the skeleton is not in the middle of the object. Caused by the used 8-topology the outer side of a curved object is much more eroded than the inner side. At last the produced skeleton has sometimes a 1 pixel thickness in terms of the 4-topology but tracking the skeleton is not always unambiguous in the 8-topology (Fig. 2 (f)). Due to this reason further thinning steps are necessary.

2.3   Extensions of the New Algorithm

To overcome the problems described above the algorithm needs to be enhanced. The problems at image borders are mainly caused by a 1 pixel frame of background points. Because it is a special effect of the segmentation process the frame is converted to object pixels and reconverted at the end of the thinning process.

To treat single background points inside an object in the first iteration special masks, shown in Fig. 3 are used. To reduce the object up to its midline the thinning method is combined with a distance map. A distance map can be approximated by an iterative erosion containing the distances of object pixels to their nearest borders. Using the 8-topology when eroding a binary image yields a maximum norm. An erosion based on the 4-topology gives distance values corresponding to the sum of the components of the distance vector. An Euclidian norm can be approximated by an erosion based on the 4-topology and the 8-topology alternately. The first step of the algorithm remains unchanged but at the second step only the marked points are erased that are not maximal in the 8-topology. In this way objects can be widely reduced to its midline. But plateaus in the distance map (that are often close to bifurcations) cause that small areas greater than 1 pixel remain. An example can be seen in Fig. 4 (c). Now the object has to be eroded with the known masks given in Fig. 1 ignoring the distance map until no more points can be deleted. The result of the method

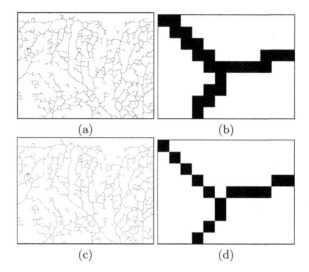

Fig. 5. Results of thinning method after erosion conditioned by distance map and after erosion without respecting distance map (a), subimage (b), (c) result after erasion of all simple points, (d) subimage of (c).

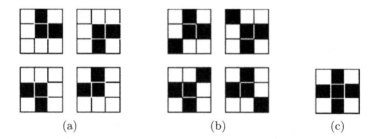

Fig. 6. The 3 × 3 masks that are used to find redundant points: (a) The points in the middle are redundant, (b) and (c) the points in the middle belong to a bifurcation and are not redundant.

up to this point is a skeleton of the object similar to that of the former method, the difference though is that the skeleton is positioned in the middle of the object. In Fig. 5 (a) the result is presented. In detail one can see that sometimes the skeleton is 1 pixel thin in the 4-topology but more than 1 pixel thin in the 8-topology (Fig. 5 (b)). That means that much more simple points exist that have to be deleted.

For finding and deleting these simple points another set of masks is used. All points that match the condition of the masks in Fig. 6 (a) are simple points and can be erased while points that match a mask of Fig. 6 (b) or Fig. 6 (c) belong to a bifurcation of the skeleton and are not simple points. These points are not to be deleted. After erasion of all simple points there is a nearly perfect skeleton of an object whose lines are well positioned in the middle of the object, as well

Expand image by 1 pixel of object points at the edges of the image		
Compute distance map of the image		
FOR $x \in [0, XSIZE)$, $y \in [0, YSIZE)$		
	IF	f_{xy} object point
	THEN	erosion according to Fig. 3 and distance map
	FOR $x \in [0, XSIZE)$, $y \in [0, YSIZE)$	
		IF f_{xy} object point
		THEN erode f_{xy} according to Fig. 1 and distance map
UNTIL no pixel else can be deleted		
	FOR $x \in [0, XSIZE)$, $y \in [0, YSIZE)$	
		IF f_{xy} object point
		THEN erode f_{xy} according to Fig. 1 ignoring the distance map
UNTIL no pixel else can be deleted		
	FOR $x \in [0, XSIZE)$, $y \in [0, YSIZE)$	
		IF f_{xy} simple point according to Fig. 6
		THEN delete f_{xy}
UNTIL no pixel else can be deleted		
Remove 1 pixel of object points at the edges of the image		

Fig. 7. Structure of the new thinning algorithm

as the objects endings are preserved in the skeleton and the skeleton is poor in artefacts. The final result is shown in Fig. 5 (c) as a whole and in Fig. 5 (d) in detail. Fig. 7 gives a structural overview of the new thinning algorithm.

3 Results

The results in Fig. 5 demonstrate that the new method yields a skeleton that preserves the topology of the object. In addition it is rather smooth, poor in artefacts and it is 1 pixel thin in terms of the 8-topology. The requirement on thinning methods to preserve end points of an object should form Y-like skeleton endings. Instead of this the skeleton ends in a single line at a distance of about a vessel radius from the vessel border. This is an advantage in analysing objects like blood vessels.

To measure the robustness of the method to rotation a synthetic image has been rotated by 45 and 90 degrees and the resulting images have been thinned too. As one can see in Fig. 8 our thinning method is invariant to rotation by 45 degrees. The different course of the skeleton at the lower end of skeleton in Fig. 8 (e) is caused by border noise originated in the rotation process. It also demonstrates that border noise can locally modify the course of the skeleton.

In the next step the results of our approach are compared to a method described in [5]. Fig. 9 shows the different results of the two methods. In most cases the position of the skeleton points differ about 1 or 2 pixels. Only skeleton points close to bifurcations can differ more caused by plateaus in the distance map. In case of blood vessel images the differences in skeletons are as low as in

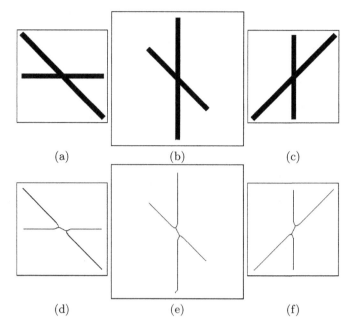

Fig. 8. Influence of rotation to the thinning method: (a) synthetic image, (b) image after beeing rotated by 45 degrees, (c) image after rotation by 90 degrees, (d), (e), (f) thinning results of (a), (b), (c).

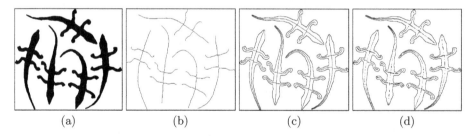

Fig. 9. Comparison of thinning methods: (a) image (from [5]), (b) result of mask based method, (c) result of [5], (d) comparison of (b) and (c) (identical points invisible)

the example above (Fig. 10). In addition the result of our proposed approach contains less artefacts than the skeleton of [5].

The processing time depends quadratically on the image size and the number of object points. At every iteration it is first tested whether a point is an object point or not. Then, the mask operation is processed only on object points. Because of local processing the method is rather fast. A typical blood vessel image of size 752×576 and nearly 40 percent object pixel takes approximately 1.3 sec processing time on a PC with Pentium III, 933 MHz processor.

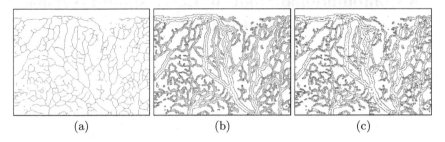

(a)   (b)   (c)

Fig. 10. Thinning results of Fig. 2 (c): (a) result of mask based method, (b) result of [5], (c) comparison of (a) and (b) (identical points invisible)

4   Summary

In this paper we presented a morphological thinning method that consists of iterative conditional parallel erosion. The erosion scheme is defined by a set of mask operations and is combined with a distance map. Due to this combination it is enforced that the skeleton is positioned in the middle of the object. For that reason it combines the advantages of morphological and distance map based methods. The computational time is rather fast and the resulting skeleton image contains only little artefacts. As a result of the last thinning step the skeleton of an object is exactly 1 pixel thin in terms of the 8-topology.

References

1. B. Steckemetz. Adaptive Skelettierung handgeschriebener Zeichen. In *Tagungsband Mustererkennung*. DAGM, Springer Verlag, 1997.
2. Donath, K., Wolf, M., Höper, J., Niemann, H., and Plaßwilm, L. (1999). Zeitliche Analyse der Angiogenese im extraembryonalen Gefäßsystem des Hühnerembryos. In Förstner, W., Buhmann, J. M., Faber, A., and Faber, P., Hrsg., *DAGM-Symposium*, Informatik Aktuell, S. 381–388. Springer. Mustererkennung 1999, 21. DAGM-Symposium, Bonn, 15.–17. September 1999, Proceedings.
3. Bernard, T. M. and Manzanera, A. (1999). Improved low complexity fully parallel thinning algorithm. In *Proc. Int. Conf. on Image Analysis and Processing (ICIAP)*, S. 215–220, Venice, Italy. IEEE Computer Society.
4. Manzanera, A., Bernard, T., Prêteux, F., and Longuet, B. (2002). n-dimensional skeletonization: a unified mathematical framework. *Journal of Electronic Imaging*, 11(1):25–37.
5. Ogniewicz, R.L. and Kübler, O. (1995). Hierarchic voronoi skeletons. In *Pattern Recognition* 28:343–359.

A Computational Model of Early Auditory-Visual Integration

C. Schauer and H.-M. Gross

Dept. of Neuroinformatics, Ilmenau Technical University, D-98684 Ilmenau, Germany

Abstract. We introduce a computational model of sensor fusion based on the topographic representations of a "two-microphone and one camera" configuration. Our aim is to perform a robust multimodal attention-mechanism in artificial systems. In our approach, we consider neurophysiological findings to discuss the biological plausibility of the coding and extraction of spatial features, but also meet the demands and constraints of applications in the field of human-robot interaction. In contrast to the common technique of processing different modalities separately and finally combine multiple localization hypotheses, we integrate auditory and visual data on an early level. This can be considered as focusing the attention or controlling the gaze onto salient objects. Our computational model is inspired by findings about the inferior colliculus in the auditory pathway and the visual and multimodal sections of the superior colliculus. Accordingly it includes: a) an auditory map, based on interaural time delays, b) a visual map, based on spatio-temporal intensity difference and c) a bimodal map where multisensory response enhancement is performed and motor-commands can be derived. Along with our experiments, questions arise about the spatial and temporal nature of audio-visual information: Which precision or what shape of receptive fields are suitable for grouping different types of multimodal events? What are useful time windows for multisensory interaction? These questions are rarely discussed in the context of computer vision and sound localization, but seem to be essential for the understanding of multimodal perception and the design of appropriate models.

1 Introduction

In recent years a lot of promising work on the problem of spatial hearing has been published – many investigations and models of auditory perception exist from neurobiology to psychoacoustics [3,2]. However, although numerous applications in robotics and human-machine interaction are imaginable, only a few working examples are known. There might be different reasons for that: on the one hand, the models normally can include only a few details of the complex neural coding and processing mechanisms in the real auditory system. On the other hand, when aiming at localization systems working in everyday environments, many acoustic effects arising from very different acoustic characteristics must be faced.

In computer-vision the situation is different. The field is established and a huge number of models and applications exists - biologically motivated approaches or technical solutions of specific application problems. It is surprising, that multimodal approaches are relatively seldom, even though artificial vision systems provide processing of motion, color or other object specific features and the mechanisms of spatial hearing and vision

B. Michaelis and G. Krell (Eds.): DAGM 2003, LNCS 2781, pp. 362–369, 2003.
© Springer-Verlag Berlin Heidelberg 2003

complement one another quite obviously. For us, the simulation of early auditory-visual integration is promising significant advantages in the orientation behavior of mobile robots [4]. Furthermore, some remarkable publications on the neurophysiological background of multisensory integration [10], [11] inspire new solutions for computational models.

Parts of the model described here, are comparable to the system by Rucci, Edelmann and Wray [7], because a direct structural realization of neural mechanisms is used instead of abstract statistical methods. In contrast to Rucci's system, the emphasis of our work is not placed on the problem of self-calibration and adaption but on robustness and real-world capability. For this reason, also the feasibility of significant and reproducible experiments is discussed in this article.

2 Modelling Binaural Sound Localization

In contrast to visual perception, hearing starts with one–dimensional, temporal signals, whose phasing and spectrum are essential for the localization. To evaluate spatial information of a sonic field, the auditory system utilizes acoustic effects caused by a varying distance between the sound source and the two ears and the shape of the head and body. We can categorize these effects in intensity differences and time delays. In [2] a comprehensive study of sound localization based on different types of binaural and monaural information is presented, including findings about the localization blur: The achieved precision in the horizontal plane corresponds conspicuously to the relation of azimuth angle variation and interaural intensity differences (ITDs) – a hint for the importance of ITD processing. The assumption, that many localization tasks could be solved just by calculating ITDs and the detailed functional and structural description of the ITD processing neural circuits has been the starting point of our modeling.

2.1 Binaural Model Concept

Our work on real–world–capable ITD processing is similar to Lazzaro's neuromorphic auditory localization system [6], but follows a more pragmatic approach. In our simulations, we use digital algorithms for the preprocessing and coincidence detection within the auditory patterns, as well as an Amari-type dynamic neural field for the evaluation of ambiguous localization hypothesis [8]. The model includes the following stages:

1. Microphone signals are filtered by a cochlear model (all–pole–gammatone filter) and coded into spikes (hair-cell model).
2. For every frequency channel, the spike patterns from left and right are cross–correlated (Jeffress coincidence detection model for the medial superior olive (MSO) [5]) - the time–code of binaural delay is transformed into a place code, representing interaural phase differences.
3. The resulting pattern is projected onto a non–tonotopic representation of ITDs and thus of azimuthal locations of sound sources (Model of the Inferior Colliculus, IC). As the result of a winner-take-all (WTA) process, only one direction will be dominant at a time.
4. With the help of a special microphone configuration (see fig. 1, left), a simple estimation of interaural spectral differences determines the in front or behind orientation. This way, a 360°-map of horizontal directions is formed.

2.2   Performance of the Sound Localization

Performance tests included all sorts of common sounds (clicks, hand claps, voices, pink noise) and were performed outdoors (without echoes) and in an empty, acoustically disadvantageous (echoic) lecture hall. In quiet situations (background noise < -30dB), 100% of the test signals were localized correctly within the accuracy of the discrete system. In additional tests in a shopping center (less echoic, signal-noise ratio 3-5dB) command–words and hand–claps of a person were detected with a probability of 81% and a precision of +/- 10° (90% within +/- 20°). To demonstrate the ability of detecting even moving natural stimuli, the processing of a 12 word long sentence is shown (figures 1), where the tracked speaker position is travelling once around the microphones (performed in the lecture hall without background noise).

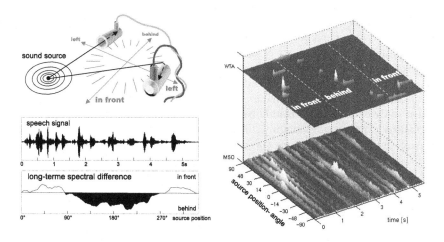

Fig. 1.   Left: Microphone configuration and 360-degree localization of a speaker moving as described in the text. **Right:** Visualization of the IC output (bottom) and the resulting activity in the WTA (top).

3   Concept for a Sub-cortical Auditory-Visual Integration

Usually, spatial perception and attention has multimodal character, whereas hearing and vision seem to be complementary strategies. Other than the auditory system, vision is based on a receptor, that is already providing topologically organized information and the question becomes in which way objects of interest manifest themselves in the continuous visual representation? In the context of human-robot interaction, we have named feature candidates like pure intensity, motion, color or contour. In contrast to the low-level auditory-space processing in the midbrain, we must now distinguish between *cortical object recognition* and *low-level multi-sensor fusion*. Firstly, we clarify the term "low-level": Since visual features do not have interrelations with characteristic frequencies, the first stage for a visual-auditory integration can be found, following the projections from the non-tonotopical spatial maps in the extern IC. Investigations on the mainly visually, but also auditory (via ICx) innervated, superior colliculus (SC), provide evidence for a merging of the sensor modalities and the forming of multisensory spatial maps [10]. Visually sensitive neurons found here, are not or less specialized for color or orientation of contours but respond to broadband intensity and certain velocities of moving stimuli (changes in intensity). We use these findings as a basis for our multi-modal model, although we also consider to integrate higher-level features as an option in concrete applications. According to [11], at least the following properties of the representation and integration of multiple sensory inputs in the SC had to be considered in the model architecture:

Superficial SC (SCs) is responsive only to visual and especially to moving stimuli. Counterpart of a retinotopically ordered map in SCs is a one-dimensional map of horizontally arranged intensity differences, provided by a wide-angle vision system. Presumed, that auto-motion is omitted during sensory recording, the intensity differences are coding scene motion.

(i) Deep layers of the SC (SCd) respond to visual, somatosensory, auditory and multimodal stimuli. (ii) visual receptive fields (RF) are significantly larger than in SCs. In the model, we propose convergent visual projections from SCs to SCd, where also the auditory input from ICx is received. According to the field of vision, the RFs of the visual projections might cover just a part of the resulting multisensory map.

Most SCd multisensory neurons display response enhancement when receiving spatially and temporally coincident stimuli but show response depression if simultaneous stimuli are spatially separated. This actual property of multisensory integration can be realized by a WTA-type network with both auditory and visual afferents and global inhibition. Competing features inhibit each other, aligned stimuli excite one another.

Maximal enhancement occurs with minimally effective stimuli. Especially for a strong bimodal or unimodal activation, the WTA response is limited by global inhibition and by the sigmoidal output of the neurons. With a suitable set of network parameters, the combination of weak stimuli should show a greater enhancement than adding a second activation to a WTA process, that is already *saturated* by one strong stimuli.

In SCd overlapping multisensory and motor-maps initiate overt behavior. We are going to use the multisensory map to code turn reflexes of a robotic head toward the acoustic or visual stimulus; small moves if the stimuli originate almost from the center, and stronger ones if "something" is to be seen on or heard from the side.

Different modality-specific RFs have to be aligned to allow response enhancement, even if eyes and/or ears can be moved separately. If so, there has to be also an exclusively visual map in SCd, controlling eye movement. This is consistent with the known models of saccade generation [9]. To achieve map alignment every eye-specific motor-command must cause an adjustment in the auditory map. In the model, this is realized by a controlled change of the weights of the ICx–SCd projection (fig. 2).

Similar to [7], we use a modification of the network-model of the auditory inferior colliculus to realize the multimodal map. A nonlinear notation can be given as a bimodal version of the standard dynamic field of Amari-type [1]:

$$\tau \frac{d}{dt} z(r,t) = -z(r,t) + c_A x_A(r,t) + c_V x_V(r,t)$$

$$-c_i \int y(z(r,t))dr + c_n \int w(r-r')y(z(r',t))dr'$$

The state $z(r,t)$ of a neuron at position r is depending on three components: the weighted bimodal inputs x_A and x_V, global inhibition according to the integrated network output and lateral feedback from neighboring positions r'. All neurons have sigmoidal output, calculated by the Fermi-function: $y(z(r,t)) = (1 + exp(-\sigma \cdot z(r,t)))^{-1}$.

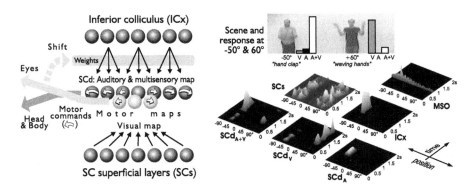

Fig. 2. Left: A simplified and universal model of the superior colliculus, which satisfies the properties, mentioned in the text. Further simplifications can be made, if no separate camera turns are possible (no separate SCd visual map and static ICx-SCd-projections) or if an omnidirectional camera is used (modified SCs-SCd projection). **Right:** The representation of exemplary bimodal (hand clap) and simultaneous unimodal stimuli (waving hands) is shown for the auditory, visual and multimodal maps (MSO denotes the binaural cross-correlator). To evaluate response enhancement, the SCd-map is computed three times: with only visual (V), only auditory (A) and bimodal input (A+V).

4   Experiments and Benchmarks

4.1   Database Concept for Flexible Audio-Visual superposition

Since we are not processing highly specific features but modelling early stage mechanisms, the effects and properties of our simulations have to be basic and universally valid. The question, how to prove the general validity of the model in diverse and real situations, is a critical point, not only in this study. A common technique is to use recordings or realtime experiments in a restricted environment (lights and noise-bursts in a dark, anechoic chamber) for a detailed analysis. However, the relevance of those analysis to real situations must be doubt for several reasons: In reality, the stimuli are not point-like and, simply depending on the situation and the distance to the observer, occur in very different shapes, characteristics and dynamics. Another practice, which is widely used in the fields of neuroinformatics and artificial intelligence, is to generate simulations of the environment. Virtual experiments can be repeated and varied easily, but have the drawback of providing less complexity than real sensory inputs.

To overcome this dilemma, we combine recordings of real situations and off-line simulations in a novel approach. Separate recordings of sounds and visual scenes are stored in a database and can be assembled to randomly arranged but reasonable situations. The type of stimuli and scenes targets typical situations in man-machine-interaction, while the database can be extended for another purpose or to reproduce other simple multimodal setups (e.g. such as in [7]). Up to now, the visual stimuli include local motion (gestures, single hand-claps, waving hands) and translations (people walking by, getting closer or away). Since motion coded by intensity differences is the only visual cue in the model, the experiments become widely independent from object color, illumination or background texture. For the acoustic database, we recorded different words and claps and reproduced them from a number of angles in a lecture hall ($\approx 300 m^2, 1 sec$ reverberating time). Yet the current database, including five persons, 14 visual and 10 acoustic events offers a combinational variety, that is suitable for reproducible statistical interpretations. To share ideas and experiences, the data are public available from `http://cortex.informatik.tu-ilmenau.de/~schauer` , where also a more detailed description of the experimental setup is provided.

4.2 Results

The novel database concept enables a new method of testing and evaluating our model, already in respect to real applications. Beside single experiments, it is possible to inquire benchmarks and statistical analysis. In the context of our simulations, we define a benchmark as a number of repetitions of a multimodal experiment, where certain temporal and/or spatial parameters of the scene vary. For every scene, the multimodal part of the model is simulated three times: with only visual, auditory and multimodal input. Based on these results, the amount of response enhancement can be measured in a similar way to neurophysiological recordings as $((CM - SM_{max}) \cdot 100)/SM_{max}$, where CM is the combined-modality response and SM_{max} is the response to the most effective single-modality stimulus [10]. The response itself is the temporal integration of the activity at one position in the spatial map. With the help of benchmark tests, it was possible to demonstrate major properties of the sensory representation in our biologically inspired model:

Response enhancement is performed for correlated multimodal stimulation. (fig. 3) The amount of response enhancement and the spatial disparities and effective time windows in which this effect occurs, are plausible compared to biological perception and can also be adjusted to the demands of specific applications. E.g. the spatial window for grouping auditory and visual stimuli is depending on the minimum object distance and can be realized by applying large receptive fields.

Response depression occurs for simultaneous but spatially separated events. In the model, this property is based on the global inhibitory mechanism of the WTA-network. In a corresponding benchmark (not plotted) the depression ranges from 10-60%.

Maximal enhancement occurs with minimally effective stimuli. It was shown, that a typical WTA-process is suitable to cause an inverse proportionality of single modality effectiveness and multimodal response enhancement. (fig. 4)

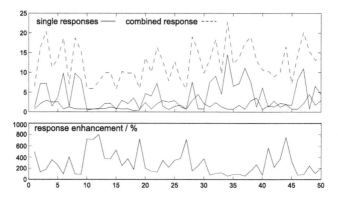

Fig. 3. Benchmark of 50 different multimodal events (clapping/waving hands and simultaneous speech as described in 4.1). The activity at the center-position of the auditory stimulus is shown. Response enhancement was observed in all scenes and ranges from 70-800%.

5   Conclusions

Based on a robust sound localization and scene motion, simply coded by temporal intensity differences, it was possible to demonstrate essential properties of sub-cortical sensory integration by simulating a dynamic neural field of Amari type with bimodal inputs. Response enhancement, response depression and the relation of maximum enhancement to least effective single modality stimuli where shown.

Further, the proposed concept of generating virtual audio-visual experiments with the help of a database of real-world scenes enables a wide range of new analysis. The spatial and temporal parameters of early multisensory integration (time-windows, receptive fields) can now be discussed by means of statistical benchmarks, already in the context of real situations and concrete applications. Along with the first simulations, we gained new insights in the mechanisms of early saliency or attention. An example is the interpretation of the very large receptive fields in the SCd, that are necessary for grouping even spatially separated stimuli, if multimodal events occur close to the observer. If, e.g. command words and gestures are processed, a person's head and hands are represented in noticeable different directions, but contributing to one multimodal event. In this situation, a high spatial resolution in the auditory and visual representations would be counterproductive. In general one can assume, that the reliability of a multimodal activation is much more important than a high localization precission (as observed e.g. during saccade generation in the superficial SC).

Although it is imaginable to perform also the initiation of motor commands and map shifting on the base of the databank, we strive for a realtime capable implementation on an experimental robotic platform and tests in real man-machine communication. The practical aspect of the application of the model is an expected significant advantage in the detection and tracking of users interacting with the mobile robot.

This work was supported by Deutsche Forschungsgemeinschaft, grant to GK 164,1-96.

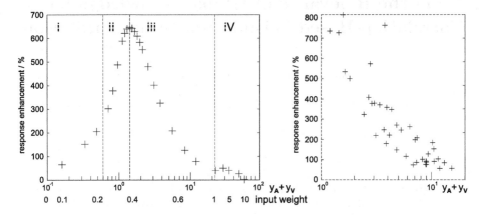

Fig. 4. Ineffective single-modality stimuli should produce the strongest response enhancement. **Left:** An experiment with correlated stimuli was repeated 26 times with varying input-weights of the bimodal WTA-network. The single-modality responses $y_A + y_V$ are plotted against the amount of response enhancement in the corresponding multimodal experiment. The WTA-topology and the sigmoidal output of the Amari-neurons causing four characteristic intervals: I) subthreshold range, additive combination of very weak responses, II) beginning of WTA-type behavior, III) normal WTA-process, saturation for multimodal stimulation only, IV) saturation, even for single-modality activation. **Right:** The neurophysiologic plausible condition, where single-modality activation and response enhancement are inversely proportional (interval III) was realized in the benchmark (compare fig.3)

References

1. Amari, S. *Dynamics of pattern formation in lateral inhibition type neural fields.* Biological Cybernetics 27:77–87, 1977.
2. Jens Blauert. *Spatial Hearing..* MIT Press, 1996.
3. G. Ehret and R.Romand The Central Auditory System. Oxford University Press, 1997.
4. Gross, H.-M., Boehme, H.-J. PERSES – a Vision-based Interactive Mobile Shopping Assistant. in: Proc. IEEE SMC 2000, pp. 80–85.
5. L.A. Jeffress. A place theory of sound localization. *Journal of Comperative Physiological Psychology*, 41:35–39, 1948.
6. John Lazzaro and Carver Mead. A silicon model of auditory localization. Neural Computation, 1(1):41–70, 1989.
7. Rucci, M., Wray, J., Edelman, G.M. Robust localization of auditory and visual targets in a robotic barn owl. Robotics and Autonomous Systems 30, 181–193, 2000.
8. Schauer, C., Zahn, Th., Paschke, P., Gross, H.-M. Binaural Sound Localization in an Artificial Neural Network. in: Proc. IEEE ICASSP 2000, pp. II 865–868.
9. Schiller, P.H. A model for the generation of visually guided saccadic eye movements. in: Models of the visual cortex, D. Rose, V.G. Dobson (Eds). Wiley, 1985, pp 62–70
10. Stein, B.E. and Meredith, M.A. The Merging of the Senses. The MIT Press, 1993.
11. M. T. Wallace, L. K. Wilkinson, B. E. Stein. Representation and Integration of multisensory Inputs in Primate Superior Colliculus. Journal of Neurophysiology. Vol. 76, No.2: 1246–1266, 1996

On the Relevance of Global Knowledge for Correlation-Based Seismic Image Interpretation

Melanie Aurnhammer and Klaus Tönnies

Computer Vision Group, Otto-von-Guericke University, Postfach 4120
39016 Magdeburg, Germany
{aurnhamm,klaus}@isg.cs.uni-magdeburg.de

Abstract. Matching horizons across faults in seismic data is an application problem arising from the field of structural geology. Automating this task is difficult because of the small amount of local information typical for seismic images. In this paper, we examine the hypothesis that the problem can only be solved satisfactorily by introducing global knowledge in addition to local features. Furthermore, an extension of the current approach is proposed, which aims at computing a throw value for every pixel at a fault.

1 Introduction

The interpretation of seismic images is an area in which computer vision and pattern recognition methods are used with increasing success. Nonetheless, several tasks of structural interpretation are still performed manually. Structural interpretation comprises the localisation and interpretation of *faults*, tracking of uninterrupted seismic *horizons* and correlating, i.e. matching these horizons across faults. Horizons indicate boundaries between rocks of different lithology, while faults are discrete fractures across which there is measurable displacement of strata. The amount of vertical displacement associated with a fault at any location is termed the *throw* of the fault.

While tracking of uninterrupted horizon segments has been automated satisfactorily by using low-level image processing methods, automatic interpretation of fault patterns on seismic sections poses many problems, especially those of matching horizons across faults. Horizon matching and thereby determining geologically valid assignments is an important but time consuming, as well as highly subjective, task of structural interpretation. Earlier approaches to solve this problem [1,2] suffered from using local image information only. In [3], we presented an approach, which solved the problem for a certain class of faults (normal faults) by introducing global knowledge into the interpretation process. A geological model was developed, based on local and global measurements as well as on local and global constraints. Results confirmed the suitability of the approach and methods chosen, although in two of fourteen cases, no geologically valid solution could be found. We believe this to be due to the particular unreliability of at least parts of the seismic data. Furthermore, the definition of horizons

B. Michaelis and G. Krell (Eds.): DAGM 2003, LNCS 2781, pp. 370–377, 2003.

was difficult because of noise or rapid changes of geology. In cases, where the data is of poor quality, an approach which requires fewer input horizons could improve the reliability of matchings. Moreover, detailed fault interpretation would benefit from a throw value computed for every pixel at a fault line. We call this a *continuous* approach, while matching defined horizons is referred to as *discrete* approach.

As for the discrete case, a solution to the continuous matching problem is admissible only if it is geologically valid. The most promising strategy to fulfill this requirement is, to build a continuous solution upon the result of the discrete matching, since it will then follow the geological model defined in [4]. We expect that neither in the discrete nor in the continuous case it is sufficient to rely on local image information only.

In this paper, we show the relevance of introducing a geological model into the matching process. We first examine the reliability of the local image information, and then describe the calculation of the local measurement for the discrete approach. Various experiments are reported, which examine the significance of local as well as global knowledge. Furthermore, a strategy for the generation of an appropriate initial solution for a continuous process is proposed.

2 Local Attributes

2.1 Image Information

Reflectors in seismic images usually correspond to horizons which indicate boundaries between rocks of markedly different lithology. It is theoretically possible to relate the reflection amplitude, or grey value, to the amount of the acoustic impedance change between boundaries, and to determine whether the reflection originates from an interface with a positive or negative reflection coefficient [5]. In seismic images, the sign of the reflection coefficient or *polarity* results from the grey value. Usually, dark values refer to negative, and light values to positive polarity. Since an individual seismic reflection is only defined by its amplitude and polarity, a correlation of reflections according to those attributes is insufficient. Furthermore, the seismic trace is usually a composite of the reflections at each acoustic impedance contrast. The reflections interfere if the seismic pulse is longer than the separation between some of these contrasts. Hence, there is no straightforward one-to-one relationship between the composite seismic trace and the acoustic boundaries [5]. It is thus more appropriate to analyse reflector sequences rather than single reflectors. Reflector sequences are distinguishable by characteristic patterns which can usually be found on either side of a fault. In general, they are relatively constant over some distance. Thus, character permits correlation of reflections, even across faults.

2.2 Cross-Correlation Coefficient

Comparing two similar functions or traces, one of which is delayed in time (vertical axis) relative to the other, is a well known problem at many processing stages of seismic data. Cross-correlation (CC) is the measurement which is usually employed to solve this task. The main advantage of using CC is its insensitivity to local differences in the amplitudes of the two waveforms, compared to other methods [6]. This is an important characteristic in regard to seismic data, since the same horizon often shows differences in reflection amplitude or grey value on different sides of the fault. Furthermore, CC is especially useful when the data quality is poor [7].

Formally, the CC $P_{xy}(L)$ between two functions of finite length x_i and y_i ($i = 1, 2, \ldots, n$) can be defined as

$$P_{xy}(L) = \sum_{i=1}^{n-L} x_{i+L} y_i \quad (-m < L < +m),$$ (1)

where L is the lag or displacement of x_i relative to y_i and m the maximum lag value of the function.

The CC function is normalised by dividing by the geometric mean of the autocorrelation values at zero shift of the two traces:

$$P_{xy}(L)_{\text{norm}} = \frac{P_{xy}(L)}{\sqrt{P_{xx}(0) P_{yy}(0)}}.$$ (2)

Estimating the CC function by considering grey value functions whose length is equal to the fault length, does not constitute a reasonable method. This is due to the behaviour of a fault, which is characterised by a change of throw along the fault. The fault throw typically increases from zero, at the upper end of the fault plane, to a maximum in the central portion of the fault, followed by a decrease to zero at the lower limit of the fault plane. For this reason, it can only be assumed, that the throw remains approximately constant over a restricted neighbourhood.

These theoretical considerations are supported by experiments, one of which is shown exemplarily for one fault (see Figure 1). The CC function displayed in Figure 2(a) was calculated for different lags in both directions, using a window size equal to the fault length[1]. Within this region, the throw, which corresponds to the lag, varies between five and sixteen pixels. As expected, the CC function shows no clear indication for correlation.

In case of computing CC for predefined horizons, the problem arising from throw changes is solved by computing the measurement for windows of several pixels above and below the horizons.

2.3   Computing Cross-Correlation for Defined Horizons

The CC coefficient is applied in order to calculate a measurement for the similarity of horizon pairs (HPs), i.e. one horizon segment from either side. The calculation of the CC coefficient for each possible HP is performed on averaged

---

[1] Here, the fault length is defined by the distance from top to lowest horizon.

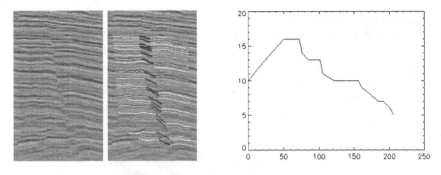

Fig. 1. Test fault with correlated horizons and resulting discrete throw function

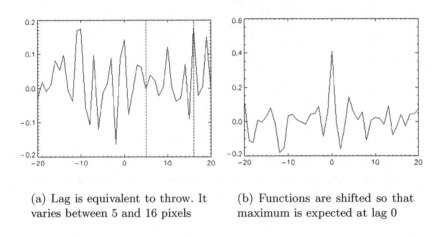

(a) Lag is equivalent to throw. It varies between 5 and 16 pixels

(b) Functions are shifted so that maximum is expected at lag 0

Fig. 2. CC functions calculated for (a) unscaled and (b) scaled grey values

amplitudes in direction of the particular horizon segment, over a neighbourhood, or window, of several pixels above and below this horizon (see Figure 3).

To estimate the parameter settings, experiments were performed on seven representative but simple test faults from four different data sets.

The decision on the appropriateness of a parameter is made according to the number of correct correlations concerning the optimal solution: the CC coefficients for left horizons, which belong to a HP contained in the solution, and all possible right counterparts are calculated. A correlation is correct, if the HP which actually belongs to the solution shows the maximum CC coefficient. False correlations are those, where the maximum CC coefficient corresponds to any other pair.

An appropriate range for averaging the grey values in horizon direction was found between three and eight pixels. In the following experiments, the grey values are averaged over five pixels.

Experiments showed, that computing the CC coefficient at a small distance from the fault leads to slightly better results compared to those obtained at the closest horizon pixel to the fault. This is probably due to distortions which may be present in the vicinity of the fault. Appropriate values for this distance ranged between three and ten pixels. From this range, the value of five pixels was chosen for the following experiments.

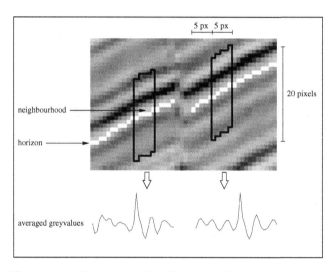

Fig. 3. Illustration of grey value function generation for calculation of CC

Function Scaling: Cross-correlation is extremely sensitive to the *stretching* of one of the two functions [6]. However, the strata often are unequally compressed on different sides of a fault, which yields the above mentioned changes of fault throw. In order to compensate for possible unequal compression inside a window, the CC is calculated for stepwise scaled functions of one side of the fault. Among the various CC values $P_{xy}(L)_{\text{norm}}$ thus obtained, the maximum is chosen. The local similarity $S_{l,r}$ of two horizon segments l and r is defined as their maximum normalised CC coefficient:

$$S_{l,r} = \max_{r \in R} \{P_{xy}(L)_{\text{norm}}\}. \tag{3}$$

The scaling range $R = \{+s, \dots, -s\}$ depends on the window size w. One of the averaged grey value functions is enlarged or reduced in steps of one pixel. For each direction, s is calculated using expression

$$s = \text{round}(\frac{1}{10}w), \tag{4}$$

for $w = (5, 10, 15, \dots, 50, 55, 60)$. This means that the function is scaled by $\{+1, \dots, -1\}$ pixel for $w = 5$ to $w = 10$, $\{+2, \dots, -2\}$ pixel for $w = 15$ to

$w = 20$ and so on. Scaling in steps of five pixels was found to be sufficient in the present case. Experiments showed, that increasing the scaling range beyond the range defined above leads to distortions of the CC values and thus deteriorates the results. Figure 4 compares the rate of correct assignments for CC coefficients calculated from scaled and unscaled functions. This rate is the average from the seven test faults. Scaling yielded better results, especially for window sizes above 15 pixels, although the difference between scaled and unscaled functions is not significant.

Window Size: The optimal window size is a compromise between a too small window, which leads to ambiguous results, and a too large one, where the throw change distorts the CC values.

Figure 4 shows the averaged percentage of correct assignments as a function of window size. Standard deviation values are between 0.13 and 0.28 for the scaled function and between 0.2 and 0.29 for the unscaled one. Reasonable window sizes range from about 15 to 40 pixels. The maximum value (66%) resulting from the scaled calculation was obtained for a window size of 30 pixels.

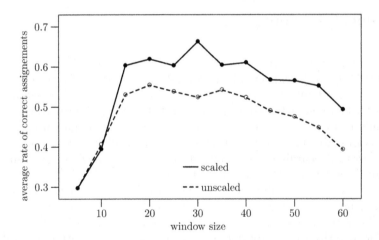

Fig. 4. Comparison of correct assignment rate of scaled and unscaled CC calculation for different window sizes. Shown is the averaged rate from seven test faults

2.4 Assessment of Local Measurement for Strata Matching

The hypothesis, that a solely local feature based approach is insufficient to solve the problem of matching strata across faults was corroborated by the experiments performed in Section 2.2 and 2.3.

It was shown exemplarily for one fault, that calculating the CC coefficients for a window size equal to the fault length did not yield an indication for correlation for a certain lag due to the variation of fault throw. In order to find matching horizons and therewith corresponding throw values, the CC coefficient was calculated for grey value functions of restricted length, where the throw is expected to be approximately constant. The average rate of correct assignments thus obtained for the seven test faults was 66% at maximum. Other test faults, which were not considered in this parameter selection, showed values far below this rate, e. g. only 6% in one case, or 37% for the fault shown in Figure 1. The experiments described in order to find a common window size appropriate for all data sets and faults tested, indicated that a suitable size range actually exists. Scaling one of the functions with a constant factor yielded improvements of the reliability of the CC coefficients, although the difference was not significant. If however, the true scaling factors, i.e. the fault throw function, were known in advance, we expect the results to be improved. Theoretically, the CC function should show a clear indication for correlation, if one of the functions is transformed in order to equalise the differences in strata compression on both sides.

3   Global Attributes

The global knowledge which was introduced into the discrete matching process was derived from the expected behaviour of the fault throw function. Estimating the throw of a fault is complicated by the fact, that faults are often not contained to their complete extent in a data set. Important information concerning the fault throw, such as amount and location of maximum displacement, or expectations about the throw gradient, is not available. Nonetheless, certain characteristics regarding the behaviour of the fault throw can be found. In our geological model [4], these are described by a measure of displacement variation and several constraints. Generating an initial solution for the continuous matching problem by interpolating the throw values obtained from the discrete correlations has the advantage, that this global knowledge is already included. In order to verify the appropriateness of such an initial solution, several experiments were performed. First, an appropriate interpolation of the discrete throw values was investigated. An appropriate polynomial should have far less degrees of freedom than the number of HPs, but should nonetheless be flexible enough to model the throw function. Moreover, the higher the degree of freedom, the higher the probability, that the function also follows artefact peaks or throughs. We compared polynomials from third to sixth degree to scale one of the two grey value functions for which the CC coefficients were calculated. The best results were obtained for 4th to 6th degree polynomials. The CC function shown in Figure 2(b) was obtained by using a 5th degree polynomial. An indication of correlation is attained at the correct lag (0.41 for lag=0), clearly separated from other local maxima.

With regard to the implementation of a continuous approach, an interesting question is, if an adequate interpolation of the fault throw function is possible with less HPs. Our experiments indicated, that reducing the number of HPs to a great extent (up to 60-70%), still allows a correlation-based matching. For the test fault shown in Figure 1, using only the seven HPs (37%) for which a correct correlation (see Section 2.3) was obtained, yielded the global maximum for the expected lag, although not clearly separated from other local maxima. This result was achieved even though only one HP from the lower ten was included.

4 Conclusion and Outlook

It was shown, that local knowledge, although relevant, is not sufficient to find geologically valid matchings of strata across a fault. The geological model designed for the discrete problem can be transferred to the continuous case by interpolation of the discrete solution. Since the number of HPs for throw function interpolation can be substantially reduced, a process is proposed, where only a few reliable HPs are used to generate the initial solution. These HPs can be either automatically or manually matched. The reliability of the initial solution can be estimated by recalculating the CC coefficient after transformation of one of the greyvalue functions by the interpolated fault throw function. Future work includes the investigation of such feedback loop as well as optimisation of the initial solution.

Acknowledgements. We would like to acknowledge Shell for the seismic data and fruitful discussions.

References

1. Kemp, L.F., Threet, J.R., Veezhinathan, J.: A neural net branch and bound seismic horizon tracker. In: 62nd Annual International Meeting, Expanded Abstracts, Houston, USA, Society of Exploration Geophysicists (1992)
2. Alberts, P., Warner, M., Lister, D.: Artificial neural networks for simultaneous multi horizon tracking across discontinuities. In: 70th Annual International Meeting, Expanded Abstracts, Calgary, Canada, Society of Exploration Geophysicists (2000)
3. Aurnhammer, M., Tönnies, K.: The application of genetic algorithms in structural seismic image interpretation. In Gool, L.V., ed.: Proceedings Pattern Recognition. Volume 2449 of Lecture Notes in Computer Science., Zurich, Switzerland, 24th DAGM Symposium, Springer Verlag (2002) 150–157
4. Aurnhammer, M., Tönnies, K.: Horizon correlation across faults guided by geological constraints. In: Proceedings of SPIE. Volume #4667., San Jose, California, USA (2002) 312–322
5. Badley, M.E.: Practical seismic interpretation. D. Reichel, Boston (1985)
6. Anstey, N.A.: Correlation techniques – a review. Geophysical Prospecting **12** (1964) 355–82
7. Telford, W.M., Geldart, L.P., Sheriff, R.E.: Applied Geophysics. Cambridge University Press (1990)

Automatic Pixel Selection for Optimizing Facial Expression Recognition Using Eigenfaces

Carmen Frank and Elmar Nöth

Lehrstuhl für Mustererkennung,
Universität Erlangen-Nürnberg,
Martensstraße 3, 91058 Erlangen, Germany,
{frank,noeth}@informatik.uni-erlangen.de
http://www5.informatik.uni-erlangen.de

Abstract. A new direction in improving modern dialogue systems is to make a human-machine dialogue more similar to a human-human dialogue. This can be done by adding more input modalities, e.g. facial expression recognition. A common problem in a human-machine dialogue where the angry face may give a clue is the recurrent misunderstanding of the user by the system. This paper describes recognizing facial expressions in frontal images using eigenspaces. For the classification of facial expressions, rather than using the whole image we classify regions which do not differ between subjects and at the same time are meaningful for facial expressions. Using this face mask for training and classification of *joy* and *anger* expressions of the face, we achieved an improvement of up to 11% absolute. The portability to other classification problems is shown by a gender classification.

1 Introduction

Dialogue systems nowadays are constructed to be used by a normal human being, i.e. a naive user. Neither are these users familiar with "drag and drop" nor do they want to read thick manuals about a lot of unnecessary functionality. Rather modern dialogue systems try to behave similar to a human-human dialogue in order to be used by such naive users. But what does a human-human dialogue looks like?

A human being uses much more input information than the spoken words during a conversation with another human being: the ears to hear the words and the vocal expression, the eyes to recognize movements of the body and facial muscles, the nose to smell where somebody has been, and the skin to recognize physical contact. In the following we will concentrate on facial expressions. Facial expressions are not only emotional states of a user but also internal states affecting his interaction with a dialogue system, e.g. helplessness or irritation.

At the moment, there are several approaches to enhance modern dialogue systems. The dialogue system *SmartKom* introduced in [Wah01] which is funded by the BMBF[1] is also one of the new powerful dialogue systems. It is a multimodal

---

[1] This research is being supported by the German Federal Ministry of Education and Research (*BMBF*) in the framework of the SmartKom project under Grant 01 IL 905 K7. The responsibility for the contents of this study lies with the authors.

B. Michaelis and G. Krell (Eds.): DAGM 2003, LNCS 2781, pp. 378–385, 2003.

multimedial system which uses speech, gesture and facial expression as input channels for a human-machine dialogue. The output is a combination of images, animation and speech synthesis.

One idea of facial expression recognition is to get as soon as possible a hint for an angry user in order to modify the dialogue strategies of the system and to give more support. This prevents the users from getting disappointed up to such an extent that they would never ever use the system again. If a system wants to know about the users internal state by observing the face, it first has to localize the face and then recognize the facial expression.

The task of facial expression recognition is to determine the emotional state of a person. A common method is to identify facial action units (AU). These AU were defined by Paul Ekman in [Ekm78]. In [Tia01] a neural-network is used to recognize AU from the coordinates of facial features like lip corners or the curve of eye brows. To determine the muscle movement from the optical flow when showing facial expressions is the task in [Ess95]. It is supplemented by temporal information to form a spatial-temporal motion energy model which can be compared to different models for the facial expressions. In [Kir90] eigenspaces and face symmetry are used to characterize a human face.

2   Algorithm

We propose a method where only pixels that are significant for facial expressions are used to create an eigenspace for facial expression recognition. These significant pixels are selected automatically by a training set of face images showing facial expressions. First we give a short introduction to standard eigenspaces. Then we show their disadvantages and introduce our face mask as improvement.

2.1   Introduction to Eigenspaces

Eigenspace methods are well known in the topic of face recognition (e.g. [Tur91], [Yam00], [Mog94]). In a standard face recognition system, one eigenspace for each person is created using different images of this person. Later, when classifying a photo of an unknown person, this image is projected using each of the eigenspaces. The reconstruction error of the principal component representation is an effective indicator of a match.

To create an eigenspace with training images a partial Karhunen-Loéve transformation, also called principal component analysis (PCA) is used. It is a dimensionality reduction scheme that maximizes the scatter of all projected samples, using N sample images of a person $\{x_1, x_2, \ldots, x_N\}$ taking values in an n-dimensional feature space. Let μ be the mean image of all feature vectors. The total scatter matrix is then defined as

$$S_T = \sum_{k=1}^{N} (x_k - \mu)(x_k - \mu)^T. \tag{1}$$

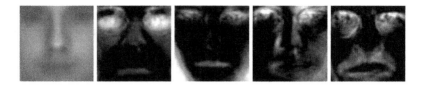

Fig. 1. The leftmost image is the average image of all training images for the *anger* eigenspace. The following images are some of the high order eigenvectors (eigenfaces) of this eigenspace, which model brightness of eyes, face shape, lightning and lips.

In PCA, the optimal projection W_{opt} to a lower dimensional subspace is chosen to maximize the determinant of the total scatter matrix of the projected samples,

$$W_{opt} = arg \max_{W} |W^T S_T W| = [w_1, w_2, \ldots, w_m] \qquad (2)$$

where $\{w_i | i = 1, 2, \ldots m\}$ is the set of n-dimensional eigenvectors of S_T corresponding to the set of decreasing eigenvalues. These eigenvectors have the same dimension as the input vectors and are referred to as Eigenfaces.

In the following sections we assume that high order eigenvectors correspond to high eigenvalues. Therefore high order eigenvectors hold more relevant information.

2.2   Disadvantages of Standard Eigenspaces

An advantage and as well a disadvantage of eigenspace methods is their capability of finding significant differences between the input samples which need not be significant for the classification problem. This feature enables eigenspace methods to model a given sample of a n-dimensional feature space in an optimal way using only a m-dimensional space.

But if one has significant differences between training samples not relevant for separating the classes, nevertheless they appear in the high order eigenvalues and maybe fudge the classifying result. An example for such differences of training samples is lighting. Training samples created under different lighting conditions constitute an eigenspace which model the light in high order eigenvectors. In Figure 1 the first five eigenvectors (often called eigenfaces) from an *anger* eigenspace can be seen modeling light and face contour but not facial expressions. Therefore in face recognition often the first p eigenvectors are deleted as described in [Bel96].

2.3   Eigenfaces for Facial Expression Recognition

When using eigenfaces for facial expression recognition of unknown faces, one possibility is to calculate one eigenspace for each facial expression from a labeled database of different persons.

The classification procedure corresponds to that of face recognition: project a new image to each eigenspace and select the eigenspace which best describes

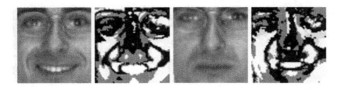

Fig. 2. The first image is the *smile* face followed by the difference when projecting this image to *smile* and *anger* eigenspace. The next images are the *anger* face and its difference image.

the input image. This is accomplished by calculating the residual description error.

In addition to the disadvantage mentioned above, a problem for facial expression classification is that the person itself, whose facial expression should be classified, is unknown.

Each person uses a different smile. Each person has a different appearance of the neutral face. But each smile of each person should be classified as *smile*. And even facial expressions result from very subtle changes in the face and therefore do not show up in the high order eigenvectors.

2.4   Adapting Eigenfaces for Facial Expression Recognition

In order to deal with this fact we tried to eliminate parts of the face with a high level of changes between different persons which do not contribute to facial expressions. To find out which parts of the face are unnecessary for classifying facial expression, we also use an eigenspace approach.

Imagine we have a training set F_κ of l samples y_i with similar characteristics for each class Ω_κ, $\kappa \in 1, \ldots k$. Thus there is different illumination, different face shape etc. in each set F_κ. Reconstructing one image with each of our eigenspaces results in k different samples. The reconstructed images do not differ in characteristics like illumination, because this is modeled by each eigenspace. But they differ in facial expression specific regions, such as the mouth area.

So we can obtain a mask vector $\boldsymbol{m}$ as the average of difference images using a training set S. For a two class problem this is done in the following way,

$$\boldsymbol{m} = \frac{1}{|S|} \sum_{y_i \in S} V_1^T (\boldsymbol{y}_i - \boldsymbol{\mu}_1) - V_2^T (\boldsymbol{y}_i - \boldsymbol{\mu}_2) \tag{3}$$

where $|S|$ stands for the cardinality of set S and V_κ^T is the eigenspace for class κ. In Figure 2 the *smile* and *anger* face of a man are projected to both eigenspace and the resulting difference images are shown. Before training an eigenspace, we now delete vector components (in this case pixels) from all training samples whose corresponding component of the mask vector $\boldsymbol{m}$ is smaller than a threshold θ. The threshold is selected heuristically at the moment. The same components must be deleted from an image before classification. A positive side effect is the reduction of feature dimension. The face mask used for our experiments (see. Figure 3) eliminates about 25% of all pixels.

Fig. 3. The first image is an average of faces projected to *smile* and *anger* eigenspaces. This image binarised with a threshold of $\theta = 210$ is the next to the right. All *white* pixels are deleted before further computation. The next two images are equivalent, but trained for gender classification. The used threshold is $\theta = 165$.

Fig. 4. Three persons from AR-Face Database showing *smile* and *angry* facial expressions.

3   Data

All experiments described in this article are performed using the AR-Face Database [Mar98]. From this database we selected one image per person showing a *smile* or *angry* facial expression. This results in 270 images altogether: 32% with glasses and 17% with facial hair. The whole set was split into 4 parts, 3 parts were used for training and one for testing in a leave one out method. No normalization was done. The tip of the nose, marked by a naive person, served as a reference point to cut the face from the whole image.

Samples of this database are displayed in Figure 4.

4   Experiments

4.1   Facial Expression Mask

The first task is to generate a mask which emphasizes regions of the face important for facial expressions and deletes other regions. We use a set of training images, to create one *anger-* and one *smile*-eigenspace. The same set of images is used to create a mask using equation 3.

This means in detail: project and reproject one image with each eigenspace, subtract the resulting images, calculate an average image over all difference images created from the training set.

Using a threshold θ the mask image is converted to a binary image. Preliminary experiments showed 210 to be a suitable value when using 1 byte of color information for each channel. Such a binarised mask with the corresponding average image can be seen in Figure 3.

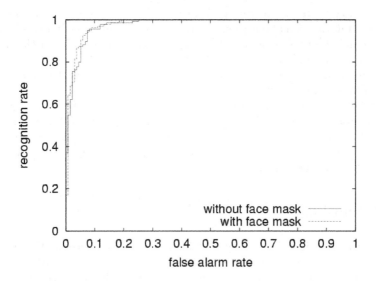

Fig. 5. Recognition rate compared to false alarm rate when using grey level images and a threshold of 210.

4.2 Facial Expression Classification

The images used for the experiments are similar to the faces in Figure 4 and have a size of 64 × 64 pixels. The classes used were *anger* and *smile*.

To get an idea of the obtained improvement by the face mask, we show both ROC-curves in one chart, see Figure 5. When using *grey level* information of an image the improvement is about 11% points for a low false alarm rate. For *rgb* images we achieve an improvement of 5%. The total recognition rates are 95% for *rgb* and 93% for *grey level* images.

To prove the portability of our method to other classification problems, we implemented a female/male classifier. The recognition rates achieved without facial masks were 94% for a medium false alarm rate. The face masks obtained an improvement of 2% absolute.

5 Application

The knowledge about a users internal state is important to a modern personalized dialogue system. The possible internal user state not only include anger and happiness but also helplessness or confusing. An example application for giving useful information to an automatic dialogue system by analyzing facial expression is a dialogue about current television program. A happy face of a user when getting information about a thriller indicates an affectation for thriller. From now on this user can be lead to a happy mood when thriller are presented to him first while information about other genres is presented afterwards.

Up to now there are no results from naive persons using a dialogue system which uses information about their emotional state. The reason for this is that on the one hand the users must not know about this functionality of the dialogue system in order to show natural behavior. On the other hand they should be familiar with the system because the dialogue must be as similar as possible to a human-human interaction.

In Wizard-of-Oz experiments the users seemed not to be confused by the facial camera, they forgot being filmed during the dialogue. The questionnaires which are filled out after each dialogue showed the users are not aware of facial expressions influencing the dialogue. They are content with the system and would like to use it an other time.

6   Conclusion

Our experiments show that significant information for discriminating facial expressions can not be found in the high order eigenvectors of standard eigenspaces. Moreover fudging information is represented by the high order eigenvectors. This is avoided by using masked faces for the eigenspace training. The used facial mask is automatically trained from a set of faces showing different expressions. It emphasizes discriminating facial regions and fades out unnecessary or mistakable parts.

Using this face mask for training and classification of *joy* and *anger* expressions of the face, we achieve an improvement of 11% when using grey level images. The described method for data selection to train eigenspaces for facial expression recognition can be used for other classification task, too. A separate face mask is necessary, because different features of faces appear at different positions in a face. When using this method for gender classification it results to an improvement of 2%.

The next steps for us will be to increase the recognition rates for the rgb case by a more detailed mask and the application of the mask method to the detection of faces using eigenspace methods.

7   Remarks

There are lots of differences between facial expressions. E.g. neither does each smile result from the same positive emotional state of a person nor does each person express a positive emotional state with the same smile. A smile may express love to someone else but a slightly different smile says 'I am sorry'.

The same is true for anger. And especially anger is an emotional state which is expressed in very different manners by different individuals. Some form wrinkles at the forehead, others nearly close their eyes, knit their eyebrows or press the lips together.

But *angry* is besides *helplessness* the most important state for an automatic human-machine dialogue system a user can be in. The anger of a user gives a hint for problems in communication which should be solved by the dialogue system.

Of course it would be nice to know that a user is happy and satisfied with the system but in this case no system reaction is necessary.

The *angry* and *neutral* state of a person are those states which are most difficult to discriminate. A human person produced 50% false alarms and 95% recognition rate when classifying *anger* vs. *neutral* faces from the described database. The reason for this high false alarm rate is that, as mentioned above anger is expressed in very different ways and people often hide anger. The classification of facial expressions of a familiar person is much easier for the human as well as for an automatic system.

The recognition rates for the classification of *angry* and *neutral* user states are much lower than for *angry* and *smile*. Using a mask with a threshold $\theta = 135$ for grey level images it is 70%.

References

[Bel96]   Belhumeur, P.; Hespanha, J.; Kriegman, D.: *Eigenfaces vs. Fisherfaces: Recognition Using Class Specific Linear Projection*, in *European Conference on Computer Vision '96*, 1996, S. 45–58.

[Ekm78]   Ekman, P.; Friesen, W.: *The Facial Action Coding System: A Technique for the Measurement of Facial Movement*, in *Consulting Psychologists Press, Palo Alto, CA*, 1978.

[Ess95]   Essa, I.; Pentland, A.: *Facial Expression Recognition Using a Dynamic Model and Motion Energy*, in *Proceedings of the Fifth International Conference on Computer Vision*, 1995, S. 360–367.

[Kir90]   Kirby, M.; Sirovich, L.: *Application of the Karhunen-Loève Procedure for the Characterization of Human Faces*, *TPAMI*, Bd. 12, Nr. 1, 1990, S. 103–108.

[Mar98]   Martinez, A.; Benavente., R.: *The AR Face Database*, Purdue University, West Lafayette, IN 47907–1285, 1998.

[Mog94]   Moghaddam, B.; Pentland, A.: *Face Recognition Using View–Based and Modular Eigenspaces*, in *Vismod, TR-301*, 1994.

[Tia01]   Tian, Y.; Kanade, T.; Cohn, J.: *Recognizing Action Units for Facial Expression Analysis*, *IEEE Transactions on Pattern Analysis and Machine Intelligence (PAMI)*, Bd. 23, Nr. 2, 2001, S. 97–115.

[Tur91]   Turk, M.; Pentland, A.: *Face Recognition Using Eigenfaces*, in *Proceedings of Computer Vision and Pattern Recognition*, 1991, S. 586–591.

[Wah01]   Wahlster, W.; Reithinger, N.; Blocher, A.: *SmartKom: Multimodal Communication with a Life–Like Character*, in *Eurospeech 2001*, 2001, S. 1547–1550.

[Yam00]   Yambor, W. S.; Draper, B. A.; Beveridge, J. R.: *Analyzing PCA–based Face Recognition Algorithms: Eigenvector Selection and Distance Measures*, in *Second Workshop on Empirical Evaluation Methods in Computer Vision*, 2000.

Robust Image Sequence Mosaicing

Birgit Möller, Denis Williams, and Stefan Posch

Institute of Computer Science
Martin-Luther-University Halle-Wittenberg
06099 Halle / Saale (Germany)
{moeller,williams,posch}@informatik.uni-halle.de

Abstract. Mosaicing is a technique to efficiently condense the static information of an image sequence within one extended mosaic image. The core of mosaicing is to estimate a global transformation between images due to the global camera motion. This is usually accomplished by either matching segmented image features or exploiting all iconic image data directly within a featureless approach. In this paper we propose to combine aspects from both techniques where we abandon to segment features, however select pixels to be used for parameter estimation based on structural image data and information about independently moving scene parts. While this results in a speed up of the estimation process the main focus is to improve robustness with respect to ambiguities arising from homogeneous image regions and to motion in the scene.

1 Introduction

Image sequences can be represented efficiently using *mosaic images*. Within a mosaic the information of all images of the sequence is fused thus extending the camera's viewing angle by memorizing all parts of a scene that have ever been present in at least one image. Mosaics are generated by first estimating parameters of an appropriate motion model, e.g. a 2D-projective transformation in case of pure rotational motion including zooming as in our setup. Estimation is usually either based on corresponding image features (*feature-based*) or directly on intensity information (*featureless*). Given appropriate parameters the images are then integrated into the mosaic by fusing their intensity information. Computation of mosaics can be performed either offline or online. In the first case mosaicing is based on the whole sequence and a mosaic is available only after all images have been acquired. In the second case each image is processed instantaneously and a constantly evolving mosaic is available at any time.

Most mosaicing techniques are restricted to static scenes since large independently moving objects in the scene might disrupt the parameter estimation process and cause integration errors in the mosaic image. However, since static scenes cannot be assumed in any case, methods are required to handle dynamic scenes also. Irani et al. [1] introduced an approach where multiple mosaic representations are used to detect and track different independently moving scene parts without explicitly representing dynamic data. In contrast, our approach

B. Michaelis and G. Krell (Eds.): DAGM 2003, LNCS 2781, pp. 386–393, 2003.

yields a complete online scene representation by separating static and dynamic data. The static scene parts are integrated into one mosaic image while the dynamic information, basically given in terms of trajectories of detected moving objects, is represented separately, after a detailled analysis has been performed (sec. 3.1, [2]). Thus the formerly mentioned integration errors can be avoided, but the parameter estimation still might fail. To solve this problem, in this work we present an online approach for robust image registration in the presence of moving objects in the scene. The parameter estimation is focussed on a small but significant subset of pixels, similar to the work of Mégret et al. [3], however, contrary to that approach, not exclusively selected based on motion data, which is extracted during the distinction of static and dynamic image regions, but also derived from intensity information in single images. In this way the disrupting influence of independently moving scene parts as well as homogeneous regions is reduced. In the work of Ben-Ezra et al. [4] dominant motion estimation combined with selection of pixels is used for motion segmentation. As our goal encompasses more than just motion segmentation (we generate a complete scene representation), additional and more stable information about moving image regions is available and can be propagated over time leading to more accurate parameters. In conclusion, on the one hand no image features are segmented and matched, while on the other hand only relevant pixels are taken into account, resulting in a *hybrid* approach combining aspects of both feature-based and feature-less approaches.

2   Parameter Estimation

As outlined above the first class of algorithms for parameter estimation is based on image features, e.g. corners or edges. Transformation parameters between two images are computed from a set of pairs of corresponding features. Ben-Ezra et al. [5] introduced an approach where feature points are matched against possibly corresponding lines thus no explicit point correspondences are required although still appropriate feature points have to be extracted. Algorithms of the second class work directly on the image intensity information. Parameter estimation is accomplished by minimizing a suitable error function (e.g. the squared intensity difference [6] in the overlapping area of the images) with regard to the underlying motion model.

   Our approach for estimating robust transformation parameters is based on the featureless *projective flow* algorithm [7]. A projective reconstruction between two images is determined calculating the optical flow between both images constrained by a suitable motion model m_α. The optical flow is given by the well known *brightness constancy constraint equation*

$$v_x I_x + v_y I_y + I_t = 0$$

where I_x, I_y and I_t denote the image derivatives in x, y and time t. Thus, expressing the displacement vector $\boldsymbol{v} = [v_x, v_y]^T$ in terms of the motion model

m_α and summing up the values of the constraint equation for *all* valid pixels in the overlapping area of both images, the following error function results:

$$o(\alpha) = \sum_{x,y}((m_\alpha(x) - x)I_x + (m_\alpha(y) - y)I_y + I_t)^2$$

For minimization $o(\alpha)$ is differentiated with respect to the unknown parameters α and the resulting equations are solved.

Since employing a projective motion model for m_α yields a non-linear system of equations, the optimization is performed based on a pseudo-perspective model, which serves as a good approximation for the desired projective transformation. In this case a linear equation system results, which is solved using the gaussian method. The projective parameters can then be calculated directly from a minimal set of point correspondences given through the pseudo-perspective transformation. The whole optimization process is embedded into an iterative framework which runs over several image resolution levels.

3   Dynamic Scenes

As mentioned above most image registration techniques are restricted to image sequences of static scenes where motion is induced only by the active camera. In that case parameters of a suitable motion model can be reconstructed and all images be registered into a common mosaic frame. In case of dynamic scenes, when large independently moving objects are present in the scene, two types of problems arise. First the parameter estimation might fail due to moving objects concealing the camera motion that should be reconstructed. Secondly, even if the parameter estimation succeeds moving objects cause integration errors in the mosaic image since the same object is projected onto different positions in each registered frame and thus its image in the mosaic is blurred.

To overcome these problems in our approach static and dynamic scene information is separated. In a first step independently moving objects are detected and their dynamic information is extracted, as described in the following paragraph. Once moving image parts are known, these on the one hand affect the selection of significant pixels for parameter estimation (section 4) and are on the other hand excluded from the integration process to avoid blurring. Integration is usually done by fusing, e.g. averaging, the intensity information of all image pixels projected onto the same mosaic pixel. If motion information is available, only static pixels are taken into account. Thus a mosaic of the static scene background is generated which serves as reference for both motion detection and parameter estimation. In contrast to [3], where an offline approach for generating background mosaics of dynamic scenes was introduced, we primarily focus on online aspects aiming to provide a mosaic image at any time during processing of the sequence (i.e. only integrating the images available at a given point in time). Furtheron we don't restrict the selection of suitable pixels for parameter estimation to the use of motion data, but also include structural information.

3.1 Motion Detection and Tracking

In this paragraph the motion detection and tracking algorithms are briefly outlined while details are given in [2].

Given a correct projective transformation between two images, in our case the background mosaic and the current sequence image, independently moving objects are detected by calculating pixelwise intensity residuals between the registered images. Pixels where this residual exceeds a certain threshold are classified as moving. Since even in static image regions single residuals larger than the chosen threshold might appear (e.g. due to image noise) the calculation is averaged in a neighborhood of each pixel usually sized 3 x 3 or 5 x 5.

Based on this pixel classification, dynamic information of moving objects which is not represented in the mosaic of the scene background, is extracted by tracking these objects over time. For this purpose regions are segmented from the motion data. To reduce image noise regions exhibiting a size below a given threshold are excluded in further considerations. The remaining regions are grouped into connected components which are tracked based on size, position and intensity histograms. Tracking components and not regions allows robust tracking despite variance in segmentation. The center of mass positions of tracked components yield trajectory data for each moving object which is sufficient to characterize its dynamic behaviour within the processed image sequence. Together with the mosaic this dynamic information yields a complete representation of the scene. Furtheron trajectories yield clues for online verification of the motion data. E.g., when formerly moving objects become static or static objects start moving (and accordingly the mosaic representation of the static scene parts and the motion data need to be updated), the trajectories of these objects exhibit considerable changes within the variance of their trajectory point positions. Thus, detecting such changes and updating the motion data based on these results, pixel selection and with it parameter estimation is always based on a reliable set of pixels which is chosen by optimally exploiting the currently available information.

4 Pixel Selection

The *hybrid approach* we use to estimate perspective projections is based on a featureless method [7] and the observation that not all pixels involved in the optimization process contribute equally to a good result. Some pixels contain more information than others, some may even lead to wrong parameters, e.g. when the pixel is part of a moving object. Suitable selection of *relevant pixels* improves the parameter estimation and reduces the calculation time, provided the selection itself is not too expensive with respect to computational resources. Relevance is based on motion between images and on structure within images as described in the following.

4.1   Relevant Pixels

The overall aim is to estimate parameters for the motion induced by the active camera. Moving objects in the scene induce a different motion than the static background. If the parameter estimation expects only one single motion (as [7] does), all pixels are supposed to comply to this global motion. However, a pixel belonging to a moving object (*moving pixel*) does not agree with this global motion and thus deteriorates the parameters estimated. Therefore, moving pixels are excluded from the estimation process.

Since *moving pixels* are identified during the motion detection process (see 3.1), motion information is only available for previous, already processed images of the sequence. Thus exclusion of pixels is based solely on the motion detected in the previous image.

Besides motion information also the gray level information of single images is exploited. The more "structure" an image contains in the vicinity of a pixel, the easier it is to find the corresponding position in the subsequent image. Conversely for pixels lying in homogeneous regions it is much harder to find the right match. A good measure for the amount of structure at a given pixel is the gradient norm of the image. Therefore we introduce a *relevance measure R*, that is set to the gradient norm for each *not moving* pixel.

The optimization process of the parameter estimation is, however, not based on point correspondences but on image derivatives. In the resulting linear equations the influence of a pixel is proportional to the magnitude of the derivatives at that position. Thus, pixels in homogeneous regions have little influence on the estimation process anyway, and since the values of their derivatives are mainly due to noise in the image this influence introduces mostly errors. So selecting pixels with high derivatives corresponds to selecting the ones with the most influence resulting in a faster parameter estimation due to the reduced number of pixels.

This measure is used to select as *relevant* all pixels with R above a threshold θ chosen depending on the maximal value (usually we use $\theta = 0.15 \cdot \max_{\boldsymbol{x}}\{R(\boldsymbol{x})\}$ which leaves us with about 8-27% of the pixels of the images in the example shown below). This way the number of selected pixels can vary according to image content.

4.2   Initialization

As we have no motion information for the first image to be processed we cannot exclude *moving pixels*. If there is too much (object-)motion between the first two frames of the image sequence the parameter estimation will fail. So this situation is to be avoided, either by being sure there are no moving objects (or only few small ones) in the first two frames, by providing motion information for the first frame or by providing correct perspective parameters for the transformation between the first two frames so the estimation can start one frame later.

Fig. 1. Six images out of 689 of an example image sequence.

5   Results

The proposed algorithms have been evaluated on various image sequences. In this section, results for one exemplary sequence are presented (Fig.1), where a person is moving in front of a whiteboard while writing on it. As already stated, the overall goal is to represent this sequence by integrating the static background parts (e.g. whiteboard, table and wall) into a mosaic and extracting the dynamic information of the person in addition, where the second aspect is not further considered for the purpose of this paper.

Fig. 2. From left to right: reference mosaic, current image and motion map. Note: The motion detection is sensitive enough to also find the shadow of the depicted person.

In this example the scene is initially static, thus correct parameters can be calculated as argued in section 4.2. Once these are given, independently moving objects are detected for each new image with regard to the current mosaic representation (Fig.2). The resulting moving regions are used twice: once during image integration and the second time within the pixel selection process for the next image (as described in section 4).

Relevant pixels resulting from thresholding the gradient image, as proposed in 4.1, are shown in Fig.3. As can be seen in the final mosaic image (Fig.5), in this way a representation of the static scene background is generated covering information from all 689 images of the sequence. This incremental evolving mosaic is available anytime during processing of the sequence and provides also information about areas of the scene which are currently occluded by the moving person. The moving regions are correctly detected and excluded from integration. They are represented separately in a correspondence graph (see [2]) which is not described here as already mentioned.

The necessity for pixel selection as proposed in this paper is demonstrated in Fig.4. The estimation process fails completely due to erroneous information

Fig. 3. Left motion map, middle gradient image, and on the right the resulting relevant pixels.

introduced by pixels excluded with our approach. In other image sequences including motion this effect often occurs either as serious as shown in the example rendering mosaicing completely impossible or inducing a gradual shift of parameters estimated that leads to a significant degradation of image quality.

Fig. 4. Parameter estimation without pixel selection. Reference image (left), current image (middle), and distorted image after transformation (right).

As explained in section 4.1, the number of pixels selected for the parameter estimation varies depending on the contents of the current image. Basically the time needed for estimating parameters is reduced with decreasing number of selected pixels, typically we achieve a speed up of about 20 %, if only 10 to 25 % of the total number of image pixels are selected. However, in the presence of many erroneous moving pixels, which for example occur when inaccurate parameters are provided, only very few pixels might be selected as relevant. In such a case parameter estimation becomes difficult due to a lack of available image information and the algorithm then performs increasingly more iterations. This leads to higher computation times despite the large reduction of pixels considered. Thus, to ensure a robust estimation, an appropriate lower bound for the number of selected pixels is required, which is not included so far.

Finally it has to be mentioned that the quality of the calculated parameter set depends on the distribution of the selected pixel subset. If it is distributed non-uniformly over the image, a correct parameter estimation might be impossible. Therefore additional constraints for ensuring a uniform pixel distribution are necessary.

Fig. 5. The resulting mosaic for the whole sequence.

6   Conclusion

We presented an online approach for robust mosaicing of image sequences. By separating static and dynamic information and focussing the parameter estimation on a subset of relevant pixels, chosen based on structural data as well as motion information, it becomes possible to extract a mosaic based background representation from all images of a sequence. Although additional computation is necessary to select relevant pixels the total amount of time spent estimating parameters is reduced. However, one has to ensure that enough relevant pixels are selected as outlined in the previous section. The proposed algorithm can easily be modified to work with other featureless methods for estimating image transformations, and it can also be extended to include further pixel relevance measures, e.g. color information or texture-based features.

References

1. Irani, M., Rousso, B., Peleg, S.: Computing occluding and transparent motions. International Journal of Computer Vision **12** (1994) 5–16
2. Möller, B., Posch, S.: Detection and tracking of moving objects for mosaic image generation. In: Pattern Recognition, Proc. of 23rd DAGM Symposium. LNCS 2191 (2001) 208–215
3. Mégret, R., Saraceno, C., Kropatsch, W.: Background mosaic from egomotion. International Conference on Pattern Recognition **1** (2000) 571–574
4. Ben-Ezra, M., Peleg, S., Rousso, B.: Motion segmentation using convergence properties. ARPA Image Understanding Workshop (1994) 1233–1235
5. Ben-Ezra, M., Peleg, S., Werman, M.: Robust, real-time motion analysis. DARPA Image Understanding Workshop (1998)
6. Irani, M., Anandan, P., Hsu, S.: Mosaic based representations of video sequences and their applications. In: Proceedings of International Conference on Computer Vision. (1995) 605–611
7. Mann, S., Picard, R.: Video orbits of the projective group: A new perspective on image mosaicing. Technical Report 338, MIT Media Laboratory Perceptual Computing Section (1996)

Gibbs Probability Distributions for Stereo Reconstruction

Dmitrij Schlesinger

Dresden University of Technology
schles@ics.inf.tu-dresden.de

Abstract. A new approach for stereo reconstruction is proposed. This approach is based on a Gibbs probability distribution for surfaces in 3D space. The problem of stereo reconstruction is formulated then as a Bayes decision task. The main difference compared with known methods is the use of a more realistic cost function. In case of stereo reconstruction this function can be designed in some natural way, taking into account the properties of the surface model used. The proposed method solves the Bayes decision task approximately by a Gibbs Sampler. Learning of unknown distribution parameters is included as well, using the Expectation Maximization algorithm.

1 Introduction

Actually many methods are known which deal with stereo reconstruction. One important and interesting direction we would like to refer is formed by those approaches, which use a-priori knowledge of the object (object surface) to be reconstructed. In the last few years, promising results were obtained especially by methods, which express stereo reconstruction problem in terms of energy minimization tasks (see e.g. [1]).

On the other hand energy minimization tasks are in fact a special case (namely the maximum a-posteriori decision) of more general Bayes decision tasks. Obviously, Bayes classification depends in general not only on the probability model, but on the used cost function too. It means, that the design of appropriate cost functions is as important as the development of more accurate (probability) models. This aspect was seemingly overseen so far. In this paper we would like to improve this situation by using both the modeling of surface to be reconstructed and the design of suitable cost function.

2 The Model

Our main assumption is that all considered surfaces can be represented by functions $z : \mathbb{R}^2 \to \mathbb{R}$, which assign depth $z(x,y)$ for each pair (x,y) of world coordinates. Let the processed volume be discrete, i.e. modeled by an orthogonal 3D lattice, where each triple (i,j,k) of integer coordinates corresponds to a

B. Michaelis and G. Krell (Eds.): DAGM 2003, LNCS 2781, pp. 394–401, 2003.
© Springer-Verlag Berlin Heidelberg 2003

point in 3D space. The "discrete version" of the function z can be viewed as a mapping $f : \mathbb{N}^2 \to \mathbb{N}$, that assigns exactly one value k for each pair (i, j).

Let $\mathcal{G}(R, E)$ be a graph with the set of nodes R, where each node r corresponds to exactly one pair (i, j) (and vice versa). Furthermore, we define the set of states $K = \{1, 2, \ldots, k_{max}\}$ as the set of all possible values of coordinate k. A mapping f can be understood as a labeling $f : R \to K$ of $\mathcal{G}$. We define the a-priori probability distribution of labelings as Gibbs distribution of second order:

$$p(f) \sim \prod_{(rr') \in E} g_{rr'}\big(f(r), f(r')\big)$$

The set of edges E is defined by the neighborhood relation on the set of pairs (i, j). We assume the four-neighborhood (other neighborhood structures can be used as well), thus a pair of nodes (r, r') is declared to be an edge if the corresponding pairs (i, j) and (i', j') fulfill $|i - i'| + |j - j'| = 1$.

The parameters of the distribution – the functions $g_{rr'} : K \times K \to \mathbb{R}$ – should be chosen taking into account the properties of the reconstructed surface. Here we consider the regular case only, assuming the same function for all edges, denoted by $g(k, k')$. In this paper we will use the following so called "hard function":

$$g(k, k') = \begin{cases} 1 & \text{if } |k - k'| \leq \delta, \\ 0 & \text{otherwise} \end{cases} \tag{1}$$

In this model surfaces have zero probability, if they contain "jumps" of k-coordinate (in neighboring nodes) greater than some predefined constant δ. Other possible functions are for example: $g(k, k') = \exp\big(-(k - k')^2/\sigma\big)$ – i.e. the bigger the jump the less probable it is; the Potts model – i.e. the surface is assumed to be piece-wise constant; etc.

Furthermore we assume, that the conditional probability of a stereo image pair (let us denote it by X), given the labeling f, can be written as

$$p(X \mid f) = \prod_{r \in R} q_r\big(X, f(r)\big) \tag{2}$$

where q_r are some local functions $q_r : K \to \mathbb{R}$ (for given images X). Let us consider this in more detail.

As usual for stereo reconstruction problems, two views of an 3D object are given. We call them the left and the right image. Assuming a known epipolar geometry (i.e. internal parameters of cameras and their locations), two transformations T_l and T_r are given, which map world points (r, k) into points of the left and right images respectively. Let $A(r, k)$ be a dissimilarity measure for corresponding pixels $p_l = T_l(r, k)$ and $p_r = T_r(r, k)$. It can be defined, for example, as the square difference of gray-values $\big(I_l(p_l) - I_r(p_r)\big)^2$. In addition, small neighborhoods of pixels p_l and p_r can be used to make it more robust. The dissimilarity measure can be considered as a kind of feature, extracted from a stereo pair. Thus the tuple of values $A(r, k)$, $\forall (r, k)$ for a given stereo pair is the observation X in (2). We define the local functions q_r as

$$q_r(k; \lambda) = C \cdot \frac{1}{\lambda^l} \cdot \exp\left[-\frac{A(r, k)}{\lambda}\right] \qquad (3)$$

where C is the normalizing constant, l is an empirical parameter and λ is an unknown parameter to be estimated. Such a choice of these functions follows from some simple coloring model of surface and the assumption, that the left and right images are produced independently – using the simplest model of Gaussian noise – given the surface f and its coloring. The parameter λ in (3) corresponds (up to scale) to the dispersion of noise. The value of parameter l is estimated empirically.

Consequently the joint probability distribution can be written as

$$p(f, X; \lambda) \sim \prod_{(r,r') \in E} g\big(f(r), f(r')\big) \cdot \prod_{r \in R} \frac{1}{\lambda^l} \exp\left[-\frac{A\big(r, f(r)\big)}{\lambda}\right] \qquad (4)$$

Supposing a known parameter value for λ, it seems to be reasonable to define the stereo reconstruction problem as a Bayes decision task. An often used choice is the maximum a-posteriori decision (MAP) – it corresponds to the formulation of stereo reconstruction as energy minimization task. In fact it follows from a very primitive cost function $C(d, f) = 1 - \delta(d, f)$, where the decision $d \in K^R$ is a labeling and δ is the Kronecker symbol. In this case the penalty for misclassification does not depend on the number of misclassified nodes. A better choice would be an additive cost function $C(d, f) = \sum_r c\big(d(r), f(r)\big)$, that assigns some penalty for each node. Let us denote by D the set of decisions for a node (thus the decision d is a mapping $d : R \to D$). It can be easy seen, that in this case the Bayes decision should be computed as

$$d^*(r) = \arg\min_{d(r) \in D} \sum_{k \in K} p\big(f(r) = k \mid X; \lambda\big) \cdot c\big(d(r), k\big) \qquad (5)$$

for each node $r \in R$ independently.

Let us consider now the local cost function $c\big(d(r), k\big)$. A simple choice might be, for example, again the delta function $c\big(d(r), k\big) = 1 - \delta\big(d(r), k\big)$ with $D = K$ (thus d is again a labeling). The penalty for a labeling d is then the number of misclassified nodes. The Bayes decision for each node is the state with highest a-posteriori probability.

Especially for the stereo reconstruction problem the local cost function $c\big(d(r), k\big)$ can be improved as follows. One can use the fact, that the set of states is naturally ordered – the set of states is really the set of z-coordinates. Thus the set of decisions D can be defined as the set of real values in a range $[1, k_{max}]$. Hence, the cost function can be designed in a manner, that it would depend on the distance between the decision and the "true" state. A simple choice is, for example, the square distance $\big(d(r) - k\big)^2$. The Bayes decision in this case is the mean value of all states $k \in K$:

$$d^*(r) = \sum_{k=1}^{k_{max}} p\big(f(r) = k \mid X; \lambda\big) \cdot k \tag{6}$$

Let us consider now the question, whether it is possible to learn the unknown parameter λ of the conditional probability distribution (2). To do this, we follow the Maximum Likelihood approach, i.e. we maximize the probability of the observation X with respect to λ:

$$p(X; \lambda) = \sum_f p(f, X; \lambda) \to \max_\lambda \tag{7}$$

In summary, the following tasks are to be solved:

 - The parameter λ should be estimated using (7).
 - The marginal probabilities $P\big(f(r) = k \mid X; \lambda\big)$ should be calculated.
 - The Bayes decision should be made by (6).

3   Approximate Solution

To maximize (7) we use the EM-algorithm [2,5,8] and maximize iteratively

$$\sum_f \alpha(f) \cdot \ln p(f, X; \lambda) - \sum_f \alpha(f) \cdot \ln \frac{p(f, X; \lambda)}{\sum_{f'} p(f', X; \lambda)}$$

which coincides with (7) if $\alpha(f) \geq 0$ and $\sum_f \alpha(f) = 1$. Each iteration consists of two steps. In the first step (E-step) α is chosen so that the second term reaches its maximum (with respect to $p(f, X; \lambda)$) at the given actual $p^{(n)}(f, X; \lambda^{(n)})$:

$$\alpha^{(n)}(f) = p^{(n)}(f \mid X; \lambda^{(n)}) \tag{8}$$

In the second step (M-step) the first term is maximized with respect to $p(f, X; \lambda)$ for the fixed α obtained in the E-step:

$$\sum_f \alpha^{(n)}(f) \cdot \ln p(f, X; \lambda) \to \max_\lambda \tag{9}$$

Let us consider the M-step in detail. We substitute (8) for α and (4) for p in (9). Avoiding all terms which do not depend on λ we obtain:

$$\arg\max_\lambda \sum_f p^{(n)}\big(f \mid X; \lambda^{(n)}\big) \cdot \sum_r \ln q_r\big(f(r); \lambda\big) =$$

$$\arg\max_\lambda \sum_r \sum_k p^{(n)}\big(f(r) = k \mid X; \lambda^{(n)}\big) \cdot \ln q_r(k; \lambda)$$

Finally substituting (3) we obtain the solution

$$\lambda^{(n+1)} = \frac{1}{|R| \cdot l} \sum_r \sum_k A(r, k) \cdot p^{(n)}\big(f(r) = k \mid X; \lambda^{(n)}\big) \tag{10}$$

One can see, that the main difficulty in both recognition task (5) and learning task (10) is the calculation of the marginal a-posteriori probabilities $p\big(f(r) = k\,|\,X;\lambda\big)$. Actually we do not know any algorithm, that computes these values exactly. To perform the EM-algorithm (as well as the final Bayes decision task) we estimate these probabilities using the Gibbs Sampler (see e.g. [4]). The main idea of this approach is to *generate* labelings according to the probability distribution $p(f\,|\,X;\lambda)$. This can be done by cycling through the nodes of the graph many times and generating each time a new state k for the current node r according to the conditional probability distribution

$$p\big(f(r) = k\,|\,f(R \setminus \{r\}), X; \lambda\big) \;\sim\; q_r(k;\lambda) \cdot \prod_{r':(r,r')\in E} g\big(k, f(r')\big) \qquad (11)$$

During this process the states k at each node r are observed with probabilities $p\big(f(r) = k\,|\,X;\lambda\big)$. Strictly speaking, this holds only if the number of generating steps (11) goes to infinity and if the generating process is ergodic. It is easy to show, that the process is ergodic for the hard function (1) if $\delta > 0$.

Another question is, how many times the generating step should be performed in order to obtain a safe statistic for the estimation of marginal probabilities. Unfortunately, the answer of this question is very pessimistic. In [6] an algorithm is described, that samples labelings exactly according to the given probability distribution. Its computational time is indeed not acceptable in our case (many thousands of nodes and up to typically 20-30 states).

Nevertheless it is possible to obtain subjectively good results using a significantly smaller number of generating steps as would be theoretically correct. Some experience shows, that the labelings with high a-posteriori probabilities are usually not far from the labeling with the maximum a-posteriori probability. Therefore it makes sense to initialize the generating process by the MAP decision. Fortunately, the MAP decision in the case of hard function (1) (as well as for many other functions g, which are often used for the stereo reconstruction) can be obtained exactly [3,7].

In addition it should be noted, that the location of the maximum a-posteriori decision does not depend on the parameter λ, if the hard function is used. This allows to estimate a reasonable initial value of λ for the learning process (10) by maximizing the joint probability (4) of the MAP decision with respect to λ. In other words, we substitute the optimization task $p(X;\lambda) \to \max_\lambda$ by the task $p(f^*, X; \lambda) \to \max_\lambda$, where f^* is the MAP decision. Solving this maximization task we obtain

$$\lambda^{(0)} = \frac{1}{|R| \cdot l} \sum_r A\big(r, f^*(r)\big)$$

as the initial value for the learning process (10).

4   Experiments

First of all, we do not claim, that the described approach works better than all other methods for all cases. An obvious reason is the very simple surface model,

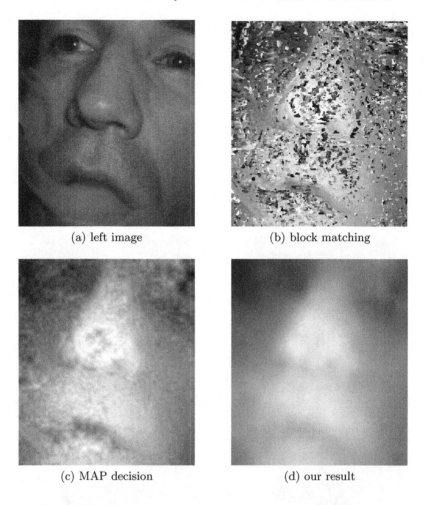

(a) left image

(b) block matching

(c) MAP decision

(d) our result

Fig. 1. Example "Smoker"

that does not take into account, for instance, some lighting details, physical properties of the surface, occlusions etc. In addition, the following should be noted. An often used criteria for comparison of stereo reconstruction algorithms is the number of misclassified pixels. In fact it corresponds to the penalty for misclassification using the additive delta cost function. In this work the problem is posed in qualitatively another way, namely as minimization of risk using the square distance as cost function. A reasonable rating measure for such algorithms might be a *spatial distance* between two surfaces (defined in a suitable way). Strictly speaking, the same measure should be used both for design of Bayes strategy and for rating the method. Thus methods, which use different criteria for optimization, are not quantitatively comparable in principle. Therefore we do not compare our results with any known results (a lot of which can be found in literature). We refer only to MAP-decisions to show, that the use of

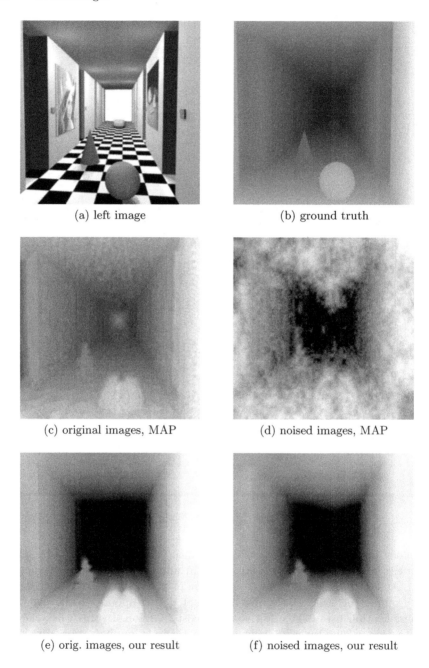

(a) left image

(b) ground truth

(c) original images, MAP

(d) noised images, MAP

(e) orig. images, our result

(f) noised images, our result

Fig. 2. Example "Corridor"

an additive cost function gives a significant *subjective* improvement with regard to the formulation as energy minimization task.

In fig. 1 an example is given. We added the result of the simplest Block Matching method just to give the impression, that the problem is really not trivial. The results obtained by the MAP decision and the decision for additive cost function are shown in 1(c) and 1(d).

The next feature we would like to note is the high robustness of the method. To illustrate this we use an artificial example shown in fig. 2. In this experiment the original left and right images were contaminated by noise of variance 100. It can be seen, that the result obtained by the proposed approach is almost not changed, whereas the MAP decision is strongly corrupted.

5 Conclusions

We have shown, that the use of a suitable cost function significantly improves results of stereo reconstruction with regard to the formulation as energy minimization task.

Although the results seem to be promising, many questions appear, both theoretical and practical. From the theoretical viewpoint, the most intriguing question is, whether it is possible to compute the needed marginal probability distributions exactly. Though this problem is NP-complete in general it would be interesting to search for solvable subclasses. From the practical viewpoint, it seems to be useful to extend the surface model (at the moment a very simple model is used). An interesting direction is to apply the method for other applications, for example, for motion analysis.

References

1. Y. Boykov, O. Veksler, and R. Zabih. Fast approximate energy minimization via graph cuts. In *ICCV*, pages 377–384, 1999.
2. A. P. Dempster, N. M. Laird, and D. B. Durbin. Maximum likelihood from incomplete data via the EM algorithm. *Journal of the Royal Statistical Society*, 39:185–197, 1977.
3. B. Flach. Strukturelle Bilderkennung: Habilitationsschrift. In German, 2003.
4. Stuart Geman and Donald Geman. Stochastic relaxation, Gibbs distributions, and the Bayesian restoration of images. *IEEE Transactions on Pattern Analysis and Machine Intelligence*, 6(6):721–741, 1984.
5. Schlesinger M.I. and Hlaváč V. *Ten Lectures on Statistical and Structural Pattern Recognition*. Kluwer Academic Publishers, Dordrecht, May 2002.
6. James Gary Propp and David Bruce Wilson. Exact sampling with coupled markov chains and applications to statistical mechanics. *Random Structures Algorithms*, 9(1):223–252, 1996.
7. M.I. Schlesinger and B. Flach. Some solvable subclasses of structural recognition problems. In Tomáš Svoboda, editor, *Czech Pattern Recognition Workshop 2000*, pages 55–62, 2000.
8. Michail I. Schlesinger. Connection between unsuprevised and supervised learning in pattern recognition. *Kibernetika*, 2:81–88, 1968. In Russian.

Partial Optimal Labeling Search for a NP-Hard Subclass of (max,+) Problems

Ivan Kovtun

Dresden University of Technology
kovtun@ics.inf.tu-dresden.de

Abstract. Optimal labeling problems are NP-hard in many practically important cases. Sufficient conditions for optimal label detection in every pixel are formulated. Knowing the values of the optimal labeling in some pixels, as a result of applying the proposed algorithm, allows to decrease the complexity of the original problem essentially.

1 Introduction

Labeling problems play a significant role in computer vision. In the present paper labeling problems are formulated as (max,+) problems. A subconvex subclass of (max,+) problems is introduced. Many image recognition problems lead to (max,+) problems. For instance, energy minimization, image segmentation by texture features, three-dimensional object reconstruction on the basis of stereoimages, noisy image restoration and other.

For the first time the (max,+) problem was formulated in the paper [8] in 1976. In the papers [8] and [11] an algorithm based on the substitution of the (max,+) problem by an auxiliary linear programming problem is proposed. The algorithm takes the decision itself whether the solution of the auxiliary linear programming problem leads to the solution of the (max,+) problem or not. Thus, the algorithm returns either the solution of (max,+) problem or the answer "no answer". In [9] and [10] a subclass of the solvable (max,+) problems is determined and it is shown that for this subclass the algorithm proposed in [8,11] always finds the solution (the answer "no answer" never appears). These problems belong to the subconvex subclass of (max,+) problems.

A new branch of algorithms for solving (max,+) problems was formed in works [3,4,6]. These algorithms are based on a reduction of the initial problem to a min-cut problem. At that the class of solvable (max,+) problems was not expanded: only a subset of subconvex (max,+) problems is solvable by proposed algorithms.

Thus, a rather well investigated subclass of the (max,+) problems that can be solved in polynomial time arises. Namely, a subset of subconvex (max,+) problems. At the same time there are practically significant subclasses of the (max,+) problems that are known to be NP-hard. Therefore, a number of investigations were devoted to a searching for approximative algorithms [5,2,7,1].

B. Michaelis and G. Krell (Eds.): DAGM 2003, LNCS 2781, pp. 402–409, 2003.

However, the exact solution of the problem in some separately taken pixels is of interest as well.

This paper presents sufficient conditions for making decision about the optimal labeling in each pixel individually. At that the special label "no label" is allowed. The proposed algorithm is applied for a NP-hard subclasses of (max,+) problems namely the Potts model. It can be also generalized to arbitrary (max,+) problems.

2   The Basic Definitions

Basic definitions are introduced in this section. Later we operate with such notions as *a vision field, a pixel, a labeling, a label set, a structure of the vision field, an order of the structure and neighboring pixels*. After the definition of *a labeling quality* the (max,+) problem is formulated in general form as the problem of searching for the labeling with an optimal quality.

Let *a vision field* T be an arbitrary finite set. The elements of the vision field are called *pixels*. One of the most frequently encountered examples of a vision field is a rectangular area of a two-dimensional integer lattice $\{(i,j) \,|\, 0 \le i < I, 0 \le j < J\}$. Let *a labeling* of the vision field T be a function $k_T : T \to \{1, 2, \ldots, l\}$. The set $\{1, 2, \ldots, l\}$ is called *a label set* and denoted by the symbol L. A restriction of this function on a subset $\tau \subseteq T$ of the vision field is denoted by k_τ $(k_\tau : \tau \to L)$, and the value of the function k_T in the pixel t is denoted by k_t. Let *a structure of the vision field* T be a set $\Im \subseteq 2^T$ of subsets of the vision field T. Note that $\Im$ does not necessarily contain all subsets of the vision field. Let *the order of the structure* be a maximum cardinality of the elements of the structure $\Im$, i.e. $\max_{\tau \in \Im} |\tau|$. Usually but not necessarily the order of the structure is two. Pixels t and t' are called *neighboring* according to the structure $\Im$ if there exists a subset $\tau \in \Im$ that contains both pixels $\{t, t'\} \subseteq \tau$. Let us denote the set of all labelings of the part τ of the vision field by $L^\tau = \{k_\tau | k_\tau : \tau \to L\}$. A function $g_\tau : L^\tau \to R$ is given for every subset $\tau \in \Im$ of the structure. This function assigns a real number to every labeling $k_\tau : \tau \to L$. Let *the quality of the labeling* $k_T : T \to L$ be the number

$$Q(k_T) = \sum_{\tau \in \Im} g_\tau(k_\tau). \tag{1}$$

The (max,+) problem consists in maximization of the quality function $Q()$ and determination of the appropriate labeling $k_T^* = \arg \max_{k_T} Q(k_T)$.

3   A Known Polynomially Solvable Subclass of (max,+) Problems

Let us suppose that the label set L is a completely ordered set: $1 < 2 < \cdots < l$. A partial ordering can be defined on the set of label pairs $(l, l') \in L \times L$. Namely, for every two label pairs (r, r') and (l, l') their maximum $(r, r') \vee (l, l') = (r \vee l, r' \vee l')$ and minimum $(r, r') \wedge (l, l') = (r \wedge l, r' \wedge l')$ are defined in a natural way. In the same way a partial ordering can be defined on the set of all labelings. For each pair of labelings k_T and k'_T we denote by $k_T \bigvee k'_T$ their maximum and by $k_T \bigwedge k'_T$ their minimum.

A function $Q : L^T \to R$ is called **subconvex** if the following condition is fulfilled for arbitrary labelings k_T and k'_T:

$$Q(k_T) + Q(k'_T) \le Q(k_T \bigvee k'_T) + Q(k_T \bigwedge k'_T). \tag{2}$$

We call a (max,+) problem subconvex if its quality function is subconvex.

An equivalent definition of subconvex function $Q : L^T \to R$ is based on the notion of discrete derivation: $\forall k_T : T \to L, k_t < l$:

$$Q'_t(k_1, \ldots, k_t, \ldots, k_n) = Q(k_1, \ldots, k_t + 1, \ldots, k_n) - Q(k_1, \ldots, k_t, \ldots, k_n).$$

The function $Q : L^T \to R$ is **subconvex** if and only if its second derivative $Q''_{tt'}(k_T) \ge 0$ is not negative for every two neighboring pixels t and t' $(t \ne t')$ and an arbitrary labeling $k_T : T \to L$ $(k_t < l, k_{t'} < l)$.

All solvable (max,+) problems known so far are subconvex. It is already proved that a subconvex (max,+) problem is solvable in polynomial time if it fulfills one of the following conditions:

1. The order of the vision field structure is two [8,11,9,10,1,3,4].
   Then the quality function (1) takes the following form

   $$Q(k_T) = \sum_{\{t\} \in \Im} q_t(k_t) + \sum_{\{t,t'\} \in \Im} g_{t,t'}(k_t, k_{t'}). \tag{3}$$

   Verification of the subconvexity condition comes down to the verification of the subconvexity of every function $g_{t,t'}$ independently: $\forall r, r' \in L \setminus \{l\}$:

   $$g_{t,t'}(r+1, r'+1) + g_{t,t'}(r, r') \ge g_{t,t'}(r+1, r') + g_{t,t'}(r, r'+1).$$

2. The order of the structure is three and the number of labels is two [6].

The question of polynomial solvability for an arbitrary subconvex (max,+) problem remains open.

From the subconvexity condition (2) it follows that if k^*_T and k^{**}_T are solutions of a subconvex (max,+) problem then $k^*_T \bigvee k^{**}_T$ and $k^*_T \bigwedge k^{**}_T$ are also solutions of the same problem. Hence, one can define **the highest** and **the lowest** optimal labelings in the following way:

$$\overset{\smile}{k}_T = \bigvee_{k^*_T = \arg \max_{k_T} Q(k_T)} k^*_T, \qquad \overset{\frown}{k}_T = \bigwedge_{k^*_T = \arg \max_{k_T} Q(k_T)} k^*_T.$$

It can be shown that computational complexity of searching for the lowest as well as the highest optimal labelings is the same as for an arbitrary optimal labeling.

The following lemma describes a property of the subconvex (max,+) problems.

Lemma 1. *Let* $\widehat{k_T} = \bigwedge\limits_{k_T^* = \arg\max\limits_{k_T} Q(k_T^*)} k_T^*$ *be the lowest optimal labeling for some*

subconvex problem and k_T *be an arbitrary labeling satisfying the condition:*

$$k_T \bigwedge \widehat{k_T} \neq \widehat{k_T} \tag{4}$$

Then the quality of the labeling k_T *is strictly less than the quality of the maximum of the labelings* k_T *and* $\widehat{k_T}$:

$$Q(k_T) < Q(k_T \bigvee \widehat{k_T}).$$

Proof. Let us rewrite the inequality (2) for labelings k_T and $\widehat{k_T}$

$$Q(k_T) + Q(\widehat{k_T}) \leq Q(k_T \bigwedge \widehat{k_T}) + Q(k_T \bigvee \widehat{k_T}) \tag{5}$$

The condition (4) together with the definition of the lowest optimal labeling leads to the inequality:

$$Q(k_T \bigwedge \widehat{k_T}) < Q(\widehat{k_T}). \tag{6}$$

We obtain the statement of the lemma by adding the inequalities (5) and (6).

4   The Main Result

We consider (max,+) problems with a structure of order two. In this case the quality function has the form (3), at that the functions q_t are arbitrary and the functions $g_{t,t'}(r, r') = \begin{cases} C_{t,t'} \geq 0, \ r = r', \\ 0, \quad\quad r \neq r'. \end{cases}$ This problem is not subconvex for more than two labels. Moreover, it is NP-hard (see [1]).

Let us build an auxiliary subconvex (max,+) problem for the given (max,+) problem. The exact solution of this auxiliary problem gives the optimal labels for the initial problem in some pixels.

This **auxiliary problem** is constructed in the following way:

1. The vision field T, the structure $\Im$ and the label set L are the same as in the initial problem.
2. Let us fix an arbitrary label $s \in L$.
3. Let us completely order labels in each pixel in the following way. The label s becomes the highest. Independently in each pixel one of the rest labels l_t^s whose quality $q_t(l_t^s)$ is maximal ($l_t^s = \arg\max\limits_{l \in L \setminus \{s\}} q_t(l)$) becomes the lowest.
4. The quality function of the auxiliary problem is

$$Q^s(k_T) = \sum_{\{t\} \in \Im} q_t(k_t) + \sum_{\{t,t'\} \in \Im} g_{t,t'}^s(k_t, k_{t'}),$$

where

$$g_{t,t'}^s(r,r') = \begin{cases} C_{t,t'}, & r = s, r' = s, \\ C_{t,t'}, & r \neq s, r' \neq s, \\ 0, & otherwise. \end{cases} \qquad (7)$$

The constructed auxiliary problem is subconvex and its lowest solution $\widehat{k_T^s}$ can be found in polynomial time.

Theorem 1. *An arbitrary solution of the initial problem* $k_T^* = \arg\max\limits_{k_T} Q(k_T)$

satisfies the following condition: $k_T^* \bigwedge \widehat{k_T^s} = \widehat{k_T^s}$.

In other words the lowest optimal labeling for the initial problem in each pixel is not lower than the label in the corresponding pixel of the auxiliary problem solution ($\forall t \in T : k_t^* \wedge \widehat{k_t^s} = \widehat{k_t^s}$). The theorem allows to reduce the number of labels in each pixel. It is necessary to examine only those labels $l \in L$ in the pixel t that lie not lower than the label $\widehat{k_T^s}$: $L_t = \{l \in L : l \bigwedge \widehat{k_t^s} = \widehat{k_t^s}\}$. In particular, the set of remaining labels L_t can consist only of the highest label $\widehat{k_t^s} = s$. In this case the value of any optimal labeling of the initial problem in the pixel t equals s.

The algorithm based on the theorem consists in execution of the following three steps for every label $s \in L$:

1. Construction of the auxiliary problem for the label s;
2. Searching for the lowest solution $\widehat{k_T^s}$ of the auxiliary problem;
3. If $\widehat{k_t^s} = s$ then $k_t^* = s$.

Proof. We will conduct the proof of the theorem in the following way: we construct for any labeling k_T, such that $k_T \bigwedge \widehat{k_T^s} \neq \widehat{k_T^s}$ a labeling with better quality. Namely, $Q(k_T \bigvee \widehat{k_T^s}) > Q(k_T)$.

Let us consider an arbitrary labeling k_T, satisfying the condition $k_T \bigwedge \widehat{k_T^s} \neq \widehat{k_T^s}$. It follows from the lemma 1 that

$$0 < Q^s(k_T \bigvee \widehat{k_T^s}) - Q^s(k_T). \qquad (8)$$

If $\widehat{k_t^s} \neq s$ then $\widehat{k_t^s} = l_t^s$. Otherwise one can construct a new labeling with the same quality, which is lower than $\widehat{k_T^s}$. Therefore, the lowest labeling $\widehat{k_T^s}$ of the auxiliary problem can take only two values in every pixel: $\widehat{k_t^s} \in \{s, l_t^s\}$.

The following inequality follows from formula (7) and aforesaid:

$$g_{t,t'}^s(k_t \vee \widehat{k_t^s}, k_{t'} \vee \widehat{k_{t'}^s}) - g_{t,t'}^s(k_t, k_{t'}) \leq g_{t,t'}(k_t \vee \widehat{k_t^s}, k_{t'} \vee \widehat{k_{t'}^s}) - g_{t,t'}(k_t, k_{t'}) \qquad (9)$$

Using inequalities (8) and (9) we obtain:

$$0 < Q^s(k_T \bigvee \widehat{k_T^s}) - Q^s(k_T) =$$

$$= \sum_{t\in T} q_t(k_t \vee \widehat{k_t^s}) + \sum_{\{t,t'\}\in \Im} g_{t,t'}^s(k_t \vee \widehat{k_t^s}, k_{t'} \vee \widehat{k_{t'}^s}) - \left(\sum_{t\in T} q_t(k_t) + \sum_{\{t,t'\}\in \Im} g_{t,t'}^s(k_t, k_{t'})\right) =$$

$$= \sum_{t\in T}\left(q_t(k_t \vee \widehat{k_t^s}) - q_t(k_t \vee \widehat{k_t^s})\right) + \sum_{\{t,t'\}\in \Im}\left(g_{t,t'}^s(k_t \vee \widehat{k_t^s}, k_{t'} \vee \widehat{k_{t'}^s}) - g_{t,t'}^s(k_t, k_{t'})\right) \le$$

$$\le \sum_{t\in T}\left(q_t(k_t \vee \widehat{k_t^s}) - q_t(k_t \vee \widehat{k_t^s})\right) + \sum_{\{t,t'\}\in \Im}\left(g_{t,t'}(k_t \vee \widehat{k_t^s}, k_{t'} \vee \widehat{k_{t'}^s}) - g_{t,t'}(k_t, k_{t'})\right) =$$

$$= Q(k_T \bigvee \widehat{k_T^s}) - Q(k_T).$$

Thus, $Q(k_T) < Q(k_T \bigvee \widehat{k_T^s})$ which was to be proved.

5   Experimental Verification of the Algorithm

The following three experiments demonstrate our approach for segmentation and stereoreconstruction problems. In all cases the vision field is a rectangular area of the integer-valued lattice $T = \{(i,j)|0 \le i < I, 0 \le j < J\}$.

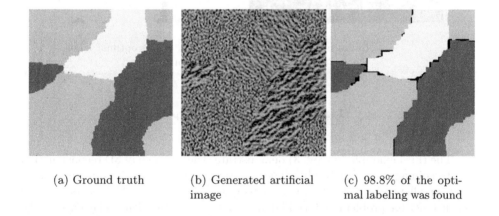

(a) Ground truth   (b) Generated artificial   (c) 98.8% of the opti-
                              image   mal labeling was found

Fig. 1. Segmentation of the artificial image

The structure is $\Im = \{\{(i,j),(i+1,j)\} \subset T, \{(i,j),(i,j+1)\} \subset T\}$. The quality function has the form (3) with the functions

$$g_{t,t'}(r,r') = \begin{cases} C \ge 0 & r = r', \\ 0 & r \ne r'. \end{cases}$$

This problem is NP-hard if the number of labels is greater than two (see [1]).

The first two examples (see fig. 1 and 2) demonstrate applicability of the algorithm for texture segmentation. In the first example an image with three textures was generated using a Markov Random Field model (fig. 1(b)). Due to this fact the real segmentation (fig. 1(a)) is known. The second example (fig. 2) demonstrates texture segmentation of a real image (fig. 2(a)). The number $q_t(k)$ defines a probability that pixel t belongs to the k-th ($k \in \{1, 2, 3\}$) texture. Figures 1(c) and 2(b) present the results of the optimal labeling search. Black color is used to mark those pixels where answer "no label" was obtained.

(a) Initial image   (b) 98.4% of the optimal label-
                                 ing was found

Fig. 2. Segmentation of the airphoto

The third example (see fig. 3) demonstrates the problem of 3D reconstruction by stereoimagepairs (fig. 3(a,b)). The qualities $q_t(k)$ are found in some reasonable way for all pixels t and 20 possible disparities ($k \in \{1, ..., 20\}$). Then the 3D reconstruction problem is formulated as a (max,+) problem. The part of the optimal labeling found by our approach is shown in the figure 3(c). Again black color is used to mark those pixels where answer "no label" was obtained.

Of course, the quality of reconstruction can be improved using a more thorough choice of the numbers $q_t(k)$, however, it is not a goal of our research.

6   Conclusion

We have shown in this paper that the exact solution can be found at least partially even for NP-hard (max,+) problems. Experimental results show the possibility to restore the optimal labeling for almost all pixels.

(a) Left picture   (b) Right picture   (c) 93.6% of the op-
                                                        timal labeling was
                                                        found

Fig. 3. Reconstruction of three-dimensional scene by the pair of stereoimages

References

1. Y. Boykov, O. Veksler, and R. Zabih. Fast approximate energy minimization via graph cuts. *IEEE Transactions on Pattern Analysis and Machine Intelligence*, 23(11):1222–1239, 2001.
2. S. Geman and D. Geman. Stochastic relaxation, gibbs distributions, and the bayesian restoration of images. *IEEE Trans. on PAMI*, 6(6):721–741, 1984.
3. D. M. Greig, B. T. Porteous, and A. H. Seheult. Exact maximum a posteriori estimation for binary images. *J. Royal Statistical Soc., Series B*, 51(2):271–279, 1989.
4. Hiroshi Ishikawa and Davi Geiger. Segmentation by grouping junctions. In *IEEE Computer Society Conference on Computer Vision and Pattern Recognition*, 1998.
5. S. Kirkpatrick, C. D. Gellatt, Jr., and M. P. Vecch. Optimization by simulated annealing. *Science*, 220(4598):671–680, 1983.
6. Vladimir Kolmogorov and Ramin Zabih. What energy functions can be minimized via graph cuts. In A. Heyden et al., editor, *ECCV 2002*, number 2352 in LNCS, pages 65–81, Berlin Heidelberg, 2002. Springer-Verlag.
7. Stan Z. Li. *Markov Random Field Modeling in Image Analysis*. Computer Science, Workbench, Springer, 2001.
8. M. I. Schlesinger. Syntax analysis of two dimensional visual signals with noise. *Cybernetics, Kiev*, 4:113–130, 1976. in russian.
9. M. I. Schlesinger and B. Flach. Some solvable subclass of structural recognition problems. In Tomas Svoboda, editor, *Czech Pattern Recognition Workshop 2000*, pages 55–61, Praha, February 2000. Czech Pattern Recognition Society.
10. M. I. Schlesinger and B. Flach. Analysis of optimal labelling problems and their applications to image segmentation and binocular stereovision. In Franz Leberl and Andrej Ferko, editors, *Proceedings East-West-Vision 2002 (EWV'02)*, pages 55–60. International Workshop and Project Festival on Computer Vision, Computer Graphics, New Media, 2002.
11. M. I. Schlesinger and V. K. Koval. Two dimensional programming in image analysis problems. *Automatics and Telemechanics, Moscow*, 2:149–168, 1976. in russian.

Extraction of Orientation from Floor Structure for Odometry Correction in Mobile Robotics

Christof Schroeter, Hans-Joachim Boehme, and Horst-Michael Gross

Fachgebiet Neuroinformatik,
Technische Universitaet Ilmenau
{christof.schroeter,hans-joachim.boehme,
horst-michael.gross}@tu-ilmenau.de

Abstract. We are presenting a method for correcting odometry readings of a robot for increased accuracy of position estimation. Our method uses a simple pragmatic approach and exploits the distinct structure of the floor in our experimental area. By continually extracting orientation information from the floor view, we are able to correct the heading component of odometry, thereby eliminating the major source for position errors. Compared to other approaches the solution is computationally inexpensive. Our experiments show that by employing our correction method we are able to significantly increase position accuracy and consistently map paths up to several hundred meters.

1 Introduction

Self-localization is a basic task in any autonomous robot application. Knowledge of position is a pre-requisite to any sensible navigation behaviour. Most robots are equipped with some sort of odometry sensors (like wheel encoders) for measuring their own motion. Using dead-reckoning, these measurements can be used by the robot to localize itself relative to a reference point. Due to the nature of dead-reckoning the resulting position estimates are prone to a variety of errors, and accuracy is decreasing over time. In our PERSES project [4], we developed a simple approach for correcting the orientation component of odometry readings by exploiting the special floor structure found in the environment we are using for development and experiments, a home depot.

This paper is structured as follows. In section 2 we motivate the use of our orientation correction method and discuss related topics such as scan matching, landmark navigation and SLAM. Section 3 shows in detail the implementation of our floor image processing and correction of odometry data. Section 4 contains experimental results and proves the vast improvement in position estimation, enabling us to consistently map an area of $40 * 40\text{m}^2$ without additional localization techniques.

2 Localization

In our PERSES project, we are developing an interactive artificial shopping assistant that will act as a guide and mobile information terminal for customers in a store environment. Current experimental platform is a RWI B21r robot. To be able to act autonomously,

B. Michaelis and G. Krell (Eds.): DAGM 2003, LNCS 2781, pp. 410–417, 2003.
© Springer-Verlag Berlin Heidelberg 2003

the robot must localize itself within its environment. The B21r is equipped with wheel encoders to keep track of its own position by dead-reckoning. Odometry is widely used in robotics because it is inexpensive, allows high sampling rates and provides good short-term accuracy. However, the fundamental idea of integration of incremental motion information inevitably leads to the accumulation of errors. Error sources can be divided into 2 categories: systematic and non-systematic errors. Examples for systematic errors are inaccurate drive geometry (wheel diameters etc.) and finite encoder resolution, while non-systematic errors are introduced by uneven floors, slipping or external forces (interaction with external bodies) [1]. While some of these errors can be corrected by carefully adjusting system parameters [2], the overall effect of deviation in position estimation is unbounded if no external reference is used. Particularly, the accumulation of orientation error causes large position errors. An example is shown in Fig. 1 (left). Here the robot traveled a straight path of 30 meters, turning by 180° at the end and returning to the starting point. Due to increasing orientation error, the straight legs appear bent and the end point is virtually located 10 m from the start.

Advanced localization techniques have been an area of intensive research for a long time and a number of different methods have been developed.

2.1 Scan Matching

In scan matching, features are extracted from readings of range measuring sensors and matched to obtain displacement between measuring positions [6]. Most applications use laser scanners for their high accuracy and reliability. Sonar sensors have been used too, but results are generally less accurate due to the higher variance of sonar measurements. For robust results from matched scans this method still depends on a position hypothesis from odometry. Because we are strongly focusing on visual sensing and aiming towards a low-cost platform, regarding the potentially significant cost increase by equipping a robot with a 2D laser scanner, we are hesitant to rely on scan matching.

2.2 Landmark Navigation, Monte Carlo Localization

Another possibility of tracking the position of a robot is by localizing itself relative to known landmarks in the environment. Landmarks can be detected by range sensors or visual input. Usually the robot needs to maintain its position between landmark observations by odometry. Newer methods, like Monte-Carlo-Localization (MCL), perform probabilistic localization by estimating a probability distribution over the state space [3, 5]. This distribution is updated with motion (odometry) and environment observations. Both landmark navigation and MCL need a map of their environment. In order to build this map, knowledge of respective positions is needed, so either method is not fit for mapping previously unknown terrain.

2.3 SLAM

The chicken-and-egg problem of mapping and localization is adressed by a still relatively new method called Simultaneous Localization and Mapping (SLAM). In SLAM, mapping and localization are not seen as separate tasks, but solved together. This is derived from the observation that the 2 problems depend on each other. The base of SLAM is an extended state space that contains position and map. A probability distribution over this common state space is maintained that converges with motion and observations [8]. Most successful applications are using laser scanners, while visual SLAM and adaption to arbitrarily large environments are subjects of ongoing research.

Here, our aim was to develop a pragmatic solution to consistent map building that is computationally efficient and does not need costly sensoric equipment. Furthermore, our experimental observations show that odometry errors of our experimental platform B21r mainly occur in the orientation component of odometry data. While drive range measurements are reasonably accurate, the growing and unpredictable error in orientation causes mapping to fail completely without a means of correction. Looking for a source of reference, we found the floor pattern in our experimental area contains easily recognizable features that provide (partial) orientation information.

The floor consists of square pieces of 30 cm by 30 cm. While the pieces themselves are only slightly textured, the lines between them show a strong contrast (Fig. 1 right). Orientation of these pieces is consistent over the whole store area. The idea of our method is to detect the main orientation of the lines between pieces and use them as reference for recalibrating odometry at each motion step.

We have experimented with deriving displacement directly from the floor observations, but due to the narrow field of view we would need a very high update frequency for robustly finding corresponding points between subsequent pictures.

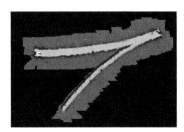

Fig. 1. Left: The map shows the effects of heading error in odometry (light areas mark free space, dark areas mark obstacles), right: tiled structure on the floor of our experimental area, a home depot

3   Floor-Based Odometry Correction

To obtain images of the floor we use a camera dedicated to this purpose only. This camera is attached at a height of 1.40m and protruding, looking down vertically, so that it is seeing about 50cm of ground space in front. Images are captured at the relatively low resolution of 192 * 143 pixels for fast processing. We use grayscale images because color yields no further information about orientation.

3.1   Processing the Floor Image

Figure 2 (top left) shows that the image is distorted radially, which is visible in the slight curving of straight lines around the center of the image.

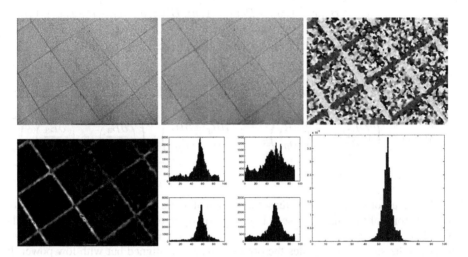

Fig. 2. Top row from left to right: initial image as captured from the camera, image after radial correction, angle of local orientations (gray values coding orientation angles in a range of -90° to 90°), bottom row: power of local orientations (smoothed by box filter), histograms for the 4 sectors (see text for explanation), overall histogram showing strong peak at main orientation

To correct this, each pixels distance to the center of the image is increased by the formula

$$r_{new} = r_{old} * (1 + r_{old}^2 * k)$$

with an empirically determined radial correction factor $k = 2 * 10^{-6}$. This is a very simple approach to correcting camera abberation, but it's sufficient for our problem. Figure 2 (top center) depicts the corrected image.

The next step is to calculate local orientation for each pixel. This is done by applying an orientation tensor (inertia tensor method) as described in [7].
In detail, this consists of the following steps:

1. Bandpass filtering of the image by applying binomial filters of different sizes.

$$B_1 = image \otimes binom(3 * 3)$$

$$B_2 = B_1 \otimes binom(5 * 5)$$

$$B_3 = 3.0 * (B_1 - B_2)$$

2. Calculate local x- and y-gradients as difference of direct neighbours

$$
\begin{aligned}
\bigtriangledown B_3(x,y) &= \left(\frac{\partial B_3(x,y)}{\partial x}, \frac{\partial B_3(x,y)}{\partial y} \right)^T \\
&= (B_3(x-1,y) - B_3(x+1,y), B_3(x,y-1) - B_3(x,y+1))^T
\end{aligned}
$$

3. Calculate angle and power of local orientation at each image point

$$
2\phi = atan\left(2 * \frac{\partial B_3}{\partial x} * \frac{\partial B_3}{\partial y}, \left(\frac{\partial B_3}{\partial x}\right)^2 - \left(\frac{\partial B_3}{\partial y}\right)^2 \right)
$$

$$
power = \left(\left(\frac{\partial B_3}{\partial x}\right)^2 - \left(\frac{\partial B_3}{\partial y}\right)^2 + 4 * \frac{\partial B_3}{\partial x} * \frac{\partial B_3}{\partial y} \right) * \left(\left(\frac{\partial B_3}{\partial x}\right)^2 + \left(\frac{\partial B_3}{\partial y}\right)^2 \right)^{-1}
$$

The result of the orientation tensor are fields of angle and power of local orientation for each point of the image. As seen in Fig. 2 (top right, bottom left), at the edges of the tiles there are strong local orientations with angles aligned to direction of these edges while on the surface of the tiles the orientations are unaligned but with low power. In a histogram of local orientations, weighted with respective power, the maximum will show the robot orientation with respect to the main orientation of the floor. While the orientation tensor output contains a range of -90° - +90° , the actual information that can be gathered is only an angle in the range 0° - 90° . Due to the square tiles images rotated by a multiple of 90° are indistinguishable. This corresponds to the histogram having 2 (dependent) maxima, one originating from vertical lines, the other from horizontal ones. Each angle k < 0° corresponds to an angle k + 90° in the orientation tensor output, therefore all these values are simply mapped into the 0° - 90° range by adding 90°.

Situations may occur where the robot encounters objects lying in its path or steers near towards immobile objects, like e.g. goods shelfs. In such cases, it may happen that the view of the floor camera is partly occupied by objects occluding the floor, leading to unpredictable local orientations in a part of the image and disturbing the histogram. To avoid errors resulting from such a situation the image is split into 4 sectors (upper right, upper left, lower right, lower left) and histograms are evaluated for each sector separately. This is based on the expectation that in most cases an object will only cover one sector. The histograms are smoothed by a box-filter, then for each sector the main orientation is determined by the maximum in the sector-specific histogram. If one of these 4 values is outlying, the respective sector is discarded, the remaining sectors are merged into a common histogram by multiplication and the maximum of this histogram is regarded as main orientation in the image.

Problems may occur when the floor structure is widely obscured by large objects or strong light/shadow contrasts introduce misleading edges. Ideally this will result in the histogram having no strong maximum, in which case no correction will be applied until the floor is visible again. However, situations may occur where objects in the image lead to a wrong orientation. Since we only use this correction approach during map building by joysticking, the human operator is responsible for avoiding such critical situations.

3.2   Re-calibrating Odometry

Given the true orientation of the robot, we can now correct odometry readings. In our architecture, sensor readings from wheel encoders are already translated into a position in low-level processing and sent to the high-level software as (x,y,ϕ)-triplets. These low-level routines always use the orientation measured by odometry and therefore calculate wrong (x,y)-positions when the true orientation is different. This means application level software must not only adjust the orientation component, but also calculate the true position change between 2 odometry data readings and update position. To this purpose, the last odometry reading is stored together with the corrected position and the angle difference between odometric orientation and visual orientation is maintained continually. When receiving a new odometry position, the difference between current and previous believed position is calculated as the driven path, rotated by the known odometry orientation error and added to the last corrected position. Correction over 2 steps is shown in Figure 3. The method simplifies by implying all the rotation error that occurs in one step is aquired at the starting point of this particular step. This seems sufficient for very small steps (updates are done with a distance of a few cm only). Experimentation with more sophisticated but computationally expensive models only showed marginal differences.

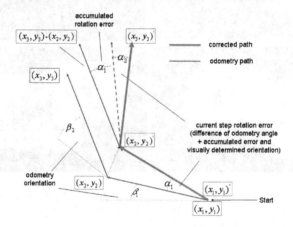

Fig. 3. Principle of correcting odometry with reference orientation

Now with a good estimate of the true position of the robot, we can build maps by generating local maps from sonar range readings and incorporating them into a global map. For this purpose we use the grid map approach and update formula from [9].

4   Results

We tested our method by driving closed loops of different size in our home depot experimental area. By exactly returning to the starting point, we were able to determine the error in localization.

In the first experiment (Fig. 4 top row) we drove through 2 hallways with an overall path length of about 55 meters. Without correction the end position yielded by odometry was about 7 m from the real position (left). With correction (right), the difference between real and estimated position is about 10 cm in either x- and y-direction of the reference frame. After driving the same loop back in the opposite directon the error still was no larger than 12 cm in either direction. The second pair of maps (Fig. 4 bottom row) shows an experiment with a slightly longer path of about 120 m. Here without correction the error was more than 12 m. With correction, however, the position after driving that path was 8 cm in x- and 30 cm in y-direction, and after driving the same path back to the starting point again, it was 30 cm and 40 cm. Overall repeated experiments show that we can assume a total position difference of about 20 cm for each 50 m of driven path. These remaining errors are introduced by inaccuracies in the visual orientation as well as from errors in odometry range measurement.

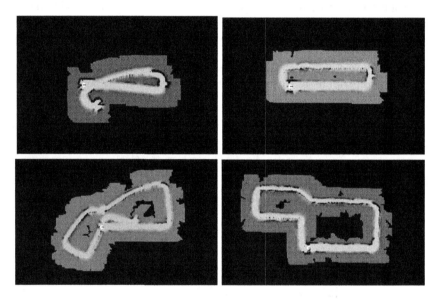

Fig. 4. Comparison of maps with uncorrected and corrected odometry, top left: closed path of 55 m length, without correction, right: same with correction, bottom left: closed path of 120 m without correction, right: same with correction

Finally Figure 5 shows the result of mapping an area of about 30% of the whole store. Here, after a total path length of 350 m, the effects of the remaining position error become visible in the map (2 neighbouring hallways appear too near together leaving no room for the goods shelf between). The total error was 0.9 m in both directions. To avoid the accumulating of errors, we still need to re-calibrate robot position after driving some hundred meters. To this purpose, we will choose some reference points and measure their respective positions, so we can set exact position in regular intervals when crossing such a point while joysticking the robot around. Once a map is generated, we do not rely on correct odometric information anymore because we can then employ another localization method based on that map as explained in section 2.2.

Fig. 5. Here we mapped a significant part of the home depot area

5   Conclusions

We developed and tested an approach to vision-based odometry correction by extracting orientation from floor images. The implementation exploits the strong structure we find in our experimental area, but with specific pre-processing it may be able to adapt to other recognizable patterns. Although we cannot completely negate the long-term effect of inaccurate odometry, we showed that it is possible to build maps without the necessity of further sensors or special preparation of the environment. Our future interest, however, lies in visual SLAM (Simultaneous Localization And Mapping) and we expect to be able to build consistent maps without the need for odometry correction and to gain flexibility in arbitrary environments for our robots.

References

1. J.Borenstein, H.R.Everett, and L.Feng. Where am I? - Sensors and Methods for Mobile Robot Positioning. Technical report, University of Michigan, 1996.
2. J.Borenstein and L.Feng. Measurement and correction of systematic odometry errors in mobile robots. *IEEE Trans. on Robotics and Automation*, 12(5), 1996.
3. F.Dellaert, D.Fox, W.Burgard, and S.Thrun. Monte carlo localization for mobile robots. In *Proc. of the 1999 IEEE Intl. Conf. on Robotics and Automation (ICRA)*, 1999.
4. H.-M.Gross and H.-J.Boehme. Perses - a vision-based interactive mobile shopping assistant. In *Proc. of the IEEE Intl Conf. on Systems, Man and Cybernetics (IEEE-SMC 2000*, pp 80–85, 2000.
5. H.-M.Gross, A.Koenig, H.-J.Boehme, and C.Schroeter. Vision-based monte carlo self-localization for a mobile service robot acting as shopping assistant in a home store. In *Proc. of the 2002 IEEE/RSJ Intl. Conf. on Intelligent Robots and System (IROS2002)*, pp 265–262, 2002.
6. J.-S.Gutmann and C.Schlegel. Amos: Comparion of scan matching apporaches for self-localization in indoor environments. In *Proc. of the 1st Euromicro Workshop on Advanced Mobile Robots (EUROBOT '96)*, 1996.
7. B.Jaehne. *Practical Handbook on Image Processing for Scientific Applications.* CRC Press LLC, Boca Raton, Florida, 1997.
8. M.Montemerlo, S.Thrun, D.Koller, and B.Wegbreit. FastSLAM:A factored solution to the simultaneous localization and mapping problem. In *Proc. of the AAAI Natl. Conf. on Artificial Intelligence*, 2002.
9. Hans Moravec. Sensor fusion in certainty grids for mobile robots. *AI Magazine*, 9(2):61–77, 1988.

On Consistent Discrimination between Directed and Diffuse Outdoor Illumination

Artur Ottlik and Hans-Hellmut Nagel

Institut für Algorithmen und Kognitive Systeme
Fakultät für Informatik der Universität Karlsruhe (TH)
76128 Karlsruhe, Germany
{ottlik|nagel}@iaks.uni-karlsruhe.de

Abstract. This investigation studies the contrast across boundaries of shadows which are cast by moving vehicles or selected stationary objects in a traffic scene onto the road surface. If a sufficient fraction of this subset of hypothetical shadow contours is overlapped by strong edge elements, such a finding is usually taken as a cue that *directed* sunshine illuminates the traffic scene. Otherwise, *diffuse* illumination is assumed. Experiments with different illumination states of a traffic scene indicate that such a conclusion appears justified in many cases. It is demonstrated, however, that much more complicated situations may occur which need detailed inferences in order to arrive at a consistent interpretation.

1 Introduction

Model-based tracking of road vehicles in video sequences can be improved by taking into account the shadow which a vehicle casts onto the road plane. Such an approach requires, however, that it is known whether diffuse or directed daylight illumination prevailed at the time when each image frame had been recorded. Figure 1 illustrates shadow contours, generated by a 3D-model-based tracking approach and overlayed (in green color[1]) in addition to the projection of model segments according to the current pose estimate for the depicted vehicle (see, e. g., [1]). The left panel illustrates an example recorded while the sun shone brightly whereas the sky was covered by clouds during recording of the right panel, causing a diffuse illumination of this road scene.

Initial investigations into the exploitation of shadow contours for model-based tracking relied on the user to provide interactively the required knowledge about type and direction of illumination. Frequent evaluations of new and/or long image sequences, especially of outdoor scenes, make it increasingly cumbersome for a user to estimate the prevailing illumination conditions and to provide these estimates interactively to the model-based tracking system. Not surprisingly, attempts have been reported to estimate the illumination conditions automatically, based on the image frame to be evaluated currently [4]. Another recently published approach checks whether or not a shadow contour – cast hypothetically by a tall mast onto the road plane – is covered by edge elements sufficiently well

---

[1] Difficult to see in printed version; please inspect PDF-version.

B. Michaelis and G. Krell (Eds.): DAGM 2003, LNCS 2781, pp. 418–425, 2003.
© Springer-Verlag Berlin Heidelberg 2003

Fig. 1. The left panel shows an image frame recorded while the sun shone brightly whereas the sky was covered by clouds during recording the frame shown in the right panel.

in order to justify the conclusion that the expected shadow is present indeed and thus provides a cue for directed illumination [2].

The latter approach may occasionally result in 'false alarms', for example if edge segments of a moving vehicle passing across the hypothetical shadow contour accidentally align with it. This may generate enough edge elements in the image to let the 'shadow edge coverage' exceed a predefined threshold – see Figure 2. Some temporal continuity requirement may be introduced in order

Fig. 2. The left panel shows frame 774 of an image sequence recorded with overcast sky, without extended shadows as expected in such a case. The center panel shows image frame No. 776 where an accidental alignment of a fastback with the hypothetical shadow contour of the tall mast causes a 'false (directed sunshine) alarm'. The tracking process attempts, therefore, to include vehicle shadows into the pose update process. The rightmost panel reproduces frame 778 of this same sequence where this 'false alarm' did no longer occur and matching switched back to the treatment of shadow contours induced by a *diffuse* illumination.

to avoid such unjustified short switches between illumination states. Experience has shown, however, that this does not solve the problem: on windy days with broken clouds, the illumination state for outdoor scenes may change within about one tenth of a second. Such a period is of the same order as that attributable to accidental alignments of fast moving image structures with those due to shadow-casting. Search for a *consistent* interpretation of potential shadow contours within as large a fraction of the field of view as possible promises a more robust approach. Investigations towards such a solution will be reported in the sequel.

2   A Daylight Illumination Discrimination Approach

It appears useful to specify as precisely as possible the boundary conditions for the approach to be studied. This will facilitate a later diagnosis whether unsatisfactory results should be attributed to a potential implementation error, to numerical difficulties, to a suboptimal tuning of parameters, or to inappropriate assumptions. In principle, *model-based* tracking excludes other alternatives as potential explanations for observed failures or insufficiencies. It thus becomes possible to trace down *systematically* the root causes for unsatisfactory results in order to remove them.

Fig. 3. Frame 135 from the image sequence `dtneu04`. The red square around the vehicle in the center indicates the cropped image area which is shown in Figure 4.

2.1   Enumeration of the a priori Knowledge Exploited

It is assumed that the following knowledge is available to the system:

1. The road traffic scene is recorded by a single, stationary B/W-video camera.
2. All roads within the field of view of the recording camera are situated within the *same* plane of the depicted scene.
3. Internal parameters of the camera and its pose relative to the road plane.
4. The geographical coordinates (longitude and latitude) of the recorded scene, the date, and the time of day are known for each recorded image frame. Due to the increasing availability of Global Position System (GPS) data, this requirement does no longer constitute a severe bottleneck. Based on these data, the direction can be calculated from which the sun illuminates the scene, provided it is not occluded by clouds.

Fig. 4. These panels show a zoom onto a vehicle at frame 135 in the sequence `dtneu04`. As can be seen in the right panel, many edge elements have been assigned to the shadow segment.

Fig. 5. A zoom onto a vehicle at frame 640 in the sequence `dt_kont01`. The object model is overlayed in the center panel. The right panel illustrates the test for the hypothetical shadow of this vehicle. Bright pixel indicate the (comparatively small number of) edge elements which fit well to the segments of the hypothetical shadow boundary.

5. Boundaries of visible lanes are known in the 3D scene.
6. For each vehicle, its *corresponding* 3D polyhedral vehicle model is known.
7. Position, height, and diameter of masts carrying traffic lights, traffic indicator boards, or lamps are known in the form of approximating cones and/or polyhedra.
8. 3D polyhedral models are known for other opaque bodies within the field of view of the recording camera to the extent that such bodies may occlude significantly any vehicle to be tracked.

Note that we just exploit knowledge required for model-based tracking; *no additional assumptions are introduced*. It is assumed further that a procedure is available which can decide whether or not an edge element *overlaps* a model segment projected into the image plane. Then, either the category *diffuse* or the category *directed* has to be assigned to the illumination condition which prevailed while the current image frame had been recorded.

Fig. 6. Contour segments of models of various masts projected into the image plane and overlayed to frame 176 from sequence dt_kont01.

2.2   Outline of the Estimation Algorithm (Current Version)

For each image frame, the following steps are executed:

1. Determine the regions corresponding to the image of a road.
2. Use ray-tracing to determine for each road pixel whether it is visible from the camera or not (i. e. occluded by a vehicle or another opaque body).
3. Determine for each road pixel, which is visible to the camera, whether it is visible from the current direction of the sun (illuminated) or not (shadowed).
4. Aggregate hypothetically *shadowed road* pixels into regions, *provided* they are visible to the recording camera.
5. Determine the contour of each visible hypothetically shadowed road region.
6. Exclude contour segments where such a hypothetical shadow region touches the silhouette of a shadow-casting body.
7. Determine for each edge element whether it overlaps a visible boundary segment between a shadowed road region and one hypothetically illuminated directly by the sun.
8. Determine a figure-of-merit like the fraction of the total length of visible shadow-road boundaries overlapped by edge elements (*shadow/road boundary coverage (S/RBC)*).

A first approach will compare this S/RBC with a threshold in order to distinguish between diffuse (S/RBC below threshold) and directed (S/RBC at or above threshold) illumination conditions.

3   Experimental Results

Figure 3, recorded in bright sunshine, shows an entire frame from which the window presented in Figure 4 has been cropped. The left panel of Figure 4 shows an enlarged window around a fastback. The center panel shows the same window, overlayed by a projection of the polyhedral model for this vehicle at the current best estimate for the vehicle pose. The right panel is similar to the

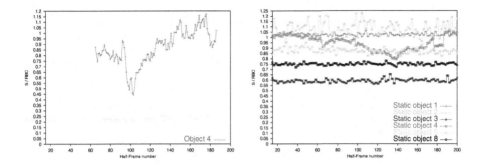

Fig. 7. Left panel: the S/RBC for vehicle *object_4* as a function of (half-)framenumber in the sequence `dtneu04` recorded in bright sunshine. Right panel: The S/RBC for the masts illustrated in Figure 6, again as a function of the framenumber in the same sequence `dtneu04`. In both panels, the S/RBC almost always exceeds a value of 0.55.

center one, but includes the shadow/road boundary. It is clearly discernible that this shadow/road boundary exhibits enough contrast to give rise to numerous strong edge elements. The left panel of Figure 5 shows an enlarged window around a fastback from frame 640 of sequence `dt_kont01` recorded at the time of an *overcast sky*. The right panel corresponds to the right one in Figure 4, including the hypothetical shadow/road boundary expected if the sun would actually shine directly onto this scene: only few edge elements overlap these shadow/road boundaries. In addition to moving objects, the procedure outlined above has been applied to images of tall masts which cast elongated shadows across the scene as illustrated by Figure 6. In case of directed sunshine, results obtained for a vehicle (see left panel of Figure 7) and for several tall masts as illustrated in the right panel of Figure 7 provide evidence as expected: the S/RBC exceeds in general 0.55, in most cases even 0.7. Analogous evidence has been obtained for diffuse illumination as demonstrated in Figure 8, provided accidental alignment of shadow contours with *unmodelled* scene components are excluded. The dependency of S/RBCs during strong temporal changes of illumination conditions are well illustrated by Figure 9.

4   Discussion and Outlook

It turned out that many *component* algorithms which have been gradually incorporated into a model-based road vehicle tracking system can be easily combined in order to provide a much more consistent and robust estimate of current illumination conditions. Care has been taken to explicate the conditions which have to be satisfied in order to apply the approach outlined and illustrated in the preceding sections.

Although this approach appears to work fine in case all these seemingly innocuous assumptions are satisfied, it can be upset, e. g., by trees which occlude part of the road with many leafless branches. These branches will cause numerous

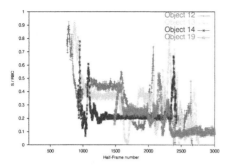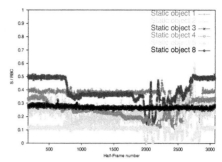

Fig. 8. S/RBCs (left panel: vehicles; right panel: masts) recorded under *diffuse* illumination in sequence dt_kont01. Whereas S/RBCs for the mast shadows consistently remain below 0.6, S/RBCs for vehicle shadows exceed this value during the beginning and end of this sequence. These 'excess' S/RBC values are due to accidental alignment of shadow contours with *unmodelled* tree branches and lane markings.

edge elements in practically all orientations with the consequence that enough of them overlap an hypothetical shadow cast onto the road behind these trees. Such areas thus have to be detected and excluded from any attempt to estimate the illumination state.

Another surprising finding has been that even a comparatively small scene like the one illustrated in Figure 3 can be covered by multiple small clouds with fuzzy boundaries such that directed and diffuse illumination coexist in close neighborhood. It thus is no longer possible in general to assume a *single* daylight illumination state even for such a small scene.

Obviously, a number of additional situations may occur where the list of assumptions enumerated in Section 2.1 is still incomplete. For example, we did not treat the case where large buildings outside the field of view can cast a shadow onto visible parts of the road. In these cases, some vehicles may exhibit strong evidence for directed illumination whereas other ones, driving within areas shadowed by these buildings, give evidence to the contrary. It remains to be seen to which extent such situations can be handled by introducing a corresponding hypothesis, possibly bound to a well delimited part of the scene. In fortunate circumstances, at least a rough estimate of the shadow-casting parts of such buildings may be obtained, in particular if the temporal variation of their shadows with the time of day can be evaluated more closely. Other sources of inconsistent evidence appear possible, for example effects due to a wider range of weather conditions as studied, e. g., in [3]. Nevertheless, the approach described in this contribution appears to provide a good starting point towards gradual improvement of illumination estimation for road traffic scenes in daylight.

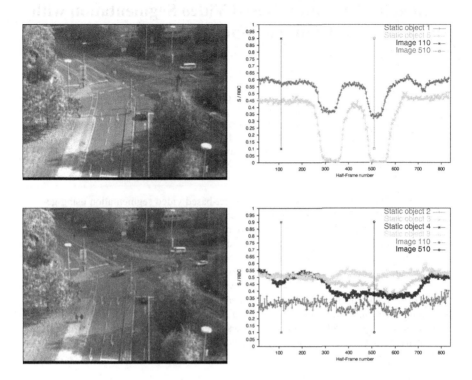

Fig. 9. The 'Shadow/Road Boundary Coverage (S/RBC)' illlustrated during quickly changing illumination conditions. The left panel in the top row shows frame 110 of image sequence dt_kont03a at a time where bright sunshine illuminated most of the depicted scene. The left panel in the bottom row shows frame 510 recorded 8 seconds later when the sky had become partially clouded. The top right panel plots the S/RBC for the two center masts with strong changes of shadow contours on the road. The bottom right panel shows S/RBCs for other masts where the shadows do not change that markedly during the recording period.

References

1. D. Koller, K. Daniilidis, and H.-H. Nagel: *Model-Based Object Tracking in Monocular Image Sequences of Road Traffic Scenes.* International Journal of Computer Vision **10**:3 (1993) 257–281.
2. H. Leuck and H.-H. Nagel: *Model-Based Initialisation of Vehicle Tracking: Dependency on Illumination.* In: Proc. 8th International Conference on Computer Vision (ICCV 2001), 9–12 July 2001, Vancouver/BC, Canada, Vol. I, pp. 309–314.
3. S.G. Narasimhan and S.K. Nayar: *Vision and the Atmosphere.* International Journal of Computer Vision **48**:3 (2002) 233–254.
4. I. Sato, Y. Sato, and K. Ikeuchi: *Illumination from Shadows.* IEEE Transactions on Pattern Analysis and Machine Intelligence PAMI-25:3 (2003) 290–300.

Genetic Algorithm-Based Video Segmentation with Adaptive Population Size

Se Hyun Park[1], Eun Yi Kim[2*] and Beom-Joon Cho[1]

[1]Division of Computer Engineering, College of Electronic and Information, Chosun Univ.,
375 Susuk-dong, Dong-gu, Gwangju, Korea
sehyun@chosun.ac.kr
[2]College of Internet and Media, Konkuk Univ.,
1 Hwayang-dong, Gwangjin-gu, Seoul, Korea
eykim@kkucc.konkuk.ac.kr

Abstract. This paper presented a novel object-based video segmentation using genetic algorithms. The novelty of the approach is that the population size is not constant, but motion dependent. The population size depends on the degree of the motion. In our approach, the video segmentation is performed by two steps: initial segmentation and temporal tracking. Once the objects constituting the scenes, which are tracked through the whole video sequence. Then, the temporal tracking is carried out by chromosomes that evolve using distributed genetic algorithms (DGAs). Each chromosome has its own population size according to its motion amounts, and independently evolves using local evolutionary rules. The proposed method was tested with well-known video sequences, and the results confirmed its effectiveness in segmenting a video sequence.

1 Introduction

Video segmentation, as related to the extraction and tracking of independently moving objects in a video sequence, has been the subject of intensive research due to its importance in a variety of applications, including vision systems, pattern recognition, video compression, and so on [1-3]. In particular, there has been a growing interest in video sequence segmentation mainly due to the development of MPEG-4 and MPEG-7. In these visual coding standard, a video sequence is considered to be composed of independent objects, called video object planes (VOPs), so that is processed object-by-object. Therefore, to support these content-based functionalities, each frame of the video sequence must first be segmented into semantic objects.

Until now, various techniques and algorithms have been proposed to resolve these issues. These methods can be categorized into three basic techniques according to the information they use for segmentation: spatial segmentation; motion segmentation; spatiotemporal segmentation. Among these, the third technique uses both spatial and temporal information (i.e., color and motion), has become a recent focus of intensive research and would seem to produce a more meaningful segmentation. The spatio-temporal segmentation step divides the first frame in a sequence into video objects forming the scene. And then temporal tracking step segments the subsequent frame, and establishes the temporal correspondence between the same video objects in the sequence.

---

* The corresponding author: Tel. +82-2-450-4135

B. Michaelis and G. Krell (Eds.): DAGM 2003, LNCS 2781, pp. 426–433, 2003.

Recently, genetic algorithms based video segmentation has been proposed [1, 2]. In particular, the techniques presented in [1] can automatically extract and track semantic objects in video sequence. The method improves the computational time as well as the quality of the segmentation results. However, it is still slow when applied to real-time video applications, such as video coding and video surveillance. There are several factors that influence the computational time, including the label size, crossover rates, mutation rates, and population size (i.e., window size). In particular, the population size has a significant influence on both the speed and the performance of the object-tracking method. The segmentation with larger window size retains the temporal correspondence of the same object between successive frames [2]. That is to say, larger window size is required for tracking successfully objects with faster motion. However, it requires more computational time. Besides, the method applies fixed window size to all other objects though each object has different motion, and so the computational time is wasted. One idea to solve this problem is that genetic algorithms with different window sizes are applied to different video objects. Once objects are produced by the initial segmentation method, they are separately updated by DGAs with different widow sizes in direct proportion to the amount of motion involved.

This paper presents GA-based video segmentation with adaptive population size. The population size of the approach depends on the degree of the motion. This proposed method consists of two parts: initial segmentation and temporal tracking. The initial segmentation is used to segment the two initial frames into semantic objects and is performed using video segmentation method that is presented in [1]. In temporal tracking, a motion vector for each object should first be estimated to decide the window size of DGAs, and then each object is projected into next frame based on the motion. The projected object is then assigned to DGAs with different widow sizes in direct proportion to the amount of motion involved. In order to update a video object, each object is updated by chromosomes that evolve using DGAs. The proposed method was tested with several well-known video sequences, and the experimental results confirm its effectiveness in segmenting a video sequence.

2 Proposed Method

This paper presents object-based video segmentation using genetic algorithms. Fig. 1 shows outline of the proposed method. The proposed method consists of two parts: initial segmentation and temporal tracking. The first issue deals with separating the moving objects from the background. The second issue deals with segmenting and tracking the video objects in the successive frames. This is performed based on the assumption that the current segmentation is likely to be very similar to the previous one, hence the segmentation results of the current frame is successively obtained using the segmentation result of the previous frame. Temporal tracking is performed by chromosomes that evolve using DGAs. The chromosomes are initialized with the spatial segmentation result of the previous frame, thereafter only unstable chromosomes corresponding to the moving objects parts are evolved by crossover and mutation. Moreover, chromosomes have the different population sizes according to their motion amounts. This ensures the coherence between the successive segmentations, and it identifies the different video objects composing the scene throughout the video sequence. As well as, it allows for reduction of the computational time and for improvement of the segmentation quality.

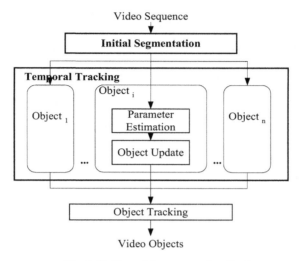

Fig. 1. Outline of the proposed method

2.1 Initial Segmentation

Initial segmentation stage is used to define the objects consistuting the scene. It consists of three steps: spatial segmentation, motion detection, and video object extraction. The spatial segmentation divides frames in the video sequence into regions with accurate boundaries and is performed by chromosomes that evolve using distributed genetic algorithms (DGAs). The motion detecton produces a CDM that dictates the foreground and background using the adaptive threshold presented in [4]. In video object extraction, video object planes are created by combination of the spatial segmentation results and CDM. The details of respective steps are described in [1].

2.2 Temporal Tracking

Temporal tracking consists of three steps: parameter estimation, object update, and object tracking. Prior to track the changed information between the successive frames, the population sizes of DGAs are determined. And then, each object is updated by chromosomes that evolve using modified DGAs. The chromosomes are started from the result of the previous frame, and only unstable chromosomes corresponding to boundaries of an object are evolved. This update is also applied to background object and then segments background into new regions included by new object. Thereafter, the updated video objects are tracked on consecutive frames in object tracking phase.

2.2.1 Parameter Estimation

In DGAs, a small-sized population reduces the computational time, yet results in premature convergence as insufficient samples are provided in the search space. In contrast, a large-sized population can provide more information to search for better solutions, as the population contains more representative solutions within the search space. However, higher computational costs are involved with a large-sized population, along with a potentially unacceptably slow rate of convergence. From the viewpoint of video, it would seem to be reasonable that the larger population sizes are given to the chromosomes corresponding to the moving objects, than ones corresponding to the background. This mechanism allows for the same representative solutions while reducing the computational cost.

Each chromosome has its own motion vector based on the corresponding object. Then, the motion vector of an object Q is determined as follows.

$$\left(W_{t,i,x}, W_{t,i,y}\right) = \left(\max\left(\alpha \left| C_x(Q_{t-1,i}) - C_x(Q_{t-2,i}) \right|, 3 \right), \quad \max\left(\alpha \left| C_y(Q_{t-1,i}) - C_y(Q_{t-2,i}) \right|, 3 \right) \right),$$

where $Q_{t,i}$ is i^{th} object in t^{th} frame, and $W_{t,i,x}$ and $W_{t,i,y}$ are x- and y-component of window size to segment $Q_{t,i}$, respectively. And, and $C(\cdot)$ is the function computing the center of an object. The term α is a constant that controls the weight of the window size relative to an object motion, and it is determined. In addition, the minimum value of window size is fixed to 3. The window size is determined on the assumption that the motion of an object between successive frames is similar to one between the previous frames. Hence, the window size is set to all pixels of the projected object as illustrated in Fig. 2.

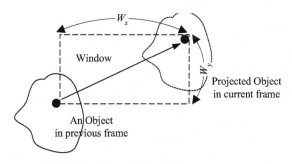

Fig. 2. Decision of the window size

2.2.2 Object Update

As a video object moves through a video sequence, it might rotate or change its shape. To allow for this, the video object must be spatially and temporally updated every frame, thus object update is performed in two steps: spatial update and temporal update.

The spatial update of objects is performed by chromosomes that evolve using modified DGAs. The DGAs have the different evolutionary rules as well as the different population sizes. Unlike the standard DGAs, the chromosomes are started with the segmentation results of the previous frame, and only chromosomes corresponding to the actually moving objects are evolved by mating operators. The modified DGAs are described in Fig. 3. At time t ($t > 0$), the system receives the input frame F_t, $C_{t-1,i}$, and $W_{t,i}$, that is, the current frame, the segmentation result of ith object in the previous frame, and the window size in proportion to the amount of motion of ith object, respectively. Starting with the segmentation results of the previous frame, chromosomes in i^{th} object are then evolved through iteratively performed selection and genetic operators. In the selection process, the chromosomes are updated to new chromosomes, $C'_{t,i}$. Thereafter, the Decision Module classifies the chromosomes into stable chromosomes, $S\_C_{t,i}$, or unstable chromosomes, $U\_C_{t,I}$, according to their fitness values. In the current frame, the chromosomes in i^{th} object are sorted in an increasing order based on their fitness values. Only unstable chromosomes are evolved by crossover and mutation. In Fig. 3, $U\_C'_{t,i}$ and $U\_C''_{t,i}$ are chromosomes evolved by crossover and mutation, respectively. $S\_C_{t,i}$ is then delayed for τ, the time taken for the genetic operators within a generation. These operators are iteratively performed until the stopping criterion is satisfied. The stopping criterion is denined in [2].

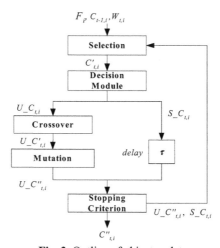

Fig. 3. Outline of object update

To temporally update moving objects, a change detection mask (CDM) is produced by adaptive thresholding and historical information. CDM is firstly obtained by adaptively thresholding the intensity difference between two consecutive frames. And then the results are verified and compensated by historical information, to enhance the coherent segmentation results of moving objects. Here, the *history information* of a pixel means whether or not the pixel belongs to the moving object parts in the previous frame. If it belongs to part of a moving object in the previous frame and its label is the same as one of the corresponding pixel in the previous frame, the pixel is marked as the foreground area in the current frame.

2.2.3 Object Tracking

The last step is to establish the correspondence between the same video. Then, the natural correspondence is a key of proposed object-tracking method. The *natural correspondence* means those regions making up an object retain their label values through the whole video sequence. Therefore, temporal linkages between same objects in the successive frames can be established by this natural correspondence.

In the following, the object K in the current segmentation results $VOP(t)$ represents a *child*, while the object P which was previously detected represents a *parent*. The object $K = \{K_i \mid i \in \Lambda\}$ and $P = \{P_i \mid i \in \Lambda\}$ are composed of regions taking specific values in the label set Λ.

As such, the natural correspondence between a child and a parent is only established if the following condition is satisfied:

$$Sim(K, K^*) \geq \theta_{N\_C}, \tag{1}$$

where

$$K^* = \arg \max_{P \in VOP(t-1)} Sim(K, P) \quad \text{and} \tag{2}$$

$$Sim(K, P) = -\frac{\sum_{i \in \Lambda} \mid num(K_i) - num(P_i) \mid^2}{\sum_{i \in \Lambda} \mid num(K_i) \mid}. \tag{3}$$

In (1), θ_{N_C} is the threshold, which is fixed at -200, regardless of the input video sequence, K' is the parent that has the most similar label distribution and similar size to K, and $Sim(\cdot, \cdot)$ is the function computing the similarity between P and K. The similarity between two VOPs is measured relative to two measures: 1) the label distribution of the regions forming the VOPs and 2) the size of the regions corresponding to the specific labels in the VOPs. If there is a significant difference between the sizes of the regions assigned to a label in two VOPs, the similarity value is decreased. Plus, if the difference between the labels of the regions forming the parent and the child is increased, the similarity is also decreased. In summary natural correspondence between P and K is only established if they consist of regions with similar sizes and labels.

3 Experimental Results

To assess the validity of the proposed method, it was tested with several different data and the results were compared with Kim *et al.*'s method [2]. They proposed a GA-based segmentation method that can automatically extract and tracks moving objects. The feature of that work is to provide the chromosomes corresponding to the moving objects parts with more opportunity to be evolved by mating operators. Kim *et al.* proved their work can be enhance the performance relative to speed and segmentation quality rather than standard GAs. However, their work has a limit to establish the natural correspondence of same objects between the successive frames, because it use a fixed population sizes.

Our aim is to develop a GA-based video segmentation method that can improve the performance than other existing GA-based segmentation method. Accordingly, our results were compared with ones of Kim *et al.* Then, to evaluate the quality of the segmentations, the evaluation function F was used, which was also used by Kim *et al.* [2] and Liu *et al.* [5]. Liu *et al.* originally propose the evaluation function. The smaller the value of F, the better the segmentation results. Two methods were tested with several video sequences, and compared each other. However, due to space constraints, only two results for *Claire* and *Table Tennis* were showed in this section.

The parameters used in experiments were as follows: the stability threshold was set at 99.9%, the stability number at 50, the maximal stability at 100%, the maximum number of generations at 1000, the label size at 64, crossover and mutation rate 0.1 and 0.005, respectively. Finally, the window size was fixed to 5×5 in Kim *et al.*'s method, while it was not constant in our method.

Fig. 4 shows the result for *Claire*. Since the body of the woman stays almost immobile during most of the sequence, this is a typical example of where a visually important object can be lost due to the lack of decisive information in certain frames. Fig. 4(a) shows the original frame at time 90 and 96, and the corresponding segmentation results are shown in Fig. 4(b). And Figs. 4(c) and (d) show the regions colored in accordance with its label, and extracted moving VOPs. As shown in Fig. 4(c), those regions corresponding to the same objects are colored with the same color, thereby establishing a natural correspondence between the same objects. In addition, Fig. 4(d) shows that the proposed method clearly compensated for the lack of motion information as both the woman and the background were robustly identified in all the frames.

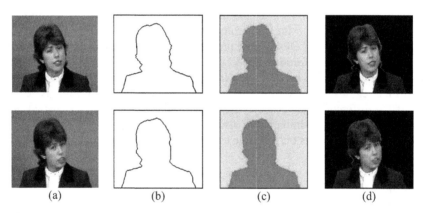

(a)   (b)   (c)   (d)

Fig. 4. Segmentation results for *Claire*. (a) Original frames, (b) Segmentation results, (c) Colored region according to their label values, (d) VOPs for moving objects.

To fully demonstrate the validity of the proposed methods for object extraction and tracking, they were applied to a video sequence with more than two objects. Fig. 5 shows the object extraction and tracking results for *Table Tennis*. As you can see, the boundaries of extracted VOPs were virtually perfect, and VOPs were correctly tracked through the successive frames. Fig. 5(a) shows the original frame and the corresponding segmentation results are shown in Fig. 5(b). And Figs. 5(c), (d) and (e) show the regions colored in accordance with its label, and extracted moving VOPs. As shown in Fig. 5(c), those regions corresponding to the same objects are colored with the same color, thereby establishing a natural correspondence between the same objects.

Table 1 summarized the performance comparisons of two methods when segmenting the sequence *Claire* and *Table Tennis*. These comparisons show that the proposed method could improve both the quality of the segmentation results and the convergence speed. Consequently, the proposed method demonstrated a superior perform-ance when compared with other DGA-based algorithms.

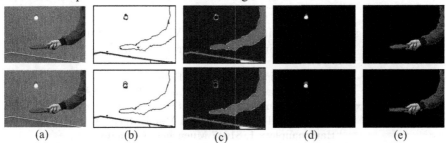

| (a) | (b) | (c) | (d) | (e) |

Fig. 5. VOPs generation results for Table Tennis. (a) Original frames, (b) Segmentation results, (c) Colored region according to their label values, (d) VOPs for ball, (e) VOPs for the arm.

Table 1. Performance comparisons

Methods	Video Sequences	Average no. of generations to segment a frame	Average time taken to segment a frame	Average value of the uniform evalua-tion functions
Kim *et al.*'s	Claire	26.01	2.63	52.43
method	Table Tennis	24.42	6.76	39.48
Proposed	Claire	18.23	1.12	44.24
method	Table Tennis	21.68	4.55	35.94

4 Conclusion

This paper presented GA-based video segmentation with adaptive population size. The population size of the approach depends on the degree of the motion. This pro-posed method consisted of two parts: initial segmentation and temporal tracking. The initial segmentation was used to segment the two initial frames into semantic objects. In temporal tracking, each object was updated and tracked through a whole video sequence. The experimental results confirmed its effectiveness in segmenting a video sequence.

Acknowledgement. This work was supported by Korea Research Foundation Grant (KRF-2002-003-D00337)

References

1. Hwang, S. W., Kim, E. Y., Park, S. H., Kim, H. J.: Object extraction and tracking using genetic algorithms. International Conference on Image Processing 2001, (2001) 383-386
2. Kim, E. Y., Hwang, S. W., Park, S. H., Kim, H. J.: Spatiotemporal segmentation using ge-netic algorithms. Pattern Recognition, Vol. 34. (2001) 2063-2066.
3. Meier, T., Ngan, K. N.: Video segmentation for content-based coding. IEEE Trans. Circuits Syst. Video Technol., Vol. 9, No. 8. (1999) 1190-1203.
4. Habili, N., Moini, A., Burgess, N.: Automatic thresholding for change detection in digital video. in Proc. SPIE, Vol. 4067. (2000) 133-142.
5. Liu, J., Yang, Y. H.: Multiresolution color image segmentation. IEEE Trans. Pattern Anal. Machine Intell., Vol. 16, No. 7. (1994) 689-700.

Component Fusion for Face Detection in the Presence of Heteroscedastic Noise

Binglong Xie[1], Dorin Comaniciu[1], Visvanathan Ramesh[1],
Markus Simon[2], and Terrance Boult[3]

[1] Siemens Corporate Research
755 College Road East, Princeton, NJ 08540, USA
{binglong.xie, dorin.comaniciu, visvanathan.ramesh}@scr.siemens.com
[2] Information and Communication Mobile, Siemens AG
Haidenauplatz 1, 81617 Muenchen, Germany
markus.simon@siemens.com
[3] Computer Science and Engineering Dept., Lehigh University
19 Memorial Drive West, Bethlehem, PA 18015, USA
tboult@cse.lehigh.edu

Abstract. Face detection using components has been proved to produce superior results due to its robustness to occlusions and pose and illumination changes. A first level of processing is devoted to the detection of individual components, while a second level deals with the fusion of the component detectors. However, the fusion methods investigated up to now neglect the uncertainties that characterize the component locations. We show that this uncertainty carries important information that, when exploited, leads to increased face localization accuracy. We discuss and compare possible solutions taking into account geometrical constraints. The efficiency and usefulness of the techniques are tested with both synthetic and real world examples.

1 Introduction

It is known that component-based face detection can yield better performance than global approaches when pose and illumination variations and occlusions are considered[9,5,6,11]. While pose and illumination significantly change the global face appearance, since the components are smaller than the whole face, they are less prone to these changes. The component detectors can accurately locate the face components as well. This information should be used to register and normalize the face to a "standard" one, which is appropriate for face recognition. Also, component-based methods can be used to build a detector that can handle partial occlusions [6,11]. Component-based methods have been also successfully used in other areas, such as people detection [8].

In [5], Heisele et al present a component-based face detector with a two-level hierarchy of Support Vector Machine (SVM) classifiers [2]. The face components are detected independently with the trained SVMs at the first level, and at the second level, a single SVM checks if the geometric locations of the components

B. Michaelis and G. Krell (Eds.): DAGM 2003, LNCS 2781, pp. 434–441, 2003.

comply with a face. However, only the largest responses from the component detectors are used when checking the validity of the geometry. Also, SVMs are slow and it should be very challenging to employ them in real-time systems.

In [10], Viola and Jones employ 4 types of rectangular features and use AdaBoosting [4] to automatically build the strong classifier from feature-based weak classifiers. They compute the integral image (similar to the summed area table in [3]) to accelerate the computation of features. Their paper reports a high detection rate, a low false detection rate and the boosted face detector works in real-time.

This paper introduces a new framework for component fusion in the context of the face detection task. Fusion relies on modeling the noise as heteroscedastic and is constrained by a geometric face model. To achieve real-time performance, we employ AdaBoosting when training component detectors. However, our framework is open to various types of component detectors, e.g., SVMs.

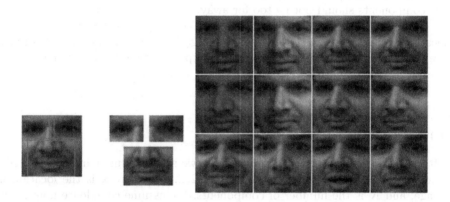

Fig. 1. Left: the components of a face. The left eye component and right eye component are 36 by 28 pixels. The lower face component is 52 by 40 pixels. **Right:** Face examples. The first row and the second row are frontal and turning left faces respectively with 4 different illumination settings.The third row shows faces with different expressions.

2   Component Detectors

In our work, we use 3 components for a face. All the faces are aligned to a 64 by 64 pixel image. We then use three rectangles to cut 3 components, left eye, right eye and lower face, as shown in Figure 1 (left).

Our face database has 1862 faces. The images were taken with 5 poses (frontal, turning left, turning right, tilting up, and tilting down) and 4 illumination conditions(dark overall, lighting from left, lighting from right, and bright overall). There are also some faces with different expressions. Figure 1 (right) shows some examples from the database. We collected more than 6000 pictures as negative examples for detector training.

The AdaBoosting theory states that by adding weak classifiers one can obtain better strong classifiers. However in practice this might not be true, since the weak classifiers are often correlated. To deal with this issue, we use a modified AdaBoosting method that trains the component detectors such that the trained strong classifier is verified to be empirically better at each boosting step.

3   Component-Based Face Model

Suppose we have a probabilistic face model, where each component position has some uncertainty. With the uncertainties, the face model is flexible to describe a variety of possible faces. Assuming Gaussian distributions, in the face model we have a set of 2D points with means $\mathbf{m}_i$, and covariance matrices C_i, $i = 1, 2, ..., N$, where N is the number of components. The face model is a constraint that the components should comply with the geometrical configurations, e.g., the components should not be too far away (see Figure 2 (left)).

The face model is trained from known face examples. We know the exact locations of the components in each training face example, so we can estimate the mean and covariance matrix of each component from these locations.

4   Component Fusion

4.1   Problem Formulation

After the component detectors are trained, we scan the input image to get the component confidence maps, $A_i(\mathbf{x})$, $i = 1, 2, ..., N$, where $\mathbf{x}$ is the location in image, and N is the number of components. We assume confidence map $A_i(\mathbf{x})$ is normalized across all the components.

With the face model $\{\mathbf{m}_i, C_i\}_{i=1,2,...,N}$, the overall face likelihood is:

$$L = \prod_{i=1}^{N} \left[A_i(\mathbf{x}_i) \frac{1}{|2\pi C_i|^{\frac{1}{2}}} \exp\left(-\frac{1}{2} (\mathbf{x}'_i - \mathbf{m}_i)^T C_i^{-1} (\mathbf{x}'_i - \mathbf{m}_i) \right) \right] \qquad (1)$$

where $\{\mathbf{x}'_i\}$ are rigidly transformed from $\{\mathbf{x}_i\}$ into the face model space, subject to rotation, translation and scaling.

Note the simple maxima of individual component detector responses are not necessarily best choices for component locations under face model constraints. Our goal is to find the best component localization $\{\mathbf{x}_i\}$ with maximal L. We can do exhaustive search with all $A_i(\mathbf{x})$ but that is too expensive.

Since the shape of $A_i(\mathbf{x})$ is often smooth and Gaussian-like, we use a Gaussian shape to approximate it. In other words, the underlying noise model is assumed heteroscedastic, i.e., the noise is both anisotropic and inhomogeneous. We can identify the local maximum as $s_i = A_i(\boldsymbol{\mu}_i)$, where $\boldsymbol{\mu}_i$ is the location of maximum and considered the center of the Gaussian shape. Matei [7] gives a non-parametric method to estimate the "covariance" matrix Q_i in a area B around $\boldsymbol{\mu}_i$:

$$Q_i = \frac{\sum_{\mathbf{x} \in B} \left[A_i(\mathbf{x}) \, (\mathbf{x} - \boldsymbol{\mu}_i) \, (\mathbf{x} - \boldsymbol{\mu}_i)^T \right]}{\sum_{\mathbf{x} \in B} A_i(\mathbf{x})} \tag{2}$$

Then the confidence map can be rewritten:

$$A_i(\mathbf{x}) = s_i \frac{1}{|2\pi Q_i|^{\frac{1}{2}}} \exp\left(-\frac{1}{2} \, (\mathbf{x}_i - \boldsymbol{\mu}_i)^T \, Q_i^{-1} \, (\mathbf{x}_i - \boldsymbol{\mu}_i) \right) \tag{3}$$

Therefore,

$$\ln L = \sum_{i=1}^{N} \left[\ln s_i - \frac{1}{2} \ln \left(|2\pi Q_i| \, |2\pi C_i| \right) \right] - \frac{1}{2} d^2 \tag{4}$$

where

$$d^2 = \sum_{i=1}^{N} |\mathbf{x}_i' - \mathbf{m}_i|^2_{C_i} + \sum_{i=1}^{N} |\mathbf{x}_i - \boldsymbol{\mu}_i|^2_{Q_i} \tag{5}$$

$$= \sum_{i=1}^{N} (\mathbf{x}_i' - \mathbf{m}_i)^T C_i^{-1} (\mathbf{x}_i' - \mathbf{m}_i) + \sum_{i=1}^{N} (\mathbf{x}_i - \boldsymbol{\mu}_i)^T Q_i^{-1} (\mathbf{x}_i - \boldsymbol{\mu}_i) \tag{6}$$

In order to maximize L one should minimize d^2. When d^2 is computed for an observation, L or $\ln L$ can be thresholded to make a detection or rejection decision.

4.2 Least Square Fitting

For the beginning, let us simplify the problem so that we only have fixed-point face model $\{\mathbf{m}_i\}$ and fixed-point observations $\{\mathbf{x}_i\}$, for example, taking the means of the face model and maxima of the confidence maps.

Suppose we find the scaling factor s, the rotation R and translation $\mathbf{x}_0$, so that an observation point $\mathbf{x}$ can be mapped to a point $\mathbf{x}'$ in model space.

$$\mathbf{x}' = sR(\mathbf{x} - \mathbf{x}_0) \tag{7}$$

where, the rotation matrix R is a function of θ:

$$R = \begin{pmatrix} \cos\theta & \sin\theta \\ -\sin\theta & \cos\theta \end{pmatrix} \tag{8}$$

Our goal is to minimize the sum of squared error d^2 by choosing the right s, R and $\mathbf{x}_0$:

$$d^2 = \sum_{i=1}^{N} |\mathbf{x}_i' - \mathbf{m}_i|^2 \tag{9}$$

By taking the partial derivatives of Equation (9) with respect to θ, s and $\mathbf{x}_0$, and setting them to zeros (denoting $\mathbf{m}_i = (m_i, n_i)^T$ and $\mathbf{x}_i = (x_i, y_i)^T$), we get the solution:

$$\theta = \arctan \frac{\sum m_i \sum y_i - \sum n_i \sum x_i - N \sum (m_i y_i - n_i x_i)}{\sum m_i \sum x_i + \sum n_i \sum y_i - N \sum (m_i x_i + n_i y_i)} \tag{10}$$

$$s = \frac{N \sum (\mathbf{m}_i^T R \mathbf{x}_i) - (\sum \mathbf{m}_i^T) R (\sum \mathbf{x}_i)}{N \sum (\mathbf{x}_i^T \mathbf{x}_i) - (\sum \mathbf{x}_i^T)(\sum \mathbf{x}_i)} \tag{11}$$

$$\mathbf{x}_0 = \frac{1}{N} \sum \mathbf{x}_i - \frac{1}{sN} R^T \sum \mathbf{m}_i \tag{12}$$

Using the above solution, we can evaluate Equation (9) to get the least square error. A smaller d^2 suggests a larger similarity between the observation and model geometrical configurations. This simple method does not take the individual component confidences into consideration, nor the heteroscedastic model of the noise.

4.3   Fitting Points to a Probabilistic Model

Within this section assume that we have a probabilistic model of 2D points $\{\mathbf{m}_i, C_i\}_{i=1,2,...,N}$. We want to match the observed points $\mathbf{x}_i$ to the model. This case has been analyzed by Cootes and Taylor[1], and here is the summary.

An observation point $\mathbf{x}$ can be mapped to a point $\mathbf{x}'$ in model space:

$$\mathbf{x}' = R\mathbf{x} + \mathbf{t} \tag{13}$$

where, $\mathbf{t} = (t_x, t_y)^T$ and the scaling and rotation matrix R is

$$R = \begin{pmatrix} a & -b \\ b & a \end{pmatrix} \tag{14}$$

Let us denote $\mathbf{a} = (a, b)^T$, and the goal is to find the best $\mathbf{a}$ and $\mathbf{t}$ to minimize the Mahalanobis distance:

$$d^2 = \sum_{i=1}^{N} |\mathbf{x}'_i - \mathbf{m}_i|_{C_i}^2 = \sum_{i=1}^{N} (R\mathbf{x}_i + \mathbf{t} - \mathbf{m}_i)^T C_i^{-1} (R\mathbf{x}_i + \mathbf{t} - \mathbf{m}_i) \tag{15}$$

Taking the partial derivatives of Equation (15) with respect to $\mathbf{a}$ and $\mathbf{t}$, and setting them to zeros, we get the solution:

$$\begin{pmatrix} \mathbf{a} \\ \mathbf{t} \end{pmatrix} = \begin{pmatrix} \sum C_i^{-1} Y_i, & \sum C_i^{-1} \\ \sum Y_i^T C_i^{-1} Y_i, & \sum Y_i^T C_i^{-1} \end{pmatrix}^{-1} \begin{pmatrix} \sum C_i^{-1} \mathbf{m}_i \\ \sum Y_i^T C_i^{-1} \mathbf{m}_i \end{pmatrix} \tag{16}$$

where, $Y_i = (\mathbf{x}_i, J\mathbf{x}_i)$ and

$$J = \begin{pmatrix} 0 & -1 \\ 1 & 0 \end{pmatrix} \tag{17}$$

4.4   Matching Probabilistic Observations to a Probabilistic Model

With the model $\{\mathbf{m}_i, C_i\}$ and observation $\{\boldsymbol{\mu}_i, Q_i\}$, $i = 1, 2, ..., N$, we want to find the best choices of component locations $\mathbf{x}_i$, and the associated transformation $\mathbf{a}$ and $\mathbf{t}$ to minimize the combined Mahalanobis distance d^2 in Equation (6), where $\mathbf{x}'_i$ is a function of $\mathbf{x}_i$, $\mathbf{a}$ and $\mathbf{t}$ according to Equation (13). Unfortunately, it is hard to find the close form solution to this problem, because the partial derivatives are not linear with respect to $\mathbf{x}_i$, $\mathbf{a}$ and $\mathbf{t}$.

We can use two strategies to solve this optimization problem. One employs numerical optimization methods, such as Levenberg-Marquardt or Newton iterative optimization, which require iterations before convergence.

The other approximates the solution. Notice in Equation (6) there are two terms. The first term is the Mahalanobis distance in the model space, and the second term is the Mahalanobis distance in the observation space. If we pick $\boldsymbol{\mu}_i$ as the solution for $\mathbf{x}_i$ (this is the first approximation of the solution, though very rough), and use Section 4.3 to match $\boldsymbol{\mu}_i$ to the probabilistic model $\{\mathbf{m}_i, C_i\}_{i=1,2,...,N}$, we end up a biased minimization d^2_{obs} of Equation (6) where the second term is zero. On the other hand, if we pick $\mathbf{m}_i$ as the matched points $\mathbf{x}'_i$ in the model space, and use Section 4.3 to match $\mathbf{x}'_i$ back to the observation $\{\boldsymbol{\mu}_i, Q_i\}_{i=1,2,...,N}$ (denote that the choices in the observation space are $\mathbf{x}''_i$), we end up another biased minimization d^2_{mod} of Equation (6) where the first term is zero. The real minimization must be a tradeoff between these two biased ones. The second approximation of the solution we choose is then the equal average:

$$\mathbf{x}_i = \frac{\boldsymbol{\mu}_i + \mathbf{x}''_i}{2} \tag{18}$$

Further more, we can refine the equal average to get the third approximation, the weighted average approximation, by using the Mahalanobis distances in weighting the average:

$$\mathbf{x}_i = \boldsymbol{\mu}_i + \frac{d^2_{obs}}{d^2_{obs} + d^2_{mod}}(\mathbf{x}''_i - \boldsymbol{\mu}_i) \tag{19}$$

The advantage of the approximations is that they are fast. If the solutions are close to the real minimum, the approximations are more favorable for real-time face detection systems.

5   Experiments

5.1   Synthetic Data

In this experiment, we assume a face model where the centers of the left eye, right eye and lower face components are:

$$\mathbf{m}_1 = \begin{pmatrix} 17.5 \\ -13.5 \end{pmatrix} ; \mathbf{m}_2 = \begin{pmatrix} 45.5 \\ -13.5 \end{pmatrix} ; \mathbf{m}_3 = \begin{pmatrix} 31.5 \\ -43.5 \end{pmatrix} \tag{20}$$

and the associated covariance matrices are:

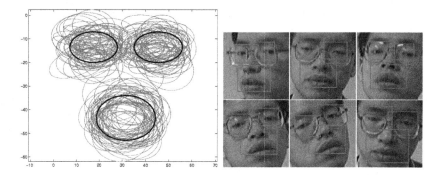

Fig. 2. Left: Face model and 50 examples of the observation distributions. The thick ellipses are the model distribution. The thin ellipses are the randomly generated observation distributions. **Right**: Real world face detection examples from a video with different poses.

$$C_1 = \begin{pmatrix} 18 & 0 \\ 0 & 7 \end{pmatrix} ; C_2 = \begin{pmatrix} 18 & 0 \\ 0 & 7 \end{pmatrix} ; C_3 = \begin{pmatrix} 27 & 0 \\ 0 & 15 \end{pmatrix} \tag{21}$$

We randomly generate observation data by adding noise to both the means and covariance matrices of the components in the face model. A 0-mean Gaussian noise with a standard deviation of 4 pixels is added to both x and y directions of the means, and the covariance matrices are also added with a 0-mean Gaussian noise with a standard deviation of 3. The face model and observation examples are shown in Figure 2 (left).

Figure 3 (left) shows the d^2 computed with various approximations. The observation mean approximation has large errors. The equal average and weighted average approximations are very close to the true d^2 obtained by Levenberg-Marquardt optimization. Figure 3 (right) shows the distance error of the best match for each component in average in the observation space. We can see small but noticeable displacement errors for the equal and weighted average methods, compared to Figure 3 (left). This suggests that the when d^2 is close to the minimum, the d^2 surface is quite flat, which is because of the fact that we have relatively large covariances in the face model and observation examples.

5.2   Real World Examples

With AdaBoosting component detectors, our current face detection system runs comfortably at frame rate on a standard laptop with 640 by 480 image size. We tested our techniques with real world examples. Figure 2 (right) shows some examples of handling pose changes. We are currently evaluating the performance of the system on standard face databases.

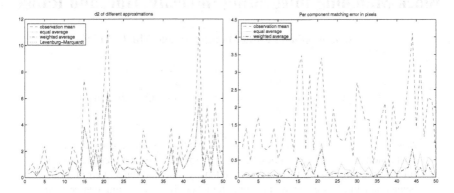

Fig. 3. Left: d^2 from various approximations. **Right**: Both the weighted and average approximations have small localization errors. The x axis is the sample number index in the above graphs.

6   Conclusion

This paper presented a statistical fusion framework for component-based face detection. The framework is tested with component face detectors trained using AdaBoosting, running in real-time. Our work is effective with both synthetic and real world experiments. We do not model the cross-component correlations and this could be part of future work.

References

1. T. Cootes and C. Taylor. Statistical models of appearance for computer vision. Technical report, University of Manchester, September 1999.
2. Corinna Cortes and Vladimir Vapnik. Support-vector networks. *Machine Learning*, 20(3):273–297, 1995.
3. F. Crow. Summed-area tables for texture mapping. In *Proceedings of SIGGRAPH*, volume 18, pages 207–212, 1984.
4. Yoav Freund and Robert E. Schapire. Experiments with a new boosting algorithm. In *International Conference on Machine Learning*, pages 148–156, 1996.
5. B. Heisele, T. Serre, M. Pontil, and T. Poggio. Component-based face detection. In *CVPR01*, pages I:657–662, 2001.
6. T.K. Leung, M. C. Burl, and P. Perona. Finding faces in cluttered scenes using random labeled graph matching. In *Fifth Intl. Conf. on Comp. Vision*, June 1995.
7. Bogdan Matei. Heteroscedastic errors-in-variables models in computer vision. Ph.D. Dissertation, Rutgers, the State University of New Jersey, May 2001.
8. A. Mohan, C. Papageorgiou, and T. Poggio. Example-based object detection in images by components. *IEEE Trans. on PAMI*, 23(4), 2001.
9. C. Papageorgiou and T. Poggio. A trainable system for object detection. *IJCV*, 38(1):15–33, June 2000.
10. P. Viola and M. Jones. Robust real-time face detection. In *ICCV01*, page II: 747, 2001.
11. K. Yow and R. Cipolla. Feature-based human face detection. *IVC*, 15(9):713–35, 1997.

Block Matching Integrating Intensity, Hue, and Range

Seok-Woo Jang[1], Marc Pomplun[1], and Min C. Shin[2]

[1] Computer Science, University of Massachusetts at Boston, USA
{swjang, marc}@cs.umb.edu
[2] Computer Science, University of North Carolina at Charlotte, USA
mcshin@uncc.edu

Abstract. In this paper, we propose a new block matching algorithm that extracts motion vectors from consecutive range data. The proposed method defines a matching metric that integrates intensity, hue and range. Our algorithm begins matching with a small matching template. If the matching degree is not good enough, we slightly expand the size of a matching template and then repeat the matching process until our matching criterion is satisfied or the predetermined maximum size has been reached. As the iteration proceeds, we adaptively adjust weights of the matching metric by considering the importance of each feature.

1 Introduction

Block matching techniques have been widely used in areas such as video compression, motion estimation, video coding and video conferencing [1]. In block matching, a present frame of a sequence is first divided into N×N square blocks of pixels. For each block of a present frame, we look for the block of pixels that is most similar to it within a search area in the previous frame, according to a predetermined matching criterion. The relative positions of the two blocks define a motion vector associated with the present block. The collection of all motion vectors defines a motion field.

In order to reduce the computational time, many of the block matching techniques are concerned with how to define a search area in which to look for a candidate block. Some examples are the full search algorithm [2], the three-step search algorithm [3] and the four-step search algorithm [4]. The full search algorithm exhaustively examines all locations in the search area and provides the best solution. The three-step search algorithm uses a uniformly allocated search pattern [3]. The four-step search algorithm employs center-biased checking point patterns and halfway-stop techniques for fast block motion estimation [4]. On the other hand, the accuracy of block matching is another important criterion, because it determines the quality of the resulting motion vectors. Especially in the areas of motion estimation like moving object detection and tracking, it is more important to extract accurate motion vectors than to estimate those quickly, since the tracking is usually performed in a predicted small search area of an image, not within the whole image area.

Also, most block matching algorithms just consider the difference of gray intensities of corresponding blocks when they compute the degree of match. This criterion for block matching may be acceptable for the case of video coding, since the primary concern of coding is to reduce the temporal redundancy between successive frames.

B. Michaelis and G. Krell (Eds.): DAGM 2003, LNCS 2781, pp. 442–449, 2003.
© Springer-Verlag Berlin Heidelberg 2003

However, when we need an accurate estimation of block motion vectors as in video conferencing where interpolation is sometimes needed to improve the image quality based on motion, it may cause a problem. For instance, adjacent blocks may show similar intensities though their internal structures are different. Then, the intensity-based matching metric may choose as a candidate any of the blocks, resulting in inaccurate block motion vectors.

In this paper, to resolve these limitations, we propose a new block matching algorithm that extracts motion vectors from consecutive range data. We will discuss range data in detail in the next section. The proposed algorithm defines a matching metric that integrates intensity, hue and range features. The degree of overall match is computed as the weighted sum of matches of individual features. Our algorithm begins matching with a small matching template. If the matching degree is not good enough, we slightly expand the size of a matching template and then repeat the matching process until our matching criterion is satisfied or the predetermined maximum size has been reached. As the iteration proceeds, we adaptively adjust the weights of the matching metric by using the entropy of each feature in the search area, so that we may discriminate features according to the distinctiveness of features of an involved block.

2 Range Data

Range data is very useful in motion estimation and understanding because of improved quality of subsequent motion analysis as well as expanded data usability [5]. In a range image, the distances to points imaged are recorded over a quantized range. For instance, range value zero may mean a distance of 0 to 2.5 cm, range value one a distance of 2.5 cm to 5.0 cm, ... , range value 255 a distance of 637.5 cm to 640 cm. For display purposes, the distances are often coded in gray scale, such that the darker a pixel is, the closer it is to the camera. A range image may also be displayed using a arbitrary color for each quantized distance for easy viewing of isodistance quantization bands. The data acquired by a range camera is often referred to as being 2.5-D in nature, as opposed to 3-D. This is to differentiate this type of device from other sensors, such as a magnetic resonance image, which can acquire measurements in a complete 3-D grid, whereas range images only provide depth information about the visible surfaces of objects [6].

An image sequence captured from a real environment includes many areas which have different depth from the camera. In a 2-D image, a gray-scale or color of imaged points is recorded, but the depths of the points are ambiguous, whereas a range image includes the distances to imaged points. In this paper, we use range data to improve the accuracy of block matching. Our block matching algorithm uses range as one feature for defining the matching metric. The details will be discussed in the next section.

3 Matching Metric

Given a block of size N × N pixels, the block motion estimation looks for the best matching block within a search area. One can consider various criteria as a measure of the match between two blocks [7]. We claim that the intensity difference between two blocks by itself may not provide an accurate estimation of block motion, since it does not consider the internal structure of the local scene. We suggest involving multiple features in a matching metric. The similarity between blocks is then taken to be the weighted sum of the similarities in their individual features.

When multiple features are used in a matching metric, one has to take into consideration the following two issues. The first is the issue of normalizing the scale of features. If one of the features has a wide range of possible values compared to the other features, it will have a large effect on the total similarity and the decisions will be based primarily upon this single feature. To overcome this problem, it is necessary to apply scaling factors to the features before computing the similarities. The second issue is how to properly weight the features according to their importance. Depending on the context of a block, some features may be more informative than others. If some prior knowledge of the relative importance of the features is available, the features could be weighted according to their importance or desired contribution.

In this paper, we define the displaced block similarity (DBS) as a matching degree between two blocks as in (1).

$$
DBS(i, j; u, v; n) = \alpha(n) \cdot F_{\text{inten}}(i, j; u, v; n) + \beta(n) \cdot F_{\text{hue}}(i, j; u, v; n)
$$
$$
+ \gamma(n) \cdot F_{\text{range}}(i, j; u, v; n) \tag{1}
$$

$$
F_{\text{inten}}(i, j; u, v; n) = \left(1 - \frac{1}{n^2} \sum_{y=0}^{n-1} \sum_{x=0}^{n-1} \left| \frac{I_t(i+x, j+y) - I_{t-1}(i+u+x, j+v+y)}{I_{\max}} \right| \right) \times 100
$$

$$
F_{\text{hue}}(i, j; u, v; n) = \left(1 - \frac{1}{n^2} \sum_{y=0}^{n-1} \sum_{x=0}^{n-1} \left| \frac{H_t(i+x, j+y) - H_{t-1}(i+u+x, j+v+y)}{H_{\max}} \right| \right) \times 100
$$

$$
F_{\text{range}}(i, j; u, v; n) = \left(1 - \frac{1}{n^2} \sum_{y=0}^{n-1} \sum_{x=0}^{n-1} \left| \frac{R_t(i+x, j+y) - R_{t-1}(i+u+x, j+v+y)}{R_{\max}} \right| \right) \times 100
$$

In (1), F_{inten}, F_{hue} and F_{range} denote intensity, hue and range features, respectively. The index n denotes the size of a block template, (i,j) denotes the starting position of a current block in a present image, and (u,v) denotes the corresponding disparity between two blocks. I_t and I_{t-1} denote intensity values of the current frame and the previous frame, respectively. H_t and H_{t-1} denote hue values, and R_t and R_{t-1} denote range values. $I_{\max}$, $H_{\max}$ and $R_{\max}$ denote the maximum values of the three features. $\alpha(n)$, $\beta(n)$ and $\gamma(n)$ denote weights for intensity, hue and range features, respectively, at the size of block template n. The details of weight adjustment will be discussed in the next section. The displaced block similarity is formed as the weighted sum of the similarities of individual features, and has values from 0 to 100. The candidate block that maximizes $DBS(i,j;u,v;n)$ is selected as the best matched block and the corresponding displacement (u,v) becomes the motion vector of the block $(i,j;n)$.

Our block matching algorithm employs an evaluation function that examines matching degrees of candidate blocks to determine the appropriateness of the size of a block template. This function is designed with the following considerations: First, we consider the distinctiveness of the best match. When the degree of the best match is considerably higher than those of its neighbor candidates, we say that the match is distinctive and the corresponding size of a block is proper. However, if the degree of the best match is close to those of its neighbor candidates, it may indicate that the candidate blocks are within a large homogeneous region. We then suspect the inappropriateness of the size of a block template and therefore expand it and repeat the matching procedure. The second consideration is when to stop expanding the size. We use a simple criterion, namely expanding stops when the distinctiveness of the best match does not improve any further even if we expand the size.

In order to formalize the above idea in the form of an equation, we define the evaluation function $\Phi(i,j;n)$ as in (2). In (2), $(i^*, j^*; n)$ is the position where the best match occurs for the block template at (i,j) of size n. We denote as $DT(i,j;n)$ the distinctiveness of the best match, which is the minimal difference between matching degrees of the best match and its neighbor candidates. The index (l,m) denotes the positions of neighbors of the best match. $GD(i,j;n)$ denotes the gradient of the

$$\Phi(i, j;n) = \max\left[\frac{e_1 + TH(i, j;n)}{e_2 + GD(i, j;n)}\right] \times \frac{e_1 + TH(i, j;n)}{e_2 + GD(i, j;n)} \tag{2}$$

$$TH(i, j;n) = T_{PK} - DT(i, j;n)$$

$$GD(i, j;n) = DT(i, j;n) - DT(i, j;n-1)$$

$$DT(i, j;n) = \min_{-1 \le l, m \le 1}\left[DBS(i^*, j^*;n) - DBS(i+l, j+m;n)\right]$$

distinctiveness with respect to size, which is computed by subtracting the distinctiveness evaluated at size $n-1$ from the distinctiveness evaluated at size n. $TH(i,j;n)$ denotes the subtraction of the distinctiveness $DT(i,j;n)$ from the threshold T_{pk}. e_1, and e_2 are constants that control the speed of convergence. The evaluation function $\Phi(i,j;n)$ is so constructed that it has a positive value only when the distinctiveness is not greater than the threshold of T_{pk} and the gradient of the distinctiveness is positive.

4 Weight Adjustment

To determine the weights of each feature, we use the entropy of the corresponding feature in the search area under consideration. Entropy is a statistical measure of uncertainty and is often used as a suitable criterion for optimum feature selection [8]. It is a good measure of dispersion of feature values in a search area. We adopt this concept in the design of weights in (1). Features that increase the uncertainty in a given search area are considered more informative than those that have the opposite effect, since the high uncertainty of a feature implies the high possibility that a candidate block may have a different feature value from other blocks in the search area. This criterion is equivalent to emphasizing features that show large interclass dissimilarities. Thus, we assign heavy weights to features that have large values of uncertainty, and light weights to features that have small values of uncertainty. Since the process of assigning weights is performed for each block of a present frame, it is reasonable to expect that the resulting DBS will yield more accurate motion vectors.

We compute weights of features as the normalized entropies as in (3), so that they have values from 0 to 1 and the sum of them becomes 1.

$$\alpha(n) = \frac{E_{inten}}{E_{inten} + E_{hue} + E_{range}} \tag{3}$$

$$\beta(n) = \frac{E_{hue}}{E_{inten} + E_{hue} + E_{range}}$$

$$\gamma(n) = \frac{E_{range}}{E_{inten} + E_{hue} + E_{range}}$$

In (3), E_{inten}, E_{hue} and E_{range} denote the entropies of the intensity, hue and range features and they are defined as in (4). Here, $P(\cdot)$ denotes the probability density of the feature value which is to be evaluated in a given search area. W denotes the search area in which to look for the current block.

$$E_{inten} = -\sum_{i,j \in W} P(I(i,j)) \log P(I(i,j)) \tag{4}$$

$$E_{hue} = -\sum_{i,j \in W} P(H(i,j)) \log P(H(i,j))$$

$$E_{range} = -\sum_{i,j \in W} P(R(i,j)) \log P(R(i,j))$$

5   Experimental Results and Conclusions

In this section, we evaluate the performance of the proposed block matching algorithm in terms of the accuracy of resulting motion vectors. Fig. 1 shows two adjacent frames in a sequence of test images. In this sequence, the camera is stationary and a person is moving his hand upward. The size of each individual frame is 320×240 pixels quantized uniformly to 8 bits.

To compare the performance of our approach with those of other approaches, we also implemented the full search method, the three-step search method and the four-step search method. Fig. 2 depicts motion vectors for Fig. 1 obtained using these methods. As may be noticed, all the methods may obtain quite accurate results in the area where the intensity difference is distinctive. However, in areas where adjacent blocks show similar intensities, our method shows superior results. It is confirmed that hue and range features as well as the intensity feature are used and the corresponding size of a block template is expanded in those areas.

Fig. 3 illustrates the sizes of block templates over the whole blocks in the proposed method. The horizontal axis represents indices of horizontal positions of blocks, and the vertical axis those of vertical positions. In Fig 3, value 0 means (N+0)×(N+0) block template, value 1 (N+1)×(N+1) block template, and so on. We can clearly see that the size of block templates is expanded in areas where adjacent blocks have similar feature values.

(a) Input image at t   (b) Input image at t+Δt

Fig. 1. Test image sequence

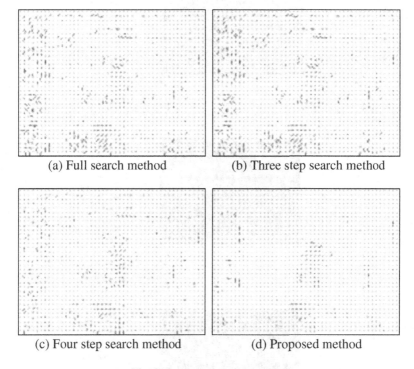

(a) Full search method   (b) Three step search method

(c) Four step search method   (d) Proposed method

Fig. 2. Estimated motion vectors

Fig. 4 depicts the values of α, β and γ at each block. They have different values depending on the distinctiveness of each feature. We can easily see that which feature is more informative in images than others with Fig. 4.

In summary, we have presented in this paper a new block matching algorithm that extracts motion vectors from range images using multiple features. Our algorithm defines a matching metric that integrates intensity, hue and range. We have employed

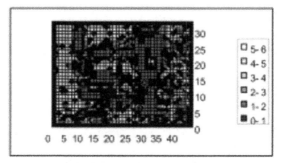

Fig. 3. Sizes of block templates

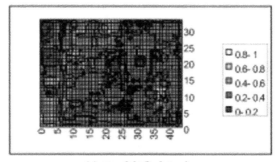

(a) α. weight for intensity

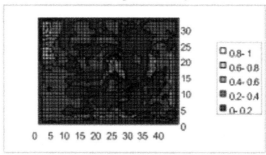

(b) β. weight for hue

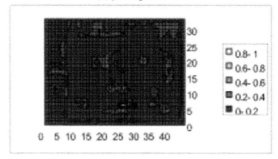

(c) γ. weight for range

Fig. 4. Value of α, β and γ

the evaluation function that examines matching degrees of candidate blocks to determine the appropriateness of the size of a block template. As the iteration proceeds, we also adaptively adjust weights of the matching metric by considering the importance of features. Experimental results show that our algorithm outperforms other algorithms in terms of accuracy of the estimated motion vectors, though our algorithm requires some computational overhead.

For future work, since the entropy measure needs a large amount of computation, we will adopt a simplified version that preserves the main idea of the uncertainty. Furthermore, our block matching algorithm needs to be applied to various types of range images including camera motions and moving objects.

References

1. Xuan Jing, Ce Zhu and Lap-Pui Chau, Smooth Constrained Motion Estimation for Video Coding, Signal Processing, Vol. 83, Issue 3 (2003) 677–680
2. B. Liu and A. Zaccarin, New Fast Algorithms for the Estimation of Block Motion Vectors, IEEE Trans. on Circuits and Systems for Video Technology, Vol. 3, No. 2 (1994) 438–441
3. R. Li, B. Zeng et al, A New Three-Step Search Algorithm for Block Motion Estimation, IEEE Trans. on Circuits and Systems for Video Technology, Vol. 4, No. 4 (1994) 438–441
4. Lai-Man Po and Wing-Chung Ma, A Novel Four-Step Algorithm for Fast Block Motion Estimation, IEEE Transactions on Circuits and Systems for Video Technology, Vol. 6, No. 3 (1996) 313–317
5. Leonid V. Tsap and Min C. Shin, Improving Quality and Speed of Range Data for Communication, IEEE International Workshop on Cues in Communication, Kauai, Hawaii, (2001) .
6. Adams Hoover et al, An Experimental Comparison of Range Image Segmentation Algorithm, IEEE Trans. on Pattern Analysis and Machine Intelligence, Vol. 18, No. 7 (1996) 673–689
7. Ramesh Jain et al, Machine Vision, McGraw-Hill (1995)
8. Jing Gong, Liyuan Li and Weinan Chen, Fast Recursive Algorithms for Two-Dimensional Thresholding, Pattern Recognition, Vol. 31, No. 3 (1998) 295–300

Geometric Segmentation and Object Recognition in Unordered and Incomplete Point Cloud

Sung Joon Ahn, Ira Effenberger, Sabine Roth-Koch, and Engelbert Westkämper

Fraunhofer IPA, Nobelstr. 12, 70569 Stuttgart, Germany
{sja,ime,sar,wke}@ipa.fraunhofer.de

Abstract. In applications of optical 3D-measurement techniques segmentation and outlier elimination in point clouds is a tedious and time-consuming task. In this paper, we present a very robust and efficient procedure of segmentation, outlier elimination, and model fitting in point clouds. For an accurate and reliable estimation of the model parameters, we apply orthogonal distance fitting (ODF) algorithms that minimize the square sum of the geometric error distances. The model parameters are grouped and simultaneously estimated in terms of form, position, and rotation parameters, hence providing a very advantageous algorithmic feature for segmentation and object recognition. We give an application example for the proposed procedure which is applied to an unordered and incomplete point cloud containing multiple objects taken by laser radar.

1 Introduction

In recent years noticeable progress of optical 3D-measurement techniques has been achieved through interdisciplinary cooperation of optoelectronics, image processing, and close-range photogrammetry. Among the diverse optical 3D-measuring devices, the laser radar is capable of measuring millions of dense 3D-points in a few seconds under various measuring conditions such as object surface material, measuring range, and ambient light [7,10]. An application example of laser radar is the digital documentation of an engineering plant which mainly consists of simple geometric elements such as plane, sphere, cylinder, cone, and torus.

In contrast to the recent progress of 3D-measurement techniques, the advances of software tools for 3D-data processing have been virtually stagnated. In practice, the segmentation and outlier elimination in point clouds is the major bottleneck of the overall procedure and is usually assisted by human operator. Thus, considering the remarkable performance of the advanced 3D-measuring devices, the development of a flexible and efficient software tool for 3D-data processing with high accuracy and high automation degree is very urgent in many engineering fields.

With regard to software tools for 3D-data processing, least-squares model fitting plays a fundamental role in estimating the object model parameters of a point cloud. Among the various error measures, the *shortest distance* (named as geometric distance, orthogonal distance, or Euclidean distance in the literature) between the model feature and the given point is widely accepted as the best error measure for segmentation and model fitting of dimensional data [1,6,9]. In fact, the use of the geometric error measure

B. Michaelis and G. Krell (Eds.): DAGM 2003, LNCS 2781, pp. 450–457, 2003.

is prescribed by a recently ratified international standard for testing the data processing softwares for coordinate metrology [4,8].

In this paper, we present an efficient object recognition procedure (an interactive procedure between segmentation, outlier elimination, and model fitting in unstructured and incomplete point clouds) using the geometric error measure not only for distinguishing between the inliers and the outliers of a model feature but also for estimating the model parameters. The procedure is triggered by clicking a seed point in the point cloud and providing a simple low-level model type. After a proper model feature has been recognized and determined, the membership points of the model feature are cleared from the point cloud. The clicking and clearing cycle is to be repeated until no more object structure is visible in the point cloud. As the results of the overall procedures we get a list of the recognized objects and their model parameter values.

2 Curves and Surfaces in Space

An analytic curve/surface in 2D/3D-space can be mathematically described in explicit, implicit, or parametric form. It must be pointed out that the explicit features are the subset of the implicit and of the parametric features. Since the explicit features are axis-dependent and single-valued, their use in applications is limited, e.g., a full circle/sphere cannot be described in explicit form. Moreover, with diverse applications handling dimensional models or objects, the usual description form of a curve/surface is the implicit or the parametric form [5]. Hence our main interest is concentrated on the use of the implicit and the parametric features.

2.1 Rigid Body Motion

Generally, a model feature is arbitrarily located and oriented in space. And, the rigid body motion of model feature is of great interest for the applications of computer vision, motion analysis, robotics, and visualization. Thus, a model description and model fitting algorithm will be very advantageous for applications, if the model parameters $\mathbf{a}$ are grouped and estimated in terms of form $\mathbf{a}_g$, position $\mathbf{a}_p$, and rotation parameters $\mathbf{a}_r$

$$\mathbf{a}^T \triangleq (\mathbf{a}_g^T, \mathbf{a}_p^T, \mathbf{a}_r^T) = (a_1, \dots, a_l, X_o, Y_o, Z_o, \omega, \varphi, \kappa) \ . \tag{1}$$

The *form parameters* $\mathbf{a}_g$ (e.g., the three axis-lengths a, b, c of an ellipsoid) represent the shape and size of the standard (canonical) model feature defined in model coordinate frame xyz

$$\begin{cases} f(\mathbf{a}_g, \mathbf{x}) = 0 & : \text{implicit feature} \\ \mathbf{x}(\mathbf{a}_g, \mathbf{u}) & : \text{parametric feature} \ . \end{cases} \tag{2}$$

The form parameters are invariant to the rigid body motion of model feature. The *position parameters* $\mathbf{a}_p$ and the *rotation parameters* $\mathbf{a}_r$ describe the rigid body motion of model feature in reference coordinate frame XYZ

$$\mathbf{X} = \mathbf{R}_{\omega,\varphi,\kappa}^{-1}\mathbf{x} + \mathbf{X}_o \quad \text{or} \quad \mathbf{x} = \mathbf{R}_{\omega,\varphi,\kappa}(\mathbf{X} - \mathbf{X}_o) \ . \tag{3}$$

We characterize the form parameters as *intrinsic parameters* and the position/rotation parameters as *extrinsic parameters* of model feature according to their context. A model feature is then to be identified and classified with its intrinsic parameters, independent of the varying extrinsic parameters, i.e., even after a rigid body motion. The functional interpretation and treatment (3) of the extrinsic parameters is basically the same to all model features in 2D/3D-space.

2.2 Model Hierarchy

By utilizing the parameter grouping, we can build an hierarchical interface between model types (Fig. 1). For example, a sphere, the generalization of a point in 3D-space, is a special instance of an ellipsoid that is again a special instance of a superellipsoid. The hierarchical model interface facilitates an efficient and advantageous parameter initialization and model selection in the model fitting process. The initial parameter values from fitting a low-level model type to the same point set preconditions a stable convergence of the orthogonal distance fitting (ODF) [2,3], because the parameter values and the geometric error distances experience no abrupt changes with model transition. In other words, the two model features before and after model transition look the same (e.g., transition from sphere to ellipsoid) or at least similar (e.g., transition from 3D-circle to torus). Remarkably, the ODF problems of the most primitive model types in the model hierarchy can be solved in closed form (line/plane fitting) or their initial parameter values can be determined in closed form (circle/sphere fitting). This means that the overall procedure of the iterative fitting of many a model feature can be automatically carried out by using the internally successively supplied initial parameter values.

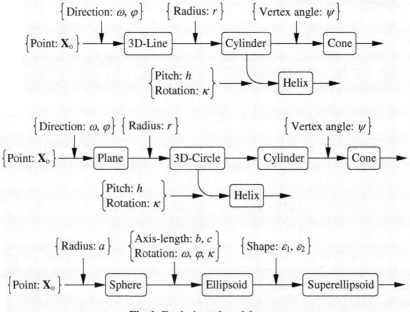

Fig. 1. Evolution of model types.

2.3   Region of Interest

In order to exclude the plain outliers not only from the further time-consuming operations but also from distorting the results of model fitting, we apply the two-fold criterion for the region of interest (ROI) to the measurement points by utilizing the parameter grouping (1) and the properties of the implicit model description (2).

First, we restrict the measurement point domain within a box with a safety margin t containing the interest portion of the model feature (2) defined in frame xyz. For example, the domain box of an ellipse can be defined in frame xy as below (Fig. 2):

$$|x_i| \leq a + t \quad \text{and} \quad |y_i| \leq b + t .$$

Provided with the rotation matrix $\mathbf{R}$ and the position $\mathbf{X}_o$ of the model feature, we need only a few multiplications for computing the coordinates $\mathbf{x}_i = \mathbf{R}(\mathbf{X}_i - \mathbf{X}_o)$ of a measurement point in model frame xyz. By applying the domain box criterion, the *potential* measurement points of the model feature can be screened from a large set of measurement points at a minimal computing cost.

Regarding now the measurement points lying inside the domain box, we consider the point $\mathbf{x}_i$ as an *inlier candidate* of the model feature, if $\mathbf{x}_i$ lies yet between two iso-features of (2), $f(\mathbf{a}_g, \mathbf{x}) - \text{const} = 0$ with $\text{const}_{in} < 0$ and $\text{const}_{out} > 0$, respectively. Otherwise, $\mathbf{x}_i$ will be considered rather as a plain outlier. For an ellipse (Fig. 2), we use

$$\text{const}_{out} = f(\mathbf{a}_g, \mathbf{x}_{out}) \quad \text{with} \quad \mathbf{x}_{out} = \begin{cases} (a + t, \, 0)^T & : a < b \\ (0, \, b + t)^T & : a \geq b \end{cases}, \quad \text{and}$$

$$\text{const}_{in} = f(\mathbf{a}_g, \mathbf{x}_{in}) \quad \text{with} \quad \mathbf{x}_{in} = \begin{cases} (\max(a/2, \, a - t), \, 0)^T & : a < b \\ (0, \, \max(b/2, \, b - t))^T & : a \geq b . \end{cases}$$

The time-consuming determination of the shortest distance points on the model feature from each measurement point, which is necessary for the further outlier elimination (see Section 3.2) and the succeeding ODF model fitting, is to be carried out only for the *inlier candidates* lying inside the narrow ROI of the *current* model feature. The two-fold ROI criterion excluding the plain outliers not only makes the low-cost search for the inlier candidates possible but also preconditions a robust and reliable model fitting.

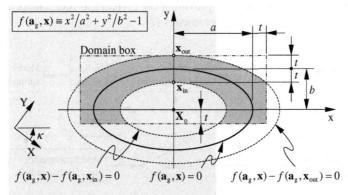

Fig. 2. Example of the ROI (shaded with half tone) of a semi-ellipse in XY-plane with $a \geq b$.

3   Segmentation and Model Fitting in Point Clouds

We describe a semi-automatic object recognition scheme "Click & Clear" (Fig. 3) in point clouds, an interactive procedure between segmentation, outlier elimination, and model fitting, in which the parameter grouping (1) and the algorithmic features of the ODF algorithms [2,3] play an important role.

3.1   Orthogonal Distance Fitting and Model Selection

The ODF of a model feature (2)–(3) to a set of given points in space estimates the model parameters by minimizing the performance index

$$\sigma_0^2 \triangleq (\mathbf{X} - \mathbf{X}')^{\mathrm{T}} \mathbf{P}^{\mathrm{T}} \mathbf{P} (\mathbf{X} - \mathbf{X}') \quad \text{or} \quad \sigma_0^2 \triangleq \mathbf{d}^{\mathrm{T}} \mathbf{P}^{\mathrm{T}} \mathbf{P} \mathbf{d} \ , \tag{4}$$

where $\mathbf{X}^{\mathrm{T}} = (\mathbf{X}_1^{\mathrm{T}}, \dots, \mathbf{X}_m^{\mathrm{T}})$ and $\mathbf{X}'^{\mathrm{T}} = (\mathbf{X}_1'^{\mathrm{T}}, \dots, \mathbf{X}_m'^{\mathrm{T}})$ are the coordinate row vectors of the m given points and of the m corresponding points on the model feature, respectively. Moreover, $\mathbf{d} = (d_1, \dots, d_m)^{\mathrm{T}}$ is the distance column vector with $d_i = \|\mathbf{X}_i - \mathbf{X}_i'\|$ and, $\mathbf{P}^{\mathrm{T}} \mathbf{P}$ is the weighting or error covariance matrix. Interested readers are referred to [2,3] for a detailed description of the ODF algorithms for implicit and parametric features, which estimate the model parameters $\mathbf{a}$ in terms of the three parameter groups $\mathbf{a}_\mathrm{g}$, $\mathbf{a}_\mathrm{p}$, and $\mathbf{a}_\mathrm{r}$ (1). The ODF algorithms in [2,3] are very versatile and efficient from the viewpoint of implementation and application to a new model type because we only need to provide the first and the second derivatives of the standard model feature (2) that has usually a few form parameters $\mathbf{a}_\mathrm{g}$ without involvement of the position $\mathbf{a}_\mathrm{p}$ and the rotation parameters $\mathbf{a}_\mathrm{r}$. Another powerful algorithmic feature of the ODF algorithms in [2,3] for processing a point cloud with a large number of data points is that the computing cost and the memory space usage are proportional to the number of data points.

Choosing the proper model type as such the decision between sphere and ellipsoid for a set of given points is a relevant issue for many applications. The ODF algorithms in [2,3] provide very helpful information about the quality of the estimation results, among others, the square sum σ_0^2 (4) of the geometric error distances and the parameter covariance matrix. The index σ_0^2 indicates the overall performance of the model selection and model fitting. And, the parameter covariance matrix allows a qualitative insight into the estimated model parameters by providing the correlation coefficients and standard deviations of the estimated model parameters [2].

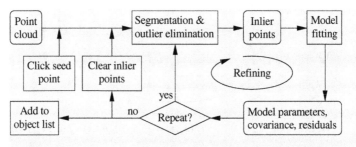

Fig. 3. Object recognition scheme "Click & Clear" in point cloud.

3.2   Segmentation and Object Recognition

The "Click & Clear" procedure (Fig. 3) starts with selecting a seed point in the point cloud and providing a low-level model type (e.g., sphere) by the user. If necessary, before repeating the model refining cycle in Fig. 3, the model type can be internally changed upwards or downwards in the model hierarchy shown in Fig. 1, e.g., from sphere to ellipsoid, or vice versa. The detailed procedure is described in the following:

1. Pick the seed point and provide a low-level model type, e.g., sphere.
2. Initialize the model parameters through model fitting to a small portion of the point cloud around the seed point. Also initialize the safety margin t of ROI (see Section 2.3) for the initialized model feature, e.g., $t = r/2$ for sphere.
3. Determine the shortest (geometric) error distances d_i of each inlier candidate lying inside the ROI of the *current* model feature and, evaluate the rms error distance $\sigma_{ROI} = \sqrt{\frac{1}{m} \sum_{i=1}^{m} d_i^2}$, where m is the number of the inlier candidates.
4. Considering the inlier candidates inside the ROI, determine the set of inliers yet having the geometric error distances of $d_i \leq \alpha_{threshold} \cdot \sigma_{ROI}$, where $\alpha_{threshold}$ is the outlier threshold factor ($2.0 \leq \alpha_{threshold} \leq 3.0$ works well). Optionally, if there is no membership change between the current and the old set of inliers, go to step 9.
5. Fit the model feature to the inlier set. If the resultant standard error deviation σ_{inlier} is smaller than the given error size concerning the accuracy of the used measuring device, go to step 9.
6. Update the safety margin $t \leftarrow \alpha_{growing} \cdot \alpha_{threshold} \cdot \sigma_{inlier}$ of ROI, where $\alpha_{growing}$ is the growing factor of ROI ($1.0 \leq \alpha_{growing} \leq 1.2$ works well).
7. If necessary, change the model type, e.g., from sphere to ellipsoid, or vice versa.
8. Repeat from the third step.
9. Clear the inliers from the point list and, add the model type and its parameter values to the object list.
10. If necessary, repeat from the first step.

3.3   Experimental Results

For an experimental example for the proposed procedure "Click & Clear", a point cloud of about 18,300 points (Fig. 4) taken from multiple object surfaces by a laser radar [7] is segmented and recognized (Fig. 5). Strategically, in order to reduce the overall computing and user working cost, the recognition of simple model features (e.g., plane and sphere) is to precede the recognition of complex model features. In particular, the plane recognition is computationally inexpensive (plane fitting is a noniterative task) and identifies generally a large portion of the point cloud in the early phase of the overall procedure (Fig. 5a and Fig. 5b). Consequently, the cost of the succeeding procedures for recognition of complex objects can be reduced. The initial parameter values, which are supplied from the model fitting to a small but well-conditioned portion of the point cloud around the seed point, are generally adequate for a stable and robust object recognition thanks to the narrow ROI criteria and the robust ODF algorithms. Even when the initial parameter values are falsified (Fig. 5a and Fig. 5c), the proposed procedure in Section 3.2 leads the object recognition to the correct results (Fig. 5b and Fig. 5d).

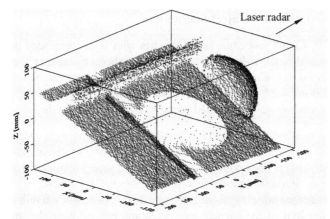

Fig. 4. Unordered and incomplete point cloud (about 18,300 points) taken by laser radar.

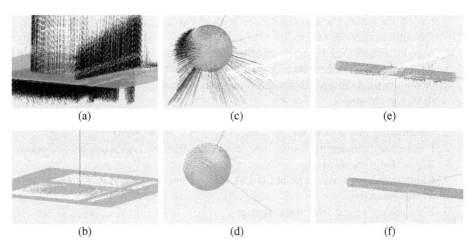

Fig. 5. Results of the object recognition (segmentation and model fitting) in the point cloud shown in Fig. 4. Distance error bars are four times elongated. (a), (c), and (e) Initial states of the single model fittings; (b), (d), and (f) Segmented point clusters and the fitting results; (a) and (b) Plane, (c) and (d) sphere, (e) and (f) cylinder recognition.

4   Summary and Discussion

One of the ultimate goals of computer vision is the fully automatic recognition of multiple objects in the real world, which might be reachable through a well-conducted analysis of all the available information such as point cloud, object surface texture/color, and object database. On the way to this goal, we have developed a semi-automatic procedure "Click & Clear" for the object recognition in point clouds, in which the parameter grouping (1) and the ODF algorithms play a fundamental role. The use of the geometric error measure is indispensable for an accurate and reliable outlier elimination and model fitting, although the required computing costs are relatively high. In order to save computing time, we introduced the two-fold criterion that inexpensively defines the narrow ROI of model feature by utilizing the parameter grouping (1) and the properties of the implicit model description (2). The plain outliers are efficiently excluded not only from the further time-consuming operations but also from distorting the model fitting. In summary, thanks to the narrow ROI definition and the robust ODF algorithms, the overall procedures of the object recognition "Click & Clear" in point cloud were able to be carried out with a minimal user interaction. We demonstrated on real measurement data the outstanding performance of the procedure "Click & Clear" applied to unordered and incomplete point clouds.

The next working steps towards a fully automatic object recognition and reconstruction would be the use of the object surface image and the application of the parameter constraints [2] between multiple objects. The object surface image (the gray image or the point reflectance image of object surfaces) is usually taken simultaneously with the point cloud by the optical 3D-measuring devices [7,10]. Because a locally homogeneous region in the surface image hints at a locally smooth object surface, we can use the associating point set with the homogeneous image region as the seed point set for the object recognition in Fig. 3. In addition, if the range of the probable model types representing the objects taken in point clouds is a priori known, the object recognition could be automatically carried out at a bounded computing cost, because a relatively small database of model types is due to be scanned for the proper model type for the point set containing the seed point set. Furthermore, the application of the additional geometric constraints to the object model parameters (e.g., relative/absolute constraints on shape, size, position, and rotation of multiple objects) will enhance the qualitative contents of the resultant list of the recognized objects and their model parameters.

References

1. Adcock, R.J.: Note on the method of least squares. The Analyst **4** (1877) 183–184
2. Ahn, S.J., Rauh, W., Cho, H.S., Warnecke, H.-J.: Orthogonal Distance Fitting of Implicit Curves and Surfaces. IEEE Trans. Pattern Analy. and Mach. Intell. **24** (2002) 620–638
3. Ahn, S.J., Rauh, W., Westkämper, E.: Fitting of Parametric Space Curves and Surfaces by Using the Geometric Error Measure. Lect. Notes Comput. Sc. **2249** (2002) 548–556
4. Drieschner, R., Bittner, B., Elligsen, R., Wäldele, F.: Testing Coordinate Measuring Machine Algorithms: Phase II. BCR Report no. EUR 13417 EN, Commission EC, Luxemburg (1991)
5. Farin, G., Hoschek, J., Kim, M.-S.: Handbook of Computer Aided Geometric Design. Eds., Elsevier Science, Amsterdam (2002)
6. Hastie, T.: Principal curves and surfaces. PhD Thesis, SLAC Report-276, Stanford Linear Accelerator Center, Stanford University, CA (1984)
7. Heinz, I., Mettenleiter, M., Härtl, F., Fröhlich, C.: 3-D Ladar for Inspection of Real World Environments. Proc. 5th Conf. Optical 3-D Measurement Techniques, Vienna (2001) 10–17
8. ISO 10360-6:2001: Geometrical Product Specification (GPS) - Acceptance test and reverification test for coordinate measuring machines (CMM) – Part 6: Estimation of errors in computing Gaussian associated features. ISO, Geneva (2001)
9. Pearson, K.: On Lines and Planes of Closest Fit to Systems of Points in Space. The Philosophical Magazine: Ser. 6 **2** (1901) 559–572
10. Ullrich, A., Reichert, R., Schwarz, R., Riegl, J.: Time-of-flight-based 3-D imaging sensor with true-color channel for automated texturing. Proc. 5th Conf. Optical 3-D Measurement Techniques, Vienna (2001) 2–9

Real-Time Inspection System for Printed Circuit Boards

Kang-Sun Choi, Jae-Young Pyun, Nam-Hyeong Kim,
Byeong-Doo Choi, and Sung-Jea Ko

Korea University, Anam-Dong Sungbuk-Ku, Seoul, Korea,
kschoi@dali.korea.ac.kr

Abstract. In this paper, we present a real-time PCB inspection system which can detect defects including the breaks in the wires and short circuit. The proposed inspection algorithm is based on referential matching between the stored reference image and the test (observed) image and is significantly faster when compared to existing algorithms. In the proposed method, block matching with half-pixel precision is performed to solve the translational and rotational misalignment in referential matching. We also present an image processing algorithm for compensating for the non-uniformity of the illumination source. In order to reduce the computational complexity, we optimize the proposed algorithm using the Single Instruction Multiple Data (SIMD) instructions implemented in Intel Pentium IV, so called the Streaming SIMD Extensions 2 (SSE2).

1 Introduction

As the density of circuit patterns becomes finer, especially in the circuit boards used for computers and wireless communication systems, pattern inspection by human takes a great deal of time and is not reliable due to inevitable human errors. Meanwhile, existing automatic optical inspection (AOI) systems have proved their efficiencies in detecting defects of the PCB [1,2,3,4].

In this paper, we present a fast PCB inspection method based on the referential method which can effectively detect the defects of the PCB on a conveyor in real time. In the proposed method, block matching with half-pixel precision is performed to solve the translational and rotational misalignment in referential matching. We also present an image processing algorithm for compensating for the non-uniformity of the illumination source. The proposed algorithm can reduce computational load and improve the parallel processing performance by using the Single Instruction Multiple Data (SIMD) instructions implemented in Intel Pentium IV, so called the Streaming SIMD Extensions 2 (SSE2).

The paper is organized as follows: In Sect. 2, we briefly introduce the manufacturing progress of the PCB and present the proposed inspection algorithms in detail. The shading correction method is also introduced to compensate for the non-constant intensity of the illumination source. The structure of the proposed inspection system is discussed and the performance of the proposed inspection system is examined using real PCBs. Finally, conclusions are given in Sect. 3.

B. Michaelis and G. Krell (Eds.): DAGM 2003, LNCS 2781, pp. 458–465, 2003.

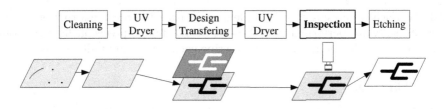

Fig. 1. The proposed manufacturing progress diagram.

2   Proposed Real-Time PCB Inspection System

Figure 1 shows the manufacturing progress of the PCB. A bare board is washed off and cleaned to remove surface oxidation and oil for better adhesion during the design transfer process. Wet boards are passed through the ultra-violet (UV) dryer. In the design transfer process, the pattern artwork is printed on the bare board as squeezing a pattern screen with etch-resist ink. The proposed PCB inspection system inspects the printed circuit pattern before the copper foil is etched, while most existing PCB inspection systems detect defects after the whole manufacturing progress is finished.

Since the proposed approach detects defects generated during the design transfer process, boards with defects can be reused after correcting defects. Screen deformation caused by thousands of squeezing may introduce successive defects at the same position.

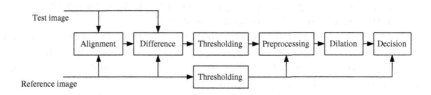

Fig. 2. Block diagram of the proposed PCB inspection system.

Figure 2 depicts the block diagram of the proposed PCB inspection system. Since the proposed inspection method is based on referential matching between the reference image and the test (observed) image, an accurate alignment reducing the translational and rotational displacement is performed. The aligned test image is subtracted from the stored reference image and the resulting difference image is converted into a binary image using a thresholding algorithm. Finally, morphological operators are applied to the resulting binary image to detect the defects. Each processing unit is implemented using the SSE2 instructions to accelerate software performance of 128-bit SIMD double-precision floating point and integer applications. Next, we describe each processing unit in detail.

2.1 Alignment

When PCBs are transported on the conveyor belt, the shift of the PCBs is inevitable. The mechanical guiding system can reduce the displacement within $2mm$ which corresponds to $\pm 0.2°$ tilt. To further reduce the translational and rotational displacement, we propose an image processing algorithm for the alignment with an half pixel accuracy.

For the proposed alignment, we first select the positions of eleven blocks of size 32×32 in the reference image, each of which includes a distinct feature pattern. To estimate the translational displacement between the reference PCB image and the test image, the full search block matching (FSBM) algorithm is used.

The proposed alignment algorithm searches a location (m_m, n_m) such that the sum of the error norms from the eleven pre-selected blocks is minimized:

$$(m_m, n_m) = \underset{m,n}{argmin} \sum_{i=1}^{11} \|X_i - Y_i(m, n)\|, \tag{1}$$

where the vectors X_i and $Y_i(m, n)$ represent the ith pre-selected block in the reference image and the ith candidate blocks in the scanned image, respectively. Each pre-selected block contains salient features in the reference image.

Since the error norm, the sum of absolute difference (SAD), is computed at every location of (m, n) in the search region, this method requires exhaustive computation which makes its practical application difficult. The SIMD instruction which compares sixteen pixels at once and returns two SAD values can significantly reduce the SAD computational load [5].

Although the rotation is fairly small, the discrepancy between the stored reference image and the test (observed) image is fairly large. Thus, the rotational alignment is also performed to compensate for this discrepancy. The following basic rotation transformation requires four floating-point multiplications and two floating-point additions for each pixel.

The floating-point computations can be significantly reduced by using the midpoint line algorithm [6] which mainly uses the integer addition, the increment by 1, and the logic justification. With the midpoint line algorithm, only the first pixel in a raster line is rotated by using (3), and the rotated coordinates of the neighboring pixel are obtained by simply adding $\cos\theta$ and $\sin\theta$, respectively, to the x and y coordinates of the previous point, i.e., $x_{i+1} = \cos\theta + x_i$ and $y_{i+1} = \sin\theta + y_i$. Since the packed arithmetic SSE instructions calculate four single-precision floating-point values simultaneously, the rotated coordinates of the neighboring pixels can be determined by a single instruction.

To measure the rotational displacement, the rotated versions of each pre-selected block, X^r, are obtained by rotating X by $0.05°$ from $0°$ to $0.3°$ and by

$-0.05°$ from $-0.05°$ to $-0.3°$. For each rotated version, the minimum SAD value ϵ_m^r and the corresponding location $(m_m^r,\ n_m^r)$ are obtained by using FSBM. The test image is rotated by the angle corresponding to the minimum SAD value among ϵ^rs and translated by the corresponding location.

Initially, we set the search range of ± 30 pixels in the horizontal direction and ± 50 pixels in the vertical direction, which corresponds to 6161 SAD operations for each block and obtain a displacement. For the rotated version, this computational load can be reduced by using a priori information, this displacement, since the location with the minimum SAD after rotation is located in the neighborhood of $(m_1,\ n_1)$ due to the tiny rotation angle. Consequently, the search range can be significantly reduced, which alleviates the computational load greatly.

Figure 3 shows the result of the alignment. To emphasize the improvement, the contrast and level of the images are modified. Figure 3(a) shows the difference image between the reference and the test image compensated by the translational alignment method only, where the misalignment is seen in the lower left corner. Figure 3(b) shows that the combination of translational and rotational alignment has improved the matching performance.

 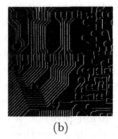

(a)   (b)

Fig. 3. Absolute difference between the reference and the test image. (a) With translational alignment only. (b) With translational and rotational alignment.

2.2   Thresholding – Binarization

In the PCB inspection system, the trace pattern of the PCB is segmented as objects of interest by a simple thresholding method. The difficulty with the thresholding method is to select an optimal threshold value. Especially when the area scan camera is used, it is difficult to acquire images of uniform intensity due to the nonuniform characteristics of the lighting source and camera lens. Figure 4 shows an example of the non-uniformity of illumination which is obtained by scanning a copper foil of a cleaned bare board prior to any manufacturing process. It is seen that the illumination (or brightness) even in the "cleaned copper" image varies with position.

To solve this problem, we propose an shading correction algorithm to compensate for the non-constant intensity of the light source. This algorithm uses an

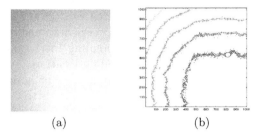

(a)   (b)

Fig. 4. The non-uniformity of illumination. (a) The image of a copper foil of a cleaned bare board. (b) The intensity contour line of (a).

adaptive threshold for binarizing images as follows: We first select five regions $R_1, \cdots, R_5$ in the image as shown in Fig. 5(a). For these regions, we calculate the average gray levels m_is from the cleaned copper image and the threshold values T_is from the reference image. Figures 5(b) and 5(d) show regions R_2 of the "cleaned copper" and PCB reference images, respectively. The minimum and the maximum are selected from each of sets $\{m_i\}$ and $\{T_i\}$. We denote the minimum and the maximum of $\{m_i\}$ ($\{T_i\}$) by m_{min} and m_{max} (T_{min} and T_{max}). The "cleaned copper" image is transformed into the shade-corrected image using an intensity transformation, $s = T(r)$, as shown in Fig. 5(f), where r and s are the intensity of pixels before and after processing, respectively. Each pixel value of the shade-corrected image is used as the adaptive threshold for binarization of the corresponding pixel of the reference image.

In this binarization process, a threshold image is generated by the above algorithm for the shade correction and each pixel value of the input image is compared with the collocated pixel value in the threshold image. To compare the collocated pairs fast, our SSE2 implementation reads and binarizes 16 pixel values at a time as shown in the following codes. The first 2 lines load 16-pixel values from the adaptive threshold and the input images, respectively. Using the "psubusb" and "pcmpeqb" instructions, when the input is greater than the associated threshold, "FFh" is set the corresponding position in the register "XMM4", otherwise "00h".

```
movdqu  XMM7, XMMWORD PTR [ecx] // #1
movdqu  XMM0, XMMWORD PTR [eax] // #2
xorpd   XMM4, XMM4              // #3

movdqa  XMM6, XMM7              // #4
psubusb XMM6, XMM0              // #5
pcmpeqb XMM4, XMM6             // #6
```

Figure 5(h) shows a result of the proposed thresholding method using the shading correction algorithm. It is seen that the proposed method produces a better result in binarizing the image.

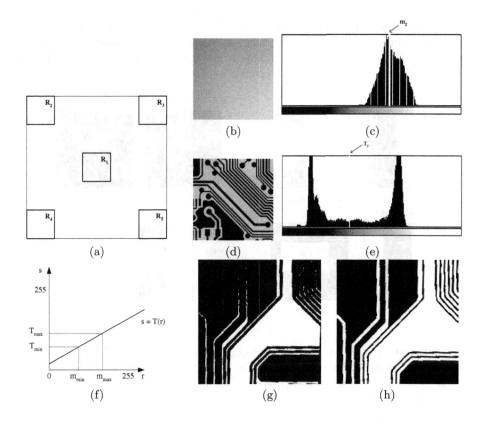

Fig. 5. Shading correction. (a) Regions of interest. (b) An example of region R_2 in the clean image. (c) The histogram and the mean value of (b). (d) An example of region R_2 in the reference image. (e) The histogram and the threshold value of (d). (f) Gray-level transformation function. (g) Binarized Region R_2 without shading correction. (h) Binarized Region R_2 with shading correction.

2.3 Detecting Defects

Figure 6 presents the proposed method of detecting open and short circuit errors in the test image. Figures 6(a) and 6(b) are subimages of the reference and test images, respectively. The difference image between these two images is shown in Fig. 6(c). The difference image in Fig. 6(c) and the reference image in Fig. 6(a) are processed by the proposed thresholding algorithm described in the previous subsection. The resultant binary images are shown in Figs. 6(d) and 6(e). In Fig. 6(d), the "white" object is a defect candidate. The difference image in Fig. 6(d) is dilated by a morphological dilation operator and the result is shown in Fig. 6(f). The images in Figs. 6(e) and 6(f) are laid overlapping each other. The overlaid image is shown in Fig. 6(g). To determine whether the dilated defect candidate in Fig. 6(f) is a real defect or not, we count the number of cross points by tracking the boundary of the dilated candidate using the 8 directional chain code method as shown in Fig. 6(g). The cross point represents the change of intensity values in the binary reference image along the boundary of the dilated candidate. If the number of cross points is greater than three for the candidate, the dilated defect candidate is considered as a real defect.

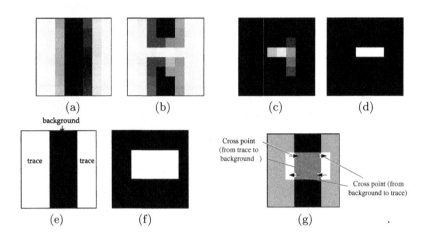

Fig. 6. Defect decision process. (a) A part of the reference image. (b) The corresponding part of test image. (c) Difference image. (d) Binarized difference image. (e) Binarized image of (a). (f) Dilated image. (g) Overlaid image.

2.4   Implementation

Figure 7(a) shows the proposed inspection system consisting of 4 area-scan camera units arranged in parallel, 4 vision computers with Pentium IV processor, a host computer, and an illumination system. Figure 7(b) shows the graphic user interface (GUI) of the proposed system.

When the conveyor belt moves at 7 m/min, to inspect a PCB of size 303 × $509mm^2$, each camera unit of 1008 × 1018 pixel resolution captures a field of view (FOV) of 80 × 80 mm^2 seven times every 0.685 second. Thus, 28 images from each PCB are processed by the four vision computers in real time.

Figures 7(c) shows that the proposed system detects defects in a real test PCB. The upper part of the image has open-circuits in horizontal traces, and the other part contains short defects within double horizontal traces. The proposed system can not only indicate the position of detected defects, but also mark open-circuits and short-circuits with diamond and square signs at those points, respectively.

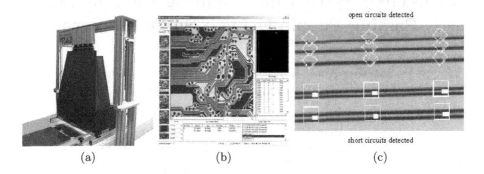

(a)   (b)   (c)

Fig. 7. Automatic inspection system for printed circuit board. (a) Cameras and illumination equipments. (b) Graphic user interface (GUI). (c) Inspection resulting image where a square and a diamond represent short- and open-circuits, respectively.

3 Conclusion

We presented the fast PCB inspection system based on the referential method which can detect the defects of the PCB on a conveyor in real time. A fast alignment reducing the translational and rotational displacement was efficiently implemented using the SSE2 instructions. To compensate for the non-uniformity of illumination, we also proposed the shading correction algorithm with the adaptive threshold. Experimental result showed that the proposed inspection system can be detect both the open-circuit and short-circuit defects effectively.

References

1. Moganti, M., Dagli, C., Tsunekawa, S.: Automatic PCB inspection algorithms: A survey. Computer Vision and Image Understanding. **63** (1996) 287–313
2. Moganti, M.: A subpattern level inspection system for printed circuit boards. Computer Vision and Image Understanding. **70** (1998) 51–62
3. Hara, Y., Akiyama, N., Karasaki, K.: Automatic inspection system for printed circuit boards. IEEE Trans. on Pattern Analysis and Machine Intelligence. **PAMI-5** (1983) 623–630
4. Szolgay, P., Tömördi, K.: Analogic algoritms for optical detection of breaks and short circuits on the layouts of printed circuit boards using cnn. International Joural of Circuit Theory and Applications. **6** (1999) 103–116
5. Block-matching in motion estimation algorithms using Pentium 4 processor SSE2 instructions. Tech. Rep. **AP-940** Intel
   ftp://download.intel.com/design/perftool/cbts/appnotes/sse2/ w_me_alg.pdf.
6. Xuede, C., Sewei, L., Xiaobu, Y., Ling, C., Beikai, Z.: Midpoint line algorithm for high-speed high-accuracy rotation of images. IEEE International Conference on Systems, Man and Cybernetics. **4** (1996) 2739–2744

Real-Time System for Counting the Number of Passing People Using a Single Camera

Jae-Won Kim[1], Kang-Sun Choi[1], Byeong-Doo Choi[1],
Jae-Yong Lee[2], and Sung-Jea Ko[1]

[1] Department of Electronics Engineering, Korea University,
Anam-Dong, Sungbuk-Ku, Seoul, Korea
{jwkim, kschoi, bdchoi, sjko}@dali.korea.ac.kr
[2] Nextreaming Corporation,
Yeoksam-Dong, Kangnam-Ku, Seoul, Korea
jlee@nextreaming.com

Abstract. In this paper, we propose a real-time people counting system with a single camera for security inside the building. The camera is hung from the ceiling of the door so that the image data of the passing people are not fully overlapped. The implemented system recognizes people movement along various directions. To track people even when their images are partially overlapped, the proposed system analyzes the captured image and estimates important feature information. Then each bounding box enclosing each person in the tracking region are tracked. The convex hull of each individual obtained by the proposed algorithm provides more accurate tracking information. Through extensive tests in various environments, the proposed system exhibits the correct people counting results of over 96%.

1 Introduction

Real-time people flow information is very useful source for security application as well as people management such as pedestrian traffic management, tourist flows estimation. To track and count moving people is considered important for the office security or the marketing research. Many of such measurements are still carried out on manual works of persons. Therefore it is necessary to develop the automatic method of counting the passing people.

Several attempts have been made to track pedestrians. Segen and Pingali [1] introduced a system in which the pedestrian silhouette is extracted and tracked. The system runs in real-time, however, the algorithm is too heavy to track many people simultaneously and can not deal well with temporary occlusion. Masoud and Papanikolopoulos [2] developed a real-time system in which pedestrians were modeled as rectangular patches with a certain dynamic behavior. The system had robustness under partial or full occlusions of pedestrians by estimating pedestrian parameters. Rossi and Bozzoli [3] avoided the occlusion problem by mounting the camera vertically in their system in order to track and count passing people in a corridor, but assumed that people enter the scene along

B. Michaelis and G. Krell (Eds.): DAGM 2003, LNCS 2781, pp. 466–473, 2003.
© Springer-Verlag Berlin Heidelberg 2003

only two directions (top and bottom side of the image). Terada [4] proposed a counting method which segmented the human region and road region by using the three dimensional data obtained from a stereo camera. However, this system also assumed only simple movement of pedestrians.

In this paper, we propose a real-time people counting system with a single camera for security inside the building. The camera is hung from the ceiling of the door so that the image data of the passing people are not fully overlapped. The implemented system recognizes people movement along various directions. To track people even when their images are partially overlapped, the proposed system analyzes the captured image and estimates several feature information. Then each bounding box enclosing each person in the tracking region are tracked. The approximated convex hull of each individual in the tracking area is obtained to provide more accurate tracking information. This paper is organized as follows: Section 2 describes the system architecture of the proposed people counting system. In Sec. 3, the people counting and tracking algorithms are given in detail. Finally, Section 4 presents the experimental results and conclusion.

2   System Architecture

Figure 1 shows a scene of the passing people through the security door inside the building. There are incoming and outgoing individuals in the scene. A single camera unit is hung from the ceiling of the door so that the passing people can be observed and tracked in a tracking area in front of the door. The images captured by the camera are processed and the number of the passing people is calculated.

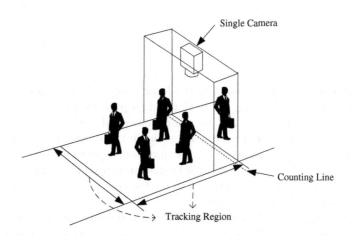

Fig. 1. Scene of the door

To cope with inherently dynamic phenomena (people enter the scene, move across the field of view of the camera, and finally cross the counting line), the people tracking and counting problem has been decomposed into the following three steps: [3]

(Step 1). Determine whether any potentially interesting objects have entered into the scene (Alerting phase);
(Step 2). Track their motion until the counting line is reached (Tracking phase);
(Step 3). Establish how many people correspond to tracked objects (Interpretation phase).

The proposed system provides the graphic user interface (GUI) to define the alerting area, the tracking area, and the counting line as shown in Fig. 2.

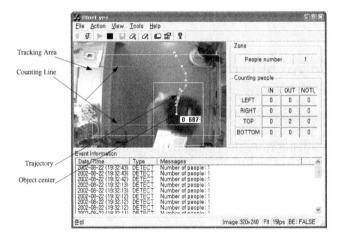

Fig. 2. The graphic user interface of the proposed system

Figure 3 illustrates the flow chart of the proposed algorithm. Background subtraction and thresholding are performed to produce difference images. The difference image is preprocessed by a morphological opening operator (erosion followed by dilation) to remove small clusters in the image. Then, each object is matched the corresponding object in the previous captured image by comparing their center positions. This tracking information is used for counting people. As shown in Fig. 2, the proposed system shows the trajectories and traffic information of incoming and outgoing people.

The proposed algorithm uses two types of difference images. These two difference images contain different information of newly incoming objects. The up flow generates a background-subtracted image where moving objects appear. However, if the pattern of moving object is similar to that of background, the

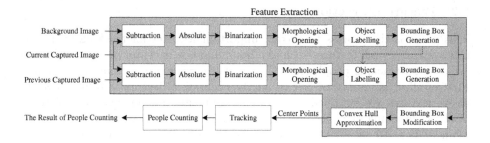

Fig. 3. Main steps in the proposed people counting system

moving object can not be distinguished. The other difference image is obtained by subtracting two successive images. This image can provide motion (boundary) information of moving object even when the moving object is similar to the background. However, when the object stays at a position, the motion information does not appear. On the other hand, when the object moves fast, the boundary information is blurred and incorrect.

3   Proposed Algorithm

3.1   Background Estimation

The background estimation method affects the performance of the system. Since lighting conditions vary in time, the background image is updated using a very slow recursive function to capture slow changes in the background. Background subtraction has been used by many to extract moving objects in the scene [1], [5], [6], [7]. To obtain more accurate background, we propose an adaptive background estimation algorithm which has robustness under the change of illumination as follows:

First, the system determines whether moving objects exist in a current image by comparing the current image with the previous captured image. If there is no moving object, a new background image is obtained by averaging three images including the previous background image, the current background image, and the current captured image.

This background estimation method deals well with the gradual change of illumination, but can not deal with the abrupt large change of illumination occurred in the whole image. To overcome this problem, we compensate the average intensity level of the illumination. From the background image and the current captured image, the average intensity levels of the four blocks each of which is located at the corner of the images are measured. The intensity difference between the corresponding intensity levels of two images is calculated and applied to the current background image to compensate the abrupt change of intensity if moving objects exist in the current image.

3.2   Feature Extraction

This phase is the process to extract important features for tracking people. In this system, several features such as a bounding box, a center point, and an area are used for tracking people since these features are more invariant and reliable. First of all, it is important to extract the accurate object mask from which the above features are obtained. Since many segmented regions exist in the result of object labelling, it is necessary that related segments are merged into object main bodies. To satisfy this demand, we propose bounding box-based feature extraction algorithm as follows:

First, after object labelling is performed with a subtracted image between a background image and a current captured image, each labelled object is determined whether it is a main body or a part of the body by means of the area feature. The part of the body is merged into the closest main body. Then, the bounding box of each merged object which is the smallest rectangle surrounding the object is obtained. In order to obtain more accurate object mask, object labelling is performed with a subtracted image between a previous image and a current image using the bounding box obtained above. Through this process, we can obtain more accurate bounding box considering the movement of moving people. Figure 4(a) shows the bounding box surrounding a binarized object mask after above process.

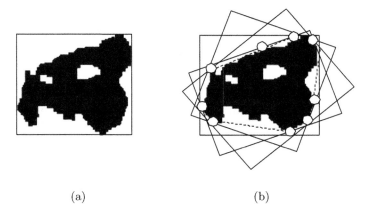

(a)   (b)

Fig. 4. Object extraction (a) Mask and its associated bounding box (b) Convex hull approximation

However, it is necessary to extract more accurate object features since these object masks have holes in each object. Thus, the simple convex hull of the object inside the bounding box is approximated. As shown in Fig. 4(b), 24 points of an approximated convex hull are found by rotating the bounding box at the every angle of 15 degrees. Through the convex hull approximation, we can estimate a center point not affected by the hole in the extracted object mask. Although we extract feature information, they are not always good enough when occlusion of people occurred in the captured image. In addition, a vertically mounted camera does not always guarantee non-overlap of objects. Therefore, to overcome this problem, separation of each person can be achieved by using the past tracking information about the bounding boxes.

3.3   Object Tracking

For the approximated convex hull of each merged object, the corresponding convex hull in the previous captured image is searched for by comparing their center positions. In the object tracking algorithm, the center point of convex hull verified as a pedestrian in the previous image is predicted in the current image by analyzing the past velocity information of the moving object as

$$\hat{v}(t + 1) = (1 - a)v(t) + a\hat{v}(t), \tag{1}$$

where a is a damping coefficient, $v(t)$ and $\hat{v}(t+1)$ are the measured displacement vector at time t and the predicted displacement vector at time t + 1, respectively.

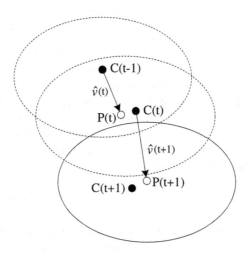

Fig. 5. Object tracking using motion prediction method

Figure 5 shows the procedure of the object tracking method using motion prediction. First, the next position P(t + 1) of the current object at time t is estimated by shifting the current actual center point C(t) by $\hat{v}(t+1)$. Then, the system defines the circular search range centered on P(t + 1) with the predefined radius and searches for an object whose center point is inside the circular search range. In Fig. 5, C(t + 1) represents the center point of the detected object.

The tracking information is updated by linking the information of the detected object to the information of the tracked object. From $C(t + 1)$, this procedure is iterated. After this procedure, tracking information is fed back to the feature extraction procedure in order to perform more accurate extraction of object features.

3.4 People (Object) Counting

In the proposed people counting system, four counting lines are pre-defined. For each counting line, incoming and outgoing of people are determined and counted. These counting lines are located to the any place in the tracking area and (de)activated according to some cases. People counting is performed when a person crosses the counting line(s). In Fig. 2, only top and bottom counting lines were activated and an woman is moving down.

4   Experiments and Conclusion

The proposed people counting system was implemented to operate at about 15 frames per second and use an analog CCD camera. The experiments were performed to demonstrate the performance of the proposed people counting system. These experiments were carried out using several tests. The CCD camera was set 2.5m above the floor which is conventional height of a ceiling in many buildings. Although this situation can introduce the false warning, the bounding box representation which allows partial object occlusion reduces the false warning. Correct people counting results of 96% were obtained and the performance of the proposed people counting system improved as the height of the camera became higher. This result shows that the proposed people counting system guarantees the performance enough for security. Table 1 shows the detail specification of the proposed people counting system.

However, there are some problems in the proposed people counting system. First, the influence of shadows was not considered because we assume that a single camera and lightings are hung from the ceiling of the door. And when moving people are almost near other people, the segmentation of people is not operated perfectly. Thus, the proposed people counting system is not suitable where many people are moving at the same time. But, we provide the false warning system to cope with ambiguous situation where people are so close or an object is so big. In the further research, we will deal with these problems to improve the performance.

In this paper, we have described an implementation method for the people counting system which detects and tracks moving people using a fixed single camera. To track people even when their images are partially overlapped, the proposed system estimates a bounding box enclosing each person and tracks the bounding box. The simple convex hull of each person in the tracking area is approximated to provide more accurate tracking information.

Table 1. Detail specification of the proposed people counting system

Specifications	Detail information
Test Running System	Pentium III 1GHz
Processing Ability (Frame per second)	15 - 30 fps (It shows the best performance at 15 fps)
Counting Line	4 direction incoming/outgoing (Left, Top, Right, Bottom)
Tracking Area Setting (Rectangle)	Yes
Notification - Event (To notify ambiguous objects)	Yes
Motion Detection - Event	Yes
Still Image Storage (If events exists)	Yes (JPEG File Format)

References

1. Segen, J., Pingali, S.: A camera-based system for tracking people in real time. IEEE Proc. Of Int. Conf. Pattern Recognition. **3** (1996) 63–67
2. Masoud, O., Papanikolopoulos, N. P.: A novel method for tracking and counting pedestrians in realtime using a single camera. IEEE Trans. on Vehicular Tech. **50** (2001) 1267–1278
3. Rossi, M., Bozzoli, A.: Tracking and counting moving people. IEEE Proc. of Int. Conf. Image Processing. **3** (1994) 212–216
4. Terada, K., Yoshida, D., Oe, S., Yamaguchi, J.: A counting method of the number of passing people using a stereo camera. IEEE Proc. of Industrial Electronics Conf. **3** (1999) 1318–1323
5. Baumberg, A., Hogg, D.: Learning flexible models from image sequences. Proc. Eur. Conf. Computer Vision. **1** (1994) 229–208
6. Smith, C., Richards, C., Brandt, S. A., Papanikolopoulos, N. P.: Visual tracking for intelligent vehicle-highway systems. IEEE Trans. on Veh. Technol. **45** (1996) 744–759
7. Cai, Q., Aggarwal, J. K.: Tracking human motion using multiple cameras. Proc. 13th Int. Conf. Pattern Recognition. (1996) 68–72

Multiple Classifier Systems for the Recognition of Orthoptera Songs

Christian Dietrich, Friedhelm Schwenker, and Günther Palm

Department of Neural Information Processing
University of Ulm - D-89069 Ulm, Germany
{dietrich, schwenker, palm}@neuro.informatik.uni-ulm.de

Abstract. The classification of bioacoustic time series is topic of this paper. In particular, we discuss the combination of local classifier decisions from several feature spaces with static and adaptable fusion schemes, e.g. averaging, voting and decision templates. We present static fusion schemes and algorithms to calculate decision templates, and demonstrate the behaviour of both approaches to bioacoustic applications, the classification of insect songs. Results of these algorithms are presented for species of crickets and katydids. Both families are members of the insect order *Orthoptera*.

Keywords: multiple classifier systems, bioacoustics

1   Introduction

The classification of sounds of species is a fundamental challenge to study animal vocalizations [5]. Many of these studies are based on manual inspection and labeling of sound spectra, which relies on agreement between human experts. Recently, pattern recognition approaches including machine learning techniques have been used for automatic classification of animal vocalizations.

Grigg et. al. [5] implemented a software system based on Quinlans C 4.5 decision tree algorithms in order to classify the vocalizations of 22 species of frogs occuring in northern Australia. Kogan and Margoliash discussed in [8] dynamic time warping and hidden Markov models [13] for the automated classification of bird songs (four zebra finches *(Taeniopygia guttata)* and four indigo buntings *(Passerina cyanea)*). In Murray et. al. [11] Kohonen's self organizing neural networks have been used to analyse vocalizations of false killer whales *(Psendorca crassidens)*.

We focus on the automated classification of *Orthoptera* songs based on local features, i.e. on sequences of locally derived feature vectors. These feature vectors serve as inputs of fuzzy-k-nearest neighbour classifiers [2]. In order to classify a time series, for each local feature vector a soft decision is calculated through the classifier. Then these local decisions are combined to an overall decision. This type of decision fusion is called *temporal fusion*. Temporal fusion is the combination of a sequence of decisions calculated in different parts of the time series into a single decision. A large number of combining schemes for temporal

B. Michaelis and G. Krell (Eds.): DAGM 2003, LNCS 2781, pp. 474–481, 2003.
© Springer-Verlag Berlin Heidelberg 2003

classifications exists: combining local class decisions, voting the soft classifier outputs, and combining the real valued outputs of each class [14].

For the combination over the feature space the decisions of multiple classifiers are combined. *Static combining paradigms* [2] where the classifier outputs are simply combined through a fixed fusion mapping and *adaptable combining paradigms* [9] where an additional fusion layer is trained through a second supervised learning procedure are proposed and discussed.

Training a multiple classifier system with an adaptable fusion mapping can be considered as a two phase learning problem:

1. Building the *Classifier Layer* consisting of a set of *first level classifiers* where each classifier is trained on a specific training set $\mathcal{R}$.
2. Training of the *Fusion Layer* performing a mapping of the classifier outputs (soft or crisp decisions) into the set of desired class labels by using a data set called validation set $\mathcal{V}$.

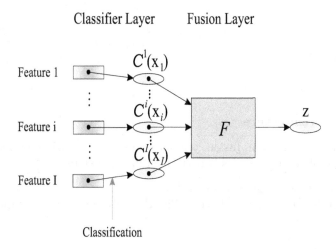

Fig. 1. Two layer architecture consisting of a classifier layer and an additional fusion layer. The combination of the classifier decisions of the individual classifiers $C^1, ..., C^I$ is accomplished in the fusion layer.

So, the overall classifier system (see Figure 1) is a two layer architecture very similar to layered neural networks, with a two layer structure such as multilayer perceptrons and radial basis function networks.

2   Classification Fusion of Local Features

In this Section we propose static and trainable fusion architectures for the combination of local decisions. The situation is illustrated in Figure 2 where a window

W^j covering a small part of the time series $s(t)_{t=1}^T$ is moved over the whole time series. Each time series is labeled with its corresponding class label $\omega \in \Omega$, $\Omega = \{1, ..., L\}$. For each window W^j, $j = 1, ..., \mathcal{J}$ a set of I features $\mathbf{x}_i(j) \in \mathbb{R}^{D_i}$, $i = 1, ..., I$ and $D_i \in \mathbb{N}$, is extracted from the time series. Typically $\mathcal{J}$, the number of time windows varies from time series to time series. For a time series $s(t)_{t=1}^T$ this leads to I feature streams $\mathbf{x}_i(j)_{j=1}^{\mathcal{J}}$ of constant length.

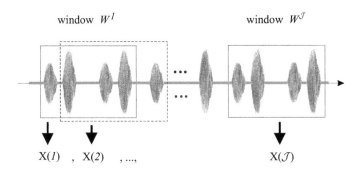

Fig. 2. A set of I features $X(j) = (\mathbf{x}_1(j), ..., \mathbf{x}_I(j))$ is extracted from the j-th local time window W^j.

2.1   CFT-Architecture

In the CFT (classification, fusion, temporal integration) fusion architecture the classification of the time series is performed in three steps:

1.) Classification of single feature vectors (C-step)
   For each feature $i = 1, ..., I$ a classifier $\mathcal{C}^i$ is given through a mapping

$$\mathcal{C}^i : \mathbb{R}^{D_i} \to \Delta \qquad (1)$$

   where the set Δ is defined through

$$\Delta := \{(\mathbf{y}_1, ..., \mathbf{y}_L) \in [0, 1]^L | \sum_{l=1}^{L} \mathbf{y}_l = 1\}. \qquad (2)$$

   Thus, for each local time window W^j, I classifications $\mathcal{C}^1(\mathbf{x}_1(j)), ..., \mathcal{C}^I(\mathbf{x}_I(j))$ are made for the individual features $\mathbf{x}_1(j), ..., \mathbf{x}_I(j)$.
2.) Decision fusion of the local decisions (F-step)
   For each time window W^j the I classification results are combined into a local decision $\mathbf{z}^j \in \Delta$ through a fusion mapping $\mathcal{F} : \Delta^I \to \Delta$

$$\mathbf{z}^j := \mathcal{F}(\mathcal{C}^1(\mathbf{x}_1(j)), ..., \mathcal{C}^I(\mathbf{x}_I(j))), \quad j = 1, ..., \mathcal{J} \qquad (3)$$

   which calculates the fused classification result based on I decisions.

3.) Temporal fusion of decisions over the whole time series (T-step)
The combination of the local decisions of the whole set of time windows W^J, $J = 1, ..., \mathcal{J}$ is given through

$$\mathbf{z}^o := \mathcal{F}(\mathbf{z}^1, ..., \mathbf{z}^{\mathcal{J}}) \tag{4}$$

hereby $\mathcal{F} : \Delta^{\mathcal{J}} \rightarrow \Delta$ is an aggregation rule.

Different aggregation rules may be assumed for the integration of classifier decisions over time (see Eq. 4) and the combination of classifier decisions over the feature space (see Eq. 3). For simplicity we do not discriminate between fusion over time and fusion over the feature space. Let us assume that N is the number of classifiers which have to be combined. For the temporal integration $N = \mathcal{J}$ and $\mathcal{F} : \Delta^{\mathcal{J}} \rightarrow \Delta$ is proper fusion mapping, whereas for decision fusion over the feature space $N = I$ and $\mathcal{F} : \Delta^{I} \rightarrow \Delta$ is the applied mapping. The combination of the individual classifiers $\mathcal{C}^1, ..., \mathcal{C}^N$ by averaging the classifier decisions is known to be robust and is applied in many applications [14]. It is simply given by

$$\mathcal{F}(\mathbf{z}^1, ..., \mathbf{z}^N) := \frac{1}{N} \sum_{n=1}^{N} \mathbf{z}^n. \tag{5}$$

Majority voting returns a crisp decision as a binary coded unit vector which is defined through

$$\mathcal{F}(\mathbf{z}^1, ..., \mathbf{z}^N)_l := \begin{cases} 1 & , l = \underset{\omega \in \Omega}{\mathrm{argmax}} \left(\sum_{n=1}^{N} \mathbf{z}_\omega^n \right) \\ 0 & , \text{otherwise} \end{cases} . \tag{6}$$

2.2   Decision Templates

The concept of decision templates (DTs) is a simple, intuitive, and robust aggregation idea that evolved from the *fuzzy template* which is introduced by KUNCHEVA, see [9,10]. Let $\Omega = \{1, ..., L\}$ be again the set of class labels, and $\mathcal{C} : \mathbb{R}^D \rightarrow \Delta$ be a *probabilistic classifier* mapping (see Eq. 2). We assume that the classifier mapping $\mathcal{C}$ is trained through a supervised training procedure on a finite training set $\mathcal{R} \subset \mathbb{R}^D \times \Omega$ with patterns $(\mathbf{x}^\mu(J)_{J=1}^{\mathcal{J}^\mu}, \omega^\mu)$ of feature streams and corresponding class labels ω^μ.

In order to train the fusion layer, the previously trained classifier is applied. For a trained classifier $\mathcal{C}$, *decision templates* $\mathcal{T}^\omega$ for each class $\omega \in \Omega$ can be calculated by the mean of the local classifier outputs $\mathcal{C}(\mathbf{x}^\mu(\cdot))$ for inputs $\mathbf{x}^\mu(\cdot)$ of class ω [10]:

$$\mathcal{T}^\omega := \frac{1}{|\mathcal{V}^\omega|} \sum_{\mathbf{x}^\mu(J) \in \mathcal{V}^\omega} \mathcal{C}(\mathbf{x}^\mu) \tag{7}$$

Here $\mathcal{V}^\omega$ is a finite validation set of $\mathbb{R}^D \times \{\omega\}$. Then the decision template $\mathcal{T}^\omega \in \Delta$ may be interpreted as characteristic classifier output for the inputs

$\mathbf{x}^{\mu}(\cdot)$ of $\mathcal{V}^{\omega}$. In the context of decision templates the classifier output $\mathcal{C}(\mathbf{x}(\jmath))$ is also called local *decision profile* of classifier $\mathcal{C}$ and input $\mathbf{x}(\jmath)$ [9]. In order to improve the overall classifier ensemble performance particularly for a multi-class pattern recognition problem $(L > 2)$, instead of classifying objects based on a single feature, a set of I different features is used. A typical approach to deal with I features is to build I classifiers, i.e. one classifier per feature space (see Figure 1), and to combine the I classifier outputs into a final decision[3,10]. In the case of I input features with classifier mappings $\mathcal{C}^i : \mathbb{R}^{D_i} \to \Delta, i = 1, ..., I$ the *decision template* $\mathcal{T}^{\omega}$ of class ω is given by a $(I \times L)$-matrix

$$\mathcal{T}^{\omega} := \begin{bmatrix} \mathcal{T}_1^{\omega} \\ \vdots \\ \mathcal{T}_I^{\omega} \end{bmatrix} \in \Delta^I. \tag{8}$$

Hereby $\mathcal{T}_i^{\omega} \in \Delta$ is the decision template of the i-th feature space $\mathbb{R}^{D_i}$ and target class ω. The local decision profile $\mathcal{P}^{\jmath}$ for an input $X(\jmath) = (\mathbf{x}_1(\jmath), ..., \mathbf{x}_I(\jmath))$ is given by the individual classifier outputs of the I previously trained classifiers

$$\mathcal{P}^{\jmath}(X(\jmath)) = [\mathcal{C}^1(\mathbf{x}_1(\jmath)), ..., \mathcal{C}^{\mathcal{J}}(\mathbf{x}_{\mathcal{J}}(\jmath))]^T \in \Delta^I. \tag{9}$$

The classification of time series with decision templates works as follows:

Algorithm $\omega^* = \mathrm{DT}((X(\jmath))_{\jmath=1}^{\mathcal{J}}, (\mathcal{T}^{\omega})_{\omega=1}^{L})$
    foreach $\jmath = 1, ..., \mathcal{J}$
(a) $\mathcal{P}^{\jmath} = [\mathcal{C}^1(\mathbf{x}_1(\jmath)), ..., \mathcal{C}^I(\mathbf{x}_I(\jmath))]^T$
        foreach $\omega \in \Omega$
(b) $\mathbf{z}_{\omega}^{\jmath} = \mathcal{S}(\mathcal{P}^{\jmath}, \mathcal{T}^{\omega})$
        end
    end
(c) $\mathbf{z} = \mathcal{F}(\mathbf{z}^1, ..., \mathbf{z}^{\mathcal{J}})$
(d) $\omega^* = \underset{\omega}{\mathrm{argmax}}(\mathbf{z}_{\omega})$

Algorithm DT: Classification of time series $(X(\jmath))_{\jmath=1}^{\mathcal{J}}$ consisting of $\mathcal{J}$ local feature vectors with decision templates.

The classifiers $\mathcal{C}^1, ..., \mathcal{C}^I$ are applied to calculate the local decision profile $\mathcal{P}^{\jmath}$, see step (a). Then for each class $\omega \in \Omega$ a local class membership value $\mathbf{z}_{\omega}^{\jmath}$ based on a similarity measure $\mathcal{S}$ between the decision profile $\mathcal{P}^{\jmath}$ and the decision template $\mathcal{T}^{\omega}$ is calculated (see step (b) in Algorithm DT and Eq. 10). After temporal integration of local decisions (see step (c)) the class with the maximum membership ω^* is the final decision, see step (d).

The most popular similarity measure is based on the normalized squared Euclidean distance (L2-norm) or more general, it is based on the normalized L_p-norm $|| \cdot ||_p$ and is defined by

$$S_p(\mathcal{P}, \mathcal{T}^\omega) := 1 - \frac{1}{2I} \sum_{i=1}^{I} ||\mathcal{P}_{i,\cdot} - \mathcal{T}_{i,\cdot}^\omega||_p \quad \in [0,1]. \qquad (10)$$

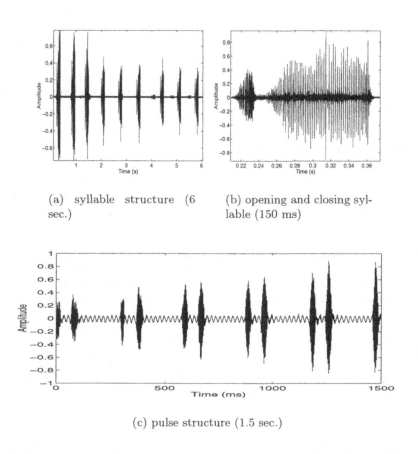

(a) syllable structure (6 sec.)

(b) opening and closing syllable (150 ms)

(c) pulse structure (1.5 sec.)

Fig. 3. Typical time amplitude pattern of the stridulatory signals of the katydid species *Ephippiger ephippiger* in 2 different time resolutions (see Figure (a) and (b)). Time amplitude pattern of the cricket species *Noctitrella glabra* (see Figure (c)).

3   Application

We present results achieved with the proposed multiple classifier algorithms to bioacoustic data. The data set consists of sound patterns from 31 different species of crickets and 22 different species of katydids with the recordings of 6 to 12 individuals per species. These recordings are provided from Ingrisch [7], Nischk

[12] and Heller [6] and are part of a specimen-based multimedia database, bringing together data from different sound archives (see (http://www.dorsa.de). Sound patterns are stored in the WAV-format (sampling rate ranges from 44.1 kHz to 500 kHz, 16 Bit sampling accuracy).

The *Orthoptera* songs consist of sequences of sound patterns called syllables (see Figure 3(b)). Based on these syllables (sequences of so-called pulses, see Figure 3(c)) the *Orthoptera* species are classified [12]. On- and off-sets of the pulses are determined through the short time energy of the signal and two threshold functions to get the relevant parts of the signal [4]. Time windows $\mathcal{W}^j$, $j = 1, ..., \mathcal{J}$ are aligned at the on-sets and the off-sets of the pulses in order to calculate pulse lengths, pulse distances, pulse frequencies, time encoded signals, and energy contours of pulses [2].

4   Results and Discussion

Because of the limited data sets the K-fold cross validation test [1] with 5 cross validation cycles has been performed. The classification results for the proposed fusion schemes are given in Table 1. The basic conclusion of our experiments is

Table 1. Error rates for the CFT fusion architecture and the DT fusion scheme in percent. Hereby $\frac{a}{b}$ denotes that in the CFT fusion architecture decision fusion is applied with aggregation rule a, whereas the temporal combination is applied by aggregation rule b. Averaging (AVR) and majority voting (VOT) are the applied aggregation rule.

data set	$\frac{AVR}{AVR}$	$\frac{AVR}{VOT}$	$\frac{VOT}{AVR}$	$\frac{VOT}{VOT}$	DT
crickets	12.32	13.41	13.08	14.16	10.49
katydids	23.18	27.06	28.26	31.64	17.01

that that the membership estimates of the individual classifiers are important for the combination of the classifiers because the combination with majority voting (see Eq. 6) typically performs not as good as the combination with averaging (see Eq. 5). By training the decision fusion mapping with the decision templates approach the classifier performance was improved in comparison to the combination with the CFT fusion architecture. Finally, and independent from these questions of fundamental research, the classifier system described here could be implemented into *Rapid Assessment tool*, to detect, classify and monitor tropical biodiversity.

Acknowledgment. DORSA (www.dorsa.de) forms part of the Entomological Data Information System (EDIS) and is funded by the German Ministry of

Science and Education (BMBF). We are greatful to Klaus Riede (ZFMK Bonn, Germany), Sigfrid Ingrisch (ZFMK Bonn, Germany), Frank Nischk and Klaus Heller for providing their sound recordings, suggestions and discussions.

References

1. C. M. Bishop. *Neural Networks for Pattern Recognition.* Oxford University Press, New York, 1995.
2. C. Dietrich, F. Schwenker, and G. Palm. Classification of time series utilizing temporal and decision fusion. In J. Kittler and F. Roli, editors, *Multiple Classifier Systems*, pages 378–387. Springer, 2001.
3. C. Dietrich, F. Schwenker, and G. Palm. Decision templates for the classification of bioacoustic time series. In H. Bourland et. al., editor, *Proceedings of IEEE Workshop on Neural Networks and Signal Processing*, pages 159–168, 2002.
4. C. Dietrich, F. Schwenker, K. Riede, and G. Palm. Classification of bioacoustic time series utilizing pulse detection, time and frequency features and data fusion. *www.informatik.uni-ulm.de/pw/berichte* Ulmer Informatik-Berichte 2001–04, University of Ulm, 2001.
5. G. Grigg, A. Taylor, H. Mc Callum, and G. Watson. Monitoring frog communities: An application of machine learning. In *Proceedings of Eighth Innovative Applications of Artificial Intelligence Conference, Portland Oregon*, pages 1564–1569. AAAI Press, 1996.
6. K. G. Heller. *Bioakustik der Europäischen Laubheuschrecken. Ökologie in Forschung und Anwendung.* Margraf, Weikersheim, 1988.
7. S. Ingrisch. Taxonomy, stridulation and development of Podoscirtinae from Thailand. *Senckenbergiana biologica*, 77:47–75, 1997.
8. J. A. Kogan and D. Margoliash. Automated recognition of bird song elements from continous recordings using dynamic time warping and hidden markov models: A comparative study. *Journal of the Acoustical Society of America*, 103(4):2185–2196, 1998.
9. L. I. Kuncheva. Using measures of similarity and inclusion for multiple classifier fusion by decision templates. *Fuzzy Sets and Systems*, 122(3):401–407, 2001.
10. L. I. Kuncheva, J. C. Bezdek, and R. P. W. Duin. Decision templates for multiple classifier fusion. *Pattern Recognition*, 34(2):299–314, 2001.
11. S. O. Murray, E. Mercado, and H. L. Roitblat. The neural network classification of false killer whale *(pseudorca crassidens)* vocalizations. *Journal of the Acoustical Society of America*, 104(6):3626–3633, 1998.
12. F. Nischk. *Die Grillengesellschaften zweier neotropischer Waldökosysteme in Ecuador.* PhD thesis, University of Köln, Germany, 1999. Memorandum UCB/ERL–M89/29 (in German).
13. N. Rabiner and L. Y. Juang. *Fundamentals of Speech Recognition.* Prentice-Hall, New Jersey, 1993.
14. D. M. J. Tax, M. van Bruecklen, R. P. W. Duin, and J. Kittler. Combining multiple classifiers by averaging or by multiplying? *Pattern Recognition*, 33:1475–1485, 2000.

A Region Based Seed Detection for Root Detection in Minirhizotron Images

Gregor Erz* and Stefan Posch

Martin-Luther-University Halle-Wittenberg, Institute of Computer Science
D-06099 Halle, Germany, {erz,posch}@informatik.uni-halle.de

Abstract. Automatic analysis of plant root images is very important for the analysis of root architecture and morphology as requested by ecological, agronomic and biological studies. Extending the approach in [1] we improve the detection of special root parts called seeds which are expanded to complete roots in a subsequent step. Replacing the original contour based seed detection by a region based one allows us to take more global information into account. As the seed detection influences the overall performance strongly the such acquired improvements benefit the whole root detection significantly.

1 Introduction

Examining and modelling plant growth in ecological, agronomic and biological studies requires quantitative information about root architecture and morphology. Roots do not only serve as mechanical anchors of the plant, but are very important in nutrient uptake as well. Taking advantage of destruction free examination using transparent tubes (minirhizotrons) in conjunction with endoscopes the minirhizotron technique ([3]) is widely used for root inspection. The images acquired by this method are usually recorded on a VCR and digitized later. Unfortunately it is a very time consuming task to analyze them, e.g. to measure a roots length or its area.

Automatic detection of roots in minirhizotron images is therefore an important task in machine based analysis of such material. Some techniques for finding roots in these images are already known (e.g. [1], [4]). Most aim at generating a binary image for each minirhizotron image where pixels are labeled either to be on a root or not. In this paper we expand our approach [1] by adding an alternative technique for seed detection, which is one of the two main phases of this method. Section 2 gives a tense overview of the system, subsequently the new seed detection is described in detail and results are presented in section 4.

2 Overview

The outline of our approach to detect roots in minirhizotron images is as follows: First, the image of interest is extracted from our database and appropriate

---

* This work is supported by the Deutsche Forschungsgemeinschaft (DFG).

B. Michaelis and G. Krell (Eds.): DAGM 2003, LNCS 2781, pp. 482–489, 2003.

preprocessing steps are applied, namely low pass filtering via median, sobel edge detection and optional sub-sampling. The first main phase is to detect at least one *seed* for each root projected into the image. A seed is defined as a rather small, distinct part of the root, which is clearly identifiable as partial root and has a shape close to a rectangle (e.g. contains no branchings). It is described by two pixel chains located on the contour of the root projection. The rational behind this approach is the fact, that in most images only small parts of each root are clearly separable from the background (composed of soil, pebbles and defilement) using intensity information only.

After detecting these seeds, each is expanded in the second phase using a more sophisticated A*-search to complete the partial root taking the shape of the hypothesized root into account as well. The resulting roots are represented as a binary image, which is stored along with relevant attributes (e.g. number of roots per image, length, area) in the database for further analysis as advised by the biological application.

3   Seed Detection

Applied to low gradient images, the previously employed contour based seed detection often fails to detect seeds on valid root regions. It thus fails to meet two important requirements:

1. at least one seed per root should be detected
2. only a moderate number of wrong seeds should be detected

To address this problem we decided to use a more globally oriented region based approach. The main idea is to apply varying thresholds to the image and select from the resulting regions suitable *seed regions*. Seed regions are likely to be parts of roots and therefore are subsequently used to extract (approximately rectangular) seeds which we are interested in.

Figure 1 illustrates the steps of this method. The seed regions are acquired using a number of different thresholds thus coping with locally varying intensities and subsequently judged by a seed criterion (see subsection 3.1). An example for one thresholded image is depicted in figure 1(b). From the boundary of a valid seed region a set of pixel *chains* is computed that roughly parallel the main axis of the region (figure 1(d)). Combining these chains into *chain pairs* (figure 1(e)) and adapting their length will produce several *protoseeds* per region (figure 1(f)). These are used to calculate the final seeds employing an A*-search.

It is to be noted, that such a threshold based approach has proven to be too simple minded to detect complete roots due to the complexity and inhomogeneities of minirhizotron images. This is noted e.g. in [2] and, after all, was the motivation for our contour based A*-algorithm in [1]. However, when detecting seed regions we are content with retrieving one subpart of the root region only, which shows to be robustly feasible using thresholds. Having the option of employing other region segmentation algorithms (e.g. watershed or region growing) we use the one described as it works fast and very well for our purpose.

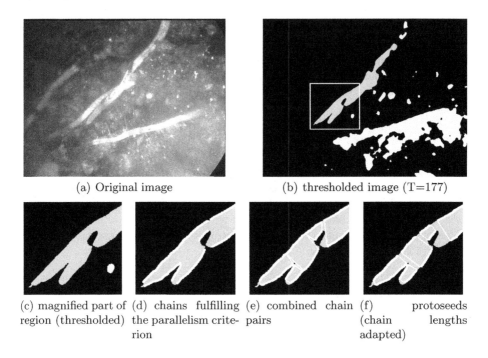

(a) Original image   (b) thresholded image (T=177)

(c) magnified part of region (thresholded)   (d) chains fulfilling the parallelism criterion   (e) combined chain pairs   (f)   protoseeds (chain lengths adapted)

Fig. 1. Creation of Seeds

3.1   Seed Regions

The selection of a suitable threshold to compute seed regions is not trivial, especially as histograms of minirhizotron images are usually not bi- or even multi-modal. With each root region generally having its own optimal threshold this problem is aggravated. We therefore employ various thresholds and select valid seed regions using contraints as described in the following.

Constraints and Seed Criterion. As we expect seeds to be longish and of a certain minimum size, we constrain the width W, the length L and the area A of the region. All of them must meet some minimum requirements in size to distinguish seeds from small pebbles for example. W and L are approximated using the square root of the eigenvalues (i.e. the standard deviation) computed via PCA. To express some kind of compactness of a seed the ratio $\frac{W}{L}$ is taken into consideration. It is scale invariant and required to be less than a threshold θ_O. Taking sub-sampled images into account, W, L and A are compared against a quantity related to the resolution of the image. Using the diagonal length Λ of the image yields the following size constraint:

$$(W > \theta_W \cdot \Lambda) \wedge (L > \theta_L \cdot \Lambda) \wedge (A > \theta_A \cdot \Lambda^2)$$

Since a seed region usually has a smooth boundary we use an approximation for the curvature energy E of the regions border. It is calculated using the second derivative of the parametric description of the region border P_i, $i\epsilon\{1, ..., N\}$ and compared against an upper threshold θ_E.

$$(\frac{\partial^2}{\partial x^2} + \frac{\partial^2}{\partial y^2})\boldsymbol{P}_i \quad with \quad \boldsymbol{P}_i = (x_i, y_i)$$

Using discrete approximations $\Delta\boldsymbol{P_i}$ we obtain E as:

$$\theta_E > E = \sum_{i=1}^{N} \Delta\boldsymbol{P_i}$$

Combining all these criteria allows us to assess seed regions that are hypothesized by the dynamic thresholding described next.

Dynamic Thresholding. To find all regions fulfilling this seed criterion one can test all possible thresholds. To address efficiency, however, we decided to make use of a special feature a root region usually has: it is surrounded by high gradient magnitudes. This means that small changes of the threshold do not change the seed region considered significantly.

We therefore proceed as follows: a number P of equidistant thresholds T_i

$$T_i = \frac{256}{P} \cdot i \quad i\epsilon\{0, ..., P-1\}$$

for the initial interval $[0, 255]$[1] is computed and the image binarized applying each threshold. Regions found at T_i and fulfilling the seed criterion are selected[2] and processed separately to find the optimal threshold. This is done by refining the search with P new thresholds T_k within the interval $[T_{i-1}, T_{i+1}]$.

$$T_k = \frac{(T_{i+1} - T_{i-1})}{P} \cdot k + T_{i-1} \quad k\epsilon\{0, ..., P-1\}$$

Increasing[3] thresholds will decrease the width-to-length ratio because the impact of the absolute change is relatively higher on the width. This is true up to the point where the region breaks up or disappears which results in a sudden rise of $\frac{W}{L}$. Therefore the width-to-length ratio aids in finding the optimal threshold which is designated to have minimal $\frac{W}{L}$. A new refined interval for further examination is created recursively with the last one being scanned with a stepwidth of one.

P should be chosen according to the images that are to be processed. If image contrast is high we successfully used P=8 but images of low contrast require larger P. It is important to note that even for P=64 a significant speedup can be achieved compared to a brute force approach in the case where few regions are present only which is typical for our application. Results for P=32 and P=64 as well as P=8 are presented in chapter 4.

---

[1] for 8 bit gray level images

[2] If the same region is found more than once for different T_i the one with the lowest width-to-length ratio is processed further.

[3] This is true for bright roots and dark backgrounds and reversed in the other case which is equally treated by this approach due to symmetric searching.

3.2   Creating Chains

A protoseed is represented by two pixel chains that consist of seed region border pixels. By selecting pixels from that border we will now create chains that will aid in the creation of protoseeds subsequently (section 3.3).

Parallelism Criterion. In many cases the seed regions do not have the rectangular form required for a seed due to branching off, crossing roots and occluding objects. Therefore, from one seed region several protoseeds will be created genererally. The corresponding subparts of the seed region feature highly parallel contours. Thus, we formulate a parallelism criterion that pixels must fulfil to be accepted as members of a chain representing these subparts. Let n be the orientation of the region and e the approximated tangent direction of the pixel considered, both normalized to length 1. Then validity results from:

$$|n \cdot e| > \theta_{par}$$

If a set of at least N_{mcl} neighbouring pixels is found valid they are combined into one potential chain of a protoseed. Since all pixels of this chain are roughly parallel to the regions orientation, the chains itself are approximately parallel, too.

Distinguishing Left and Right Chains. To determine the boundary of a seed region inner-boundary-tracing is used. Since we do not alter the order of the boundarys pixels the resulting chains are oriented accordingly. Therefore, a protoseed will always be composed of two antiparallel chains (see figure 2(a)).

To simplify protoseed creation a chain is labeled to be 'left' or 'right' of the region. Chains with a direction c being antiparallel to the seed regions orientation n are called 'right'. By this definition a chain will be called 'left' if $n \cdot c > 0$ and 'right' otherwise.

3.3   Protoseed Generation

Protoseeds are created by combining the correct 'left' and 'right' chain into one pair and adapting their length.

Projective Chain Pair Matching and Length Adaption. At first all combinations of two chains are considered. Obviously, potential matches are required to overlap when projected onto the regions main axis. Given the 'left' chain L in figure 2(b) for example, all overlapping 'right' chains R_i, $i\epsilon\{1,2,3\}$, must be considered as possible protoseed counterparts. The correct one is

1. on the opposing side of the region (not fulfilled for R_3 in figure 2(b)) **and**
2. has the smallest distance to L.

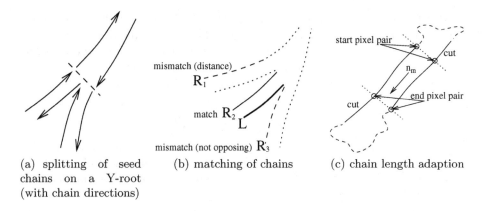

(a) splitting of seed chains on a Y-root (with chain directions)   (b) matching of chains   (c) chain length adaption

Fig. 2. Creating seeds from chains

Having found a matching pair the lengths of both chains have to be adapted. To this end the common main axis n_m is computed as the average of both chain directions c_l and c_r and the projections of both chains onto n_m are intersected. Finally all pixels are discarded from both chains, which do not project onto this intersection (see figure 2(c) for an illustration).

Aligning Seeds. The protoseeds we produced so far were selected by thresholding without any gradient information. However, the subsequent A*-algorithm to expand seeds (called root detection in [1]) relies heavily on the gradient magnitudes in the image. Therefore, we will now 'align' the detected seed chains to the maximum gradient. This is done by employing the identical A*-algorithm used for root detection to connect the start pixel pair with the end pixel pair of the protoseed (see figure 2(c)). All A* parameters for this initial search are chosen identical to the subsequent root detection. This forces the aligned chain pair to locations with high gradient magnitudes while preserving the shape as roughly parallel. The results of this search are the final seeds.

4   Results

Both seed detections were evaluated using two sets of minirhizotron images. The first set to which we will refer as *set A* was already used in [1] for evaluation. It consists of 32 images featuring an overall of 48 root regions. Only one image does not have a root region at all. The second set labeled as *set B* is composed of 367 images chosen randomly from our database with a total of 2276 images. It contains 110 regions in 77 images and 290 images without any root. Both sets were created by our co-operation partners at the University of Bielefeld using different plants and setups.

In figure 3 two images are given as an example. Detected seeds are colored in white with the original image reduced in brightness for better inspection. As obvious from figure 3(c) the contour based seed detection fails to detect the correct root region but produces a number of incorrect seeds. In the example of figure 3(e) and 3(f), both algorithms detect at least one seed on the root projected and are thus equivalent with regard to our requirements for seed detection as defined in section 3. This is despite the fact, that the region based technique generates two seeds of bigger extent, since we expect the subsequent root detection to correctly extend a seed to cover the complete root in both cases. No incorrect seeds are found by the region based seed detection in either example. All results were obtained using the parameters in table 1 and are summarized in table 2 for both sets. The given parameters were found experimentally and prove to be not sensitive against perturbations.   As root regions are to be detected,

(a) original image   (b) new seed detection   (c) old seed detection

(d) original image   (e) new seed detection   (f) old seed detection

Fig. 3. Examples: an image from set A (upper) and set B (lower)

Table 1. Parameters used to obtain the given results

parameter	θ_L	θ_W	θ_O	θ_A	θ_E	θ_{par}	N_p	N_{mcl}
value	0.143	0.01	0.33	0.002	8.5	0.92	5	9

we count each root with a least one seed detected as correct in table 2. The percentages listed refer to the total number of roots in the column *correct* and to all seeds detected in the column *additional*. Wrong seeds (i.e. false alarms), which are not located on root regions, are counted in this column. The new seed detection performs superior for set A regarding additional seeds detected. Only for P=8 it misses one seed region which is found by the contour based detection. In all other cases it performs equally or better. For set B a significant improvement with regard to correctly detected seeds can be noticed. About twice to three times as many correct seeds are detected by the new seed detection as are by the contour based method. The number of additional seeds, however, is lower

Table 2. Detected regions (*correct*) or seeds (*additional*) for both sets

	set A				set B			
Algorithm	correct	in %	additional	in %	correct	in %	additional	in %
[1]	38	79.17%	131	53.47%	25	22.73%	650	95.03%
TS (P= 8)	37	77.08%	0	0%	57	51.82%	196	41.88%
TS (P=32)	38	79.17%	51	24.4%	87	79.09%	572	57.72%
TS (P=64)	39	81.25%	63	28.5%	92	83.64%	670	52.26%

for P=8 and P=32 only. This is due to the generation of approximately 4 seeds per seed region (127 wrong seed regions were detected using P=32 for example). However, incorrect seeds are very unlikely expanded by the root detection using the A*-algorithm and can thus be easily discarded after expansion.

5   Conclusion

In this paper we described a new approach to detect root seeds in minirhizotron images. This new seed detection is based on a more globally oriented technique using dynamic thresholding to determine optimal thresholds for each seed region which is part of a projected root. From these seed regions a number of pixel chain pairs is generated and combined into protoseeds. They provide a start and end point for a contour aligning A*-search. The seeds found by this search are located on high gradient magnitudes in the image and are suitable for the subsequent root expansion. The new seed detection gives better results regarding the specific requirements. This is true especially for images featuring low gradient magnitudes. Both seed detections are completely interchangeable in the context of the whole root detection process described by [1].

Acknowledgement. We gratefully acknowledge the cooperation with our project partners S. Breckle and H. Anlauf from the University of Bielefeld for fruitful discussions and the images provided.

References

1. M. Jankowski: *Automatische Detektion von Wurzelsystemen in Minirhizotron-Bildern*, Bielefeld, 1995
2. A. L. Smit et al. (Eds.): *Root Methods*, Springer-Verlag, Heidelberg, 2000
3. G.H. Bates: *A device for the observation of root growth in the soil*, London 1937, Nature 139:966–967
4. A. J. M. Smucker, J. Ferguson, W. P. DeBruyn, R. K. Belford, J. T. Ritchie: *Image Analysis of Video-Recorded Plant Root Systems*, in *Minirhizothrons Observation Tubes: Methods and Applications for Measuring Rhizosphere Dynamics*, No. 50, ASA Special Publications, 1987, p. 67–80.

Image Retrieval Using Local Compact DCT-Based Representation

Štěpán Obdržálek[1] and Jiří Matas[1,2]

[1] Center for Machine Perception, Czech Technical University, Prague, CZ
[2] Centre for Vision Speech and Signal Processing, University of Surrey, Guildford, UK

Abstract. An image retrieval system based on local affine frames is introduced. The system provides highly discriminative retrieval of rigid objects under a very wide range of viewing and illumination conditions, and is robust to occlusion and background clutter. Distinguished regions of data dependent shape are detected, and local affine frames (coordinate systems) are obtained. Photometrically and geometrically normalised image patches are extracted and used for matching.
Local correspondences are formed either by direct comparison of photometrically normalised colour intensities in the normalised patches, or by comparison of DCT (discrete cosine transform) coefficients of the patches. Experimental results are presented on a publicly available database of real outdoor images of buildings. We demonstrate the effect of the number of DCT coefficients that are used for the matching. Using the DCT, excellent results with a retrieval performance of 100% in rank 1 are achieved, and memory usage is reduced by a factor of 4.

1   Introduction

The widespread availability of digital images, and the increasing ease of their acquisition, distribution and storage, give rise to miscellaneous applications demanding reliable retrieval of images from digital databases. Many approaches addressing the problem of image retrieval were introduced, the most common being those using global descriptors of whole images, like colour histograms [1,2], texture [3], shape [4], or colour invariants [5,6]. For a comprehensive survey, see [7]. We leave aside the problems of connecting the user's query specification to the image representation (the problem known as the 'semantic gap'), and focus on the class of retrieval problems where the query is formed by an image of (a part of) the object of interest. We assume that the query object may cover only a fractional part of the database image and that it may be viewed from a significantly different viewpoint and under different illumination.

Variations in an object's appearance caused by viewpoint and environment changes are generally complex. Objects with intricate shapes change their overall look dramatically even for small differences in viewpoints. To simplify the situation, we assume that these variations, although complex in general, can be reasonably well approximated by simpler transformations at local scale. Geometric image deformations are locally approximated by 2D affine transformations, photometric changes by affine transformations of individual RGB channels.

The proposed approach is based on robust, affine and illumination invariant detection of local affine frames (local coordinate systems). Local correspondences between the

---

* The authors were supported by European Union under project IST-2001-32184, by Czech Ministry of Education under project LN00B096, and by CTU grant No. CTU0307013.

B. Michaelis and G. Krell (Eds.): DAGM 2003, LNCS 2781, pp. 490–497, 2003.

query and database images are established by a direct comparison of measurements in local image patches with shape and colour normalised according to the affine frames. The method compares well with the state of the art. Object recognition and retrieval results on standard public image databases COIL-100 (mostly man-made 3D objects, no object occlusion nor background clutter) and FOCUS (planar logos, no occlusion but significant background clutter) are superior to any published results. The experiments are described in detail in [8,9].

The presented image retrieval system is motivated by a real application: the localisation of an user in an outdoor environment. The system handles real outdoor images where the illumination varies due to weather changes, where objects are occluded, and where the background is cluttered. As the size of the database of known objects increases, the memory requirement of the object representation becomes important. We use the discrete cosine transform (DCT) to efficiently encode the local intensity information. The memory usage is thereby reduced by a factor 4, while the retrieval performance is maintained or even slightly improved.

The rest of the paper is organised as follows. In Section 2 we present an overview of the retrieval process and briefly discuss the concepts of distinguished regions and local affine frames. Section 3 details how images are represented by a set of local measurements, and in Section 4 experimental results are presented. Finally, Section 5 presents the conclusions.

2   Overview of the Retrieval Process

The outline of the proposed retrieval process is as follows (the first three steps are visualised in Fig. 1):

1. For every database and query image compute distinguished regions.
2. Construct local affine frames on the regions.
3. Generate intensity representations of local image patches normalised according to the local affine frames.
4. Generate discrete cosine transformation (DCT) representations of the normalised local patches.
5. Establish correspondences between frames of query and database images, by computing the euclidean distance between the local image intensities or their DCT coefficients, and by finding the nearest match.
6. An estimate of the match score is based on the number and quality of the established local correspondences.

In the rest of this Section we briefly introduce the concepts of the first two steps, the distinguished regions and the local affine frames. Remaining steps are discussed in the following sections.

Distinguished Regions (DRs) are image elements (subsets of image pixels), that posses some distinguishing property that allows their repeated and stable detection over a range of image formation conditions. In this work we exploit a new type of distinguished regions introduced in [10], the *Maximally Stable Extremal Regions* (MSERs). This type of distinguished regions has a number of attractive properties: 1. invariance to affine and perspective transforms, 2. invariance to monotonic transformation of image intensity,

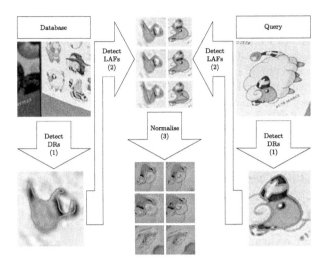

Fig. 1. Block diagram: obtaining the local, affine invariant image descriptors.

3. computational complexity almost linear in the number of pixels and consequently near real-time run time, and 4. since no smoothing is involved, both very fine and coarse image structures are detected. We do not describe MSERs here; the reader is referred to [10] which includes a formal definition of MSERs and a detailed description of the extraction algorithm.

Local affine frames (LAFs, local object-centered coordinate systems) allow normalisation of image patches into a canonical frame, and enable direct comparison of photometrically normalised intensity values, eliminating the need for invariants. For every distinguished region, multiple frames are computed. The actual number of the frames depends on the region's complexity. While simple elliptical regions have no stable frames detected, regions of complex non-convex shape may have tens of frames associated. Robustness of our approach is thus achieved by 1. selecting only stable frames and 2. employing multiple processes for frame computation. A detailed description of the local affine frame constructions is given in [9] and [8].

3   Image Representation

Images are represented by sets of local measurements. Since local affine frames are established, there is no need for geometrically invariant descriptors of local appearance. Any measurement taken relative to the frame is affine invariant.

Geometry. The affine transformation between the canonical frame with origin $O = (0,0)^T$ and basis vectors $e_1 = (1,0)^T$ and $e_2 = (0,1)^T$ and an established frame F is described in homogenous coordinates by a 3 by 3 matrix $\mathbf{A}_F = \begin{pmatrix} a_1 & a_2 & a_3 \\ a_4 & a_5 & a_6 \\ 0 & 0 & 1 \end{pmatrix}$. The image area (defined in terms of the affine frame) where the local measurements are taken from is referred to as a measurement region (MR). The choice of MR shape and size is

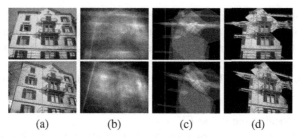

(a)   (b)   (c)   (d)

Fig. 2. Coverage of images. (a) original query and database images, (b) image coverage by local patches, whiter area – more overlapping patches, (c) image patches where correspondences between the images were found (including mismatches), (d) image area covered by the corresponding patches.

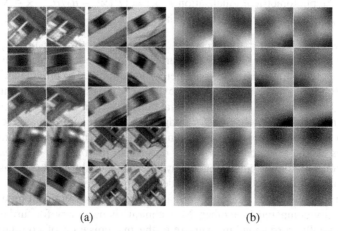

(a)   (b)

Fig. 3. Examples of correspondences established between frames of query (left columns) and database (right columns), for the image pair from Figure 2. (a) geometrically and photometrically normalised image patches, (b) the same patches reconstructed from 10 DCT coefficients per colour channel.

arbitrary. Our choice is to use a square MR centered around a detected LAF, specifically an image area spanning $\langle -2, 3 \rangle \times \langle -2, 3 \rangle$ in the frame coordinate system. See Figure 2 for an example of how an image is covered by measurement regions.

Photometry. Our model assumes a linear camera (ie. a camera without gamma-correction) and that no specular reflections are present in the local patches. The combined effect of different scene illumination and camera and digitiser settings (gain, shutter speed, aperture) can be then represented by affine transformations of individual colour channels. The transformation of intensities in colour channels between two corresponding patches I and I' is considered in the form:

$$\begin{pmatrix} r' \\ g' \\ b' \end{pmatrix} = \begin{pmatrix} m_r & 0 & 0 \\ 0 & m_g & 0 \\ 0 & 0 & m_b \end{pmatrix} \begin{pmatrix} r \\ g \\ b \end{pmatrix} + \begin{pmatrix} n_r \\ n_g \\ n_b \end{pmatrix}$$

The constants $m_r, n_r, m_g, n_g, m_b, n_b$ differ for individual correspondences. This model agrees with the monochromatic reflectance model [11] and is an affine extension of the diagonal model, commonly used in colour constancy problems. To achieve invariance to affine photometric variations and to enable direct intensity comparison, the patch intensities are transformed into a canonical form: the intensities in individual colour channels are affinely transformed to have zero mean and unit variance.

Normalisation Procedure. The normalisation of a local image patch proceeds in four steps:

1. Establish a local affine frame F.
2. Compute the affine transformation $\mathbf{A}_F$ between the canonical coordinate system and F.
3. Express the intensities of the LAF's measurement region in the canonical coordinate system $I'(\mathbf{x}) = I(\mathbf{A}_F \mathbf{x})$, $\quad \mathbf{x} \in \mathrm{MR}$ with some discretisation.
4. Apply the photometric normalisation $\hat{I}'(\mathbf{x}) = (I'(\mathbf{x}) - \mu)/\sigma$, $\quad \mathbf{x} \in \mathrm{MR}$ where μ is the mean and σ is the standard deviation of I' over the MR.

The twelve normalisation parameters $(a_1 \ldots a_6, m_r, n_r, m_g, n_g, m_b, n_b)$ are stored along with the normalised intensity measurement. When considering a pair of patches for a correspondence, these twelve parameters are combined to provide the local transformation (both geometric and photometric) between the images. Constraints can be put here on the transformation to prune potential matches. Typical constraints may include: allowing only small scale changes for images taken from approximately constant distance from the objects, rejecting significant rotations when upright camera and object orientations can be assumed, allowing for only small illumination changes for images taken in a controlled environment, and many others. If the runtime conditions are known, the unconstrained invariance can so be traded for higher discriminativity.

Intensity representation. After the normalisation, any measurement on a local patch can be directly compared to another. No technique is necessary for further alignment of the potentially corresponding pairs (e.g. the maximisation of correlation over an unknown rotation). To establish correspondences between patches, we can use directly the underlying intensity function. The normalised MR content is stored in a discretised form as an array of 15×15 pixels, and the correlation coefficient is used as the similarity measure of two patches. See Figure 3a for an example of pairs of normalised patches.

Discrete Cosine Transformation. Patch description by a discretised intensity function is high-dimensional. In many pattern recognition problems (eg. in face recognition) the Karhunen-Loeve (KL) transformation is used to reduce the feature dimensionality without significant deterioration of the recognition performance. The KL transformation has drawbacks though. Mainly, it depends on the second-order statistics of the training data, ie. the training (database) images have to be known in advance.

For the dimensionality reduction we therefore use the discrete cosine transformation (DCT) instead of the Karhunen Loeve transformation. The DCT has the following desirable properties:

- For uniformly distributed data, the DCT approximates the Karhunen-Loeve transformation [12].
- Fast algorithms exist that computes DCT with $O(n \log n)$ time complexity.
- Due to the widespread use of DCT in image and video compression domain (JPEG, MPEG, etc.), hardware implementations of DCT are widely available.
- Unlike the KL transformation, DCT does not require a training set.

Fig. 4. Example of database images. Five images are present for every of the 201 buildings.

Keeping only low frequency DCT coefficients, the high frequencies are neglected. Local patches differing only in the high frequencies become indistinguishable. On the other hand, the high frequencies are corrupted by image noise and by small misalignments caused by inexact frame detection. The DCT is thus less sensitive to the imprecisions present in the normalised patches, as is experimentally verified in Section 4. The number of DCT coefficients that should be used depends on the discriminativity required, ie. basically on the database size. In Section 4, we experimentally show how the number of the DCT coefficients affect the retrieval performance. In Figure 3b an example is shown of what information is preserved if 10 DCT coefficients per colour channel are used. The image patches are the same as in Figure 3a.

4 Experiments

Dataset. The experiments were conducted on a set of images of 201 different buildings in Zurich, Switzerland. The dataset was kindly provided by ETH Zurich and is publicly available [13]. The database consists of five photographs of every of the 201 buildings. The photographs are taken from different viewpoints but under approximately constant illumination conditions. The database contains 1005 images in total, the image resolution is 320×240 pixels. Examples of the database images are shown in Figure 4. A separate set of 115 query images is provided. For every query image, there are exactly five matching images of the same building in the database. Not all the database buildings have corresponding queries, the number of queries per building ranges from 0 to 5. Query and database images differ in viewpoint, variations in the illumination are present, but rare. Examples of corresponding query and database images are shown in Figure 5.

Experimental Protocol. 115 query images were matched against 1005 database images, ie. 115575 matches were evaluated in total. For every query image, the R closest database images were retrieved. The recall rate r_R was evaluated, which is defined as $r_R = \frac{n_R}{N}$, where n_R is the number of correct answers in the first R retrieved images, and N the number of all possible correct answers. In our case, when every query has 5 corresponding images in the database, $N = \min(R, 5)$.

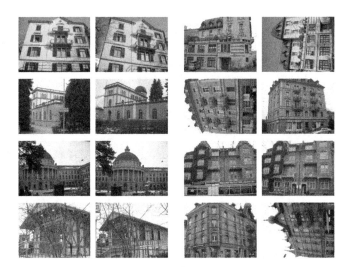

Fig. 5. Examples of corresponding query (left columns) and database (right columns) images. The image pairs exhibit occlusion, varying illumination and viewpoint and orientation changes.

Table 1. Summary of experimental results.

Method	Average recall r_R					Memory
	r_1	r_2	r_3	r_4	r_5	usage
direct intensity	98.3%	96.6%	93.6%	89.1%	81.9%	1300 MB
DCT 6 coeffs	99.1%	98.3%	95.7%	91.1%	84.0%	290 MB
DCT 10 coeffs	99.1%	98.7%	96.8%	92.2%	85.0%	370 MB
DCT 15 coeffs	100.0%	99.1%	97.4%	92.8%	85.4%	470 MB
HPAT [14]	86.1%					

Results. The two local patch representations (see Sect. 3) are compared, ie. the directly stored intensities versus the DCT coefficients. The results are summarised in Table 1. For both methods, recall r_R is shown for $R = 1 \ldots 5$. The recall r_1 is equivalent to the percentage of correct images retrieved in rank 1. The last column shows the memory required to store the representation of the whole database of 1005 images. The last line in Table 1 shows the results published in [14].

Summary. Generally, the proposed retrieval system performed well, obtained results were superior to results published in [14]. The retrieval performance was, or was close to, 100% in the first rank. The DCT representation performed slightly better than the direct intensity representation. We believe that this is due to the DCT properties discussed in Section 3 – the insensitivity to image noise and small frame misalignments. Regarding the memory requirements, the DCT representation is much more compact. The memory usage is reduced to circa 20–30% depending on the number of DCT coefficients stored.

5   Conclusions

In this paper, an image retrieval system based on local affine frames (object-centered coordinate systems) was presented. The system is robust to object occlusion and background clutter, and allows retrieval of objects in images taken from significantly different viewpoints. Normalised image patches are extracted, and photometrically and geometrically normalised according to the detected frames. Local matches are formed both by direct comparison of photometrically normalised colour intensities in the normalised patches, and by comparison of DCT (discrete cosine transform) coefficients of the patches. Both representations allow for robust and selective matching, providing excellent retrieval performance. Experimental results obtained on a publicly available image dataset of buildings were superior to other published results. Retrieval performance of 100% in rank one was achieved when the local image patches were represented by 15 DCT coefficients in every colour channel. The DCT representation performed better in terms of recall rate and required about 5 times less memory storage than representation by the intensities of the normalised patches.

References

1. Swain, M., Ballard, D.: Color indexing. In: International Journal of Computer Vision, vol. 7, no. 1. (1991) 11–32
2. Finlayson, G.D., Chatterjee, S.S., Funt, B.V.: Color angular indexing. In: ECCV. (1996) 16–27
3. Liu, F., Picard, R.W.: Periodicity, directionality, and randomness: Wold features for image modeling and retrieval. IEEE PAMI **18** (1996) 7–733
4. Mokhtarian, F., Abbasi, S., Kittler, J.: Robust and efficient shape indexing through curvature scale space. In: In Proceedings of British Machine Vision Conference, Edinburgh, UK. (1996) 53–6
5. Mindru, F., Moons, T., Gool, L.V.: Recognizing color patterns irrespective of viewpoint and illumination. In: CVPR99. (1999) 368–373
6. Tuytelaars, T., Gool, L.V.: Content-based image retrieval based on local affinely invariant regions. In: Proc. Visual '99: Information and Information Systems. (1999) 493–500
7. Smeulders, A.W.M., Worring, M., Santini, S., Gupta, A., Jain, R.: Content-based image retrieval at the end of the early years. IEEE PAMI **22** (2000) 1349–1380
8. Obdržálek, Š., Matas, J.: Object recognition using local affine frames on distinguished regions. In: The British Machine Vision Conference (BMVC02). (2002)
9. Obdržálek, Š., Matas, J.: Local affine frames for image retrieval. In: The Challenge of Image and Video Retrieval (CIVR2002). (2002)
10. Matas, J., Chum, O., Urban, M., Pajdla, T.: Robust wide baseline stereo from maximally stable extremal regions. In Rosin, P.L., Marshall, D., eds.: Proceedings of the British Machine Vision Conference. Volume 1., London, UK, BMVA (2002) 384–393
11. Healey, G.: Using color for geometry-insensitive segmentation. Journal of the Optical Society of America **6** (1989) 86–103
12. Jain, A.K.: Fundamentals of Digital Image Processing. Prentice Hall, Inc., Englewood Cliffs, New Jersey 07632 (1986)
13. Shao, H., Svoboda, T., Van Gool, L.: ZuBuD — Zurich Buildings Database for Image Based Recognition. Technical Report 260, Computer Vision Laboratory, Swiss Federal Institute of Technology (2003)
14. Shao, H., Svoboda, T., Tuytelaars, T., Van Gool, L.: Hpat indexing for fast object/scene recognition based on local appearance. In: International Conference on Image and Video Retrieval. (2003) To appear.

Variance Component Estimation in Performance Characteristics Applied to Feature Extraction Procedures

Marc Luxen

Institute for Photogrammetry, University of Bonn, Germany
luxen@ipb.uni-bonn.de http://www.ipb.uni-bonn.de/~marc/

Abstract. This paper proposes variance component estimation (VCE) for empirical quality evaluation in computer vision. An outline is given for the scope of VCE in the context of quality evaluation. The principle of VCE is explained and the approach is applied to results of low level feature extraction. Ground truth is only partly needed for estimating the precision, accuracy and bias of extracted points and straight lines. The results of diverse feature extraction modules are compared.

1 Introduction

Performance evaluation is essential for systems development. Building computer vision systems requires clear documentation of the quality of each algorithm.

This paper deals with algorithms resulting in quantities (e.g. lengths, angles, probabilities) which have a probability density function that can be parameterized by first and second order moments. Characterizing such algorithms can be based on the results on multiple data sets, either exploiting mutual constraints between different results or using ground truth, e. g. when using simulated data. Both scenarios are useful. We propose variance component estimation (VCE) for determining the quality in both cases (cf fig. 1).

VCE estimates parameters of the distribution of observed values from the residuals of a maximum likelihood estimation. Together with additional parameters in the estimation it is able to determine (1) the internal precision, (2) the external accuracy and (3) the bias, all three measures being the classical triad for characterizing measurement. In case of repeated observations the VCE simplifies, in case of given ground truth the estimation of the bias simplifies.

The paper is organized as follows: Section 2 defines "precision", "accuracy" and "bias" as concepts for specifying quality. Section 3 proposes VCE for estimating these measures based on the results of parameter estimation. In Section 4, VCE is specialized to the case of estimating the quality of feature extraction procedures for point and line extraction and in section 5, the approach is applied to the output of diverse point and edge extraction modules. The paper closes with a discussion and an outlook.

Notation. We use Euclidean and homogeneous representation of entities in 2D. Euclidean entities are denoted with slanted letters, e. g. x and homogeneous

B. Michaelis and G. Krell (Eds.): DAGM 2003, LNCS 2781, pp. 498–506, 2003.

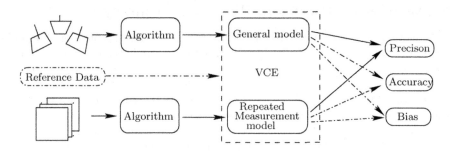

Fig. 1. Estimating precision, accuracy and bias by VCE in general and repeated measurement model.

entities are denoted with upright shaped letters, e. g. $\mathbf{x}$. Stochastic entities $\underline{\mathbf{x}}$ are underscored. "True" values $\widetilde{\mathbf{x}}$ are marked with a tilde and expectation values $\bar{\mathbf{x}}$ are marked with a bar. Estimated entities $\hat{\mathbf{x}}$ are labeled with a hat. Uncertainty of entities is represented by covariance matrices Σ_{xx}, containing variances $\sigma_{xx} \doteq \sigma_x^2$ and covariances σ_{xy}.

2 Precision, Bias, and Accuracy

In the following, processing results by applying an algorithm to data is interpreted as an observation process: The result of an algorithm is modeled as a stochastic variable $\underline{p}$ (observation) with mean $\bar{p} = E(\underline{p})$ and covariance matrix Σ_{pp}. We assume that true values $\widetilde{p}$ exist, representing the perfect result on given noisy data and use the following terms for characterization:

Precision. The *precision* of an observation $\underline{p}$ is defined as the variance of $\underline{p}$. It is represented by the covariance matrix

$$\Sigma_{pp} = E[(\underline{p} - \bar{p})(\underline{p} - \bar{p})^\mathsf{T}]$$

and covers stochastic errors of the observation process.

Bias. The *bias* b of an observation $\underline{p}$ is the deviation

$$b = \widetilde{p} - \bar{p}$$

of the expectation value $\bar{p}$ from the true value $\widetilde{p}$. It covers systematic errors of the observation process.

Accuracy. The *accuracy* of an observation $\underline{p}$ is the variance of the observation $\underline{p}$ referring to the true value $\widetilde{p}$. It is represented by the matrix of second moments

$$^a\Sigma_{pp} = E[(\underline{p} - \widetilde{p})(\underline{p} - \widetilde{p})^\mathsf{T}]$$

and covers both, systematic and stochastic errors of the observation process.

The relation between precision accuracy, and bias is given by (cf [8])

$$^a\Sigma_{pp} = \Sigma_{pp} + bb^\mathsf{T}. \tag{1}$$

3   Estimating Precision, Bias, and Accuracy

This section presents a two step procedure for estimating the bias, precision and accuracy. In the first step, parameter estimation is carried out in a linear model which links the expectation values of the observations mutually and together with unknown parameters. In this model, the biases of the observations are treated as additional unknowns. Maximum likelihood estimation leads to optimal estimates for the biases and the other model parameters. In the second step, VCE is carried out based on the estimated observation residuals of step 1. This leads to optimal estimates for precision and accuracy of the observations.

3.1   Step 1: Parameter Estimation for Estimating the Bias

The most simple case of parameter estimation in a linear model is the well known Gauß Markoff model

$$E(\boldsymbol{y}) = \sum_i \beta_i \boldsymbol{a}_i = \boldsymbol{A}\boldsymbol{\beta}, \tag{2}$$

where the goal is estimating unknown parameters $\boldsymbol{\beta} = (\beta_i)$ from given data $\boldsymbol{y} = (\boldsymbol{p}_1^\mathsf{T}, \dots, \boldsymbol{p}_N^\mathsf{T})^\mathsf{T}$ via a given coefficient matrix $\boldsymbol{A} = (\boldsymbol{a}_i)$. For estimating the unknown parameters, the expectation values $E(\boldsymbol{y})$ of the observations $\boldsymbol{y}$ are formulated as a linear combination of the known vectors $\boldsymbol{a}_i$. A best unbiased estimation $\hat{\boldsymbol{\beta}}$ for the unknown weights β_i is obtained by minimizing the variance $V(\hat{\boldsymbol{\beta}})$ under $E(\hat{\boldsymbol{\beta}}) = \tilde{\boldsymbol{\beta}}$ (cf [8]).

If in (2) the unknown biases of the observations are introduced as additional parameters, the parameter estimation procedure may be used for optimally estimating the biases. This requires a measurement setup that reveals sufficient information for estimating the biases together with the other parameters.

3.2   Step 2: Variance Component Estimation for Estimating Precision

Variance component estimation (VCE) is a technique for estimating the precision of observations by analyzing the estimated residuals of the observations. For this purpose, systems with high redundancy are required.

Analogous to the Gauß-Markoff-Model (2), the model of VCE component estimation is given by

$$E(\Sigma) = \sum_c \sigma_{0,c}^2 \Sigma_c^{(0)},$$

where $\Sigma_c^{(0)}$ are given matrices and the goal is estimating the unknown variance factors $\sigma_{0,c}^2$. Here it is the expectation value $E(\Sigma)$ of the covariance matrix Σ of observations that is formulated as linear combination of given matrices $\Sigma_c^{(0)}$. A best estimation for the variance factors $\sigma_{0,c}^2$ is obtained by minimizing $V(\hat{\Sigma})$. For estimating the unknown variance factors, the expectation value $E(\Sigma)$ of the covariance matrix Σ is approximated by $\Sigma_0 = \sum_c \Sigma_c^{(0)}$.

The principle of VCE can be sketched as follows: Let $\hat{\boldsymbol{y}}$ be the vector containing the estimated expectation values of the observations $\boldsymbol{y}$ and let $\hat{\boldsymbol{\varepsilon}} = \hat{\boldsymbol{y}} - \boldsymbol{y} =$

$\boldsymbol{Dy}$ with $\boldsymbol{D} = \boldsymbol{I} - \boldsymbol{A}(\boldsymbol{A}^{\mathsf{T}}\Sigma_0^{-1}\boldsymbol{A})^{-1}\boldsymbol{A}^{\mathsf{T}}\Sigma_0^{-1}$ (cf [8]) be the vector of the estimated observation residuals resulting from parameter estimation in a Gauß Markoff model. In the case of a diagonal covariance matrix $\Sigma_0 = \mathrm{Diag}\,(\sigma_i^2)$, the estimated variance factor of the observations is given by

$$
\hat{\sigma}_0^2 = \frac{\hat{\boldsymbol{e}}^{\mathsf{T}}\Sigma_0^{-1}\hat{\boldsymbol{e}}}{R} = \underbrace{\frac{\hat{e}_1^2/\sigma_1^2 + \hat{e}_2^2/\sigma_2^2 + \ldots + \hat{e}_k^2/\sigma_k^2}{r_1 \;\; + \;\; r_2 \;\; + \ldots + \;\; r_k}}_{\to \hat{\sigma}_{01}^2} \;+\; \underbrace{\frac{\hat{e}_{k+1}^2/\sigma_{k+1}^2 + \ldots + \hat{e}_K^2/\sigma_K^2}{r_{k+1} \;\;\;\; + \ldots + \;\; r_K}}_{\to \hat{\sigma}_{02}^2},
$$

(3)

where r_i is the contribution of observation i to the total redundancy R. If different variance factors $\sigma_{0,1}^2$ and $\sigma_{0,2}^2$ are expected for e.g. two different types of observations, the fraction in (3) can formally be partitioned into two parts. Analyzing each part leads to separate estimations $\hat{\sigma}_{0,i}^2$ and $\hat{\sigma}_{0,2}^2$ of the variance factors σ_{01}^2 and σ_{02}^2.

For a general covariance matrix Σ_0, best estimations $\hat{\sigma}_{0,c}^2$ of the variance components $\sigma_{0,c}^2$ are given by (cf. [1], [8])

$$
\hat{\sigma}_{0,c}^2 = \frac{\hat{\boldsymbol{e}}^{\mathsf{T}}\Sigma_0^{-1}\Sigma_c^{(0)}\Sigma_0^{-1}\hat{\boldsymbol{e}}}{\mathrm{tr}(\Sigma_0^{-1}\boldsymbol{D}\Sigma_c)},
$$

$tr(\#)$ denoting the trace operator. The estimated covariance matrix of observations is given by

$$
\hat{\Sigma} = \sum_c \hat{\Sigma}_c \qquad \text{with} \qquad \hat{\Sigma}_c = \hat{\sigma}_{0,c}^2 \Sigma_c^{(0)}.
$$

Observe that the estimated covariance matrix $\hat{\Sigma}$ depends on the approximation Σ_0. Therefore VCE is applied iteratively with $\Sigma_0^{(\nu+1)} = \sum_c \hat{\Sigma}_c^{(\nu)}$ and $\hat{\Sigma}_c^{(\nu)} := (\hat{\sigma}_{0,c}^2)^{(\nu)}\hat{\Sigma}_c^{(\nu-1)}$. In the case of convergence, it holds $(\hat{\sigma}_{0,c}^2)^{(\nu)} \to 1$ for all factors $\sigma_{0,c}^2$.

3.3 Special Case: Repeated Measurement with Ground Truth Available

In the case that an algorithm is applied to N noisy versions of a data set, resulting in the observations $(\boldsymbol{p}_{1n}, \ldots, \boldsymbol{p}_{In})$ on the nth data set, and that ground truth $\tilde{\boldsymbol{p}}_{in}$, $i \in \{1, \ldots, I\}$ is available, parameter estimation and VCE lead to the following trivial results:

Bias. If the observations are weighted equally, the estimated expectation value of N observations $\boldsymbol{p}'_{in}$ is given by their mean $\hat{\boldsymbol{p}}_i = \frac{1}{N}\sum_{n=1}^{N}\boldsymbol{p}_{in}$. With the true value $\tilde{\boldsymbol{p}}_i$ of the observations $\boldsymbol{p}_{in}$, the bias of observations $\boldsymbol{p}_{in}$ is obtained by

$$
\boldsymbol{b}_{p_i} = \hat{\boldsymbol{p}}_i - \tilde{\boldsymbol{p}}_i \qquad \text{with} \qquad \hat{\boldsymbol{p}}_i = \frac{1}{N}\sum_{n=1}^{N}\boldsymbol{p}_{in}.
$$

(4)

Precision. The estimated covariance matrix and therefore the precision of the observations are given by

$$
\hat{\Sigma}_{p_i p_i} = \frac{1}{N-1}\sum_{n=1}^{N}(\boldsymbol{p}_{in} - \hat{\boldsymbol{p}}_i)(\boldsymbol{p}_{in} - \hat{\boldsymbol{p}}_i)^{\mathsf{T}}.
$$

(5)

Accuracy is obtained by replacing in (5) the estimated point coordinates $\hat{p}_i$ are replaced by their error free values $\tilde{p}_i$, leading to the matrix of second moments

$$^a\widehat{\Sigma}_{p_ip_i} = \tfrac{1}{N-1}\sum_{n=1}^{N}(p_{in} - \tilde{p}_i)(p_{in} - \tilde{p}_i)^\mathsf{T} \tag{6}$$

If the sum (6) is taken not over n but over i, j and divided by $(I-1)$, where I is the total number of observations in image n, then the mean accuracy of the observations in image n is obtained.

4   Precision, Accuracy, and Bias of Points and Straight Lines

4.1   Representation of Points and Straight Lines in 2D

Points. A point in 2D and its uncertainty is represented by its Euclidean coordinate vector $x = (x, y)^\mathsf{T}$ and its 2×2 covariance matrix Σ_{xx}, given by

$$\Sigma_{xx} = \begin{pmatrix} \sigma_x^2 & \sigma_{xy} \\ \sigma_{xy} & \sigma_y^2 \end{pmatrix} = R_\psi \begin{pmatrix} \sigma_r^2 & 0 \\ 0 & \sigma_t^2 \end{pmatrix} R_\psi^\mathsf{T} \text{ with } R_\psi = \begin{pmatrix} \cos(\psi) & -\sin(\psi) \\ \sin(\psi) & \cos(\psi) \end{pmatrix}.$$

Herein, σ_r^2 and σ_t^2 are the variances of the point in the two main directions of its confidence ellipse; ψ represents the direction of the main semi-axis of the confidence ellipse in the image coordinate system. (cf. fig. 2).

In homogeneous coordinates, an uncertain point is represented by a 3×1 coordinate vector **x** and its rank 2 covariance matrix Σ_{xx}, for example

$$\mathbf{x} = (x^\mathsf{T}, 1)^\mathsf{T} \text{ and } \Sigma_{xx} = \text{Diag}\,(\Sigma_{xx}, 0). \tag{7}$$

Straight lines. Following ([3]), straight lines $l = (\phi, d)^\mathsf{T}$ in 2D are represented by their normal direction ϕ and their distance d to the origin of the image coordinate system (cf fig. 2). With the coordinates $\begin{pmatrix} s \\ d \end{pmatrix} = \begin{pmatrix} -\sin(\phi) & \cos(\phi) \\ \cos(\phi) & \sin(\phi) \end{pmatrix} \begin{pmatrix} x_g \\ y_g \end{pmatrix}$ of the center of gravity (x_g, y_g) of the line in the uv-coordinate system of fig. 2, the uncertainty of the line is given by the covariance matrix (cf [3])

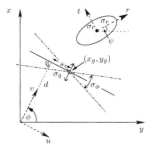

$$\Sigma_{ll} = \begin{pmatrix} 1 & 0 \\ s & 1 \end{pmatrix} \begin{pmatrix} \sigma_\phi^2 & 0 \\ 0 & \sigma_q^2 \end{pmatrix} \begin{pmatrix} 1 & 0 \\ s & 1 \end{pmatrix}^\mathsf{T}.$$

Fig. 2. Representation of uncertain points and straight lines in 2D.

Herein, σ_ϕ^2 denotes the variance of the line direction and σ_q^2 is the variance representing the uncertainty of the center of gravity in the direction across the line.

With the 3×1 vector $\mathbf{a} = (\sin(\phi), -\cos(\phi), t)^{\mathsf{T}}$, homogeneous coordinates $\mathbf{l}$ of the line and their 3×3 covariance matrix Σ_{ll} of rank 2 are given by (cf [7])

$$\mathbf{l} = (\sin(\phi), \cos(\phi), -s)^{\mathsf{T}} \quad \text{and} \quad \Sigma_{\mathrm{ll}} = \sigma_\phi^2 \, \mathbf{aa}^{\mathsf{T}} + \sigma_d^2 \operatorname{Diag}(0,0,1). \tag{8}$$

Observe that the covariance matrix Σ_{ll} can be decomposed into a sum of a matrix that only depends on the uncertainty σ_ϕ^2 of the direction and a matrix that only depends on the uncertainty σ_q^2 of the center of gravity across the line.

4.2 Procedures for Estimating Bias, Precision, and Accuracy of Extracted Points and Straight Line Segments

According to the explanations in section 3, we follow two approaches to estimating the bias, precision and accuracy of points and straight line segments provided by feature extraction procedures.

1. Parameter estimation and VCE in a general model without ground truth at hand
2. Estimating bias, precision and accuracy from repeated measurement with ground truth at hand

General approach.   Given homologous points and straight lines extracted from $N \geq 2$ projective images of an object, in a first step bundle adjustment for camera orientation is carried out (cf [6]). The biases of the observed points and line segments are treated as additional unknowns and they are optimally estimated together with the camera orientation parameters.[1] In the second step, VCE is carried out for estimating the precision. Accuracy is estimated using (1).

Within the VCE procedure, we assume stochastic independence of points and straight lines and decompose the covariance matrix Σ of the observations $\mathbf{y}$ into

$$\Sigma = \sigma_{0,x'}^2 \underbrace{\begin{pmatrix} \Sigma_{x'x'} & 0 \\ 0 & 0 \end{pmatrix}}_{\Sigma_1^{(0)}} + \sigma_{0,\phi}^2 \underbrace{\begin{pmatrix} 0 & 0 \\ 0 & \Sigma_{l'l',\phi} \end{pmatrix}}_{\Sigma_2^{(0)}} + \sigma_{0,q}^2 \underbrace{\begin{pmatrix} 0 & 0 \\ 0 & \Sigma_{l'l',d} \end{pmatrix}}_{\Sigma_3^{(0)}}$$

with the unknown variance factors $\sigma_{0,x'}^2$, $\sigma_{0,\phi}^2$ and $\sigma_{0,q}^2$. The first matrix $\Sigma_1^{(0)}$ represents the uncertainty of points. It contains the $3I \times 3I$ block diagonal matrix $\Sigma_{x'x'} = \operatorname{Diag}(\Sigma_{x_1'x_1'}, \dots, \Sigma_{x_I'x_I'})$ with the elements given by (7), assuming independent observations of equal precision $\sigma_x = \sigma_y = 1$ and $\sigma_{xy} = 0$.

The $3J \times 3J$ structure matrices $\Sigma_2^{(0)}$ and $\Sigma_3^{(0)}$ represent the uncertainty of lines. Their sub-matrices $\Sigma_{l'l',\phi} = \operatorname{Diag}(\Sigma_{l_1'l_1',\phi}, \dots, \Sigma_{l_J'l_J',\phi})$ and $\Sigma_{l'l',q} = \operatorname{Diag}(\Sigma_{l_1'l_1',q}, \dots, \Sigma_{l_J'l_J',q})$ are obtained from (8) with $\sigma_\phi = 1[\mathrm{rad}]$, $\sigma_q = 1[\mathrm{pel}]$.

---

[1] In the case of a planar object, bundle adjustment can be replaced by estimating planar homographies between the object and the images (cf [7]), including the biases as additional unknowns.

Repeated measurement approach. Given points and straight lines extracted from N noisy versions of the same image and having ground truth at hand, bias, precision and accuracy of the points and straight lines is estimated by employing the equations (4), (5) and (6) with points parameterized by $\boldsymbol{x} = (x, y)^\mathsf{T}$ and lines parameterized by $\boldsymbol{l} = (\phi, d)^\mathsf{T}$.

5   Experiments

Primarily, our experiments are intended to verify the usability of our approach for evaluating the precision, accuracy and bias of points and straight lines. Secondary, we wanted to compare the quality of feature extraction modules on various levels of image noise.

5.1   Experimental Setup

In the experiment, we involved the Harris corner detector (cf [5]), the Förstner window operator (cf [2]) and the Förstner point operator (cf [2]) as procedures for point extraction and the feature extraction software FEX (cf [3]) and the Schickler - Operator (cf [9]) as procedures for straight line extraction. Each operator was applied to 11 synthetic image pairs, each consisting of two noisy versions of the 500×500 image that is shown in

Fig. 3. Test Image

fig. 5. On a dark background, the image contains 25 bright squares in various rotations. The side length of each square is $50[pel]$ and the image contrast is $\varDelta g = 85[gr]$. Image noise σ_n was chosen in 12 steps in the range of $\sigma_n \in \{0,\ 0.7,\ 1.4,\ 2.8,\ 4.2,\ 5.7,\ 7.1,\ 8.8,\ 11.3,\ 16.7,\ 30.2\}[gr]$.

The tuning parameters σ_1 and σ_2 (cf [3]) of each operator were chosen to $\sigma_1 = 1.0$ and $\sigma_2 = 3.0$ for point extraction and $\sigma_1 = 1.0$ and $\sigma_2 = 2.0$ for straight line extraction. Only the noisiest image was smoothed with $\sigma_1 = 2.0$.

VCE was used in the general approach for estimating the precision of extracted points and lines. Accuracy and bias were analyzed using the repeated measurement approach with ground truth.

5.2   Results

The experiment proves the usability of VCE for estimating precision, bias and accuracy of points and straight lines. The results of VCE in the general and in the repeated measurement approach are consistent and plausible and allow a comparison of feature extraction modules with regard to precision, bias and accuracy.

Quality of points. In fig. 4, the estimated precision, accuracy and bias of points is depicted as function of the image noise σ_n.

For noise in the range $0 - 8[gr]$, the Harris operator and the Förstner window operator have the same characteristic in precision, accuracy and bias. This is to be expected because their theory is very similar. Bias and accuracy are about 3–4 pixels and thus quite bad – a fact that is plausible because both opera-

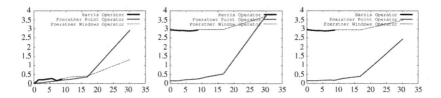

Fig. 4. Noise dependence of precision, accuracy and bias of points from the Harris corner detector (thick), the Förstner window operator (thin) and the Förstner point operator (dashed). *Left:* Precision $\hat{\sigma}_p = \sqrt{\sigma_{x'x'} + \sigma_{y'y'}}$ [pel]. *Center:* Accuracy $^a\hat{\sigma}_p = \sqrt{^a\hat{\sigma}_{x'x'} + {}^a\hat{\sigma}_{y'y'}}$ [pel]. *Right:* Bias $\hat{b} = \sqrt{^a\hat{\sigma}_p^2 - \hat{\sigma}_p^2}$ [pel]. In each graph, the first axis is labeled with the standard deviation $\sigma_n[gr]$ of the image noise.

tors do not provide optimal *points* but *optimal positions of search windows* for point extraction (cf [2]). For larger noise ($\sigma_n > 8$), in our example no points are detected by the Harris operator.

For image noise in the range of $\sigma_n < 16$ [gr], the Förstner point operator provides points with accuracy $^a\sigma_p < 0.5[pel]$. In this noise range, precision bias and accuracy increase nearly linearly with the noise. The bias is small ($< 0.3[pel]$). Larger noise worsens heavily the quality of the results.

Quality of straight lines. The estimated quality of the results of line extraction is depicted in fig. 5. Referring to precision, accuracy and bias of extracted features, for lower noise ($\sigma_n < 17[gr]$) the feature extraction FEX is superior to the Schickler operator both in precision and accuracy. For noise $\sigma_n > 17[gr]$, precision and accuracy decrease heavily. This is caused by the fact that with increasing noise straight lines are broken up into smaller pieces with worse quality. Concerning the uncertainty of the center of gravity of lines in the direction across the line, both FEX and the Schickler operator behave similar and the uncertainty increases linearly with increasing noise.

6   Conclusions and Outlook

In this paper we have proposed VCE for estimating the quality of results drawn from computer vision algorithms. The application area of VCE in the context of quality evaluation has been outlined and its basic principles have been explained. After a specialization to the case of repeated measurement, VCE was carried out exemplarily for estimating the precision, accuracy and bias of points and straight lines.

The results are consistent and plausible and show the usability of VCE for evaluating quality. A more meaningful investigation of precision, accuracy and bias of feature extraction modules will have to take into account synthetic and real images of various quality and content. Furthermore, investigating precision, accuracy and bias of features is not enough for characterizing feature extraction algorithms (cf [4]). We also will evaluate other properties of feature extraction extraction algorithms, especially the coverage of lines, and the effect onto relations between features needed for grouping.

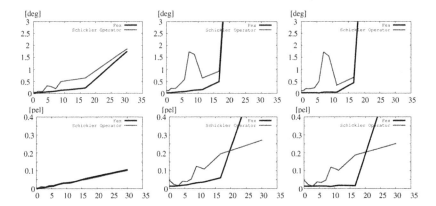

Fig. 5. Noise dependence of precision, accuracy and bias of lines from FEX and from the Schickler-Operator. **Top row:** Uncertainty in line direction *Left:* Precision $\hat{\sigma}_\phi$. *Center:* Accuracy $^a\hat{\sigma}_\phi$. *Right:* Bias $\hat{\sigma}_\phi = \sqrt{^a\hat{\sigma}_\phi^2 - \hat{\sigma}_\phi^2}$. **Bottom row:** Uncertainty of the center of gravity across the line. *Left:* Precision $\hat{\sigma}_d$. *Center:* Accuracy $^a\hat{\sigma}_d$. *Right:* Bias $\hat{\sigma}_d = \sqrt{^a\hat{\sigma}_d^2 - \hat{\sigma}_d^2}$. In each graph, the first axis is labeled with the standard deviation σ_n [gr] of the image noise.

Acknowledgement. This work has been supported by the German Research Council (DFG).

References

1. W. Förstner. Ein Verfahren zur Schätzung von Varianz- und Kovarianzkomponenten. Allgemeine Vermessungsnachrichten, 11–12: 446–453, 1979.
2. W. Förstner and E. Gülch. A Fast Operator for Detection and Precise Location of Distinct Points, Corners and Centres of Circular Features. In *Proceedings of the Intercommission Conference on Fast Processing of Photogrammetric Data, Interlaken*, pages 281–305, 1987.
3. C. Fuchs. *Extraktion polymorpher Bildstrukturen und ihre topologische und geometrische Gruppierung.* DGK, Bayer. Akademie der Wissenschaften, Reihe C, Heft 502, 1998.
4. C. Fuchs, F. Lang, and W. Förstner. On the Noise and Scale Behaviour of Relational Descriptions. In Eder Ebner, Heipke, editor, *Int. Arch. f. Photogr. and Remote Sensing, Vol. 30, 3/2*, volume XXX, pages 257–267, 1994.
5. C. G. Harris and M. Stephens. A Combined Corner and Edge Detector. In *4th Alvey Vision Conference*, pages 147–151, 1987.
6. R. Hartley and A. Zisserman. *Multiple View Geometry.* Cambridge University Press, 2000.
7. S. Heuel. *Statistical Reasoning in Uncertain Projective Geometry for Polyhedral Object Reconstruction.* PhD thesis, Institut für Photogrammetrie, Bonn Univ., 2002.
8. K. R. Koch. *Parameter Estimation and Hypothesis Testing in Linear Models.* Springer, Berlin, 2nd edition, 1999.
9. W. Schickler and T. Läbe. *Interne Programmdokumentation.* Institut für Photogrammetrie, Universität Bonn, Nussallee 15, 53115 Bonn, 2002.

A New Distance Measure for Probabilistic Shape Modeling

Wei-Jun Chen and Joachim M. Buhmann

Rheinische Friedrich Wilhelms Universität
Institut für Informatik III, Römerstr. 164
D-53117 Bonn, Germany
{chen, jb}@cs.uni-bonn.de

Abstract. The contour of a planar shape is essentially one-dimensional signal embedded in 2-D space; thus the orthogonal distance, which only considers 1-D (norm) deviation from suggested models, is not rich enough to characterize the description quality of arbitrary model/shape pairs. This paper suggests a generalized distance measure, called *Transport Distance*, for probabilistic shape modeling. B-Spline primitives are used to represent models. The probability of a hypothetical model for a shape is determined on the basis of the new distance measure. Experiments show that an optimization procedure, which maximize the model probability, generates robust and visually pleasing geometric models for data.

1 Introduction

The automatic estimation of geometric structures from shape data plays an important role in computer vision, since explicit analytic functions rather than point sets provide compact and analytically tractable representations of contours or surfaces. We assume in this paper that contour data are given as a chain code of a set of points in $\mathbb{R}^2$. Analytic representations of shapes can be flexibly incorporated in information systems for image segmentation, image compression, network transmission, object recognition, scientific visualization, virtual reality, content-based image/video retrieval, etc.[2].

Despite significant efforts, problems related to analytic shape representations remain still open. One key problem which has to be solved for geometric shape modeling is the question how to estimate the description quality of a hypothetical model for given data. Normally the *orthogonal distance*, which measures only deviations in normal direction of the geometric structure[1], is employed to estimated the description error. Similarity of shape, however, is not adequately captured by the orthogonal distance and we, therefore, replace this concept by an alternative deformation measure, the *transport distance*. In the new framework a data point on the contour is considered to be generated by moving a model point along a path either completely inside of the contour or completely outside of the contour. The restriction of the transport path to the interior or the exterior of the shape is supposed to model a topological constraint to ensure invariance to articulation of shapes like limb pose of animals and humans. The

B. Michaelis and G. Krell (Eds.): DAGM 2003, LNCS 2781, pp. 507–514, 2003.

most likely model is determined by the total transport of all model points to their corresponding contour points under the deformation constraint. This concept of shape modeling solves two conceptual problems which are related to the usage of orthogonal distance in probabilistic shape modeling: (i) construction of the model/data point correspondences; (ii) likelihood calculation from a point based distance measure.

As shown in Fig.1(b), it is difficult to decide if the individual data points on the tail part is a correct image of model points after orthogonal mapping. To avoid such poor correspondences, heuristic knowledge, such as high curvature point, inflexion points, stable scale etc. [3,5] are widely used to partition a shape into simple pieces, for which the orthogonal distance might be psychophysically motivated for piecewise model reconstruction. However, techniques using orthogonal distance together with heuristic shape partitioning exhibit the following two disadvantages: First, they almost always need some empirical thresholds or manual adjustments of parameters to compute the heuristic knowledge [5]. Second, they rarely provide a full optimization framework for shape model estimation [6], since it usually is difficult to formulate heuristic knowledge as model costs.

Many methods compute the likelihood based on the orthogonal distance from all available data points. Since the number of data points is sensitive to the noise, the likelihood is also noise dependent if all the data points are treated equally. Normalization only makes sense when the noise are homogeneously distributed along the contour. Weighing data points according to their local features, such as curvature, density, etc., faces difficulties in scale selection and weighing strategy. Alternative methods compute the likelihood from sampled model points [4]. But there are still problems in sampling ratio determination as well as distance measure for arbitrary model points. All these disadvantages are cured in the proposal to use the transport distance rather than the orthogonal distance for modeling shape deformation.

2   Related Works

For shape modeling techniques which use orthogonal distance together with heuristic knowledge based shape partitioning, readers might refer to the articles by Lindeberg and Li [3], and Bengtsson and Eklundh [5].

Splines are popularly adopted in geometric shape modeling [2]. Cham and Cippolla [4] suggested the *Potential for Energy-Reduction Maximization* (PERM) strategy to guide the new control points insertion in BSpline based shape modeling, but it is not transparently guided by the distance measure. Their paper discusses the data sampling problem in details.

Without the pre-process of data partitioning, Kern and Werman [7] have rebuilt the geometric structure of explicit functions of $y = f(x)$ or $z = f(x, y)$ using a fully Bayesian approach. Their work is distinguished from this paper since our targets are implicit 2-D functions.

3   Transport Probability

In this section, we will define the transport distance between two arbitrary $\mathbb{R}^2$ points and the transport probability between two curve segments.

Transport Path: Given two $\mathbb{R}^2$ points, o_s and o_t, one oriented and non-self-intersecting curve segment connecting them, is named a *transport path*, $\mathcal{A}(o_s, o_t; \boldsymbol{\alpha})$, from o_s to o_t, where $\boldsymbol{\alpha}$ specifies the curve segment in $\mathbb{R}^2$.

Transport Region: Given two oriented and non-self-intersecting $\mathbb{R}^2$ curve segments, $\mathcal{C}_s$ and $\mathcal{C}_t$, a region will be bounded by them if $\mathcal{C}_s$ and $\mathcal{C}_t$ connect the same point-pair and $\mathcal{C}_s$ does not intersect $\mathcal{C}_t$. (The intersecting cases will be discussed in next section.) This region together with its boundary, is called the *transport region*, $\mathcal{R}_{ts}$, for given $\mathcal{C}_s$ and $\mathcal{C}_t$. $\forall o_{cs} \in \mathcal{C}_s$ and $\forall o_{ct} \in \mathcal{C}_t$, $\exists \mathcal{A}(o_{cs}, o_{ct}; \boldsymbol{\alpha}) \subset \mathcal{R}_{ts}$. Assuming that $\mathcal{C}_s$ has curve length l_s, $o_{cs} \in \mathcal{C}_s$ can be parameterized by its arclength position u_s, where $0 \leq u_s \leq l_s$.

Path Bundle and Transport Front: Our target is to measure the deformation distance of $\mathcal{C}_t$ from $\mathcal{C}_s$. Instead of constructing the one-to-one mapping between these two curve segments, we map the transport region, $\mathcal{R}_{ts}$, onto $\mathcal{C}_s$ while assuming that $\mathcal{R}_{ts}$ can be generated by transporting individual points $o_{cs} \in \mathcal{C}_s$. Once $\mathcal{R}_{ts}$ is generated, $\mathcal{C}_t$ will be obtained. It is assumed that there is a set of maps $\{h\} = \mathcal{H}_{ts}$, in which $h \in \mathcal{H}_{ts}$ maps individual points $o_r \in \mathcal{R}_{ts}$ to (u_h, v_h), where u_h denotes the index of individual paths, and v_h denotes the positions on a path. To ensure that the mapping is unique and continuous, the following conditions are proposed to constrain $\mathcal{H}_{ts}$:

1. **one-to-one-mapping-condition**: $\forall o_r \in \mathcal{R}_{ts}$, there exists a mapping h : $o_r \mapsto (u_h, v_h)$ $u_h \geq 0$ and $v_h \geq 0$. $o_r' \neq o_r$ iff $(u_h', v_h') \neq (u_h, v_h)$;
2. **source-condition**: all $o_{cs} \in \mathcal{C}_s$ will be mapped to $(u_h = u_s, v_h = 0)$;
3. **no-breaking-path-condition**: $\forall o_r = (u_h, v_h) \in \mathcal{R}_{ts}$, $\forall \epsilon > 0$, $\exists o_r' \in \mathcal{R}_{ts}$: $o_r' = (u_h, v_h')$ holds $0 \leq v_h - v_h' < \epsilon$. This condition ensures that all $o_r \in \mathcal{R}_{ts}$ are transported from $\mathcal{C}_s$;
4. **continuity-condition**: $\forall o_r \in \mathcal{R}_{ts}$, $\forall \epsilon > 0$, $\exists \delta > 0$ determining an open ball $\mathcal{N}_e(o_r, \delta) \subset \mathbb{R}^2$, such that $o_r' : o_r' \in \mathcal{N}_e \cap \mathcal{R}_{ts}$ holds $\sqrt{(u_h - u_h')^2 + (v_h - v_h')^2} < \epsilon$. This condition ensures that within $\mathcal{R}_{ts}$, u_h and v_h are differentiable;
5. **target-condition**: $\forall o_r = (u_h, v_h) \in \mathcal{R}_{ts}$, $\exists o_{ct} \in \mathcal{C}_t : o_{ct} = (u_h, v_h^{(t)})$ satisfying $v_h \leq v_h^{(t)}$, so that every path leads to $\mathcal{C}_t$;
6. **locally-Euclidean-condition**: $\forall o_r \in \mathcal{R}_{ts}$, $\exists \delta > 0$ determining an open neighborhood $\mathcal{N}_e(o_r, \delta) \subset \mathbb{R}^2$, such that all $o_r' \in \mathcal{N}_e \cap \mathcal{R}_{ts}$ can be parameterized by a locally *Cartesian* coordinate system as $o_r' = (u_e', v_e')$ (and $o_r = (u_e, v_e)$). The *Euclidean* distance of o_r' from o_r is then measured as $d_e(o_r', o_r) = \sqrt{(u_e' - u_e)^2 + (v_e' - v_e)^2}$. Moreover, there should exist two scalar factors, $w_u = \lim_{\delta \to 0}(u_h' - u_h)/(u_e' - u_e) = du_h/du_e$ and $w_v = \lim_{\delta \to 0}(v_h' - v_h)/(v_e' - v_e) = dv_h/dv_e$. So that within $\mathcal{N}_e$, the *Euclidean* distance measure can be approximated by u_h and v_h.

Given $h \in \mathcal{H}_{ts}$, $\mathcal{R}_{ts}$ is decomposed as a set of transport paths

$$h : \mathcal{R}_{ts} \mapsto \mathcal{D}_{ts}^{(h)} = \{\mathcal{A}_r^{(h)}(u_h)|0 \le u_h \le l_s\} \tag{1}$$

where $\mathcal{A}_r^{(h)}(u_h) = \{o_r | h : o_r \mapsto (u_h, v_h)\}$ is a transport path which originates from $o_{cs}(u_s) = (u_h, 0)$ on $\mathcal{C}_s$, and ends at $o_{ct}(u_t) = (u_h, v_h^{(t)})$ on $\mathcal{C}_t$. $\forall u_h \ne u_h'$ holds $\mathcal{A}_r^{(h)}(u_h) \cap \mathcal{A}_r^{(h)}(u_h') = \emptyset$. The set $\mathcal{D}_{ts}^{(h)}$ is called a *path bundle* of $\mathcal{R}_{ts}$. Each value of v_h determines a *transport front*, $\mathcal{F}_r^{(h)}(v_h) = \{o_r | h : o_r \mapsto (u_h, v_h)\}$. $\forall v_h' \ne v_h$ holds $\mathcal{F}_r^{(h)}(v_h) \cap \mathcal{F}_r^{(h)}(v_h') = \emptyset$.

Transport Distance: Given two $\mathbb{R}^2$ points, a *transport distance* between them, $V(o_s, o_t; \boldsymbol{\alpha})$, is defined as the curve length of a particular transport path $\mathcal{A}(o_s, o_t; \boldsymbol{\alpha})$. We have $V(o_s, o_t; \boldsymbol{\alpha}) = \int_{\mathcal{A}(o_s, o_t; \boldsymbol{\alpha})} dv$ where v denotes the arclength measure.

Probability Density from Stepwise Transport: It is assumed that the probability density of a transport path, $p(\mathcal{A}(o_s, o_t; \boldsymbol{\alpha}))$, only depends on its transport distance according to a continuous distribution $p(v_d; \boldsymbol{\theta})$, where v_d is a random variable and $\boldsymbol{\theta}$ denotes a parameter vector. Defining $p_{log}'(v_d; \boldsymbol{\theta}) = d(\log p(v_d; \boldsymbol{\theta}))/dv_d$, the negative logarithm of $p(\mathcal{A}(o_s, o_t; \boldsymbol{\alpha}))$ can be calculated by

$$-\log p(\mathcal{A}(o_s, o_t; \boldsymbol{\alpha})) = -\int_{\mathcal{A}(o_s, o_t; \boldsymbol{\alpha})} p_{log}'(v; \boldsymbol{\theta})dv - \log p(0, \boldsymbol{\theta})$$

$$= -\lim_{\Delta_a \to 0} \sum_{o_v \in \mathcal{A}(o_s, o_t; \boldsymbol{\alpha})} p_{log}'(v(o_a); \boldsymbol{\theta})\Delta_a - \log p(0, \boldsymbol{\theta}) \tag{2}$$

where v is the arclength, $\{o_v\}$ are sampled points and Δ_a is the sampling rate.

Locally Distinguishable Paths: Given a transport step Δ_v, the path bundle can be obtained by incrementally prolongating individual paths from $\mathcal{C}_s$ to nearby points in $\mathcal{R}_{ts}$. Given a resolution $\varepsilon_{re} > 0$, two transport paths, $\mathcal{A}_r^{(h)}(u_h)$ and $\mathcal{A}_r^{(h)}(u_h')$ are locally distinguishable on $\mathcal{F}_r^{(h)}(v_h + \Delta_v)$, if they satisfy one of the following two conditions: 1), they are distinguishable on the upper front $\mathcal{F}_r^{(h)}(v_h)$; 2) the *Euclidean* distance between $o_r = (u_h, v_h + \Delta_v)$ and $o_r' = (u_h', v_h + \Delta_v)$, holds $d_e(o_r, o_r') \ge \varepsilon_{re}$. Defining Δ_n as

$$\Delta_n(o_r) = \min\left(\Delta_n(o_r^{up} = (u_h, v_h)), w_u(o_r) \times \varepsilon_{re}\right), \tag{3}$$

where $o_r^{up} = (u_r, v_r)$, the closest two neighbors of $\mathcal{A}_r^{(h)}(u_h)$ on $\mathcal{F}_r^{(h)}(v_h + \Delta_v)$ will be $\mathcal{A}_r^{(h)}(u_h \pm \Delta_n(o_r))$. Given a small 1-D neighborhood, $\Delta_u \ge \Delta_n(o_r)$ around u_h, the number of locally distinguishable neighbors of $\mathcal{A}_r^{(h)}(u_h)$ will be $N_n(o_r) \approx \Delta_u/\Delta_n(o_r)$. Taking Δ_u as the sampling rate, we sample $I^{(v_h + \Delta_v)}$ points from $\mathcal{F}_r^{(h)}(v_h + \Delta_v)$ giving $\{o_r^{(i)} | i = 1, 2, ..., I^{(v_h + \Delta_v)}\}$. The total number of distinguishable stepwise transports, which are necessary to prolongate the path bundle from $\mathcal{F}_r^{(h)}(v_h)$ to $\mathcal{F}_r^{(h)}(v_h + \Delta_v)$, will be counted by

$$N_s(\mathcal{F}_r^{(h)}(v_h), \Delta_v)) \approx \sum_{i=1}^{I^{(v_h+\Delta_v)}} N_n(o_r^{(i)}) = \sum_{i=1}^{I^{(v_h+\Delta_v)}} \frac{1}{\Delta_n(o_r^{(i)})} \Delta_u. \tag{4}$$

For a fixed range of u_h, we have $N_s(\mathcal{F}_r^{(h)}(v_h + \Delta_v), \Delta_v)) \geq N_s(\mathcal{F}_r^{(h)}(v_h), \Delta_v))$.

Transport Probability for Path Bundle: Assuming that transport paths in a path bundle will be distinguished only locally, we define the stepwise probability from $\mathcal{F}_r^{(h)}(v_h)$ to $\mathcal{F}_r^{(h)}(v_h + \Delta_v)$ as

$$P_{log}^{(s)}\left(\mathcal{F}_r^{(h)}(v_h), \mathcal{F}_r^{(h)}(v_h + \Delta_v)\right) \approx p_{log}'(v_h; \boldsymbol{\theta}) \Delta_v N_s(\mathcal{F}_r^{(h)}(v_h), \Delta_v)). \tag{5}$$

Extended from Eq.2, the negative logarithm of the probability of a path bundle (which is generated from J_f stepwise prolongations) is calculated as

$$-\log P\left(\mathcal{C}_s, \mathcal{C}_t; \mathcal{D}_{ts}^{(h)}\right)$$

$$= -\sum_{j=0}^{J_f-1} P_{log}^{(s)}\left(\mathcal{F}_r^{(h)}(j\Delta_v), \mathcal{F}_r^{(h)}((j+1)\Delta_v)\right) - I^{(0)} \log p(0, \boldsymbol{\theta}) \Delta_u$$

$$\approx -\sum_{j=0}^{J_f-1} \left(\sum_{i=1}^{I^{((j+1)\Delta_v)}} \frac{1}{\Delta_n(o_r^{(i)})} \Delta_u p_{log}'(j\Delta_v; \boldsymbol{\theta}) \Delta_v \right) - I^{(0)} \log p(0, \boldsymbol{\theta}) \Delta_u$$

$$\approx -\sum_{j=0}^{J_f-1} \sum_{i=1}^{I^{((j+1)\Delta_v)}} \frac{1}{\Delta_n(o_r^{(i)})} p_{log}'(j\Delta_v; \boldsymbol{\theta}) \Delta_u \Delta_v - I^{(0)} \log p(0, \boldsymbol{\theta}) \Delta_u \tag{6}$$

According to the *locally-Euclidean-condition*, we sample points in $\mathcal{R}_{ts}$ by a sampling rate Δ_e, and calculate the negative logarithm of the probability as

$$-\log P\left(\mathcal{C}_s, \mathcal{C}_t; \mathcal{D}_{ts}^{(h)}\right)$$

$$\approx -\sum_{o_r \in \mathcal{R}_{ts}} \frac{w_u(o_r) w_v(o_r)}{\Delta_n(o_r)} p_{log}'(v_h(o_r); \boldsymbol{\theta}) \Delta_e \Delta_e - \sum_{o_r \in \mathcal{C}_s} \log p(0, \boldsymbol{\theta}) w_u(o_r) \Delta_e. \tag{7}$$

4   Probabilistic Shape Modeling

Given a closed and non-self-intersecting planar curve model $\mathcal{M}$, and a closed boundary $\mathcal{B}$, a number of intersecting points[1], $\{o_k | k = 1, 2, ..., K\} \subseteq \mathcal{M} \cap \mathcal{B}$,

---

[1] If there is no intersecting point, then global geometric transformations, i.e., scaling, rotation, or translation are needed to approximately align the model and the given boundary.

can always be found to naturally partition both the data and the model into K pieces

$$\mathcal{M} = \{M_k(o_k, o_{k+1})|k = 1, 2, ..., K\}, \tag{8}$$
$$\mathcal{B} = \{B_k(o_k, o_{k+1})|k = 1, 2, ..., K\} \tag{9}$$

where $o_{K+1} = o_1$ and the coincide piece-pair (M_k, B_k) satisfies that $M_k \setminus \{o_k, o_{k+1}\} \cap B_k \setminus \{o_k, o_{k+1}\} = \emptyset$. Thus M_k and B_k bound their *transport region* $R_k = \mathcal{R}_{ts}(M_k, C_k)$. Each region will be either fully inside the model shape, or fully outside the model shape. Given a mapping method, we will have a path bundle $h : R_k = \mathcal{R}_{ts}(M_k, B_k) \mapsto \mathcal{D}_{ts}^{(h)}(R_k)$.

As shown in Fig.1(a), there might be multiple permitted correspondences using different intersecting points. Suppose that for a particular model/shape pair, there is a set of possible correspondences $\{\gamma\} = \Gamma$. For a particular case γ, we have a region set $\{R_{\gamma,k}|k = 1, 2, ...K_\gamma\}$ with their path bundles $\{\mathcal{D}_{ts}^{(h)}(R_{\gamma,k})\}$. According to Eq.7, the description quality is then estimated from individual transport regions

$$-\log P(\mathcal{B}|\mathcal{M}) = \min_{\gamma \in \Gamma, h \in \mathcal{H}_{ts}} \sum_{k=1}^{K_\gamma} -\log P\left(M_{\gamma,k}, B_{\gamma,k}; \mathcal{D}_{ts}^{(h)}(R_{\gamma,k})\right) \tag{10}$$

5   Experimental Results

We assume that the statistical properties of transport distance between a hypothetic model and the given data are characterized by a *Gaussian*. Three experiments are designed to demonstrate our ideas. Firstly, we generate an artificial shape and try to re-model it according to a dynamic process which minimize the negative logarithms of the model/contour probability. As shown in Fig.2(a) and (b), we precisely re-built the model starting from a poor initialization. Secondly, we model a real camel shape by B-Spline primitives (Fig.2(c))(also starting from the poor circle-like initialization). Thirdly, we model a complex see-horse shape using B-Spline primitives. It is clearly demonstrated that the description quality degrades when fewer control points are used (Fig.3).

In our experiments, a dynamical process is used to modify the position of individual control points of B-Splines. All the possible modifications of a model are suggested by the transport distance based probability, which is after the construction of a path bundle for individual transport regions between the hypothetical model and the given data. Currently we rank all the transport probability of individual transport regions between model and data, and assign update priorities to corresponding model pieces. For each visual piece, 4 related B-Spline primitives can be modified since we use B-Splines of order 3.

6   Discussion and Conclusion

In this paper we focus on the problem of a distance measure and a probability definition of hypothetical models for given data. Depending on the geometric

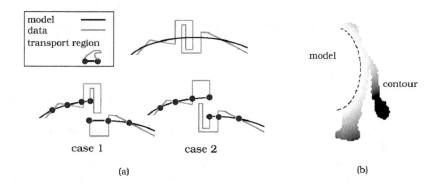

Fig. 1. transport region and transport distance: (a), complicated one to one piecewise model/data correspondences: both cases are permitted; (b), transport distance: from the model to the contour, the darker color, the longer transport distance.

Fig. 2. Experimental results(1, 2): (a), artificial data generated from b-spline model and the poor initialization; (b): precisely recovered geometric model; (c), model reconstruction of a camel shape.("+" denotes the control points of a BSpline model.)

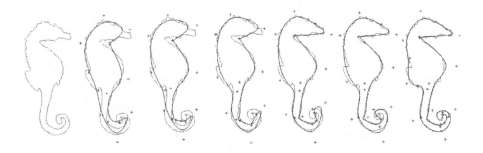

Fig. 3. Experimental results 3: model quality vs. model complexity. On the left, the source contour is shown.

properties of the input contour, the differences between the transport distance and the orthogonal distance are more or less pronounced accoring to the topological properties of individual transport regions between model and data.

Naturally we avoid the data pre-processing problem which is always required by orthogonal distance based methods when given shapes are complex. We are not arguing that heuristic knowledge is inappropriate for shape modeling, but we prefer to avoid it in the modeling process and we rather use shape related knowledge, i.e, curvature derivatives, arclength measurements, scaling, for tasks such as recognition, matching, etc. These measures are conveniently defined on the basis of analytic functions.

Although we only use a *Gaussian* assumption in experiments, other distributions can also be considered to characterize the statistical properties of transport distance. For example, if $p(v_d, \boldsymbol{\theta})$ is a *Laplace* distribution, then the area of a transport region provides the lower bound of Eq.7.

The robustness of model reconstruction originate from the fact that for a hypothetical model, its transport path bundle are determined by the topological properties of individual transport regions, which is robust to unknown small noise along the given data.

In this paper we suggest a new generalized distance measure, the transport distance, for geometric shape reconstruction. Experiments demonstrate that the transport distance can effectively characterize the model quality and guide the model selection.

The approach presented provides a suitable starting point for several further extensions: first, the tradeoff between model complexity and model quality should be thoroughly investigated; second, transport distance based shape modeling should be combined with other vision tasks such as segmentation, recognition, etc.; third, the concept of transport distance should be extended to higher dimensions such as surface modeling.

References

1. Andrew Blake and Michael Isard, *Active Contours,* Springer-Verlag, 1998
2. Sven Loncaric, "A Survey of Shape Analysis Techniques," *Pattern Recognition,* vol. 31, no. 8, pp. 983–1001, 1998.
3. Tony Lindeberg and Meng-Xiang Li, "Segmentation and Classification of Edges Using Minimum Description Length Approximation and Complementary Junction Cues," *Computer Vision and Image Understanding,* vol. 67, no. 1, pp. 88–98, 1997.
4. Tat-Jen Cham and Roberto Cipolla, "Automated B-Spline Curve Representation Incorporating MDL and Error-Minimizing Control Point Insertion Strategies," *IEEE Trans. of PAMI,* vol. 21, no. 1, pp. 49–53, 1999.
5. Ann Bengtsson and Jan-Plof Eklundh, "Shape Representation by Multiscale Contour Approximation," *IEEE Trans. of PAMI,* vol. 13, no. 1, pp. 85–92, 1991.
6. Rhodri H. Davies and Carole J. Twining and T. F. Cootes and John C. Waterton and Chris J. Taylor, "3D Statistical Shape Models Using Direct Optimisation of Description Length," *Proceeding of ECCV'02,* vol. LNCS 2352, pp. 3–20, 2002.
7. D. Keren and M. Werman, "A Full Bayes Approach to Curve and Surface Reconstruction," *Journal of Mathematical Imaging and Vision,* vol. 11, pp. 27–43, 1999.

Generating Rotation-Invariant Texture Features by Randomization of Operator Orientation

Jens Pannekamp and Engelbert Westkämper

Fraunhofer Institute for Manufacturing Engineering and Automation (IPA)
Nobelstrasse 12, 70569 Stuttgart, Germany
pannekamp@ipa.fhg.de

Abstract. Rotation-invariant texture features are generated by randomizing the orientation of the underlying texture operators. The approach is applied to texture features based on local binary patterns as well as to sum and difference histograms. Results are given for a difficult classification problem of 15 different Brodatz textures and 7 rotation angles. Due to randomization, the error rate becomes independent of the texture orientation. Moreover, the classification of periodic textures is enhanced significantly.

1 Introduction

As human beings do, machine vision systems should be able to classify textures independent of their orientation. An overview of methods for rotation-invariant texture classification is given by Pietikäinen *et al.* [7].

The basic task of texture classification consists in determining the texture class C of an input image at position P. Although quite different in implementation, most approaches share the following steps: First, an rotation-dependent operator O_φ is defined in order to extract information from neighboring pixels. Applying O_φ to a set of R evenly-spaced directions results in rotation-dependent features f_φ^{dep}. In the next step, rotation-invariant features f^{inv} are derived from f_φ^{dep} by means of normalization or integration. Alternatively, the features f_φ^{dep} are fed into an invariant classifier such as symmetric phase matched only filtering (SPMOF) [8]. In both cases, true rotation-invariance is only achieved if the inverse angular resolution $\Delta\varphi$ of O_φ is greater than $2\pi/R$. Gabor filter banks for example as given by Jain *et al.* [3] agree to this condition. For features such as local binary patterns (LBP) [6] or features based on sum and difference histograms (SUMDIF) [9] true rotation-invariance results only if $\Delta\varphi = 1/D \geqq 2\pi/R$, where D signifies the length of the displacement vector.

2 Texture Features

2.1 Local Binary Patterns (LBP)

Ojala *et al.* [5] introduced the Local Binary Pattern (LBP) texture operator shown in Fig. 1. The basic idea consists in comparing the gray-value at position

B. Michaelis and G. Krell (Eds.): DAGM 2003, LNCS 2781, pp. 515–522, 2003.

Example				Binary Image				Weights		
6	5	2		1	0	0		1	2	4
7	6	1		1		0		128		8
9	8	7		1	1	1		64	32	16

$$\text{LBP} = (10001111)_2 = 1 + 16 + 32 + 64 + 128 = 241$$

Fig. 1. Calculation of LBP for a 3×3 neighborhood ($R = 8$): After thresholding the neighborhood by the value of the center pixel, the LBP is derived as inner product with a constant weight matrix.

P with a set of R neighbors, thus creating a binary number of length R which corresponds to a local binary pattern. The LBP histogram computed over a region is used for texture description. For $R = 8$, a 256-bin histogram is obtained. Rotation-invariant histograms can be derived if all cyclic permutations of a binary LBP are mapped onto the same rotation-invariant pattern LBPROT [7] [6]. In this way, rotation-invariance is generated by means of normalization.

The discriminating power of LBP/LBPROT histograms can be significantly increased by using a multipredicate approach: Histograms are not only calculated for neighbors with distance $D = 1$ to the central pixel P but for multiple distances D.

LBP/LBPROT histograms are classified by means of a log-likelihood or distance classifier.

2.2 Sum and Difference Histograms (SUMDIF)

Unser [9] introduced sum and difference histograms for texture description as an alternative to the widespread co-occurrence matrices [2]. The advantages are savings in computation time and more reliable estimates of the (1-dimensional) histograms. Like co-occurrence matrices, sum and difference histograms are calculated for a specific displacement vector v with orientation φ and length D over an image region.

Typical texture features (SUMDIF) derived from the histograms are mean, variance, energy, correlation, entropy, contrast, homogeneity, cluster shade and

Table 1. The number of LBP rises exponentially with the number of operator orientations R. If LBPs emanating from rotation or mirroring are not to be distinguished, the number of LBPROTs is reduced.

No. of orientations R	Inverse angular resolution $\Delta\varphi$	No. of LBP	No. of LBPROT	No. of mirror-symmetric LBPROT
4	90.0 °	16	6	6
8	45.0 °	256	36	30
12	30.0 °	4096	352	224
16	22.5 °	65536	4116	2250

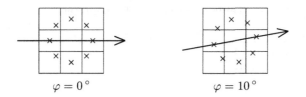

$\varphi = 0°$ $\varphi = 10°$

Fig. 2. The randomization of operator orientation is demonstrated for LBP/LBPROT with $R = 8$.

cluster prominence. Histograms and features SUMDIF may be calculated for a set of R evenly spaced orientations. Rotation-invariant features SUMDIFROT are obtained as moments (mean, variance) of features SUMDIF over the R orientations. Thus, invariance is achieved by integration.

As with LBP/LBPROT, a multipredicate approach improves on the discriminating power. A normal distribution classifier [1] is suggested for classification.

3   Randomization

As stated above, true rotation invariance requires the inverse angular resolution $\Delta\varphi$ to be greater than $2\pi/R$:

$$\Delta\varphi \geqq 2\pi/R \tag{1}$$

For LBPROT and SUMDIFROT, the inverse angular resolution is given by $\Delta\varphi = 1/D$ corresponding to the inverse angular resolution of a pixel at distance D. Thus, features calculated for $D = 1$ and $R = 8$ can be considered as rotation-invariant ($\Delta\varphi = 1 \geqq 0.79$). If LBPROT or SUMDIFROT are calculated for an increased predicate, eg. $D = 3$, condition (1) no longer holds for $R = 8$ ($\Delta\varphi \approx 0.33 \ngeqq 0.79$). Increasing the number of orientations R is an obvious choice for restoring the inequality. Unfortunately, there are limitations for increasing R. For LBP, the number of patterns LBP rises exponentially with R (cf. Tab. 1), thus leading to sparsly populated histograms. For SUMDIF on the other hand, the calculation of large numbers of histograms becomes computationally inefficient. Typical values for D such as $D = 5$ would necessitate the evaluation of more than 30 orientations.

Instead of adjusting the number of operator orientatons R, we propose to increase the inverse angular resolution $\Delta\varphi$ by randomizing the operator orientation O_φ: Every time a histogram entry for LBPROT or SUMDIF is calculated, the orientation of O_φ is offset by a random angle from the interval $[-\pi/R, \pi/R]$. Figure 2 displays the randomization of operator orientation for LBP/LBPROT. Additionally, it may be considered to calculate more than one histogram entry for each position P in order to obtain statistically more reliable histograms. Due to the random orientation and interpolation effects the extracted binary pattern resp. sum/difference of gray values might take different values.

Table 2. Overview of experiments.

Experiment	Texture feature	No. of features	Classifier
A	LBPROT ($R = 8$, $D = 1$)	36	Log-Likelihood
B	LBPROT ($R = 8$, $D = 1$)	36	Distance
C	LBPROT ($R = 12$, Mirror Invariance, $D = 1$)	224	Distance
D	LBPROT ($R = 12$, Mirror Invariance, $D = 1, 2, 4, 6$)	896	Distance
E	LBPROT ($R = 12$, Mirror Invariance, $D = 1, 2, 4, 6$, Randomized)	896	Distance
F	SUMDIFROT ($R = 12$ for $D = 1 - 6$, Randomized)	8 out of 270	Normal Distribution

For an efficient implementation one might deterimine the random orientation and neighbor positions for each histogram entry in advance. They can be re-used for every region to extract the texture properties.

4   Experiments

The textures for the experiments originate from Pietikäinen *et al.* [7]. They comprise 15 different Brodatz textures in 7 rotation angles. For each rotation angle and texture 64 samples of size 32×32 pixels are provided. Samples of rotation angle $0\,°$ were used for training while samples of rotation angles $30\,°$, $60\,°$, $90\,°$, $120\,°$, $150\,°$ and $200\,°$ were used as test data.

Six experiments with different settings are compared (Tab.2). Experiment A shows the best result of Pietikäinen using only local binary patterns and serves as reference experiment. Experiments B–F were implemented by our group. Each experiment improves upon the feature extraction or classification in order to reduce error rates. Experiment B replaces the log-likelihood- by a distance-classifier. In Experiment C, the number of neighbors is increased from $R = 8$ to $R = 12$. At the same time, mirrored patterns are considered to be equivalent, thus limiting the number of histogram bins to 224, cf. Tab. 1. Experiment D introduces a multipredicate approach. Finally, experiment E uses randomized orientations for the LBPROT. Experiment F is based on a completely different approach. Here, features SUMDIFROT are extracted from sum and difference histograms and classified by a normal distribution classifier. Moreover, feature selection [4] is applied in order to reduce the number of features from 270 to 8, keeping only the features with the highest power of discrimination.

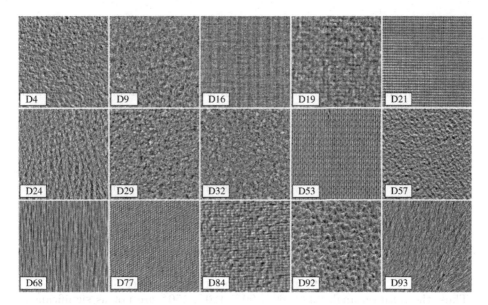

Fig. 3. Original Brodatz images from which the training and test samples of size 32×32 pixels were taken.

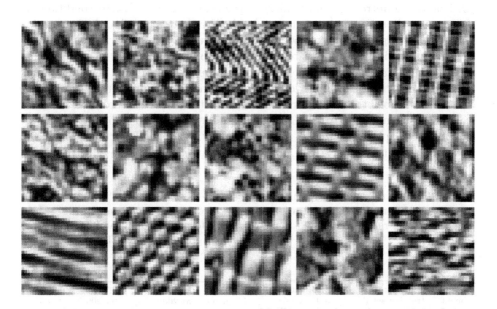

Fig. 4. A sample of size 32×32 pixels is displayed for each of the 15 textures.

5   Results and Discussion

In Tab. 3 overall error rates (averaged over all textures and all rotation angles) are shown. From experiment A to F, the error rate could be reduced from 47.7 % to 7.7 % proving the effectiveness the of proposed modifications. Moreover, the modest increase in error rates from training to test set demonstrate the rotation-invariance of all features. Every single modification in the feature extraction or the classification process (B: distance classifier, C: increased no. of neighbors, D: multipredicate approach, E: randomization, F: features SUMDIFROT) lowered the error rates. The largest reduction was due to the introduction of the multipredicate approach (C → D) whereas the randomization seems to be less important (D → E).

A different rating arises if only textures with rotation angle 200 ° are considered (Tab. 4). Now, the largest drop in error rate occurs from experiment D to E due to randomization. A careful examination of the experimental setup reveals that the rotation angle 200 ° is particularly meaningful. Using $R = 12$ neighbors for LBPROT corresponds to an intrinsic rotation invariance of $360°/12 = 30°$. Thus, the rotation angles 30 °, 60 °, 90 °, 120 °, 150 ° are not as significant as 200 ° for the verification of rotation-invariance.

Figure 5 underlines these findings. Additionally, it shows a near-constant error rate over the rotation angles for all experiments except for experiment D. Due to the introduction of enlarged predicates ($D = 1, 2, 4, 6$) condition (1) for true rotation-invariance no longer holds. Error rates rise sharply for rotation angles not being multiples of $360°/R = 30°$. True rotation invariance is restored by the randomization of operator orientation in experiment E.

The importance of the randomization is emphasized by another observation. Texture D21 shows a near periodic structure making it much more error-prone to small rotations than the more stochastic textures. For texture D21, the error rate drops from 60.9 % to 0.0 % through randomization, cf. Tab. 4!

Table 5 displays the results of experiment F in detail. The confusion matrix reveals that 5 textures (D16, D53, D68, D77 and D93) are classified perfectly.

Table 3. Error rates (%) on training and test set. Each introduced modification reduces the error rates.

Table 4. Error rates (%) on test set for textures with rotation angle 200 °. Here, the effect of randomization (D → E) is much greater than in Tab. 3, especially for the periodic texture D21.

Experiment	Error rate on training set (%)	Error rate on test set (%)
A	not available	47.7
B	37.7	41.3
C	35.2	39.5
D	14.7	22.5
E	16.7	19.7
F	5.7	7.7

Experiment	All Textures at 200 °	Texture D21 only at 200 °
A	not available	not available
B	43.5	71.9
C	42.1	76.6
D	35.9	60.9
E	21.0	0.0
F	6.8	0.0

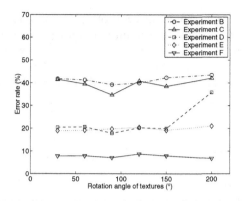

Fig. 5. Error rates on test set for different rotation angles.

On the other hand 3 textures (D19, D29, D92) account for 58 % of the misclassifications. Considering the similarity of these textures in Fig. 4 points up the the difficulty of the given classification task.

Table 5. Confusion matrix for experiment F. The test data for each class is made up of 384 subimages.

True class	\multicolumn{15}{c}{Predicted class}														
	D4	D9	D16	D19	D21	D24	D29	D32	D53	D57	D68	D77	D84	D92	D93
D4	361	5	0	0	0	13	0	0	0	5	0	0	0	0	0
D9	11	344	0	5	0	11	8	5	0	0	0	0	0	0	0
D16	0	0	384	0	0	0	0	0	0	0	0	0	0	0	0
D19	0	0	0	323	0	1	6	1	0	2	0	0	2	49	0
D21	0	0	0	0	383	0	0	0	0	0	0	0	0	0	1
D24	7	17	0	0	0	350	1	0	0	9	0	0	0	0	0
D29	14	1	0	13	0	0	314	13	0	0	0	0	5	24	0
D32	1	1	0	3	0	0	17	348	0	0	0	0	0	14	0
D53	0	0	0	0	0	0	0	0	384	0	0	0	0	0	0
D57	7	0	0	0	0	14	0	0	0	363	0	0	0	0	0
D68	0	0	0	0	0	0	0	0	0	0	384	0	0	0	0
D77	0	0	0	0	0	0	0	0	0	0	0	384	0	0	0
D84	0	0	0	6	0	0	23	0	0	0	0	0	355	0	0
D92	2	0	0	79	0	0	38	8	0	0	0	0	1	256	0
D93	0	0	0	0	0	0	0	0	0	0	0	0	0	0	384

6   Conclusion

It has been demonstrated that real rotation invariance presumes the inverse angular resolution $\Delta\varphi$ to be greater than $360°/R$, with R specifying the number of operator orientations. For texture features such as standard LBPROT or SUMDIFROT this condition is only fulfilled for small displacement vectors v of moderate length D. The randomization of operator orientation has been proposed as an efficient approach to obtain true rotation invariance, even for large predicates. Its applicability has been demonstrated for texture features LBPROT and SUMDIFROT. Especially, for near-periodic textures the error rate could be reduced significantly. The approach can easily be extended to other texture features.

References

1. K. Fukunaga. *Introduction to Statistical Pattern Recognition*. Academic Press, New York, 1990.
2. R. M. Haralick, K. Shanmugam, and I. Dinstein. Textural features for image classification. *IEEE Trans. Systems, Man, and Cybernetics*, 3(6):610–621, November 1973.
3. A. Jain and F. Farrokhnia. Unsupervised texture segmentation using Garbor filters. *Pattern Recognition*, 24:1167–1186, 1991.
4. A. Jain and D. Zongker. Feature selection: Evaluation, application, and small sample performance. *IEEE Trans. Pattern Analysis and Machine Intelligence*, 10(2):153–158, February 1997.
5. T. Ojala, M. Pietikäinen, and D. Harwood. A comparative study of texture measures with classification based on feature distributions. *Pattern Recognition*, 29:51–59, 1996.
6. T. Ojala, M. Pietikäinen, and T. Mäenpää. Multiresolution gray-scale and rotation invariant texture classification with local binary patterns. *IEEE Trans. Pattern Analysis and Machine Intelligence*, 24(7):971–987, July 2002.
7. M. Pietikäinen, T. Ojala, and Z. Xu. Rotation-invariant texture classification using feature distributions. *Pattern Recognition*, 33:43–52, 2000. http://www.ee.oulu.fi/research/imag/texture/.
8. A. Teuner, O. Pichler, and B. J. Hosticka. Unsupervised texture segmentation of images using tuned matched Gabor filters. *IEEE Trans. Image Processing*, 4:863–870, 1995.
9. M. Unser. Sum and difference histograms for texture classification. *IEEE Trans. Pattern Analysis and Machine Intelligence*, 8(1):118–125, January 1986.

Estimation of Skill Levels in Sports Based on Hierarchical Spatio-Temporal Correspondences

Winfried Ilg[1], Johannes Mezger[2], and Martin Giese[1]

[1] Laboratory for Action, Representation and Learning
Department for Cognitive Neurology, University Clinic Tübingen, Germany
{wilg,giese}@tuebingen.mpg.de
[2] Graphical-Interactive Systems, Wilhelm Schickard Institute for Computer Science
University Tübingen, Germany

Abstract. We present a learning-based method for the estimation of skill levels from sequences of complex movements in sports. Our method is based on a hierarchical algorithm for computing spatio-temporal correspondence between sequences of complex body movements. The algorithm establishes correspondence at two levels: whole action sequences and individual movement elements. Using Spatio-Temporal Morphable Models we represent individual movement elements by linear combinations of learned example patterns. The coefficients of these linear combinations define features that can be efficiently exploited for estimating continuous style parameters of human movements. We demonstrate by comparison with expert ratings that our method efficiently estimates the skill level from the individual techniques in a "karate kata".

1 Introduction

The analysis of complex movements is an important problem for many technical applications in computer vision, computer graphics, sports and medicine (see reviews in [6] and [10]). For several applications it is crucial to model different styles of movements, for example to quantify the movement disorders in medical gait analysis, or for the classification and description of different skill-levels in sports. In the literature different methods for the parameterization of styles of complex movements have been proposed, e.g. based on hidden Markov models [2][13], principal component analysis [15][1] or fourier coefficients [12].

An efficient method for the synthesis of movements with different styles is the linear combination of example trajectories. Such linear combinations can be defined efficiently on the basis of spatio-temporal correspondence. The technique of Spatio-Temporal Morphable Models (STMMs) defines linear combinations by weighted summation of spatial and temporal displacement fields that morph the prototypical movement trajectories into a reference pattern. This method has been successfully applied for the generation of cyclic movements in computer graphics (motion morphing [3],[14]) as well as for the recognition of movements and movement styles from trajectories in computer vision [8].

To generalize the method of linear combination for complex sequences containing many complex movements we extend the basic STMM algorithm by introducing a second

B. Michaelis and G. Krell (Eds.): DAGM 2003, LNCS 2781, pp. 523–531, 2003.

hierarchy level that represents motion primitives. Such primitives correspond to parts of the approximated trajectories, e.g. techniques in a sequence of karate movements. These movement primitives are then modeled using STMMs by linearly combining example movements. This makes it possible to learn generative models for sequences of movements with different styles. We apply this hierarchical algorithm to model sequences of complex karate movements and to estimate the skill levels of different actors based on the trajectory information obtained by motion capturing.

2   Algorithm

An overview of the hierarchical algorithm is shown in figure 1. The next sections describe the extraction of the movement elements and the modeling of the individual elements by STMMs.

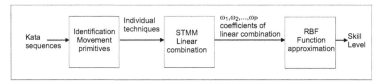

Fig. 1. Schematic description of the method and data flow. First, individual techniques are identified and segmented using invariant key features. Then the segmented techniques are represented by linear combination of prototypical example trajectories using STMMs. The resulting linear coefficients $\omega_1 \dots \omega_P$ are mapped onto the estimated skill level with RBF networks that are trained with expert ratings for the skill levels of each individual karate technique.

2.1   Identification of Movement Primitives

For the identification of movement primitives within a complex movement sequence an appropriate description of the spatio-temporal characteristics of the individual movement elements must be found that is suitable for a robust matching with stored example templates. Based on such features spatio-temporal correspondence between new movement sequences and stored example sequences can be established on a coarse level. The underlying features must be invariant against changes of the style of the individual movements elements. Different elementary spatio-temporal and kinematic features, like angular velocity [5][11] or curvature and torsion of the 3D trajectories [4] have been proposed in the literature. The key features of our algorithm are zeros of the velocity in few "characteristic coordinates" of the trajectory $\zeta(t)$. For the matching process, which is based on dynamic programming, we represent the features by discrete events. Let m be the number of the motion primitive and r the number of characteristic coordinates of the trajectory. Let $\kappa(t)$ be the "reduced trajectory" of the characteristic coordinates that takes the values κ_i^m at the velocity zeros[1]. The movement primitive is then characterized

---

[1] Zero-velocity is defined by a a zero of the velocity in at least one coordinate of the reduced trajectory.

by the vector differences $\Delta \kappa_i^m = \kappa_i^m - \kappa_{i-1}^m$ of subsequent velocity zeros (see fig. 2).

Fig. 2. Illustration of the method for the automatic identification of movement primitives: (a) In a first step all key features κ_i^s are determined. (b) Sequences of key features from the sequences (s) are matched with sequences of key features from the prototypical movement primitives (m) using dynamic programming. A search window is moved over the sequence. The length of the window is two times the number of key features of the learned movement primitive. The best matching trajectory segment is defined by the sequence of feature vectors that minimizes $\sum_j \|\Delta \kappa_i^s - \Delta \kappa_j^m\|$ over all matched key features. With this method spatio-temporal correspondence at a coarse level is established.

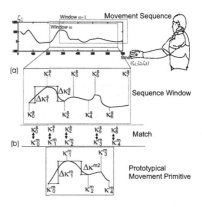

A robust identification of movement primitives in noisy data with additional or missing zero-velocity points κ_i^s can be achieved by dynamic programming. The purpose of the dynamic programming is an optimal sequence alignment between the key features of the prototypical movement primitive $\kappa_0^m \dots \kappa_q^m$ and the key features of a search window $\kappa_0^s \dots \kappa_p^s$ (see fig. 2b). This is accomplished by minimizing a cost function δ that is given by the sum of $\|\Delta \kappa_i^s - \Delta \kappa_j^m\|$ over all matched key features. A more formal description of the algorithm is given in [9].

2.2 Morphable Models for Modeling Movement Primitives

The technique of *Spatio-Temporal Morphable Models* [7],[8] is based on linearly combining the movement trajectories of prototypical motion patterns in space-time. Linear combinations of movement patterns are defined on the basis of spatio-temporal correspondences that are computed by dynamic programming [3]. Complex movement patterns can be characterized by trajectories of feature points. The trajectories of the prototypical movement pattern p can be characterized by the time-dependent vector $\zeta_p(t)$. The correspondence field between two trajectories ζ_1 and ζ_2 is defined by the spatial shifts $\xi(t)$ and the temporal shifts $\tau(t)$ that transform the first trajectory into the second. The transformation is specified mathematically by the equation:

$$\zeta_2(t) = \zeta_1(t + \tau(t)) + \xi(t) \tag{1}$$

By linear combination of spatial and temporal shifts the Spatio-Temporal Morphable Model allows to interpolate smoothly between motion patterns with significantly different spatial structure, but also between patterns that differ with respect to their timing. The correspondence shifts $\xi(t)$ and $\tau(t)$ are calculated by solving an optimization problem that minimizes the spatial and temporal shifts under the constraint that the temporal shifts define a new time variable that is always monotonically increasing. For further details about the underlying algorithm we refer to [7],[8]. Signifying the spatial and temporal shifts between prototype p and the reference pattern by $\boldsymbol{\xi}_p(t)$ and $\tau_p(t)$, linearly combined spatial and temporal shifts can be defined by the two equations:

$$\boldsymbol{\xi}(t) = \sum_{p=1}^{P} w_p\, \boldsymbol{\xi}_p(t) \qquad \tau(t) = \sum_{p=1}^{P} w_p\, \tau_p(t) \tag{2}$$

The weights w_p define the contributions of the individual prototypes to the linear combination. We always assume convex combinations with $0 \leq w_p \leq 1$ and $\sum_p w_p = 1$. After linearly combining the spatial and temporal shifts the trajectories of the morphed pattern can be recovered by morphing the reference pattern in space-time using the spatial and temporal shifts $\boldsymbol{\xi}(t)$ and $\tau(t)$. The space-time morph is defined by equation (1) where $\boldsymbol{\zeta}_1$ is the reference pattern and $\boldsymbol{\zeta}_2$ has to be identified with trajectory of the linearly combined pattern.

Fig. 3. A Snapshot from motion capturing karate movements with 11 cameras. The subjects had 41 markers and perform the karate kata "Heian Shodan"

3   Experiments

We demonstrate the function of the algorithm by modeling movement sequences from martial arts. Using a motion capture system (VICON 612) with 11 cameras we captured the movements of 7 actors performing the karate kata "Heian Shodan". 14 movement sequences (two sequences per actor) were captured at a sampling frequency of 120 Hz using 41 passively reflecting markers. The actors had different belt levels (Kyu degrees) in karate (Shotokan) (see tab. 1). The kata was decomposed into 20 movement primitives (karate techniques). The total duration of the whole sequences was between 25 and 35 s ($\doteq$ 3000-4200 captured frames). Each individual technique was rated by an expert on a scale from 0 to 10.

3.1   Identification of Individual Techniques

The individual techniques were extracted automatically from the kata sequences using the method described in section 2.1. For the representation of the relevant key features we

Table 1. Official belt levels (Kyu degrees) of the seven actors and average of the expert ratings for the individual techniques $\bar{r}_{exp}$ on a scale from 0 to 10 (0 signifying optimal performance, and 10 signifying worst performance).

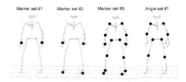

actor	den	mar	tho	joh	ste	chr	joa
Kyu	7	6	5	5	3	2	1
$\bar{r}_{exp}$	8.1	7.0	6.0	4.2	2.2	1.9	0.9

Fig. 4. Visualization of different feature sets used for the analysis. Feature sets #1-#3 were based on selected 3D markers. Feature set #4 is based on joint angles. The black dots illustrate the positions of the selected markers respectively joints.

have examined different feature sets based on 3D markers and joint angles (fig. 4). The prototypes for the identification of individual techniques were generated from manually segmented trajectories. As prototypes we used techniques from individual actors and also the averages over all actors generated by time alignment using STMMs. Fig. 5 shows the error measure δ for all frames for a kata sequence using one particular prototypical movement primitive for matching.

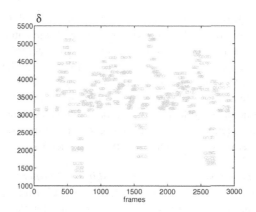

Fig. 5. Results of the automatic segmentation for one sequence identifying one technique for actor (chr) using the prototypical movement primitive generated by a 3 movements average $3av$. The diagram shows the distance measure of the dynamic programming method, δ, for different matches of the corresponding movement primitive over the whole sequence. The circles mark the times of the matched key feature κ_i^m in the sequence (see fig. 2). Each match of a whole movement primitive is illustrated by a row of circles with the same δ. The number of circles corresponds to the number of key features of the movement primitive. There are three distinct minima in the δ-function corresponding to a technique that occurs multiple times in the kata with slightly different rotation steps. The movement primitive (with the correct rotation step) corresponds to the smallest minimum of the error function that occurs at frame 595.

The results of the automatic segmentations are as follows: Out of the 280 individual techniques in the data set 96% were correctly classified. The best segmentation results were obtained using prototypes generated by averaging the trajectories of all actors. Using an average of three actors including a beginner, a medium skilled karateka, and a master, we obtained comparable results. In general, using prototypes generated by averaging we obtained significantly better segmentations than for prototypes that were derived from individual actors. Segmentation errors typically arise when the same technique occurs multiple times in different contexts in the kata. Such errors can be easily removed by taking into account the overall sequence of the techniques in the kata. The best segmentation performance was obtained with marker set # 1. The reason for this result might be that the movements of the feet during many of the techniques were very similar. Our segmentation algorithm was sensitive enough to detect if actors forgot individual movements during the kata.

3.2   Modeling of Movement Element by Linear Combination

In the next step, the segmented movement elements were approximated by linear combinations of prototypical movement primitives. The weights of these linear combinations are useful (1) for actor identification, if the movement comes from an actor in the prototype set (2) for the estimation of skill levels of actors, which is not in the prototype set.

Actor identification.   Based on the representation by linear combinations a robust actor identification can be realized. The STMM is trained with the automatically segmented movements from all actors. A new movement sequence from actor (tho), that was not part in the training set, is approximated by the linear combination of the training movement sequences. Fig. 6.a shows that the linear coefficients $\omega_{p,i}$ peak exactly for the weight of the prototype (tho). In addition, the estimated weight of this prototype is close to one for all techniques. This actor identification works for both types of feature sets (3D markers and joint angles). The identification is thus not based on the specific kinematic structure of the actor, but rather on specific spatio-temporal characteristics.

Coefficients of linear combination as basis for skill level estimation.   The linear coefficients can also be used as basis for the estimation of skill levels. For this purpose the mapping between the linear coefficients and an estimate for the skill level is learned (sec. 3.3). The coefficients reflect the weighting of the specific spatio-temporal characteristics of the prototypes for the rated movement pattern. We evaluated the method using a leave-one-out paradigm. The STMM was trained with the automatically segmented movements from a set of six prototypes excluding the actor that performed the test sequence. Fig. 6.b shows a typical example of the estimated coefficients $\omega_{p,i}$ for a new actor. Interestingly, the weight estimations for the different movement primitives are similar even though the actor was not in the training set. This indicates correlations in movement styles of different actors that are similar for different movement elements.

3.3   Skill-Level Estimation on Segments

For the estimation of the skill-levels based on the linear coefficients $\omega_{p,i}$ (eq. 2) we used RBF networks. For each karate technique a separate network was trained that realizes the

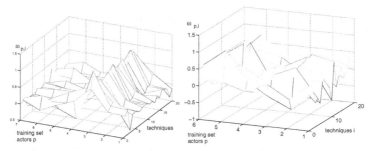

Fig. 6. Left panel: Coefficients $\omega_{p,i}$ of the linear combination that approximates a new sequence of actor *tho*. The weight corresponding to this actor has the index $p = 3$. (The tested sequence was not in the training set for the STMM). Right panel: Coefficients $\omega_{p,i}$ of linear combination approximating a sequence of the actor *joh* after the STMM has been trained with a set of six prototypes excluding actor *joh*. Consistently, for most movement primitives high coefficients arise for $p = 5$ and $p = 2$.

mapping $RBF_p^i : [\omega_1 \ldots \omega_P] \rightarrow r_{est}^{p,i}$, where $r_{est}^{p,i}$ denotes the estimate. The networks were trained with the coefficient vectors for the prototypes $p_1 \ldots p_P$ and the expert ratings.

Fig. 7 (left panel) shows a comparison between the estimated skill levels and the expert ratings for all techniques of a single actor. The right panel shows the averaged deviations $\Delta_i = (\sum_{p \in \mathcal{P}} |r_{est}^{p,i} - r_{exp}^{p,i}|)/\#\mathcal{P}$ for all techniques i averaged over all actors. The figure shows that the reliability varies over the movement primitives. A possible explanation is that the techniques vary with respect to their difficulty. Very simple techniques might not so well differentiate between different skill levels as more difficult ones.

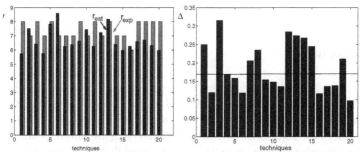

Fig. 7. Left panel: Comparison between the estimates r_{est} of the skill level obtained from the individual techniques and the expert ratings r_{exp} for one actor (mar). The averages of the estimated and the real skill levels are quite similar (6.3 vs. 7.0). In particular for techniques that were not executed correctly larger deviations arise. Right panel: Reliability of the skill-level estimates from the different kata techniques. Techniques with $\Delta_i < 0.2$ were used to compute the averaged skill-level.

For the further analysis the techniques with a reliability $\Delta_i < 0.2$ were determined. Only the estimates of the RBF networks trained with these techniques were combined into a final skill level estimate by computing the average of their outputs.

The overall reliability of the proposed method was then tested with a new data set with sequences from the 7 actors using only the previously selected techniques. The results of the skill-level estimation based on different feature sets and segmentation methods compared with the expert ratings are shown in figure 8 and table 2. The estimates have exactly the same monotonic order as the expert ratings and match them closely in the range of the lower skill levels. Larger deviations occur for some actors with higher ranks (ste and chr). The estimates of the extreme skill levels are shifted towards less extreme values, likely a consequence of the lack of training data outside the range between these extremes.

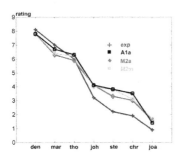

Fig. 8. Comparison of the averaged expert ratings (exp) with the automatically estimated ratings using different feature sets (see table 2) for all actors. The automatic estimates obtained with different feature sets are very similar.

Table 2. Comparison between the belt level (Kyu), expert rating averaged over all techniques $\bar{r}_{exp}$, and the estimated skill levels for different sets of features. Results are shown for automatic and manual segmentation of the movement primitives ($m \doteq manual, a \doteq automatic$). Based on the estimate $\bar{r}_{A1}^a$ an estimated belt level Kyu$_{est}$ was computed by linear transformation using the extreme skill values (1. and 7. Kyu) as reference points.

actor	den	mar	tho	joh	ste	chr	joa
Kyu	7	6	5	5	3	2	1
Kyu$_{est}$	7.0	5.9	5.5	3.5	3.2	2.9	1.0
$\bar{r}_{exp}$	8.1	7.0	6.0	4.2	2.2	1.9	0.9
$\bar{r}_{M2}^m$	7.8	6.3	5.9	4.1	3.3	3.0	1.6
$\bar{r}_{M2}^a$	7.8	6.4	6.2	4.0	3.8	3.1	1.7
$\bar{r}_{A1}^a$	7.8	6.7	6.3	4.1	3.8	3.5	1.4

4   Discussion

We have presented a learning-based method for the quantification of movement styles in sequences of movements that works on small data sets. The proposed method is based on establishing spatio-temporal correspondence between learned prototypical example sequences and new trajectories exploiting a hierarchical algorithm for the computation of spatio-temporal correspondence. We demonstrated that this technique is suitable for person recognition from individual movement primitives, and for the estimation of skill levels from sequence of complex movements in sports.

Compared to related methods for the representation of movement styles in computer vision and computer graphics (see section 1) the proposed method seems to be interesting for the following reasons: (1) As demonstrated in this paper it works with very small data sets. We applied principle component analysis on the same trajectories using the same type of neural networks and obtained less accurate estimates of the skill level. (2) The coefficients of the STMM are often intuitive to interpret, as shown in figure 6. (3) A further advantage of the proposed method, which applies also to some other techniques, is that representation of movement sequences by linear combinations of learned examples is also suitable for synthesis of movement sequences with defined styles [9]. Future work will have to test the proposed method on bigger data sets.

Acknowledgments. This work is supported from the Deutsche Volkswagenstiftung. We thank H.P. Thier, B. Eberhardt, W. Strasser, H.H. Bülthoff and the Max Planck Institute for Biological Cybernetics for additional support.

References

1. A. F. Bobick and J. Davis. An appearance-based representation of action. In *Proceedings of the IEEE Conference on Pattern Recognition*, pages 307–312, 1996.
2. M. Brand. Style machines. In *SIGGRAPH*, 2000.
3. A. Bruderlin and L. Williams. Motion signal processing. In *SIGGRAPH*, pages 97–104, 1995.
4. T. Caelli, A. McCabe, and G. Binsted. On learning the shape of complex actions. In *International Workshop on Visual Form*, pages 24–39, 2001.
5. A. Galata, N. Johnson, and D. Hogg. Learning variable lenth markov models of behavior. *Journal of Computer Vision and Image Understanding*, 81:398–413, 2001.
6. D.M. Gavrila. The visual analysis of human movement: a survey. *Journal of Computer Vision and Image Understanding*, 73:82–98, 1999.
7. M. A. Giese and T. Poggio. Synthesis and recognition of biological motion pattern based on linear superposition of prototypical motion sequences. In *Proceedings of IEEE MVIEW 99 Symposium at CVPR, Fort Collins*, pages 73–80, 1999.
8. M.A. Giese and T. Poggio. Morphable models for the analysis and synthesis of complex motion patterns. *International Journal of Computer Vision*, 38(1):59–73, 2000.
9. W. Ilg and M.A. Giese. Modeling of movement sequences based on hierarchical spatial-temporal correspondence of movement primitives. In *Workshop on Biologically Motivated Computer Vision*, pages 528–537, 2002.
10. T. B. Moeslund. A survey of computer vision-based human motion capture. *Journal of Computer Vision and Image Understanding*, 81:231–268, 2001.
11. T. Mori and K. Uehara. Extraction of primitive motion and discovery of association rules from motion data. In *Proceedings of the IEEE International Workshop on Robot and Human Interactive Communication*, pages 200–206, 2001.
12. M. Unuma, K. Anjyo, and R. Takeuchi. Fourier principles for emotion-based human figure animation. In *SIGGRAPH*, pages 91–96, 1995.
13. A. D. Wilson and A. F. Bobick. Parametric hidden markov models for gesture recognition. *IEEE Transactions on Pattern Analysis and Machine Intelligence*, 21(9):884–900, 1999.
14. A. Witkin and Z. Popovic. Motion warping. In *SIGGRAPH*, pages 105–108, 1995.
15. Y. Yacoob and M. J. Black. Parameterized modeling and recognition of activities. *Journal of Computer Vision and Image Understanding*, 73(2):398–413, 1999.

Determining Position and Fine Shape Detail in Radiological Anatomy

Georg Langs[*1], Philipp Peloschek[2], and Horst Bischof[3]

[1] Pattern Recognition and Image Processing Group 183/2
Vienna University of Technology
langs@prip.tuwien.ac.at
[2] Department of Diagnostic Radiology
University of Vienna
philipp.peloschek@univie.ac.at
[3] Institute for Computer Graphics and Vision
University of Technology Graz
bischof@icg.tu-graz.ac.at

Abstract. In this paper a method is proposed that identifies bone positions and fine structure of bone contours in radiographs by combining active shape models (ASM) and active contours (snakes) resulting in high accuracy and stability. After a coarse estimate of the bone position has been determined by neural nets, an approximation of the contour is obtained by an active shape model. The accuracy of the landmarks and the contour in between is enhanced by applying an iterative active contour algorithm to a set of gray value profiles extracted orthogonally to the interpolation obtained by the ASM. The neural nets obtain knowledge about visual appearance as well as anatomical configuration during a training phase. The active shape model is trained with a set of training shapes, whereas the snake detects the contour with fewer constraints and decreases the influence of a priori knowledge in a controlled manner. This is of particular importance for the assessment of pathological changes of bones like erosive destructions caused by rheumatoid arthritis.

1 Introduction

Rheumatoid arthritis is an incurable disease leading to disability and increased mortality. The accurate determination of its progression is a decisive factor during treatment and clinical studies. In particular the quantification of erosive destructions of bony contours in hand radiographs provides valuable information [12]. An automation is highly desirable by means of objectivity, accuracy and reproducibility of quantification results.

Active shape models (ASM) [2] are a frequently used tool in medical image analysis. They efficiently search images with a flexible and compact model using a priori knowledge derived from training data. It is possible to recognize objects with high variation in shape and appearance. The result provides a parametric description of the identified shape.

---

[*] This research has been supported by the Austrian Science Fund (FWF) under grant P14445-MAT

B. Michaelis and G. Krell (Eds.): DAGM 2003, LNCS 2781, pp. 532–539, 2003.
© Springer-Verlag Berlin Heidelberg 2003

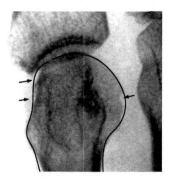

Fig. 1. Metacarpal bone with erosive changes (arrows) and result of an ASM search.

Despite their high speed, generality and robustness against bad initialization [11] ASM segmentation algorithms face certain drawbacks: (1) ASMs are based on distinct and recognizable features that have to be trained. (2) In order to avoid an over-constrained model of shape variation the training set has to be sufficiently large. Since during training the landmarks have to be annotated manually, this is costly and time consuming. (3) Due to the linearity of the model it is not capable of reconstructing severe pathological changes like erosions caused by rheumatoid arthritis. Non-linear shape models have been introduced in [4], though these models are more flexible the first two problems remain.

Active contours (Snakes) [6] on the other hand adapt even to fine structures, require no training but are very sensitive to inaccurate initialization [11]. They adapt to image content by iteratively solving an energy minimizing problem influenced by external and internal forces. By applying non-conservative external force fields the convergence of snakes to *contour concavities* is enhanced. In [13] *gradient vector flow* is utilized to generate a force field of this kind.

In this paper we introduce an approach that reduces drawbacks of both methods by combining the advantages of ASMs and snakes. *ASM driven snakes* enhance the result of ASMs and provide high accuracy and robustness, while the size of the necessary set of samples for ASM training can be decreased. The method not only enhances the accuracy of landmark detection of a standard ASM but identifies contour lines in between ASM landmarks. The approximation of fine shape details is restricted only by parameters of the inner force field of a snake. This is in contrast to [5]. A priori knowledge is used only with respect to the gray level neighborhood of the landmarks while the tie of the final result to the shape model is gradually decreased. These are crucial properties in detection of pathologic changes like bone erosions, since they cannot be modeled accurately with ASMs. In Fig. 1 a bone in a hand radiograph showing erosive destructions and the result of an ASM search are depicted. The ASM result does not adapt to the erosions.

The paper is organized as follows: In section 2 methods are outlined and the algorithm is explained in detail, in section 3 results of experiments are reported and in section 4 a conclusion and a brief outlook to future research are given.

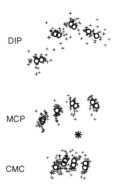

Fig. 2. Output space $\mathbb{R}^2$ of LLM nets that detect joint locations of a hand. Crosses: training sets for LLM nets on DIP-, MCP and CMC joints of 2nd finger to 5th finger. For each net a pair of circles indicates the present positions of the output units $\mathbf{w}_{1,2}^{out}$.

2   Methods

The utilized methods will be described briefly, followed by a detailed description of the *ASM driven snakes* algorithm.

Local Linear Mapping Nets. A local linear mapping is a smooth mapping from $\mathbb{R}^n \rightarrow \mathbb{R}^m$ [10]. In order to approximate a nonlinear function $f : \mathbb{R}^n \rightarrow \mathbb{R}^m$ the input space is partitioned into domains $D_i \subset \mathbb{R}^n$ where the function f is replaced by a local linear approximation $f_i : D_i \rightarrow \mathbb{R}^m$. The partition $\{D_i : i \in I\}$ as well as the linear functions f_i are obtained during a training phase. A set of input units $\{\mathbf{w}_i^{in}\} \in \mathbb{R}^n$ and a corresponding set of output units $\{\mathbf{w}_i^{out}\} \in \mathbb{R}^m$ are initialized randomly and are subject to an updating process during training. The update is performed based on training examples in the form of pairs $(\mathbf{x}_{train}, \mathbf{y}_{train}) \in \mathbb{R}^n \times \mathbb{R}^m$. In each step the input unit $\mathbf{w}_s^{in}$ with the smallest Euclidean distance to $\mathbf{x}_{train}$ is chosen as a reference vector in the input space. The according local linear function f_s is defined with respect to the output unit $\mathbf{w}_s^{out}$. This results in a Voronoi triangulation of the input space that adapts to the distribution of the training samples. Fig. 2 shows the output space used in this work.

Active Shape Models. We apply a standard ASM algorithm [3,2] in order to estimate the bone contour. An active shape model S represents a shape as a set of labeled points (landmarks) $x = (x_1, x_2, \ldots, x_{n_a})$. The *pose* i. e. effects of scaling, rotation and translation $x = L(s, \phi)x' + X_c$ are treated in the alignment procedure. After determining a mean shape $\bar{x}$ the modes m_i of variation i. e. the deformations of the shape are found by applying principal component analysis to the deviations of the training samples $dx_i = x_i - \bar{x}$. The matrix $M = (m_1, m_2, \ldots, m_t)$ built by the first t modes can be used to approximate any shape in the training set by building a sum $x = \bar{x} + Mb$ weighted by $b = (b_1, b_2, \ldots, b_t)$.

In order to model the gray level neighborhoods of the landmarks x_i for each model landmark x_i, a one dimensional profile g_{ij} is extracted from the training image j. It has length n_p, is centered at the point x_i and is orthogonal to the curve passing through

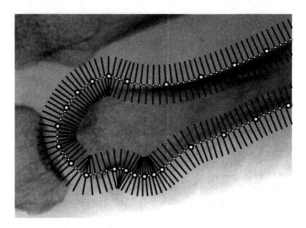

Fig. 3. Cutout of a bone detected by an ASM. Profiles orthogonal to the spline interpolation of the landmarks (represented by larger circles) are depicted.

the landmarks. Information about the gray level neighborhood for each landmark in the model is represented by $g_i = 1/n \sum_{j=1}^{n} g'_{ij}$ i.e. the mean of the derivatives of $\{g_{ij} | j = 1, \ldots, n_t\}$.

During the search for a shape x in an input image, suggested movements for each approximated model point $\hat{x}_i$ are calculated based on a convolution of the actual gray level profile and g_i resulting in a cost function. After the points have been moved pose and shape parameters are adjusted so that $\hat{x} = (\hat{x}_1, \hat{x}_2, \ldots, \hat{x}_{n_a})$ is represented by the model S. The procedure is iterated until it converges. The result is a set of points $\hat{x} = (x_1, x_2, \ldots, x_{n_a})$ being an estimation of the landmark positions in the image.

Snakes and gradient vector flow. A snake [6,13] $x(s) = [x(s), y(s)]$ is a curve that moves through the spatial domain of an image $P(x, y)$ to minimize an energy functional controlled by internal force field formed by weighting parameters α and β representing tension and rigidity of the curve and an external force field. The external force field is based on an edge map $f(x, y) = -E_{ext}(x, y)$ derived from the image. The snake satisfies the force balance equation $F_{int} + F_{ext} = 0$ where $F_{int} = \alpha x'' - \beta x''''$ and $F_{ext} = -\nabla E_{ext}$. A stable state of the curve is reached iteratively[6].

A gradient vector flow (GVF) field [13] is a non-conservative vector field $v(x, y) = [u(x, y)v(x, y)]$ that minimizes the energy functional

$$\int \int \mu(u_x^2 + u_y^2 + v_x^2 v_y^2) + |\nabla f|^2 |v - \nabla f|^2 dx dy. \tag{1}$$

It is nearly equal to the gradient of the edge map $v \approx \nabla f$ if ∇f is large, and has low variation in homogenous regions of f.

2.1 The ASM Driven Snakes Algorithm

The proposed algorithm proceeds in the following main steps roughly divided into a coarse initialization phase and a increasingly fine determination of the bone contour:

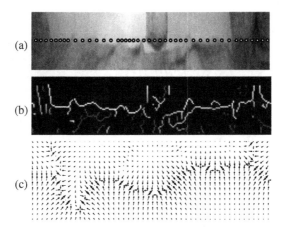

Fig. 4. (a) The set of gray level profiles P from extracted orthogonally to the ASM result, (b) edge map f. (c) detail of vector field v

1. Coarse Identification of the Shape Position. A coarse initialization of the ASM is achieved by an artificial neural network (in particular a LLM-net) which detects the positions of fingertips and joints in a radiograph. It is based on outputs of Gabor jets i.e. sets of Gabor filters applied to different windows extracted from the image and on anatomical information. It calculates position estimates for the joints. The method is similar to an approach used in [10] and can be generalized to other anatomical structures in a straightforward way. For details please refer to [8,7].

2. ASM search. The shape is represented by landmarks $x = (x_1, x_2, \ldots, x_{n_a})$. An ASM search on the input image I results in an estimate of the landmark positions $\hat{x}^1 = (\hat{x}_1^1, \hat{x}_2^1, \ldots, \hat{x}_{n_a}^1)$. The ASM has been trained on a set of training samples.

3. Extraction of Profiles. The positions of the landmarks $\hat{x}_i^1 \in \hat{x}^1$ are interpolated by a cubic spline. This yields a fine approximation of the entire contour parameterized by the square root of chord-length [9] based solely on the landmark positions. Gray level profiles p_i with length m are extracted from the image. They are orthogonal to the spline interpolation and build a matrix $P = [p_1, p_2, \ldots, p_n]$. Fig.3a shows their original positions in a cutout of I around a metacarpal bone. We view $P(x, y)$ with $(x, y) \in [0, n] \times [0, m]$ as a continuous distribution of gray values. Fig.4a depicts the matrix P resulting from Fig.3 with landmarks $\hat{x}_i$ being projected into the new domain. The spline interpolation in between the ASM landmarks i.e. the first estimate of the contour is positioned at points $s_1^{ASM} = (x, y)_{i=1,\ldots,n} : (x, y)_i = (i, m/2)$ in $P(x, y)$.

4. Generation of the Edge Map. A weighted edge map $f(x, y)$ (Fig. 4b) is generated based on the matrix P.

$$f(x, y) := sign(c(x, y)) *^{\cdot} (\tau c(x, y) + \eta(a_b(x) \star dP(x, y)/dy) + \gamma o(x, y)) \quad (2)$$

where $*^{\cdot}$ denotes pixel-wise multiplication. $c(x, y)$ is the accumulation of outputs of a sequence of Canny edge detectors [1] $C(x, y, \sigma, t)$ with pairs of varying hysteresis thresholds $t = t_1, t_2, \ldots, t_c$ applied to $P(x, y)$. It forms a fundament for the weighted

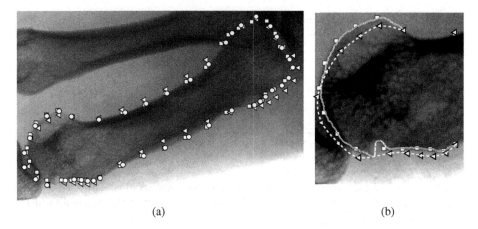

(a)   (b)

Fig. 5. (a) □ : manually assigned landmarks; landmarks detected by an △ ASM and by ○ ASM driven snakes; (b) Contour in between landmarks, dashed line: detected by ASM; solid line: detected by ASM driven snakes.

edge map. $a_b(x)$ are generated by interpolating values of neighboring profiles g_i and g_j with $i \leq x < j$. The convolution $(a_b(x) \star dP(x, y)/dy)$ corresponds to the similarity of the derivative of the profiles extracted from the input image and an interpolation of the derivatives of profiles to be found by the ASM. The binary function $o(x, y) \in \{0, 1\}$ equals 1 iff the point (x, y) is part of an edge that crosses s_1. The parameters α, β control the influence of the initial estimate s_1^{ASM} on the new estimate by means of the inner force field that controls the elasticity of the snake. γ controls the effect of the estimate s_i on s_{i+1}. Increasing α and β causes a higher similarity in direction but prevents fitting of fine structure. γ determines the force dragging s_{i+1} to connected edges that cross s_i. η steers the influence of the visual appearance information stored in the ASM whereas τ controls the similarity to an edge detector with gradually lower weighted branchings.

5. Snake search. By generating a GVF vector field v (Fig. 4c) from f and applying the standard iterative snake algorithm (Sec. 2) a new approximation of the transformed shape and contour positions in between landmarks in P is derived. The active contour is initialized on the position of s_1 and converges to a new estimation of the contour and the set of landmarks s_2 that differs from s_1 orthogonally to the ASM result.

6. Back projection. The resulting points are back projected on the image.

Steps 4 and 5 can be iterated with varying parameters for the active contour by generating a GVF force field and fitting a new active contour s_{i+1} based on s_i. By increasing elasticity of succeeding snakes they gradually adapt to finer structures.

3   Experiments

We evaluated the method with respect to (1) improved accuracy of landmarks represented by the ASM and (2) accuracy of the located contour in between landmarks.

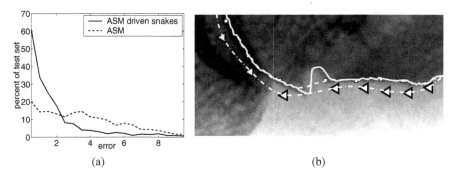

Fig. 6. (a) Error distribution orthogonal to the contour for landmarks found by ASM and ASM driven snakes. (b) Results: dash-dotted line: ASM search; solid line: ASM driven snake with high elasticity; dashed line: low elasticity.

Experimental Setup. Tests were performed on hand radiographs with and without erosive changes. The edge length of a pixel is $0.0846mm$. The ASMs were initialized randomly with varying initialization error. The performance of *ASM* and *ASM driven snakes* were evaluated with two ASM training sets T_{15} (15 training samples) and T_{30} (30 training samples). Each bone was represented by 42 landmarks. The test set consisted of 10 manually assigned shapes.

Results. The median joint position error achieved by the initializing LLM-nets on images with reduced resolution (10%) is $2.77mm$.

The ASM driven snakes decrease landmark position error only orthogonally to the contour. With T_{30} the median orthogonal landmark position error was reduced from originally 3.7 pixels to 1.33(36%) pixels by 3 suceeding snakes with increasing elasticity. In Fig. 5a true landmarks, landmarks found by an ASM and landmark positions improved by ASM driven snakes are depicted. The percentage of landmarks lying within a 3 pixel error corridor around the true shape was increased from 40% to 75%. Fig. 6a shows the distribution of landmark position errors orthogonal to the contour.

The median error of an ASM trained with T_{15} is 3.78 pixels, training with T_{30} decreased the error to 3.71 pixels, ASM driven snakes based on T_{15} achieve a median error of 1.45 pixels. Thus ASM driven snakes allow for reduction of training set size. Structures within the bone that have higher contrast than the actual bone contour can lead to a deterioration of accuracy. This can be overcome to some extend by increasing the size of the profiles $a_b(x)$ in Eq. 2. Fig. 5b shows the result of an ASM (dashed line) compared to the result with ASM driven snakes (solid line) on the joint region of a bone. The ASM driven snake adapts well to the erosion.

In Fig. 6b the result of an ASM search (dash-dotted line) and two snakes with different elasticity parameters (dashed and solid line) are depicted. Both perform equal on the healthy bone contour but differ at the erosion. Therefore, this method can be used for quantitative assessment of bone erosions. Preliminary experiments using a simple classifier on features derived from the ASM and the snakes show promising results.

4   Conclusion

A method to identify bone contours in radiographs by applying a combination of active shape models and active contours based on automated initialization by local linear mapping nets is introduced. The advantages of both methods i. e. robustness with respect to coarse initialization and high accuracy even on contours hard or impossible to model are preserved. The contour search is initialized by a local linear mapping net method that learns visual appearance as well as anatomical configuration of the hand during a training phase. The presented algorithm is generalizable to other anatomical structures. The work is of particular interest for the automated quantification of erosive destructions caused by rheumatoid arthritis. Future research will focus on the analysis of the derived contour description that makes direct feature extraction possible. An automated discrimination of pathological changes is work in progress and shows promising results.

References

1. F. J. Canny. A computational approach to edge detection. *IEEE Trans. Pattern Analysis Machine Intelligence*, 8(6):679–698, 1986.
2. Timothy F. Cootes, A. Hill, Christopher J. Taylor, and J. Haslam. The use of active shape models for locating structures in medical images. *Image and Vision Computing*, 12(6):355–366, 1994.
3. Timothy F. Cootes, C. J. Taylor, D. H. Cooper, and J. Graham. Training models of shape from sets of examples. In *Proc. British Machine Vision Conference*, pages 266–275, Berlin, 1992. Springer.
4. Daniel Cremers, Timo Kohlberger, and Christoph Schnorr. Nonlinear shape statistics in mumford-shah based segmentation. In *ECCV (2)*, pages 93–108, 2002.
5. G. Hamarneh and T. Gustavsson. Combining snakes and active shape models for segmenting the human left ventricle in echocardiographic images. *IEEE Computers in Cardiology*, 27:115 –118, 2000.
6. M. Kass, A. Witkin, and D. Terzopoulos. Snakes: Active contour models. *International Journal on Computer Vision*, 1:321–331, 1988.
7. Georg Langs, Horst Bischof, and Philipp L. Peloschek. Automatic quantification of destructive changes caused by rheumatoid arthritis. Technical Report PRIP-TR-79, Pattern Recognition and Image Processing Group, Vienna University of Technology, 2003.
8. Georg Langs, Philipp Peloschek, and Horst Bischof. Locating joints in hand radiographs. In *Proceedings of Computer Vision Winter Workshop CVWW*, pages 97–102, 2003.
9. Eugene T.Y. Lee. Choosing nodes in parametric curve interpolation. *Computer-Aided Design*, 21:363–370, 1989.
10. C. Noelker and H. Ritter. Detection of fingertips in human hand movement sequences. In *Proceedings of the International Gesture Workhop, LNCS1371*, pages 209–218, 1997.
11. T. Nopola, A. Järvi, E. Svedström, and O. Nevalainen. Segmenting bones from wristhand radiographs. Technical Report TUCS Technical Report No. 371, Turku Centre for Computer Science, 2000.
12. Désirée van der Heijde. Structural damage in rheumatoid arthritis as visualized through radiographs. *Arthritis Res*, 4(2):29–33, 2002.
13. Chenyang Xu and Jerry L. Prince. Snakes, shapes and gradient vector flow. *IEEE Transactions on image Processing*, 7(3):359–369, March 1998.

Solutions for Model-Based Analysis of Human Gait

Roman Calow, Bernd Michaelis, and Ayoub Al-Hamadi

Otto-von-Guericke University Magdeburg
Institute for Electronics, Signal Processing and Communications (IESK)
PO box 4120, D-39016 Magdeburg, Germany
Roman.Calow@E-Technik.uni-magdeburg.de

Abstract. The analysis-by-synthesis concept is applied in markerless human gait analysis. Human locomotion is approximated by means of adaptive tracking with a 3D model that moves in exactly the same manner as the subject in front of the cameras. This paper focuses on two particular problems: (1) the inverse mapping of pixels from the synthetic image back to the surface of the 3D model, and (2) the acquisition of initial values for automatic initialization of the 3D model for subsequent reliable tracking. Some interesting initialization constraints arise when the analysis-by-synthesis concept is applied in medical human gait analysis. The moving subject is segmented with an improved dual difference technique, which uses the gradient norms of real camera images. The most important assumption is that human gait is almost completely periodic. This allows a much more robust approach whereby the keyframe animation technique serves to synthesize artificial motion patterns using approximately correct joint angles.

1 Introduction

Medical gait analysis finds application in the diagnosis of many diseases. Gait analysis is also widely used in sports medicine. Simultaneously acquired frame sequences, taken with a series of calibrated cameras, contain useful information for motion analysis. Image analysis is still a very laborious task, but can be considerably automated by means of marker-based systems. However, the use of markers and other contacting devices has been criticized because of their impact on the motion patterns of subjects. A markerless system for automatic image processing would therefore be welcomed.

Much has been published on the topic of markerless gait analysis [1]. An actual development is remote person identification simply using statistical image information. Other approaches use a model to perform extensive search operations in state space. The model-based approach is often used to reconstruct the exact temporal behavior of the subject's body from the state variables $\mathbf{\Phi}(t)$ (translation and angle of joint) and other model parameters $\mathbf{A}$ (joint clearances, shape, etc.). $\mathbf{\Phi}(t)$ and $\mathbf{A}$ determine the concrete pictorial reproduction and the shape of the 3D human model [2] $M(\mathbf{\Phi}(t), \mathbf{A}, i)$. i is the index of a chosen point. Relevant medical values can be derived from the plot of $\mathbf{\Phi}(t)$. They can serve

B. Michaelis and G. Krell (Eds.): DAGM 2003, LNCS 2781, pp. 540–547, 2003.

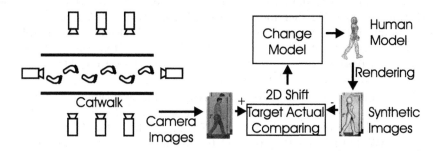

Fig. 1. Left: Acquisition with multiple cameras, right: analysis-by-synthesis loop [5]

as starting points for the calculation of forces and moments [3]. The model can be compared with the real person in 2D or 3D space. 2D images are generally easier to evaluate. In our experimental setup (similar Fig. 1), images from several cameras was used. For a camera c, the following nonlinear generic model is used.

$$p_c(t, i) = P_c(M(\mathbf{\Phi}(t), \mathbf{A}, i)) \tag{1}$$

Eq. (1) must be inverted by means of automatic linearization [4]. The images are processed with the analysis-by-synthesis iteration procedure as shown in Fig. 1. The procedure is described very well in [5], it can be used for point clouds and rendered surfaces. This procedure makes all 3D animation and computer graphics procedures [6][2] accessible for image processing [7] that have been developed up to the present time. Missing or incorrect model information represent discrepancies between synthetically generated images and real captured camera images. These deviations have to be minimized by iterative parameter adaptation of the model. This procedure is illustrated in a simplified control loop in Fig. 1. In gait analysis the deviations are mainly 2D shift vectors between camera image and synthetic image $p_c(t, i)$. The deviations may be evaluated in 3D scene space as well as in the 2D images. While the former is difficult, in the later only the 2D shift between camera image and synthetic image needs to be detected with a reliable method such as (Optical flow [8], Block matching [9], or other matching algorithms [10]).

2   Inverse Mapping Problem

How should the 2D shift vectors in the images be applied to the 3D model? The corresponding points $p_c(t, i)$ in the model have to be moved along the 2D shift vectors to their target points in the real camera image by changing $\mathbf{\Phi}(t)$. After model synthesis it is normally not clear (due to self-occlusion) which pixel in the synthetic image corresponds to which visible surface element in the 3D model.

The point i on the model surface, that can influence the position of the point in the image, is needed therefore for every 2D shift vector. In simple models the image points may be projected back onto the model. However, in complex 3D models with many mutually occluding surfaces, a choice must be made between a number of possible points, and visibility tests are necessary. These tests can be run with some extra analytic processing.

The z-buffer algorithm offers a relatively simple solution to the occlusion problem [6]. In occlusion situations only those image elements nearest to the observer will be rendered by the z-buffer algorithm. OpenGL(R) [11] with PFD_DRAW_TO_BITMAP were used to capture the synthetic images. Thus, the z-buffer algorithm can be applied for image analysis. The 3D model is typically only rendered once for the realistic photographic image while the visibility of each pixel is tested over a z-buffer.

The z-buffer may also be used for image analysis. The complete scene is rendered again without illumination and interpolation attributes, and every surface element is rendered this time with its unique color, or gray value. In this second scene image the origin of every pixel on the 3D model can be ascertained with the color of the pixel. In the simplest case each surface triangle is rendered with its own color. The first triangle with (R=0, G=0, B=1), for example, the second triangle with R=0, G=0, B=2), and so forth. We can thus represent 256*256*256=16777216 different surface elements with the three RGB colors. The rendered image therefore contains the indices for the surface elements. It is designated the index buffer (see Fig. 2). The coding of surface position is still quite inaccurate, because all pixels in a triangle, for instance, are of the same color. The vertices of a triangle lie in the same plane. We can compute the point of intersection between a plane and the pixel ray precisely by conventional means, albeit at a cost. We can obtain a good approximation by rendering the scene a third time. Rendering system interpolation is enabled this time and a characteristic color gradient with the three primary colors (red, green and blue) is assigned to each triangle. The result is the interpolation buffer. The color gradient of each triangle is given by the color value of its vertices V_1(R=255, G=0,B=0), V_2(R=0,G=255,B=0) and V_3(R=0,G=0,B=255). The same approach can be applied to lines. Besides the model primitives for every pixel in the synthetic

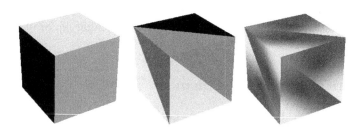

Fig. 2. Left: Cube in synthetic image, center: index buffer, right: interpolation buffer

image, the approximate position of the each pixel within the primitive (triangle, or line) can now be estimated: the sum of colors scanned (R,G,B) is normalized and used to interpolate the position within the triangle (see Fig. 2).

$$r = R/(R+G+B) \qquad g = G/(R+G+B) \qquad b = B/(R+G+B) \quad (2)$$

The three floating point numbers (r,g,b) can be used as interpolation coefficients. The 3D position $\boldsymbol{P}$ of the projected pixel is now determined by linear combination of the 3D coordinates of the three vertices $\boldsymbol{V}_1, \boldsymbol{V}_2, \boldsymbol{V}_3$.

$$\boldsymbol{P} = r \cdot \boldsymbol{V}_1 + g \cdot \boldsymbol{V}_2 + b \cdot \boldsymbol{V}_3 \quad (3)$$

The accuracy of the method is limited by the interpolation procedure. Triangles should be kept small, so that they only cover a few pixels in the image.

3   Initialization

Good starting points for the 3D model parameters and state variables are needed, because the relationships between these values and shift vectors in the image are nonlinear. Surface models of humans can be generated with commercial body scanners [12]: the parameters $\mathbf{A}$, fixed for a subject, are determined. Approximate values for the state variables $\boldsymbol{\Phi}(t)$ are required. As described in the literature the analysis of arbitrary motion is a complex task. To simplify motion analysis in clinical gait analysis the following assumptions are made:

1. The background of each camera remains stationary.
2. Only one test person moves in a restricted measurement envelope.
3. Only approximately periodic gait is measured.
4. The head of the subject is always upright and its appearance doesn't change.
5. The subject moves in his sagittal plane.

A hybrid top-down and bottom-up recognition strategy is possible with the 3D model. At first the moving subject is separated from the stationary background (bottom-up). There are only slight variations in the appearance of head and shoulder, so that this part of the body can be used to calculate the translation of the subject. The approximate 3D trajectory of the head may be calculated, if the head position in each time slice and every camera channel is known. Supposition 5 allows us to compute the approximate orientation of the subject from the trajectory. The translation of the subject in the images is compensated by resampling the images. This facilitates the reconstruction of the subject's leg motion. The position of the legs is an important feature for the reconstruction of the walking cycle. The system searches for keyframes showing the subject with maximum opening between legs. Model parameters for intermediate time slices are interpolated with the keyframe technique from computer animation [6]. It is assumed that there is a mean walking cycle $\bar{\boldsymbol{\Phi}}(t)$ that approximately represents many subjects. The model cycle, whose phase best fits the subject cycle phase, is synchronized now with the subject cycle (top down).

The subject is segmented by the gradient-dual-difference (GDD) algorithm, similar to the algorithm from [13]. With Eq. (4) a positive gradient norm G_t is computed from camera image I_t. The following applies to every pixel:

$$G_t = \sqrt{\left(\frac{dI_t}{dx}\right)^2 + \left(\frac{dI_t}{dy}\right)^2} \tag{4}$$

$$V_t' = (G_t - G_{t+1}) - (G_{t-1} - G_t) = -G_{t+1} - G_{t-1} + \underline{2 \cdot G_t} \tag{5}$$

$$V_t = Max(V_t', V_{thresh}) - V_{thresh} \tag{6}$$

Three successive frames and there processing path are shown in Fig. 3. In

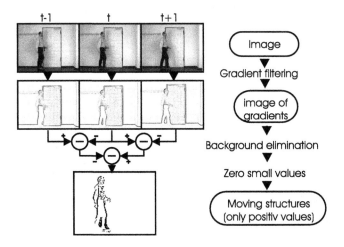

Fig. 3. Gradient-dual-difference (GDD) algorithm

contrast to the first algorithm [13], the gradient norms are processed first in every sequence time slice. The static gradient norms of the background will be eliminated by the first differences $(G_t - G_{t+1})$ and $(G_{t-1} - G_t)$. As shown in Eq. 5, V_t' is calculated with negative values of the dynamic gradient norms at time G_{t-1} and G_{t+1}. On the other hand, moving gradient norms of time G_t will be made double positive. Negatives and very small foreground edges V_t' are suppressed with a positive threshold V_{thresh}. Foreground moving gradient norms V_t are thus obtained.

Pixels $V_t(x, y)$ of the foreground edge images in time slice t form the basis for analysis of the head position. The mass $m_t(y)$ and the (line) center of gravity $s_t(y)$ of the foreground gradient norms are calculated now for each line y. x is the column of line and w the width.

$$m_t(y) = \sum_{x=0}^{w} V_t(x, y) \qquad s_t(y) = \frac{1}{m_t(y)} \sum_{x=0}^{w} V_t(x, y) \cdot x \tag{7}$$

The absolute values in the following are given for standard resolution frames (760 x 578). They may have to be adapted. Beginning at the top, the system checks whether the mass $m_t(y)$ of foreground edges in 50 successive lines exceeds a given threshold. If this is true for at least 45 out of 50 lines the head has probably been found and the search can be stopped. The average over the 45 centers of gravity is computed and results in a good approximation of the actual head position. The search also confirms the presence or absence of a subject in the checked frame. The search range can be restricted by reducing the number of lines and/or columns to prevent false interpretations. However, this procedure is too inaccurate to establish the translation of the subject, and it can only confirm that the center of gravity lies with the silhouette of the subject. Good approximate values for the search ranges of the known accurate matching techniques have been generated [8][9][10].

When the head positions are defined in all cameras, the head position in 3D space and in each time slice may be estimated using simple triangulation [14]. Assuming the subject walks in his sagittal plane, the approximate orientation of the subject can be computed from his 3D head trajectory. The front portion of the body model now points in the direction of motion. When the position and orientation of the subject have been defined, the camera showing the subject from the side can be selected from the set of cameras in use. This is the master camera. And it is primarily responsible for detecting the walking cycle.

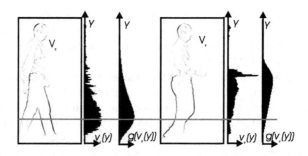

Fig. 4. Left: Time slice t=0 (double support phase); right: time slice t=9 (single leg stance) right of each image: unfiltered line variance $v_t(y)$, smoothed line variance

The phase position of the walking cycle is estimated now. The approach is similar to that in [15]. The task is complete, when the time slices in the sequence showing the subject with his legs open are known. Fig. 4 shows two foreground gradient images from the 'travelling' camera. On the left, a subject with open legs, and on the right with legs closed. A variance criterion $v_t(y)$ was calculated for each line y.

$$v_t(y) = \sum_{x=0}^{w} V_t(x,y) \cdot (x - m_t(y))^2 \tag{8}$$

The result and a smoothed version (Gauss filter) is shown on the left near each foreground gradient image in Fig. 4. The variance criterion for one image line (highlighted) is used to detect the walking phase. An approximately periodic

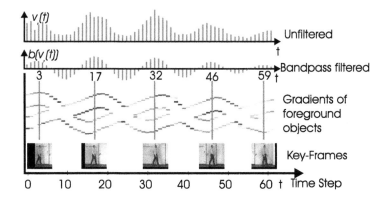

Fig. 5. Variance criterion of one line and extracted keyframes

signal is generated with respect to time, with some local maxima in the time slices where the subject opened his legs. Therefore, the signal is filtered with a band pass filter. To ensure no phase shift, filtering in the frequency domain is recommended [16]. The window for the Fast Fourier Transformation (FFT) should be at least twice as long as the frame sequence, otherwise the beginning and end of the sequence will influence each other. The pass band of the filter can be calculated with the minimum and maximum walk cycle frequencies. The keyframes are detected after back transformation to the spatial domain. The left leg is in front in every second maximum, the right leg in intermediate maxima. The key states of a typical gait pattern $\bar{\Phi}(t)$ are synchronized with the keyframes captured in this manner. Now the 'in-betweens' can be interpolated [6] and used as good initial values. Alternatively a 1D complex Gabor filter may be used to compute the local phase of gait in each time slice. This made interpolation very smart and simple. The resulting model moves with a typical gait pattern synchronized with the frame sequence. Finally, the precise amplitudes of the leg motion $\Phi(t)$ are determined, and model parameters $\mathbf{A}$ may be corrected if necessary. The analysis-by-synthesis concept is used for this purpose.

4   Conclusion

The analysis-by-synthesis concept seems to be suited for medical gait analysis. Widespread non-linearities and ambiguities due to occlusion make the application difficult. The system has to be correctly initialized and the inverse mapping problem effectively solved in order to reliably track typical gait. The proposed solution for inverse mapping using the z-buffer and additional rendering of individual patches with different colors gives good results and allows unique assignment. For the initialization of the given problem, one can assume that the sequences are repeated more or less periodically. The same apples to the state variables. Thus the one-off laborious solution for a 'standard gait' forms the basis of the approach. Period adaptation, determination of the relative starting time, and parameter scaling offer meaningful initial values for the state variables, and enable the linearized model to be used for tracking. For real world applications with more structured background some foreground gradients may be lost. Regardless a good result may be expected, the variance criterium with gaussian smoothing (vertical) and band pass filtering (in time) made initialization robust.

Acknowledgement. This work was supported by EU grant 0046KE0000, BMBF/LSA grant 0028IF0000 and grant BMBF 03i0404A.

References

1. Moeslund, T.B., Granum, E.: A Survey of Computer Vision-Based Human Motion Capture (2001), Computer Vision and Image Understanding: CVIU
2. Lander, J.: Over My Dead, Polygonal Body (October 1999), Game Developer Magazine, Source code Skeletal Deformation in OpenGL, http://www.darwin3d.com/gdm1999.htm
3. Winter, D. A.: Biomechanics and motor control of human movement (1990), Wiley-Interscience, USA
4. Wachter, S.: Verfolgung von Personen in monokularen Bildfolgen (1997), Vice Versa
5. Koch, R.: Dynamic 3D Scene Analysis through Synthesis Feedback Control (1993), IEEE Trans. Patt. Anal. Mach. Intell., analysis and synthesis, Vol. 15 (6) 556–568
6. Foley, D. J., v. Dam, A. v., Feiner, S. K., Hughes, J. F.: Computer Graphics: Principles and Practice (1997), Addison-Wesley
7. Stevens, M. R., Beveridge, J. R.: Integrating Graphics and Vision for Object Recognition (2001), Kluver Academic Publishers
8. Black, M. J.: The Robust Estimation of Multiple Motions: Parametric and Piecewise-Smooth Flow Fields (1996), Computer Vision and Image Understanding Vol. 63, No. 1, January 75–104
9. Mecke, R.: Grauwertbasierte Bewegungsschätzung in monokularen Bildsequenzen unter besonderer Berücksichtigung bildspezifischer Störungen (1999), Shaker Verlag
10. Thayananthan, A., Stenger, B., Torr, P.H.S., Cipolla, R.: Shape Context and Chamfer Matching in Cluttered Scenes, Proc. Conf. Computer Vision and Pattern Recognition, Madison, USA, June 2003
11. Shreiner, D.: OpenGL(R) Reference Manual, see first: http://www.opengl.org/
12. VITRONIC Dr.-Ing. Stein Bildverarbeitungssysteme: http://www.vitus.de/
13. Kameda, Y., Minoh, M.:A Human Motion Estimation Method using 3-successive video frames (1996), Proceedings of International Conference on Virtual Systems and Multimedia'96, 135–140
14. Luhmann, T.: Nahbereichsphotogrammetrie: Grundlagen, Methoden und Anwendungen (2000), Wichmann Verlag
15. Collins, R. T., Gross, R., Shi, J.: Silhouette-based Human Identification from Body Shape and Gait, (2002) Conference on Face and Gesture
16. Frigo, M., Johnson, S. G.: FFTW manual online, http://www.fftw.org/

Robust Hand–Eye Calibration of an Endoscopic Surgery Robot Using Dual Quaternions

Jochen Schmidt, Florian Vogt*, and Heinrich Niemann

Lehrstuhl für Mustererkennung, Universität Erlangen-Nürnberg
Martensstr. 3, 91058 Erlangen, Germany
{jschmidt,vogt,niemann}@informatik.uni-erlangen.de

Abstract. This paper presents an approach for applying a dual quaternion hand–eye calibration algorithm on an endoscopic surgery robot. Special focus is on robustness, since the error of position and orientation data provided by the robot can be large depending on the movement actually executed. Another inherent problem to all hand–eye calibration methods is that non–parallel rotation axes must be used; otherwise, the calibration will fail. Thus we propose a method for increasing the numerical stability by selecting an optimal set of relative movements from the recorded sequence. Experimental evaluation shows the error in the estimated transformation when using well–suited and ill–suited data. Additionally, we show how a RANSAC approach can be used for eliminating the erroneous robot data from the selected movements.

1 Introduction

In this paper we present an approach for the practical aspects in terms of robustness of hand–eye calibration using an endoscopic surgery robot. Especially, we address two problems: how to choose the data that is used in the calibration algorithm such that the numerical stability increases, and how to use a RANSAC approach for outlier detection and removal.

A common drawback of all hand–eye calibration algorithms, which is inherent to the problem itself, is that at least two motions are necessary where the rotations have non–parallel rotation axes. Consequently, numerical stability can be increased by selecting the data accordingly. Additionally, outlier detection and removal is essential, since the position and orientation data provided by the robot arm is unreliable when substantial changes in the direction of movement are executed. A RANSAC approach [6] is used for this purpose.

The application area is the reconstruction of high–quality medical light fields [12]. The hand–eye transformation has to be estimated every time when the camera head is mounted anew on the endoscope optics, which is done before each operation because it has to be sterilized. Therefore, an algorithm that works automatically and stably without human interaction is desirable.

A vast amount of literature is available on the topic of hand–eye calibration. The classical way is to solve for rotation first, and then for translation [9,11]. In [7] an

---

* This work was partially funded by the Deutsche Forschungsgemeinschaft (DFG) under grant SFB 603/TP B6. Only the authors are responsible for the content.

B. Michaelis and G. Krell (Eds.): DAGM 2003, LNCS 2781, pp. 548–556, 2003.

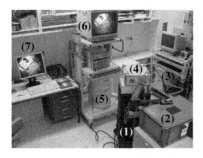

Fig. 1. Left: experimental setup. (1) AESOP 3000, (2) "patient", (3) camera head and endoscope, (4) light source, (5) computer, (6) video–endoscopic system (original image), (7) second monitor (computer image/light field). Right: original image as seen by the camera.

algorithm is proposed that solves for both simultaneously using nonlinear optimization, while Daniilidis [3,4] is the first who presented a linear algorithm for simultaneous computation of the hand–eye parameters. This was the main reason why we chose this algorithm as a basis for our work.

The paper is organized as follows: Sect. 2 describes the AESOP 3000 robot system as well as the method formerly used for estimating the unknown hand–eye transformation between robot plug and camera. In Sect. 3 we give a short introduction to hand–eye calibration methods, with special focus on the dual quaternion approach proposed by Daniilidis. How to make the hand–eye calibration robust enough for practical purposes is described in Sect. 4. Experimental results are given in Sect. 5.

2   The Robot System

We use the *Computer Motion Inc.* AESOP 3000 (cf. Fig. 1, left, no. (1)) endoscopic surgery robot. Images are grabbed directly from the endoscopic camera. The robot arm has seven degrees of freedom (one translational and six rotational), which are provided by the robot before and after each image is taken; the data is averaged for further processing. The complete experimental setup is shown in Fig. 1 (left). A calibration pattern is used to estimate the intrinsic camera parameters [10]. Radial and tangential lens–distortion coefficients are computed in order to undistort the (highly distorted) endoscopic images. Given these seven values, the position and orientation (pose) of the endoscope plug can be computed from the known kinematics, but not the pose of the tip of the endoscope. Up to now, the unknown transformation from plug to camera was estimated as follows: The distance from plug to endoscope–lens was measured by hand, while the orientation of the optics with respect to the plug was calculated in two steps. Since the camera head is not fixed at the endoscope optics but is mounted anew before each operation, the rotation between head and optics had to be computed. This was done by detecting a notch at the optics border (cf. Fig. 1, right). Usually a 30° optics is used, i.e. the angle had to be taken into account when computing the final transformation. Then the relative movement between two images using a calibration pattern was computed and the plug–angle was optimized such that the relative movement calculated by the kinematics equaled the real one. This method has some drawbacks: First of all, measuring by hand is arduous and inaccurate. Also, notch detection requires using additional low-level image processing methods instead of data already available and is only possible if an optics is used that actually has a notch, which is not the case for all endoscope optics. These drawbacks are eliminated by using a robust hand–eye calibration method as described in the following sections.

3   Hand–Eye Calibration

3.1   Overview

Given rigid displacements between the movements of a robot arm and the movements of a camera mounted on that arm, the unknown rigid transformation between arm and camera has to be computed, which is the same for all arm/camera movement pairs. This is known as hand–eye calibration. These circumstances are shown in the following commutative diagram; robot arm poses are denoted by A, camera poses by C at two time steps i and k. The unknown hand–eye transformation is denoted by R_{HE} and t_{HE}.

$$
\begin{array}{ccc}
A_k & \xrightarrow{R_{HE},t_{HE}} & C_k \\
{\scriptstyle R_{Aik},t_{Aik}} \uparrow & & \uparrow {\scriptstyle R_{Cik},t_{Cik}} \\
A_i & \xrightarrow{R_{HE},t_{HE}} & C_i
\end{array}
\tag{1}
$$

The hand–eye parameters R_{HE} and t_{HE} can be recovered from the following equation induced by the commutativity of diagram (1):

$$
\begin{pmatrix} R_{HE} & t_{HE} \\ 0_3^T & 1 \end{pmatrix} \begin{pmatrix} R_{Aik} & t_{Aik} \\ 0_3^T & 1 \end{pmatrix} = \begin{pmatrix} R_{Cik} & t_{Cik} \\ 0_3^T & 1 \end{pmatrix} \begin{pmatrix} R_{HE} & t_{HE} \\ 0_3^T & 1 \end{pmatrix}
\tag{2}
$$

which can be decomposed into two separate equations:

$$
R_{HE} R_{Aik} = R_{Cik} R_{HE}
\tag{3}
$$

$$
(I_3 - R_{Cik}) t_{HE} = t_{Cik} - R_{HE} t_{Aik}
\tag{4}
$$

These are the well–known hand–eye equations, which were first published in [9,11]. Numerous solutions for solving (3) and (4) have been proposed, e. g., [9,11,7,3]. The classical way is to first solve (3) for R_{HE}, and then (4) for t_{HE}. In [7] an algorithm is proposed that solves for R_{HE} and t_{HE} simultaneously using nonlinear optimization, while Daniilidis [3,4] is the first who presented a linear algorithm for simultaneous computation of the hand–eye parameters. Besides the well–founded theory and good performance, this was the main reason why we chose the dual quaternion algorithm for our application. Additionally, using this algorithm it is possible to show how numerical stability of hand–eye calibration in general is increased by selecting optimal relative movement pairs as described in Sect. 4.1. Therefore, we will now give a summary of the dual quaternion algorithm.

3.2   Dual Quaternions: A Unified Representation of Rotation and Translation

Quaternions. Quaternions are a commonly used representation for rotations in 3–D, hence we will not go into much detail here; for details see, e. g., [5,8].

A quaternion h is defined as $h = w + xi + yj + zk$ with $w, x, y, z \in \mathbb{R}$, where w is the real part and x, y, z are the imaginary parts. For the imaginary units, the following equation holds: $i^2 = j^2 = k^2 = ijk = -1$. Often a quaternion is written as a 4–D vector $h = (w, x, y, z)$ or $h = (w, v)$, where v is a 3–vector containing the imaginary parts. Just as the multiplication of two unit complex numbers defines a rotation in 2–D, a multiplication of two unit quaternions yields a rotation in 3–D. Let p be a 3–D point to be rotated, a a rotation axis with $|a| = 1$, and θ the angle of rotation around this axis. Define the following two quaternions:

$$h = \left(\cos \frac{\theta}{2}, \sin \frac{\theta}{2} \cdot a \right), \quad p' = (0, p) \quad . \tag{5}$$

Then

$$p'_{\text{rot}} = h p' \overline{h} \quad , \tag{6}$$

where p'_{rot} is the rotated point and $\overline{h}$ is the conjugate of h.

Dual Quaternions. As quaternions are a representation for 3–D rotations, dual quaternions treat rotations *and* translations in a unified way.

Dual Numbers Dual numbers were proposed by Clifford in the 19th century [2]. They are defined by $\hat{z} = a + \varepsilon b$, where $\varepsilon^2 = 0$. When using vectors for a and b instead of real numbers, the result is a dual vector.

Dual Quaternions A dual quaternion $\hat{h}$ is defined as a quaternion, where the real and imaginary parts are dual numbers instead of real ones, or equivalently as a dual vector where the dual and the non–dual part are quaternions: $\hat{h} = h + \varepsilon h'$. Just as unit quaternions represent rotations, unit dual quaternions contain rotation and translation [3]. In the dual quaternion representation of R and t, the non–dual part h is defined as in (5), and the dual part as

$$h' = \left(-\frac{t^T a}{2} \sin \frac{\theta}{2}, \frac{1}{2} \left(t \times (\sin \frac{\theta}{2} \cdot a) + \cos \frac{\theta}{2} \cdot t \right) \right) \quad . \tag{7}$$

Using the dual quaternion representation, the hand–eye calibration formulas (3) and (4) and can be written in a concise way, very similar to (6):

$$\hat{h}_c = \hat{h} \hat{h}_r \overline{\hat{h}} \quad , \tag{8}$$

where $\hat{h}_r$ encodes the movement of the robot arm and $\hat{h}_c$ the movement of the camera.

3.3   Algorithm

This section gives an overview over a linear algorithm for hand–eye calibration using dual quaternions presented by Daniilidis in [3,4]. Starting from (8) he derives a linear system of equations which has to be solved for h and h':

$$A \begin{pmatrix} h \\ h' \end{pmatrix} = 0 \quad . \tag{9}$$

Since each movement pair $(\hat{h}_r, \hat{h}_c)$ results in 6 equations, for n motions A is a $6n \times 8$ matrix having rank 6.

Note that at least two motions of the robot arm/camera *with different rotation axes* are necessary for reconstructing the rigid hand–eye transformation. This is a general result [1,11], i. e. it is not specific to the dual quaternion algorithm.

Solving (9) using Singular Value Decomposition (SVD) with $A = U \Sigma V^{\mathrm{T}}$ results in two zero singular values, or nearly zero singular values in the case of noisy data. The two–dimensional solution space is spanned by the column vectors v_7 and v_8 of V that correspond to the zero singular values, i. e. $\left(h \; h' \right)^{\mathrm{T}} = \lambda_1 v_7 + \lambda_2 v_8$. The two remaining unknowns λ_1 and λ_2 can be computed by using the additional constraint that $\hat{h}$ is a unit dual quaternion. The recovery of the actual hand–eye transformation, i. e. R_{HE} and t_{HE}, from $\hat{h}$ is easy: The rotation matrix can be computed directly from the non–dual part h of $\hat{h}$ (cf. e. g., [8]). The translation vector is given by $t_{\mathrm{HE}} = 2h'\overline{h}$ (cf. [3]).

4   Hand-Eye Calibration of an Endoscopic Surgery Robot

In this section we are going to describe how the numerical stability of hand–eye calibration can be increased by selecting robot/camera movement pairs in an optimal way. Additionally, elimination of outliers using a RANSAC approach is presented.

4.1   Selection of Movement Pairs for Increased Numerical Stability

For reconstructing the rigid transformation from robot arm to camera using hand–eye calibration, at least two motions with *different* rotation axes are necessary (cf. Sect. 3.3).

As probably in most applications, in endoscopic surgery, robot arm movements are usually continuous, which means that translation and rotation of neighboring frames are similar and the rotation axes are not very different. Hence it is usually suboptimal to process the arm/camera positions in their temporal order. It is much better to select the data such that relative movements are used for calibration that actually fulfill the requirement above. As an optimality criterion we propose to use the scalar product between the rotation axes of two camera movements. Let a_{ij} and a_{kl} be the normalized rotation axes of two relative movements from frame i to j and from k to l, respectively. Then

$$s_{ij,kl} = |a_{ij}^{\mathrm{T}} a_{kl}| \tag{10}$$

gives a value of one for parallel rotation axes and zero for orthogonal axes, where the latter are the ones that are suited best for hand–eye calibration. Note that camera and not robot arm data should be used at this point, since the camera was calibrated accurately using a calibration pattern, while the data provided by the robot is still corrupted by outliers and hence unreliable. Also, it is important for practical purposes, that the rotation axes of relative movements are well–defined. For small rotations, the axis changes its direction considerably, and two axes may be almost orthogonal even if the movement pair is ill–suited for hand–eye calibration. Therefore, we recommend a pre–selection of those relative movements, where the rotation matrix differs from identity. In our implementation, we use the rotation angle θ for pre–selection (cf. Sect. 5). An additional benefit of this step is that the amount of data for the following pairwise rating decreases and thus computation time as well.

Selection of the best pairs increases the numerical stability of the hand–eye calibration, which can be easily seen if we examine at the condition number of matrix A in (9). This matrix is of rank six if non–parallel axes are used, and of rank five if parallel axes are used. Now consider the ratio of the largest singular–value of A and the sixth singular–value: The system is ill–conditioned in the case of parallel axes (the condition number becomes infinite in the worst case), and the condition gets better (i. e. the sixth singular value is much greater than zero) if the axes are non-parallel.

If the goal is an optimal data set consisting of m movement pairs, the problem can be formulated as follows: Let C denote the set of all movement pairs possible; find a subset M of C such that the following criterion is minimized:

$$s_M = \sum_{(ij,kl)\in M} s_{ij,kl} \quad , \tag{11}$$

where s_M denotes the rating of M. Better pairs in the sense of low absolute ratings s_M lead to lower condition numbers and thus higher numerical stability. In general, this means that $s_{ij,kl}$ has to be computed for all possible movement pairs (but of course not necessarily be stored) in order to get the optimal subset M. Our experiments showed that this is actually possible if the number of frames is not too high; e. g., even for 100 frames and a pre–selection as described above, computation of the optimal subset takes only a few seconds on a state–of–the art PC. For n frames, the algorithm is of complexity $O(n^4)$: The total number of all relative movements is $n(n+1)/2$; if m movements are left after pre–selection, the total number of pairs is $m(m+1)/2$. For the worst case, i. e. $m = n(n+1)/2$, this results in $m(m+1)/2 = (n^4 + 2n^3 + 3n^2 + 2n)/8 = O(n^4)$.

4.2 Eliminating Outliers

The AESOP 3000 robot provides pose information, which is usually accurate (cf. Fig. 2). Nevertheless, experiments showed that in some cases, especially when the direction of movement changes substantially, pose information is very unreliable (note the peaks in Fig. 2). This is only a local problem, since the experiments also showed that the pose–error does not sum up during the movement of the arm. Thus it is necessary to detect the positions where those changes occur, so that they can be removed from the data used for hand–eye calibration. Possible methods for outlier elimination are:

 - Remove the positions where the changes in direction of translation of the robot arm are very high.
 - Follow an iterative approach and use all data in the first iteration; for the second iteration remove those positions that have very high errors when comparing the hand–eye transformed robot poses with the data from the calibrated endoscope.

Table 1. Mean error per frame for old method and hand–eye calibration, once with best movement pairs, once for pairs in temporal order. For the Euler angles, the error is given in degrees, for the rotation in norm of the difference quaternion, and for the translation in mm.

Method/Sequence	Euler x	Euler y	Euler z	Quaternion	Translation
ALF1, old method	0.289	0.279	0.246	0.00477	0.675
ALF1, hand–eye, best	0.219	0.386	0.245	0.00495	0.897
ALF1, hand–eye, temporal order	0.941	0.729	0.675	0.0135	10.7
ALF2, old method	0.259	0.264	0.352	0.00495	0.910
ALF2, hand–eye, best	0.218	0.272	0.288	0.00433	1.15
ALF2, hand–eye, temporal order	0.502	0.834	1.50	0.0161	10.85

– Apply a RANSAC [6] approach; use the same error measure as in the item above.

Since the most promising approach is the last one, we are going to describe now how to apply RANSAC for outlier removal:

1. Choose m random samples from the movement pairs selected as described in Sect. 4.1, where each sample consists of $e = 2$ movements, the minimum number required for hand–eye calibration.
2. For each sample i: Compute $R_{\mathrm{HE}i}, t_{\mathrm{HE}i}$.
3. Apply the hand–eye transformation to the robot arm poses and compute the error between the transformed arm poses and the calibrated camera poses for each relative movement. Determine the number of consistent pairs.
4. Keep the largest set of consistent pairs.
5. After all samples are evaluated: Re–compute $R_{\mathrm{HE}i}$ and $t_{\mathrm{HE}i}$ using *all* consistent pairs of the largest set.

The probability P that in at least one sample *all* e elements are inliers is given by $P = 1 - (1 - (1 - \epsilon)^e)^m$, where ϵ is the estimated outlier–rate. If this equation is solved for m we get the minimum number of samples that should be chosen. For $P = 0.99$, $e = 2$, and an estimated outlier–rate of $\epsilon = 20\%$ we get $m \approx 4.51$, i. e. at least 5 samples should be used.

5   Experiments

For evaluation of accuracy and robustness of the dual quaternion hand–eye calibration algorithm with the extensions for movement pair selection and outlier elimination, we present here the results on endoscopic image sequences with different movement paths. Instead of a real patient, a box with a hole for the endoscope that is inlaid with newspaper and printed OP–images of the abdomen was used. An example image (without calibration pattern) is shown in Fig. 1 (right).

Table 1 shows the errors for the two sequences *ALF1* (55 frames) and *ALF2* (100 frames) for the former method used, for the best movement pairs using the hand–eye method, and for the hand–eye algorithm where the relative movements were used in temporal order. The error per frame was computed between the actual endoscope poses

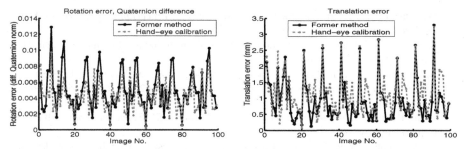

Fig. 2. Sequence *ALF2*. Left: Error in rotation measured in norm of the difference quaternion. Right: Error in translation measured in norm of the difference vector.

(from the calibration pattern) and the poses computed by applying the hand-eye transformation to the robot arm data. Comparison of the errors of the best pairs and pairs in temporal order shows impressively the influence of pair selection: When using the temporal order, the hand–eye algorithm fails; when using the best pairs, the error is comparable to the former method described in Sect. 2, but without its drawbacks, in particular completely automatically. Before the selection of pairs rated using (10), we pre–selected those relative movements, where the rotation angle θ was between $10°$ and $170°$ for sequence *ALF1*, and between $15°$ and $165°$ for *ALF2*. For *ALF1* we used 30% (absolute: 36531) of all possible pairs left after pre–selection, for *ALF2* 10% (absolute: 1720). Figure 2 depicts plots of the relative error in frame–to–frame movement for the *ALF2* sequence in rotation (measured in norm of the difference quaternion) and translation for the former non–automatic method described in Sect. 2 and for the robust hand–eye calibration method. Noticeable are the distinct peaks: These are exactly the frames where the robot position data is very erroneous, which is the case if the movement direction changes considerably. Remember also, that no nonlinear refinement was used yet, which would result in even better performance.

6   Conclusion

We presented an approach for selecting the relative robot/camera movements such that hand–eye calibration can be performed in a numerically stable way. Outlier removal is very important in our application as well, which is the use of an endoscopic surgery robot, since the robot position data is unreliable when movements such as substantial direction changes are executed. We showed how to use RANSAC to accomplish this goal. Although we applied a dual quaternion hand–eye calibration algorithm, these problems are not specific to it, but inherent to the hand–eye calibration problem itself. We showed experimentally the benefit of movement pair selection compared to the straightforward approach of using relative movements in temporal order.

References

1. H. Chen. A Screw Motion Approach to Uniqueness Analysis of Head–Eye Geometry. In *Proc. of CVPR*, pages 145–151, Maui, Hawaii, June 1991.

2. William Clifford. Preliminary Sketch of Bi–quaternions. *Proceedings of the London Mathematical Society*, 4:381–395, 1873.
3. K. Daniilidis. Hand-Eye Calibration Using Dual Quaternions. *International Journal of Robotics Research*, 18:286–298, 1999.
4. K. Daniilidis. Using the Algebra of Dual Quaternions for Motion Alignment. In G. Sommer, editor, *Geometric Computing with Clifford Algebras*, chapter 20, pages 489–500. Springer-Verlag, 2001.
5. Oliver Faugeras. *Three-Dimensional Computer Vision: A Geometric Viewpoint*. MIT Press, Cambridge, MA, 1993.
6. M. A. Fischler and R. C. Bolles. Random sample consensus: a paradigm for model fitting with applications to image analysis and automated cartography. *Communications of the ACM*, 24:381–385, 1981.
7. R. Horaud and F. Dornaika. Hand-Eye Calibration. *International Journal of Robotics Research*, 14(3):195–210, 1995.
8. J. Schmidt and H. Niemann. Using Quaternions for Parametrizing 3–D Rotations in Unconstrained Nonlinear Optimization. In *Vision, Modeling, and Visualization 2001*, pages 399–406, Stuttgart, Germany, November 2001. AKA/IOS Press, Berlin, Amsterdam.
9. Y. Shiu and S. Ahmad. Calibration of Wrist Mounted Robotic Sensors by Solving Homogeneous Transform Equations of the Form $AX = XB$. *IEEE Trans. on Robotics and Automation*, 5(1):16–29, February 1989.
10. R. Y. Tsai. A Versatile Camera Calibration Technique for High–Accuracy 3D Machine Vision Metrology Using Off–the–Shelf TV Cameras and Lenses. *IEEE Journal of Robotics and Automation*, RA–3(4):323–344, August 1987.
11. R. Y. Tsai and R. K. Lenz. A New Technique for Fully Autonomous and Efficient 3D Robotics Hand/Eye Calibration. *IEEE Trans. on Robotics and Automation*, 5(3):345–358, June 1989.
12. F. Vogt, S. Krüger, D. Paulus, H. Niemann, W. Hohenberger, and C. H. Schick. Endoskopische Lichtfelder mit einem kameraführenden Roboter. In *7. Workshop Bildverarbeitung für die Medizin*, pages 418–422, Erlangen, March 2003. Springer-Verlag.

Real-Time Recognition of 3D-Pointing Gestures for Human-Machine-Interaction

Kai Nickel and Rainer Stiefelhagen

Interactive Systems Laboratories
Universität Karlsruhe (TH), Germany
{nickel,stiefel}@ira.uka.de

Abstract. We present a system capable of visually detecting pointing gestures and estimating the 3D pointing direction in real-time. We use Hidden Markov Models (HMMs) trained on different phases of sample pointing gestures to detect the occurrence of a gesture. For estimating the pointing direction, we compare two approaches: 1) The line of sight between head and hand and 2) the forearm orientation. Input features for the HMMs are the 3D trajectories of the person's head and hands. They are extracted from image sequences provided by a stereo camera. In a person-independent test scenario, our system achieved a gesture detection rate of 88%. For 90% of the detected gestures, the correct pointing target (one out of eight objects) was identified.

1 Introduction

In the concept of multi modal user interfaces, users are able to communicate with computers using the very modality that best suits their current request. Apart from mouse or keyboard input, these modalities include speech, handwriting or gesture. Among the set of gestures intuitively performed by humans when communicating with each other, pointing gestures are especially interesting for applications like smart rooms, virtual reality or household robots. The detection of pointing gestures is particularly useful in combination with speech recognition, as they can help to resolve ambiguities and specify parameters of location in verbal statements ("Switch *that* light on!").

In this paper, a pointing gesture is defined as a movement of the arm towards a pointing target. This is why we chose the trajectory of the hand as input feature for the gesture models. Our system was designed to function in natural environments, to operate in real-time, and to be person- and target-independent. The system performs three tasks:

- color- and range-based tracking of head and hands to gain input features for the gesture models;
- classification of the trajectories by means of a combination of Hidden Markov Models (HMMs) in order to detect pointing gestures in natural movements;
- determination of the pointing direction.

B. Michaelis and G. Krell (Eds.): DAGM 2003, LNCS 2781, pp. 557–565, 2003.

1.1 Related Work

There are numerous approaches for the extraction of body features by means of one or more cameras. In [1], Wren et al. demonstrate the system *Pfinder*, that uses a statistical model of color and shape to obtain a 2D representation of head and hands. Azarbayejani and Pentland [2] describe a 3D head and hands tracking system that calibrates automatically from watching a moving person. An integrated person tracking approach based on color, dense stereo processing and face pattern detection is proposed by Darrell et al. in [3].

Hidden Markov Models have been used for years in continuous speech recognition [10], and have also been applied successfully to the field of gesture recognition. In [4], Starner and Pentland were able to recognize hand gestures out of the vocabulary of the *American Sign Language* with high accuracy. Becker [5] presents a system for the recognition of *T'ai Chi* gestures based on head and hand tracking. In [6], Wilson and Bobick propose an extension to the HMM framework, that addresses characteristics of parameterized gestures, such as pointing gestures. Jojic et al. [7] describe a method for estimating the pointing direction in dense disparity maps.

2 Tracking of Head and Hands

In our approach we combine stereoscopic range information and skin-color classification in order to achieve a robust tracking performance. The setup consists of a fixed-baseline stereo camera connected to a standard PC. A commercially available library (see [8]) calculates a dense disparity map made up of pixel-wise disparity values, and provides 3D coordinates for each pixel (Fig. 1b). A histogram-based model represents the distribution of human skin color in the chromatic color space. In order to initialize and maintain the model automatically, we search for a person's head in the disparity map of each frame. Following an approach proposed in [3], we first look for a human-sized connected region, and then check its topmost part for head-like dimensions. Pixels inside the head region contribute to the skin-color model.

a. Left camera image   b. Disparity map   c. Skin color map

Fig. 1. In the disparity map, the brightness of a pixel is associated with its distance to the camera. In the skin color map, dark pixels represent hight skin color probability.

In order to find potential *candidates* for the coordinates of head and hands, we search for connected regions in the morphologically filtered skin-color map. For each region, we calculate the centroid of the associated 3D pixels. If the pixels belonging to one region vary strongly with respect to their distance to the camera, the region is split by applying a k-means clustering method. We thereby separate objects that are situated on different range levels but accidentally merged into one object in the 2D image.

The task of tracking consists in finding a good hypothesis s_t for the positions of head and hands at time t. The decision is based on the current observation O_t (the 3D skin-pixel clusters) and the hypothesis for the preceding frame s_{t-1}. With each new frame, all combinations of the clusters' centroids are evaluated to find the hypothesis s_t that maximizes the product of the following 3 scores:

- The *observation score* $P(O_t|s_t)$ is a measure for the extent to which s_t matches the observation O_t. $P(O_t|s_t)$ increases with each pixel that complies with the hypothesis.
- The *posture score* $P(s_t)$ is the prior probability of the posture. It is high if the posture represented by s_t is a frequently occurring posture of a human body. To be able to calculate $P(s_t)$, a model of the human body was built from training data.
- The *transition score* $P(s_t|s_{t-1})$ is a measure for the probability of s_t being the successor of s_{t-1}. It is higher, the closer the positions of head and hands in s_t are to their positions in s_{t-1}.

Our experiments indicate that by using the method described, it is possible to track a person robustly, even when the camera is moving and when the background is cluttered. The tracking of the hands is affected by occasional dropouts and misclassifications. Reasons for this can be temporary occlusions of a hand, a high variance in the visual appearance of hands and the high speed with which people move their hands. Due to the automatic updates of the skin-color model, the system does not require manual initialization.

3 Detection of Pointing Gestures

When looking at a person performing pointing gestures, one can identify three different phases in the movement of the pointing hand:

- Begin (B): The hand moves from an arbitrary starting position towards the pointing target.
- Hold (H): The hand remains motionless at the pointing position.
- End (E): The hand moves away from the pointing position.

We examined pointing gestures performed by different persons, and measured the length of the separate phases. The average length of a pointing gesture was 1.8 sec. Among the three phases, the hold phase shows the highest duration variance (from 0.1sec up to 2.5sec).

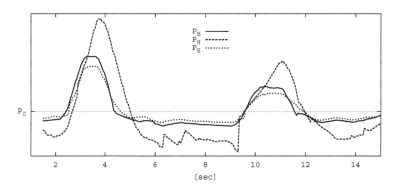

Fig. 2. Output probabilities of the phase-models during a sequence of two pointing gestures

For estimating the pointing direction, it is crucial to detect the hold phase precisely. Therefore, we model the three phases separately: Three dedicated HMMs (M_B, M_H, M_E) were trained exclusively on data belonging to their phase. We choose the same HMM topology (3 states, left-right) for each of the three models. For each state, a mixture of 2 Gaussian densities represents the output probability. To get a reference value for the output of the phase models, we train a *null model* M_0 on short feature sequences ($0.5sec$) which do *not* belong to a pointing gesture. For M_0, we choose an ergodic HMM with 3 states and 2 gaussians per state. The models were trained with hand-labeled BHE-phases using the Baum-Welch reestimation equations (see [10]).

3.1   Classification

As we want to detect pointing gestures on-line, we have to analyze the observation sequence each time a new frame has been processed. The length of the BHE-phases varies strongly from one gesture to another. Therefore, we classify not only one, but a series of subsequences $s_{1..n}$, each one starting at a different frame in the past and ending with the current frame t_0 (see also [5]). The lengths of the sequences are chosen to be within the minimum/maximum length of a pointing gesture. For each of the phase models, we search for the subsequence $\hat{s}_{B,H,E}$ that maximizes the probability of being produced by the respective model. As $P(\hat{s}|M_0)$ represents the probability, that $\hat{s}$ is *not* part of a pointing gesture, we use it to normalize the phase-models output probabilities:

$$\hat{s}_{B,H,E} = argmax\ logP(s_{1..n}|M_{B,H,E}) \tag{1}$$
$$P_{B,H,E} = logP(\hat{s}_{B,H,E}|M_{B,H,E}) - logP(\hat{s}_{B,H,E}|M_0)$$

In order to detect a pointing gesture, we have to search for three subsequent time intervals that exhibit high output probabilities P_B, P_H and P_E. Ideally, the respective model would significantly dominate the other two models in its

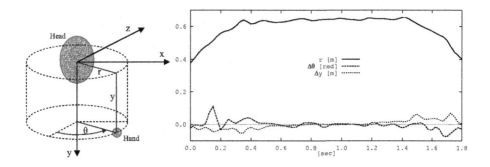

Fig. 3. The hand position is transformed into a cylindrical coordinate system. The plot shows the feature sequence of a typical pointing gesture.

interval. But as Fig. 2 shows, M_H tends to dominate the other models in the course of a gesture. That is why we detect a pointing gesture whenever we find three points in time, $t_B < t_H < t_E$, so that

$$P_E(t_E) > P_B(t_E) \wedge P_E(t_E) > 0 \qquad (2)$$
$$P_B(t_B) > P_E(t_B) \wedge P_B(t_B) > 0$$
$$P_H(t_H) > 0$$

3.2 Features

We evaluated different transformations of the feature vector, including carte-sian, spherical and cylindrical coordinates[1]. In our experiments it turned out that cylindrical coordinates of the hands (see Fig. 3) produce the best results for the pointing task. The radius r represents the distance between hand and body, which is an important feature for pointing gesture detection. Unlike its counter-part in spherical coordinates, r is independent of the hand's height y. The origin of the coordinate system is set to the center of the head, to achieve invariance with respect to the person's location. Since we want to prevent the model from adapting to absolute hand positions – as these are determined by the specific pointing targets within the training set – we use the *deltas* (velocities) of θ and y instead of their absolute values. The final feature vector is $(r, \Delta\theta, \Delta y)$.

3.3 Estimation of the Pointing Direction

We explored two different approaches to estimate the direction of a pointing gesture: 1) the line of sight between head and hand and 2) the orientation of the forearm. The estimate of the pointing direction is based on the mean value of

---

[1] See [11] for a comparison of different feature vector transformations for gesture recognition.

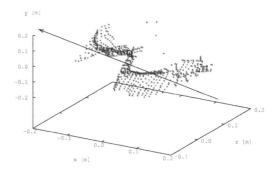

Fig. 4. The first principal component (depicted by an arrow) of the 3D-pixel cloud around the hand is used as an estimate for the forearm orientation.

the head and hand measurements (resp. forearm measurements) within the hold phase of the respective gesture.

In order to identify the orientation of the forearm, we calculate the covariance matrix C of the 3D-pixels within a 20cm radius around the center of the hand. The eigenvector v^1 with the largest eigenvalue (first principal component) of C denotes the direction of the largest variance of the data set. As the forearm is an elongated object, we expect v^1 to be a measure for the direction of the forearm (see Fig. 4). This approach assumes that no other objects are present within the critical radius around the hand, as those would influence the shape of the point set[2].

4   Experiments and Results

In order to evaluate the performance of our system, we prepared an indoor test scenario with 8 different pointing targets (see Fig. 5). Ten test persons were asked to imagine the camera was a household robot. They were to move around within the camera's field of view, every now and then showing the camera one of the marked objects by pointing on it. In total, we captured 206 pointing gestures within a period of 24 min.

4.1   Pointing Direction

The head-hand line and the forearm line were evaluated on hand-labeled H-phases in order to avoid errors caused by the gesture detection module. Nevertheless, an error was induced by the stereo vision system as the camera's coordinates did not comply perfectly with the manual measurements of the target positions. Table 1 summarizes the results. The good results of the head-hand

---

[2] We found that in the hold phase, this pre-condition is satisfied, as the distance between hand and body and between hand and target object is generally sufficient.

Table 1. Accuracy of the pointing direction: a) average angle between the extracted pointing line and the ideal line between hand and target, b) the percentage of gestures for which the correct target (1 out of 8) was identified.

	Avg. error angle	Target identified
Head-hand line	14.8°	99.1%
Forearm line	42.8°	69.6%

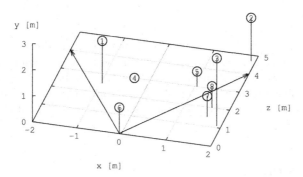

Fig. 5. Positions of the 8 targets in the test scenario. The minimum distance between two targets was 50cm. The arrows depict the camera's field of view.

line indicate that most people in our test set intuitively relied on the head-hand line (and not the forearm line) when pointing on a target. The test persons were pointing with an outstretched arm almost every time, thus reducing the potential benefit even of a more accurate forearm measurement[3].

4.2   Gesture Detection

Two measures were used to determine the quality of the gesture detection:

- the detection rate (*recall*) is the percentage of pointing gestures detected correctly,
- the *precision* of the gesture detection is the ratio of the number of correctly detected gestures to the total number of detected gestures (including false positives).

We performed the evaluation with the *leave-one-out* method to make sure that the models were evaluated on sequences that were not used for training. Here, we measured the quality of the extracted pointing direction using the head-hand line on automatically detected H-phases. See Table 2 for the results.

While the detection rate is similar in both cases (88%), the person-dependent test set has a lower number of false positives compared to the person-independent

---

[3] Unlike the relatively stable head position, the forearm measurements vary strongly during the H-phase.

K. Nickel and R. Stiefelhagen

Table 2. Evaluation of the quality of pointing gesture detection. The person-independent results are the average results on ten subjects. For the person-dependent case, average results on three subjects are given (see text for details).

	Detection rate (Recall)	Precision	Avg. error angle	Target identified
person-dependent	88.2%	89.3%	12.6°	97.1%
person-independent	87.6%	75.0%	20.9°	89.7%

test set, resulting in a higher classification accuracy. In addition, the estimation of the pointing direction is more accurate in the person-dependent case, so that 97% of the targets were identified correctly. This indicates that it is easier to locate the H-phase correctly when the models are trained individually for each subject. However, even in the person-independent case, 90% of the targets were identified correctly.

5 Conclusion

We have demonstrated a real-time[4] 3D vision system which is able to track a person's head and hands robustly, detect pointing gestures, and to estimate the pointing direction. By using dedicated HMMs for different gesture phases, high detection rates were achieved even on defective trajectories. In an evaluation, our system achieved a gesture detection rate of 88%. For 90% (97% person-dependent) of the gestures, the correct pointing target could be identified. For estimating the pointing direction, we compared the line of sight between head and hands and the forearm orientation. With an average error of 14.8°, the head-hand line turned out to be a good estimate for the pointing direction.

Acknowledgements. We would like to thank Christian Fuegen for insightful discussions on the use of HMMs. Also thanks to everybody who participated in our data collection. This research is partially supported by the German Research Foundation (DFG) as part of the Sonderforschungsbereich 588 "Humanoide Roboter".

References

1. Wren, C., Azarbayejani, A., Darrell, T., Pentland, A.: Pfinder: Real-Time Tracking of the Human Body. IEEE Transaction on Pattern Analysis and Machine Intelligence, Vol. 19, No. 7, 1997.
2. Azarbayejani, A., Pentland, A.: Real-time self-calibrating stereo person tracking using 3-D shape estimation from blob features. Proceedings of 13th ICPR, 1996.

---

[4] The system runs at 10-15 FPS on a 2.4GHz Pentium PC.

3. Darrell, T., Gordon, G., Harville, M., Woodfill, J.: Integrated person tracking using stereo, color, and pattern detection. IEEE Conference on Computer Vision and Pattern Recognition, Santa Barbara, CA, 1998.
4. Starner, T., Pentland, A.: Visual Recognition of American Sign Language Using Hidden Markov Models. M.I.T. Media Laboratory, Perceptual Computing Section, Cambridge MA, USA, 1994.
5. Becker, D.A.: Sensei: A Real-Time Recognition, Feedback and Training System for T'ai Chi Gestures. M.I.T. Media Lab Perceptual Computing Group Technical Report No. 426, 1997.
6. Wilson, A.D., Bobick A.F.: Recognition and Interpretation of Parametric Gesture. Intl. Conference on Computer Vision ICCV, 329–336, 1998.
7. Jojic, N., Brumitt, B., Meyers, B., Harris, S., Huang, T.: Detection and Estimation of Pointing Gestures in Dense Disparity Maps. IEEE International Conference on Automatic Face and Gesture Recognition, Grenoble, France, 2000.
8. Konolige, K.: Small Vision Systems: Hardware and Implementation. Eighth International Symposium on Robotics Research, Hayama, Japan, 1997.
9. Yang, J., Lu, W., Waibel, A.: Skin-color modeling and adaption. Technical Report of School of Computer Science, CMU, CMU-CS-97-146, 1997.
10. Rabiner, L.R.: A Tutorial on Hidden Markov Models and Selected Applications in Speech Recognition. Proc. IEEE, 77 (2), 257–286, 1989.
11. Campbell, L.W., Becker, D.A., Azarbayejani, A., Bobick, A.F., Pentland, A.: Invariant features for 3-D gesture recognition. Second International Workshop on Face and Gesture Recognition, Killington VT, 1996.

Pose Estimation of Cylindrical Fragments for Semi-automatic Bone Fracture Reduction

S. Winkelbach [1], R. Westphal[1], and T. Goesling [2]

[1] Institute for Robotics and Process Control, Technical University of Braunschweig,
Muehlenpfordtstr. 23, 38106 Braunschweig, Germany
`{s.winkelach, r.westphal}@tu-bs.de`
`http://www.cs.tu-bs.de/rob/`

[2] Department of Trauma Surgery, Hannover Medical School,
Carl-Neuberg-Str. 1, 30625 Hannover, Germany
`goesling.thomas@mh-hannover.de`

Abstract. We present an approach for estimating the relative transformations between fragments of a broken cylindrical structure in 3d. To solve this problem, we first measure the orientation and position of the cylinder axes for each fragment by an adapted kind of Hough Transformation. The cylinder axes are an important feature for separation of fractured areas and for calculation of an initial reposition solution (constraining 4 DOFs). After these processing steps, we compute the relative transformations between corresponding fragments by using well-known surface registration techniques, like 2d depths correlation and the ICP (Iterative Closest Point) algorithm. One goal of our project is to use the proposed method for estimation of relative transformations between fragments of fractured long bones for computer aided and semi-automatic bone alignment and fracture reduction in surgery.

1 Introduction and Related Work

Axis detection and registration of fragments of a broken cylinder has an important field of application in computer aided and semi-automatic bone alignment and fracture reduction in surgery. A usual kind of therapy is the adjustment of femur fragments by closed medullary nailing. Apart from many advantages, like avoiding additional surgical trauma to the already traumatized area, this minimally invasive method has the disadvantage, that it often results in an imprecise reposition. This frequently leads to physiological stress, dysfunction, premature joint deterioration and pain. One goal of our project is the avoidance of these complications by utilizing a force-torque controlled robot with haptical feedback for the semi-automatic alignment and reduction of femoral shaft fractures. Before the robot-assisted surgery can take place, it is important to determine the reposition parameters in a preoperative planning step. Especially the final positions of the bone fragments must be computed as precise as possible and with preferably as few as possible interventions of the surgeon. This complex registration problem makes it necessary to develop and apply several image

B. Michaelis and G. Krell (Eds.): DAGM 2003, LNCS 2781, pp. 566–573, 2003.
© Springer-Verlag Berlin Heidelberg 2003

processing techniques and make up a complex processing chain. In addition, to all intents and the purpose outlined above, these techniques are also important and useful in many other applications.

Our approach can be divided into two parts: First, analysing cylindrical structures and detecting their cylinder axes by an adapted kind of Hough transformation and simultaneous detection of fractured surfaces. And second, solve the '3d-puzzle-problem' by pairwise matching the fragments to estimate their relative transformations. Detection of cylindrical and tubular structures in 3d-data (range data in most cases) is a frequently treated problem in computer vision and medical imaging. One possibility is to fit cylinder models to a set of points and minimize an error function e.g. [1]. Other approaches take advantage of the fact, that cylindrical surface normals lie on a circle in a gaussian sphere representation [2,3]. In [4] segmentation of tubular structures is achieved by using an randomized Hough transformation for high dimensional parameter spaces, combined with a Kalmann filter. This approach tries to segment generalized cylinders with an elliptical cross section and a free-form curve.

The second challenge is to reconstruct the structure by matching their broken fragments. This reassembling problem has been addressed rarely in literature. Publication [5] solves this problem without using any features or information about the final model. This takes place by searching a relative pose of one fragment with a minimal distance to an other one in an 7 DOF search space. However, by distinguishing between fracture surface and intact cylinder surface we can use well-known surface registration techniques like range data correlation e.g.[6] or the Iterative-Closest-Point algorithm (ICP) introduced in [7]. An interesting comparison of different efficient ICP variants is given in [8].

2 System Overview

2.1 Data Acquisition and Fragment Extraction

Due to the fact that the main application of our method was 'bone alignment', we solely consider 3d computer tomography volumes as input data, but the method certainly is applicable to many other data types as well. At first we segment and label the relevant fragments of the fractured bone. After that, a sub-voxel accurate reconstruction of the bone surface takes place by using the well-known marching cube algorithm [9]. This algorithm produces a closed triangle mesh of the fragment surfaces, which will be processed in the following.

2.2 Cylinder Axes and Fracture Surface Recognition

For estimating the axes of cylindrical structures in 3d, we use a two step Hough-like voting mechanism.

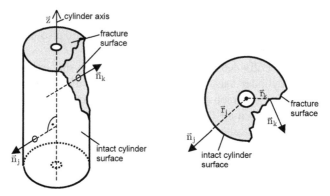

Fig. 1. (*Left*): Schematic view of a fragmented cylinder. Normals $\vec{n}_j$ of intact surface vertices are perpendicular to the cylinder axis $\vec{z}$ ($\vec{n}\perp\vec{z}$ - criterion). (*right*):Upper view of the same scene. Normals $\vec{n}_j$ of intact surface vertices are collinear to their radius-vectors $\vec{r}_j$ ($\vec{n}\parallel\vec{r}$ - criterion).

2.2.1 Detecting Cylinder Axis Orientation

The first step is based on the fact, that all normals $\vec{n}_i$ of an intact cylindrical surface are perpendicular to the cylinder axis (herein after called $\vec{n}\perp\vec{z}$ - criterion; see Fig. 1 *left*). For each surface normal $\vec{n}_i$ we accumulate the orientation of all perpendicular vectors $\{\vec{a} \mid \vec{a} \perp \vec{n}_i\}$ in an 2d accumulation buffer A. Spherical coordinates (φ,θ) of $\vec{a}$ are used as buffer indices.

$$A(\varphi,\theta) = \sum_i A_i(\varphi,\theta) \qquad\qquad ; \; \varphi,\theta \in \{0°...180°\} \qquad (1)$$

$$A_i(\varphi,\theta) = \begin{cases} 1 \text{ if } \vec{a}(\varphi,\theta) \perp \vec{n}_i \\ 0 \text{ else} \end{cases} \quad \text{with} \quad \vec{a}(\varphi,\theta) = \begin{pmatrix} \sin\theta \cdot \cos\varphi \\ \sin\theta \cdot \sin\varphi \\ \cos\theta \end{pmatrix} \qquad (2)$$

By this, cylindrical surfaces are forming clusters (local maxima) in A and the coordinates of a cluster specify the orientation of the requested cylinder axis.

Certainly, this mathematical definition is unsuitable for an efficient implementation. Therefore we use the following iterative algorithm:

1.   initialize the accumulation buffer $A(\varphi,\theta)$ with 0

2.   for every vertex with surface normal $\vec{n}_i = \left(n_{i,x}, \quad n_{i,y}, \quad n_{i,z}\right)$

      for every $\varphi \in \{0°...180°\}$

$$\theta := \arctan\frac{-n_{i,z}}{n_{i,x}\cos(\varphi) + n_{i,y}\sin(\varphi)}$$

$$A(\varphi,\theta) := A(\varphi,\theta) + 1$$

3.   find the most voted cluster (global maximum (φ_m,θ_m)) in A
    $\Rightarrow$ direction vector of cylinder axis $\vec{z} = \vec{a}(\varphi_m,\theta_m)$

In our experiments we use a buffer size of 180 x 180. This method turned out to be very robust against noise; it is also applicable if the cross section of the cylinder is not a circle. In other words we can detect the axis orientation of a subset of the generalized cylinder class, where the extrusion path is a straight line and the extruded curve remains almost constant over the path (like long bone shafts).

2.2.2 Identifying Fractured Areas

After calculating the orientation of the cylinder axis, it is possible to identify and mark vertices of major fractured areas by verifying the $\vec{n} \perp \vec{z}$ - criterion. Certainly we accept slight deviations regarding real noisy data. The only exception to this identification rule are fractured areas running parallel to the axis.

2.2.3 Detecting Cylinder Axis Origin

The second step is based on the fact that all normals $\vec{n}_i$ of an intact cylindrical surface are collinear to their radius-vectors $\vec{r}_i$ (herein after called $\vec{n} \| \vec{r}$ - criterion; see Fig. 1 *right*). This holds under the assumption, that the cylinder cross section is a real circle. In non-circular cases it might be better to use the center of mass. The following algorithm assumes, that all fragments are already aligned axially, whereas the cylinder axes are oriented in z-direction.

For each vertex $v_i = (v_{i,x}, v_{i,y}, v_{i,z})$ with surface normal $n_i = (n_{i,x}, n_{i,y}, n_{i,z})$ we accumulate the projection of a line containing v_i and $v_i + n_i$ to an image plane B which is perpendicular to the cylinder axis.

$$B(x,y) = \sum_i B_i(x,y) \quad ; x \in \{x_{min}...x_{max}\}; y \in \{y_{min}...y_{max}\} \tag{3}$$

$$B_i(x,y) = \begin{cases} 1 \text{ if } \begin{pmatrix} v_{i,x} - x \\ v_{i,y} - y \end{pmatrix} \| \begin{pmatrix} n_{i,x} \\ n_{i,y} \end{pmatrix} \\ 0 \text{ else} \end{cases} \tag{4}$$

Iterative algorithm:
1. initialize the accumulation buffer $B(x,y)$ with 0
2. for every vertex $\vec{v}_i$ with normal $\vec{n}_i$

$$\text{add a line with origin } \begin{pmatrix} v_{i,x} \\ v_{i,y} \end{pmatrix} \text{ and direction } \begin{pmatrix} n_{i,x} \\ n_{i,y} \end{pmatrix} \text{ to } B(x,y)$$

3. find the most voted cluster (global maximum (x_m, y_m)) in B

$$\Rightarrow \text{ origin of the cylinder axis } \vec{p} = (x_m, y_m, 0)$$

In our experiments a buffer size of 200 x 200 turned out to be sufficient.

2.2.4 Identifying Further Fractured Areas

Now the most remaining unidentified fractured areas can by located by testing the $\vec{n} \| \vec{r}$ - criterion for each vertex. By checking both criteria, more than 90% of fractured areas are detectable in general. Remaining undetected fractured areas have the same alignment like a potential cylinder surface. They only could be found by using additional features, like the cylinder radius or local surface smoothness. But we omit these additional tests, because we want to allow a slight diameter variation along the cylinder axis and we want to be almost robust against smoothness-degrading noise.

2.3 Surface Registration

After the processing steps described above, all fragments can be aligned axial and matched pairwise by registrating their fracture surfaces. A correctly determined cylinder axis constrains 4 DOFs of the relative transformation between each pair. Relative rotation around and translation along the cylinder axis are still unknown. To estimate the rotation we use a special kind of image correlation: For each pair, we generate two orthographic Z-buffers (resp. range maps) Z_1, Z_2 with size M x N of the fractured surfaces, whereas the image plane is perpendicular to the cylinder axis. By pre-transforming all vertices to polar coordinate space, a rotation around the cylinder axis correspond to a shift in φ -direction (see Fig. 2).

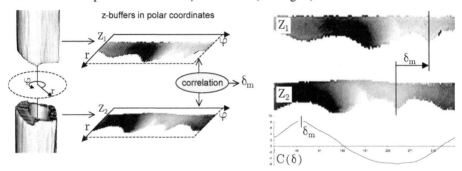

Fig. 2. (*Left*): Schematic view of fragment matching by z-buffer correlation. (*right*): Z-buffers Z_1, Z_2 in polar coordinates of both bone fragments and their correlation function $C(\delta)$

This enables us to find a rotation with the best match by searching the maximum of the periodic cross correlation between both z-buffers.

The standard unnormalized 2d cross correlation of two images A, B with mean values μ_a, μ_b is defined as

$$C(u,v) = \sum_{y=0}^{M} \sum_{x=0}^{N} (A(x,y) - \mu_a) \cdot (B(x - u, y - v) - \mu_b)$$ (5)

This simple form is not suitable for our problem, because we only want to allow image shift in one direction and furthermore we have to consider invalid pixels without underlying surface. Regarding this, we use the following modified 1d correlation function, which only calculates the correlation of overlapping valid image regions

$$C(\delta) = \sum_{r=0}^{M} \sum_{\varphi=0}^{N} (Z_1(\varphi,r) - \mu_1(\delta)) \cdot (Z_2(\varphi - \delta,r) - \mu_2(\delta)) \cdot m(\varphi,r,\delta)$$ (6)

with a binary function $m(\varphi,r,\delta)$, which indicates overlapping valid regions

$$m(\varphi,r,\delta) = \begin{cases} 1 \text{ if } Z_1(\varphi,r) \text{ and } Z_2(\varphi - \delta, r) \text{ are object pixels} \\ 0 \text{ if } Z_1(\varphi,r) \text{ or } Z_2(\varphi - \delta, r) \text{ is a background pixel} \end{cases} \qquad (7)$$

and δ-dependent mean values

$$\mu_n(\delta) = \frac{1}{\sum_{r=0}^{M}\sum_{\varphi=0}^{N} m(\varphi,r,\delta)} \cdot \sum_{r=0}^{M}\sum_{\varphi=0}^{N} Z_n(\varphi,r) \cdot m(\varphi,r,\delta) \qquad (8)$$

The maximum of $C(\delta)$ yields the rotation with the best match with the exception of some special cases where a lower local maximum is the proper one. Therefore we store the relative transformations of all possible matches in a table and verify them in a final stage. It is easy to determine the last unknown relative translation along the cylinder axis by calculating the contact distance.

This z-buffer correlation results in a satisfying matching for most common fractures; but the accuracy is heavily dependent on the precision of the axis. Therefore we use these results just as initial pose for a subsequent ICP matching [7] in order to improve the accuracy. It turned out, that the unmodified ICP algorithm, as well as the suggested variants of [8], often fail to find the correct solution and worsens the results in many cases. To avoid this problem, we slightly modify the algorithm by appending an additional axis-constraint, which inhibits the fragment to rotate far out of axially parallel alignment.

3 Experimental Results

For experimental evaluation we applied our approach to CT scans of real human femur fractures as well as to artificial femurs and plastic cylindrical models from [11] with diverse types of simple, wedge and complex fractures. Analysis of accuracy in the case of real femurs is only feasible by comparing the computed reposition results with virtual manual repositions of the reconstructed bone fragment surfaces.

The accuracy of the whole processing chain (fragment segmentation, surface reconstruction, axis estimation and surface registration) affects the total reposition precision and must be considered.

The first row of Fig. 3 shows a broken human femur shaft with a simple fracture in its accidental pose (a1); after axis alignment with segmented fractured areas (a2); and the reposition result (a3). About 99% of fractured areas are identified properly and the estimated fragment axes show an angular deviation of less than one degree. The graphs (a4) and (a5) visualize the accumulation buffers of our axis orientation and origin detection algorithm. As can be seen, the fragment surfaces form conspicuous clusters. The noise in (a5) is raised due to the non-circular cross section of the femur; thus detection of the cylinder origin might be less robust. The second and third row of

Fig. 3 illustrate fracture detection, axis estimation and matching results of two broken cylindrical bone models.

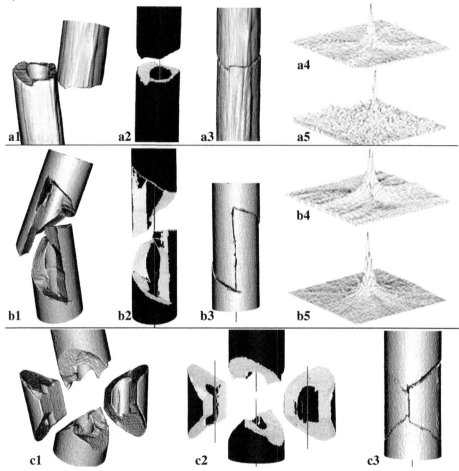

Fig. 3. (*a*) Real human femur with simple fracture; (*b*) Cylindrical bone model with a spiral fracture; (*c*) Cylindrical bone model with a complex fracture; (*a1-c1*) accidental pose; (*a2-c2*) axial aligned fragments and segmented fractured areas; (*a3-c3*) matching result; (*a4,b4*) cluster for axis orientation of the lower fragment; (*a5,b5*) cluster for axis origin of the lower fragment

In a nutshell, our approach yields an accuracy of about one degree of angular deviation in simple cases, and even for the majority of complex fractured cases it achieves an accuracy of below four degrees of angular deviation. Under most conditions the translational error is far less than the transversal CT slice distance. This holds under the premise, that all significant bone fragments, which connect both bone endings, yield enough 'analysable' surface for reposition. See [12] for additional results and a demonstration of our reposition software.

4 Conclusions

It turned out, that our approach for estimating the relative transformations between fragments of a fractured long bone is a very robust and accurate tool for computer aided and semi-automatic bone alignment and fracture reduction in surgery. The method is even applicable, if the femurs of both legs are broken; methods using mirror symmetrical relations [10] are useless in these cases. Moreover, we achieve a better reposition precision and fracture reduction by considering the whole fragment surface, than simple landmark based methods do. The next step is to transfer the reposition parameters to a robot system which will take over the task of exact repositioning and stable retention. Due to this, we expect better reposition results, a reduction of radiation exposure of surgeons, and a reduction of surgery time and cost. Extensive promising studies in collaboration with medical partners for this kind of robot assisted fracture reduction already have been completed and are subject of further publications.

References

1. Faber, P., Fisher, B.: A Buyer's Guide to Euclidean Elliptical Cylindrical and Conical Surface Fitting. In: Proc. 12th BMVC, Manchester, UK (2001), pp. 521–530
2. Hebert, M., Ponce, J.: A New Method for Segmenting 3-D Scenes into Primitives. In: ICPR, IEEE 6th Int. Conf. on Pattern Recognition, Vol. 2, (1982), pp 836–838
3. Chaperon, T., Goulette, F.: Extracting cylinders in full 3D data using a random sampling method and the Gaussian image. Workshop Vision, Modeling, and Visualization 2001, Stuttgart, Germany (2001)
4. Behrens, B., Rohr, K., Stiehl, H. S.: Using an Extended Hough Transformation Combined with a Kalmann Filter to Segment Tubular Structures in 3D Medical Images. Workshop Vision, Modeling, and Visualization 2001, Stuttgart, Germany (2001)
5. Papaioannou, G., Karabassi, E.-A., Theoharis: T., Reconstruction of Three-Dimensional Objects through Matching of Their Parts. IEEE Transact. on PAMI, Vol. 24, No. 1, (2002)
6. Benjemaa, R., Schmitt, F.: Fast Global Registration of 3D Sampled Surfaces Using a Multi-Z-Buffer Technique. In: Proc. IEEE Int. Conf. on Recent Advances in 3D Digital Imaging and Modeling, Ottawa, Canada (1997), pp. 113–120
7. Besl, P. J., McKay, N. D.: A Method for Registration of 3-D Shapes. IEEE Transact. on PAMI, Vol. 14, No. 2, (1992), pp. 239–256
8. Rusinkiewicz, S., Levoy, M.: Efficient Variants of the ICP Algorithm. In: Proc. IEEE Int. Conf. on Recent Advances in 3D Digital Imaging and Modeling, Québec City, Canada (2001), pp. 145–152
9. W.E. Lorensen, H.E. Cline, Marching cubes: A high resolution 3D surface construction algorithm, Computer Graphics 21:4 (1987), pp. 163–169.
10. Ron, O., Joskowicz, L., Simkin, A., Milgrom, C.: Computer-Based Periaxial Rotation Measurement for Aligning Fractured Femur Fragments. 4th International Conference on Medical Image Computing and Computer-Assisted Intervention. Utrecht, The Netherlands (2001)
11. Synbone AG, Clavadelerstrasse, 7270 Davos, Switzerland, http:\\www.synbone.ch
12. Project overview and video demonstration: http://www.cs.tu-bs.de/rob/femur.html

Pose Estimation of Free-Form Surface Models

Bodo Rosenhahn, Christian Perwass, and Gerald Sommer

Institut für Informatik und Praktische Mathematik
Christian-Albrechts-Universität zu Kiel
Olshausenstr. 40, 24098 Kiel, Germany
{bro,chp,gs}@ks.informatik.uni-kiel.de

Abstract. In this article we discuss the 2D-3D pose estimation problem of 3D free-form surface models. In our scenario we observe free-form surface models in an image of a calibrated camera. Pose estimation means to estimate the relative position and orientation of the 3D object to the reference camera system. The object itself is modelled as a two-parametric surface model which is represented by Fourier descriptors. It enables a low-pass description of the surface model, which is advantageously applied to the pose problem. To achieve the combination of such a signal-based model within the geometry of the pose scenario, the conformal geometric algebra is used and applied.

1 Introduction

Pose estimation itself is one of the oldest computer vision problems. It is crucial for many computer and robot vision tasks. The problem is finding a rigid motion, which fits object models with image data. One main question is, how to represent objects, and the wide variety of literature deals with different entities concerning simple point or line correspondences up to general free-form contours. Pioneering work was done in the 80's and 90's by Lowe [7], Grimson [6] and others. These authors use point correspondences. More abstract entities can be found in [17,2]. In the literature we find circles, cylinders, kinematic chains or other multi-part curved objects as entities. Works concerning free-form curves can be found in [4,15]. Contour point sets, affine snakes, or active contours are used for visual servoing in these works. A free-form surface model can be represented for example as parametric form, implicit surface, superquadric, etc. An overview of free-form representations can e.g. be found in [3], though the focus of this work is on object recognition and not on pose estimation.

Pose estimation means to estimate the relative position and orientation of a 3D object to a reference camera system: We assume a 3D object model and the extracted silhouette of the object in an image of a calibrated camera. The aim is to find the rotation R and translation t of the object, which leads to the best fit of the reference model with the extracted silhouette. To relate 2D image information to 3D entities we interpret a point on the 2D silhouette as a projection ray in space, gained through projective reconstruction from the image point. This idea will be used to formulate the pose estimation problem in a 3D scenario. Our recent work concentrates on modeling objects by using features of

B. Michaelis and G. Krell (Eds.): DAGM 2003, LNCS 2781, pp. 574–581, 2003.

the object [12] (e.g. corners, edges, kinematic chains) and on modeling objects by using free-form contour models [11]. Instead, we now deal with 3D free-form surface models of objects. This is the next step of generalization of our existing algorithms and leads to the possibility of modeling more natural objects.

2   The Pose Problem in Conformal Geometric Algebra

This section concerns the formalization of the free-form pose estimation problem in conformal geometric algebra. Geometric algebras are the language we use for the pose problem and the main argument for choosing this language is its possibility of coupling projective, kinematic and Euclidean geometry by using a conformal model. Besides, it enables a coordinate-free and dense symbolic representation. In this work we will only present basic principles of geometric algebras to give an idea of the rich properties of geometric algebras. A more detailed introduction to geometric algebras can be found in [13,14].

The main idea of geometric algebras $\mathcal{G}$ is to define a product on basis vectors which extends a linear vector space V of dimension n to a linear space of dimension 2^n with rich subspace structure. The elements are so-called multivectors as higher order algebraic entities in comparison to vectors of a vector space as first order entities. A geometric algebra is denoted as $\mathcal{G}_{p,q}$ with $n = p + q$. Here p and q indicate the numbers of basis vectors which square to $+1$ and -1, respectively. The product defining a geometric algebra is called *geometric product* and is denoted by juxtaposition, e.g. uv for two multivectors u and v. Operations between multivectors can be expressed by special products, called *inner* ·, *outer* ∧, *commutator* × and *anticommutator* $\overline{\times}$ product. The idea behind conformal geometry is to interpret points as *stereographically projected* points. This means augmenting the dimension of space by one. The method used in a stereographic projection is visualized for the 1D case in the left image of figure 1: Points x on the line e_1 are mapped to points x' on the unit circle by intersecting the line

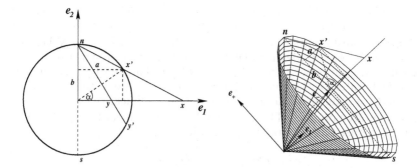

Fig. 1. Left: Visualization of a stereographic projection for the 1D case: Points on the line e_1 are projected on the (unit) circle and vice versa. Right: Visualization of the homogeneous model for a stereographic projection in the 1D case. All stereographic projected points are on a cone, which is a null cone in the Minkowski space.

spanned by the *north pole* n and x with the circle. The basic formulas for projecting points in space on the hypersphere and vice versa are for example given in [10]. Using a homogeneous model for stereographic projected points means to augment the coordinate system by a further additional coordinate whose unit vector now squares to minus one. In 1D this leads to a cone in space, which is visualized in the right image of figure 1. This cone is spanned by the original coordinate system, an augmented dimension for the stereographic projection and an homogeneous dimension. This space is chosen to have a Minkowski metric and leads to a representation of any Euclidean point on a null cone (1D case) or a null hypercone (3D case). In [14] it is further shown that the conformal group of $\mathbb{R}^n$ is isomorphic to the Lorentz group of $\mathbb{R}^{n+1,1}$ which has a spinor representation in $\mathcal{G}_{n+1,1}$. We will take advantage of both properties of the constructed embedding which are the representation of points as null-vectors and the spinor representation of the conformal group.

The conformal geometric algebra $\mathcal{G}_{4,1}$ (CGA) [8,13] is suited to describe conformal geometry. The point at infinity, $\mathbf{e} \simeq n$, and the origin, $\mathbf{e}_0 \simeq s$, are special elements of the representation which are used as basis vectors instead of $\mathbf{e}_+$ and $\mathbf{e}_-$ because they define a null space in the conformal geometric algebra. A Euclidean point $x \in \mathbb{R}^3$ can be represented as a point $\underline{x}$ on the null cone by taking $\underline{x} = x + \frac{1}{2}x^2\mathbf{e} + \mathbf{e}_0$. The multivector concepts of geometric algebras then allow to define entities like points, lines, planes, circles or spheres. Rotations are represented by rotors, $\mathbf{R} = \exp\left(-\frac{\theta}{2}l\right)$. The parameter of a rotor $\mathbf{R}$ is the rotation angle θ applied to a unit bivector l which represents the dual of the rotation axis. The rotation of an entity can be performed by its spinor product $\underline{X}' = \mathbf{R}\underline{X}\widetilde{\mathbf{R}}$. The multivector $\widetilde{\mathbf{R}}$ denotes the reverse of $\mathbf{R}$. A translation t can be expressed in a similar manner with a translator, $\mathbf{T} = \exp\left(\frac{\mathbf{e}t}{2}\right)$. A rigid body motion can be expressed as a screw motion [9]. The motor $\mathbf{M}$ describing a screw motion has the general form $\mathbf{M} = \exp(-\frac{\theta}{2}(n + \mathbf{e}m))$, with a unit bivector n and an arbitrary 3D vector m. The pair $(\theta n, \theta m)$ in the exponential term is also called a *twist* [2].

Constraint equations for pose estimation

Now we start to express the 2D-3D pose estimation problem for pure point correspondences: *a transformed object point has to lie on a projection ray, reconstructed from an image point.* Let $\underline{X}$ be a 3D object point given in CGA. The (unknown) transformation of the point can be described as $\mathbf{M}\underline{X}\widetilde{\mathbf{M}}$. Let x be an image point on a projective plane. The projective reconstruction of an image point in CGA can be written as $\underline{L}_x = \mathbf{e} \wedge \mathbf{O} \wedge x$. The line $\underline{L}_x$ is calculated from the optical center $\mathbf{O}$, the image point x and the vector $\mathbf{e}$ as the point at infinity. The line $\underline{L}_x$ is given in a Plücker representation. Collinearity can be described by the commutator product. Thus, the 2D-3D pose problem for a point $\underline{X} \in \mathbb{R}^{4,1}$ can be formalized as constraint equation in CGA,

$$(\mathbf{M}\underline{X}\widetilde{\mathbf{M}}) \times (\mathbf{e} \wedge \mathbf{O} \wedge x) = 0.$$

Constraint equations which relate 2D image lines to 3D object points or 2D image lines to 3D object lines can be expressed in a similar manner. Note: The constraint equations in the unknown motor $\mathbf{M}$ express a distance measure which has to be zero. The minimization of that distance leads to estimates of the pose.

Fourier descriptors in CGA

Fourier descriptors are often used for object recognition [5] and affine pose estimation [1] of closed contours. We are now concerned with the formalization of

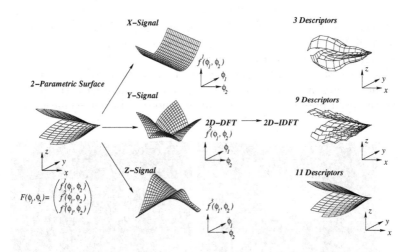

Fig. 2. Visualization of surface modeling and approximation by using three 2D Fourier descriptors.

3D Fourier descriptors in CGA. We assume a two-parametric surface of the form

$$F(\phi_1, \phi_2) = \sum_{i=1}^{3} f^i(\phi_1, \phi_2) \mathbf{e}_i.$$

This means, we have three 2D functions $f^i(\phi_1, \phi_2) : \mathbb{R}^2 \to \mathbb{R}$ acting on the different base vectors $\mathbf{e}_i$. For a discrete number of sampled points, $f^i_{n_1, n_2}$, ($n_1 \in [-N_1, N_1]; n_2 \in [-N_2, N_2]; N_1, N_2 \in \mathbb{N}$) on the surface, we can now interpolate the surface by using a 2D discrete Fourier transform (2D-DFT) and then apply an inverse 2D discrete Fourier transform (2D-IDFT). The surface can therefore be approximated as a series expansion

$$F(\phi_1, \phi_2) \simeq \sum_{i=1}^{3} \sum_{k_1=-N_1}^{N_1} \sum_{k_2=-N_2}^{N_2} \mathbf{p}^i_{k_1,k_2} \exp\left(\frac{2\pi k_1 \phi_1}{2N_1+1} \mathbf{l}_i\right) \exp\left(\frac{2\pi k_2 \phi_2}{2N_2+1} \mathbf{l}_i\right)$$

$$= \sum_{i=1}^{3} \sum_{k_1=-N_1}^{N_1} \sum_{k_2=-N_2}^{N_2} \mathbf{R}^{k_1,\phi_1}_{1,i} \mathbf{R}^{k_2,\phi_2}_{2,i} \mathbf{p}^i_{k_1,k_2} \widetilde{\mathbf{R}^{k_2,\phi_2}_{2,i}} \widetilde{\mathbf{R}^{k_1,\phi_1}_{1,i}}.$$

Here we have replaced the imaginary unit $i = \sqrt{-1}$ with three different rotation axes, represented by the bivectors $\mathbf{l}_i$, with $\mathbf{l}_i^2 = -1$. The complex Fourier series coefficients are contained in the vectors $\mathbf{p}^i_{k_1,k_2}$ that lie in the plane spanned by $\mathbf{l}_i$. We will call them phase vectors. These vectors can be obtained by a 2D-DFT of the sample points $f^i_{n_1,n_2}$ on the surface,

$$\boldsymbol{p}^i_{k_1,k_2} = \frac{1}{(2N_1+1)(2N_2+1)}$$

$$\sum_{n_1=-N_1}^{N_1} \sum_{n_2=-N_2}^{N_2} f^i_{n_1,n_2} \exp\left(-\frac{2\pi k_1 n_1}{2N_1+1} l_i\right) \exp\left(-\frac{2\pi k_2 n_2}{2N_2+1} l_i\right) \mathbf{e}_i.$$

This is visualized in figure 2: a two-parametric surface can be interpolated and approximated by using the estimated 2D Fourier descriptors.

Pose estimation of free-form surfaces

So far we have introduced the basic constraint equations for pose estimation and the surface representation of objects. We now continue with the algorithm for silhouette based pose estimation of surface models. In our scenario, we assume

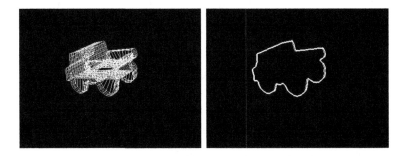

Fig. 3. Left: The projected surface model on a virtual image. Right: The estimated 3D silhouette of the surface model, back projected in an image.

to have extracted the silhouette of an object in an image. To compare points on the image silhouette with the surface model, the idea is to work with those points on the surface model which lie on the outline of a 2D projection of the object. This means we work with the 3D silhouette of the surface model with respect to the camera. To obtain this, the idea is to project the whole surface on a virtual image. Then the contour is calculated and from the image contour the 3D silhouette of the surface model is reconstructed. This is visualized in figure 3. The contour model is then used within our contour based pose estimation algorithm [11]. We are applying an ICP-algorithm [16]. Since the aspects of the surface model are changing during the ICP-cycles, a new silhouette will be estimated after each cycle to deal with occlusions within the surface model.

Solving a set of constraint equations for a free-form contour with respect to the unknown motor $\boldsymbol{M}$ is a non-trivial task, since a motor corresponds to a polynomial of infinite degree. In [12] we presented a method which does not estimate the rigid body motion on the Lie group $SE(3)$, but the parameters which generate their Lie algebra $se(3)$, comparable to the ideas, presented in [2]. This means we linearize and iterate the equations. It corresponds to a gradient descent method in the 3D space. The algorithm for pose estimation of surface models is summarized in figure 4.

Surface based pose estimation
```
 ┌   Reconstruct projection rays from image points
 │ ╱ Project low-pass object model in virtual image
 │╱  Estimate 3D silhouette
 │
```
Apply contour based pose estimation algorithm
```
    ┌   ╱ Estimate nearest point of each ray to the 3D contour
    ┤ ᴘᴄᴵ Use the correspondence set to estimate contour pose
    └   ╲ Transform contour model
   ╲ Transform surface model
 └   Increase the low-pass approximation of the surface model
```

Fig. 4. The algorithm for pose estimation of surface models.

3   Experiments

Figure 5 shows different approximation levels of the surface model of a car. The approximations are achieved by using not all phase vectors of the surface model, but a subset leading to a low-pass description of the surface model. The object model itself consists of $69 \times 21 \approx 1450$ 3D points. In 3D it has a height, width and depth of $11cm \times 21cm \times 10cm$ and is used for the experiments in figures 6 and 7.   The convergence behavior of the algorithm is shown in figure 6. As

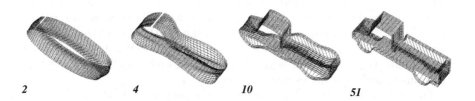

2   4   10   51

Fig. 5. Different approximation levels of the surface model. In the examples, 2, 4, 10 and 51 Fourier descriptors are used.

Table 1. Time performance of the implemented modules. Note, the 2D-DFT and the 2D-IDFT are calculated once at the beginning of the image sequence.

Module	Time (ms)	Module	Time (ms)	Module	Time (ms)
2D-DFT	700ms	Image processing	12 ms	ICP-cycle	50 ms
2D-IDFT	12ms - 700 ms	3D silhouette	20 ms		

can be seen, we refine the pose results by using a low-pass approximation of the surface and by adding successively higher frequencies during the iteration. This is basically a multi-resolution method and helps to avoid getting stuck in local minima during the iteration.

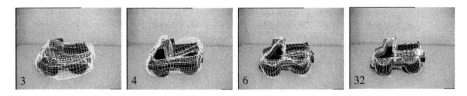

Fig. 6. Pose results of the low-pass contours during the ICP cycle.

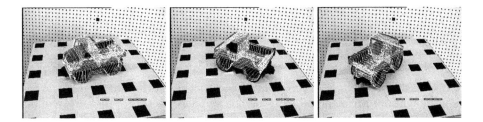

Fig. 7. Different pose results of the object model.

Figure 7 shows different pose results obtained with our algorithm. Note, that our algorithms are even able to deal with non-homogeneous background and with camera noise. We implemented the sources in C++. The computing time of the different involved modules is summarized in table 1. These values are obtained with a Linux 2GHz machine. As can be seen, the 2D-DFT and 2D-IDFT are the bottleneck for the time performance. Therefore, the 2D-DFT and the 2D-IDFT is only estimated once at the beginning of the algorithm and the data is copied and transformed with the estimated rigid motion.

The overall computing times vary with the number of ICP-cycles and is for this object model around 400 ms for each image. We tested the algorithm on different image sequences containing up to 600 images.

4 Discussion

In this work we present a novel approach for free-form surface pose estimation. Free-form surfaces are modelled by three 2D Fourier descriptors and low-pass information is used for approximation. The estimated 3D silhouette is then combined with the pose estimation constraints. The coupling of geometry with signal theory is achieved by using the conformal geometric algebra. In this language we are able to fuse concepts, like complex numbers, Plücker lines, twists, Lie algebras and Lie groups in a compact manner. The experiments show the basic properties of the algorithm and future work will concentrate on collecting more experiences with this approach, making stability experiments, etc.

Acknowledgements. This work has been supported by DFG Graduiertenkolleg No. 357 and by EC Grant IST-2001-3422 (VISATEC).

References

1. Arbter K. and Burkhardt H. Ein Fourier-Verfahren zur Bestimmung von Merkmalen und Schätzung der Lageparameter ebener Raumkurven. *Informationstechnik*, Vol. 33, No. 1, pp. 19–26, 1991.
2. Bregler C. and Malik J. Tracking people with twists and exponential maps. *IEEE Computer Society Conference on Computer Vision and Pattern Recognition*, Santa Barbara, California, pp. 8–15 1998.
3. Campbell R.J. and Flynn P.J. A survey of free-form object representation and recognition techniques. *Computer Vision and Image Understanding (CVIU)*, No. 81, pp. 166–210, 2001.
4. Drummond T. and Cipolla R. Real-time tracking of multiple articulated structures in multiple views. In *6th European Conference on Computer Vision, ECCV 2000, Dubline, Ireland*, Part II, pp. 20–36, 2000.
5. Granlund G. Fourier preprocessing for hand print character recognition. *IEEE Transactions on Computers*, Vol. 21, pp. 195–201, 1972.
6. Grimson W. E. L. Object Recognition by Computer. *The MIT Press, Cambridge, MA*, 1990.
7. Lowe D.G. Solving for the parameters of object models from image descriptions. In *Proc. ARPA Image Understanding Workshop*, pp. 121–127, 1980.
8. Li H., Hestenes D. and Rockwood A. Generalized homogeneous coordinates for computational geometry. In [14], pp. 27–52, 2001.
9. Murray R.M., Li Z. and Sastry S.S. A Mathematical Introduction to Robotic Manipulation. *CRC Press*, 1994.
10. Needham T. Visual Complex Analysis. *Oxford University Press*, 1997
11. Rosenhahn B., Perwass Ch. and Sommer G. Pose estimation of 3D free-form contours in conformal geometry In *Proceedings of Image and Vision Computing (IVCNZ) D. Kenwright (Ed.)*, New Zealand, pp. 29–34, 2002.
12. Rosenhahn B. and Sommer G. Adaptive Pose Estimation for Different Corresponding Entities. In *Pattern Recognition, 24th DAGM Symposium, L. Van Gool (Ed.)*, Springer-Verlag, Berling Heidelberg, LNCS 2449, pp. 265–273, 2002.
13. Rosenhahn B. and Sommer G. Pose Estimation in Conformal Geometric Algebra Part I: The stratification of mathematical spaces. Part II: Real-Time pose estimation using extended feature concepts. *Technical Report 0206*, University Kiel, 2002.
14. Sommer G., editor. Geometric Computing with Clifford Algebra. *Springer Verlag*, 2001.
15. Stark K. A method for tracking the pose of known 3D objects based on an active contour model. *Technical Report TUD / FI 96 10*, TU Dresden, 1996.
16. Zang Z. Iterative point matching for registration of free-form curves and surfaces. *IJCV: International Journal of Computer Vision*, Vol. 13, No. 2, pp. 119–152, 1999.
17. Zerroug, M. and Nevatia, R. Pose estimation of multi-part curved objects. *Image Understanding Workshop (IUW)*, pp. 831–835, 1996

IR Pedestrian Detection for Advanced Driver Assistance Systems

M. Bertozzi[1], A. Broggi[1], M. Carletti[1], A. Fascioli[1], T. Graf[2], P. Grisleri[1], and M. Meinecke[2]

[1] Dipartimento di Ingegneria dell'Informazione
Università di Parma – Parma, I-43100, ITALY
{bertozzi,broggi,fascal,grisleri}@ce.unipr.it
[2] Electronic Research
Volkswagen AG – Wolfsburg, D-38436, GERMANY
{thorsten.graf,marc-michael.meinecke}@volkswagen.de

Abstract. This paper describes a system for pedestrian detection in infrared images implemented and tested on an experimental vehicle. A specific stabilization procedure is applied after image acquisition and before processing to cope with vehicle movements affecting the camera calibration. The localization of pedestrians is based on the search for warm symmetrical objects with specific size and aspect ratio. A set of filters is used to reduce false detections. The final validation process relies on the human shape's morphological characteristics.

1 Introduction

The capability of observing the world through visual information is a strong requirement for future driver assistance systems since their dues are getting more complex. Especially, driver assistance systems dedicated to reduce the number of fatalities and severities of traffic accidents impose several requirements on the sensorial system. One of the major and challenging tasks is the detection and classification of pedestrians.

Naturally, the use of visual cameras is a promising approach to cope with the demands of pedestrian detection. Several different image processing methods and systems have been developed in the last years, including shape-based methods [5, 6], texture- and template-based methods [7, 8], stereo [9], as well as motion clues [10, 11]. All these methods have to overcome the difficulties of different appearances of pedestrians in the visual domain caused mainly by e.g. clothes and illumination changes.

In order to facilitate the recognition process and to enable the detection of pedestrian in dark environments passive infrared (*IR*) cameras have come into focus [3]. Some first pedestrian detection systems [1, 2] for IR images and videos have been developed demonstrating the potential and benefits that IR cameras can provide.

In this paper we present a new pedestrian detection method employing IR cameras. This method can be divided into the following steps: (*i*) pitch angle compensation, (*ii*) localization of warm symmetrical objects with specific size and aspect ratio, (*iii*) refinement process utilizing an additional set of filters to decrease the number of false positives, and (*iv*) final validation based on human shape morphological characteristics to build the list of pedestrians appearing in the scene. Although the proposed method

B. Michaelis and G. Krell (Eds.): DAGM 2003, LNCS 2781, pp. 582–590, 2003.

exploits only single images and performs no tracking, experimental results demonstrate the robustness and stability of the proposed method.

In the following section considerations on the IR domain are provided; section 3 presents the problem analysis and design choices; section 4 describes the approach and algorithm; finally section 5 discusses the results and concludes the paper with some final consideration.

2   Characterization of IR Domain

Images in the IR domain convey a type of information very different from images in the visible spectrum. In the IR domain the image of an object relates to its temperature and the amount of heat it emits but is not affected by illumination changes.

Generally, the temperature of people is higher than the environmental temperature and their heat radiation is sufficiently high compared to the background. Therefore, in IR images pedestrians are bright and sufficiently contrasted with respect to the background, thus making IR imagery suited to their localization. Other objects which actively radiate heat (cars, trucks...) have a similar behavior; however people can be recognized thanks to their shape and aspect ratio.

One major point in favor of IR cameras is the independency to lighting changes: IR cameras can be used in day-time or night-time with no or little difference extending vision beyond the usual limitations of day-light cameras. Moreover, the absence of colors or strong textures eases the processing towards interpretation. Furthermore, the problem of shadows is greatly reduced.

Nevertheless, the problem of detecting humans in IR images is far from being trivial.

Conditions of high temperature or strong sun heating can decrease the temperature's differential in the scene modifying the thermal footprint of bodies. In addition, in case of strong external heat radiation, clothes that people wear can have different thermal behavior depending on their type and color, thus introducing textures to the image.

Conversely, in case of low external temperature, clothes can significantly shield the heat emission and only parts of the body can be perceivable. Another problem, even if less critical than in the visible domain, is represented by objects carried by people.

The problems mentioned above make the detection of pedestrians harder. Nevertheless, the IR domain seems to be promising and justifies deep investigation.

3   Problem Analysis and Design Choices

Two issues have to be defined when designing the system: the *setup of the vision system*, considering physical and aesthetical automotive requirements and the *target*, i. e. the desired range of pedestrians' height and width. Moreover, the algorithm has to be designed considering that the input data are low resolution digital images.

Setup of the vision system: the mapping between image pixels and world coordinates has to be known for a correct localization. The calibration is performed on a flat stretch of road by placing markers at known distances up to 40 m; the relation between 3D coordinates of these points and the corresponding pixels in the image was used to compute camera orientation.

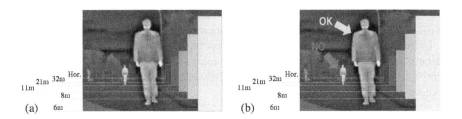

Fig. 1. Detection range: (*a*) sizes of BBs for 170 cm tall pedestrians at different distances; (*b*) the feasible distance range for a 170 cm tall pedestrian (green).

These parameters are then used for computing the relationships between 3D coordinates and image pixels, under the assumption of a flat road in front of the vision system. While being a strong assumption, in the area close to the vehicle (up to 20 m) it is supposed to hold even in presence of hills or bumps. In the faraway area, some errors in the calibration may occur, thus generating less confident results.

Detection distance range: the presence of a pedestrian is checked in different-sized bounding boxes (*BBs*) placed in different positions in the image.

Indeed, not all possible BBs need to be checked, mainly due to computational time and detail content. In fact, tiny BBs enclosing faraway pedestrians feature a very low information content and may be easily confused with other road participants or infrastructures that present similar thermal characteristics.

Thus, it is imperative to define a BBs' size-range for which the detection can lead to a sufficiently accurate result. In this work the considered sizes are: 12×28 pixels for the smallest BB and 42×100 for the largest one. In addition, a specific size and aspect ratio are used to define targets. The size of a pedestrian has been fixed to the following values: height 180 cm $\pm 10\%$ and width 60 cm $\pm 10\%$. These two choices lead to a limited detection area in front of the vehicle, as described in the following.

Fig. 1.a shows distances from 6 m to 32 m assuming a flat road. The image displays two pedestrians at different distances from the acquisition sensor. Also sizes of BBs for a 170 cm tall pedestrian at different distances are shown.

Fig. 1.b shows the size of the BBs that are examined (green), and highlights which pedestrian cannot be detected; the distance range in which a 170 cm tall pedestrian can be detected is shown as well (red). The detection distance range can be computed as a function of pedestrian height specification and the BBs height range [12]. With the setup and design choices used for this work, the distance range is 7 m $\div$ 20 m.

4   Algorithm Description

The algorithm is divided into three parts: (*i*) image stabilization for pitch angle compensation, (*ii*) localization of areas of interest (attentive vision) and generation of possible candidates based on symmetry, (*iii*) filtering of candidates to remove errors, based on non-pedestrian characteristics, (*iv*) validation of candidates on the basis of a match with a simple morphological model. The last part is currently under development and its results need to be validated by further investigation.

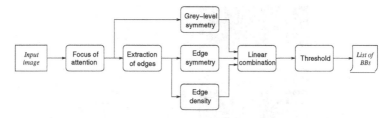

Fig. 2. Scheme of the low-level phase.

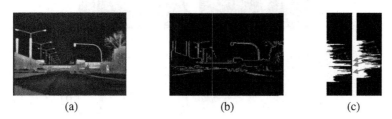

(a)   (b)   (c)

Fig. 3. (*a*) Source image, (*b*) edges in the interesting area, (*c*) correlation between two subsequent histograms.

4.1 Image Stabilization

Vehicle oscillations are generally present during driving and are due to road roughness; although filtered by the dumper system, they are perceived by the camera. Since the pedestrian recognition application relies on correct camera calibration, vertical oscillations need to be compensated. A software image stabilizer is preferable with respect to optical/mechanical ones because it requires less hardware resources.

Stabilization is regarded as a prefiltering and applied after image acquisition and before the actual image processing.

From the analysis of different video sequences, four types of movements in the images have been identified.

Perspective movements: when the vehicle is moving on a straight flat road, due to perspective, each frame resembles a zoomed version of the previous.

Horizontal translation: when the vehicle is steering, objects move horizontally.

Vertical translation: when the vehicle is driving uphill or downhill, objects move vertically. This is also the case when approaching high obstacles such as overbridges.

Vertical oscillations: road imperfections or artifacts (rough road or speed bumpers) are the main cause of vertical oscillations. A procedure devoted to compensate the last type of movements is presented.

The image stabilizer evaluates the movements of objects' horizontal borders, which generally –in absence of oscillations– move continuously and slowly towards the top of the image. Two consecutive frames are compared and the vertical offset between them is computed. The oscillation is compensated by shifting the new image in the opposite direction. In the following the main steps are presented.

Focus of Attention: in order to ignore the vertical movements of edges present in the image when approaching tall structures (e.g. overbridges) only the central stripe of the image is processed.

586   M. Bertozzi et al.

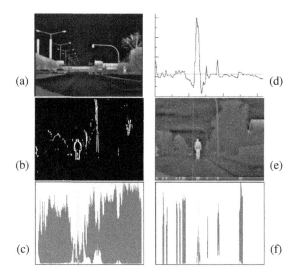

Fig. 4. Computation of symmetries and focus of attention: (*a*) original image; (*b*) vertical edges image; (*c*) symmetries of grey levels (red) and vertical edges (green), density of vertical edges (yellow), their combination (white); (*d*) histogram of grey levels together with its global (red) and local (green) average; (*e*) positions of possible vertical symmetry axes (green); (*f*) histograms are computed only in correspondence with the green dashes.

Edge Extraction: horizontal edges are extracted in the area of interest by means of a classical Sobel filter. The grey-level resulting image is then thresholded using an adaptive threshold.

Fig. 3.a presents a frame of a test sequence while fig. 3.b shows the result of horizontal edge detection in the interesting area.

Histogram Computation: a row-wise histogram is computed on the edge image. The histogram is checked whether appropriate information is available or not. In case of a low quantity of information (e.g a uniform scene) the procedure is stopped and stabilization disabled.

Correlation Evaluation: the changes in the shape of the histogram from one frame to the following allow to determine the offset between them. This is achieved through the convolution between the current histogram and a reference one, which is dynamically updated. Fig. 3.c shows two histograms in a sequence; the red arrows point out the correlation between the highest peaks. The computation of the offset is straightforward.

A set of filters are used to remove abrupt variations and low frequency components of oscillations which generally result from perspective effects of road objects. Another filter is used to progressively reduce the offset in a sequence, bringing the horizon back to its original position.

Image Shift: the vertical offset computed so far is then used to shift the current frame before processing.

4.2 Candidates Generation and Filtering

The low-level part of the algorithm, depicted in fig. 2, is mainly based on the computation of symmetries. The input image is processed to focus the attention on interesting regions, then vertical edges are extracted. Both input and vertical edges images are searched for symmetrical areas, with specific aspect-ratio and size/perspective constraints. The density of edges in these areas is also considered.

The original input image is shown in fig. 4.a; fig. 4.b depicts a binary image containing the vertical edges, and fig. 4.c shows a number of histograms computed by selecting, for each vertical symmetry axis, the BB having the maximum: symmetry of grey levels (red), symmetry of vertical edges (green), and density of vertical edges (yellow). The white histogram presents a combination of all the above; the pedestrian presents high local peaks in all histograms.

Considerations generally true for images in the IR domain permit to reduce the number of symmetry axes to be examined, thus avoiding the need of an exhaustive search. Since pedestrians are warmer than the background, a filter has been defined to eliminate symmetry axes in cold image areas. For this purpose, a histogram encoding the presence of white (hot) pixels is computed; its local average (computed on a small window) as well as its overall average are also computed (fig. 4.c). The low-pass filter is used to smooth the histogram and remove small peaks close to high peaks, while the overall average is used to mask out histogram peaks in cold areas.

Thus, vertical symmetry axes intersecting the green portions of the bottom of the image are considered, while the remaining ones (intersecting red dashes) are neglected (figs. 4.d and 4.e).

Candidates are generated by thresholding the resulting histogram. Each over-threshold peak corresponds to a BB containing the shape of a potential pedestrian. This list is then passed on to next phase of the processing which is in charge of selecting and possibly removing false positives.

The candidates are filtered on the basis of specific features of human artifacts that may have been highlighted as potential pedestrians in the previous step. In other words, specific filters have been designed to remove: BBs centered on poles, road signs, buildings, and other artifacts that present high symmetry and BBs that feature a reduced amount of edges in the upper and lower part, since pedestrians are characterized by a uniform distribution of edges.

The edges within a BB are used to compute a vertical histogram. This operation is performed for each BB. The shape of the vertical histogram is used to filter the BBs (fig. 5).

Each surviving BB is then resized and reduced in height and width in order to fit the internal presence of edges. The BBs that have been resized too much are then removed, while the other BBs are again filtered in order to eliminate: BBs that –due to this resize operation– would represent pedestrians that are too faraway (fig. 6.a, arrow 1), BBs that do no longer meet perspective constraints (fig. 6.a, arrow 2), and BBs that do no longer meet the original assumptions on aspect ratio (fig. 6.a, arrow 3).

Fig. 5. Filters relying on specific features of artifacts. For each BB the vertical histogram of edges is displayed on top of it. The arrows point discarded BBs.

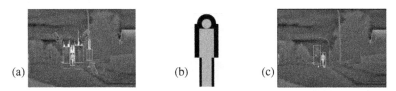

Fig. 6. (*a*) Elimination of BBs following the resize step; (*b*) the simple model encoding morphological characteristics of a pedestrian, (*c*) the match with the model allows to validate a pedestrian and to discard a false positive.

4.3 Validation of Candidates

The following paragraph describes the preliminary results of the ongoing research.

Each surviving BB is validated through the match with a simple model encoding morphological and thermal characteristics of a pedestrian.

Fig. 6.b shows the model that is used for the match; the model is resized according to the size of the BB, and then matched with the gray level original image. A vote is given and the candidates which present a vote lower than a threshold are discarded.

In fig. 6.c the votes relative to two BBs are displayed: the highest represents an actual pedestrian, while the lowest one represents a tree. Even if the tree has a shape that resembles a human, the filter is able to discard it.

5 Discussion of Results and Conclusions

Fig. 7 shows a few results of pedestrian detection in IR images. The two horizontal green lines encode the detection distance range in which pedestrians are searched for ($7\ m \div 20\ m$), while the horizontal white line encodes the horizon when the flat road and no vehicle pitch assumptions are met. Results are encoded as BBs superimposed onto the original images. They highlight pedestrians within the distance range only.

The result shows that the system is able to detect one or more pedestrians even in presence of a complex background. The major critical situations, presented in fig. 8, are: (*i*) in presence of a complex background, artifacts or objects other than pedestrians are occasionally detected (fig. 8.a); (*i*) the algorithm does not miss the detection of a pedestrian but miscalculates the exact position or size of the BB, thus corrupting the distance estimation (fig. 8.b); (*iii*) walking pedestrians are occasionally not detected due to aspect ratio constraints (see fig. 8.c); anyway in the following frame of the sequence

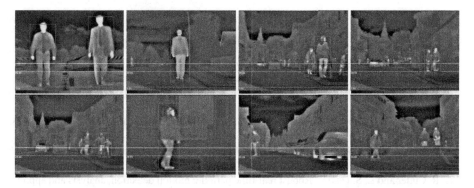

Fig. 7. Results of pedestrian detection in different situations: with complex or simple scenario or with one or more pedestrians. The distance (meters) is displayed below the boxes. The two horizontal green lines encode the range in which pedestrians are searched for, while the horizontal white line encodes the horizon.

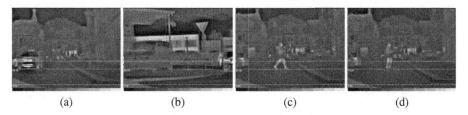

(a)   (b)   (c)   (d)

Fig. 8. Situation in which the algorithm fails: (*a*) a false positive is found due to a complex background, (*b*) a wrong distance is computed, (*c*) a walking pedestrian is misdetected when it does not met the aspect-ratio constraints, while it is correctly detected in the following frame (*d*).

(fig. 8.d) the same pedestrian is correctly detected, thus a tracking could be used to solve this case.

The algorithm developed so far proves to be effective in different situations although it employs only single images. In order to increase the reliability and robustness of the system appropriate tracking procedures will be added and validated by carrying out extensive tests in different weather conditions.

References

1. H. Nanda and L. Davis, "Probabilistic Template Based Pedestrian Detection in Infrared Videos," in *Procs. IEEE Intelligent Vehicles Symposium 2002*, June 2002.
2. F. Xu and K. Fujimura, "Pedestrian Detection and Tracking with Night Vision," in *Procs. IEEE Intelligent Vehicles Symposium 2002*, June 2002.
3. Y. L. Guilloux and J. Lonnoy, "PAROTO Project: The Benefit of Infrared Imagery for Obstacle Avoidance," in *Procs. IEEE Intelligent Vehicles Symposium 2002*, June 2002.
4. T. Tsuji, H. Hattori, M. Watanabe, and N. Nagaoka, "Development of Night-vision System ," *IEEE Trans. on Intelligent Transportation Systems*, vol. 3, pp. 203–209, Sept. 2002.
5. M. Bertozzi, A. Broggi, A. Fascioli, and M. Sechi, "Shape-based Pedestrian Detection," in *Procs. IEEE Intelligent Vehicles Symposium 2000*, pp. 215–220, Oct. 2000.

6. D. M. Gavrila and J. Geibel, "Shape-Based Pedestrian Detection and Tracking," in *Procs. IEEE Intelligent Vehicles Symposium 2002*, June 2002.

7. C. Curio, J. Edelbrunner, T. Kalinke, C. Tzomakas, and W. von Seelen, "Walking Pedestrian Recognition," *IEEE Trans. on ITS*, vol. 1, pp. 155–163, Sept. 2000.

8. M. Oren, C. Papageorgiu, P. Sihna, E. Osuna, and T. Poggio, "Pedestrian Detection using Wavelet Templates," in *Procs. IEEE Conf. on Computer Vision and Pattern Recognition*, (San Juan, Puerto Rico), pp. 193–199, 1997.

9. L. Zhao and C. Thorpe, "Stereo- and Neural Network-based Pedestrian Detection," in *Procs. IEEE Intl. Conf. on Intelligent Transportation Systems'99*, pp. 298–303, Oct. 1999.

10. B. Heisele and C. Wöhler, "Motion-based Recognition of Pedestrians," in *Procs. IEEE Intl. Conf. on Pattern Recognition*, pp. 1325–1330, June 1998.

11. R. Cutler and L. S. Davis, "Robust real-time periodic motion detection, analysis and applications," *IEEE Trans. on PAMI*, vol. 22, pp. 781–796, Aug. 2000.

12. M. Bertozzi, A. Broggi, T. Graf, P. Grisleri, and M. Meinecke, "Pedestrian Detection in Infrared Images," in *Procs. IEEE Intelligent Vehicles Symposium 2003*, June 2003. in press.

Color-Based Object Tracking in Multi-camera Environments

Katja Nummiaro[1], Esther Koller-Meier[2], Tomáš Svoboda[2],
Daniel Roth[2], and Luc Van Gool[1,2]

[1] Katholieke Universiteit Leuven, ESAT/PSI-VISICS, Belgium,
{knummiar,vangool}@esat.kuleuven.ac.be
[2] Swiss Federal Institute of Technology (ETH), D-ITET/BIWI, Switzerland,
{ebmeier,svoboda,vangool}@vision.ee.ethz.ch

Abstract. This paper presents a multi-view tracker, meant to operate
in smart rooms that are equipped with multiple cameras. The cameras
are assumed to be calibrated[1]. In particular, we demonstrate a virtual
classroom application, where the system automatically selects the camera
with the 'best' view on the face of a person moving in the room. Real-
time object tracking, which is needed to achieve this, is implemented
by means of color-based particle filtering. The use of multiple model
histograms for the target (human head) results robust tracking, even
when the view on the target changes considerably like from the front
to the back. Information is shared between the cameras, which adds
robustness to the system. Once one camera has lost the target, it can
be reinitialized with the help of the epipolar constraints suggested by
the others. Experiments in our research environment corroborate the
effectiveness of the approach.

1 Introduction

Intelligent environments like 'smart rooms' pose several research challenges, such
as object/people tracking, face/gesture recognition, and speech analysis. There
is a rich variety of applications at stake, like surveillance, human-computer in-
terfacing, video conferencing, industrial monitoring, and tele-training.

In this paper we focus on the autonomous processing of visual information
based on a network of calibrated cameras. Each camera system comprises a
recognition and tracking module which locates the target in the observed scene.
Both modules operate on color distributions, where the target model includes a
description of the changes of its colors with viewpoint. To document interesting
events on-line, an automated virtual editor is included in the central server,
which produces a single video stream out of the different camera outputs by
systematically selecting the one with the 'best' view. Figure 1 illustrates the
system architecture of our multi-camera setup.

For the integration of the multiple cameras, the ViRoom (Visual Room)
system by Doubek *et al.* [4] is used. The modular architecture is constructed

---

[1] The full calibration is used, but the mutual epipolar geometry would be sufficient.

B. Michaelis and G. Krell (Eds.): DAGM 2003, LNCS 2781, pp. 591–599, 2003.
© Springer-Verlag Berlin Heidelberg 2003

from low-cost digital cameras and standard computers running under Linux. It also supports consistent, synchronized image acquisition. The ViRoom has fixed cameras, whereas our smart room has cameras which are mounted on pan-tilt heads. Therefore, we have extended the ViRoom software with automatic camera control in order to keep the target in the center of view.

Currently, the research area of multi-camera systems is very active [2,7,8,12]. For instance, a flexible multi-camera system for low bandwidth communication is presented by Comaniciu *et al.* [2]. Based on color tracking the target on the current image can be transmitted in real-time with high resolution. Khan *et al.* [7] describe an interesting approach to track people with multiple cameras that are uncalibrated. When a person enters the field of view of one camera, the system searches for a corresponding target in all other cameras by using previously compiled field of view lines. Krumm *et al.* [8] describe an approach for tracking in an intelligent environment, using two calibrated stereo cameras that provide both depth and color information. Each measurement from a camera is transformed into a common world coordinate system and submitted to a central tracking module.

The work most closely related to ours is that of Trivedi *et al.* [12], where an overall system specification for an intelligent room is given. The 3D tracking module operates with multiple cameras and maintains a Kalman filter for each object in the scene. In comparison, we use a more general representation of the probability distribution of the object state which allows to initialize this distribution along the epipolar lines when an object enters the field of view of a camera. In our system the best view is selected according to the quality of the tracking results for the individual cameras while Trivedi *et al.* utilize the motion of the tracked target. We also introduce the use of multiple target histogram based on color distributions in tracking.

The outline of this paper is as follows. Section 2 presents a short review of the color-based tracking technique. In Section 3 the multiple target models used for the tracking are explained. Section 4 presents the exchange of information in the camera network while Section 5 explains the selection of the optimal camera view. In Section 6 some experimental results are presented and finally, Section 7 concludes the paper.

2   Tracking

Robust real-time tracking of non-rigid objects is a challenging task. Color histograms provide an efficient feature for this kind of tracking problems as they are robust to partial occlusion, are rotation and scale invariant and computationally efficient. The fusion of such color distributions with particle filters provides an efficient and robust tracker in case of clutter and occlusion. Particle filters [5] can namely represent non-linear problems and non-Gaussian densities by propagating multiple hypotheses simultaneously.

The color-based particle filter [9,10] approximates the posterior density by a set of weighted random samples $\{(\mathbf{s}_t^{(n)}, \pi_t^{(n)})\}_{n=1}^N$ conditioned on the past ob-

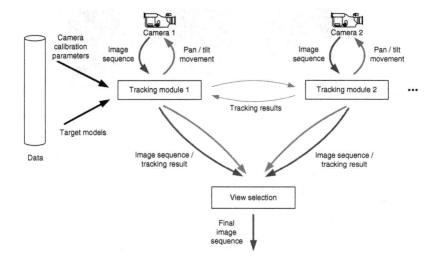

Fig. 1. The sketch of the system architecture with multiple cameras.

servations. Each sample **s** represents one hypothetical state of the object, with a corresponding discrete sampling probability π, where $\sum_{n=1}^{N} \pi^{(n)} = 1$. The tracked object state is specified by an elliptical region

$$\mathbf{s} = \{x, y, \dot{x}, \dot{y}, H_x, H_y, \dot{H}\} \qquad (1)$$

where x, y represent the location of the ellipse, $\dot{x}, \dot{y}$ the motion, H_x, H_y the length of the half axes and $\dot{H}$ the corresponding scale change.

In order to compare the histogram of such a hypothesized region $p_{\mathbf{s}^{(n)}}$ with the target histogram q from an initial model, a similarity measure based on the Bhattacharyya coefficient [1,3,6]

$$\rho[p_{\mathbf{s}_t^{(n)}}, q] = \sum_{u=1}^{m} \sqrt{p_{\mathbf{s}_t^{(n)}}^{(u)} q^{(u)}} \qquad (2)$$

is used, where m represents the number of bins for the histograms.

3   Multiple Target Models

To support multiple cameras, a color adjustment (that was already part of the ViRoom software [4]) is applied during the calibration. Another consideration when working with multiple cameras, is using more than one histogram for the target model. For example, when a person walks around in the smart room, camera may at one time have the face in its field of view, and later the back of

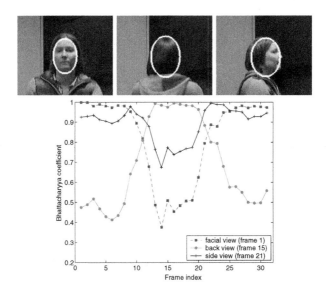

Fig. 2. Top row: The three main views and histogram regions for the target model (frames 1, 15 and 21). Bottom row: The plotted Bhattacharyya values from a 360° turning head sequence, using the different target models (facial, side and back view) and comparing them to the facial region (frame 1).

the head. The color distributions will probably be quite different in these cases, and this correspondence can be established with the multiple cameras.

Three characteristic head images, one from the front, one from the side and one from the back are selected as initial target models and the corresponding histograms $q = \{q_f, q_s, q_b\}$ are stored. During the tracking, the similarity measures to these three histograms are included in the object state. By using a linear stochastic model for the propagation, the Bhattacharyya coefficients for the next frames can be estimated. Rapid changes of these coefficients are therefore avoided. Fig. 2 shows the evolution of the Bhattacharyya coefficients with respect to the three characteristic views shown in the top row as the head gradually turns around. As can be seen, the Bhattacharyya coefficients change smoothly with the viewing angle.

The initial samples of the particle filter for each camera are spread over the whole image or are strategically placed at positions where the target is expected to appear in case such knowledge is available. A target is recognized on the basis of the three Bhattacharyya coefficients, where the best matching model is taken as the target model. By calculating the mean value μ and the standard deviation σ of the Bhattacharyya coefficient for elliptic regions over all the positions of the background in the initialization step, we define the appearance condition as

$$\rho[p_{\mathbf{s}_t^{(n)}}, q] > \mu + 2\sigma. \tag{3}$$

This indicates a 95% confidence that a sample does not belong to the background. If a fraction $b \cdot N$ of the samples shows a high enough correspondence to one of the target histograms the object is considered to be found and the tracking process is started. The parameter $b = 0.1$ has been proven sufficient in our experiments and is called the 'kick-off fraction'. During tracking, the target model of each camera is adapted as described in our earlier work [9].

4   Exchanging Information across Cameras

Exchanging information across the cameras is important to increase the robustness of the tracking. Such information exchange can take different forms. For instance, cameras could come to a consensus about which (different) side of a face they also see and ensure that these sides are consistent. We are currently implementing this aspect. Here we describe another type of collaboration, that has to do with the area where the targets are expected in the different views, i.e. with the (re)initialization of the individual trackers. In case one or a few cameras have lost the target, the other cameras can provide strong indications where to look based on their epipolar geometry. Epipolar geometry is used in two different ways: 1) During initialization when one of the target models matches an object, 2) When the object is temporally lost due to clutter, occlusions or other difficult tracking conditions.

Initialization: When an object is detected in one camera, we try to initialize it in the other cameras. For this purpose, the epipolar lines are calculated that correspond to the estimated target location. Samples are then placed stochastically around these lines and the velocity components are chosen from Gaussian distributions. If the object is already visible in more than one camera, the samples are distributed around the intersection of the corresponding epipolar lines.

Reinitialization: If less than $b \cdot N$ of the samples fulfill the appearance condition which is explained in Eq. 3, we consider the object to be lost. In this case, we use the epipolar lines and their intersections to reinitialize an object during tracking. A fraction of the samples are then spread around the epipolar lines of the other cameras while the remaining samples are propagated normally.

5   Best View Selection

Faces of people are among the most important targets to be tracked in smart rooms. For applications, where images are transmitted to another location, it will also be important to make an appropriate selection among the views that are available. Accordingly, we have developed an automated virtual editor which creates a video stream by switching to the best view on the face of a person who is freely walking around. Camera hand-over is controlled on the basis of the tracking results by evaluating the Bhattacharyya coefficient (see Eq. 2) of the mean state of each tracker

Fig. 3. The best view selection according to the Bhattacharyya coefficients of the individual trackers is shown. The small images at the bottom show the tracking results of the individual camera trackers as white ellipses. The numbers represent the corresponding Bhattacharyya coefficients. In the top row the used target model and the output of the virtual editor are displayed.

$$\rho[p_{E[S]}, q_f] = \sum_{u=1}^{m} \sqrt{p_{E[S]}^{(u)} q_f^{(u)}} \tag{4}$$

$$E[S] = \sum_{n=1}^{N} \pi^{(n)} \mathbf{s}^{(n)}. \tag{5}$$

As the Bhattacharyya coefficient represents a similarity measure with respect to the target histogram, the virtual editor always chooses the camera view which provides the highest Bhattacharyya coefficient for the face histogram (the characteristic frontal view). Figure 3 illustrates the best view selection on the basis of the individual Bhattacharyya coefficients.

6   Results

In this section the experimental results demonstrate the capabilities and limitations of our distributed tracking system. All images are captured from live video streams and have a size of 160×120 pixels. The application runs at 5-8 frames per seconds — without any special optimization — on Pentium III PCs at 1GHz under Linux where each of the three cameras are attached to their own computer. The capability of the virtual editor is illustrated in Figure 4. It can be seen that the camera hand-over automatically chooses the best front view of the tracked face even if it is partly occluded.

The initialization plays an important role in the multi-camera tracker. When there are several potential targets in the neighborhood of the epipolar lines, a wrong object can be selected. Such a scene is shown in Figure 5. In the top row, the situation is still handled correctly as the target is occluded in the middle

Fig. 4. The virtual editor automatically chooses the best front view of the tracked face.

Fig. 5. The initialization step can cause problems in tracking, if there are several equally good candidates in the vicinity of the epipolar lines.

camera and not initialized. In the second row, the target is not localized correctly whereas in the third row a wrong target is selected. In both cases, the target is occluded in two cameras, so that the samples are spread along an epipolar line and not around an intersection point. Robustness can certainly be increased with more cameras. On the other hand, applications with crowds in the fields of view will also then pose critical problems.

7 Conclusion

As cameras get cheaper, PCs more powerful, and information traffic more congested, the interest in technology that better supports virtual meetings increases. This paper proposed a multi-camera setup that actively tracks a person. As cameras may see different parts of the head at different times, these changes are supported for through a target model that contains a choice of different color histograms, each corresponding to an interval of viewing angles. The tracker of each camera dynamically chooses the model that matches best. These choices are fed into a 'virtual editor', that selects the camera yielding the best view of the face.

Information exchange between the individual trackers is currently only used for the (re)initialization process by applying epipolar geometry. We will push this integration further by implementing a multi-view tracker that combines the geometric and photometric information coming from all cameras in order to process a single, 3D state rather than individual image-by-image states. Furthermore, we will enhance the virtual editor. The camera selection should generate a video stream that is maximally informative and pleasant to watch, avoiding too many short cuts. In addition, the Bhattacharyya coefficient will be combined with alternative decision rules. We also plan to interpolate between available views, in order to create a virtual camera. A meeting setup with multiple people is another interesting extension. The virtual editor should be able to locate the person who is the center of attention at any given time.

Acknowledgment. The authors gratefully acknowledge support by the European Commission project STAR (IST-2000-28764) and the NCCR project IM2, funded by the Swiss National Science Foundation SNF. We thank Petr Doubek and Stefaan De Roeck for the multi-camera set-up, and Bart Vanluyten and Stijn Wuyts for including the active cameras.

References

1. F. Aherne, N. Thacker and P. Rockett, *The Bhattacharyya Metric as an Absolute Similarity Measure for Frequency Coded Data*, Kybernetika, pp. 1–7, Vol. 32(4), 1997.
2. D. Comaniciu, F. Berton and V. Ramesh, *Adaptive Resolution System for Distributed Surveillance*, Real-Time Imaging, pp. 427–437, Vol. 8, 2002.
3. D. Comaniciu, V. Ramesh and P. Meer, *Real-Time Tracking of Non-Rigid Objects using Mean Shift*, CVPR, pp. 142–149, Vol. 2, 2000.
4. P. Doubek, T. Svoboda and L. Van Gool, *Monkeys – a Software Architecture for ViRoom – Low-Cost Multicamera System*, ICVS, pp. 386–395, 2003.
5. M. Isard and A. Blake, *CONDENSATION – Conditional Density Propagation for Visual Tracking*, International Journal on Computer Vision, pp. 5–28, Vol. 1(29), 1998.
6. T. Kailath, *The Divergence and Bhattacharyya Distance Measures in Signal Selection*, IEEE Transactions on Communication Technology, COM-15(1) pp. 52–60, 1967.
7. S. Kahn, O. Javed and M. Shah, *Tracking in Uncalibrated Cameras with Overlapping Field of View*, PETS, 2001.
8. J. Krumm, S. Harris, B. Meyers, B. Brumitt, M. Hale and S. Shafer, *Multi-Camera Multi-Person Tracking for EasyLiving*, International Workshop on Visual Surveillance, pp. 3–10, 2000.

9. K. Nummiaro, E. Koller-Meier and L. Van Gool, *An Adaptive Color-Based Particle Filter*, Journal of Image and Vision Computing, pp. 99–110, Vol 21(1), 2003.
10. P. Pérez, C. Hue, J. Vermaak and M. Gangnet, *Color-Based Probabilistic Tracking*, ECCV, pp. 661–675, 2002.
11. T. Svoboda, H. Hug and L. Van Gool, *ViRoom – Low Cost Synchronised Multi-camera System and its Self-Calibration*, DAGM, pp. 515–522, 2002.
12. M.M. Trivedi, I. Mikic and S.K. Bhonsle, *Active Camera Networks and Semantic Event Databases for Intelligent Environments* Proceedings of the IEEE Workshop on Human Modelling, Analysis and Synthesis, 2000.

Improving Children's Speech Recognition by HMM Interpolation with an Adults' Speech Recognizer

Stefan Steidl, Georg Stemmer, Christian Hacker, Elmar Nöth, and
Heinrich Niemann*

Universität Erlangen-Nürnberg, Lehrstuhl für Mustererkennung, Martensstraße 3,
D-91058 Erlangen, Germany
`stefan.steidl@informatik.uni-erlangen.de`

Abstract. In this paper we address the problem of building a good
speech recognizer if there is only a small amount of training data available. The acoustic models can be improved by interpolation with the
well-trained models of a second recognizer from a different application
scenario. In our case, we interpolate a children's speech recognizer with
a recognizer for adults' speech. Each hidden Markov model has its own
set of interpolation partners; experiments were conducted with up to
50 partners. The interpolation weights are estimated automatically on a
validation set using the EM algorithm. The word accuracy of the children's speech recognizer could be improved from 74.6 % to 81.5 %. This
is a relative improvement of almost 10 %.

1 Introduction

Traditionally, automatic speech recognition has been focusing on adults' speech
while speech of children has been ignored almost completely. Nevertheless, the
economic market for children's speech recognizers is growing. You just have
to think of the huge number of children having already mobile phones which
could be controlled via speech or of toys with speech recognition like SONY's
entertainment robot AIBO. Unfortunately using a speech recognizer for adults
to recognize children's speech yields only very poor results, because children's
speech differs too much from adults' speech. One possible solution of this problem
is the collection of large amounts of children's speech data what is expensive and
time-consuming. Furthermore, finding test persons is much more difficult with
children than with adults since the parents must agree, the children have to be
picked up and brought home again and so on.

In literature, often MLLR (maximum likelihood linear regression) or MAP
(maximum a posteriori) methods are applied to adapt a speech recognizer for
adults' speech to children's speech. Another promising technique is vocal tract

---

* A part of this work was funded by the European Commission (IST programme) in the
framework of the PF-STAR project under Grant IST-2001-37599. The responsibility
for the content lies with the authors.

length normalization (VTLN). In this paper HMM interpolation is used to solve the problem: A children's speech recognizer is trained on a small amount of children's speech and afterwards the hidden Markov models (HMMs) are interpolated with the HMMs of an adult speech recognizer in order to increase the robustness of the models. Note that HMM interpolation is not in contrast to the techniques mentioned above. Especially a combination with VTLN makes sense and will be investigated in the near future.

The following issues are addressed in this paper: What are good interpolation partners? With how many partners should be interpolated? Which HMM parameters have to be interpolated? Which method is used for interpolation? In the following we describe a data-driven algorithm to choose an optimal set of interpolation partners for each hidden Markov model. The number of interpolation partners is optimized on a validation set and varies from one to 50. The parameters of the semi-continuous HMMs are interpolated linearly. The interpolation weights are estimated automatically on the basis of a validation set using the EM algorithm.

The idea to interpolate HMMs which have been trained on different datasets in order to achieve robust models is not new. For instance, K. Livescu [3] uses HMM interpolation to combine recognizers for non-native and native speech. Interpolation has also been employed for the same purpose by L. Mayfield Tomokiyo in [4]. Both approaches have in common that a single interpolation weight is shared by all HMMs and each hidden Markov model has only one *fixed* interpolation partner.

2   Interpolation of Hidden Markov Models

This paper focuses on the interpolation of semi-continuous hidden Markov models. In the following it is assumed that all HMMs share one common codebook consisting of K Gaussian densities. As each speech recognizer comes up with its own codebook, both codebooks have to be merged first. A greedy algorithm is used which selects sequentially the best pair $(\mathcal{N}_1, \mathcal{N}_2)$ of Gaussian densities and merges them into a new density $\mathcal{N}_3$ by taking the average of the density parameters. In our case only a simple mapping of the densities was performed. As a distance measure in order to choose the best pair of densities the increase of the entropy ΔH between the original densities $\mathcal{N}_1$ and $\mathcal{N}_2$ with their a priori probabilities p_1 and p_2 on the one hand and the resulting density $\mathcal{N}_3$ on the other hand is used:

$$\Delta H = (p_1 + p_2) \cdot H(\mathcal{N}_3) - \big(p_1 \cdot H(\mathcal{N}_1) + p_2 \cdot H(\mathcal{N}_2)\big) . \tag{1}$$

The entropy H of a Gaussian density $\mathcal{N}(\boldsymbol{x}|\boldsymbol{\mu}, \boldsymbol{\Sigma})$ is calculated as follows:

$$H(\mathcal{N}) = \int \mathcal{N}(\boldsymbol{x}) \cdot \ln \big(\mathcal{N}(\boldsymbol{x})\big) \, \mathrm{d}\boldsymbol{x} = \frac{1}{2} \ln \big((2\pi e)^D \cdot |\boldsymbol{\Sigma}|\big) . \tag{2}$$

D is the dimension of the feature vector $\boldsymbol{x}$. The algorithm is iterated until each density is merged. More details and extensions of the algorithm can be found in

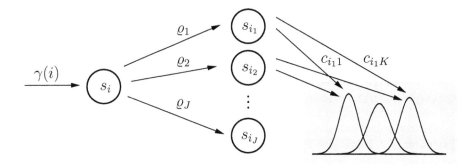

Fig. 1. The linear interpolation problem (3) can be interpreted as a hidden Markov model

[7]. In the next two sections, we describe the linear interpolation method and the estimation of the interpolation weights using the EM algorithm [6]. Afterwards the algorithm to choose the best interpolation partners is presented.

2.1   Linear Interpolation

We consider the general case of J interpolation partners. All J hidden Markov models are assumed to have the same number of states. The K mixture weights c_{ik} of the HMM state s_i are interpolated with the mixture weights c_{ijk} of the interpolation partners $s_{i_2}, \ldots, s_{i_J}$ as follows, where we set $s_{i_1} = s_i$ and $c_{i_1k} = c_{ik}$:

$$\forall k: \quad \hat{c}_{i_k} = \varrho_1 \cdot c_{i_1k} + \ldots + \varrho_J \cdot c_{ijk} \quad \text{with} \sum_{j=1}^{J} \varrho_j = 1 \ . \tag{3}$$

In a second step the transition probabilities a_{ij} of state i are interpolated with the same interpolation weights ϱ_j.

2.2   Estimation of the Interpolation Weights

As each state of each HMM which has to be interpolated has its own set of interpolation weights ϱ_j, a tremendous number of parameters has to be estimated. This is done automatically on the basis of a validation set using the EM algorithm. The estimation formulas for the interpolation weights are based on [6, p. 305].

In order to use the EM algorithm to estimate the weights the problem (3) is interpreted as a discrete hidden Markov Model as shown in Fig. 1 [1]. As before, state $s_i = s_{i_1}$ is interpolated with the states s_{i_2} to s_{i_J}. The interpolation weights ϱ_j are interpreted as the transition probabilities from state s_i to the states s_{i_j}. The mixture weights c_{ijk} correspond to the output probabilities $b_{i_j}(k)$. The EM algorithm is an iterative parameter estimation technique which calculates new values of the parameters on the basis of existing estimates. The probability

$P(s_{i_j} \mid k, s_i, \boldsymbol{\varrho})$ is the probability of being in state s_{i_j} if the output is codeword k and an existing set of estimates $\boldsymbol{\varrho}$ is given. It's calculated as follows:

$$P(s_{i_j} \mid k, s_i, \boldsymbol{\varrho}) = \frac{P(s_{i_j}, k \mid s_i, \boldsymbol{\varrho})}{P(k \mid s_i, \boldsymbol{\varrho})} = \frac{\varrho_j \cdot c_{i_j k}}{\sum_{j=1}^{J} \varrho_j \cdot c_{i_j k}} . \tag{4}$$

Using this equation you can calculate the transition probabilities ϱ_j.

$$\varrho_j = P(s_{i_j} \mid s_i, \boldsymbol{\varrho}) = \sum_{k=1}^{K} P(k \mid s_i, \boldsymbol{\varrho}) \cdot P(s_{i_j} \mid k, s_i, \boldsymbol{\varrho}) \tag{5}$$

In order to get new estimates of the transition probabilities the term $P(k \mid s_i, \boldsymbol{\varrho})$ in (5) is replaced with the probability $\zeta(i, k) = P(s_i, k | \boldsymbol{X}, \boldsymbol{\lambda})$ which is calculated on the validation set.

$$\tilde{\varrho}_j = \sum_{k=1}^{K} \zeta(i, k) \cdot \frac{\varrho_j \cdot c_{i_j k}}{\sum_{j=1}^{J} \varrho_j \cdot c_{i_j k}} \tag{6}$$

Due to this replacement the new estimates of the transition probabilities have to be normalized to meet the condition $\sum_{j=1}^{J} \varrho_j = 1$.

$$\hat{\varrho}_j = \frac{\tilde{\varrho}_j}{\sum_{j=1}^{J} \tilde{\varrho}_j} \tag{7}$$

The algorithm stops if the estimates of the transition probabilities don't change anymore. With the following measure of quality [6, p. 305] the success of the HMM interpolation can be evaluated quickly without having to re-compute the likelihood $P(\boldsymbol{X}|\boldsymbol{\lambda})$ of the validation set:

$$\ell(\varrho_1, \dots, \varrho_J) = \log \prod_{k=1}^{K} \left(\sum_{j=1}^{J} \varrho_j \cdot c_{i_j k} \right)^{\zeta(i,k)} \tag{8}$$

$$= \sum_{k=1}^{K} \zeta(i, k) \log \left(\sum_{j=1}^{J} \varrho_j \cdot c_{i_j k} \right) . \tag{9}$$

2.3 Determination of the Interpolation Partners

We now can interpolate any hidden Markov Model with an arbitrary set of interpolation partners. The time required to calculate the interpolation weights and the amount of data available for a robust estimation of the interpolation weights is the only limiting factor to the number of interpolation partners. We found it reasonable to restrict the number of partners to at most 50 for our experiments. This raises the question which HMMs are good interpolation partners. In a first pass we therefor interpolate each HMM of the first speech recognizer with all

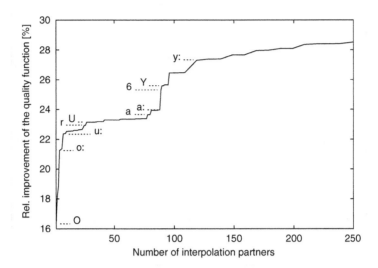

Fig. 2. Results of the interpolation of the monophone o: with the first n $(1 \leq n \leq 250)$ interpolation partners of the n-best list in terms of the relative improvement of the quality function. The marks indicate where new core phones appear for the first time, they are labeled with the name of the new core phone in SAMPA notation [5]

models of the second recognizer individually and evaluate the improvement of the quality function (9). In doing so you obtain a list of n possible interpolation partners. Figure 2 shows the results of the interpolation of the monophone o: with the first n $(1 \leq n \leq 250)$ interpolation partners of the n-best list in terms of the relative improvement of the quality function. Two aspects become evident: Firstly, choosing only the first 50 interpolation partners yields only a suboptimal result. Secondly, the graph shows noticeable steps. These steps are caused by HMMs which represent polyphones[1] with identical core phone and similar right and left context. In Fig. 2 marks indicate where new core phones appear for the first time, they are labeled with the name of the new core phone in SAMPA notation [5]. Similar HMMs yield nearly the same result if they are interpolated separately. But in combination the results can't be improved any further. Hence it makes sense not to choose the first n entries of the n-best list, but to choose only those polyphones whose distance to the interpolation partners which are already chosen is larger than a given threshold. As a distance measure the Kullback-Leibler divergence between corresponding HMM states (10) is used.

$$d(s_i, s_j) = \sum_{k=1}^{K} c_{ik} \cdot \log \frac{c_{ik}}{c_{jk}} \qquad (10)$$

---

[1] Polyphones are the generalization of the well-known concepts of bi- or triphones and allow a variable-sized context.

Table 1. Partitioning of the children's speech corpus for the training of the speech recognizer and for the interpolation of the hidden Markov models

Task	Speakers	Texts
Training Speech Recognizer	40	*Zürcher Lesetest*
	6 of 40	*Nordwind und Sonne*
HMM Interpolation	6 - 40	*Nordwind und Sonne*
Evaluation	20	*Nordwind und Sonne*

3 Speech Database

In this paper we describe the interpolation of a speech recognizer for children with a recognizer for adults. The children's speech corpus consists of read speech of 62 children (29 male and 33 female) at the age of 10 to 12 years. The pupils read four different German texts: *Nordwind und Sonne (The North Wind and the Sun)* and three texts of the reading test *Zürcher Lesetest* [2]. Each text is about 90 words long. The vocabulary consists of 227 entries. Altogether 3.5 hours of read children's speech are available.

To train the adults' speech recognizer a subset of the recordings of the VERB-MOBIL Project [8] was used. It consists of 28 hours of spontaneous dialogues between humans in German (11,762 turns of 610 dialogues). The vocabulary contains 6825 entries.

4 Experimental Results

4.1 Baseline Recognizer

As an adults' speech recognizer we use the VERBMOBIL recognizer for spontaneous speech. Its codebook consists of 500 densities. On the VERBMOBIL test set a word accuracy of 76.1 % is achieved using a 4-gram language model. If this recognizer is used to recognize children's speech (vocabulary reduced to *Nordwind und Sonne*, no language model) a word accuracy of 61.9 % is achieved.

In order to obtain a baseline system for children's speech we retrained this recognizer using the texts of the *Zürcher Lesetest* of 40 children. The testing of the recognizer and the evaluation of the HMM interpolation is performed with the text *Nordwind und Sonne* of the remaining 20 children. The data of the speakers of the training set reading *Nordwind und Sonne* is used for HMM interpolation. In order to include polyphones of the *Nordwind und Sonne* text in the model inventory of the children's speech recognizer the corresponding recordings of 6 of the 40 training speakers are added to the speech recognizer's training data. Table 1 shows the partitioning of the children corpus. The speakers of the training and test sets are disjoint. To evaluate the effects of the HMM interpolation we don't use any language model. Our baseline speech recognizer yields a word accuracy of 74.6 %.

Table 2. Results of the HMM interpolation with a varying number of interpolation partners

Experiment	Word Accuracy
Baseline	74.6 %
1 partner	79.2 %
5 partners	79.8 %
10 partners	80.1 %
20 partners	**80.9 %**
30 partners	80.7 %
40 partners	**80.9 %**
50 partners	80.8 %

4.2 HMM Interpolation

In the experiments described in this paper we interpolate our baseline recognizer for children's speech with the VERBMOBIL recognizer for adults' speech. The first group of experiments evaluates the optimal number of interpolation partners. The method to choose the interpolation partners is described in Sect. 2.3. The full validation set consisting of 40 speakers reading *Nordwind und Sonne* is used. Table 2 shows the results of these experiments. With only one interpolation partner, the word accuracy of our speech recognizer can be improved from 74.6 % to 79.2 %. As expected, you get even better results with more interpolation partners. The maximum of 80.9 % is reached with 20 resp. 40 partners. This is equivalent to a relative improvement of 8.4 %.

The second group of experiments evaluates the influence of the size of the validation set used to calculate estimates of the interpolation weights. The experiments are conducted with 20 and with 50 interpolation partners. Table 3 shows the results. It could be expected that you will need a large validation set to get robust estimates of the interpolation weights. Fortunately, this is not the case. The size of the validation set has only little influence on the HMM interpolation. The best results are achieved with even a small validation set consisting of only 6 resp. 12 speakers. Using 50 interpolation partners, a maximal word accuracy of 81.5 % is reached. Compared to the baseline system, this is a relative improvement of 9.2 %. The fact that a relatively small validation set is sufficient is an important result because if a large validation set was required it could have been better to use this data for training of the (baseline) speech recognizer instead for interpolating the hidden Markov models. Further experiments on other speech data will show whether this is a fortunate coincidence or not.

5   Conclusion and Outlook

Our experiments show two things: Firstly, if a speech recognizer has poorly trained models because of a lack of training data it can be improved by interpolating its models with the models of a second speech recognizer although the speech databases of both recognizers are different. Our new approach to choose

Table 3. Results of the HMM interpolation with 20 and with 50 partners and a varying number of speakers in the validation set

Partners	Validation Set	Word Accuracy
20 partners	6 speakers	**81.4 %**
	12 speakers	81.1 %
	18 speakers	80.7 %
	24 speakers	81.0 %
	30 speakers	80.8 %
	40 speakers	80.9 %
50 partners	6 speakers	81.3 %
	12 speakers	**81.5 %**
	18 speakers	81.3 %
	24 speakers	81.1 %
	30 speakers	81.4 %
	40 speakers	80.8 %

a different set of interpolation partners with up to 50 partners for each model is successful. This method is more promising than the HMM interpolation with only one fixed partner. A direct comparison between both methods is still missing. Secondly, adults' speech can help to recognize children's speech although both kinds of speech differ quite much. In our concrete case, the word accuracy of our children's speech recognizer could be improved by almost 10 %. Further experiments combining our approach with VTLN will be carried out. Due to the fact that all children read the same four texts, it would be better to add the validation set to the training of the baseline recognizer. We therefore plan to redo the experiments using a new children corpus with a much bigger vocabulary.

References

1. Jelinek, F. and Mercer, R. L.: Interpolated Estimation of Markov Source Parameters from Sparse Data. In: Gelsema, E. S., Kanal, L. N. (eds.): Pattern Recognition in Practice. North Holland Publishing Co., Amsterdam (1980) 381–397
2. Linder, M. and Grissemann, H.: Zürcher Lesetest. 6th edn. Testzentrale Göttingen, Robert-Bosch-Breite 25, 37079 Göttingen (2000), http://www.testzentrale.de
3. Livescu, K.: Analysis and Modeling of Non–Native Speech for Automatic Speech Recognition. Master Thesis, Massachusetts Institute of Technology (1999)
4. Mayfield Tomokiyo, L.: Recognizing Non–Native Speech: Characterizing and Adapting to Non–Native Usage in LVCSR. PhD Thesis, Carnegie Mellon University (2001)
5. SAMPA – Computer Readable Phonetic Alphabet.
   http://www.phon.ucl.ac.uk/home/sampa/home.htm
6. Schukat-Talamazzini, E. G.: Automatische Spracherkennung – Grundlagen, statistische Modelle und effiziente Algorithmen. Vieweg (1995)
7. Steidl, S.: Interpolation von Hidden Markov Modellen. Diploma Thesis (in German), Chair for Pattern Recognition, University of Erlangen-Nuremberg (2002)
8. Wahlster, W.: Verbmobil: Foundations of Speech-to-Speech Translation. Springer (2000)

Image Sequence Analysis in Environmental and Live Sciences

B. Jähne[1,2]

[1] Research Group Image Processing, Interdisciplinary Center for Scientific
Computing, Heidelberg University, Im Neuenheimer Feld 368, 69120 Heidelberg
[2] Institute for Environmental Physics, Heidelberg University
Im Neuenheimer Feld 229, 69120 Heidelberg
Bernd.Jaehne@iwr.uni-heidelberg.de

Abstract. Image sequence processing techniques are essential to study
dynamical processes such as exchange, growth, and transport processes.
In this survey paper, a generalized framework for the estimation of the
parameters of dynamic processes including motion fields is presented.
Some examples from environmental and live sciences illustrate how this
framework helped to tackles some key questions that could not be solved
without taking and analyzing image sequences.

1 Introduction

In computer vision motion fields are mostly required to explore 3-D space and
dynamic scenes. Thus one of the most important tasks is the reconstruction of
3-D structure and motion fields ("structure from motion"). Mostly only opaque
rigid objects are studied and the requirements for absolute accuracy are not
that stringent because the estimates of the velocity field are integrated into an
action-perception cycle. As long as this cycle converges, the accuracy is sufficient.

For scientific applications the focus shifts from motion field to the processes
causes change and motion in image sequences. Thus the most important task
here is not the determination of motion field itself but the estimation of parameters of dynamic processes and the distinction between different models. The
problem is, however, that dynamic processes such as chemical reactions, dispersion or growth processes also change the objects and thus also their intensities in
image sequences. Thus both motion and dynamical processes do change intensities and it is no longer possible to estimate the motion field or the parameters
of dynamic processes separately. Consequently, it is required to extend motion
analysis to a more general approach that allows the estimation of the parameters
of dynamic processes including the motion field. Such kind of problems occur
also in computer vision when the motion field has to be estimated in a scene
with changing illumination. Therefore it can be expected that computer vision
will benefit form the application to scientific problems by a general solution to
the problem of motion estimation under varying illumination conditions.

This survey paper consists of two main parts. In the first part (Sect. 2), a
generalized framework for the estimation of parameters of dynamic processes
including the motion field is presented. In the second part (Sect. 3), it is shown

B. Michaelis and G. Krell (Eds.): DAGM 2003, LNCS 2781, pp. 608–617, 2003.
© Springer-Verlag Berlin Heidelberg 2003

with some examples from environmental and live sciences that this new technique helped to answer some key problems in basic sciences.

Most of the results reported in this paper were gained within an interdisciplinary research unit at the University of Heidelberg [1]. The research group image processing at the Interdisciplinary Center for Scientific Computing cooperated with application groups from the Institute for Environmental Physics, the Institute for Botany, the Kirchhoff Institute for Physics, the Institute of Physiology and the German Cancer Research Center. Given the wide range of applications from satellite imaging with spectroscopic image sequences to high-resolution 3-D light microscopy, it is obvious that the methods developed are general enough to be useful for other applications as well.

2 A Generalized Framework for the Estimation of Dynamic Processes

2.1 Optimization Approach to Motion Estimation

In this section, well-known low-level motion estimators are represented in a generalized optimization approach that is suitable to be extended to the estimation of additional parameters. We start from the basic fact that motion appears as oriented structures in space-time images (Fig. 1). In the direction of motion the gray values do not change. Therefore the scalar product of a vector $p = [u, v, 1]$ in the direction of motion is perpendicular to the spatiotemporal gradient $\nabla_{xt} g$ is zero.

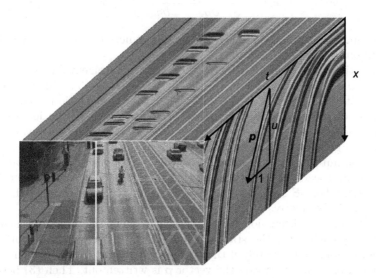

Fig. 1. Image sequence with a traffic scene as a space-time image. On the right side of the cube a yt slice marked by the vertical white line in the xy image is shown, while the top face shows an xt slice marked by the horizontal line (after [2]).

In order to find this direction and thus the velocity field $\boldsymbol{u}(\boldsymbol{x}, t)$, the following error functional can be minimized [2]:

$$e(\boldsymbol{x}, \boldsymbol{u}) = \int w(\boldsymbol{x}' - \boldsymbol{x}, t' - t) \left\| \boldsymbol{\nabla}_{xt} g^T \boldsymbol{p} \right\| \mathrm{d}^N x' \mathrm{d}t' \to \min \qquad (1)$$

The spatiotemporal window function $w(\boldsymbol{x}' - \boldsymbol{x}, t' - t)$ determines the area in space and time over which the averaging takes place. For the sake of a compact notation, windowed integrals as in (1) are abbreviated by

$$\int w(\boldsymbol{x}' - \boldsymbol{x}, t' - t) \left\| \ldots \right\| \mathrm{d}^N x' \mathrm{d}t' = \overline{\left\| \ldots \right\|} \qquad (2)$$

Then (1) reduces to

$$e(\boldsymbol{x}, \boldsymbol{u}) = \overline{\left\| \boldsymbol{\nabla}_{xt} g^T \boldsymbol{p} \right\|} \to \min. \qquad (3)$$

Mostly an L_2-norm (least squares) is used. Then in (3) the data term contained in the spatiotemporal gradient and the parameters to be estimated can be separated yielding

$$e_2(\boldsymbol{x}, \boldsymbol{u}) = \boldsymbol{p}^T \boldsymbol{J} \boldsymbol{p} \quad \text{with} \quad \boldsymbol{J} = \overline{\boldsymbol{\nabla}_{xt} g \boldsymbol{\nabla}_{xt} g^T}. \qquad (4)$$

The symmetric tensor $\boldsymbol{J}$ is known as the structure tensor and has the components

$$\boldsymbol{J}_{pq}(\boldsymbol{x}, t) = w(\boldsymbol{x}, t) * \left(\frac{\partial g(\boldsymbol{x}, t)}{\partial p} \frac{\partial g(\boldsymbol{x}, t)}{\partial q} \right) \quad \text{with} \quad p, q \in \{\boldsymbol{x}, t\}. \qquad (5)$$

In this equation, the integral over the window function (see (2)) is written as a convolution operation.

The estimation of motion therefore reduces to an eigenvalue analysis of the tensor $\boldsymbol{J}$ and the eigenvector to the smallest eigenvalue [3]. This eigenvector is oriented into the direction of motion. (The eigenvalue solution is equivalent to a rotation of the coordinate system to principle axes.) In the ideal case of a constant motion in a noise-free image sequence, the smallest eigenvalue is zero, because the gray values do not change at all in this direction.

The computation of the structure tensor is straightforward. It can be performed as a cascade of linear convolution and (nonlinear) point operations as $\mathcal{B}(\mathcal{D}p \cdot \mathcal{D}q)$, where $\mathcal{B}$ and $\mathcal{D}$ are a smoothing filter of the shape of the window function and a derivative filter into the directions p and q.

For the further discussion it is important to note that the approach formulated here incorporates the standard idea of the preservation of optical flow. This can be seen immediately if the spatiotemporal gradient is split up into the spatial and temporal part and the vector $\boldsymbol{p}$ is written out. Then (3) becomes

$$e(\boldsymbol{x}, \boldsymbol{u}) = \overline{\left\| \frac{\partial g}{\partial t} + \boldsymbol{u} \boldsymbol{\nabla} g \right\|} \to \min. \qquad (6)$$

2.2   Extension to the Dynamic Processes

The extension of (3) and (6) for other processes that change gray values is straightforward. The term in the norm contains an equation for conservation of gray vales:

$$\frac{\partial g}{\partial t} + \boldsymbol{u}\nabla g = 0. \tag{7}$$

When there is only motion, temporal changes can only be caused by moving spatial gradients. Other terms that change gray values just add additional terms. The most important processes encountered in scientific applications are briefly discussed here:

Source term. A source term (as, e. g., a heat source density observed in thermal image sequences) directly results in a temporal change of the gray values:

$$\frac{\partial g}{\partial t} + \boldsymbol{u}\nabla g = s. \tag{8}$$

First order chemical reaction. A first order chemical reaction (we assume that the gray value in an image is proportional to the concentration of a chemical species) or any other relaxation process causes a temporal decay of the concentration proportional to the rate constant λ and the concentration g:

$$\frac{\partial g}{\partial t} + \boldsymbol{u}\nabla g = -\lambda g. \tag{9}$$

A term of this form constitutes also an elegant solution for motion estimation with changing illumination using a multiplicative illumination model. Here λ has the meaning of a temporal rate of change of the illumination [4].

Diffusion process. A diffusion process causes the concentration to spread out according to the instationary diffusion equation [5]:

$$\frac{\partial g}{\partial t} + \boldsymbol{u}\nabla g = D\Delta g. \tag{10}$$

Forces. Forces $\boldsymbol{F}$ applied to moving objects cause an acceleration $\boldsymbol{a} = [a, b]^T$ of the motion according to the law of Newton, $\boldsymbol{F} = m\boldsymbol{a}$. A direct estimation of acceleration is possible if not a constant but an accelerated velocity field is modeled according to

$$\frac{\partial g}{\partial t} + (\boldsymbol{u} + \boldsymbol{a}t)\nabla g = 0 \tag{11}$$

Deformations. Deformation of objects result in a spatially changing motion field. In first order, such a motion field can be described by a deformation matrix

$$A = \begin{bmatrix} a_{11} & a_{12} \\ a_{21} & a_{22} \end{bmatrix} \tag{12}$$

resulting in

$$\frac{\partial g}{\partial t} + (\boldsymbol{u} + \boldsymbol{Ax})\boldsymbol{\nabla}g = 0 \tag{13}$$

This matrix contains all possible elementary 2-D deformations: rotation, dilation, stretching, and shear [6]. If not all four degrees of freedom are possible for a certain process, deformations can be restricted. For a homogeneous growth process, e. g., when a plant part is known to grow homogeneously in all directions, the matrix $\boldsymbol{A}$ reduces to a scalar growth parameter r.

The essential point with all these extensions is that all parameters to be estimated appear as linear factors with terms that can be estimated from the data. Therefore the processes can be combined and it is possible to collect all parameters to be estimated in a parameter vector $\boldsymbol{p}$ and all data terms in a data vector $\boldsymbol{d}$. In the case of a complex process composed of terms with relaxation, diffusion, acceleration, and homogeneous growth, we end up with

$$\begin{aligned}
e_2(\boldsymbol{x}, \boldsymbol{u}) &= \boldsymbol{p}^T \boldsymbol{J} \boldsymbol{p} \quad \text{and} \quad \text{with} \quad \boldsymbol{J} = \overline{\boldsymbol{d}\boldsymbol{d}^T} \\
\boldsymbol{d} &= [g_x, g_y, g, g_x x + g_y y, t g_x, t g_y, x g_x + y g_y, g_t]^T, \\
\boldsymbol{p} &= [u, v, \lambda, -D, a, b, r, 1]^T.
\end{aligned} \tag{14}$$

In this specific example, the structure tensors generalizes to an 8×8 tensor containing derivatives of gray values up to second order. In addition products with coordinate values x, y, and t appear. These are not global coordinates but local coordinates centered around the center of the window.

From the above consideration, it is obvious that this approach can be extended to any type of dynamic processes that can be described by partial differential equations that are linear in the parameters to be estimated. Therefore only nonlinear processes cannot be handled with this approach.

The eigenvalue analysis gives only unbiased results if the error of all elements of the data vector are equal. While this is at least approximatively true for the estimation of the motion fields, it is no longer true if other terms with higher derivatives or terms without errors are contained in the data vector. Then it is required to apply equilibrization techniques that scale the individual elements in the data vector so that all elements have equal errors. Alternatively, mixed ordinary least squares (OLS) and total least squares (TLS) techniques can be used. For further details, see [7].

2.3 Rank-Deficit Generalized Structure Tensors

When the model describes the underlying dynamic process observed by an image sequence, the structure tensor has just one small eigenvalue in the ideal case, i. e., its rank is one lower than its dimension. If this is the case, all parameters can be estimated. In most cases, however, the rank will be lower.

This is already the case when just the motion field is estimated. At a straight edge, e.;g., the rank of the structure tensor is 1 and only the velocity component perpendicular to the edge can be determined ("aperture problem"). With higher-dimensional generalized structure tensors, it can be expected, that rank-deficit tensors appear even more often.

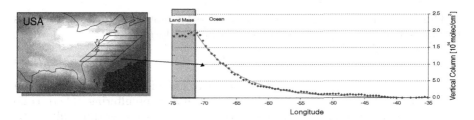

Fig. 2. Example for the stationary decay curve along a latitudinal section through a NO_2 plume at the eastern shore of the US (after [8]).

This is illustrated with an interesting example, where the combination of motion and a first-order chemical reaction results in a stationary gray value pattern. We assume a constant motion in x direction and a first-order decay rate λ. Then according to (9), a stationary profile occurs when

$$u\frac{\partial g}{\partial x} = -\lambda g \quad \text{or} \quad g = g_0 \exp[-(\lambda/u)x]. \tag{15}$$

Such stationary profiles are indeed observed in satellite image sequences of tropospheric NO_2 concentration when plumes generated at the east coast of the USA are transported to the North Atlantic Ocean by westerly winds. Over the ocean there are no sources and the NO_2 concentrations decay exponentially due to the combined action of transport and a first-order decay process.

On the other side, it is often possible to estimate parameters of dynamic processes even when it is impossible to estimate the full motion field. A simple example of this kind is the estimation of the diffusion coefficient of a homogeneous diffusion process at a straight edge. Because of the isotropy of the diffusion process, the blurring of the edge with time in just one direction is sufficient to estimate the diffusion coefficient, whereas only the component of the velocity perpendicular to the edge can be determined.

2.4 Optimal Filtering

From the discussion in Sect. 2.1 and 2.2 and (14) it appears that good filters for motion estimation require perfect derivative operators. Fortunately, this is not true. A more closer look reveals that a surprisingly general class of filters can be used for the estimation of motion.

Because moving objects appear as oriented structures in image sequences, any operation on the gray values of image sequences that does not change the orientation of spatiotemporal patterns still will give the same velocity field. Therefore any common linear prefiltering of the image sequence with a mask $b(x,t)$ does not change the estimated parameters. This can also be seen from the Fourier transform of the data vector in (14). A common filter applied to all terms (including the original gray value) results only in a common factor that does not change the direction of the data vector.

This basic fact has far-reaching consequences for motion estimation. It means that any set of filters with transfer functions of the form

$$d(\boldsymbol{k}) = \mathrm{i}k_p^q B(\boldsymbol{k}), \tag{16}$$

provides suitable filter set. The index p refers to any of the directions x, y, and t. The set of filters in (16) thus includes the common prefiltering. There is no restriction to the common filter $B(\boldsymbol{k})$. As long as it is a smoothing filter, the derivative filters remain derivative filters. They are just replaced by regularized filter kernels. The common filter can have, however, any transfer function. Then they are no longer necessarily derivative filters. It is interesting to note that the same conclusion can be reached by a completely different train of thoughts as discussed in [9].

The wide degree of freedom for filters opens innovative ways to optimize classes of filters given the frequency distribution of noise and signals in the image sequence. It is not surprising that standard derivative filters show considerable errors in the estimation of the direction of the gradient. According to Sect. 2.1, unbiased motion estimates, however, require unbiased estimates of the direction of the gradient. The Sobel filter, for example, shows deviations in the direction of the gradient up to $5°$ [6]. A filter with the same shape as the Sobel filter

$$\boldsymbol{D}_{x,\mathrm{opt}} = \boldsymbol{D}_x * \boldsymbol{B}_y * \boldsymbol{B}_t, \quad \boldsymbol{D}_x = \frac{1}{2}[1,0,-1], \quad \boldsymbol{B}_{y,t} = [p/2, 1-p, p/2]^T \tag{17}$$

shows a maximum error in the direction of the gradient of only $0.4°$ with $p = 6/16$ (Sobel: $p = 1/4$) [10,11] under the assumption of isotropic Gaussian noise in the image sequence.

2.5   Generalized Regularization

Because of the sparse local information contained in image sequences, regularization approaches are required to compute dense motion fields. For the estimation of the parameters of dynamic processes, regularization becomes even more important, because more parameters have to be estimated from the same amount of data. Since the early work of [12] about global regularization, significant progress has been made. In a recent invited paper [13] showed the equivalence between variational approaches and anisotropic diffusion and developed a design principle for rotationally invariant anisotropic regularizers.

It is straightforward to extend these concepts to the joint estimation of motion fields and parameters of dynamic processes because the form of the equations remains the same, only the number of parameters to be estimated has increased according to the model for the dynamic process.

In general, a spatiotemporal regularizer that constrains the parameter field is given by

$$\left\| \boldsymbol{d}^T \boldsymbol{p} \right\| + R(\boldsymbol{\nabla}_{xt} p_k) \to \min, \tag{18}$$

where $R(\boldsymbol{\nabla} p_k)$ is a generally nonlinear function of the spatiotemporal gradient of all elements of the parameter vector. Using a regularizer that is simply a sum of squared gradients of all elements of the parameter vector $\alpha^2 \sum_k |\nabla_{xt} p_k|^2$ is a simple extension of the homogenous global regularizer used by [12]. There are three ways to vary and thus optimize the estimate of parameters of dynamic models and in each step homogeneous, inhomogeneous, or anisotropic diffusion can be used:

- Direct regularization (prefiltering) of the image sequence data as described in Sect. 2.4 in order to obtain an optimal unbiased estimate of the data vector given the statistics of noise and signal in the image sequence.
- Convolution by the window function results in a 'local' solution, where the width and shape of window function determines the degree of local averaging.
- The use of a regularizer functional R as in (18) finally leads to 'Globally' constrained solution.

3   Application Examples

In this survey paper only a few application examples can be shown (Fig. 3–5). A detailed discussion of more applications can be found in [1].

a

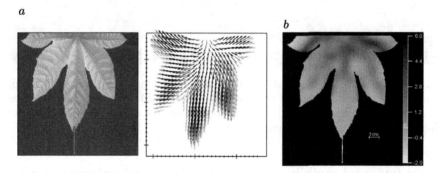

Fig. 3. a Leaf of a castor-oil plant and flow field due to growth; b growth rate (divergence of the motion field); the scale for the divergence ranges from -2.0 to 6.0 permille/min.

4   Directions for Future Research

Although a general framework for the estimation of dynamic processes from image sequences is available and has help to solve some key problems in environmental and live sciences, there are still many open research problems. Among them are:

Efficient algorithms. Efficient algorithms are required for widespread application.

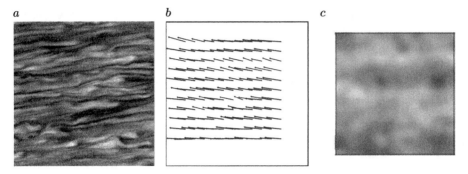

Fig. 4. Analysis of infrared image sequences of the ocean surface **a** Example image with a sector of about $1\,m \times 1\,m$; **b** Flow field. **b** Heat flux density at the surface (source term according to (8)).

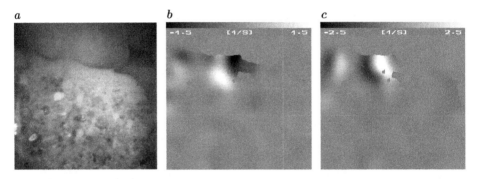

Fig. 5. Example for the study of flow in sediments. **a** One of the images of the flow of sand particles in the sediment observed with an embedded endoscope. **c** Divergence and **d** rotation of the vector field as a color overlay on the original image; a color scale is included at the top of each image.

Sparse temporal sampling. As all optical-flow based techniques, the techniques described in this paper require temporally densely sampled image sequences. In many practical applications

Spherical quadrature filters. The relation between classical optical-flow based and quadrature-filter based techniques [14] and the recent extension to spherical quadrature filters [15] requires further attention.

Motion superimposition.

Nonlinear dynamic models. Another significant challenge is the extension to nonlinear dynamic models.

Acknowledgments. First of all I would like to thank all members of DFG Forschergruppe "Bildfolgenanalyse zum Studium dynamischer Prozesse", who with their enthusiasm and dedication for interdisciplinary research made it possible that this research unit was successful. Financial support for this research by the Deutsche Forschungsgemeinschaft, through the Forschergruppe FOR 240 "Bildfolgenanalyse zum Studium dynamischer Prozesse", the DFG-Graduiertenkolleg "Modellierung und Wissenschaftliches Rechnen in Mathematik und Naturwissenschaften", and the Schwerpunktprogramm SPP 1117 "Mathematische Methoden der Zeitreihenanalyse und digitalen Bildverarbeitung" (LOCOMOTOR subproject) is gratefully acknowledged. Sediment transport (Fig. 5) is being studied in a project funded by the German Federal Waterways Engineering and Research Institute (BAW), Karlsruhe.

References

1. Jähne, B., ed.: Image Sequence Analysis to Investigate Dynamic Processes. Lecture Notes in Computer Science. Springer, Berlin (2003) in preparation.
2. Jähne, B.: Spatio-temporal Image Processing. Volume 751 of Lecture Notes in Computer Science. Springer, Berlin (1993)
3. Bigün, J., Granlund, G.H.: Optimal orientation detection of linear symmetry. In: Proc. ICCV'97, Washington, DC, IEEE Computer Society (1987) 433–438
4. Haussecker, H.W., Fleet, D.J.: Computing optical flow with physical models of brightness variation. IEEE Trans. PAMI **23** (2001) 661–673
5. Crank, J.: The Mathematics of Diffusion. 2 edn. Clarendon, Oxford (1975)
6. Jähne, B.: Digital Image Processing. 5 edn. Springer, Berlin (2002)
7. Garbe, C.S., Spies, H., Jähne, B.: Mixed OLS-TLS for the estimation of dynamic processes with a linear source term. In Gool, L.V., ed.: Pattern Recognition, Proc. 24th DAGM Symposium Zurich. Volume 2449 of Lecture Notes in Computer Science., Berlin, Springer (2002) 463–471
8. Wenig, M., Beirle, S., Hollwedel, J., Kraus, S., Leue, C., Wagner, T., Platt, U., Jähne, B.: Atmospheric emission, transport, trends and fate of tropospheric trace gases. In Jähne, B., ed.: Image Sequence Analysis to Investigate Dynamic Processes. Lecture Notes in Computer Science, Berlin, Springer (2003)
9. Mester, R.: The generalization, optimization, and information-theoretic justification of filter-based and autocovariance-based motion estimation. In: Proc. Intern. Conf. Image Processing (ICIP'03), Barcelona. (2003)
10. Scharr, H., Körgel, S., Jähne, B.: Numerische Isotropieoptimierung von FIR-Filtern mittels Querglättung. In Paulus, E., Wahl, F.M., eds.: Mustererkennung 1997 19. DAGM Symposium Braunschweig. Informatik aktuell, Berlin, Springer (1997) 367–374
11. Scharr, H.: Optimale Operatoren in der Digitalen Bildverarbeitung. Diss., Univ. Heidelberg (2000)
12. Horn, B.K.P., Schunck, B.G.: Determining optical flow. Artificial Intelligence **17** (1981) 185–203
13. Schnörr, C., Weickert, J.: Variational image motion computation: theoretical framework, problems and perspectives. In Sommer, G., Krüger, N., Perwasser, C., eds.: Mustererkennung 2000. Informatik Aktuell, Berlin, Springer (2000) 476–487
14. Granlund, G.H., Knutsson, H.: Signal Processing for Computer Vision. Kluwer, Dordrecht (1995)
15. Felsberg, M.: Disparity from monogenic phase. In van Gool, L., ed.: Pattern Recognition, 24th DAGM Symposium. Volume 2449 of Lecture Notes in Computer Science., Berlin, Springer (2002) 248–256

Author Index

Lecture Notes in Computer Science

For information about Vols. 1–2710
please contact your bookseller or Springer-Verlag